T0346336

CHILDBIRTH

*Changing Ideas and Practices in Britain and
America 1600 to the Present*

Series Editor
PHILIP K. WILSON
Truman State University

Assistant Editors
ANN DALLY
*Wellcome Institute for the History of
Medicine (London)*

CHARLES R. KING
Medical College of Ohio

A GARLAND SERIES

SERIES CONTENTS

VOLUME

5

DISEASES OF PREGNANCY AND CHILDBIRTH

Edited with introductions by
PHILIP K. WILSON
Truman State University

GARLAND PUBLISHING, INC.
New York & London
1996

Library of Congress Cataloging-in-Publication Data

Childbirth : changing ideas and practices in Britain and America
1600 to the present / edited with introductions by Philip K.
Wilson.
    p.   cm.
    Includes bibliographical references.
    Contents: v. 1. Midwifery theory and practice — v. 2. The
medicalization of obstetrics: personnel, practice, and instruments — v. 3. Methods and folklore — v. 4. Reproductive science, genetics, and birth control — v. 5. Diseases of pregnancy
and childbirth.
    ISBN 0-8153-2230-5 (v. 1 : alk. paper). — ISBN 0–8153–
2231–3 (v. 2 : alk. paper). — ISBN 0–8153–2232–1 (v. 3 : alk.
paper). — ISBN 0–8153–2233–X (v. 4. : alk. paper). — ISBN 0–
8153-2234–8 (v. 5 : alk. paper)
    1. Childbirth—United States—History. 2. Childbirth—Great
Britain—History. 3. Obstetrics—United States—History. 4. Obstetrics—Great Britain—History. I. Wilson, Philip K., 1961–.
    [DNLM: 1. Obstetrics—trends. 2. Midwifery—trends.
3. Pregnancy Complications. 4. Reproduction Techniques.
5. Genetic Counseling. 6. Contraception. WQ 100C5356 1996]

RG518.U5C47 1995
618.4'0973—dc20
DNLM/DLC
for Library of Congress   96–794
                                                  CIP

CONTENTS

LIST OF ILLUSTRATIONS

SERIES INTRODUCTION

Since "most women are interested in the process of giving birth and all men have been born," it would appear, claimed Johns Hopkins University obstetrician Alan Guttmacher, that the topic of childbirth would above all other topics have "universal appeal." Birth is also one of the most individual moments in each of our lives, but although we all share the experience of being delivered, the processes of delivery have been diverse. The social gathering around the childbed common in earlier times has, for many, been replaced by a more isolated hospital bed. Maternal fears of the pain and peril of procreation have, or so prevalent historiography would have us believe, intensified with the intervention of male midwives and obstetricians bringing along new "tools" of the trade. Markedly divergent beliefs about assisting in labor have created polarized factions of attendants. Some have followed wisdom similar to what Britain's Percivall Willughby first espoused in 1640:

> Let midwives observe the ways and proceedings of nature for the production of her fruit on trees, or the ripening of walnuts or almonds, from their first knotting to the opening of the husks and falling of the nut . . . . These signatures may teach midwives patience, and persuade them to let nature alone perform her work.

Opposing factions adhered to claims similar to that of the early nineteenth-century Philadelphia midwifery professor, Thomas Denman, that belief in:

> labour, being a natural act, . . . not requiring the interference of art for either its promotion or its accomplishment . . . has, from its influence, retarded, more perhaps than any other circumstance, the progress of improvement in this most important branch of medical science.

Other comparisons among midwifery writings suggest that although expectant women may no longer avoid the same "longings and cravings" of pregnancy as did their eighteenth-century forebears, contemporary concern about exposing pregnant women and their fetuses to nicotine, alcohol, known teratogenic agents, and unwarranted stress evokes similar warnings. Indeed, as the works included in this collection illustrate, many similar concerns have been shared by expectant mothers and their labor attendants for centuries.

Although there is a substantial literature on childbirth, it typically lacks the full medical, historical, and social contextualization that these volumes provide to readers. This series attempts to fill the gap in many institutions' libraries by bringing together key articles illuminating a number of issues from different perspectives that have long concerned the expectant mother and the attendants of her delivery regarding the health of the newborn infant. Primary and secondary sources have been culled from British and American publications that focus on childbirth practices over the past three hundred years. Some represent "classic" works within the medical literature that have contributed towards a more complete understanding of pertinent topics. The series draws from historical, sociological, anthropological, and feminist literature in an attempt to present a wider range of scholarly perspectives on various issues surrounding childbirth.

Childbirth: Changing Ideas and Practices is intended to provide readers with key primary sources and exemplary historiographical approaches through which they can more fully appreciate a variety of themes in British and American childbirth, midwifery, and obstetrics. For example, general historical texts commonly claim that childbed (puerperal) fever, a disease that has claimed hundreds of thousands of maternal lives, provoked much fear throughout most of British and American history. In addition to supplying readers with historians' interpretations, *Childbirth: Changing Ideas and Practices* also provides discussions of the causes and consequences of particular cases of childbed fever taken directly from the medical literature of the nineteenth and twentieth centuries, thereby enabling a better understanding of how problematic this disorder initially was to several key individuals who, after first increasing its incidence, ultimately devised specific methods of its prevention.

The articles in this series are designed to serve as a resource for students and teachers in fields including history, women's studies, human biology, sociology, and anthropology. They will also meet the socio-historical educational needs of pre-medical and nursing students and aid pre-professional, allied health, and midwifery instructors in their lesson preparations. Beyond the content of many collections on the history of childbirth, readers frequently need access to the primary sources in order to develop their own interpretive accounts. This five-volume series expands the readily accessible knowledge base as it represents both actual experiences and socio-historical interpretations on select developments within the history of British and American childbirth, midwifery, and obstetrics.

Given the vast and expanding literature on childbirth, it is virtually impossible anymore for any single source to provide a complete coverage of such a broad topic. Selecting precisely what articles to include has been, at times, a painstaking process. We have purposefully excluded works on abortion as many of these articles have recently been reprinted elsewhere. Additionally, we have only touched upon midwifery/obstetrical education, the legal issues surrounding childbirth, marriage, sex, and the family, and genetic engineering since numerous contemporary works in print thoroughly discuss these themes. Seminal articles that are currently available in other edited collections as well as general review articles were, with a few exceptions, not considered for reprinting in this series. There are several areas, including eclampsia, the development and role of the placenta, pregnancy tests throughout history, and Native American childbirth practices, for which suitable articles are wanting. Related topics such as gynecology and gynecological diseases, pediatrics, neonatology, postnatal care and teratology, though of considerable concern to many pregnant women and health care providers, appear beyond the scope of our focus and the interest of our generalist readers. Space did not allow for me to cover childbirth from the viewpoint of what have historically been considered alternative or complementary healing professions such as herbalism, homeopathy, or osteopathy, even though thousands of healthy children have been delivered by practitioners in these professions. The exorbitant permission charges that some journals charge for reprinting their articles has prohibited us from including many important articles. Finally, we have opted not to reprint biographical articles as the typical lengthy accounts of individuals would have precluded addressing more general relevant issues.

Series Acknowledgments

I am grateful to the many individuals who offered their assistance, suggestions, and support throughout the gestation of this project. Foremost, I wish to thank my co-editors, Dr. Charles R. King and Dr. Ann Dally, both highly valued "team players" in what truly became an international collaborative creation. Their medical expertise and historiographical suggestions strengthened the content of this series. Laura Runge, my undergraduate research student and Ronald E. McNair Post-Baccalaureate Achievement Program Scholar, provided exemplary editorial assistance throughout the growth of this project. In addition, she introduced Melissa Blagg-Holcomb to our team, a truly exceptional undergraduate scholar, without whom this project would not have been completed in such a timely manner. Melissa's professional interest in nurse midwifery expanded the scope of the literature we reviewed. Our research would have been impossible without the assistance of many librarians, archivists, and other members of the research staff. In particular, I wish to thank Lyndsay Lardner (The Wellcome Institute, London), Susan Case (Clendening Medical History Library, Kansas City), and Janice Wilson (Hawaii Medical Library, Honolulu; Sterling Medical Library, New Haven, and Pickler Memorial Library, Kirksville) for their exemplary library assistance. The unfailing efforts of Sheila Swafford, in Pickler Library's Reference Department, to secure necessary material are deeply appreciated. The editors also wish to thank Jane Carver, Prof. Mark Davis, Prof. Robbie Davis-Floyd, Nancy Dellapenna, Clare Dunne, Prof. Paul Finkelman, Andy Foley, Dr. Denis Gibbs, Ferenc Gyorgyey, Gwendolyn Habel, Jack Holcomb, Charlene Jagger, Maggie Jones, Carol Lockhart, Barb Magers, Andrew Melvyn, Jean Sidwell, Prof. John Harley Warner, Prof. Dorothy C. Wertz and the staffs of the Library of the Royal Society of Medicine (London), the National Library of Medicine (Bethesda), Pickler Memorial Library (Kirksville) and Rider Drug and Camera (Kirksville) for their assistance in preparing certain parts of this series. Leo Balk of Garland Publishing, Inc., proved to be a stable sounding board during the conception stage of *Childbirth*, a role that Carole Puccino has deftly carried on throughout the later progressions of this work. I also wish to thank my colleagues at the University of Hawaii-Manoa, Yale University, and Northeast Missouri State University (soon to be Truman State University) for their support and critical commentary on this project. Northeast Missouri State University provided a Summer Faculty Research Grant which allowed for the timely completion of this project. Finally, I remain indebted to my wife, Janice, for providing astute critique, able reference library assistance, and continual support and encouragement.

Philip K. Wilson

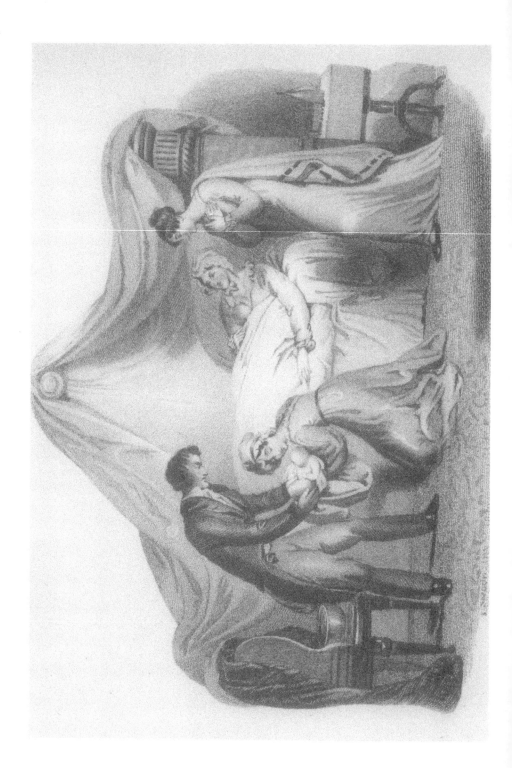

INTRODUCTION

Many cultures have, at some point in their existence, conceptualized disease within their own population as arising from some supernatural force. Afflictions were due to sorcery, breach of taboo, some spiritual presence, or loss of soul. Hippocratic writers in ancient Greece described a different concept of disease: nature, they claimed, had set the four bodily humors—blood, phlegm, black bile, and yellow bile—into balance. Diseases of pregnancy and childbirth to the Hippocratics, like other types of disease, did not derive from particular organ systems but rather from an imbalance of the bodily humors. Health care practitioners worked alongside nature to assist in re-establishing the balance.

In a recent contribution to our understanding of disease, Charles Rosenberg argued that disease "does not exist" within a culture until the people have "agreed that it does, by perceiving, naming, and responding to it." He elaborates that diseases are not merely pathological entities. Rather, they are much more complex, being

> at once a biological event, a generation-specific repertoire of verbal constructs reflecting medicine's intellectual and institutional history, an occasion of and potential legitimization for public policy, an aspect of social role and individual—intrapsychic—identity, a sanction for cultural values, and a structuring element in doctor and patient interactions.[1]

In the early 1800s, male-midwives increasingly viewed and classified pregnancy as a disease. Specifically, pregnancy was associated with potentially fatal anatomical and physiological changes. Once the medical community framed pregnancy as a pathological state, the responsibility of mediating the stages of pregnancy and childbirth literally changed hands. As physicians were professionally and culturally viewed as the caretakers of disease, parturient women, suffering from the disease of pregnancy, by necessity fell under their provenance.

"Under the popular *medical* orders of the day," so health reformer Russell Trall argued in 1850, "pregnant women are regarded as invalids." They were "bled, paragoric'd, magnesia'd, stimulated, mineralised and poisoned, just as though they were going through a regular course of fever."[2] The reformers argued, in what Regina Markell Morantz claimed was "strikingly prophetic of today's feminist critique of professional obstetric practice," that pregnancy should be viewed as a natural phenomenon rather than a disease.[3] Women should be provided substantial food and drink, and fresh air, all the while wearing comfortable, clean clothing. Childbirth, itself, was to be assisted naturally without the use of any drugs.

In today's society, as Irvine Loudon noted, "few of us have personal knowledge of a maternal death." Most women "expect not only to survive childbirth, but to do so in perfect health after a perfect and satisfying delivery of a perfect baby."[4] Until very recently, however, a woman's concern of the "risk" of possibly dying in the course of pregnancy, labor, or the puerperium (the few days following childbirth) was, according to most accounts, considerable.[5] The voluminous statistical tabulations of maternal mortality rates, as well as the less common personal diaries of women's pregnancies, document the fear that often accompanied childbirth.

Of the various diseases of pregnancy and childbirth, childbed (puerperal) fever has claimed more victims than any other pregnancy-related disease to which womankind has been subjected. Many unfortunate women began to experience chills within seventy-two hours following childbirth. Attendants typically observed a weak, rapid pulse, a quickened respiratory rate, a clammy sweat, dry mouth, and an overall malaise. Often the abdomen became distended and intensely painful—with the pain being aggravated by the mere covering of a bed sheet. The flow of lochia (i.e., postpartum vaginal discharge) typically following childbirth was often suppressed. Axillary temperatures were commonly noted up to 108° F or more. These physical findings continued to such a state that, by the seventh or eighth day, the woman often died.

In the mid-nineteenth century, Boston physician Oliver Wendell Holmes aggressively attempted to convince physicians and nurses that they were responsible for transmitting this disease to their patients. The concept of childbed fever as a contagious disease was not in the minds of many practitioners at the time. Many intra- and inter-professional challenges preceded the American acceptance of the European-born germ theory of disease. By the late 1880s, the importance of antiseptic use and aseptic technique to prevent childbed fever's spread was more readily acknowledged. In the early twentieth century, additional preventative measures, including hospital cleanliness and increased maternal care, improved the morbidity associated with childbirth, but the mortality appeared to remain comparable to that of pre-antiseptic times. Various improvements in associating specific bacteria as causative agents of specific diseases together with further developments of chemotherapy and antibiotics provided some control of the disease, but such measures, unfortunately, diminished the role of asepsis.

Despite many attempts to eradicate this childbed scourge, outbreaks still occur in British and American hospitals. Boston, New York City, and Sacramento served as hosts to four such outbreaks in American hospitals between 1965 and 1984.[6] Traditional bacterial isolation procedures following the 1965 outbreak at Boston Hospital for Women identified the most likely source of contamination as the anesthetist who was present in over one-half of the infected women's deliveries. It was found he had been harboring the infectious organism beneath a scab on the back of his hand, and that he routinely held his patient's hands during delivery for both reassurance and to prevent the parturient women from touching sterile surroundings.[7]

In 1979, conclusions from a nine-year study at the University of Illinois Medical Center in Chicago re-emphasized the importance of maintaining asepsis in the delivery room: "a fruit of hard-earned lessons that medical history has taught us at a terrible cost of lives."[8] Such measures as abandoning prophylactic antibiotics, isolating post-operative infection patients to particular staff members, compulsory hand washing between patients, and reducing the number of vaginal examinations during the early stages of childbirth were re-implemented. A significant decline in puerperal infection resulted, thus suggesting that many contemporary cases of childbed fever would be prevented if aseptic procedures were rigorously followed.

Natural childbirth has resurged as a popular practice in recent decades. Home births, according to many tabulations, have shown a considerable decrease in maternal infection. The presence of fathers and other family members during childbirth adds potentially harmful bacteria to the birth scene, but their presence, even during cesarean births, has not increased postpartum infection.[9]

Other physiological disturbances have wreaked havoc for the pregnant mother and/or the child she carried. Beliefs about a condition variably referred to as eclampsia, toxemia, or the metabolic hypertensive disorder of pregnancy—the ancient enigma of obstetrics—have changed throughout the centuries. Presently, this disease is medically viewed as a metabolic disease of late pregnancy perhaps initiated by immunological means, exacerbated by concomitant liver and kidney dysfunction and worsened by the changing hormones of pregnancy. Earlier theories about toxemia speculated that it was primarily a kidney disorder related to an imbalance of salt intake, a disease of "placental insufficiency", a nutritional deficiency, or a disease caused by an "over-distention of the uterus." A more complete history of this disease awaits an author.

The embryonic developmental disturbances related to maternal thalidomide ingestion are well known. Thousands of children, now adults, from forty-six countries bear the partial-formed limbs resulting from the sedative, tranquilizing pills which , in the late 1950s, their mothers were told had no toxic or harmful side effects if taken during pregnancy.

> Secrecy cast a long shadow in the thalidomide affair, first over the discovery of what went wrong, medically and legally, and then over publication of the truth.

After "the truth" was known,

> Some governments—but not all—took steps to screen drugs more thoroughly before they reached their populations, and also to monitor the longer-term effects of approved drugs.[10]

Richard Gillam and Barton Bernstein, in a following article, discuss the medical-legal furor which arose over the latent carcinogenic risk in daughters of mothers who took the drug diethylstilbestrol (DES) in order to prevent miscarriage.

Numerous environmental agents, from radiation and pesticides to vitamin overdose and hexachlorophene, once used as an antibacterial baby soap, have been shown to have teratogenic (i.e., fetal malforming) effects. Many Americans know the United States' Surgeon General's warning that "Smoking by pregnant women can result in fetal injury, premature birth, and low birth weight." Furthermore, people with only a vague understanding of the nature of the Fetal Alcohol Syndrome regularly gaze upon the phase "women should not drink alcoholic beverages during pregnancy because of the risk of birth defects" as stated on alcoholic beverage containers. Are these merely medical warning statements for expectant women, or are these yet another attempt to gain control over the woman's body?

This issue of bodily control resurfaced in the 1990's debate over perinatal HIV screening and testing. In a recent review of this debate, it was claimed that all too often public policy questions surrounding women's reproductive and child welfare decision-making reflect an unjustifiable adversarial framing of the relationship between women and their fetuses and children. . . . many supposed maternal-child conflicts actually are conflicts between the mother and others who presume to be better able to judge what course of action is in the infant's best interest.[11]

This volume is designed to give readers a historical context within which to better understand the role of disease and pregnancy. Pregnancy, when viewed as a disease, helped focus social concerns on needed reform. However, when societal or environmental conditions are viewed as the agents of pregnancy-related disease, it is often the woman rather than the environment who is manipulated to reduce the "risks" of disease.

Philip K. Wilson

NOTES

1. Charles E. Rosenberg, "Framing Disease: Illness, Society and History." In Charles E. Rosenberg and Janet Golden, eds., *Framing Disease: Studies in Cultural History,* (New Brunswick, N. J.: Rutgers University Press, 1992), xii–xxvi.

2. R.T. Trall, "Allopathic Midwifery," *Water-Cure Journal* 9 (1850): 9, as cited by Regina Markell Morantz in "Making Women Modern: Middle-Class Women and Health Reform in 19th-Century America." In Judith Walzer Leavitt, ed., *Women and Health in America: Historical Readings* (Madison: University of Wisconsin Press, 1984), 351, 356.

3. Morantz, "Making Women Modern," 350.

4. Irvine S.L. Loudon, "Childbirth." In W.F. Bynum and Roy Porter, eds., *Companion Encyclopedia of the History of Medicine,* 1069 (London: Routledge, 1994), vol. 2, 1069.

5. Adrian Wilson has recently challenged this "fear thesis" in "The Perils of Early Modern Procreation: Childbirth With or Without Fear," *British Journal of Eighteenth-Century Studies* 16 (Spring 1993): 1–20.

6. John Figgis Jewett, et al., "Childbed Fever—A Continuing Entity," *Journal of the American Medical Association* 206 (October 7, 1968): 344–50. M.L. Tancer, J.E. McManus, and G. Bellotti, "Group A, Type 33, β-Hemolytic Streptococcal Outbreak on a Maternity and Newborn Service," *American Journal of Obstetrics and Gyne-*

cology 103 (1969): 1028–33. Philip B. Mead, et al., "Group A Streptococcal Puerperal Infection: Report of an Epidemic," *Obstetrics and Gynecology* 32 (October 1968): 460–64. James McGreggor, Allen Ott, and Mark Villard, "An Epidemic of 'Childbed Fever'," *American Journal of Obstetrics and Gynecology* 150 (1984): 385–88.

7. J.F. Jewett, "Childbed Fever," 347.

8. Leslie Iffy, et. al., "Control of Perinatal Infection by Traditional Preventive Measures," *Obstetrics and Gynecology* 54 (October 1979): 410.

9. Stephen H. Jackson, Frederick R. Schlichting, and Russell L. Hulme, "Effects of Fathers at Cesarean Birth on Postpartum Infection Rate," *AORN Journal* 36 (1982): 976.

10. Insight Team of *The Sunday Times* of London, *Suffer the Children: The Story of Thalidomide* (New York:Viking Press, 1979), 4,2.

11. Ruth R. Faden, Gail Geller, and Madison Powers, *AIDS, Women, and the Next Generation: Towards a Morally Acceptable Public Policy for HIV Testing of Pregnant Women and Newborns* (New York: Oxford University Press, 1991), vii.

FURTHER READING

Abel, Ernest L. *New Literature on Fetal Alcohol Exposure and Effects: A Bibliography, 1983–1988.* Westport, Conn.: Greenwood Press, 1990.

Bell, Susan E. "A New Model of Medical Technology Development: A Case Study of DES." *Research in the Sociology of Health Care* 4 (1986): 1–32.

Bichler, Joyce. *DES Daughter: The Joyce Bichler Story.* New York: Avon, 1981.

Brandt, Allan M. *No Magic Bullet: A Social History of Venereal Disease in the United States since 1880.* New York: Oxford University Press, 1985.

Brewer, Thomas H. *Metabolic Toxemia of Late Pregnancy: A Disease of Malnutrition.* New Canaan, Conn.: Keats Publishing, Inc., 1982.

Carter, K. Codell and Barbara R. Carter. *Childbed Fever. A Scientific Biography of Ignaz Semmelweis.* Westport, Conn.: Greenwood Press, 1994.

Chertok, L. *Psychosomatic Methods in Painless Childbirth: History, Theory, and Practice.* New York: Pergamon Press, 1959.

Chesney, Leon C. *Hypertensive Disorders in Pregnancy.* New York:

Appleton-Century-Crofts, 1978.

Connelly, Mark Thomas. "Prostitution, Venereal Disease, and American Medicine." In *Women and Health in America. Historical Readings*, edited by Judith Walzer Leavitt, 196–221. Madison: University of Wisconsin Press, 1984.

Dobbie, B. M. Willmott. "An Attempt to Estimate the True Rate of Maternal Mortality, Sixteenth to Eighteenth Centuries." *Medical History* 26 (January 1982): 79–89.

Ettorre, Elizabeth. *Women and Substance Use.* New Brunswick, N. J.: Rutgers University Press, 1992.

Faden, Ruth R., Gail Geller, and Madison Powers. *AIDS, Women and the Next Generation: Towards a Morally Acceptable Public Policy for HIV Testing of Pregnant Women and Newborns.* New York: Oxford University Press, 1991.

Gifford, Houghton and R.L. Hullinghorst, "Poliomyelitis in Pregnancy." *American Journal of Obstetrics and Gynecology* 55 (1948): 1030–36.

Gordon, Richard E. and Katherine K. Gordon, "Social Factors in the Prediction and Treatment of Emotional Disorders of Pregnancy." *American Journal of Obstetrics and Gynecology* 77 (1959): 1074–83.

Green, C.M. "Puerperal Eclampsia." *American Journal of Obstetrics* 28 (1893): 18–44.

Guttzke, D.W., "'The Cry of the Children': The Edwardian Medical Campaign Against Maternal Drinking." *British Journal of Addiction* 79 (1984): 71–84.

Hamilton, James Alexander and Patricia Neel Harberger, *Postpartum Psychiatric Illness: A Picture Puzzle.* Philadelphia: University of Pennsylvania Press, 1992.

Heifetz, Ruth. "Women, Lead and Reproductive Hazards: Defining a New Risk." In *Dying for Work: Worker's Safety and Health in Twentieth-Century America*, edited by David Rosner and Gerald Markowitz, 160–76. Bloomington, Indiana: Indiana University Press, 1987.

Insight Team of *The Sunday Times* of London. *Suffer the Children: The Story of Thalidomide.* New York: Viking Press, 1979.

Kooser, John. "Observations on the Possible Relationship of Diet to the Late Toxemia of Pregnancy." *American Journal of Obstetrics and Gynecology* 41 (1941): 288–94.

Kundsin, Ruth B., Lawrence Falk, and Sally S. Hipp, eds. "Impact on the Fetus of Parental Sexually Transmitted Disease." *Annals of the New York Academy of Sciences* 549 (December 30, 1988): 1–264.

Lansing, Dorothy I., W. Robert Penman, and Dorland J. Davis. "Puerperal Fever and the Group B Beta Hemolytic Streptococcus." *Bulletin of the History of Medicine* 57, no.1 (Spring 1983): 70–80.

Ledger, William J., Anne M. Reite, John T. Headington. "A System for Infectious Disease Surveillance on an Obstetric Service." *Obstetrics and Gynecology* 37 (May 1971): 769–78.

Lichtendorf, Susan S. and Phyllis L. Gillis. *The New Pregnancy: The Active Woman's Guide to Work, Legal Rights, Health Care, Travel, Sports, Dress, Sex, and Emotional Well-Being*. New York: Random House, 1979.

Loudon, Irvine. "Puerperal Fever, the Streptococcus, and the Sulphonamides, 1911–1945." *British Medical Journal* 295 (1982): 485–90.

Loudon, Irvine. *Death in Childbirth. An International Study of Maternal Care and Maternal Mortality 1800–1950*. Oxford: Clarendon Press, 1992.

McGregor, Deborah Kuhn. "Female Disorders and Nineteenth-Century Medicine: The Case of Vesico-Vaginal Fistula." *Caduceus* 3, no. 1 (Spring 1987): 1–30.

Marinal, Jose G., Alan L. Scriggins, and Rudolph F. Vollman. "History of the Maternal Mortality Study Committees in the United States." *Obstetrics and Gynecology* 34 (1969): 123–38.

Potts, Charles S. "Intra-Uterine Poliomyelitis." *Archives of Neurology and Psychiatry* 221 (1929): 288–98.

Quetel, Claude. *History of Syphilis*. Cambridge: Polity Press, 1990.

Sachs, Benjamin P., Dick A.J. Brown, Shirley G. Driscoll, Erica Schulman, David Acker, Bernard J. Ransh, and John J. Jewett. "Maternal Mortality in Massachusetts." *New England Journal of Medicine* 316 (1987): 667–72.

Semmelweis, Ignaz. *The Etiology, Concept and Prophylaxis of Childbed Fever*, translated by K. Codell Carter. Madison: University of Wisconsin Press, 1983, originally published 1861.

Sims, J.M. "On the Treatment of Vesico-Vaginal Fistula." *American Journal of Medical Science*, n.s. 23 (1852): 59–82.

Smilkstein, Gabriel, et al., "Predictions of Pregnancy Complications: An Application of the Biopsychosocial Model'" *Social Science and Medicine* 18 (1984): 315–21.

Smith, D.S. and Michael S. Hindus, "Premarital Pregnancy in America 1640–1971: An Overview and Interpretation," *Journal of Interdisciplinary History* 5 (1975): 537–70.

Steiner, P.E. and C.L. Lushbaugh. "Maternal Pulmonary Embolism by Amniotic Fluid as a Cause of Obstetric Shock and Unexpected Death in Obstetrics." *Journal of the American Medical Association* 117 (1941): 1245–54, 1340–45.

Veith, Ilza. *Hysteria: The History of a Disease*. Chicago: University of Chicago Press, 1965.

Vinovskis, Maris. "An 'Epidemic' of Adolescent Pregnancy: Some Historical Considerations." *Journal of Family History* 6 (Summer 1981): 205–30.

Zagon, Ian S. and Theodore A. Slotkin. *Maternal Substance Abuse and the Developing Nervous System*. San Diego, Calif.: Academic Press, Inc., 1992.

Zimmerman, David R. *Rh: The Intimate History of a Disease and Its Conquest*. New York: Macmillan Co., Inc, 1973.

Puerperal Fever

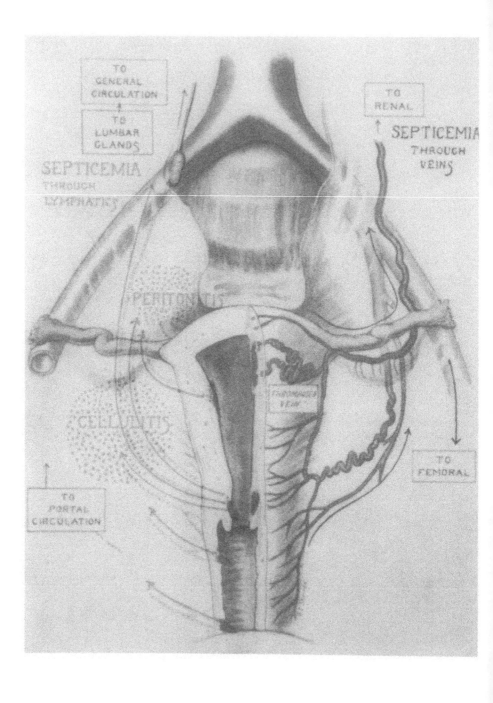

PUERPERAL FEVER IN EIGHTEENTH-CENTURY BRITAIN*

Margaret DeLacy

Even to physicians accustomed to witnessing great suffering and frequent death, puerperal fever was a particularly horrible disease. "I almost shudder with horror when I consider the excruciating torments that must rack the distressed patient under these dreadful circumstances," wrote Nathaniel Hulme, physician to the City of London Lying-in Hospital, in 1772.[1] In the same year, John Leake of the New Westminster Lying-in Hospital commented:

> If those diseases which have been found most dangerous and mortal in their effects ought principally to be considered by physicians, none will more deservedly engage their attention than the *Childbed Fever,* as there is not, perhaps, any malady ... where powerful remedies of every kind have been tried with more diligence and less success.[2]

The eighteenth century marked a new epoch in the history of this affliction. Although we have reports of four possible epidemics from the seventeenth century, the first well-documented epidemic of what was probably streptococcal puerperal fever occurred in the Hôtel-Dieu in Paris in 1745, and the first known British epidemic took place at the British Lying-in Hospital in Brownlow Street in 1760.[3] In the eighteenth century, epidemic puerperal fever was for the first time recognized as a distinct disease, and for the first time treatises were devoted to the subject. At the end of the

---

* This paper was first read at the sixty-first annual meeting of the American Association for the History of Medicine, New Orleans, Louisiana, 6 May 1988. Research for this paper was conducted with the aid of a grant from the American Council of Learned Societies for 1986–87. I would like to thank Robert Kimbrough, Chief Professor of Infectious Diseases and Assistant Chief of Medicine of Good Samaritan Hospital, Portland, for advising me on current medical views about the transmission of streptococcal infection; Judith Schneid Lewis and Irvine Loudon for advice on the argument; Mary Pauli of the Clackamas County Library, Douglas Tallman of the Multnomah County Library, Jerome DeGraff of Portland State University Library, and the staff of the National Library of Medicine for providing material; and my husband, John DeLacy, for technical assistance.

[1] Nathaniel Hulme, *A Treatise on the Puerperal Fever* ... (1772), reprinted in *Essays on the Puerperal Fever and Other Diseases Peculiar to Women Selected from the Writings of British Authors Previous to the Close of the Eighteenth Century,* ed. Fleetwood Churchill (London: Sydenham Society, 1849), p. 66. (Essays found in Churchill's collection will hereafter be noted as FC.)

[2] John Leake, *Practical Observations on the Childbed Fever* (1772), FC, p. 117.

[3] For three seventeenth-century epidemics, see James Hawley Burtenshaw, "The fever of the puerperium (puerperal infection)," *New York Med. J.,* 1904, 79: 1073–78, 1134–38, 1189–94, 1234–38, and 80: 20–25 (pp. 1137–38). August Hirsch, in his *Handbook of Geographical and Historical Pathology,* trans. Charles Creighton, vol. 2 of 3 (London: New Sydenham Society, 1885), gives a table of epidemics (pp. 422–24), which lists a fourth. Both of them note the epidemic in Paris (1664).

century the first step was taken toward understanding its etiology when Alexander Gordon demonstrated that birth attendants could be carriers.[4]

Many historians have associated the rise of puerperal fever with the rise of the male obstetrician in general and the maternity hospital in particular. In a seminal article of 1965, Thomas McKeown and R. G. Brown wrote:

> When first introduced, and for many years after ... institutional confinement had an adverse effect on mortality.... with few exceptions hospital death rates were many times greater than those for related home deliveries.... it may be asked whether results of institutional delivery at the earlier period were equally bad. There is reason to believe that they were worse.[5]

Feminists soon adopted this argument. For example, Ann Oakley commented in 1980:

> The achievements of male obstetrics over those of female midwifery are ... argued ... from the double premise of male and medical superiority. More recent investigations ... are now revealing a different picture, in which the introduction of men ... brought special dangers to mothers and babies. The easier transmission of puerperal fever in male-run lying-in hospitals is one example; the generally careless and ignorant use of technology another. In Britain in the eighteenth and early nineteenth centuries many of the male midwives' innovations were often fatal.[6]

These contentions have been accepted by many historians,[7] but the available evidence has not been fully brought to bear on this issue.

---

[4] Alexander Gordon, *A Treatise on the Epidemic Puerperal Fever of Aberdeen* (1795), FC, pp. 445–500.

[5] Thomas McKeown and R. G. Brown, "Medical Evidence Related to English Population Changes in the Eighteenth Century," in *Population in History: Essays in Historical Demography*, ed. David V. Glass and D. E. C. Eversley (1965; reprint, London: Edward Arnold, 1969), pp. 287–88.

[6] Ann Oakley, *Women Confined* (Oxford: Martin Robertson, 1980), pp. 10–12. See also Barbara Katz Rothman, *In Labour: Women and Power in the Birthplace* (London: Junction Books; New York: W. W. Norton, 1982), pp. 52–55.

[7] See Gail Pat Parsons, "The British medical profession and contagion theory: puerperal fever as a case study, 1830–1860," *Med. Hist.*, 1978, *22*: 140–41; A. Clair Siddall, "Bloodletting in American obstetric practice, 1800–1945," *Bull. Hist. Med.*, 1980, *54*: 107; Cecilia C. Mettler, *History of Medicine* (Philadelphia, Pennsylvania: Blackiston, 1947), p. 907; David Charles and Bryan Larsen, "Streptococcal puerperal sepsis and obstetric infections: a historical perspective," *Rev. Infect. Diseases*, 1986, *8*: 411; Harold Speert, *Iconographia Gyniatrica: A Pictorial History of Gynecology and Obstetrics* (Philadelphia, Pennsylvania: F. A. Davis, 1973); Jean Donnison, *Midwives and Medical Men: A History of Inter-Professional Rivalries and Women's Rights* (New York: Schocken, 1977); Lawrence D. Longo, introduction to his recent edition of Charles White's *A Treatise on the Management of Pregnant and Lying-in Women* (London: Edward and Charles Dilly, 1773; reprint, Canton, Massachusetts: Science History Publications, 1987), p. ix; and Roderick E. McGrew and Margaret P. McGrew, *Encyclopedia of Medical History* (New York: McGraw-Hill, 1985), s.v. "Puerperal Fever" (pp. 291–92).

For the opposing view, see Edward Shorter, *A History of Women's Bodies* (New York: Basic Books, 1982), and *idem*, "The Management of Normal Deliveries and the Generation of William Hunter," in *William Hunter and the Eighteenth-Century Medical World*, ed. William F. Bynum and Roy Porter (Cambridge: Cambridge University Press, 1985), pp. 371–84. Shorter's article offers compelling evidence that midwives intervened routinely in normal labor in early modern Europe, to the extent of regularly removing the placenta manually immediately following birth. It also documents the increasingly conservative management of eighteenth-century obstetricians. My own research confirms Shorter's conclusions. Shorter anticipated the present paper by suggesting that the incidence of epidemic puerperal fever should be compared with the incidence of epidemics of streptococcal pharyngitis. See also Mabel C. Buer, *Health, Wealth, and Population in the Early Days of the Industrial Revolution* (1926; reprint, New York: Howard Fertig, 1968), pp. 139–47, and Irvine Loudon, "Deaths in childbed from the eighteenth century to 1935," *Med. Hist.*, 1986, *30*: 18.

Historians have cited the appalling rates of postpartum sepsis found in nineteenth-century institutions and have claimed that eighteenth-century rates could hardly have been any better. Even when eighteenth-century rates are cited, they are often averaged over periods of many years, thus obscuring changes that took place during the course of the century. Finally, some historians have accepted McKeown and Brown's dismissal of reported rates as "frankly incredible."[8]

This paper will reassess the incidence of puerperal fever in the eighteenth century to determine the relationship between the rise of the maternity hospital and maternal mortality. Part 1 discusses problems in defining and understanding the disease. Part 2 analyzes the timing of epidemics in maternity hospitals and concludes that the connection between the rise of the maternity hospital and the appearance of epidemic puerperal fever may have been indirect: other factors may have been involved, including a change in the incidence or virulence of the pathogens that caused puerperal fever. Part 3 examines maternal mortality figures and finds that there was a general improvement in mortality rates during the course of the century— an improvement that was more marked in hospital figures than in figures for home births. Part 4 argues that the development of contagionist disease theory may have helped fend off some epidemics in maternity hospitals toward the end of the century.

WHAT IS PUERPERAL FEVER?

It is easier to understand the difficulties and confusion that confronted the eighteenth-century physician if we realize that puerperal fever is still a disease in search of a satisfactory definition. Among historians there is a working understanding that puerperal fever is similar to, if not synonymous with, postpartum infection and involves some bacterial invasion of the birth canal following childbirth. On closer examination, however, a precise delineation of the disease becomes entangled in ambiguities and complexities. Following childbirth, women may coincidentally contract fevers from diseases such as typhoid or from bladder infections which are largely unrelated to any damage to their reproductive systems. (These fevers may still partly be a result of pregnancy and birth insofar as these events may depress immunity, expose patients to cross-infection, or disturb other parts of the body.) Furthermore, postpartum infection can result from a range of infective organisms, many of which may also cause other diseases. Some of these pathogens may cause illnesses such as trembling, heart disease, and arthritis: since these ailments are usually the result of other factors, the link between them and postpartum infection was not appreciated until very recently. In some cases the initial infection is silent and the damage appears

---

[8] McKeown and Brown, "Medical Evidence," p. 289.

later, or affects the child more than the mother. Some of these organisms usually come from outside the body, but some are endogenous: they are normal inhabitants of the female genital tract or of other parts of the body. Finally, women may experience ephemeral fevers that are unrelated to any identified infection and are possibly due to hormonal changes associated with parturition and lactation.[9]

Since postpartum infection in hospitals is notoriously a nosocomial (hospital-generated) disease, researchers face a further problem in the form of the reluctance of medical personnel to admit that it exists and thus accept responsibility for causing illness. The "fudge factor" caused by the inclination to assign cases of postpartum infection to some unrelated condition finally compelled British researchers to adopt a strict definition of puerperal fever based only on symptoms: "A fever of 100.4°F [or more] over a period of 24 or more hours during the three weeks after childbirth."[10] (Americans adopted a slightly different definition.) However, what is considered a relevant period after childbirth is still a problem, as it was in the eighteenth century, and this renders different series of postpartum morbidity and mortality rates incompatible. Modern hospitals frequently send patients home within one to four days after delivery and do not keep track of them thereafter. Moreover, this definition is not based on etiology and thus includes a large number of unrelated fevers. For example, an investigation at Queen Charlotte's Hospital in 1951 found 1,423 cases of fever associated with 2,701 deliveries, but only 141 of those cases were defined as "true genital tract infections."[11] Other researchers, attempting a more precise measurement, have relied on bacterial cultures, only to experience difficulties because of the large number of positive cultures in asymptomatic patients.

Postpartum infection, in the broad sense of any genital tract infection following childbirth, was a significant cause of maternal mortality in the eighteenth century. Estimates vary, but it may well have accounted for half of all maternal deaths. Because many of the causative organisms were endogenous or very common in the environment, women were often resistant to them and only became ill if they sustained extensive damage to the birth canal or excessive trauma. Although they might be fatal, these postpartum infections were also often mild. Because their incidence depended to a large degree on what happened in the course of a particular

[9] For general works on postpartum infection, see Sebastian Faro, ed., *Diagnosis and Management of Female Pelvic Infections in Primary Care Medicine* (Baltimore, Maryland: Williams and Wilkins, 1985), and William J. Ledger, *Infection in the Female*, 2d ed. (Philadelphia, Pennsylvania: Lea and Febiger, 1986). I would like to thank Michael Collins for supplying me with copies of these works. David Charles and Thomas A. Klein, "Postpartum Infection," in *Obstetric and Prenatal Infections*, ed. David Charles and Maxwell Finland (Philadelphia, Pennsylvania: Lea and Febiger, 1973), contains useful history but is now outdated.
[10] As cited in Loudon, "Deaths in childbed," p. 25.
[11] Leonard Colebrook, "Puerperal Infection," in J. M. Munro Kerr, R. W. Johnstone, and Miles H. Phillips, eds., *Historical Review of British Obstetrics and Gynecology, 1800–1950* (London: Livingstone, 1954), p. 224. See also Joan Taylor and H. D. Wright, "The nature and sources of infection in puerperal sepsis," *J. Obstet. Gyn. Brit. Empire*, 1930, n.s. 37: 213–32.

labor, they tended to be incidental or endemic rather than epidemic.[12] Every eighteenth-century obstetrician saw many women with fevers resulting from traumatic labors or from such problems as a retained placenta. In some cases, the midwife or physician introduced the infection, in other cases it came from the woman's own body or from her home, but these infections were a part of every practice. It was the frequency of such fevers which hindered the acceptance of the theories of Oliver Wendell Holmes and Ignaz Semmelweis in the next century, since many cases of these fevers could not be traced to carriers; nor could any common precautions eliminate puerperal infections entirely.[13]

When they spoke of puerperal fever, however, most eighteenth-century authors meant more than simply any infection or fever following childbirth. They described a characteristic pattern of symptoms which delineated the most severe and frequently epidemic form of the disease. Hulme, for example, wrote that puerperal fever "is as much an original or primary disease as the ague, quinsy, pleurisy, or any other complaint."[14] It could be distinguished from after-pains, from milk fever (resulting from engorgement and an infected breast), from miliary fever (probably typhoid), from ileus, from colic, from local infections of the uterus, and from cholera. Charles White distinguished it from a "simple inflammation."[15] In 1790, Joseph Clarke distinguished puerperal fever from ephemeral fevers lasting only twenty-four hours following birth, and he further distinguished between epidemic puerperal fever and the incidental fevers that resulted from inflammation.[16] John Leake also differentiated between incidental and infectious cases.[17]

Nevertheless, considerable confusion remained. Thomas Kirkland commented that the term *puerperal fever* could be applied to any fever arising in consequence of pregnancy or delivery and occurring during the lying-in period. The fever itself was merely a symptom, not a disease, and could result from a number of different causes such as an infected uterus or an absorption of putrid effluvia from outside. He added, however, that puerperal fever should not be confused with diseases such as smallpox and typhus coincidentally contracted by women in the period after delivery.[18] John Clarke complained in 1793 that:

> the name of puerperal fever having been given indiscriminately to every febrile disease attacking women in childbed, has thus become a source of much incon-

---

[12] Shorter, *History of Women's Bodies*, chap. 6.

[13] For the importance of Group B infections see Dorothy I. Lansing, W. Robert Penman, and Dorland J. Davis, "Puerperal fever and the Group B beta hemolytic streptococcus," *Bull. Hist. Med*, 1983, 57: 70–80, and J. Wister Meigs, "Puerperal fever and nineteenth-century contagionism: the obstetrician's dilemma," *Trans. Stud. Coll. Phys. Philadelphia*, 1975, 42(3): 273–80.

[14] Hulme, *Treatise*, FC, p. 61.

[15] White, *Treatise*, ed. Longo, p. 10.

[16] Joseph Clarke, *Observations on the Puerperal Fever, more especially as it has of late occurred in the Lying-in Hospital of Dublin* (1790), FC, pp. 351 and 362.

[17] Leake, *Practical Observations*, FC, p. 153.

[18] Thomas Kirkland, *A Treatise on Childbed Fevers and the Methods of Preventing Them* (1774), FC, p. 283.

venience. Practical men, misled by this false bias, have persuaded themselves that the form of disease, which respectively they may have most frequently met with, is the only one.[19]

Some medical writers also included diseases that, to a modern eye, do not belong. Thus, Kirkland and White both seem to have confused the disease on some occasions with typhus, and many if not all of the cases in William Butter's 1775 tract seem to have been due to worms or other intestinal infections.[20] There was also fierce argument over whether peritonitis or hysteritis was the more characteristic form of the disease.

Despite this uncertainty, most authors depicted a particular cluster of symptoms that they believed distinguished puerperal fever both from other epidemic diseases such as smallpox and from less severe postpartum infections such as mastitis or uterine abscesses. A typical attack of puerperal fever occurred shortly after birth, generally on the second, third, or fourth day. The shorter the interval between birth and onset, the more dangerous the disease. It began with chills and shivering and was accompanied by a fast pulse and headache. Intense abdominal pain was frequent but not invariable. The patient usually remained conscious and often showed great fear or despair. The face was often flushed and the patient took short, quick breaths. Thomas Denman, in 1768, seems to have been the first English author to comment on the "erysipelatous appearance" of the joints.[21] There might be vomiting or suppression of the milk or lochia. The fever was dangerous, killing most of those attacked, but there was some variation in its severity. Autopsies showed large accumulations of pus and fluid in the abdominal cavity with other signs of inflammation which might extend to the lungs. Epidemics were more common during the cold months of the year.

The insistence of many experienced physicians that puerperal fever was not a simple infection, a local inflammation, or an incidental fever; the symptoms they recorded, such as the sudden onset of a high fever and flushing; the very high mortality rate, the autopsy descriptions, and the epidemic incidence—all strongly suggest that most of these cases were caused by one particular pathogen out of the many that may cause postpartum infections: the Group A beta-hemolytic streptococcus. This caused the terrifying epidemics that led obstetricians to take drastic measures and to publish their experiences. As Edward Shorter has pointed out, however, these epidemics caused fewer deaths overall than the sporadic infections that were often caused by other organisms, including Group B streptococci.

[19] John Clarke, *Practical Essays on the Management of Pregnancy and Labour; and on the Inflammatory and Febrile Diseases of Lying-in Women* (1791), FC, p. 389.

[20] William Butter, *An Account of Puerperal Fevers as they appear in Derbyshire* ... (1775): "Worms, either alive or dead, frequently come away in the stools," and "This puerperal fever is so far from being of a peculiar nature, that it is exactly analogous to the worm fever so fatal to children" (FC, pp. 337 and 343).

[21] Thomas Denman, *An Essay on the Puerperal Fever* (1768), FC, p. 48.

Severe infection with Group B strains may cause symptoms that are difficult to distinguish clinically from symptoms of infection with Group A, but Group B is usually a sporadic, rather than an epidemic, infection.[22]

The group letters were assigned in the late 1920s by Rebecca Lancefield, who also developed a way to distinguish among different strains within Group A.[23] This made it possible for researchers to investigate the differences between the Group A strains that normally cause pharyngitis and those that cause impetigo. Pharyngeal strains of Group A are now known to cause several different diseases which on a cursory inspection would appear to be unrelated. They include wound infections and septicemia, puerperal fever, sore throat, scarlet fever, erysipelas, thrombophlebitis, pneumonia, rheumatic fever and carditis, subcutaneous nodules, erythema marginatum, and chorea. While both throat and skin strains may cause kidney disease, only the pharyngial strains normally cause rheumatic fever, which was sometimes called "acute rheumatism" or "acute arthritis" in the eighteenth century. Occasionally the skin strains are found in the throat. The throat and skin strains have a different incidence. Skin strains tend to occur in warm climates and in warm months. Throat strains, on the other hand, are common in colder climates, such as that of northern Europe, and in the colder months of the year. The more virulent a strain is, the more infectious it appears to be. Scarlet fever is caused by particular strains of streptococci, but the scarlet fever strains vary in their virulence.

Because infection with any virulent strain of the Group A streptococci confers permanent immunity to that strain and may confer resistance to some less virulent strains, streptococcal pharyngitis is primarily a disease of children. If a virulent strain is of an uncommon type, however, it will attack persons of all ages. The bacteria rapidly lose virulence outside the body, and there are no significant animal hosts except for cows, who may transmit the disease in milk. To spread, the bacteria therefore require direct contact between a susceptible host and an infected person or a healthy carrier. Many people may contract subclinical infections or become healthy carriers, and most of those who experience untreated infections will continue to carry the disease for several weeks in their noses or throats. There are healthy carriers who retain the disease indefinitely, for months and maybe years, in many parts of the body, including the fingernails. Following an epidemic that attacked twenty women in the Boston Hospital in 1965, epidemiologists found that about 5 percent of the hospital staff and 10 to 15

---

[22] See nn. 12 and 13.

[23] Most of the following two paragraphs paraphrases Gene H. Stollerman's *Rheumatic Fever and Streptococcal Infection* (New York: Grune and Stratton, 1975), pp. 12–100. See also Daniel M. Musher, "The grampositive cocci: I. Streptococci," *Hosp. Prac.*, 1988, *23*: 63–76. I would like to thank Robert Kimbrough for this reference, and the Infectious Diseases Department of the Oregon Health Sciences University for supplying a copy. See also Lewis W. Wannamaker, "The Streptococcal Siren," in *Infectious Disease Review*, ed. William J. Holloway, 10th Infectious Disease Symposium (New York: Futura Publishing, 1974), pp. 167–83.

percent of the neighboring community were asymptomatic carriers of hemolytic streptococci. Of the forty hospital carriers, four had positive throat cultures for Group A and one had a positive skin lesion.[24] Because it is a contact disease, streptococcal infection is closely related to urban crowding and poor housing conditions, and the rapid transfer of the disease from person to person under such circumstances results in especially virulent epidemics.

Lancefield's work also made it possible to trace individual cases of streptococcal infection to a probable source. In the 1930s, Dora Colebrook began a series of epidemiological investigations at Queen Charlotte's Hospital. She was able to culture pathogenic strains from many sources within the hospital, including dust, surgical gowns, and bedding. Several historians read this work and concluded that hospital fomites helped transmit the infection in the past, perhaps through airborne dust particles. For example, Leonard Colebrook wrote in 1954 of "dissemination through the air in dust particles, perhaps via bedding," and added that "streptococci could remain alive in dust and retain their virulence for several weeks."[25] Hospital administrators carried on a comprehensive campaign to expunge the bacteria from clothing, dust, and air. As late as 1973, David Charles and Thomas Klein wrote in a medical textbook:

> Postpartum staphylococcal and ... streptococcal infections ... are often airborne, either in droplets or dust. Viable bacteria can remain suspended in the air for long periods in minute droplets.... Larger droplets will contaminate the floor, bedside utensils, and fomites.... Inoculated dust may linger in the ward long after the source of contamination has departed, despite conventional floor mopping and waxing.... A more effective means of control is adequate ventilation.[26]

In fact, however, Colebrook had traced most actual infections to nasopharyngial carriers, not to hospital dirt. As high a proportion as half of all carriers may be asymptomatic. Following the Second World War, Charles Rammelkamp and his associates carried out a series of studies on airmen using streptococci found in the environment. They concluded that such bacteria do not remain viable for long outside the body.[27] Current infectious disease officers recommend a hospital practice that places less emphasis on the control of fomites and more emphasis on the isolation of carriers and the washing of hands between patients. This is designed to prevent the

[24] John Figgis Jewett et al., "Childbed fever: a continuing entity," *JAMA*, 1968, *206*: 344–50.
[25] Colebrook, "Puerperal Infection," in Kerr, Johnstone, and Phillips, eds., *Historical Review*, pp. 208–9 (quote on p. 209).
[26] Charles and Klein, "Postpartum Infection," p. 257.
[27] Stollerman, *Rheumatic Fever*, p. 15; and for Rammelkamp's group, see William Perry et al., "Transmission of Group A Streptococci: I. the role of contaminated bedding," *Amer. J. Hygiene*, 1957, *66*: 85–95.

direct transmission of infection from patient to patient and from attendant to patient.[28]

The unspoken comment of many historians on the physicians of the past seems to be "If only they had washed!" In fact, however, as Gail Parsons has pointed out, physicians who were carriers could have taken baths in chloride of lime without effect. Because carriers constantly recontaminate their own hands, handwashing, although essential, is not fully effective unless it is accompanied by methods to prevent recontamination such as the wearing of masks and gloves. Even after Ignaz Semmelweis instituted handwashing with chloride in Vienna, he experienced a maternal mortality rate of more than twenty-nine per thousand. The 1965 epidemic in Boston took place "without any evident breach of technique or good practice" and was traced to a small lesion on the hand of a physician-anesthetist.[29]

Even under the very different conditions in eighteenth-century hospitals, deficiencies in institutional cleanliness were probably overshadowed as a cause of infection by the presence of carriers and the extent of crowding in the wards. Once a case was introduced into a room, it would have required great luck and extraordinary vigilance to prevent the other patients in the room from contracting the infection, particularly since patients frequently tended to each other. Closing the ward entirely may have been the only effective measure available to eighteenth-century physicians. When a medical attendant became a carrier, even that course may not have been effective. Women could also contract the disease from infected children or visitors in their own homes, and some women brought the disease into the hospital with them.

THE INCIDENCE OF EPIDEMICS

The likelihood that cases would be introduced into hospitals depended in part on the prevalence and virulence of streptococcal infections in the surrounding community. Such infections were probably not new. There are several seventeenth-century descriptions of acute arthritis, a common symptom of rheumatic fever, which is caused by streptococcal infection. Sydenham's chorea, first described in 1686, is also a complication of rheumatic fever. Seventeenth-century accounts, however, suggest that at that time scarlet fever and other pharyngeal infections were usually mild.[30]

In the eighteenth century, England contained a much higher proportion

[28] F. D. Daschner, "The transmission of infections in hospitals by staff carriers: methods of prevention and control," editorial review in *Infect. Control*, 1985, 6: 97–99. Elaine Larson, "A causal link between handwashing and risk of infection? Examination of the evidence," *Infect. Control*, 1988, 9: 28–36, draws the same conclusion after a review of 423 articles published between 1879 and 1986.

[29] Parsons, "British medical profession," p. 148; Ignaz Semmelweis, *The Etiology, Concept, and Prophylaxis of Childbed Fever*, ed., abridged, and trans. K. Codell Carter (Madison: University of Wisconsin, 1983), p. 143 (my calculation for the rate for 1847–49); Jewett et al., "Childbed fever," p. 344.

[30] Stollerman, *Rheumatic Fever*, pp. 2–3.

of young children than it does now, and its increasing population was crowding into large urban slums; these conditions favored the development and spread of virulent streptococcal epidemics. Although it seems likely that most women had become immune to common strains by the time they reached childbearing age, eighteenth-century accounts suggest that new, more virulent strains were attacking a population not yet widely immune to those strains.[31]

These accounts are ambiguous because of the difficulties in diagnosis, either contemporary or retrospective. Even with bacterial cultures, streptococcal pharyngitis may be difficult to diagnose, and in the eighteenth century it was commonly mistaken for diphtheria, typhoid and miliary fever, viral pharyngitis, and even mold poisoning. Scarlet fever is more distinctive, however, and the characteristic raspberry red rash and subsequent desquamation make a retrospective verdict of streptococcal infection probable.

There was a severe and highly fatal diphtheria epidemic in New England in the 1730s which apparently included some scarlet fever cases. There were reports from England and Scotland of similar epidemics in the same decade. When "epidemic sore throat" appeared in London in 1746, however, English physicians clearly believed they were confronting a disease previously unknown to them. John Fothergill's classic *Account of the Sore Throat Attended with Ulcers* described the English disease precisely enough to make it possible for us to conclude that it was streptococcal pharyngitis.[32] Fothergill's book also broke new ground in emphasizing the contagious nature of the disorder and in recommending a more conservative therapy, replacing extensive bleedings with prescriptions of cinchona bark and fluids.[33]

---

[31] Charles Creighton, *A History of Epidemics in Britain* (1894), 2d ed., with additional material by D. E. C. Eversley, E. Ashworth Underwood, and Lynda Ovenall, 2 vols. (London: Frank Cass, 1965), *2*: 678–744, esp. p. 685. See also R. Hingston Fox in *Dr. John Fothergill and His Friends: Chapters in Eighteenth-Century Life* (London: Macmillan, 1919). Fox comments on p. 51: "Heberden, writing in 1782, considered it highly probable that the malignant sore throat was a form of scarlet fever. And this must be our verdict today." He adds that earlier epidemics in Spain and Italy were probably diphtheria. In the eighteenth century, there were occasional scarlet fever epidemics of varying type. By the nineteenth century, they were more common (occurring every few years), and they were of greater average severity and mortality. Perhaps in Fothergill's time, Fox concludes, the disease was in the process of development.

[32] John Fothergill, *An Account of the Sore Throat Attended with Ulcers* (1748), republished as *An Account of Putrid Sore Throat* in vol. 1 of *The Works of John Fothergill, M.D.*, ed. John Coakley Lettsom (London: Charles Dilly, 1783). I would like to thank the National Library of Medicine (NLM) for supplying me with a microfilm copy of this work.

[33] *Ibid.*, esp. pp. 403–4. Fothergill was widely credited by contemporaries for encouraging milder treatments for many fevers but particularly for scarlet fever. For example, George Aspinwall wrote in 1798: "Blood-letting, purging, and the antiphlogistic regimen, in general, were formerly adopted as an universal practice; no wonder the disease proved a fatal one.... Dr. Fothergill [*sic*] wrote the first treatise on this disorder in England, and proposed a more rational method of treating the disease.... He condemned blood-letting, and the antiphlogistic regimen, till which time the lancet proved as fatal as the guillotine in the days of Robespierre." *A Dissertation on the Cynanche Maligna* (Dedham, Massachusetts: Mann and Adams), p. 5. I would like to thank the NLM for supplying a microfilm copy of this work. "How many lives were lost," William Withering asked, "until Dr. Fothergill and Dr. Wall taught us to withhold the lancet and the purge?" *An Account of the Scarlet Fever and Sore Throat* (London, 1779; 2d ed., Birmingham, 1793), quoted in Fox, *Dr. John Fothergill*, p. 53.

Was there any significance in the simultaneity of the appearance of puerperal fever epidemics in maternity hospitals and the appearance of community scarlet fever or sore throat epidemics? An epidemiologist was able to show such a relationship for the late nineteenth century. In 1879, G. B. Longstaff compiled graphs of the incidence of eighty-nine diseases for the years 1859 to 1878. Based only on the resemblance of their curves, he concluded that there was a relationship between scarlatina, erysipelas, puerperal fever, and rheumatic carditis. The relationship between puerperal fever and erysipelas was particularly close, and scarlatina was similar to the other three except that its curve anticipated theirs by about five weeks.[34] Some eighteenth-century commentators also noted that these diseases were found together: "It is a curious circumstance," wrote the obstetrician John Clarke in 1791, "that before the attack of the epidemic of lying-in women at Paris in the year 1746, in the month of January there had been an epidemic low fever, with an ulcerous sore throat."[35]

To determine whether this "curious circumstance" occurred more than once, I have compared the known epidemics of "ulcerated sore throat" and "scarlet fever" with the hospital epidemics of puerperal fever. The results, if not conclusive, are at least suggestive. For the incidence of "sore throat" I used the accounts compiled in the chapter "Scarlatina and Diphtheria" in Charles Creighton's *History of Epidemics in Britain*. I have added a few other references.

Creighton conceded that it was difficult and perhaps pointless to attempt to distinguish between scarlet fever and diphtheria in many eighteenth-century accounts, but he added that

> whether the disease were malignant scarlatina, or diphtheria, or a mixture of the two ... it was certainly new as a whole to British experience in that generation [of the middle third of the century], and, if we except the reference by Morton to certain cases which may have been sporadic, it was a disease hitherto unheard of in England since systematic medical writings began.[36]

In fact, Creighton did engage in retrospective diagnosis, and I have tried to follow his assessments. For the incidence of puerperal fever, I followed Fleetwood Churchill's introduction to the Sydenham Society's collection of eighteenth-century tracts on puerperal fever.

The accounts show that episodes of sore throat occurred in fairly well-defined epidemics. With each epidemic, physicians became more precise in their classification. London experienced such epidemics in 1746–48, 1751–52, 1755, 1770, 1772–73, 1777–78, and 1785–94. By 1796, "scarla-

---

[34] G. B. Longstaff, "On some statistical indications of a relationship between scarlatina, puerperal fever, and certain other diseases," *Trans. Epidemiol. Soc. London*, 1879, 4: 421–30. I would like to thank Leonard G. Wilson for sending me a copy of this work.

[35] Clarke, *Practical Essays*, FC, p. 418.

[36] Creighton, *History of Epidemics*, 2: 702.

tina" seems to have become endemic. There was also an epidemic at the Foundling Hospital in 1763 which may have been measles. Epidemics took place in Sheffield in 1745, in Hertfordshire, Kidderminster, and Worcester in 1748–50, possibly in Plymouth in 1750–53, in Ireland in the 1750s, in Somerset in 1757, and in Yorkshire in 1759–60. No further reports appeared until 1770 in Manchester and 1771–72 in Ipswich, followed by an epidemic in 1777–79 in the areas around London, north Scotland, the Midlands, Newcastle, and Carlisle. In 1788 sore throat was reported in Buckinghamshire. This seems to have been streptococcal pharyngitis, but a report in 1793, this time of "croup," probably referred to diphtheria. With the exception of the area around London, England seems to have escaped without a serious epidemic between the late 1780s and 1801, but there were reports of "putrid sore-throat" in the North of Scotland, including Aberdeenshire, in 1790 and 1791.[37]

We know less about Ireland. James Sims, who practiced in County Tyrone from about 1764 until 1773, claimed he had not seen one instance of the malignant ulcerous sore throat as described by authors. Nevertheless, he reported epidemics of erysipelas in 1765–67 and 1772 and of "acute rheumatism" in 1767–68. John Rutty described what seems to have been diphtheria in 1743 and 1755 but what was referred to as "scarlet fever" in the winter of 1759–60.[38]

Between 1801 and 1805 severe sore throat epidemics were reported from such areas as Cornwall, Northampton, Cheltenham, Derby, Framlingham, Lancaster, Manchester, Liverpool, Yorkshire, and Edinburgh. In Dublin such an epidemic coincided with an epidemic of puerperal fever at the Rotunda in 1803. By the mid-nineteenth century, among the infectious childhood diseases, scarlet fever had become the leading cause of death. It was particularly fatal in England's large cities and industrial areas.[39]

Puerperal fever also occurred in epidemics. These epidemics were rarely confined to a single hospital. Reports of epidemics from widely scattered places throughout the British Isles and the Continent tend to cluster in a few "bad years," which also suggests that something other than conditions in individual institutions was involved. The first reported English epidemic of puerperal fever began in June 1760 in the British Lying-in Hospital in London and lasted until the end of December. The following spring, another London lying-in hospital experienced a fatal epidemic.[40] Maternal mortality rates in the city exceeded eighteen per thousand in 1761 and

---

[37] The 1770 Manchester epidemic is from Thomas Percival, *Observations on the State of Population in Manchester* (1789), reprinted in *Population and Disease in Early Industrial England*, ed. Bernard Benjamin (n.p.: Gregg International, 1973), p. 6. All others are from Creighton, *History of Epidemics*, 2: 678–722.

[38] James Sims, *Observations on Epidemic Disorders, with remarks on nervous and malignant fevers ...* (London, 1773), pp. 57–58 and 86; for Rutty, see Creighton, *History of Epidemics*, 2: 694.

[39] Creighton, *History of Epidemics*, 2: 719–28.

[40] Unless otherwise noted, all puerperal fever epidemics are listed in FC, pp. 3–42.

1762, the highest of the century, which suggests that these hospital epidemics were part of a larger epidemic in the city (see table 2). St. Thomas's Hospital experienced an epidemic of erysipelas in 1760 so severe it was rumored to be the plague, compelling the Governors to publish denials in the newspapers.[41] Sore throat epidemics were not reported for London in those years, but there was a puerperal fever epidemic in Aberdeen in 1760 and there were reports of sore throat in Yorkshire in 1761. The next London puerperal fever epidemic began in the late fall of 1769 and continued into 1771. It affected at least three hospitals and domiciliary births in the city, as well. There were sore throat epidemics in both London and Manchester in 1769–70.

There was only one more puerperal fever epidemic reported in London during the eighteenth century, in 1787–88. John Clarke wrote of this period that "in the year [sic] 1787 and 1788, the same year in which the disease seems to have been prevalent in Dublin, it was also exceedingly general through the whole of this country, but more especially in London, and in hospitals."[42] Indeed, the decade between 1784 and 1794 was a bad one throughout Europe, with epidemics in Vienna (1784), Copenhagen (1786), Lombardy (1786–87), Poitiers (1787), Aberdeen (1789–92), again in Copenhagen (1791–92), again in Vienna (1792–93), and in Amsterdam (1793), Rouen (1793), and Stockholm (1793 and 1794).[43] These coincided with sore throat epidemics in London in 1785–94 and Buckinghamshire in 1788, "acute arthritis" in Dublin in 1787, and "sore throat" in Aberdeenshire in 1790–91.[44] The records of the Aberdeen Dispensary, which were compiled by Alexander Gordon, show a high number of cases of erysipelas and sore throat in 1791 and of scarlet fever in 1792, when compared with the following two years. Gordon himself noted the connection between puerperal fever and erysipelas.[45]

There are two further possible puerperal fever epidemics in London. Fleetwood Churchill included 1783 in his table of puerperal fever epidemics, but I have not been able to find any further references to an epidemic in that year in the text of his book, either in his introduction or the treatises that follow, several of which include historical surveys.[46] I am therefore inclined to discard this as a printer's error. I am also discarding an

---

[41] William C. Wells, "Observations on erysipelas," *Trans. Soc. Improving Med. Chir. Knowledge,* 1800, 2: 213–28, esp. 218–19.

[42] John Clarke, *Practical Essays,* FC, p. 414.

[43] Hirsch, *Handbook,* 2: 422–24. A previously unknown puerperal fever epidemic in the Vaugirard hospital in 1791 is reported in Mireille Laget, "Childbirth in Seventeenth- and Eighteenth-Century France: Obstetrical Practices and Collective Attitudes," in *Medicine and Society in France: Selections from the Annales,* ed. Robert Forster and Orest Ranum, trans. Elborg Forster and Patricia M. Ranum, vol. 6 (Baltimore, Maryland: Johns Hopkins University Press, 1980), p. 151.

[44] The "acute arthritis" in Dublin is from Joseph Clarke, *Observations,* FC, p. 354.

[45] Gordon, *Treatise,* FC, pp. 499–500.

[46] See FC, p. 31. That year saw one of the lowest maternal mortality rates for London in the century, 8.5 per thousand.

account by William Butter of the "puerperal fever" that appeared in Derbyshire between 1765 and 1775 because I do not believe from his account that he saw cases of streptococcal puerperal fever. Including these years would not affect the conclusion, however. The records of the British Lying-in also show unusually high mortality rates in 1774 and 1775: the death rate in 1773 was 6.3, but in 1774 it was 32.3 (see table 3). This followed a sore throat epidemic in London in 1772–73, and coincided with epidemics of severe puerperal fever in Paris and Dublin in 1774–75. The British Lying-in also experienced "bad years" in 1781–82 and 1784, when the mortality rate rose above twenty per thousand. This evidence is ambiguous: fourteen women died in 1781 compared with eight the previous year; with numbers this small the additional deaths could be due to bad luck or isolated fever cases. About five hundred women a year were delivered by the British Lying-in, about 3 percent of all the women delivered in the city of London.

To summarize: there were three reported London puerperal fever epidemics, in 1760–61, 1769–71, and 1787–88. Possibly there was an epidemic in 1774–75, and less possibly one in 1783. In Scotland, there were epidemics in Aberdeen in 1760 and 1789–92 and in the Edinburgh Infirmary in 1773. The London epidemic of 1760–61 coincided with "sore throat" reported in Yorkshire and Sheffield but not in London, with "scarlet fever" in Ireland, with erysipelas in a London hospital, and with the Aberdeen puerperal fever epidemic. The London epidemic of 1769–71 coincided with "sore throat" epidemics in London and Manchester. The London epidemic of 1787–88 coincided with a sore throat epidemic in London. The possible epidemic of 1774–75 followed a London sore throat epidemic in 1773. Both Aberdeen epidemics coincided with reports of sore throat, one rather far away, in North Yorkshire, the other in Aberdeenshire itself. The Edinburgh epidemic of 1773 is the exception, since there are no reports of sore throat from Scotland or even the North of England during this period. However, it may have been part of a pandemic that included sore throat in London in 1773 and puerperal fever epidemics in London, Dublin, and Paris in 1774–75. This epidemic was especially disastrous in Paris, where it attacked seven out of every twelve women who delivered and subsequently became endemic.[47]

The Rotunda in Dublin experienced between three and four epidemics in the eighteenth century, in 1767, 1774, and 1787 and 1788, depending on whether the latter two are counted as one or two epidemics.[48] As seen above, the 1774 epidemic and that of 1787–88 coincided with other puerperal fever epidemics. The 1767 epidemic coincided with reports of erysip-

---

[47] FC, pp. 8–9. The Edinburgh Infirmary also experienced an epidemic of erysipelas in 1773, but the disease did not appear in the town (FC, p. 226).

[48] O'Donel T. D. Browne, *The Rotunda Hospital, 1745–1945* (Edinburgh: E. and S. Livingstone; Baltimore: Williams and Wilkins, 1947). See also Joseph Clarke, *Observations,* FC, pp. 351–62.

elas and acute rheumatism in County Tyrone. The 1787 epidemic coincided with "acute arthritis" in Dublin. There was also an epidemic in 1803 which coincided with reports of scarlatina throughout the British Isles.[49]

The small number of hospital epidemics in the eighteenth century is in itself surprising, because the secondary literature suggests that hospital epidemics were a constant problem. I am inclined to believe that hospital epidemics of puerperal fever were in fact unusual events in Britain and did not account for a large number of deaths, and that few significant epidemics in major cities escaped comment. Comparing the London hospital reports with the total maternal mortality for the city (see below), one finds the two series to be very similar, increasing the persuasiveness of each. The London reports can also be compared with the comprehensive set of records for the Rotunda.

Comments from obstetricians of the time also suggest that puerperal fever epidemics were unusual in the eighteenth century. For example, Alexander Gordon wrote that puerperal fever was unknown in Aberdeen between the epidemics of 1760 and 1789–92, and that he was the only physician in the city who could recognize a case, because he had seen it in London.[50] Charles White, who had practiced in Manchester for more than twenty years, commented in 1773 that he had never lost a patient to puerperal fever following a natural labor, and that such fevers had greatly decreased.[51] His assertion is borne out by the fragmentary mortality data for Manchester.[52] (Both Gordon and White, however, refer to a much less dangerous affliction known in the North as "the Weed.")[53] "Happily for the Fair sex, it does not often occur," commented the statistician William Black in 1789.[54]

Some historians believe that the low hospital mortality rates from eighteenth-century British institutions were simply falsified.[55] This undoubtedly happened occasionally. White wrote of the London epidemic of 1760–61 that:

> a gentleman whose veracity I can depend on ... attended a small private lying-in hospital ... he himself delivered six women in a short time ... and they all died:

[49] FC, p. 12; Creighton, *History of Epidemics*, 2: 721.

[50] Gordon, *Treatise*, FC, pp. 445–500, esp. pp. 447–48. On Gordon, see Ian Porter, *Alexander Gordon, M.D. of Aberdeen, 1752–1799* (London: Oliver and Boyd, 1958).

[51] White, *Treatise*, ed. Longo, p. 64. On White, see J. George Adami, *Charles White of Manchester (1728–1813) and the Arrest of Puerperal Fever* (Liverpool and New York: Paul B. Hoeber, 1923), and Charles J. Cullingworth, *Charles White, F.R.S., a Great Provincial Surgeon and Obstetrician of the Eighteenth Century* (London: H. J. Glaister, 1904).

[52] White, *Treatise*, ed. Longo, p. 138; and see Percival, *Observations*, p. 7: "Puerperal diseases also decrease every year amongst us."

[53] "The Weed" seems to have been an ephemeral fever.

[54] William Black, *An Arithmetical and Medical Analysis of the Diseases and Mortality of the Human Species*, 2d ed. (London: Charles Dilley, 1789), p. 217. I would like to thank the NLM for supplying me with a microfilm copy of this work.

[55] See McKeown and Brown, "Medical Evidence," p. 289.

he was so shocked with the loss that he desired the gentleman who had the care of the hospital to deliver some of those who should next be in labour, which he did, but they met with no better fate. They buried two women in one coffin, to conceal their bad success.

White adds, however, "Several gentlemen of the faculty were invited to the hospital to inquire into the cause of this great fatality"—so apparently it was no secret to the profession.[56] Efforts at concealment became more subtle as time went on. At the beginning of the next century, a Master of the Rotunda was dismissed for sending women ill of puerperal fever home to die. Near the end of the century, American clinics simply bribed infected pregnant women to have their babies elsewhere.[57]

Nevertheless, as a group, eighteenth-century hospital statistics are in line with each other and with statistics from other sources, such as urban maternal mortality rates. Moreover, there is no reason to believe that hospital administrators were more anxious to conceal the presence of puerperal fever in the eighteenth century, when it seemed to appear inexplicably, than in the nineteenth century, when the administrators had at least some cause for suspecting that they themselves were to blame, or even in the twentieth century, when puerperal fever was universally conceded to be a preventable, nosocomial disease. Dishonesty may explain why all the figures are lower than they should be, but dishonesty is probably randomly distributed: there is no reason for believing that eighteenth-century English hospitals were unique in "fudging" their rates.

If puerperal fever epidemics appeared infrequently in British hospitals in the eighteenth century and usually coincided with the appearance of particularly virulent community streptococcal infections, then the traditional argument that puerperal fever was caused by the rise of the maternity hospital and of the male midwife with his autopsies, forceps, and dirty hands should be reconsidered. That simultaneous puerperal fever epidemics took place in widely separated places also suggests that something other than the practices of a particular physician or the cleanliness of a particular hospital was involved. It may have been a coincidence that more virulent strains of streptococci appeared in England in the second half of the eighteenth century, just about the time many maternity hospitals were established. These events may be causally linked, but probably because they are closely related to a third factor: changes in living conditions and particularly in the extent of urbanization, which made obstetrics more lucrative and hence attractive to male practitioners. The poverty and overcrowding that compelled women to enter a hospital also contributed to the virulence and infectiousness of the bacteria. The case is not conclusive, but it is sufficient to raise doubts about the traditional explanation. Maternity hospitals in the eigh-

[56] White, *Treatise,* FC, pp. 232–33.
[57] Lansing, Penman, and Davis, "Puerperal fever," p. 75.

teenth century may have magnified epidemics, but they do not seem to have caused them.

MATERNAL MORTALITY

We will now turn from consideration of the number and timing of puerperal fever epidemics to an examination of the effect of these epidemics on total maternal mortality. Was puerperal fever killing a large number of women? Was its impact on mortality rates increasing? Did an increased risk of fever make hospital deliveries much more dangerous than home births? Recent work, including articles by Irvine Loudon and Edward Shorter, has argued persuasively that during the course of the eighteenth century the overall maternal mortality rate fell substantially, and that this trend was due in large part to improvements in obstetrical care.[58] It seems evident that this overall reduction could not have occurred without a reduction in the rate of postpartum infection. My own research fully bears out Shorter's assertion that birth attendants, whether male or female, were intervening less frequently in normal labor and were intervening more successfully in preternatural labor. It seems likely that this resulted not only in fewer deaths during labor but also in fewer deaths from infection following labor.

The overall trend can be seen in maternal mortality rates for the city of London. From the Bills of Mortality, Audrey Eccles obtained a rate of 21 per thousand in the second half of the seventeenth century.[59] Estimates from the Bills of Mortality reveal a rate of about 15 per thousand in the first decade of the eighteenth century, about 13 per thousand in the middle of the century, and about 9 per thousand in the last decade of the century (table 1).[60] This picture is not atypical for England as a whole or for Europe, although there were, of course, local variations. Some healthy villages with skilled midwives had achieved rates as low as 4 per thousand much earlier, but rates of between 10 and 20 per thousand were common, as was a decline by the end of the century. For example, Shorter has found a rate of 12 per thousand in Berlin before 1784, falling after that to 7.[61] Sweden had a death rate of between 8 and 10 per thousand in the second half of the century.[62] Manchester had a slightly better record: its rate, as reported by Charles White,

---

[58] See n. 7.

[59] Audrey Eccles, "Obstetrics in the seventeenth and eighteenth centuries and its implications for maternal and infant mortality," *Bull. Soc. Social Hist. Med.,* 1977, *20:* 8–11, cited in Shorter, *History of Women's Bodies,* pp. 98–99, and Loudon, "Deaths in childbed," pp. 13–14.

[60] My calculations are from William Heberden, *Observations on the Increase and Decrease of Different Diseases, and Particularly of the Plague* (London, 1801), reprinted in Benjamin, ed., *Population and Disease in Early Industrial England* (see appendix and table notes).

[61] Shorter, *History of Women's Bodies,* pp. 98–99. Shorter has added estimates for abortive and stillborn births to the denominator for this series.

[62] Ulf Högberg and Stig Wall, "Secular trends in maternal mortality in Sweden from 1750 to 1980," *Bull. World Health Org.,* 1986, *64:* 79–84.

was under 10 per thousand in the 1750s and 5.1 per thousand in 1771.[63] Edinburgh's rate was 14 in the 1750s and 6 in the 1790s.[64] By the mid-nineteenth century, the rate throughout Europe and Great Britain was between 4 and 5 per thousand.[65]

It is difficult to see how rates that low could be achieved without frequent and successful medical intervention, by either midwives or obstetricians. Loudon estimated that the death rate in unattended deliveries might have been between 25 and 30 per thousand deliveries.[66] Shorter does not provide a clear estimate, but his data suggest a higher rate. By the end of the eighteenth century the reported mortality rate for all deliveries was one-third to one-sixth that amount. Even when we allow for substantial inaccuracies in the rates, therefore, both the trend and the absolute magnitude suggest that the obstetrical revolution was contributing to improved outcomes. As Loudon commented:

> How was it possible for maternal mortality rates as low or lower than the national rates of the 1920s and early 1930s to be achieved before the introduction of anaesthesia, antisepsis, or twentieth-century methods? The answer is probably that the management of normal labour, and of the common complications, although remarkably poor at the beginning of the eighteenth century, was remarkably good ... at the end.[67]

In hospitals, however, the story was very different. Continental hospitals in the nineteenth century were very dangerous places. The worst record was possibly that of the Paris Maternité, which in the years between 1861 and 1864 achieved an astounding maternal mortality rate of 184 per thousand.[68] Women must have been desperate indeed to face a nearly one-in-five chance of dying in each labor. Other European hospitals also experienced in bad years rates well in excess of one hundred per thousand, and in 1866 the average rate for a large number of European hospitals was 34.2 per thousand. Thus, a "typical" maternity patient in the mid-nineteenth century faced a chance of dying in hospital approximately seven times greater than the risk she would encounter in a home delivery. Nineteenth-century British hospital maternal mortality rates were considerably lower

---

[63] White, *Treatise*, ed. Longo, p. 138. White divided the deaths of mothers in childbirth by the figure for christenings without adding in an estimate for children dead before christening, the "abortive and stillbirth" figure. That is why his figure for London is slightly higher than Shorter's. Longo, in his introduction to White's *Treatise*, has printed a useful table of White's data (pp. xvi–xvii). The table includes a figure for the Manchester infirmary, but as far as I can tell from the text, White's figures for the infirmary are for all infirmary patients and have nothing to do with maternal mortality.

[64] Shorter, *History of Women's Bodies*, p. 99.

[65] William Gilliatt, "Maternal Mortality—Still-birth and Neonatal Mortality," in Kerr, Johnstone, and Phillips, *Historical Review*, pp. 264–65.

[66] Loudon, "Deaths in childbed," p. 18.

[67] *Ibid.*

[68] Gilliatt, "Maternal Mortality," in Kerr, Johnstone, and Phillips, *Historical Review*, pp. 264–65; Burtenshaw, "Fever of the puerperium," p. 1191 (for maternal mortality at the Maternité); Buer, *Health, Wealth, and Population*, p. 270.

than this, but they still rose on occasion to between 30 and 80 per thousand.[69]

The question is whether, as McKeown and Brown argued, hospital mortality rates in the eighteenth century were no better and probably much worse than these nineteenth-century rates. Was the advent of the hospital itself responsible for these tragic events? Charles White believed that hospitals did indeed increase the risk to mothers. In his *Treatise on the Management of Pregnant and Lying-in Women* (1773) he commented that "the fatality that attends the patients in some of the lying-in hospitals greatly exceeds that of any private practice, at least any that I have been acquainted with."[70] White then provided mortality figures for four unnamed London hospitals, figures that have been widely cited by historians. My tentative identifications of these hospitals are in parentheses in what follows. "A public lying-in Hospital" (Westminster Hospital) had a rate of 25.7 between 1767 and 1772. "Another Hospital" (the British Lying-in) had a rate of 21.5 for the period between 1749 and 1770 but 39.3 for 1770 itself. "Another Hospital" (possibly the Middlesex Hospital Lying-in wards) had a rate of 19.5 for 1747–72 and 35.4 for 1771. The last (the General Lying-in Hospital in Store Street) had a rate of 7.6 for 1767–72.[71] White, however, was writing immediately after the epidemic of 1770–71, which was one of the worst years of the century for the hospitals. His longer-term rates of about 20 per thousand may be compared with rates for the city of London and the Rotunda of between 10 and 15 per thousand for the middle of the century. This suggests that in London, hospital deliveries were somewhat more dangerous than home births in the 1760s and 1770s, but the figures are heavily weighted by the epidemics of 1760 and 1770–71 and tell us little about comparative risk in other years. There is a further difficulty with White's figures: his figure of 35 women of 890 who died in 1770, a figure that is also quoted by Fleetwood Churchill for the British Lying-in. "Another Hospital from its first institution in November 1749" can only be the British Lying-in, but the numbers themselves are considerably at variance with those of the hospital's own reports, which were published by William Heberden.[72] These are 28 dead of 472 delivered in 1770. Since the British Lying-in never had as many patients in one year as 890, White either is in error or is combining data from various years.

Additional information can be obtained from other sources. William Heberden published rates taken from the reports of the British Lying-in Hospital, which opened in 1749. These can be compared with rates for the city of London, the Rotunda in Dublin, and the Vienna Hospital maternity

[69] Gilliatt, "Maternal Mortality," in Kerr, Johnstone, and Phillips, *Historical Review*, pp. 261–63, 265.
[70] White, *Treatise*, ed. Longo, p. 135.
[71] *Ibid.*
[72] "The Account of the Women Delivered, and Children Born, in the British Lying-in Hospital from ... 1749 ... 1801," in Heberden, *Observations*, pp. 39–41.

wards. Annual figures are also available for the City of London Lying-in Hospital after 1790 (see table 1; see appendix for my sources).

How credible are these rates? The London rates are based on the "childbed" rates compiled from the London Bills of Mortality by William Heberden, a close friend of Fothergill's.[73] Heberden published maternal mortality rates as a percentage of all deaths: he did not give the total number of maternal deaths. I have recalculated them to give the maternal death rate in proportion to the number of christenings. All contemporary authors complained about the inadequacy of the London data. The main complaint was that the "searchers" who assigned the cause of death did not know what they were doing and came up with strange diagnoses such as "rising of the lights." There were also, however, intractable technical problems having to do with shifts in the urban population, undercounting of Dissenters (particularly in the case of christenings), and the removal of many infants from the city. Several authors complained that cases of postpartum infection were frequently misdiagnosed as other diseases such as measles. Despite these shortcomings, the London figures do at least provide an internally consistent long series.

The London figures compare the number of maternal deaths to the number of christenings. Multiple births increased the number of christenings relative to the number of mothers (the rate of multiple births at the British Lying-in was about twelve per thousand; applied to the entire city, that rate would yield about two hundred additional births). On the other hand, the large number of stillbirths and neonatal deaths lowered the number of christenings relative to the number of mothers, as did the rapid removal of infants from the city and the avoidance of Anglican christenings by Dissenters. Black estimated the "abortive and stillbirth" figure at about seven hundred a year, which would reduce the death rate in table 1 by a little less than one death per thousand. Both the practice of removing infants from London and the avoidance of christenings seem to have increased in the course of the century. It seems likely, therefore, that the real reduction in the rates in this period would have been greater than the recorded change.

---

[73] Heberden, *Observations*. There are significant discrepancies between Table I, "Of the Annual Christenings and burials in London for each Year of the Eighteenth Century; Together with the Proportion out of every Thousand, who have died by Bowel Complaints, Small Pox, Palsy, Measles, or Childbirth—from the Bills of Mortality," and Table II, "Of Ten different Articles extracted from the London Weekly Bills of Mortality, shewing their Variations every Week for Ten Years."

James Young, "Journals, 1800–1950," in Kerr, Johnstone, and Phillips, *Historical Review*, on pp. 324–25, supplies a series taken from the *London Medical and Physical Journal* for 1816 (vol. 36), which in turn took them from the Bills of Mortality. This supplies ten-year average mortality rates for London. Comparing these figures with my calculations from Heberden's annual rates yielded rates that were very similar to those of Heberden, but slightly lower. The difference varied, but it averaged about 0.6 per thousand births. No details are supplied, but this discrepancy is presumably because the *London Medical and Physical Journal* series used the same data as Heberden but added a figure for the "stillborn and abortive" births. I would like to hear from anyone who can account for the discrepancies in Heberden's rates, correct the Bills of Mortality figures for maternal mortality, or supply additional data.

Table 1. Maternal Mortality, Four Maternity Hospitals and London
(Five-Year Averages: Deaths)

	British Lying-in (deaths per 1,000 births)	City of London Lying-in (deaths per 1,000 deliveries)	Rotunda, Dublin (deaths per 1,000 deliveries)	Vienna Maternity (deaths per 1,000 births)	London (deaths per 1,000 christenings)
1750–54	32.5		15.1*		12.8
1755–59	14.7		14.9		13.2
1760–64	30.7		14.3		16.7
1765–69	11.4		14.8		12.7
1770–74	20.6		8.6		12.2
1775–79	15.3		8.0		11.4
1780–84	19.2				9.6
1785–89	12.4		12.3	5.7	10.5
1790–94	3.9	5.3	10.7	10.7	9.3
1795–99	3.0	4.6	6.0	9.2	9.0
1800–1804	4.6**	5.6	14.1	8.5	9.4‡
1805–1809		4.1	6.4	7.2	9.4
1810–14			14.0	16.9	9.1‡
1815–19			13.1	19.9	
1820–24			14.1	33.9	
1825–29			17.0	54.1	
1830–34		6.8†	7.5	52.9	
1835–39		17.3†	17.0	60.6	
1840–44		7.6†	10.4	100.8	
1845–49		27.7†	19.1	55.6	

SOURCES: The London figures are my calculations from Heberden, *Observations*, whose figures are from the London Bills of Mortality. See also appendix.

* 1758–59

** Figure for 1800–1807 from Buer, *Health, Wealth, and Population.*

† Figures for 1830–49 from *138th Report of the City of London Lying-in Hospital.*

‡ London Bills of Mortality for 1801–10 and 1811–14 from Young, "Journals," Kerr, Johnstone, and Phillips, *Historical Review*, p. 325.

23

Whatever their inadequacies, these rates are comparable to those of Edinburgh in the 1750s which were quoted by a modern demographer, somewhat higher than those of Edinburgh in the 1770s and 1790s, and higher than those of Manchester and Northampton which were quoted by Charles White.[74] When these rates are compared year by year with those of the British Lying-in, a complex story emerges (tables 2 and 3). From 1751 until 1755 the British Lying-in rates were much higher than those for the city: overall they were about twice as high. From 1756 until 1788 they fluctuated far more than did the city rates. In many years they were similar to or lower than city rates, but in epidemic years they rose much higher.

Although the average death rate was higher in the British Lying-in, most of the excess mortality was due to increased mortality in the years 1760–61, 1770, 1774–75, 1781–82, and 1784. If we use non-epidemic years as a guide to the overall level of obstetrical care at the hospital, then for most of the second half of the century it was comparable to that in the city as a whole. Even in its worst years, the British Lying-in had a good record compared with that of nineteenth-century hospitals.

There is some evidence that the British Lying-in and other hospitals took higher-risk cases. A report of 1805 commented, "Women who are the most deformed or who are in very bad health, in general take the most pains to procure letters of admission. . . . Many would have died of disease, if they had not been with child."[75] And John Clarke noted:

> It has been remarked, in the way of objection to lying-in hospitals, that the disease has not been so frequent among the poorer classes of women, who are delivered at their own habitations; but it is to be remembered that their situation is hardly ever so distressed as that of those who are the general objects of charity in hospitals; —women without a home, without friends, without husbands, without protection, and without the common necessaries of life before they were admitted.[76]

City death rates also increased in epidemic years, but not nearly by the same amount, increasing by about 5 per thousand instead of by 50. The epidemics of 1760–61, 1770, and 1787 appear clearly in the rates (table 2). Some of this increase is due to the very high rates of death in the hospitals in epidemic years. Between about 15,000 and 19,000 children were christened in London each year. Each 15 to 20 hospital deaths, therefore, would push the overall city death rate up by 1 per thousand. In the 1760 epidemic,

---

[74] Shorter, *History of Women's Bodies*, pp. 98–99.

[75] Cited in Buer, *Health, Wealth, and Population*, p. 145.

[76] John Clarke, *Practical Essays*, FC, p. 433. See also *An Account of the British Lying-in Hospital for Married Women . . . 1749–1763* (London: C. Say, 1763): "Of the 121 women who have died in the Hospital, most of them came in not only under Circumstances of Distress and Poverty, in common with the Rest of the Patients, but also afflicted with dangerous Disorders, exclusive of their State of Pregnancy" (p. 15). Like the other maternity hospitals, the British Lying-in officially barred women with contagious diseases.

Table 2. Maternal Mortality, London
(Deaths per Thousand Christenings)

1701	14.3	1725	14.1	1750	15.8	1775	10.8
1702	14.2	1726	13.1	1751	12.0	1776	11.2
1703	14.1	1727	12.3	1752	10.6	1777	12.2
1704	16.7	1728	12.9	1753	11.4	1778	10.1
1705	17.8	1729	14.6	1754	14.6	1779	12.7
1706	15.4	1730	15.6	1755	13.7	1780	11.5
1707	16.0	1731	14.6	1756	12.1	1781	12.3
1708	15.4	1732	12.5	1757	12.7	1782	8.1
1709	14.0	1733	17.2	1758	13.1	1783	8.5
1710	14.5	1734	15.5	1759	14.2	1784	7.9
1711	13.2	1735	11.6	1760	15.9	1785	9.3
1712	13.3	1736	12.4	1761	18.4	1786	11.3
1713	11.1	1737	16.8	1762	18.2	1787	12.5
1714	17.6	1738	16.1	1763	17.1	1788	10.1
1715	16.1	1739	16.2	1764	14.1	1789	9.7
1716	13.2	1740	15.2	1765	15.3	1790	7.9
1717	13.1	1741	17.4	1766	12.5	1791	8.6
1718	14.3	1742	15.0	1767	11.0	1792	10.4
1719	15.9	1743	11.9	1768	13.3	1793	9.9
1720	14.8	1744	13.0	1769	11.2	1794	9.8
1721	16.4	1745	14.2	1770	16.0	1795	8.1
1722	16.0	1746	13.1	1771	10.5	1796	10.8
1723	15.2	1747	14.2	1772	10.9	1797	11.1
1724	12.7	1748	14.3	1773	11.6	1798	8.1
		1749	13.1	1774	12.2	1799	7.1
						1800	8.8

SOURCES: My calculations from Heberden, *Observations,* whose figures are from the London Bills of Mortality. See also appendix.

24 women died in the British Lying-in Hospital alone, thus contributing to some of the increase in the overall mortality rate. In the epidemic of 1770, John Leake found from the Bills of Mortality that the number of deaths in childbed rose by about one-third, or about 100 deaths, to a total of 272, and that this increase largely occurred between December and May—a typical pattern for streptococcal infections.[77] This raised the city's death rate from 11 to 16 per thousand. According to Heberden's summary of the British Lying-in reports, 28 died there of 472 delivered. This number represented a hospital death rate of nearly 60 per thousand and contributed about 1.6 per thousand to the city's mortality rate. There can be no question that a hospital epidemic could cause death rates to soar within the hospital to levels far above the average in the community.

[77] Leake, *Practical Observations,* FC, p. 125.

25

Table 3. Maternal Mortality, British Lying-in Hospital
(Deaths per Thousand Born)

1750	16.9	1765	15.8	1780	14.1	1795	3.2
1751	35.2	1766	16.7	1781	26.4	1796	1.6
1752	32.0	1767	7.0	1782	23.3	1797	4.8
1753	34.8	1768	5.1	1783	8.4	1798	3.5
1754	36.8	1769	12.2	1784	25.2	1799	1.9
1755	24.0	1770	59.1	1785	13.5	1800	0
1756	8.1	1771	7.3	1786	14.8		
1757	14.5	1772	6.6	1787	15.7		
1758	15.1	1773	6.3	1788	17.1		
1759	12.5	1774	32.3	1789	1.7		
1760	59.9	1775	36.5	1790	11.1		
1761	30.4	1776	5.4	1791	1.6		
1762	17.6	1777	9.9	1792	1.6		
1763	23.7	1778	19.0	1793	1.7		
1764	19.0	1779	5.3	1794	3.4		

SOURCES: Heberden, *Observations*. See also appendix.

In the final years of the century, however, both the British Lying-in and the City of London Lying-in achieved a very low mortality rate (table 1). From 1790 until 1810, the City of London Lying-in Hospital rate was about 5 per thousand. Between 1791 and 1807 the rate at the British Lying-in was about 4 per thousand. These were about half the rate in London in the same period. The Rotunda achieved an average of 6.0 from 1795 to 1799, but it was unable to maintain this rate in the early nineteenth century (tables 1 and 4). The rates at the Vienna Maternity Hospital also fell to low levels for many individual years between 1786 and 1810, although epidemics in 1793 and 1795 raised the overall average for the 1790s to about 9.8 per thousand. In 1797 and 1798 the rate fell to 2.4. It is far more likely that these rates were genuine than that the management at several different hospitals simultaneously decided to falsify rates for a short time and then simultaneously decided to abandon the deception in the second decade of the nineteenth century. Such low rates could be achieved only by highly skilled obstetrical management, but they were attainable at that time. The Westminster Dispensary, which delivered women at home, had maintained an average rate of slightly under 4 per thousand since 1774.[78]

Because of the great variation in hospital rates in the course of the century, and the overall decline during the century, statements about the relative safety of hospitals and home births are not very informative when they rely on averages or on selected individual years. Overall, hospital deliveries were slightly more dangerous than those at home, but for women who had reason to believe they were at high risk and needed skilled deliv-

[78] Loudon, "Deaths in childbed," p. 16.

Table 4. Maternal Mortality, The Rotunda, Dublin

	Clarke, "Observations"				Semmelweis, *Etiology*		
Year	Delivered	Died	Deaths per 1,000 women delivered	Year	Delivered	Died	Deaths per 1,000 women delivered
1758	454	8	17.6				
1759	406	5	12.3	1784	1261	11	8.7
1760	556	4	7.2	1785	1292	8	6.1
1761	521	9	17.3	1786	1351	8	5.9
1762	533	6	11.3	1787	1347	10	7.4
1763	488	9	18.4	1788	1469	23	15.6
1764	588	12	20.4	1789	1435	25	17.4
1765	533	6	11.3	1790	1546	12	7.7
1766	581	3	5.2	1791	1602	25	15.6
1767	664	11	16.6	1792	1631	10	6.1
1768	655	16	24.4	1793	1747	19	10.8
1769	642	8	12.5	1794	1543	20	12.9
1770	670	8	11.9	1795	1503	7	4.6
1771	695	5	7.2	1796	1621	10	6.1
1772	704	4	5.7	1797	1712	13	7.5
1773	694	13	18.7	1798	1604	8	4.9
1774	681	21	30.8	1799	1537	10	6.5
1775	728	5	6.9	1800	1837	18	9.7
1776	802	7	8.7	1801	1725	30	17.4
1777	835	7	8.4	1802	1985	26	13.0
1778	927	10	10.8	1803	2028	44	21.6
1779	1011	8	7.9	1804	1915	16	8.3
1780	919	5	5.4	1805	2220	12	5.4
1781	1027	6	5.8	1806	2406	23	9.5
1782	990	6	6.1	1807	2511	12	4.7
1783	1167	15	12.9	1808	2665	13	4.8
1784	1260	11	8.7	1809	2889	21	7.2
				1810	2854	29	10.1
				1811	2561	24	9.8
				1812	2676	43	16.9
				1813	2484	62	24.9
				1814	2508	25	9.9
				1815	3075	17	5.1
				1816	3314	18	5.4
				1817	3473	32	9.2
				1818	3539	56	15.8
				1819	3197	94	29.4

NOTE: For more information on the sources, see appendix.

ery, a hospital delivery may have been a wise choice. In most years, the difference was not great. If a woman was unlucky enough to enter a hospital during an institutional epidemic she faced a considerable added risk, but such episodes were rare. Throughout the century, though particular years could be more dangerous, on average women were as safe at the Rotunda in Dublin as they would have been at home in the city of London (tables 2 and 4). By the end of the century, a London woman seems to have been considerably safer in a maternity hospital than she was at home, although the home delivery charities seem to have had an impressive record.

These low rates, as low as those of the early twentieth century, could only have been achieved by a combination of excellent obstetrical skills and the increasingly successful avoidance of puerperal fever. Some of the improvement might have been due to a decline in the prevalence of community streptococcal infections, but this seems unlikely in the case of London hospitals, since scarlatina was reported as a constant problem in the London area during the last years of the century. Overall, streptococcal infections seem to have been increasing in incidence and virulence from the middle of the eighteenth to the middle of the nineteenth century.

EIGHTEENTH-CENTURY DISEASE THEORY

There is some reason to believe that English obstetricians and hospital management committees took measures that may have helped to reduce the risk of infection or cross-infection. English hospitals in the eighteenth century did not often perform extensive surgical operations, a factor that contributed to the comparatively low rate of wound infection and erysipelas. They generally refused admission to persons suffering from contagious diseases, including scarlet fever and ulcerated sore throat, which had been classified as contagious by Fothergill in 1748. They also frequently refused admission to children, the most frequent carriers of streptococcal infections.[79] Although they had difficulty controlling an epidemic once it appeared in a hospital, they may have been effective in minimizing the risk that such infections would be introduced in the first place.

Pregnant women in England received even more protection because they were often separated entirely from other patients in specialized institutions. There is some indication that this was a deliberate policy in England and was developed by some doctors with the idea that it might help prevent cross-infection. The case of William Hunter and his associates is particularly interesting. He was one of a group of obstetricians who resigned from the Middlesex Hospital in 1749 when it refused to establish separate maternity wards or to turn over the whole hospital to maternity cases. The group then formed the British Lying-in Hospital in Brownlow Street. Ironically, it was at the latter institution that the first recorded epidemic of puerperal fever took

---

[79] See John Woodward, *To Do the Sick No Harm: A Study of the British Voluntary Hospital System to 1875* (Boston, Massachusetts: Routledge and Kegan Paul, 1974; reprint, 1978), p. 45. See also E. M. Sigsworth, "Gateways to Death? Medicine, Hospitals, and Mortality, 1700–1850," in *Science and Society, 1600–1900,* ed. Peter Mathias (Cambridge: Cambridge University Press, 1972), pp. 97–110; Guenter B. Risse, *Hospital Life in Enlightenment Scotland: Care and Teaching at the Royal Infirmary of Edinburgh* (Cambridge: Cambridge University Press, 1986), esp. pp. 287–91; and S. G. Cherry, "The hospitals and population growth: Part I, the voluntary general hospitals, mortality, and local populations in the English provinces in the eighteenth and nineteenth centuries," *Pop. Stud.,* 1980, *34:* 59–75.

place, in 1760. This seems to be one epidemic in which it is possible that the infection was introduced by an obstetrician who performed autopsies, although the epidemic was by no means confined to that hospital.[80] The experience of that terrible epidemic seems to have left a lasting impression on Hunter. One author has attributed to it Hunter's extreme conservatism in obstetrical management. We know that when he established his Great Windmill Street School in 1767 he did so on separate premises from his midwifery practice and that when he was attending Queen Charlotte he even discontinued his anatomical lectures entirely. George C. Peachey has suggested that a fear of communicating fever led Hunter to take these actions. Moreover, although he attended the birth of Charlotte's child, the actual delivery was performed by a midwife.[81]

Hunter was one of a group of four men who had been friends from their student days in Scotland, when Hunter studied with William Cullen and Cullen became a close friend of John Fothergill's at Edinburgh. Cullen went to Glasgow and then returned to Edinburgh, where he trained hundreds of physicians, while Fothergill and Hunter moved to London. In London, Hunter studied midwifery with Cullen's friend and former neighbor William Smellie, who in turn became a friend of Fothergill's.

These men became leading members of a circle of Scottish physicians, foreigners, obstetricians, and Dissenters who had not received degrees from Oxford or Cambridge and were not acceptable to the Royal College of Physicians because of their specialty, their nationality, or their religion. As a group, they held many distinctive views on the nature of fevers and particularly on the possibility of transmission through contagion. As they increasingly dominated the obstetrical profession, their views helped shape hospital practices in general, to the benefit of maternity patients.[82]

---

[80] Both Hunter and his associate Francis Sandys were distinguished anatomists. Sandys died in 1771 and Hunter retired in 1782. Following Hunter's departure, the average mortality rate at the British Lying-in dropped considerably. On Sandys, see Zachary Cope, *William Cheselden, 1688–1752* (London: E. and S. Livingstone, 1953), and John Glaister, *Dr. William Smellie and His Contemporaries: A Contribution to the History of Midwifery in the Eighteenth Century* (Glasgow: Maclehose, 1894). On Hunter, see W. F. Bynum and Roy Porter, eds., *William Hunter and the Eighteenth-Century Medical World* (Cambridge: Cambridge University Press, 1982), esp. chaps. 1 and 2, which contain extensive further citations; George C. Peachey, "William Hunter's obstetrical career," *Ann. Med. Hist.*, 1930, n.s. *2:* 476–79; *idem, A Memoir of John and William Hunter* (Plymouth, England: Brendon, 1924); John Kobler, *The Reluctant Surgeon: The Life of John Hunter* (London: Heinemann, 1960); and Judith Schneid Lewis, *In the Family Way: Childbearing in the British Aristocracy, 1760–1860* (New Brunswick, New Jersey: Rutgers University Press, 1986).

[81] Peachey, "William Hunter's obstetrical career," pp. 476–77, 478–79.

[82] In 1744, Fothergill became the first Englishman with an Edinburgh M.D. to be permitted to apply for a license to practice medicine in London from the Royal College of Physicians. (The first Scottish graduate of Edinburgh licensed was William Schaw, in 1752.) Fothergill was at the center of the unsuccessful effort by the Licentiates to obtain the privileges of Fellowship from the College. The College refused to admit the holders of Edinburgh degrees to Fellowships, which were by law reserved for the graduates of Oxford, Cambridge, and Trinity College, Dublin. Since Dissenters were excluded from Oxford and Cambridge, this boycott of Scottish degree holders effectively excluded most Dissenters from Fellowship and, until the middle of the century, from the right to practice as a physician in London at all. Obstetricians were also refused Fellowships. The prejudice against Scots, and the hardships experienced by those excluded by the medical establishment, welded the newcomers into a close community with ties to Edinburgh and other Dissenting provincial medical communities. Nearly every distinguished physician in London who was not a Fellow of the Royal College

Fothergill's emphasis on the contagious nature of some diseases, particularly streptococcal pharyngitis, has already been noted, although there is no evidence that he connected pharyngitis with puerperal fever. Cullen also emphasized the importance of contagion in many fevers and the value of conservative therapy.[83] Fothergill, his disciple John Coakley Lettsom, and his friend John Howard were constant campaigners for improved institutional hygiene: Lettsom, who was also a pupil of Cullen's, is known to have emphasized the importance of personal as well as institutional cleanliness. Lettsom and Nathaniel Hulme served as staff physicians to the City of London Lying-in Hospital, which had an admirable mortality rate of five per thousand during Lettsom's tenure at the end of the century.[84] (See table 1.)

Hunter and Smellie and their pupils trained a very large percentage of all English obstetricians, as well as many midwives. Smellie, for example, taught more than nine hundred men in the 1740s alone, along with an unknown number of women. They or their associates also served on the professional staffs of most of the London lying-in institutions. At the General Dispensary for Poor Married Women, for example, William Black and Gilbert Blane were both pupils of Cullen's, and Blane was a protégé of William Hunter's, who obtained for him his first naval appointment. The Irish-born Black was a friend of Lettsom's.[85]

At the Lying-in Charity, which delivered about five thousand patients in their homes in 1772 (more than a quarter of all the deliveries in London), twenty-seven midwives were overseen by the physician John Ford and his assistants, one of whom was Thomas Cogan.[86] Not much is known about Ford, except that he had an M.D. from St. Andrew's and was a Methodist lay preacher. Cogan, however, was not only a former Unitarian minister but also a friend of Lettsom's, with whom he founded the Royal Humane Society. He was an early member of Lettsom's Medical Society of London. In 1780, Cogan was replaced by John Sims (M.D. Edinburgh), a Quaker and

of Physicians was associated with one or more of these four men. Most had received a distinctive medical education at Edinburgh, which became even more distinctive as men like Cullen and Hamilton assumed professorships there.

[83] On Cullen's influence, see W. F. Bynum, "William Cullen and the Study of Fevers in Britain, 1760–1820," in *Theories of Fever from Antiquity to the Enlightenment*, ed. W. F. Bynum and Vivian Nutton (*Med. Hist.*, suppl. no. 1, 1981), pp. 135–47, and Guenter B. Risse, " 'Doctor William Cullen, physician, Edinburgh': a consultation practice in the eighteenth century," *Bull. Hist. Med.*, 1974, *48*: 338–51.

[84] J. Johnston Abraham, *Lettsom: His Life, Times, Friends, and Descendants* (London: William Heinemann, 1933), p. 246. I would like to thank the NLM for supplying me with microfilm copies of Lettsom's works. On Howard, see Leona Baumgartner, "John Howard and the public health movement," *Bull. Hist. Med.*, 1937, *5*: 489–508, and John E. Ransom, "John Howard on communicable diseases," *Bull. Hist. Med.*, 1937, *5*: 131–47.

[85] Herbert R. Spencer, *A History of British Midwifery, 1650–1800* (London: John Bale, Sons, and Daniellson, 1927); William Munk, *The Roll of the Royal College of Physicians of London*, 2d ed., rev. enl., vol. 2 of 7 (London: Longman, Green, Longman, and Roberts, 1861); W. B. Howell, "Dr. George Fordyce and his times" *Ann. Med. Hist.*, 1930, n.s. *2*: 281–96, William Black, *A State of facts, relative to William Black* ([Edinburgh,] 1770).

[86] Stanley A. Seligman, "The Royal Maternity Charity: the first hundred years," *Med. Hist.*, 1980, *24*: 403–18.

also a close friend of Lettsom's. Sims served as president of the Medical Society in 1783.[87]

Dissenters such as the Quakers Fothergill and Lettsom, and Scots like Alexander Gordon or the professors of midwifery at Edinburgh Thomas Young (professor from 1756 to 1780) and Alexander Hamilton (professor from 1780 to 1800), differed from their English and Anglican colleagues in that they placed less emphasis on the importance of the climate—what Sydenham had called "the epidemic constitution of the atmosphere"—and more emphasis on the possibility of specific local contagions, which were spread by contact or fomites and could be transmitted only over a short distance by air.[88] Many English physicians, such as John Leake, William Butter, and John Clarke, believed that meteorological conditions were responsible for epidemic disease. There is considerable justification for their views, since streptococcal infections do indeed have a distinctive climatic and meteorological incidence. Miasmatic doctors were generally less alert to the importance of isolating surgical cases and patients with contagious diseases, and they sometimes believed that crowding was acceptable as long as there was adequate cross-ventilation within wards.[89]

For example, the founder of the first English maternity hospital was Sir Richard Manningham, the Cambridge-educated son of a bishop. Manningham was a dedicated anti-contagionist. In 1744 he wrote a book entitled *The Plague no Contagious Disease* and in 1758 reissued it as *A Discourse Concerning the Plague and Pestilential Fevers: plainly proving, that the general productive causes of all plagues of pestilence, are from some fault in the air: or from ill and unwholesome diet: and that the air is the principal cause of spreading the infection.* This book argued that any attempt to enact a general quarantine to prevent the introduction of the plague would do more harm than good by disrupting trade and raising the price of food to the poor. There was abundant evidence, Manningham argued, that the plague was not transmitted by contact or by tainted goods: "There is not any Corruption carried from the Body of the Sick, into the Body of the

[87] Abraham, *Lettsom*, pp. 140–41. John Sims should not be confused with James Sims, who practiced in County Tyrone before settling in London.

[88] Joseph Clarke was an Edinburgh graduate and the nephew of Fothergill's close friend George Cleghorn as well as a friend of Charles White's. I have not been able to determine whether Clarke and Cleghorn were also Quakers. For Gordon, Young, and Hamilton, see FC, p. 38, and Spencer, *History of British Midwifery*, pp. 90–97. Francis Home, professor of materia medica at Edinburgh, also adopted a contagionist view of puerperal fever; see John J. Byrne, "Dr. Francis Home and puerperal sepsis," *New Eng. J. Med*, 1954, 251: 440–42. Hunter was both a Scot and a putative lapsed Unitarian, but his personal views on disease transmission, like his personal religion, are difficult to determine. In the absence of evidence to the contrary, I have assumed that John Clarke of London, who attended St. Paul's School before studying obstetrics in London, and John Leake (the son of a Glasgow curate who settled in Cumberland), who attended Bishop Auckland Grammar School and obtained his M.D. from Rheims, were Anglicans. Obstetricians and surgeons are more difficult to classify by religion than physicians since, unlike most physicians, they did not find it advantageous to attend Oxford or Cambridge.

[89] Margaret DeLacy, "Social medicine and social institutions in eighteenth-century Lancashire" (unpublished).

Sound."[90] Manningham did not explicitly apply his views to his own field of obstetrics, perhaps because epidemic puerperal fever had not yet appeared in England, but he did argue that all fevers were products of the same underlying cause, a "lentor" of the blood, and that plague was merely the most extreme result.

The English-educated John Leake believed that the original cause of puerperal fever was a "distemperature of the air" combined with a mechanical change produced in the body by delivery, although puerperal fever might at last become infectious like dysentery or ulcerous sore throat. Along with early and copious bleeding, therefore, Leake also recommended cleanliness, ventilation, and the disinfection of the air by the burning of brimstone.[91] In 1793 John Clarke argued that "plethoric" women were more susceptible to fevers and recommended that they avoid animal food, breathe pure air, and remain horizontal for some days after delivery, but he attributed epidemic puerperal fever to a constitution of the air which resulted from a long succession of seasons whose "peculiar properties ... are infinitely too subtle for our investigation."[92]

An exception must be made for the Anglican Charles White, who demanded not only perfect cleanliness but also the complete separation of parturient women from each other. White was convinced that crowded hospitals—indeed, all hospitals—were dangerous. Although he was an Anglican, White had been trained by William Hunter and was a member of a group of hospital reformers centered in Warrington and Manchester.[93] Fothergill, who came from Warrington, spent his summers nearby. White advised Joseph Clarke on the administration of the Rotunda; perhaps it was because of his advice that the wards were small. White had strongly recommended that each patient have a separate room if possible. In fact, the Rotunda had four divisions, each with one room holding seven beds and two rooms with two beds each. A separate nurse and maid was assigned to each division.

---

[90] Richard Manningham, *A Discourse Concerning the Plague* ... (London: J. Robinson, 1758), p. 18. Spencer, *History of British Midwifery*, pp. 14–18.

[91] Leake, *Practical Observations*, FC, p. 126.

[92] John Clarke, *Practical Essays*, FC, p. 416.

[93] On this group, see Thomas Percival, *Essays, Medical and Experimental* (London: Lowndes, 1770); *idem, The Works, Literary, Moral and Medical of Thomas Percival ... to which are Prefixed Memoirs of his Life and Writings*, ed. Edward Percival, 4 vols. (London: Joseph Johnson, 1807); John Aikin, *Thoughts on Hospitals* (London: Joseph Johnson, 1771); *idem, A View of the Life, Travels, and Philanthropic Labors of the Late John Howard* (Philadelphia, Pennsylvania: John Ormrod, 1794). Aikin supplied Howard with the questions about the contagiousness of the plague which he used in collecting information for his work on Lazarettos. See also Michael W. Flinn, introduction to Edwin Chadwick's *Report on the Sanitary Condition of the Labouring Population of Great Britain, 1842* (Edinburgh: Edinburgh University Press, 1965); E. P. Hennock, "Urban sanitary reform a generation before Chadwick," *Econ. Hist. Rev.*, 1957, *10*: 113–20; B. Keith Lucas, "Some influences affecting the development of sanitary legislation in England," *Econ. Hist. Rev.*, 1953–54, *6*: 290–96; Edward Mansfield Brockbank, *Sketches of the Lives and Work of the Honorary Medical Staff of the Manchester Infirmary ... 1752 to 1830* ... (Manchester: Manchester University Press, 1904); and Lucy Aikin, *Memoir of John Aikin, M.D., with a selection of his Miscellaneous Pieces* (Philadelphia, Pennsylvania: Abraham Small, 1824). I would like to thank Dickinson College, Carlisle, Pennsylvania, for supplying a copy of Lucy Aikin's work.

Both groups agreed that thorough ventilation of hospital wards was essential to prevent cross-infection: Leake, in fact, was said to refuse to remain in a room that was not supplied with fresh air. The "nonconformist" group, because it was more willing to entertain the possibility of contagion, placed a greater emphasis on the importance of separating patients and maintaining institutional and personal cleanliness. If diseases could be transmitted only in a confined area, it was much easier to interrupt their progress through cleansing than if they were due to the atmosphere of an entire city, or to a mechanical cause, like the weight of the uterus. Contagionists were more alert to the possibility of transmission from person to person by a third party, to the need for clean hands and clothing, and to the danger of crowding. Thus, Lettsom argued:

> Matters ... are constantly arising ... from all breathing animals, and putrid animal bodies, which, under certain circumstances, are capable of producing the [putrid] fevers.... These diffusive active matters, appear in some stages of these fevers, to act as ferments on the fluids, and thereby to multiply themselves, and communicate contagion amongst a number of men.... [Contagion] does not in general extend to any considerable distance, or rise to any great height.... It is apt to remain in a concentrated state on the surface of the body retaining it, and on the garments and substances which have been in vicinity to the diseased, in the same manner as odors adhere to bodies in general.[94]

The Irish-born William Black, of the General Dispensary for Poor Married Women, differentiated between inflammatory and putrid fevers. The former were both infrequent and mild. The latter, which were common and severe, were not spread by climate, season, or any sensible qualities of the atmosphere, but could be communicated by

> imperceptible emanation or contagion from one infected person to another, by personal intercourse, by the medium of polluted goods, furniture, apparel, cloaths, and houses; in all which the noxious miasma may be concentrated and lodged.... Of what elementary nature miasma and contagion consist; the analysis of their minute atoms, whether animalcules, or to us invisible emanations, I pretend not to decide.... Neither marshy miasma, nor those from human effluvia, spread to any considerable distance through the air.[95]

The predisposing causes of such fevers included crowding, filth, rotting food or animal carcasses, "putrid sores and mortifications, gangrenous inoculation through wounds of the skin," and many other factors. Black, how-

---

[94] John Coakley Lettsom, *Reflections on the General Treatment and Cure of Fevers* (London: Printed for the author by J. D. Cornish, 1772), pp. 8–15. Like most of his contemporaries, Lettsom accepted the division of fevers into intermittent (primarily caused by marsh air), putrid, and inflammatory. Inflammatory fevers were not contagious, but the "nonconformist" doctors argued that they were also infrequent by comparison with the putrid fevers. One of the fiercest debates of the century was over the question of whether puerperal fever was putrid or inflammatory. This had implications for therapy, since the common treatment for inflammatory fevers was bleeding, while the common treatment for putrid fevers was cinchona and cordials.

[95] Black, *Arithmetical and Medical Analysis*, pp. 51 and 69.

ever, like Leake, believed puerperal fever was due to inflammation and became epidemic through "some unknown quality of the atmosphere and seasons."[96] Black's Scottish colleague Gilbert Blane, better known as a naval surgeon, is described by Margaret Pelling as a leading contagionist of the early nineteenth century.[97] The Quaker physician Anthony Fothergill wrote an article on puerperal fever in 1783 which assumed the fever was highly contagious.[98]

Thomas Young, professor of midwifery at Edinburgh, believed that puerperal fever arose from a local infection. His successor, Alexander Hamilton, commented that an outbreak of puerperal fever at Edinburgh Infirmary was due to a "specific contagion from the air of the wards [which] in surgical wards … sometimes … produces almost in every wound, even the slightest, symptoms of erysipelas and even mortification."[99] Hamilton saw puerperal fever as primarily an airborne contagion, but he believed it was so contagious it could be carried by a third person. At the Rotunda, Joseph Clarke attributed puerperal fever to a local infection. He followed the advice of Young, "the only writer who has recommended measures similar to what we pursued," and carried out a ruthless cleaning program, removing patients, whitewashing and painting the wards, and replacing the bedding.[100] When, at the end of the century, Alexander Gordon made a point of refusing to discuss the atmosphere, and instead demonstrated that attendants carried contagion from house to house, his work represented the logical culmination, although in more definitive and conclusive terms, of the work of many previous British writers.

According to Ignaz Semmelweis, the chief cause of the soaring mortality rates in nineteenth-century hospitals was the teaching of pathological anatomy and the large numbers of medical students coming into the maternity wards straight from the dissecting rooms with "cadaveric matter" on their hands. Autopsies were not performed as frequently in eighteenth-century hospitals, but they did take place. Many of the cases of puerperal fever reported by physicians included autopsy reports. Autopsies could be a source of some danger to the physicians themselves, who sometimes contracted septicemia. Lettsom died from such an infection. It seems likely, however, that the communication of puerperal fever to patients from this source occurred much less frequently in the eighteenth century than in the nineteenth. Few medical students came straight from the morgue to the ward, and medical students were often banned entirely from lying-in wards. For example, both the British Lying-in and the Middlesex Hospital barred

---

[96] *Ibid.*, p. 217.

[97] Margaret Pelling, *Cholera, Fever, and English Medicine, 1825–1865* (London: Oxford University Press, 1978), p. 27.

[98] Anthony Fothergill, "An account of an improved method of treating the puerperal fever," *London Med. J.*, 1782, *3:* 411–18. Anthony was a distant cousin of John Fothergill's.

[99] Spencer, *History of British Midwifery*, p. 97.

[100] Joseph Clarke, *Observations*, FC, pp. 360 and 357.

male students.[101] In at least one case, the physician who usually performed the autopsy did not deliver patients.[102] Pathological anatomy had not yet become fashionable.

Treatises of the time say a great deal about keeping the patients and their surroundings clean but little about personal cleanliness for attendants. Nevertheless, there is some evidence that obstetricians cleansed themselves and their instruments. Smellie was criticized by a leading London midwife for delivering in a "nightgown," a costume he recommended not only because it offered a way to conceal his forceps but also because it was easy to wash.[103] As for the forceps themselves, Smellie was again roundly criticized by John Burton, a York obstetrician, for his first design, which had the blades wrapped in leather. Burton pointed out that this made it impossible to clean the blades completely. Smellie rejoined that the leather was supposed to be removed and replaced after each use, but he soon substituted more easily cleaned metal blades.[104] The contagionist belief that the source of disease tended to adhere "in a concentrated state on the surface of the body" probably encouraged physicians to wash their hands and change their clothing.[105]

We also know that British hospitals, unlike Continental ones, preferred to keep maternity patients in small wards. For example, the Edinburgh General Lying-in Hospital had seven-bed wards for ordinary patients. A woman was admitted to one ward, was carried to the delivery room, and then, still in the same bed, was carried to a separate lying-in ward. There were also six private bedrooms for women "in a dangerous situation." When they left, their bedding was removed to a drying house for two weeks.[106] All the maternity hospitals tried to bar verminous or contagious patients and controlled visitors. For example, the Westminster New Lying-in required that patients be clean and free from infection, that patients suckle their babies, and that visitors see patients in the reception hall. No visitors were permit-

[101] *Laws, Orders, and Regulations of the British Lying-in Hospital* (London: E. Cox, 1781) and *An Account of the Middlesex Hospital* (c. 1752).

[102] Hulme, *Treatise*, FC, p. 62.

[103] Spencer, *History of British Midwifery*, p. 148.

[104] Glaister, *Dr. William Smellie*. See also Gordon, *Treatise*: "The nurses and the physicians who have attended patients affected with the puerperal fever ought carefully to wash themselves and to get their apparel properly fumigated before it be put on again" (FC, p. 485).

[105] See, e.g., Louis H. Roddis, *James Lind, Founder of Nautical Medicine* (New York: Henry Schuman, 1950) pp. 105–6: "Scrupulous cleanliness, not only to the compartment but of linen and bedding, and the disinfection of the urine, sputum, or other discharges … was part of his regular routine. He recommended that the surgeon wear special clothes when on duty and was in favor of waxed linen as being least likely to become soiled. A modern touch was in urging the frequent washing of hands on the part of the surgeon…. Even more important was his injunction against the use of sponges. Lind recommended in place of sponges the use of clean linen or cotton cloths that could be thrown away or thoroughly washed…. He had his nurses and attendants wear painted canvas jackets as these could easily be washed." Lind, a Scot, was educated at Edinburgh.

[106] James Hamilton, *Select Cases in Midwifery extracted from the Records of the Edinburgh General Lying-in Hospital with Remarks* (Edinburgh: G. Mudie and Son; London: J. Johnson, 1795).

ted within one week of delivery and after that were allowed only with written permission.[107]

In the early nineteenth century, contagionist views and the efforts they encouraged again fell out of fashion. They had never been generally accepted on the Continent. English visitors frequently described their disgust at the squalor and crowding they found in Paris. "That the Parisian malady was more highly malignant ... will not appear wonderful to anyone who has ever visited that crowded receptacle of disease and contagion, the Hôtel-Dieu," commented Anthony Fothergill in 1782.[108]

As J. George Adami wrote in 1923 of British obstetricians in the late eighteenth and early nineteenth centuries, they

> first gained control over puerperal fever. They it was who introduced free ventilation and ... cleanliness ..., who laid stress upon disinfection, who ... recognised the worth of chlorine ..., who introduced the disinfection of the hands and drainage of the puerperal wound, who would have no truck with the ... atmospheric, cosmic, or telluric theory—but held to the contagious....
>
> By the early [1840s] other influences were at work.... Charles White's ... methods had lapsed, even in Manchester itself, so that ... mortality ... became a matter of the gravest concern. This ... [was due] to the diffusion of foreign, and particularly French teaching as to the nature of puerperal fever.... It was [this] ... which, in 1826, on the ground that his procedure was old-fashioned and based on "contagionism," had at Vienna forced the resignation of Professor Boër, and had led to the disastrous introduction of Professor Klein and his "anatomical" teaching into the Allegemeines Krankenhaus.[109]

Semmelweis followed Klein. When Semmelweis demonstrated that maternal mortality rates had fallen since he had introduced chlorine handwashing, his opponents argued that the improvement was due instead to the introduction of a new system of ventilation into the hospital.

Because they believed that cross-infection could be avoided if wards were adequately ventilated, miasmatists were willing to relax the rules that had barred patients with contagious diseases from eighteenth-century hospitals. Changes in policy permitted hospitals to admit a much wider spectrum of patients. It was this, and not merely the growth in urban population, that created the appalling crowding of hospitals in the nineteenth century —which in turn contributed to appalling mortality rates. One of the most dedicated of English miasmatists was Florence Nightingale, who believed that the greatest requirement for hospital design was the promotion of free ventilation. This, in turn, was favored by the creation of large wards in place of small, separate rooms. She had hoped to establish a special program for nurse midwives but was forced to discontinue the school by an unaccept-

[107] *Laws, Rules, and Orders of the Westminster New Lying-in Hospital* (London, 1793).
[108] Fothergill, *Account*, p. 415.
[109] Adami, *Charles White*, pp. 30–31, 41, and 50–51.

ably high incidence of puerperal fever in the training wards. Her experience eventually persuaded her that maternity patients should be placed in separate rooms.[110]

The shift toward miasmatism may help to explain why hospital mortality rates, which had fallen to very low levels by the end of the eighteenth century, rose steeply again in the early nineteenth century. The greater resistance to contagionism on the Continent may also explain why Continental hospitals were far more dangerous than British ones. In Paris, for example, puerperal fever became common in the 1770s and grew steadily in incidence thereafter, creating death rates unknown in Britain. Those few historians who have discovered that nineteenth-century hospital mortality rates were not better than those of the eighteenth—but far worse—have attributed the change to increasingly adventurous surgery and to crowding.[111] This nineteenth-century rise requires further investigation to evaluate the possible contributions of changing admissions policies and the steadily increasing virulence of community streptococcal infections.

In conclusion, British maternity hospitals in the eighteenth century may have magnified epidemics, but they probably did not generate them. Moreover, their record showed continual improvement during the second half of the century. By the end of the century a pregnant woman was as safe in a hospital as she was at home, and as safe as she would be at any time before the second half of this century. This comparatively low mortality was due to a combination of factors, including improved obstetrical care and a distinctive medical tradition.

APPENDIX: TABLE SOURCES

The sources for the tables herein are as follows. Figures for the British Lying-in (tables 1 and 3) are from "Account of the Women Delivered, ... 1749 to ... 1801," in Heberden, *Observations,* pp. 39–41. This gives figures for the number of women delivered and the number of children born including stillbirths and neonatal deaths. I have calculated the rates using the number born. Because of twin births this is slightly greater than the number of women delivered. Using the number of women delivered would raise the overall annual average by about 0.2 deaths per thousand. Buer, *Health, Wealth, and Population,* supplied the rate for 1800–1807 in table 1. Figures for the City of London Lying-in (table 1) are from William Gilliatt, "Maternal Mortality," in Kerr, Johnstone, and Phillips, *Historical Review,* p. 261, for 1790–1810, and from *The One Hundred Thirty-Eighth Report of the City of London Lying-In Hospital ...* (London, 1889) for 1830–1848. Figures for the Rotunda (tables 1 and 4)

---

[110] Cecil Woodham-Smith, *Florence Nightingale, 1820–1910* (New York: McGraw-Hill, 1951), pp. 304–5. See also Sydney Selwyn, "Sir James Simpson and hospital cross-infection," *Med. Hist.,* 1965, 9: 241–48.

[111] See, e.g., Woodward, *To Do the Sick No Harm,* p. 122, and Cherry, "Hospitals and Population Growth." See also Gilliatt, "Maternal Mortality," in Kerr, Johnstone, and Phillips, *Historical Review,* p. 262, and Buer, *Health, Wealth, and Population,* pp. 145–48.

are from Joseph Clarke, "Observations on some causes of the excess of the mortality of males above that of females," *London Med. J.,* 1788, *9:* 179–200, for 1758–1784, and Semmelweis, *Etiology, Concept, and Prophylaxis of Childbed Fever,* ed. Carter, pp. 142–43, for 1784–1848. Whereas Clarke specifically states that these figures are rates for the number of women actually delivered at the Rotunda (women who left before giving birth were subtracted), Semmelweis gives his Rotunda rates as percentages of "births." Since Semmelweis gives the number of "births" as 1,261 in 1784, however, and Clarke gives 1,260 as the number of "women delivered" for the same year, I believe Semmelweis's figures are actually for women delivered. Because of the incidence of twin births, Semmelweis's figure should have been higher if it was for all children born. Figures for the Vienna Maternity wards (table 1) are from Semmelweis, *Etiology,* pp. 142–43. I do not know whether this adjusts for twins. Figures for the city of London (tables 1 and 2) are my calculations from Heberden, *Observations,* for 1750–1799, and James Young, "Journals, 1800–1950," in Kerr, Johnstone, and Phillips, *Historical Review,* p. 325, for 1800–1814. In many instances I have converted the data to deaths per thousand from some other method of expressing the rate. I have also supplied five-year averages.

II.

THE CONTAGIOUSNESS OF PUERPERAL FEVER.[a]

THE POINT AT ISSUE.

——◆——

THE AFFIRMATIVE.

"The disease known as Puerperal Fever is so far contagious as to be frequently carried from patient to patient by physicians and nurses." — *O. W. Holmes*, 1843.

THE NEGATIVE.

"The result of the whole discussion will, I trust, serve, not only to exalt your views of the value and dignity of our profession, but to divest your minds of the overpowering dread that you can ever become, especially to woman, under the extremely interesting circumstances of gestation and parturition, the minister of evil ; that you can ever convey, in any possible manner, a horrible virus, so destructive in its effects, and so mysterious in its operations as that attributed to puerperal fever." — *Professor Hodge*, 1852.

"I prefer to attribute them to accident, or Providence, of which I can form a conception, rather than to a contagion of which I cannot form any clear idea, at least as to this particular malady." — *Professor Meigs*, 1852.

" . . . in the propagation of which they have no more to do, than with the propagation of cholera from Jessore to San Francisco, and from Mauritius to St. Petersburg." — *Professor Meigs*, 1854.

"I arrived at that certainty in the matter, that I could venture to foretell what women would be affected with the disease, upon hearing by what midwife they were to be delivered, or by what nurse they were to be attended, during their lying-in ; and, almost in every instance, my prediction was verified." — *Gordon*, 1795.

a Printed in 1843 ; reprinted with additions, 1855.

"A certain number of deaths is caused every year by the contagion of puerperal fever, communicated by the nurses and medical attendants." — *Farr, in Fifth Annual Report of Registrar-General of England,* 1843.

". . . boards of health, if such exist, or, without them, the medical institutions of a country, should have the power of coercing, or of inflicting some kind of punishment on those who recklessly go from cases of puerperal fevers to parturient or puerperal females, without using due precaution ; and who, having been shown the risk, criminally encounter it, and convey pestilence and death to the persons they are employed to aid in the most interesting and suffering period of female existence." — *Copland's Medical Dictionary, Art. Puerperal States and Diseases,* 1852.

"We conceive it unnecessary to go into detail to prove the contagious nature of this disease, as there are few, if any, American practitioners who do not believe in this doctrine." — *Dr. Lee, in Additions to Article last cited.*

[INTRODUCTORY NOTE.] It happened, some years ago, that a discussion arose in a Medical Society of which I was a member, involving the subject of a certain supposed cause of disease, about which something was known, a good deal suspected, and not a little feared. The discussion was suggested by a case, reported at the preceding meeting, of a physician who made an examination of the body of a patient who had died with puerperal fever, and who himself died in less than a week, apparently in consequence of a wound received at the examination, having attended several women in confinement in the mean time, all of whom, as it was alleged, were attacked with puerperal fever.

Whatever apprehensions and beliefs were entertained, it was plain that a fuller knowledge of the facts relating to the subject would be acceptable to all present. I therefore felt that it would be doing a good service to look into the best records I could find, and inquire of the most trustworthy practitioners I knew, to learn what experience had to teach in the matter, and arrived at the results contained in the following pages.

The Essay was read before the Boston Society for Medical Improvement, and, at the request of the Society, printed in the "New England Quarterly Journal of Medicine and Surgery" for April, 1843. As this Journal never obtained a large circulation, and ceased to be published after a year's existence, and as the few copies I had struck off separately were soon lost sight of among the friends to whom they were sent, the Essay can hardly be said to have been fully brought before the Profession.

The subject of this Paper has the same profound interest for me at the present moment as it had when I was first collecting the terrible evidence out of which, as it seems to me, the commonest exercise of reason could not help shaping the truth it involved. It is not merely on account of the bearing of the question, — if there is a question, — on all that is most sacred in human life and happiness, that the subject cannot lose its interest. It is because it seems evident that a fair statement of the facts must produce its proper influence on a very large proportion of well-constituted and unprejudiced minds. Individuals may, here and there, resist the practical bearing of the evidence on their own feelings or interests; some may fail to see its meaning, as some persons may be found who cannot tell red from green; but I cannot doubt that most readers will be satisfied and convinced, to loathing, long before they have finished the dark obituary calendar laid before them.

I do not know that I shall ever again have so good an opportunity of being useful as was granted me by the raising of the question which produced this Essay. For I have abundant evidence that it has made many practitioners more cautious in their relations with puerperal females, and I have no doubt it will do so still, if it has a chance of being read, though it should call out a hundred counterblasts, proving to the satisfaction of their authors that it proved nothing. And for my part, I had rather rescue one mother from being poisoned by her attendant, than claim to have saved forty out of fifty patients to whom I had carried the disease. Thus, I am willing to avail myself of any hint coming from without to offer this paper once more to the press. The occasion has presented itself, as will be seen, in a convenient if not in a flattering form.

I send this Essay again to the MEDICAL PROFESSION, without the change of a word or syllable. I find, on reviewing it, that it anticipates and eliminates those secondary questions which cannot be entertained for a moment until the one great point of fact is peremptorily settled. In its very statement of the doctrine maintained it avoids all discussion of the nature of the disease " *known as puerperal fever*," and all the somewhat stale philology of the word *contagion*. It mentions, fairly enough, the names of sceptics, or unbelievers as to the reality of personal transmission; of Dewees, of Tonnellé, of Dugès, of Baudelocque, and others; of course, not including those whose works were then unwritten or unpublished; nor enumerating all the Continental writers who, in ignorance of the great mass of evidence accumulated by British practitioners, could hardly be called well informed on this subject. It meets all the array of negative cases, — those in which disease did not follow exposure, —

by the striking example of small-pox, which, although one of the most contagious of diseases, is subject to the most remarkable irregularities and seeming caprices in its transmission. It makes full allowance for other causes besides personal transmission, especially for epidemic influences. It allows for the possibility of different modes of conveyance of the destructive principle. It recognizes and supports the belief that a series of cases may originate from a single primitive source which affects each new patient in turn ; and especially from cases of Erysipelas. It does not undertake to discuss the theoretical aspect of the subject; that is a secondary matter of consideration. Where facts are numerous, and unquestionable, and unequivocal in their significance, theory must follow them as it best may, keeping time with their step, and not go before them, marching to the sound of its own drum and trumpet. Having thus narrowed its area to a limited practical platform of discussion, a matter of life and death, and not of phrases or theories, it covers every inch of it with a mass of evidence which I conceive a Committee of Husbands, who can count coincidences and draw conclusions as well as a Synod of Accoucheurs, would justly consider as affording ample reasons for an *unceremonious dismissal* of a practitioner (if it is conceivable that such a step could be waited for), after five or six funerals had marked the path of his daily visits, while other practitioners were not thus escorted. To the Profession, therefore, I submit the paper in its original form, and leave it to take care of itself.

To the MEDICAL STUDENTS, into whose hands this Essay may fall, some words of introduction may be appropriate, and perhaps, to a small number of them, necessary. There are some among them who, from youth, or want of training, are easily bewildered and confused in any conflict of opinions into which their studies lead them. They are liable to lose sight of the main question in collateral issues, and to be run away with by suggestive speculations. They confound belief with evidence, often trusting the first because it is expressed with energy, and slighting the latter because it is calm and unimpassioned. They are not satisfied with proof; they cannot believe a point is settled so long as everybody is not silenced. They have not learned that error is got out of the minds that cherish it, as the tænia is removed from the body, one joint, or a few joints at a time, for the most part, rarely the whole evil at once. They naturally have faith in their instructors, turning to them for truth, and taking what they may choose to give them; babes in knowledge, not yet able to tell the breast from the bottle, pumping away for the milk of truth at all that offers, were it nothing better than a Professor's shrivelled forefinger.

In the earliest and embryonic stage of professional development, any violent impression on the instructor's mind is apt to be followed by some lasting effect on that of the pupil. No mother's mark is more permanent than the mental nævi and moles, and excrescences, and mutilations, that students carry with them out of the lecture-room, if once the teeming intellect which nourishes theirs has been scared from its propriety by any misshapen fantasy. Even an impatient or petulant expression, which to a philosopher would be a mere index of the low state of amiability of the speaker at the moment of its utterance, may pass into the young mind as an element of its future constitution, to injure its temper or corrupt its judgment. It is a duty, therefore, which we owe to this younger class of students, to clear any important truth which may have been rendered questionable in their minds by such language, or any truth-teller against whom they may have been prejudiced by hasty epithets, from the impressions such words have left. Until this is done, they are not ready for the question, where there is a question, for them to decide. Even if we ourselves are the subjects of the prejudice, there seems to be no impropriety in showing that this prejudice is local or personal, and not an acknowledged conviction with the public at large. It may be necessary to break through our usual habits of reserve to do this, but this is the fault of the position in which others have placed us.

Two widely-known and highly-esteemed practitioners, Professors in two of the largest Medical Schools of the Union, teaching the branch of art which includes the Diseases of Women, and therefore speaking with authority; addressing in their lectures and printed publications large numbers of young men, many of them in the tenderest immaturity of knowledge, have recently taken ground in a formal way against the doctrine maintained in this paper.[a] The

[a] *On the Non-Contagious Character of Puerperal Fever:* An Introductory Lecture. By Hugh L. Hodge, M. D., Professor of Obstetrics in the University of Pennsylvania. Delivered Monday, October 11, 1852. Philadelphia, 1852.

On the Nature, Signs, and Treatment of Childbed Fevers: in a Series of Letters addressed to the Students of his Class. By Charles D. Meigs, M. D., Professor of Midwifery and the Diseases of Women and Children in Jefferson Medical College, Philadelphia, etc., etc. Philadelphia, 1854. Letter VI.

first of the two publications, Dr. Hodge's Lecture, while its theoretical considerations and negative experiences do not seem to me to require any further notice than such as lay ready for them in my Essay written long before, is, I am pleased to say, unobjectionable in tone and language, and may be read without offence.

This can hardly be said of the chapter of Dr. Meigs's volume which treats of Contagion in Childbed Fever. There are expressions used in it which might well put a stop to all scientific discussions, were they to form the current coin in our exchange of opinions. I leave the "very young gentlemen," whose careful expositions of the results of practice in more than six thousand cases are characterized as "the jejune and fizenless dreamings of sophomore writers," to the sympathies of those "dear young friends," and "dear young gentlemen," who will judge how much to value their instructor's counsel to think for themselves, knowing what they are to expect if they happen not to think as he does.

One unpalatable expression I suppose the laws of construction oblige me to appropriate to myself, as my reward for a certain amount of labor bestowed on the investigation of a very important question of evidence, and a statement of my own practical conclusions. I take no offence, and attempt no retort. No man makes a quarrel with me over the counterpane that covers a mother, with her new-born infant at her breast. There is no epithet in the vocabulary of slight and sarcasm that can reach my personal sensibilities in such a controversy. Only just so far as a disrespectful phrase may turn the student aside from the examination of the evidence, by discrediting or dishonoring the witness, does it call for any word of notice.

I appeal from the disparaging language by which the Professor in the Jefferson School of Philadelphia would dispose of my claims to be listened to. I appeal, not to the vote of the Society for Medical Improvement, although this was an unusual evidence of interest in the paper in question, for it was a vote passed among my own townsmen ; nor to the opinion of any American, for none know better than the Professors in the great Schools of Philadelphia how cheaply the praise of native contemporary criticism is obtained. I appeal to the recorded opinions of those whom I do not know, and who do not know me, nor care for me, except for the truth that I may have uttered ; to Copland, in his "Medical Dictionary," who has spoken of my Essay in phrases to which the pamphlets of American "scribblers" are seldom used from European authorities ; to Ramsbotham, whose commendatory eulogy is all that self-love could ask ; to the "Fifth Annual Report" of the Registrar-General of England, in which the second-hand abstract of my Essay figures largely, and not without favorable comment, in an important appended paper. These testimonies, half forgotten until this circumstance recalled them, are dragged into the light, not in a paroxysm of vanity, but to show that there may be food for thought in the small pamphlet which the Philadelphia Teacher treats so lightly. They were at least unsought for, and would never have been proclaimed but for the sake of securing the privilege of a decent and unprejudiced hearing.

I will take it for granted that they have so far counterpoised the depreciating language of my fellow-countryman and fellow-teacher as to gain me a reader here and there among the youthful class of students

I am now addressing. It is only for their sake that I think it necessary to analyze, or explain, or illustrate, or corroborate any portion of the following Essay. But I know that nothing can be made too plain fo. beginners; and as I do not expect the practitioner, or even the more mature student, to take the trouble to follow me through an Introduction which I consider wholly unnecessary and superfluous for them, I shall not hesitate to stoop to the most elementary simplicity for the benefit of the younger student. I do this more willingly because it affords a good opportunity, as it seems to me, of exercising the untrained mind in that medical logic which does not seem to have been either taught or practised in our schools of late, to the extent that might be desired.

I will now exhibit, in a series of propositions reduced to their simplest expression, the same essential statements and conclusions as are contained in the Essay, with such commentaries and explanations as may be profitable to the inexperienced class of readers addressed.

I. It has been long believed, by many competent observers, that Puerperal Fever (so called) is sometimes carried from patient to patient by medical assistants.

II. The express object of this Essay is to prove that it is so carried.

III. In order to prove this point, it is not necessary to consult any medical theorist as to whether or not it is consistent with his preconceived notions that such a mode of transfer should exist.

IV. If the medical theorist insists on being consulted, and we see fit to indulge him, he cannot be allowed to assume that the alleged laws of contagion, *deduced from observation* in other diseases, shall be cited to disprove the alleged laws *deduced from observation* in this. Science would never make progress under such conditions. Neither the long incubation of hydrophobia, nor the protecting power of vaccination, would ever have been admitted, if the results of observation in these affections had been rejected as contradictory to the previously ascertained laws of contagion.

V. The disease in question is not a common one; producing, on the average, about three deaths in a thousand births, according to the English Registration returns which I have examined.

VI. When an unusually large number of cases of this disease occur about the same time, it is inferred, therefore, that there exists some special cause for this increased frequency. If the disease prevails extensively over a wide region of country, it is attributed without dispute to an *epidemic* influence. If it prevails in a single locality, as in a hospital, and not elsewhere, this is considered proof that some *local* cause is there active in its production.

VII. When a large number of cases of this disease occur in rapid succession, in one individual's ordinary practice, and few or none elsewhere, these cases appearing in scattered localities, in patients of the same average condition as those who escape under the care of others, there is the same reason for connecting the cause of the disease with the *person* in this instance, as with the *place* in that last mentioned.

VIII. Many series of cases, answering to these conditions, are given in this Essay, and many others will be referred to which have occurred since it was written.

IX. The alleged results of observation may be *set aside ;* first, because the so-called facts are in their own nature equivocal; secondly, because they stand on insufficient authority; thirdly, because they are not sufficiently numerous. But, in this case, the disease is one of striking and well-marked character; the witnesses are experts, interested in denying and disbelieving the facts; the number of consecutive cases in many instances frightful, and the number of series of cases such that I have no room for many of them except by mere reference.

X. These results of observation, being admitted, may, we will suppose, be *interpreted* in different methods. Thus the coincidences may be considered the effect of *chance.* I have had the chances calculated by a competent person, that a given practitioner, A., shall have sixteen fatal cases in a month, on the following data : A. to average attendance upon two hundred and fifty births in a year; three deaths in one thousand births to be assumed as the average from puerperal fever; no epidemic to be at the time prevailing. It follows, from the answer given me, that if we suppose every one of the five hundred thousand annual births of England to have been recorded during the last half-century, there would not be one chance in a million million million millions that one such series should be noted. No possible fractional error in this calculation can render the chance a working probability. Applied to dozens of series of various lengths, it is obviously an absurdity. Chance, therefore, is out of the question as an explanation of the admitted coincidences.

XI. There is, therefore, *some* relation of cause and effect between the physician's presence and the patient's disease.

XII. Until it is proved to what *removable condition* attaching to the attendant the disease is owing, he is bound to stay away from his patients so soon as he finds himself singled out to be tracked by the disease. How long, and with what other precautions, I have suggested, without dictating, at the close of my Essay. If the physician does not at once act on any reasonable suspicion of his being the medium of transfer, the families where he is engaged, if they are allowed to know the facts, should decline his services for the time. His feelings on the occasion, however interesting to himself, should not be even named in this connection. A physician who talks about *ceremony* and *gratitude*, and *services rendered*, and the *treatment he got*, surely forgets himself; it is impossible that he should seriously think of these small matters where there is even a question whether he may not carry disease, and death, and bereavement into any one of " his families," as they are sometimes called.

I will now point out to the young student the mode in which he may relieve his mind of any confusion, or possibly, if *very* young, any doubt, which the perusal of Dr. Meigs's Sixth Letter may have raised in his mind.

The most prominent ideas of the Letter are, first, that the transmissible nature of puerperal fever appears improbable, and, secondly, that it would be very inconvenient to the writer. Dr. Woodville, Physician to the Small-Pox and Inoculation Hospital in London, found it improbable, and exceedingly inconvenient to himself, that cow-pox should prevent small-pox; but

Dr. Jenner took the liberty to prove the fact, notwithstanding.

I will first call the young student's attention to the show of negative facts (exposure without subsequent disease), of which much seems to be thought. And I may at the same time refer him to Dr. Hodge's Lecture, where he will find the same kind of facts and reasoning. Let him now take up Watson's Lectures, the good sense and spirit of which have made his book a universal favorite, and open to the chapter on Continued Fever. He will find a paragraph containing the following sentence: "A man might say, 'I was in the battle of Waterloo, and saw many men around me fall down and die, and it was said that they were struck down by musket-balls; but I know better than that, for I was there all the time, and so were many of my friends, and we were never hit by any musket-balls. Musket-balls, therefore, could not have been the cause of the deaths we witnessed.' And if, like contagion, they were not palpable to the senses, such a person might go on to affirm that no proof existed of there being any such thing as musket-balls." Now let the student turn back to the chapter on Hydrophobia in the same volume. He will find that John Hunter knew a case in which, of twenty-one persons bitten, only one died of the disease. He will find that one dog at Charenton was bitten at different times by thirty different mad dogs, and outlived it all. Is there no such thing, then, as hydrophobia? Would one take no especial precautions if his wife, about to become a mother, had been bitten by a rabid animal, because so many escape? Or let him look at "Underwood on Diseases of Children," [a] and he will find the case of a young

[a] Philadelphia, 1842, p. 244, note.

woman who was inoculated eight times in thirty days, at the same time attending several children with small-pox, and yet was not infected. But seven weeks after-wards she took the disease and died.

It would seem as if the force of this argument could hardly fail to be seen, if it were granted that every one of these series of cases were so reported as to prove that there could have been no transfer of dis-ease. *There is not one of them* so reported, in the Lecture or the Letter, as to prove that the disease may not have been carried by the practitioner. I strongly suspect that it was so carried in some of these cases, but from the character of the very imperfect evidence the question can never be settled without further dis-closures.

Although the Letter is, as I have implied, principally taken up with secondary and collateral questions, and might therefore be set aside as in the main irrelevant, I am willing, for the student's sake, to touch some of these questions briefly, as an illustration of its logical character.

The first thing to be done, as I thought when I wrote my Essay, was to throw out all discussions of the word *contagion*, and this I did effectually by the care-ful wording of my statement of the subject to be dis-cussed. My object was not to settle the etymology or definition of a word, but to show that women had often died in childbed, poisoned in some way by their medi-cal attendants. On the other point, I, at least, have no controversy with anybody, and I think the student will do well to avoid it in this connection. If I must define my position, however, as well as the term in question, I am contented with Worcester's definition; provided always this avowal do not open another side-controversy on the merits of his Dictionary, which Dr. Meigs has not cited, as compared with Webster's, which he has.

I cannot see the propriety of insisting that all the laws of the eruptive fevers must necessarily hold true of this peculiar disease of puerperal women. If there were any such propriety, the laws of the eruptive fevers must at least be stated correctly. It is not true, for instance, as Dr. Meigs states, that contagion is " no respecter of persons ; " that " it attacks all individuals alike." To give one example: Dr. Gregory, of the Small-Pox Hospital, who ought to know, says that persons pass through life apparently insensible to or unsusceptible of the small-pox virus, and that the same persons do not take the vaccine disease.

As to the short time of incubation, of which so much is made, we have no right to decide beforehand whether it shall be long or short, in the cases we are considering. A dissection wound may produce symptoms of poisoning in six hours ; the bite of a rabid animal may take as many months.

After the student has read the case in Dr. Meigs's 136th paragraph, and the following one, in which he exclaims against the idea of contagion, because the patient, delivered on the 26th of December, was attacked in twenty-four hours, and died on the third day, let him read what happened at the " Black Assizes " of 1577 and 1750. In the first case, six hundred persons sickened the same night of the exposure, and three hundred more in three days.[a] Of those attacked in the latter year, the exposure being on the 11th of May, Alderman Lambert died on the 13th, Under-Sheriff Cox on the 14th, and many of note before the

[a] Elliotson's *Practice*, p. 298.

20th.[a] But these are old stories. Let the student listen then to Dr. Gerhard, whose reputation as a cautious observer he may be supposed to know. "The nurse was shaving a man, who died in a few hours after his entrance; he inhaled his breath, which had a nauseous taste, and in an hour afterwards was taken with nausea, cephalalgia, and singing of the ears. From that *moment* the attack began, and assumed a severe character. The assistant was supporting another patient, who died soon afterwards; he felt the pungent heat upon his skin, and was taken immediately with the symptoms of typhus."[b] It is by notes of cases, rather than notes of admiration, that we must be guided, when we study the Revised Statutes of Nature, as laid down from the curule chairs of Medicine.

Let the student read Dr. Meigs's 140th paragraph soberly, and then remember, that not only does he *infer*, *suspect*, and *surmise*, but he actually *asserts* (page 154), " there was poison in the house," because three out of five patients admitted into a ward had puerperal fever and died. Have I not as much right to draw a positive inference from " Dr. A.'s " seventy exclusive cases as he from the three cases in the ward of the Dublin Hospital? All practical medicine, and all action in common affairs, is founded on inferences. How does Dr. Meigs know that the patients he bled in puerperal fever would not have all got well if he had not bled them?

" You see a man discharge a gun at another; you see the flash, you hear the report, you see the person fall a lifeless corpse; and you *infer*, from all these circumstances, that there was a ball discharged from

[a] Rees's *Cyc.* art. " Contagion."
[b] *Am. Jour. Med. Sciences*, Feb. 1837, p. 299.

the gun, which entered his body and caused his death, because such is the usual and natural cause of such an effect. But you did not see the ball leave the gun, pass through the air, and enter the body of the slain; and your testimony to the fact of killing is, therefore, only inferential, — in other words, circumstantial. It is *possible* that no ball was in the gun; and we *infer* that there was, only because we cannot account for death on any other supposition." [a]

"The question always comes to this: Is the circumstance of intercourse with the sick followed by the appearance of the disease in a proportion of cases so much greater than any other circumstance common to any portion of the inhabitants of the place under observation, as to make it inconceivable that the succession of cases occurring in persons having that intercourse should have been the result of chance? If so, the inference is unavoidable, that that intercourse must have acted as a cause of the disease. *All observations which do not bear strictly on that point are irrelevant*, and, in the case of an epidemic first appearing in a town or district, a succession of *two cases* is sometimes sufficient to furnish evidence which, on the principle I have stated, is nearly irresistible." [b]

Possibly an inexperienced youth may be awe-struck by the quotation from Cuvier. These words, or their equivalent, are certainly to be found in his Introduction. So are the words "top not come down"! to be found in the Bible, and they were as much meant for the ladies' head-dresses as the words of Cuvier were meant to make clinical observation wait for a permit from anybody to look with its eyes and count

* Chief Justice Gibson, in *Am. Law Journal*, vol. vi. p. 123.
Dr. Alison.

on its fingers. Let the inquiring youth read the whole Introduction, and he will see what they mean.

I intend no breach of courtesy, but this is a proper place to warn the student against skimming the prefaces and introductions of works for mottoes and embellishments to his thesis. He cannot learn anatomy by thrusting an exploring needle into the body. He will be very liable to misquote his author's meaning while he is picking off his outside sentences. He may make as great a blunder as that simple prince who praised the conductor of his orchestra for the piece just before the overture; the musician was too good a courtier to tell him that it was only the tuning of the instruments.

To the six propositions in the 142d paragraph, and the remarks about " specific " diseases, the answer, if any is necessary, seems very simple. An inflammation of a serous membrane may give rise to secretions which act as a poison, whether that be a " specific " poison or not, as Dr. Horner has told his young readers, and as dissectors know too well; and that poison may produce its symptoms in a few hours after the system has received it, as any may see in Druitt's " Surgery," if they care to look. Puerperal peritonitis may produce such a poison, and puerperal women may be very sensible to its influences, conveyed by contact or exhalation. Whether this is so or not, facts alone can determine, and to facts we have had recourse to settle it.

The following statement is made by Dr. Meigs in his 142d paragraph, and developed more at length, with rhetorical amplifications, in the 134th. " No human being, save a pregnant or parturient woman, is susceptible to the poison." This statement is wholly

57

incorrect, as I am sorry to have to point out to a Teacher in Dr. Meigs's position. I do not object to the erudition which quotes Willis and Fernelius, the last of whom was pleasantly said to have " preserved the dregs of the Arabs in the honey of his Latinity." But I could wish that more modern authorities had not been overlooked. On this point, for instance, among the numerous facts disproving the statement, the " American Journal of Medical Sciences," published not far from his lecture-room, would have presented him with a respectable catalogue of such cases. Thus he might refer to Mr. Storrs's paper " On the Contagious Effects of Puerperal Fever on the Male Subject ; or on Persons not Childbearing " (Jan. 1846), or to Dr. Reid's case (April, 1846), or to Dr. Barron's statement of the children's dying of peritonitis in an epidemic of puerperal fever at the Philadelphia Hospital (Oct. 1842), or to various instances cited in Dr. Kneeland's article (April, 1846). Or, if he would have referred to the " New York Journal," he might have seen Prof. Austin Flint's cases. Or, if he had honored my Essay so far, he might have found striking instances of the same kind in the first of the new series of cases there reported and elsewhere. I do not see the bearing of his proposition, if it were true. But it is one of those assertions that fall in a moment before a slight examination of the facts ; and I confess my surprise, that a professor who lectures on the Diseases of Women should have ventured to make it.

Nearly seven pages are devoted to showing that I was wrong in saying I would not be " understood to imply that there exists a doubt in the mind of any well-informed member of the medical profession as to the fact that puerperal fever is sometimes communicated from one person to another, both directly and indirectly." I will devote seven lines to these seven pages, which seven lines, if I may say it without offence, are, as it seems to me, six more than are strictly necessary.

The following authors are cited as sceptics by Dr. Meigs : —

Dewees. — I cited the same passage. Did not know half the facts. *Robert Lee.* — Believes the disease is sometimes communicable by contagion. *Tonnellé Baudelocque.* — Both cited by me. *Jacquemier.* — Published three years after my Essay. *Kiwisch.* — Behindhand in knowledge of Puerperal Fever.[a] *Paul Dubois.* — *Scanzoni.* } Continental writers not well informed on this point.[b]

The story of Von Busch is of interest and value, but there is nothing in it which need perplex the student. It is not pretended that the disease is always, or even, it may be, in the majority of cases, carried about by attendants ; only that it is so carried in certain cases. That it may have local and epidemic causes, as well as that depending on personal transmission, is not disputed. Remember how small-pox often disappears from a community in spite of its contagious character, and the necessary exposure of many persons to those suffering from it ; in both diseases contagion is only one of the coefficients of the disease.

I have already spoken of the possibility that Dr. Meigs may have been the medium of transfer of puerperal fever in some of the cases he has briefly catalogued. Of Dr. Rutter's cases I do not know how to

[a] *B. & F. Med. Rev.* Jan. 1842.
[b] See Dr. Simpson's Remarks at Meeting of Edin. Med. Chir. Soc. (*Am. Jour.* Oct. 1851.)

speak. I only ask the student to read the facts stated
by Dr. Condie, as given in my Essay, and say whether
or not a man should allow his wife to be attended by
a practitioner in whose hands " scarcely a female that
has been delivered for weeks past has escaped an attack," " while no instance of the disease has occurred
in the patients of any other accoucheur practising in
the same district." If I understand Dr. Meigs and
Dr. Hodge, they would not warn the physician or
spare the patient under such circumstances. They
would " go on," if I understand them, not to seven, or
seventy, only, but to seventy times seven, if they could
find patients. If this is not what they mean, may we
respectfully ask them to state what they do mean, to
their next classes, in the name of humanity, if not of
science!

I might repeat the question asked concerning Dr.
Rutter's cases, with reference to those reported by Dr.
Roberton. Perhaps, however, the student would like
to know the opinion of a person in the habit of working at matters of this kind in a practical point of view.
To satisfy him on this ground, I addressed the following question to the President of one of our principal
Insurance Companies, leaving Dr. Meigs's book and
my Essay in his hands at the same time.

Question. " If such facts as Roberton's cases were
before you, and the attendant had had ten, or even
five fatal cases, or three, or *two* even, would you, or
would you not, if insuring the life of the next patient
to be taken care of by that attendant, expect an extra
premium over that of an average case of childbirth?"

Answer. " Of course I should require a very large
extra premium, if I would take the risk at all."

But I do not choose to add the expressions of indignation which the examination of the facts before him called out. I was satisfied from the effect they produced on him, that if all the hideous catalogues of cases now accumulated were fully brought to the knowledge of the public, nothing, since the days of Burke and Hare, has raised such a cry of horror as would be shrieked in the ears of the Profession.

Dr. Meigs has elsewhere invoked " Providence " as the alternative of accident, to account for the " coincidences." ("Obstetrics," Phil. 1852, p. 631.) If so, Providence either acts through the agency of secondary causes, as in other diseases, or not. If through such causes, let us find out what they are, as we try to do in other cases. It may be true that offences, or diseases, will come, but " woe unto him through whom they come," if we catch him in the voluntary or careless act of bringing them! But if Providence does not act through secondary causes in this particular sphere of etiology, then why does Dr. Meigs take such pains to reason so extensively about the laws of contagion, which, on that supposition, have no more to do with this case than with the plague which destroyed the people after David had numbered them? Above all, what becomes of the theological aspect of the question, when he asserts that a practitioner was "only *unlucky* in meeting with the epidemic cases?" (*Op. cit.* p. 633.) We do not deny that the God of battles decides the fate of nations; but we like to have the biggest squadrons on our side, and we are particular that our soldiers should not only say their prayers, but also keep their powder dry. We do not deny the agency of Providence in the disaster at Norwalk, but we turn off the engineer, and charge the Company five thousand dollars apiece for every life that is sacrificed.

Why a grand jury should not bring in a bill against a physician who switches off a score of women one after the other along his private track, when he knows that there is a black gulf at the end of it, down which they are to plunge, while the great highway is clear, is more than I can answer. It is not by laying the open draw to Providence that he is to escape the charge of manslaughter.

To finish with all these lesser matters of question, I am unable to see why a female must necessarily be unattended in her confinement, because she declines the services of a particular practitioner. In all the series of cases mentioned, the death-carrying attendant was surrounded by others not tracked by disease and its consequences. Which, I would ask, is worse, — to call in another, even a rival practitioner, or to submit an unsuspecting female to a risk which an Insurance Company would have nothing to do with?

I do not expect ever to return to this subject. There is a point of mental saturation, beyond which argument cannot be forced without breeding impatient, if not harsh, feelings towards those who refuse to be convinced. If I have so far manifested neither, it is well to stop here, and leave the rest to those younger friends who may have more stomach for the dregs of a stale argument.

The extent of my prefatory remarks may lead some to think that I attach too much importance to my own Essay. Others may wonder that I should expend so many words upon the two productions referred to, the Letter and the Lecture. I do consider my Essay of much importance so long as the doctrine it maintains is treated as a *question*, and so long as any important part of the defence of that doctrine is thought to rest on its evidence or arguments. I cannot treat as insignificant any opinions bearing on life, and interests dearer than life, proclaimed yearly to hundreds of young men, who will carry them to their legitimate results in practice.

The teachings of the two Professors in the great schools of Philadelphia are sure to be listened to, not only by their immediate pupils, but by the Profession at large. I am too much in earnest for either humility or vanity, but I do entreat those who hold the keys of life and death to listen to me also for this once. I ask no personal favor; but I beg to be heard in behalf of the women whose lives are at stake, until some stronger voice shall plead for them.

I trust that I have made the issue perfectly distinct and intelligible. And let it be remembered that this is no subject to be smoothed over by nicely adjusted phrases of half-assent and half-censure divided between the parties. The balance must be struck boldly and the result declared plainly. If I have been hasty, presumptuous, ill-informed, illogical; if my array of facts means nothing; if there is no reason for any caution in the view of these facts; let me be told so on such authority that I must believe it, and I will be silent henceforth, recognizing that my mind is in a state of disorganization. If the doctrine I have maintained is a mournful truth; if to disbelieve it, and to practise on this disbelief, and to teach others so to disbelieve and practise, is to carry desolation, and to charter others to carry it, into confiding families, let it be proclaimed as plainly what is to be thought of the teachings of those who sneer at the alleged dangers, and scout the very idea of precaution. Let it be remembered that *persons* are nothing in this matter; better that twenty pamphleteers should be silenced, or as many professors unseated, than that one mother's life should be taken. There is no quarrel here between men, but there is deadly incompatibility and exterminating warfare between doctrines. *Coincidences*, meaning nothing, though a man have a monopoly of the disease for weeks or months; or *cause and effect*, the cause being in some way connected with the person; this is the question. If I am wrong, let me be put down by such a rebuke as no rash declaimer has received since there has been a public opinion in the medical profession of America; if I am right, let doctrines which lead to professional homicide be no longer taught from the chairs of those two great Institutions. Indifference will not do here; our Journalists and Committees have no right to take up their pages with minute anatomy and tediously detailed cases, while it is a question whether or not the "black-death" of child-bed is to be scattered broadcast by the agency of the mother's friend and adviser. Let the men who mould opinions look to it; if there is any voluntary blindness, any interested oversight, any culpable negligence, even, in such a matter, and the facts shall reach the public ear; the pestilence-carrier of the lying-in chamber must look to God for pardon, for man will never forgive him.

THE CONTAGIOUSNESS OF PUERPERAL FEVER.

In collecting, enforcing, and adding to the evidence accumulated upon this most serious subject, I would not be understood to imply that there exists a doubt in the mind of any well-informed member of the medical

profession as to the fact that puerperal fever is sometimes communicated from one person to another, both
directly and indirectly. In the present state of our
knowledge upon this point I should consider such
doubts merely as a proof that the sceptic had either
not examined the evidence, or, having examined it, refused to accept its plain and unavoidable consequences.
I should be sorry to think, with Dr. Rigby, that it was
a case of "oblique vision;" I should be unwilling
to force home the *argumentum ad hominem* of Dr.
Blundell, but I would not consent to make a *question* of a momentous fact which is no longer to be
considered as a subject for trivial discussions, but to
be acted upon with silent promptitude. It signifies
nothing that wise and experienced practitioners have
sometimes doubted the reality of the danger in question; no man has the right to doubt it any longer.
No negative facts, no opposing opinions, be they what
they may, or whose they may, can form any answer to
the series of cases now within the reach of all who
choose to explore the records of medical science.

If there are some who conceive that any important
end would be answered by recording such opinions, or
by collecting the history of all the cases they could find
in which no evidence of the influence of contagion existed, I believe they are in error. Suppose a few
writers of authority can be found to profess a disbelief
in contagion, — and they are very few compared with
those who think differently, — is it quite clear that
they formed their opinions on a view of all the facts,
or is it not apparent that they relied mostly on their
own solitary experience? Still further, of those whose
names are quoted, is it not true that scarcely a single
one could by any possibility have known the half or

the tenth of the facts bearing on the subject which have reached such a frightful amount within the last few years? Again, as to the utility of negative facts, as we may briefly call them, — instances, namely, in which exposure has not been followed by disease, — although, like other truths, they may be worth knowing, I do not see that they are like to shed any important light upon the subject before us. Every such instance requires a good deal of circumstantial explanation before it can be accepted. It is not enough that a practitioner should have had a single case of puerperal fever not followed by others. It must be known whether he attended others while this case was in progress, whether he went directly from one chamber to others, whether he took any, and what precautions. It is important to know that several women were exposed to infection derived from the patient, so that allowance may be made for want of predisposition. Now if of negative facts so sifted there could be accumulated a hundred for every one plain instance of communication here recorded, I trust it need not be said that we are bound to guard and watch over the hundredth tenant of our fold, though the ninety and nine may be sure of escaping the wolf at its entrance. If any one is disposed, then, to take a hundred instances of lives endangered or sacrificed out of those I have mentioned, and make it reasonably clear that within a similar time and compass *ten thousand* escaped the same exposure, I shall thank him for his industry, but I must be permitted to hold to my own practical conclusions, and beg him to adopt or at least to examine them also. Children that walk in calico before open fires are not always burned to death; the instances to the contrary may be worth recording; but by no means if they are to be used as arguments against woollen frocks and high fenders.

I am not sure that this paper will escape another remark which it might be wished were founded in justice. It may be said that the facts are too generally known and acknowledged to require any formal argument or exposition, that there is nothing new in the positions advanced, and no need of laying additional statements before the Profession. But on turning to two works, one almost universally, and the other extensively appealed to as authority in this country, I see ample reason to overlook this objection. In the last edition of Dewees's Treatise on the "Diseases of Females," it is expressly said, "In this country, under no circumstance that puerperal fever has appeared hitherto, does it afford the slightest ground for the belief that it is contagious." In the "Philadelphia Practice of Midwifery" not one word can be found in the chapter devoted to this disease which would lead the reader to suspect that the idea of contagion had ever been entertained. It seems proper, therefore, to remind those who are in the habit of referring to these works for guidance, that there may possibly be some sources of danger they have slighted or omitted, quite as important as a trifling irregularity of diet, or a confined state of the bowels, and that whatever confidence a physician may have in his own mode of treatment, his services are of questionable value whenever he carries the bane as well as the antidote about his person.

The practical point to be illustrated is the following: *The disease known as Puerperal Fever is so far contagious as to be frequently carried from patient to patient by physicians and nurses.*

Let me begin by throwing out certain incidental questions, which, without being absolutely essential, would render the subject more complicated, and by making such concessions and assumptions as. may be fairly supposed to be without the pale of discussion.

1. It is granted that all the forms of what is called puerperal fever may not be, and probably are not, equally contagious or infectious. I do not enter into the distinctions which have been drawn by authors, because the facts do not appear to me sufficient to establish any absolute line of demarcation between such forms as may be propagated by contagion and those which are never so propagated. This general result I shall only support by the authority of Dr. Ramsbotham, who gives, as the result of his experience, that the same symptoms belong to what he calls the infectious and the sporadic forms of the disease, and the opinion of Armstrong in his original Essay. If others can show any such distinction, I leave it to them to do it. But there are cases enough that show the prevalence of the disease among the patients of a single practitioner when it was in no degree epidemic, in the proper sense of the term. I may refer to those of Mr. Roberton and of Dr. Peirson, hereafter to be cited, as examples.

2. I shall not enter into any dispute about the particular *mode* of infection, whether it be by the atmosphere the physician carries about him into the sick-chamber, or by the direct application of the virus to the absorbing surfaces with which his hand comes in contact. Many facts and opinions are in favor of each of these modes of transmission. But it is obvious that in the majority of cases it must be impossible to decide by which of these channels the disease is con-

veyed, from the nature of the intercourse between the physician and the patient.

3. It is not pretended that the contagion of puerperal fever must always be followed by the disease. It is true of all contagious diseases, that they frequently spare those who appear to be fully submitted to their influence. Even the vaccine virus, fresh from the subject, fails every day to produce its legitimate effect, though every precaution is taken to insure its action. This is still more remarkably the case with scarlet fever and some other diseases.

4. It is granted that the disease may be produced and variously modified by many causes besides contagion, and more especially by epidemic and endemic influences. But this is not peculiar to the disease in question. There is no doubt that small-pox is propagated to a great extent by contagion, yet it goes through the same periods of periodical increase and diminution which have been remarked in puerperal fever. If the question is asked how we are to reconcile the great variations in the mortality of puerperal fever in different seasons and places with the supposition of contagion, I will answer it by another question from Mr. Farr's letter to the Registrar-General. He makes the statement that "*five* die weekly of small-pox in the metropolis when the disease is not epidemic," — and adds, "The problem for solution is, — Why do the five deaths become 10, 15, 20, 31, 58, 88, weekly, and then progressively fall through the same measured steps?"

5. I take it for granted, that if it can be shown that great numbers of lives have been and are sacrificed to ignorance or blindness on this point, no other error of which physicians or nurses may be occasionally sus-

pected will be alleged in palliation of this; but that whenever and wherever they can be shown to carry disease and death instead of health and safety, the common instincts of humanity will silence every attempt to explain away their responsibility.

The treatise of Dr. Gordon of Aberdeen was published in the year 1795, being among the earlier special works upon the disease. A part of his testimony has been occasionally copied into other works, but his expressions are so clear, his experience is given with such manly distinctness and disinterested honesty, that it may be quoted as a model which might have been often followed with advantage.

"This disease seized such women only as were visited, or delivered by a practitioner, or taken care of by a nurse, who had previously attended patients affected with the disease."

"I had evident proofs of its infectious nature, and that the infection was as readily communicated as that of the small-pox or measles, and operated more speedily than any other infection with which I am acquainted."

"I had evident proofs that every person who had been with a patient in the puerperal fever became charged with an atmosphere of infection, which was communicated to every pregnant woman who happened to come within its sphere. This is not an assertion, but a fact, admitting of demonstration, as may be seen by a perusal of the foregoing table," — referring to a table of seventy-seven cases, in many of which the channel of propagation was evident.

He adds, "It is a disagreeable declaration for me to mention, that I myself was the means of carrying the infection to a great number of women." He then enumerates a number of instances in which the disease was conveyed by midwives and others to the neighboring villages, and declares that " these facts fully prove that the cause of the puerperal fever, of which I treat, was a specific contagion, or infection, altogether unconnected with a noxious constitution of the atmosphere."

But his most terrible evidence is given in these words : " I ARRIVED AT THAT CERTAINTY IN THE MATTER, THAT I COULD VENTURE TO FORETELL WHAT WOMEN WOULD BE AFFECTED WITH THE DISEASE, UPON HEARING BY WHAT MIDWIFE THEY WERE TO BE DELIVERED, OR BY WHAT NURSE THEY WERE TO BE ATTENDED, DURING THEIR LYING-IN : AND ALMOST IN EVERY INSTANCE, MY PREDICTION WAS VERIFIED."

Even previously to Gordon, Mr. White of Manchester had said, " I am acquainted with two gentlemen in another town, where the whole business of midwifery is divided betwixt them, and it is very remarkable that one of them loses several patients every year of the puerperal fever, and the other never so much as meets with the disorder," — a difference which he seems to attribute to their various modes of treatment.[a]

Dr. Armstrong has given a number of instances in his Essay on Puerperal Fever, of the prevalence of the disease among the patients of a single practitioner. At Sunderland, " in all, forty-three cases occurred from the 1st of January to the 1st of October, when the disease ceased ; and of this number forty were witnessed by Mr. Gregson and his assistant, Mr. Gregory, the remainder having been separately seen by three accoucheurs." There is appended to the London edi-

[a] *On the Management of Lying-in Women,* p. 120.

tion of this Essay, a letter from Mr. Gregson, in which that gentleman says, in reference to the great number of cases occurring in his practice, "The cause of this I cannot pretend fully to explain, but I should be wanting in common liberality if I were to make any hesitation in asserting, that the disease which appeared in my practice was highly contagious, and communicable from one puerperal woman to another." "It is customary among the lower and middle ranks of people to make frequent personal visits to puerperal women resident in the same neighborhood, and I have ample evidence for affirming that the infection of the disease was often carried about in that manner; and, however painful to my feelings, I must in candor declare, that it is very probable the contagion was conveyed, in some instances, by myself, though I took every possible care to prevent such a thing from happening, the moment that I ascertained that the distemper was infectious." Dr. Armstrong goes on to mention six other instances within his knowledge, in which the disease had at different times and places been limited, in the same singular manner, to the practice of individuals, while it existed scarcely if at all among the patients of others around them. Two of the gentlemen became so convinced of their conveying the contagion, that they withdrew for a time from practice.

I find a brief notice, in an American Journal, of another series of cases, first mentioned by Mr. Davies, in the "Medical Repository." This gentleman stated his conviction that the disease is contagious.

"In the autumn of 1822 he met with twelve cases, while his medical friends in the neighborhood did not meet with any, 'or at least very few.' He could attribute this circumstance to no other cause than his having been present at the examination, after death, of two cases, some time previous, and of his having imparted the disease to his patients, notwithstanding every precaution." [a]

Dr. Gooch says, " It is not uncommon for the greater number of cases to occur in the practice of one man, whilst the other practitioners of the neighborhood, who are not more skilful or more busy, meet with few or none. A practitioner opened the body of a woman who had died of puerperal fever, and continued to wear the same clothes. A lady whom he delivered a few days afterwards was attacked with and died of a similar disease ; two more of his lying-in patients, in rapid succession, met with the same fate ; struck by the thought, that he might have carried contagion in his clothes, he instantly changed them, and met with no more cases of the kind.[b] A woman in the country, who was employed as washerwoman and nurse, washed the linen of one who had died of puerperal fever ; the next lying-in patient she nursed died of the same disease ; a third nursed by her met with the same fate, till the neighborhood, getting afraid of her, ceased to employ her." [c]

In the winter of the year 1824, " Several instances occurred of its prevalence among the patients of particular practitioners, whilst others who were equally busy met with few or none. One instance of this kind was very remarkable. A general practitioner, in large midwifery practice, lost so many patients from puer-

[a] *Philad. Med. Journal* for 1825, p. 408.

[b] A similar anecdote is related by Sir Benjamin Brodie, of the late Dr. John Clarke. *Lancet*, May 2, 1840.

[c] *An Account of some of the most important Diseases peculiar to Women*, p. 4.

peral fever, that he determined to deliver no more for some time, but that his partner should attend in his place.   This plan was pursued for one month, during which not a case of the disease occurred in their practice.   The elder practitioner, being then sufficiently recovered, returned to his practice, but the first patient he attended was attacked by the disease and died.   A physician, who met him in consultation soon afterwards, about a case of a different kind, and who knew nothing of his misfortune, asked him whether puerperal fever was at all prevalent in his neighborhood, on which he burst into tears, and related the above circumstances.

" Among the cases which I saw this season in consultation, four occurred in one month in the practice of one medical man, and all of them terminated fatally." [a]

Dr. Ramsbotham asserted, in a Lecture at the London Hospital, that he had known the disease spread through a particular district, or be confined to the practice of a particular person, almost every patient being attacked with it, while others had not a single case.   It seemed capable, he thought, of conveyance, not only by common modes, but through the dress of the attendants upon the patient.[b]

In a letter to be found in the " London Medical Gazette " for January, 1840, Mr. Roberton of Manchester makes the statement which I here give in a somewhat condensed form.

A midwife delivered a woman on the 4th of December, 1830, who died soon after with the symptoms of puerperal fever.   In one month from this date the

[a] Gooch, *Op. cit.* p. 71.
[b] *Lond. Med. Gaz.* May 2, 1835.

same midwife delivered thirty women, residing in different parts of an extensive suburb, of which number sixteen caught the disease and all died. These were the only cases which had occurred for a considerable time in Manchester. The other midwives connected with the same charitable institution as the woman already mentioned are twenty-five in number, and deliver, on an average, ninety women a week, or about three hundred and eighty a month. None of these women had a case of puerperal fever. "Yet all this time this woman was crossing the other midwives in every direction, scores of the patients of the charity being delivered by them in the very same quarters where her cases of fever were happening."

Mr. Roberton remarks, that little more than half the women she delivered during this month took the fever; that on some days all escaped, on others only one or more out of three or four; a circumstance similar to what is seen in other infectious maladies.

Dr. Blundell says, "Those who have never made the experiment can have but a faint conception how difficult it is to obtain the exact truth respecting any occurrence in which feelings and interests are concerned. Omitting particulars, then, I content myself with remarking, generally, that from more than one district I have received accounts of the prevalence of puerperal fever in the practice of some individuals, while its occurrence in that of others, in the same neighborhood, was not observed. Some, as I have been told, have lost ten, twelve, or a greater number of patients, in scarcely broken succession; like their evil genius, the puerperal fever has seemed to stalk behind them wherever they went. Some have deemed it prudent to retire for a time from practice. In fine, that this fever may occur spontaneously, I admit; that its infectious nature may be plausibly disputed, I do not deny; but I add, considerately, that in my own family I had rather that those I esteemed the most should be delivered, unaided, in a stable, by the manger-side, than that they should receive the best help, in the fairest apartment, but exposed to the vapors of this pitiless disease. Gossiping friends, wet-nurses, monthly nurses, the practitioner himself, these are the channels by which, as I suspect, the infection is principally conveyed." [a]

At a meeting of the Royal Medical and Chirurgical Society, Dr. King mentioned that some years since a practitioner at Woolwich lost sixteen patients from puerperal fever in the same year. He was compelled to give up practice for one or two years, his business being divided among the neighboring practitioners. No case of puerperal fever occurred afterwards, neither had any of the neighboring surgeons any cases of this disease.

At the same meeting Mr. Hutchinson mentioned the occurrence of three consecutive cases of puerperal fever, followed subsequently by two others, all in the practice of one accoucheur.[b]

Dr. Lee makes the following statement: "In the last two weeks of September, 1827, five fatal cases of uterine inflammation came under our observation. All the individuals so attacked had been attended in labor by the same midwife, and no example of a febrile or inflammatory disease of a serious nature occurred during that period among the other patients of the Westminster General Dispensary, who had been at-

---

[a] *Lect. on Midwifery*, p. 395.
[b] *Lancet*, May 2, 1840.

tended by the other midwives belonging to that institution. "[a]

The recurrence of long series of cases like those I have cited, reported by those most interested to disbelieve in contagion, scattered along through an interval of half a century, might have been thought sufficient to satisfy the minds of all inquirers that here was something more than a singular coincidence. But if, on a more extended observation, it should be found that the same ominous groups of cases clustering about individual practitioners were observed in a remote country, at different times, and in widely separated regions, it would seem incredible that any should be found too prejudiced or indolent to accept the solemn truth knelled into their ears by the funeral bells from both sides of the ocean, — the plain conclusion that the physician and the disease entered, hand in hand, into the chamber of the unsuspecting patient.

That such series of cases have been observed in this country, and in this neighborhood, I proceed to show.

In Dr. Francis's " Notes to Denman's Midwifery," a passage is cited from Dr. Hosack, in which he refers to certain puerperal cases which proved fatal to several lying-in women, and in some of which the disease was supposed to be conveyed by the accoucheurs themselves.[b]

A writer in the " New York Medical and Physical Journal " for October, 1829, in speaking of the occurrence of puerperal fever, confined to one man's practice, remarks, " We have known cases of this kind occur, though rarely, in New York."

[a] *Lond. Cyc. of Pract. Med. art. " Fever, Puerperal."*
[b] *Denman's Midwifery, p. 673, 3d Am. ed.*

I mention these little hints about the occurrence of such cases, partly because they are the first I have met with in American medical literature, but more especially because they serve to remind us that behind the fearful array of published facts there lies a dark list of similar events, unwritten in the records of science, but long remembered by many a desolated fireside.

Certainly nothing can be more open and explicit than the account given by Dr. Peirson of Salem, of the cases seen by him. In the first nineteen days of January, 1829, he had five consecutive cases of puerperal fever, every patient he attended being attacked, and the three first cases proving fatal. In March of the same year he had two moderate cases, in June, another case, and in July, another, which proved fatal. "Up to this period," he remarks, " I am not informed that a single case had occurred in the practice of any other physician. Since that period I have had no fatal case in my practice, although I have had several dangerous cases. I have attended in all twenty cases of this disease, of which four have been fatal. I am not aware that there has been any other case in the town of distinct puerperal peritonitis, although I am willing to admit my information may be very defective on this point. I have been told of some ' mixed cases,' and ' morbid affections after delivery.' " [a]

In the " Quarterly Summary of the Transactions of the College of Physicians of Philadelphia " [b] may be found some most extraordinary developments respecting a series of cases occurring in the practice of a member of that body.

[a] *Remarks on Puerperal Fever*, pp. 12 and 13.
[b] For May, June, and July, 1842.

Dr. Condie called the attention of the Society to the prevalence, at the present time, of puerperal fever of a peculiarly insidious and malignant character. "In the practice of one gentleman extensively engaged as an obstetrician, nearly every female he has attended in confinement, during several weeks past, within the above limits" (the southern sections and neighboring districts), "had been attacked by the fever."

"An important query presents itself, the Doctor observed, in reference to the particular form of fever now prevalent. Is it, namely, capable of being propagated by contagion, and is a physician who has been in attendance upon a case of the disease warranted in continuing, without interruption, his practice as an obstetrician? Dr. C., although not a believer in the contagious character of many of those affections generally supposed to be propagated in this manner, has nevertheless become convinced by the facts that have fallen under his notice, that the puerperal fever now prevailing is capable of being communicated by contagion. How otherwise can be explained the very curious circumstance of the disease in one district being exclusively confined to the practice of a single physician, a Fellow of this College, extensively engaged in obstetrical practice, — while no instance of the disease has occurred in the patients under the care of any other accoucheur practising within the same district; scarcely a female that has been delivered for weeks past has escaped an attack?"

Dr. Rutter, the practitioner referred to, "observed that, after the occurrence of a number of cases of the disease in his practice, he had left the city and remained absent for a week, but on returning, no article of clothing he then wore having been used by him before, one of the very first cases of parturition he attended was followed by an attack of the fever, and terminated fatally; he cannot, readily, therefore, believe in the transmission of the disease from female to female, in the person or clothes of the physician."

The meeting at which these remarks were made was held on the 3d of May, 1842. In a letter dated December 20, 1842, addressed to Dr. Meigs, and to be found in the "Medical Examiner,"[a] he speaks of "those horrible cases of puerperal fever, some of which you did me the favor to see with me during the past summer," and talks of his experience in the disease, "now numbering nearly seventy cases, all of which have occurred within less than a twelvemonth past."

And Dr. Meigs asserts, on the same page, "Indeed, I believe that his practice in that department of the profession was greater than that of any other gentleman, which was probably the cause of his seeing a greater number of the cases." This from a professor of midwifery, who some time ago assured a gentleman whom he met in consultation, that the night on which they met was the eighteenth in succession that he himself had been summoned from his repose,[b] seems hardly satisfactory.

I must call the attention of the inquirer most particularly to the Quarterly Report above referred to, and the letters of Dr. Meigs and Dr. Rutter, to be found in the "Medical Examiner." Whatever impression they may produce upon his mind, I trust they will at least convince him that there is some reason for looking into this apparently uninviting subject.

At a meeting of the College of Physicians just men-

[a] For January 21, 1843.
[b] *Medical Examiner* for December 10, 1842.

tioned, Dr. Warrington stated, that a few days after assisting at an autopsy of puerperal peritonitis, in which he laded out the contents of the abdominal cavity with his hands, he was called upon to deliver three women in rapid succession. All of these women were attacked with different forms of what is commonly called puerperal fever. Soon after these he saw two other patients, both on the same day, with the same disease. Of these five patients two died.

At the same meeting, Dr. West mentioned a fact related to him by Dr. Samuel Jackson of Northumberland. Seven females, delivered by Dr. Jackson in rapid succession, while practising in Northumberland County, were all attacked with puerperal fever, and five of them died. " Women," he said, " who had expected me to attend upon them, now becoming alarmed, removed out of my reach, and others sent for a physician residing several miles distant. These women, as well as those attended by midwives, all did well; nor did we hear of any deaths in child-bed within a radius of fifty miles, excepting two, and these I afterwards ascertained to have been caused by other diseases." He underwent, as he thought, a thorough purification, and still his next patient was attacked with the disease and died. He was led to suspect that the contagion might have been carried in the gloves which he had worn in attendance upon the previous cases. Two months or more after this he had two other cases. He could find nothing to account for these, unless it were the instruments for giving enemata, which had been used in two of the former cases, and were employed by these patients. When the first case occurred, he was attending and dressing a limb extensively mortified from erysipelas, and went immediately to the accouchement with his clothes and gloves most thoroughly imbued with its effluvia. And here I may mention, that this very Dr. Samuel Jackson of Northumberland is one of Dr. Dewees's authorities against contagion.

The three following statements are now for the first time given to the public. All of the cases referred to occurred within this State, and two of the three series in Boston and its immediate vicinity.

I. The first is a series of cases which took place during the last spring in a town at some distance from this neighborhood. A physician of that town, Dr. C., had the following consecutive cases.

No. 1, delivered March 20, died March 24.
 " 2,   "   April 9, " April 14.
 " 3,   "   "   10, "   "   14.
 " 4,   "   "   11, "   "   18.
 " 5,   "   "   27,   May   3.
 " 6,   "   "   28, had some symptoms,
                                    [recovered.
 " 7,   "   May 8, had some symptoms,
                                    [also recovered.

These were the only cases attended by this physician during the period referred to. "They were all attended by him until their termination, with the exception of the patient No. 6, who fell into the hands of another physician on the 2d of May. (Dr. C. left town for a few days at this time.) Dr. C. attended cases immediately before and after the above-named periods, none of which, however, presented any peculiar symptoms of the disease.

About the 1st of July he attended another patient

in a neighboring village, who died two or three days after delivery.

The first patient, it is stated, was delivered on the 20th of March. " On the 19th, Dr. C. made the autopsy of a man who died suddenly, sick only forty-eight hours ; had œdema of the thigh, and gangrene extending from a little above the ankle into the cavity of the abdomen." Dr. C. wounded himself, very slightly, in the right hand during the autopsy. The hand was quite painful the night following, during his attendance on the patient No. 1. He did not see this patient after the 20th, being confined to the house, and very sick from the wound just mentioned, from this time until the 3d of April.

Several cases of erysipelas occurred in the house where the autopsy mentioned above took place, soon after the examination. There were also many cases of erysipelas in town at the time of the fatal puerperal cases which have been mentioned.

The nurse who laid out the body of the patient No. 3 was taken on the evening of the same day with sore throat and erysipelas, and died in ten days from the first attack.

The nurse who laid out the body of the patient No. 4 was taken on the day following with symptoms like those of this patient, and died in a week, without any external marks of erysipelas.

" No other cases of similar character with those of Dr. C. occurred in the practice of any of the physicians in the town or vicinity at the time. Deaths following confinement have occurred in the practice of other physicians during the past year, but they were not cases of puerperal fever. No post-mortem examinations were held in any of these puerperal cases."

Some additional statements in this letter are deserving of insertion.

"A physician attended a woman in the immediate neighborhood of the cases numbered 2, 3, and 4. This patient was confined the morning of March 1st, and died on the night of March 7th. It is doubtful whether this should be considered a case of puerperal fever. She had suffered from canker, indigestion, and diarrhœa for a year previous to her delivery. Her complaints were much aggravated for two or three months previous to delivery; she had become greatly emaciated, and weakened to such an extent that it had not been expected that she would long survive her confinement, if indeed she reached that period. Her labor was easy enough; she flowed a good deal, seemed exceedingly prostrated, had ringing in the ears, and other symptoms of exhaustion; the pulse was quick and small. On the second and third day there was some tenderness and tumefaction of the abdomen, which increased somewhat on the fourth and fifth. He had cases in midwifery before and after this, which presented nothing peculiar."

It is also mentioned in the same letter, that another physician had a case during the last summer and another last fall, both of which recovered.

Another gentleman reports a case last December, a second case five weeks, and another three weeks since. All these recovered. A case also occurred very recently in the practice of a physician in the village where the eighth patient of Dr. C. resides, which proved fatal. "This patient had some patches of erysipelas on the legs and arms. The same physician has delivered three cases since, which have all done well. There have been no other cases in this town or its vicinity recently. There have been some few cases of erysipelas." It deserves notice that the partner of Dr. C., who attended the autopsy of the man above mentioned and took an active part in it; who also suffered very slightly from a prick under the thumb-nail received during the examination, had twelve cases of midwifery between March 26th and April 12th, all of which did well, and presented no peculiar symptoms. It should also be stated, that during these seventeen days he was in attendance on all the cases of erysipelas in the house where the autopsy had been performed.

I owe these facts to the prompt kindness of a gentleman whose intelligence and character are sufficient guaranty for their accuracy.

The two following letters were addressed to my friend Dr. Storer, by the gentleman in whose practice the cases of puerperal fever occurred. His name renders it unnecessary to refer more particularly to these gentlemen, who on their part have manifested the most perfect freedom and courtesy in affording these accounts of their painful experience.

"January 28, 1843.

II. . . . "The time to which you allude was in 1830. The first case was in February, during a very cold time. She was confined the 4th, and died the 12th. Between the 10th and 28th of this month, I attended six women in labor, all of whom did well except the last, as also two who were confined March 1st and 5th. Mrs. E., confined February 28th, sickened, and died March 8th. The next day, 9th, I inspected the body, and the night after attended a lady, Mrs. B., who sickened, and died 16th. The 10th, I attended another, Mrs. G., who sickened, but recovered. March 16th, I went from Mrs. G.'s room to attend a Mrs. H., who sickened, and died 21st. The 17th, I inspected Mrs. B. On the 19th, I went directly from Mrs. H.'s room to attend another lady, Mrs. G., who also sickened, and died 22d. While Mrs. B. was sick, on 15th, I went directly from her room a few rods, and attended another woman, who was not sick. Up to 20th of this month I wore the same clothes. I now refused to attend any labor, and did not till April 21st, when, having thoroughly cleansed myself, I resumed my practice, and had no more puerperal fever.

"The cases were not confined to a narrow space. The two nearest were half a mile from each other, and half that distance from my residence. The others were from two to three miles apart, and nearly that distance from my residence. There were no other cases in their immediate vicinity which came to my knowledge. The general health of all the women was pretty good, and all the labors as good as common, except the first. This woman, in consequence of my not arriving in season, and the child being half-born at some time before I arrived, was very much exposed to the cold at the time of confinement, and afterwards, being confined in a very open, cold room. Of the six cases you perceive only one recovered.

"In the winter of 1817 two of my patients had puerperal fever, one very badly, the other not so badly. Both recovered. One other had swelled leg, or phlegmasia dolens, and one or two others did not recover as well as usual.

"In the summer of 1835 another disastrous period occurred in my practice. July 1st, I attended a lady in labor, who was afterwards quite ill and feverish;

but at the time I did not consider her case a decided puerperal fever. On the 8th, I attended one who did well. On the 12th, one who was seriously sick. This was also an equivocal case, apparently arising from constipation and irritation of the rectum. These women were ten miles apart and five from my residence. On 15th and 20th, two who did well. On 25th, I attended another. This was a severe labor, and followed by unequivocal puerperal fever, or peritonitis. She recovered. August 2d and 3d, in about twenty-four hours I attended four persons. Two of them did very well; one was attacked with some of the common symptoms, which however subsided in a day or two, and the other had decided puerperal fever, but recovered. This woman resided five miles from me. Up to this time I wore the same coat. All my other clothes had frequently been changed. On 6th, I attended two women, one of whom was not sick at all; but the other, Mrs. L., was afterwards taken ill. On 10th, I attended a lady, who did very well. I had previously changed all my clothes, and had no garment on which had been in a puerperal room. On 12th, I was called to Mrs. S., in labor. While she was ill, I left her to visit Mrs. L., one of the ladies who was confined on 6th. Mrs. L. had been more unwell than usual, but I had not considered her case anything more than common till this visit. I had on a surtout at this visit, which, on my return to Mrs. S., I left in another room. Mrs. S. was delivered on 13th with forceps. These women both died of decided puerperal fever.

"While I attended these women in their fevers, I changed my clothes, and washed my hands in a solution of chloride of lime after each visit. I attended seven women in labor during this period, all of whom recovered without sickness.

"In my practice I have had several single cases of puerperal fever, some of whom have died and some have recovered. Until the year 1830 I had no suspicion that the disease could be communicated from one patient to another by a nurse or midwife; but I now think the foregoing facts strongly favor that idea. I was so much convinced of this fact, that I adopted the plan before related.

"I believe my own health was as good as usual at each of the above periods. I have no recollection to the contrary.

"I believe I have answered all your questions. I have been more particular on some points perhaps than necessary; but I thought you could form your own opinion better than to take mine. In 1830 I wrote to Dr. Channing a more particular statement of my cases. If I have not answered your questions sufficiently, perhaps Dr. C. may have my letter to him, and you can find your answer there." [a]

"BOSTON, *February* 3, 1843.

III. "MY DEAR SIR, — I received a note from you last evening, requesting me to answer certain questions therein proposed, touching the cases of puerperal fever which came under my observation the past summer. It gives me pleasure to comply with your request, so far as it is in my power so to do, but, owing to the hurry in preparing for a journey, the notes of the cases I had then taken were lost or mislaid. The prin-

---

[a] In a letter to myself, this gentleman also stated, "I do not recollect that there was any erysipelas or any other disease particularly prevalent at the time."

cipal *facts*, however, are too vivid upon my recollection to be soon forgotten. I think, therefore, that I shall be able to give you all the information you may require.

"All the cases that occurred in my practice took place between the 7th of May and the 17th of June 1842.

"They were not confined to any particular part of the city. The first two cases were patients residing at the South End, the next was at the extreme North End, one living in Sea Street and the other in Roxbury. The following is the order in which they occurred : —

"Case 1. Mrs. —— was confined on the 7th of May, at 5 o'clock, P. M., after a natural labor of six hours. At 12 o'clock at night, on the 9th (thirty-one hours after confinement), she was taken with severe chill, previous to which she was as comfortable as women usually are under the circumstances. She died on the 10th.

"Case 2. Mrs. —— was confined on the 10th of June (four weeks after Mrs. C.), at 11 A. M., after a natural, but somewhat severe labor of five hours. At 7 o'clock, on the morning of the 11th, she had a chill. Died on the 12th.

"Case 3. Mrs. ——, confined on the 14th of June, was comfortable until the 18th, when symptoms of puerperal fever were manifest. She died on the 20th.

"Case 4. Mrs. ——, confined June 17th, at 5 o'clock, A. M., was doing well until the morning of the 19th. She died on the evening of the 21st.

"Case 5. Mrs. —— was confined with her *fifth* child on the 17th of June, at 6 o'clock in the evening. This patient had been attacked with puerperal fever, at three of her previous confinements, but the disease

yielded to depletion and other remedies without difficulty. This time, I regret to say, I was not so fortunate. She was not attacked, as were the other patients,
with a chill, but complained of extreme pain in abdomen, and tenderness on pressure, almost from the moment of her confinement. In this as in the other cases,
the disease resisted all remedies, and she died in great
distress on the 22d of the same month. Owing to
the extreme heat of the season, and my own indispo-
sition, none of the subjects were examined after death.
Dr. Channing, who was in attendance with me on the
three last cases, proposed to have a *post-mortem* examination of the subject of case No. 5, but from some
cause which I do not now recollect it was not obtained.

"You wish to know whether I wore the same clothes
when attending the different cases. I cannot positively
say, but I should think I did not, as the weather
became warmer after the first two cases ; I therefore
think it probable that I made a change of at least a
part of my dress. I have had no other case of puerperal fever in my own practice for three years, save
those above related, and I do not remember to have
lost a patient before with this disease. While absent,
last July, I visited two patients sick with puerperal
fever, with a friend of mine in the country. Both of
them recovered.

"The cases that I have recorded were not confined
to any particular constitution or temperament, but it
seized upon the strong and the weak, the old and the
young, — one being over forty years, and the youngest
under eighteen years of age. . . . If the disease is of
an erysipelatous nature, as many suppose, contagionists
may perhaps find some ground for their belief in the
fact, that, for two weeks previous to my first case of

puerperal fever, I had been attending a severe case of erysipelas, and the infection may have been conveyed through me to the patient; but, on the other hand, why is not this the case with other physicians, or with the same physician at all times, for since my return from the country I have had a more inveterate case of erysipelas than ever before, and no difficulty whatever has attended any of my midwifery cases?"

I am assured, on unquestionable authority, that "About three years since, a gentleman in extensive midwifery business, in a neighboring State, lost in the course of a few weeks eight patients in child-bed, seven of them being undoubted cases of puerperal fever. No other physician of the town lost a single patient of this disease during the same period." And from what I have heard in conversation with some of our most experienced practitioners, I am inclined to think many cases of the kind might be brought to light by extensive inquiry.

This long catalogue of melancholy histories assumes a still darker aspect when we remember how kindly nature deals with the parturient female, when she is not immersed in the virulent atmosphere of an impure lying-in hospital, or poisoned in her chamber by the unsuspected breath of contagion. From all causes together, not more than four deaths in a thousand births and miscarriages happened in England and Wales during the period embraced by the first Report of the Registrar-General.[a] In the second Report the mortality was shown to be about five in one thousand.[b] In the Dublin Lying-in Hospital, during the seven

[a] 1st Report, p. 105. [b] 2d Report, p. 73.

9780815322344

years of Dr. Collins's mastership, there was one case of puerperal fever to 178 deliveries, or less than six to the thousand, and one death from this disease in 278 cases, or between three and four to the thousand.[a] Yet during this period the disease was endemic in the hospital, and might have gone on to rival the horrors of the pestilence of the Maternité, had not the poison been destroyed by a thorough purification.

In private practice, leaving out of view the cases that are to be ascribed to the self-acting system of propagation, it would seem that the disease must be far from common. Mr. White of Manchester says, "Out of the whole number of lying-in patients whom I have delivered (and I may safely call it a great one), I have never lost one, nor to the best of my recollection has one been greatly endangered, by the puerperal, miliary, low nervous, putrid malignant, or milk fever." [b] Dr. Joseph Clarke informed Dr. Collins, that in the course of *forty-five* years' most extensive practice he lost but *four* patients from this disease.[c] One of the most eminent practitioners of Glasgow, who has been engaged in very extensive practice for upwards of a quarter of a century, testifies that he never saw more than twelve cases of real puerperal fever.[d]

I have myself been told by two gentlemen practising in this city, and having for many years a large midwifery business, that they had neither of them lost a patient from this disease, and by one of them that he had only seen it in consultation with other physicians. In five hundred cases of midwifery, of which Dr. Storer

[a] Collins's *Treatise on Midwifery*, p. 228, etc.
[b] *Op. cit.* p. 115.
[c] *Op. cit.* p. 228.
[d] *Lancet*, May 4, 1833.

has given an abstract in the first number of this Journal, there was only one instance of fatal puerperal peritonitis.

In the view of these facts, it does appear a singular coincidence, that one man or woman should have ten, twenty, thirty, or seventy cases of this rare disease following his or her footsteps with the keenness of a beagle, through the streets and lanes of a crowded city, while the scores that cross the same paths on the same errands know it only by name. It is a series of similar coincidences which has led us to consider the dagger, the musket, and certain innocent-looking white powders as having some little claim to be regarded as dangerous. It is the practical inattention to similar coincidences which has given rise to the unpleasant but often necessary documents called *indictments*, which has sharpened a form of the cephalotome sometimes employed in the case of adults, and adjusted that modification of the fillet which delivers the world of those who happen to be too much in the way while such striking coincidences are taking place.

I shall now mention a few instances in which the disease appears to have been conveyed by the process of direct inoculation.

Dr. Campbell of Edinburgh states that in October, 1821, he assisted at the post-mortem examination of a patient who died with puerperal fever. He carried the pelvic viscera in his pocket to the class-room. The same evening he attended a woman in labor without previously changing his clothes; this patient died. The next morning he delivered a woman with the forceps; she died also, and of many others who were seized with the disease within a few weeks, three shared the same fate in succession.

In June, 1823, he assisted some of his pupils at the

autopsy of a case of puerperal fever. He was unable to wash his hands with proper care, for want of the necessary accommodations. On getting home he found that two patients required his assistance. He went without further ablution, or changing his clothes; both these patients died with puerperal fever.[a] This same Dr. Campbell is one of Dr. Churchill's authorities against contagion.

Mr. Roberton says that in one instance within his knowledge a practitioner passed the catheter for a patient with puerperal fever late in the evening; the same night he attended a lady who had the symptoms of the disease on the second day. In another instance a surgeon was called while in the act of inspecting the body of a woman who had died of this fever, to attend a labor; within forty-eight hours this patient was seized with the fever.[b]

On the 16th of March, 1831, a medical practitioner examined the body of a woman who had died a few days after delivery, from puerperal peritonitis. On the evening of the 17th he delivered a patient, who was seized with puerperal fever on the 19th, and died on the 24th. Between this period and the 6th of April, the same practitioner attended two other patients, both of whom were attacked with the same disease and died.[c]

In the autumn of 1829 a physician was present at the examination of a case of puerperal fever, dissected out the organs, and assisted in sewing up the body. He had scarcely reached home when he was summoned to attend a young lady in labor. In sixteen hours she

---

[a] *Lond. Med. Gazette,* December 10, 1831.
[b] *Ibid.* for January, 1832.
[c] *London Cyc. of Pract. Med.* art. " Fever, Puerperal."

was attacked with the symptoms of puerperal fever, and narrowly escaped with her life.[a]

In December, 1830, a midwife, who had attended two fatal cases of puerperal fever at the British Lying-in Hospital, examined a patient who had just been admitted, to ascertain if labor had commenced. This patient remained two days in the expectation that labor would come on, when she returned home and was then suddenly taken in labor and delivered before she could set out for the hospital. She went on favorably for two days, and was then taken with puerperal fever and died in thirty-six hours.[b]

" A young practitioner, contrary to advice, examined the body of a patient who had died from puerperal fever; there was no epidemic at the time; the case appeared to be purely sporadic. He delivered three other women shortly afterwards; they all died with puerperal fever, the symptoms of which broke out very soon after labor. The patients of his colleague did well, except one, where he assisted to remove some coagula from the uterus; she was attacked in the same manner as those whom he had attended, and died also." The writer in the " British and Foreign Medical Review," from whom I quote this statement, — and who is no other than Dr. Rigby, — adds, " We trust that this fact alone will forever silence such doubts, and stamp the well-merited epithet of ' criminal,' as above quoted, upon such attempts." [c]

From the cases given by Mr. Ingleby, I select the following. Two gentlemen, after having been engaged in conducting the *post-mortem* examination of a case of

[a] *London Cyc. of Pract. Med.* art. " Fever, Puerperal."
[b] *Ibid.*
[c] *Brit. and For. Medical Review* for Jan. 1842, p. 112.

puerperal fever, went in the same dress, each respectively, to a case of midwifery. "The one patient was seized with the rigor about thirty hours afterwards. The other patient was seized with a rigor the third morning after delivery. *One recovered, one died.*" [a] One of these same gentlemen attended another woman in the same clothes two days after the autopsy referred to. "The rigor did not take place until the evening of the fifth day from the first visit. *Result fatal.*" These cases belonged to a series of seven, the first of which was thought to have originated in a case of erysipelas. "Several cases of a mild character followed the foregoing seven, and their nature being now most unequivocal, my friend declined visiting all midwifery cases for a time, and there was no recurrence of the disease." These cases occurred in 1833. Five of them proved fatal. Mr. Ingleby gives another series of seven cases which occurred to a practitioner in 1836, the first of which was also attributed to his having opened several erysipelatous abscesses a short time previously.

I need not refer to the case lately read before this Society, in which a physician went, soon after performing an autopsy of a case of puerperal fever, to a woman in labor, who was seized with the same disease and perished. The forfeit of that error has been already paid.

At a meeting of the Medical and Chirurgical Society before referred to, Dr. Merriman related an instance occurring in his own practice, which excites a reasonable suspicion that two lives were sacrificed to a still less dangerous experiment. He was at the examination of a case of puerperal fever at two o'clock in the afternoon. *He took care not to touch the body.* At nine o'clock the same evening he attended a woman in la-

[a] *Edin. Med. and Surg. Journal*, April, 1838.

bor; she was so nearly delivered that he had scarcely anything to do. The next morning she had severe rigors, and in forty-eight hours she was a corpse. Her infant had erysipelas and died in two days.[a]

In connection with the facts which have been stated, it seems proper to allude to the dangerous and often fatal effects which have followed from wounds received in the post-mortem examination of patients who have died of puerperal fever. The fact that such wounds are attended with peculiar risk has been long noticed. I find that Chaussier was in the habit of cautioning his students against the danger to which they were exposed in these dissections.[b] The head *pharmacien* of the Hôtel Dieu, in his analysis of the fluid effused in puerperal peritonitis, says that practitioners are convinced of its deleterious qualities, and that it is very dangerous to apply it to the denuded skin.[c] Sir Benjamin Brodie speaks of it as being well known that the inoculation of lymph or pus from the peritoneum of a puerperal patient is often attended with dangerous and even fatal symptoms. Three cases in confirmation of this statement, two of them fatal, have been reported to this Society within a few months.

Of about fifty cases of injuries of this kind, of various degrees of severity, which I have collected from different sources, at least twelve were instances of infection from puerperal peritonitis. Some of the others are so stated as to render it probable that they may have been of the same nature. Five other cases were of peritoneal inflammation; three in males. Three were

---

[a] *Lancet*, May 2, 1840.

[b] Stein, *L'Art d'Accoucher*, 1794 ; *Dict. des Sciences Médicales*, art. " Puerperal."

[c] *Journal de Pharmacie*, January, 1836.

what was called enteritis, in one instance complicated with erysipelas ; but it is well known that this term has been often used to signify inflammation of the peritoneum covering the intestines.   On the other hand, no case of typhus or typhoid fever is mentioned as giving rise to dangerous consequences, with the exception of the single instance of an undertaker mentioned by Mr. Travers, who seems to have been poisoned by a fluid which exuded from the body.   The other accidents were produced by dissection, or some other mode of contact with bodies of patients who had died of various affections.   They also differed much in severity, the cases of puerperal origin being among the most formidable and fatal.   Now a moment's reflection will show that the number of cases of serious consequences ensuing from the dissection of the bodies of those who had perished of puerperal fever is so vastly disproportioned to the relatively small number of autopsies made in this complaint as compared with typhus or pneumonia (from which last disease not one case of poisoning happened), and still more from all diseases put together, that the conclusion is irresistible that a most fearful morbid poison is often generated in the course of this disease.   Whether or not it is *sui generis*, confined to this disease, or produced in some others, as, for instance, erysipelas, I need not stop to inquire.

In connection with this may be taken the following statement of Dr. Rigby.   "That the discharges from a patient under puerperal fever are in the highest degree contagious we have abundant evidence in the history of lying-in hospitals.   The puerperal abscesses are also contagious, and may be communicated to healthy lying-in women by washing with the same sponge ; this fact has been repeatedly proved in the Vienna Hospital; but they are equally communicable to women not pregnant; on more than one occasion the women engaged in washing the soiled bed-linen of the General Lying-in Hospital have been attacked with abscess in the fingers or hands, attended with rapidly spreading inflammation of the cellular tissue." [a]

Now add to all this the undisputed fact, that within the walls of lying-in hospitals there is often generated a miasm, palpable as the chlorine used to destroy it, tenacious so as in some cases almost to defy extirpation, deadly in some institutions as the plague; which has killed women in a private hospital of London so fast that they were buried two in one coffin to conceal its horrors; which enabled Tonnellé to record two hundred and twenty-two autopsies at the Maternité of Paris; which has led Dr. Lee to express his deliberate conviction that the loss of life occasioned by these institutions completely defeats the objects of their founders; and out of this train of cumulative evidence, the multiplied groups of cases clustering about individuals, the deadly results of autopsies, the inoculation by fluids from the living patient, the murderous poison of hospitals,—does there not result a conclusion that laughs all sophistry to scorn, and renders all argument an insult?

I have had occasion to mention some instances in which there was an apparent relation between puerperal fever and erysipelas. The length to which this paper has extended does not allow me to enter into the consideration of this most important subject. I will only say, that the evidence appears to me altogether satisfactory that some most fatal series of puerperal

---

[a] *System of Midwifery*, p. 292.

fever have been produced by an infection originating in the matter or effluvia of erysipelas. In evidence of some connection between the two diseases, I need not go back to the older authors, as Pouteau or Gordon, but will content myself with giving the following references, with their dates; from which it will be seen that the testimony has been constantly coming before the profession for the last few years.

"London Cyclopædia of Practical Medicine," article *Puerperal Fever*, 1833.

Mr. Ceeley's Account of the Puerperal Fever at Aylesbury. "Lancet," 1835.

Dr. Ramsbotham's Lecture. "London Medical Gazette," 1835.

Mr. Yates Ackerly's Letter in the same Journal, 1838.

Mr. Ingleby on Epidemic Puerperal Fever. "Edinburgh Medical and Surgical Journal," 1838.

Mr. Paley's Letter. "London Medical Gazette," 1839.

Remarks at the Medical and Chirurgical Society. "Lancet," 1840.

Dr. Rigby's "System of Midwifery." 1841.

"Nunneley on Erysipelas,"— a work which contains a large number of references on the subject. 1841.

"British and Foreign Quarterly Review," 1842.

Dr. S. Jackson of Northumberland, as already quoted from the Summary of the College of Physicians, 1842.

And lastly, a startling series of cases by Mr. Storrs of Doncaster, to be found in the "American Journal of the Medical Sciences" for January, 1843.

The relation of puerperal fever with other continued fevers would seem to be remote and rarely obvious. Hey refers to two cases of synochus occurring in the

Royal Infirmary of Edinburgh, in women who had attended upon puerperal patients. Dr. Collins refers to several instances in which puerperal fever has appeared to originate from a continued proximity to patients suffering with typhus.[a]

Such occurrences as those just mentioned, though most important to be remembered and guarded against, hardly attract our notice in the midst of the gloomy facts by which they are surrounded. Of these facts, at the risk of fatiguing repetitions, I have summoned a sufficient number, as I believe, to convince the most incredulous that every attempt to disguise the truth which underlies them all is useless.

It is true that some of the historians of the disease, especially Hulme, Hull, and Leake, in England ; Tonnellé, Dugès, and Baudelocque, in France, profess not to have found puerperal fever contagious. At the most they give us mere negative facts, worthless against an extent of evidence which now overlaps the widest range of doubt, and doubles upon itself in the redundancy of superfluous demonstration. Examined in detail, this and much of the show of testimony brought up to stare the daylight of conviction out of countenance, proves to be in a great measure unmeaning and inapplicable, as might be easily shown were it necessary. Nor do I feel the necessity of enforcing the conclusion which arises spontaneously from the facts which have been enumerated, by formally citing the opinions of those grave authorities who have for the last half-century been sounding the unwelcome truth it has cost so many lives to establish.

" It is to the British practitioner," says Dr. Rigby, " that we are indebted for strongly insisting upon

[a] *Treatise on Midwifery*, p. 228.

this important and dangerous character of puerperal fever." [a]

The names of Gordon, John Clarke, Denman, Burns, Young,[b] Hamilton,[c] Haighton,[d] Good,[e] Waller,[f] Blundell, Gooch, Ramsbotham, Douglas,[g] Lee, Ingleby, Locock,[h] Abercrombie,[i] Alison,[j] Travers,[k] Rigby, and Watson,[l] many of whose writings I have already referred to, may have some influence with those who prefer the weight of authorities to the simple deductions of their own reason from the facts laid before them. A few Continental writers have adopted similar conclusions.[m] It gives me pleasure to remember, that while the doctrine has been unceremoniously discredited in one of the leading Journals,[n] and made very light of by teachers in two of the principal Medical Schools, of this country, Dr. Channing has for many years inculcated, and enforced by examples, the danger to be apprehended and the precautions to be taken in the disease under consideration.

I have no wish to express any harsh feeling with re-

---

[a] *British and Foreign Med. Rev.* for January, 1842.

[b] *Encyc. Britannica*, xiii. 467, art. "Medicine."

[c] *Outlines of Midwifery*, p. 109.

[d] *Oral Lectures*, etc.

[e] *Study of Medicine*, ii. 195.

[f] *Medical and Physical Journal*, July, 1830.

[g] *Dublin Hospital Reports* for 1822.

[h] *Library of Practical Medicine*, i. 373.

[i] *Researches on Diseases of the Stomach*, etc. p. 181.

[j] *Library of Practical Medicine*, i. 96.

[k] *Further Researches on Constitutional Irritation*, p. 128.

[l] *London Medical Gazette*, February, 1842.

[m] See *British and Foreign Medical Review*, vol. iii. p. 525, and vol. iv. p. 517. Also *Ed. Med. and Surg. Journal* for July, 1824, and *American Journal of Med. Sciences* for January, 1841.

[n] *Phil. Med. Journal*, vol. xii. p. 364.

gard to the painful subject which has come before us. If there are any so far excited by the story of these dreadful events that they ask for some word of indignant remonstrance to show that science does not turn the hearts of its followers into ice or stone, let me remind them that such words have been uttered by those who speak with an authority I could not claim.[a] It is as a lesson rather than as a reproach that I call up the memory of these irreparable errors and wrongs. No tongue can tell the heart-breaking calamity they have caused; they have closed the eyes just opened upon a new world of love and happiness; they have bowed the strength of manhood into the dust; they have cast the helplessness of infancy into the stranger's arms, or bequeathed it, with less cruelty, the death of its dying parent. There is no tone deep enough for regret, and no voice loud enough for warning. The woman about to become a mother, or with her new-born infant upon her bosom, should be the object of trembling care and sympathy wherever she bears her tender burden, or stretches her aching limbs. The very outcast of the streets has pity upon her sister in degradation, when the seal of promised maternity is impressed upon her. The remorseless vengeance of the law, brought down upon its victim by a machinery as sure as destiny, is arrested in its fall at a word which reveals her transient claim for mercy. The solemn prayer of the liturgy singles out her sorrows from the multiplied trials of life, to plead for her in the hour of peril. God forbid that any member of the profession to which she trusts her life, doubly precious at that eventful period, should hazard it negligently, unadvisedly, or selfishly! There may be some among those whom I address

[a] Dr. Blundell and Dr. Rigby in the works already cited.

who are disposed to ask the question, What course are
we to follow in relation to this matter? The facts are
before them, and the answer must be left to their own
judgment and conscience. If any should care to know
my own conclusions, they are the following; and in
taking the liberty to state them very freely and broadly, I would ask the inquirer to examine them as freely
in the light of the evidence which has been laid before him.

1. A physician holding himself in readiness to attend cases of midwifery should never take any active
part in the post-mortem examination of cases of puerperal fever.

2. If a physician is present at such autopsies, he
should use thorough ablution, change every article of
dress, and allow twenty-four hours or more to elapse
before attending to any case of midwifery. It may be
well to extend the same caution to cases of simple peritonitis.

3. Similar precautions should be taken after the
autopsy or surgical treatment of cases of erysipelas,
if the physician is obliged to unite such offices with
his obstetrical duties, which is in the highest degree
inexpedient.

4. On the occurrence of a single case of puerperal
fever in his practice, the physician is bound to consider
the next female he attends in labor, unless some weeks
at least have elapsed, as in danger of being infected
by him, and it is his duty to take every precaution to
diminish her risk of disease and death.

5. If within a short period two cases of puerperal
fever happen close to each other, in the practice of the
same physician, the disease not existing or prevailing
in the neighborhood, he would do wisely to relinquish

his obstetrical practice for at least one month, and endeavor to free himself by every available means from any noxious influence he may carry about with him.

6. The occurrence of three or more closely connected cases, in the practice of one individual, no others existing in the neighborhood, and no other sufficient cause being alleged for the coincidence, is *primâ facie* evidence that he is the vehicle of contagion.

7. It is the duty of the physician to take every precaution that the disease shall not be introduced by nurses or other assistants, by making proper inquiries concerning them, and giving timely warning of every suspected source of danger.

8. Whatever indulgence may be granted to those who have heretofore been the ignorant causes of so much misery, the time has come when the existence of a *private pestilence* in the sphere of a single physician should be looked upon, not as a misfortune, but a crime; and in the knowledge of such occurrences the duties of the practitioner to his profession should give way to his paramount obligations to society.

ADDITIONAL REFERENCES AND CASES.

Fifth Annual Report of the Registrar-General of England, 1843. Appendix. Letter from William Farr, Esq. — Several new series of cases are given in the Letter of Mr. Storrs, contained in the Appendix to this Report. Mr. Storrs suggests precautions similar to those I have laid down, and these precautions are strongly enforced by Mr. Farr, who is, therefore, obnoxious to the same criticisms as myself.

Hall and Dexter, in Am. Journal of Med. Sc. for January, 1844. — Cases of puerperal fever seeming to originate in erysipelas.

Elkington, of Birmingham, in Provincial Med. Journal, cited in Am. Journ. Med. Sc. for April, 1844.— Six cases in less than a fortnight, seeming to originate in a case of erysipelas.

West's Reports, in Brit. and For. Med. Review for October, 1845, and January, 1847.— Affection of the arm, resembling malignant pustule, after removing the placenta of a patient who died from puerperal fever. Reference to cases at Würzburg, as proving contagion, and to Keiller's cases in the Monthly Journal for February, 1846, as showing connection of puerperal fever and erysipelas.

Kneeland. — Contagiousness of Puerperal Fever. Am. Jour. Med. Sc., January, 1846. Also, Connection between Puerperal Fever and Epidemic Erysipelas. Ibid., April, 1846.

Robert Storrs. — Contagious Effects of Puerperal Fever on the Male Subject; or on Persons not Child-bearing. (From Provincial Med. and Surg. Journal.) Am. Jour. Med. Sc., January, 1846. Numerous cases. See also Dr. Reid's case in same Journal for April, 1846.

Routh's paper in Proc. of Royal Med. Chir. Soc., Am. Jour. Med. Sc., April, 1849, also in B. and F. Med. Chir. Review, April, 1850.

Hill, of Leuchars. — A Series of Cases illustrating the Contagious Nature of Erysipelas and of Puerperal Fever, and their Intimate Pathological Connection. (From Monthly Journal of Med. Sc.) Am. Jour. Med. Sc., July, 1850.

Skoda on the Causes of Puerperal Fever. (Peritonitis in rabbits, from inoculation with different morbid secretions.) Am. Jour. Med. Sc., October, 1850.

Arneth. — Paper read before the National Academy of Medicine. Annales d'Hygiène, Tome LXV. 2° Partie. (Means of Disinfection proposed by M. " Semmeliveis " (Semmelweiss.) Lotions of chloride of lime and use of nail-brush before admission to lying-in wards. Alleged sudden and great decrease of mortality from puerperal fever. Cause of disease attributed to inoculation with cadaveric matters.) See also *Routh's* paper, mentioned above.

Moir. — Remarks at a meeting of the Edinburgh Medico-Chirurgical Society. Refers to cases of Dr. Kellie, of Leith. *Sixteen* in succession, *all fatal.* Also to several instances of individual pupils having had a succession of cases in various quarters of the town, while others, practising as extensively in the same localities, had none. Also to several special cases not mentioned elsewhere. Am. Jour. Med. Sc. for October, 1851. (From New Monthly Journal of Med. Science.)

Simpson. — Observations at a Meeting of the Edinburgh Obstetrical Society. (An "eminent gentleman," according to Dr. Meigs, whose "name is as well known in America as in (his) native land." Obstetrics. Phil. 1852, pp. 368, 375.) The student is referred to this paper for a valuable *résumé* of many of the facts, and the necessary inferences, relating to this subject. Also for another series of cases, Mr. Sidey's, five or six in rapid succession. Dr. Simpson attended the dissection of two of Dr. Sidey's cases, and freely handled the diseased parts. His next four child-bed patients were affected with puerperal fever, and it was the first time he had seen it in practice. As Dr. Simpson is *a gentleman* (Dr. Meigs, as above), and as " a gentleman's hands are clean " (Dr. Meigs' Sixth Letter), it follows that a gentleman with clean hands may carry the disease. Am. Jour. Med. Sc., October, 1851.

Peddie. — The five or six cases of Dr. Sidey, followed by the four of Dr. Simpson, did not end the series. A practitioner in Leith having examined in Dr. Simpson's house, a portion of the uterus obtained from one of the patients, had immediately afterwards three fatal cases of puerperal fever. Dr. Peddie referred to two distinct series of consecutive cases in his own practice. He had since taken precautions, and not met with any such cases. Am. Jour. Med. Sc., October, 1851.

Copland. — Considers it proved that puerperal fever may be propagated by the hands and the clothes, or either, of a third person, the bed-clothes or body-clothes of a patient. Mentions a new series of cases, one of which he saw, with the practitioner who had attended them. She was *the sixth* he had had within a few days. *All died.* Dr. Copland insisted that contagion had caused these cases ; advised precautionary measures, and the practitioner had no other cases for a considerable time. Considers it *criminal*, after the evidence adduced, — which he could have quadrupled, — and the weight of authority brought forward, for a practitioner to be the medium of transmitting contagion and death to his patients. Dr. Copland lays down rules similar to those suggested by myself, and is therefore entitled to the same epithet for so doing. Medical Dictionary, New York, 1852. Article, *Puerperal States and Diseases.*

If there is any appetite for facts so craving as to be yet unappeased, — *lassata, necdum satiata,* — more can be obtained. Dr. Hodge remarks that " the frequency and importance of this singular circumstance (that the disease is occasionally more prevalent with one practitioner than another) has been exceedingly overrated."   More than thirty strings of cases, more than two hundred and fifty sufferers from puerperal fever, more than one hundred and thirty deaths appear as the results of a sparing estimate of such among the facts I have gleaned as could be numerically valued.   These facts constitute, we may take it for granted, but a small fraction of those that have actually occurred. The number of them might be greater, but " 't is enough, 't will serve," in Mercutio's modest phrase, so far as frequency is concerned.   For a just estimate of the importance of the singular circumstance, it might be proper to consult the languid survivors, the widowed husbands, and the motherless children, as well as " the unfortunate accoucheur."

LECTURES.

CHILD-BED FEVER.
BY ELLERSLIE WALLACE

Puerperal fever is a bad name, because it is indefinite. The names remittent and intermittent fever mean something fixed and well established, but puerperal fever is a disorder over whose identity the whole medical world is at present seething.

The pathology of the condition is a singular one. As a general rule the peritoneum alone is involved in the inflammatory action, but in some cases all the structures of the uterus may be inflamed; its sinuses, its veins, its absorbents, its muscular walls, and its peritoneal covering. These structures may be separately involved, or they may be all attacked at once. Nor is this all. The inflammation may involve all the cellular tissues of the pelvis; may extend to all the structures throughout the abdomen; may gain access to the pleural cavity and bring on pleurisy. In other cases, you may open the body after death and find absolutely nothing to account for that condition but some slight inflammation of the absorbent system. In still other instances an autopsy will reveal thin, diffluent, dark colored blood, entirely unfit to carry on life, together with local ecchymoses in the bowels, spleen, kidney, lung and womb, which may here and there have broken down into abscesses.

Are these all different forms of the disease? you will, with propriety, ask. Is peritonitis the only disease in one case, and are pleurisy and peritonitis the only inflammatory conditions in another? Here pelvic cellulitis only, there an involvement of all the uterine structures, and in still a third case nothing whatsoever discernible but microscopical ecchymoses throughout the pleural and abdominal cavities? Do we call the totality of these apparently widely different pathological conditions puerperal fever? Are all these different forms of septic poisoning, or does the local disease produce the constitutional systoms and so vitate the blood, or do both local disease and septic poisoning go hand in hand? This is what the profession is at present contending over.

We are like the pendulum, swinging from one extreme to the other, and like it, never at perfect rest at any point. In some cases there are some local evidences of local poisoning and in others there are none.

Is a woman to be poisoned without cause? In a healthy district of country a woman is seized with puerperal metritis, or peritonitis, or cellulitis, or pleuritis. We say at once that it is an instance of septic poisoning. Where does the septic poison come from? Let a healthy limb be cut off. Can we not have septic poisoning there as a result of the absorption of the decomposing fluids which bathe the stump?

What is the placental surface of a womb if it is not a surface denuded of epithelium and upon which a whole host of uterine sinuses open—a raw surface ready to take on auto-infection at any moment. Or the margins of the margins of the womb and the walls of the vagina may have been cracked in the process of labor—the minutest little raw spot can absorb enough poison to kill an entire army. The most terrible dissecting wound which I ever received was acquired from the prick of a needle which had been once passed into the flesh of a subject dead for only twenty-two hours. That needle prick carried enough of the poison into my system to nearly kill me. The aperture was so tiny that I could not discover it. The minute fissures produced by cracks in the walls of the womb and virgina may absorb the poisonous and decomposing lochial discharge emerging from the vagina. Or, on the other hand, the disease may be produced by hetero-infection. The woman may contract it in a laying-in hospital.

Twelve women may be waiting in the wards to be confined and may contract puerperal fever either from the nurse who has attended a patient with the disease, or from contact with a sponge used by the patient, or from the mere transmission of the poison through the air.

Notice a careful mother when one of her children is sick with scarlet fever, how sedulously she secludes it and how painstaking she is that none of its attendants shall go near any of the other children and so by chance carry to them the septic influence.

What is the nature of a septic poison? Who knows? All we can say is that these various kinds of poisons exist. The great argument against laying-in hospitals is that it is so easy to carry the puerperal poison from one woman to another. The nurse of a puerperal fever patient should have no connection with the care of another pregnant woman until her clothes are thorougly disinfected.

If I should be called to-day to see a puerperal fever patient I would get somebody to attend to the rest of my practice for the time being. I strongly believe in the contagiousness of the septic puerperal influence—in its directly contagious qualities. Professor Charles D. Meigs, a predecessor in this chair, believed in the non-contagiousness of puerperal fever until the day of his death. Handling a piece of decomposing placenta he would say, "is this the poison so potent and so terrible that all the disinfectants known cannot destroy its virulence?" No, gentlemen, they can no more wash it out than could all the waters of the sea remove the stain of blood from Lady Macbeth's hand.

Physicians, if they be not careful, may scatter the puerperal fever poison broadcast. I do most thoroughly believe in the contagiousness of the poison—no need for giving my reasons; although I well know that there are some sporadic cases which seem to generate no poison. But so great is my terror of carrying the malady that, if I see a single case, the minute I return home I take every stitch of clothes off which I wore at the time, leaving them out in the yard for a week at least, to air, take a bath, dress myself in an entirely new suit of clothes, and even then am careful not to attend another pregnant woman for at least a week.

I was taught the theory of non-contagion and I acted upon it, and I really believe that I was the direct cause of the death of two women.

Be it contagious, or be it not; be it specific, or be it only the constitutional effect of a local impression, there is certainly something in a woman's condition after confinement, which generates a susceptibility to the occurrence of specific malidies. You attend a case of labor and everything passes off favorably. Everything is well on the second day also, except that the pulse is perhaps too retentive of its speed and remains at 85, or 88, instead of dropping down to the normal. You see her again at four o'clock in the afternoon of the second day; if the pulse is still high make it a point to call at ten o'clock that same night, and if the pulse is still high and the patient complains of some chilliness, put your horse in the stable and be ready to meet the foe, for the disease almost always comes on within seventy-two hours after the delivery, but the time of its coming is very deceptive. It is apt to be preceded by exaltation of pulse, general malaise and dryness of the mouth, with a feeling of chilliness. The chill may be great or small, lasting sometimes only half an hour and sometimes still present after two hours have past. The surface is cold and the blood is driven in upon the peritonem, which has been enormously distended, and upon all the abdominal structures which are but too ready to receive a great engorgement.

The longer the chill the worse the prognosis. The flush follows the chill and lasts a shorter or longer period, and then comes the sweat. "Put a little more coal in the stove," the patient had first asked, but soon it is, "take off this blanket, I am too warm." Where the chill, fever and sweat are of short duration the chances of cure are great. In graver cases the chill is longer and more severe. During the chill the pulse is always increased in frequency, (I am speaking, of course, of puerperal peritonitis) its beat is hard and it strikes wickedly. If the pulse is hard it shows that the vital power is good. I never saw a chill which did not bring up the speed of the pulse. I remember one case where the pulse had reached 140 to the minute in only two hours, and the chill was not yet off the patient. That pulse was not corded and wiry, but rapid. Generally following, but occasionally antecedent to the chill, a spot of pain is present in the region of the left or right ovary. The pain occasionally involves both ovaries. This pain is sharp, acute and lancinating. From the ovary as a centre, a zone of inflammation begins to spread immediately, and in two hours time the whole lower part of the belly up to the umbilicus is tender. The pain is so sharp that the patient will scream out. In whichever ovary the pain begins, the other soon begins to respond. The whole belly is swollen up, forming one great tympany. The patient has to be supported and lies with her knees drawn up so as to take the weight off the very sensitive belly. The respiration becomes very difficult and runs up to 30–45 in the minute, while the pulse ranges from 125–160. The diaphragm will not descend and every inhalation gives pain. The pain radiates, first involves the hips and then runs up on the side of the chest.

The patient's face grows pallid, anxious, ghastly. The anxiety expressed is most strange and marvelous, that of cholera is not worse. I hope you will never see this fearful expression of anxiety, but if you do I am sure that it will burn itself indelibly upon your brain. Sometimes the face is inane and expressionless. Inanity, however, is apt to come later.

What is the character of the tongue? Whether the case be due to septic poisoning as in a hospital, or be one of purely sporadic origin, the tongue is white, creamy and swollen, with red edges. The tongue may become dry. Sordes on gums, tongue, or teeth is rare in puerperal peritonitis.

The fever, just as is the case with the chill, varies in severity and in duration. It may last for only half an hour, or it may go on until the vital powers are all burnt out and the patient runs into a cold collapse, with colliquative sweats and perhaps colliquative diarrhœa. In very malignant cases, the chill lasts two hours or more, and there is no stage of reaction, the patient falling into collapse immediately after the chill, and dying short of twenty-four hours.

I like a full reactive fever well. It shows that the system is still able to contend with the morbific influence. If the patient is seen early in the course of the chill, we shall not, as a general thing, have much difficulty in curing her.

The lochia may stop like a flash with the commencement of the chill, or the flow may dribble on indefinitely. If the dribbling continues the discharge is usually of a serous nature and but slightly tinged with blood. The blood which should be flowing out is locked up in the womb and is doing harm. Arrest a healthy hemorrhage in any woman by opening the window and putting on a cold napkin and the lochia will stop at once, and pain be set up in the neighborhood of the uterus.

I do not lay much stress upon the temperature of a puerperal patient as a sign of prognostic value. In no case do I attempt to isolate the symptoms in forming my prognosis, but I consider them as a whole.

The secretion of the kidneys is, as a general rule, somewhat scanty. Occasionally the bladder will lose its tone completely, and you will be obliged to catheterize the patient. This condition is rare in puerperal peritonitis, but quite common in puerperal metritis.

Suppose that the chill makes its appearance some forty hours after delivery and that the breasts stop swelling at once. The secretion of milk ceases of course, and here is another mass thrown upon the already congested womb and peritoneum. In the healthy recovery from labor, milk is a depurative to the uterine system. The breasts, as well as the uterus, are part and parcel of the reproductive organs, and are as closely to it as are the ovaries.

The puerperal patient is usually very thirsty, but be very careful how you allow her much water. Let her have a dessert-spoonful at intervals of every ten minutes. That will be fully enough for her good. If you allow the stomach to become too full of water it will bring on vomiting. This must never be allowed to happen, if it be possible to prevent it. It jars the system and dams back the blood and increases the trouble.

Thus far I have been speaking of a case where there is peritonitis with some extension of the inflammatory process into the uterine tissues and the intestines. But, in addition to this, there may be some extensive infiltration through the root of the pelvis into the cellular tissues, together with an upward inroad into the pleural cavity.

THE TREATMENT OF PUERPERAL FEVER.

Go home and get twelve books and read each through carefully, and see if you know which is the best form of treatment recommended—they all contradict each other. It stands to reason that one treatment will not always be successful, for water will not always put out fire nor quench thirst.

I believe that there is one form of treatment far superior to and much more successful than all the others.

You are called to see a case where the chill has made its appearance only an hour ago.

You certainly expect to cure, unless the patient, from the chill, runs off into a rapid collapse, with internal and external sweating and "washerwoman's hands." In such a happening as this, God only knows what remedies can cure, and all that you can do is to ease the pain by opiates and allow the poor thing to die in peace.

Ordinarily you reach the patient some four hours after her seizure. The chill has gone, and the febrile reaction is well marked. Again, you do not see the case until the twelfth or fifteenth hour of the disease, and then it is all over—the dyspnœa and tympanites are intense. If you live far away from the patient, the chances are frightfully against you.

But to go back to our first case. You see the patient about an hour after the inception of the chill. The pulse is 135 to the minute—it may be hard and strong and wiry, or it may be weak and boshy. The breath runs from twenty-five to forty times in the minute and the pain is coming on.

Tie the woman's arm up and bleed the fever out of her. Bleed her twelve, fifteen, eighteen ounces; bleed her until the pulse comes up. In this way you unlock the locked up circulation—the vessels all engorged. Do not be troubled about the patient, she can afford to lose the blood. Having bled the pulse up, now go to work and bleed it down to such a condition that the chill passes away, and that the woman breaks out into a warm prespiration. Seat the woman up in bed, put your knee behind her, or let some one hold her, and bleed her pulse down to eighty-five beats. The sunken look of the eye will pass away, the blood will return to the surface, *and the woman will take a long breath.* Then put your finger over the vein, but do not untie the arm, and, if the pulse runs right up again, take your finger away and let the blood spurt again. *That thou doest, do quickly.* Two or three ounces less of blood may be all your patient needs. Yes! she wants to go to sleep—the pain has all gone.

Lay her down in peace and give her three grains of opium. Will you now give her a good cathartic? Upon my word, you might as well put your hand inside of her abdomen and stir up the inflamed peritoneum! So give her opium and let her rest in peace. But she

annot stand opium—never could stand it. Gentlemen, she has got to take it or she will die.

I prefer the watery extract of opium to the powder. One grain of the watery extract is worth a grain and a half of the solid opium. Moreover, the extract dissolves more quickly and is better borne by the stomach, particularly in women. I should certainly use the watery extract. Then take a piece of flannel broad enough to cover the distended belly, put it in a tub of hot water, squeeze it out, rub some oil and laudanum well into it, seeing that it is kept warm, and put it on the distended surface, covering it with a bit of oiled silk or carded cotton, and over all pin a bandage around the body loosely.

According to the amount of pain which still remains, the patient should have two-thirds of a grain of the watery extract of opium, or one grain, or a grain and a half, as the case may be. Some physicians have given as much as ten grains of opium in the first two hours. This does nothing but blunt completely all the vital powers.

Together with the first dose of opium, give the patient ten or twelve grains of calomel, not as a cathartic—the opium will prevent it from acting—but to re-establish the secretion, and then do not give any more. The plan which some adopt of giving small doses of the calomel every few hours is a very bad one.

Give her also a little mik and some beef tea to drink, or a mouthful or two of water, with some delicate broth. Make every one in the house put on slippers or move about in their stocking feet. See that the doors of the rest of the house are kept either permanently open or permanently shut.

As a usual thing in twenty-four hours the woman will begin to convalesce. Then diminish the amount of opium and increase the broth.

The milk secretion may or may not return. I have known the lochia to return in a few hours.

But we will imagine another case. When you see her the woman is in a collapse with a sunken face and cold tongue. Her breath against your hand feels cold from the intensity of the congestion. Nothing can begin to cope with this congestion but opium and bleeding.

Again, you see the case in the height of the

fever, when the pulse is full and round, and the face flushed. *Headache is rare, unless some tissue of the uterus is involved, and then it is rare not to have headache.* The pain is agonizing. Every beat of the pulse is striking a blow at the woman's life ; it runs from 104-150 to the minute.

No matter whether the case be sporadic or of septic origin, you have got to bleed largely and boldly in the stage of fever. Make a large aperture in the vein and let the blood spout freely. Bleed her f ℥ xviij-xxiij. There are but few cases in which the pulse does not go down when this limit is reached, but do not stop here. In my last case I bled the woman f ℥ xxxv, and in the case before f ℥ xxxiij. The longer the fever has lasted the more blood must be drawn. I speak of that which I do know. *I know what the lancet can do in puerperal fever.* Let the test of the time to stop be when the patient can take a full breath without hurting herself. Her tongue grows moist and her lips red. Do not dare to permit fainting, for, if you do, when the patient reacts from the fainting fit, there will be a relighting of the inflammation.

I have never seen a patient recover from this disease without bleeding. Leeches are of no use. When the convalesence is well progressed unload the bowels lightly by means of a warm water enema.

Puerperal metritis differs more in quantity than quality from pueperal peritonitis. The headache is great in metritis. The pulse and temperature are not so high. The chill and fever do not last so long. The lochia may persist as a glairy discharge. In other points there is no material difference between the two conditions. Leeches may be used in metritis, with calomel and opium. Keep up the calomel until ptyalism appears. Some use blisters in metritis. I have no faith in them.

Texas Reports on Biology and Medicine
Volume 34, Numbers 2–4, 1976

RELATIVE CONTRIBUTIONS OF HOLMES AND SEMMELWEIS TO THE UNDERSTANDING OF THE ETIOLOGY OF PUERPERAL FEVER°

M. J. BUSBY AND A. E. RODIN[†]

*Department of Pathology and the Institute for the Medical Humanities
University of Texas Medical Branch, Galveston, Texas 77550*

Puerperal fever; history of medicine; Holmes; Semmelweis

INTRODUCTION

The names of Oliver Wendell Holmes and Ignaz Philipp Semmelweis are familiar ones in the history of medicine. The two physicians were among the first to understand the nature of puerperal fever, its mode of transmission, and prophylaxis of the disease. Much has been written about these men, their lives, their works, and their impact upon medical science. The books and articles which discuss the question of priority of their hypotheses do not directly compare the writings of Holmes and Semmelweis.[1] The purpose of this paper is to show the relative contributions of Holmes and Semmelweis to the understanding of the etiology of puerperal fever by comparing their writings, professional status, and possible worldwide influence.

Until the clinical use of antibiotics in the 1940's, puerperal fever, which may occur following childbirth, was a feared and familiar scourge on the obstetrical wards in hospitals of both America and Europe. Although this disease received its name only in the 17th century, it was identified as early as 400 B.C. in writings ascribed to Hippocrates. The incidence of puerperal fever reached epidemic proportions in the hospitals of the 16th, 17th, and 18th centuries. No causative agent could be proved, but various factors, such as the suppression of uterine discharge or an atmospheric miasma, were seized upon and

° Elizabeth and Chauncey Leake History of Medicine Award to Jan Busby for this study, May 31, 1975. Rec'd. for publication May 20, 1975.

† Address for reprints: Dr. A. E. Rodin, School of Medicine, Wright State University, Dayton, Ohio 45431.

[1] A complete listing of these works may be found in "Ignaz Philipp Semmelweis, An Annotated Bibliography" by Frank P. Murphy, *Bulletin of the History of Medicine*, XX (1946), pp. 692–703.

blamed alternately, albeit vigorously, by the leading medical authorities of the time.[2]

In the 18th century, physicians such as John Burton, Charles White, and Alexander Gordon came close to the truth.[3] The nature of the disease was finally exposed by Oliver Wendell Holmes in his essay of 1843, "The Contagiousness of Puerperal Fever."[4] The credit for this discovery, however, has been awarded by history to Ignaz Philipp Semmelweis. The Hungarian physician reached his conclusions in 1847 and published them in 1861.[5] As the prevailing medical opinion of the day held that puerperal fever was not contagious, it seems rather odd that Semmelweis did not cite Holmes's views to support his thesis. Nor did Holmes make any mention of the Hungarian physician in later reprints of his essay.

The intriguing question arises: Why did Semmelweis receive the credit for discovering the infectious nature of puerperal fever instead of the man whose paper had the priority of 18 years? The following discussion will attempt to provide a definitive answer.

Oliver Wendell Holmes

Oliver Wendell Holmes, 1809–1894, began his medical career in 1830 at Tremont Medical School, which later became Harvard Medical School. From 1833–1835, Holmes studied medicine in Paris and there gained a good foundation in observation and drawing correct conclusions. He returned to Harvard to receive his medical degree in 1836. In the next two years he wrote prize-winning essays on intermittent fever, neuralgia, and the direct exploration of internal organs. In 1839–1840, Holmes served as Professor of Anatomy at Dartmouth Medical College in New Hampshire. In 1842, he wrote an exposé of "Homeopathy and Its Kindred Illusions." The next year he published "The Contagiousness of Puerperal Fever." From 1847–1882, Holmes was Professor of Anatomy and Physiology at Harvard Medical School. Dur-

---

[2] Alan F. Guttmacher, "Introduction" to *Die Aetiologie, der Begriff und die Prophylaxis des Kindbettfiebers* by Ignaz Philipp Semmelweis (New York and London: Johnson Reprint Corporation, 1966), pp. xiii–xv.

[3] *Ibid.*, pp. xvi–xxi.

[4] Oliver Wendell Holmes, "The Contagiousness of Puerperal Fever," *New England Quarterly Journal of Medicine and Surgery*, I (April 1843), reprinted in *Medical Essays* (New York: Houghton, Mifflin, and Co., 1883), pp. 103–172. Hereafter cited as *Medical Essays*.

[5] Ignaz Philipp Semmelweis, *Die Aetiologie, der Begriff und die Prophylaxis des Kindbettfiebers* (Pest, Vienna, and Liepzig, 1861); reprinted in Frank P. Murphy, trans., *Medical Classics*, V–VIII (January–April, 1941), pp. 339–773. Hereafter cited as *Medical Classics*.

Oliver Wendell Holmes

Texas Rep Biol Med 41 2-4, 1976

ing these same years, he also acted as dean of the school, published three novels and a book of medical essays, and received honors and acclaim from Harvard University and his fellow physicians.[6]

Holmes made many contributions to the practice and teaching of medicine. Although his research on puerperal fever was very important, this was only one of the active physician's many interests. Holmes was not, of course, an obstetrician but a general practitioner who included obstetrics in his practice and interest. Throughout his life, however, Holmes was more well-known as a poet and wit than as a physician. Because of his humor and eloquence, Holmes was much in demand at formal speaking occasions.[7] He seemed to derive great pleasure from both his medical and literary pursuits. When asked by Canadian physician William Osler whether he derived greater satisfaction from his essay on puerperal fever or one of his most famous poems, "The Chambered Nautilus," Holmes replied: "There is more selfish pleasure to be had out of the poem—perhaps a nobler satisfaction from the life-saving labor."[8]

In 1842, Oliver Wendell Holmes had a successful private practice in Boston, Massachusetts, and was an active member of the Boston Society for Medical Improvement. This small voluntary association of local physicians met twice a month to consider papers and case presentations. In June, 1842, a subject of vital interest was presented before the society. An obstetrician, Walter Channing, announced as his topic 13 fatalities resulting from puerperal fever. During the next six months, several physicians presented numerous case histories of the disease, including those of a physician and a medical student who were both injured with a scalpel while performing an autopsy. Both became ill with puerperal fever; the student died. These reports touched off an explosive debate on the contagious nature of puerperal fever.[9]

This controversy was not new. In the 18th and 19th centuries, the accepted etiological agents for the disease were labeled either as internal or external factors. Suppression of uterine discharge was an example of an internal factor, while the development of an injurious agent called miasma—which was supposedly spread by the atmosphere

[6] Miriam Rossiter Small, *Oliver Wendell Holmes* (New York: Twayne Publishers, 1962), pp. 36, 39–41, 47–48, 51–53, 64–87.

[7] *Ibid.*

[8] Oliver Wendell Holmes, "Letter to William Osler," quoted in J. Morris Slemons, "A Cross-Light on Doctor Holmes and His Investigation of Childbirth Fever," *Western Journal of Surgery, Obstetrics, and Gynecology*, LI (April 1943), p. 170.

[9] Eleanor M. Tilton, *Amiable Autocrat* (New York: Henry Schuman, 1947), p. 170. Hereafter cited as *Autocrat*.

and to which pregnant and puerperal women were especially susceptible—represented an external factor. Three British obstetricians provided the counter-argument. In 1751, John Burton suggested a vague
association between the carelessness of attendants and the introduction
of the disease to the patient. Charles White proposed in 1773 a regimen
of room fumigation, cleanliness, fresh air, and isolation for his patients,
none of whom ever died from puerperal fever. Alexander Gordon
stated unequivocally in his 1795 "Treatise on the Epidemic Puerperal
Fever" that the disease was caused by a specific infection, although he
did not understand the true nature of the transmitted agent.[10]

Although many physicians individually came to the conclusion that
puerperal fever could be transmitted from one person to another, the
weight of medical authority as presented by leading obstetricians and
standard textbooks, came down heavily on the opposing side.[11] Nevertheless, Dr. Holmes was sufficiently stirred by the conflicting arguments to begin research on the disease. Not only did he scour medical
journals and books, but he also sought and obtained recent case histories from physicians in practice. Holmes's studies led him to a strong
conviction that puerperal fever was definitely contagious and that
"obstetricians, nurses, and midwives were active agents of infection,
carrying the dreaded disease from the bedside of one mother to that
of the next." Holmes backed up this statement with an irrefutable array
of facts and logic.[12]

The Boston Society for Medical Improvement was convinced of the
significance of this report and published it in the April, 1843, issue of
The New England Quarterly Journal of Medicine and Surgery, the
fourth issue of the only volume published. Because the circulation of
the periodical was small, the article attracted only limited attention;
however, a 2-page abstract of the 60-page original appeared in the July,
1843, issue of the *American Journal of the Medical Sciences*. The abstract elicited a stronger response, including a 10-page commentary in
the Fifth Annual Report of the Registrar-General of Great Britain. In
1852, Copland's *Medical Dictionary* gave Holmes credit for establishing the contagious nature of puerperal fever.[13]

As might be expected, Holmes's discovery did not pass unchallenged.
Two well-known, authoritative professors and obstetricians, Hugh L.
Hodge and Charles D. Meigs, assailed Holmes's work rather viciously,
the latter calling it an example of "the jejeune and fizzenless dreamings

[10] Guttmacher, "Introduction," pp. xv, xlv-xx.
[11] Tilton, *Autocrat*, p. 170.
[12] *Ibid.*, p. 171.
[13] *Ibid.*, p. 173.

Texas Rep Biol Med 14 2-4, 1956

of sophomore writers."[14] This outcry encouraged Holmes to re-publish his essay in 1855. The new introduction scornfully declared that "I had rather rescue one mother from being poisoned by her attendant, than claim to have saved forty out of fifty patients to whom I had carried the disease."[15] This paper reached a larger audience than did the 1843 article, yet its circulation was still inversely proportional to its importance as a medical document.[16]

Although there were still many who denied the transmissible nature of puerperal fever, the author of the controversial paper must have been gratified when "a reviewer of the 1857 edition of Meig's *Obstetrics* corrected him for the error to which he still clung, and cited as the final authority Dr. Oliver Wendell Holmes."[17] Other supporters of Holmes's position included Dr. Henry I. Bowditch of Boston and Dr. William Osler.[18]

Ignaz Philipp Semmelweis

In the 1840's, the etiology of puerperal fever was also becoming a subject of interest in Europe, especially Vienna, the medical capital of the world. It was here that Ignaz Philipp Semmelweis had received his medical degree. In 1846, he was appointed as an assistant in the First Clinic of the maternity department in the Allgemeine Krankenhaus, the largest maternity hospital in the world.[19]

Semmelweis was 29 years old when he first drew his conclusions about the etiology of puerperal fever. At that time his discoveries became central issue in a power struggle among the hospital's administrative staff. The vice-director of medical studies, Anton Rosas, was losing control over the medical faculty, who were led by Josef Skoda. The latter had proposed an investigation by a faculty committee of the drastically reduced mortality rate from puerperal fever in the First Clinic after Semmelweis had introduced a compulsory prophylactic routine. Klein, Semmelweis' superior, was not selected for the committee and began an opposition movement that was supported by Rosas. The vice-director feared that the committee would threaten his authority and managed to block their investigation. Semmelweis' petition for reappointment as a resident in the First Clinic became linked

[14] *Ibid.*, p. 174.

[15] Holmes, *Medical Essays*, p. 106.

[16] Thomas Franklin Currier, "A Bibliography of Oliver Wendell Holmes," ed. Eleanor M. Tilton (New York: Russell & Russell, 1953), p. 35.

[17] Tilton, *Autocrat*, p. 176.

[18] Currier, "Bibliography," p. 34.

[19] Guttmacher, "Introduction," p. xxiv.

Texas Rep Biol Med 34 2-4, 1976

Texas Rep Biol Med 11 2-1, 1956

with Skoda's fight. His petition was refused, and he was subjected to
much criticism because of his ideas on puerperal fever.[20]

In 1850, Semmelweis returned to Pest, Hungary, where he became
the director of an obstetric clinic and later a professor of midwifery at
the University of Pest. There he continued to proclaim his hypotheses
and successfully instituted prophylactic measures against puerperal
fever. In 1858, Semmelweis published his conjectures in the Hungarian
language, and in 1861, his book, *The Etiology, Concept, and Prophylaxis of Childbed Fever*, was written. Criticism and skepticism continued unabated. Four years later, Semmelweis, then 47 years old, was
confined to an insane asylum. Ironically, that same year he died of
blood poisoning as a result of an injury received while performing an
autopsy.[21]

Semmelweis' interest in puerperal fever arose from his observations
in the Allgemeine Krankenhaus. The obstetrical department was divided into 2 clinics. The First Clinic was used solely for the instruction
of medical students, the Second Clinic for midwives. For some reason,
the mortality rate in the First Clinic was usually 3 times that in the
Second Clinic. This extremely high percentage of deaths in his own
clinic, for which he could find neither cause nor cure, horrified the
Hungarian obstetrician and soon became an obsession with him.[22]

In the clinic, Semmelweis examined patients, performed autopsies,
and compiled statistics. By chance, he was in a natural experimental
situation in the hospital, with the Second Clinic serving as a control for
his observations in the First Clinic. Semmelweis concluded that the
only difference between the clinics was that medical students were in
one clinic and midwives in the other. He also found that the only
difference between these two groups and their treatment of the pa-
titions was the medical students performed autopsies on women who
had died from puerperal fever and then examined patients without
taking any measures such as changing clothes or washing their hands
in a solution stronger than soap and water. The midwives, of course,
did not perform any autopsies. Thus, the professor concluded that
puerperal fever was an infectious disease that could be caused by
transferral of "cadaveric particles" on the hands of doctors or students
going straight from autopsy to patient. To prove this theory, Semmel-

---

[20] Nikolaus Mani, "Review of Ignaz Philipp Semmelweis und die Wiener Medizinische Schule" by Erna Lesky, *Bulletin of the History of Medicine*, XL (1966),
pp. 389–390.

[21] Logan Clendening, *The Romance of Medicine* (New York: Garden City
Publishers, 1933), pp. 331–332.

[22] Semmelweis, *Medical Classics*, pp. 355–357.

Texas Rep Biol Med 31 2-4, 1973

weis enforced a routine of hand-washing with chlorinated lime. A drop in the mortality rate of the clinic soon followed.[23]

Semmelweis was supported in his deductions by Skoda and Rokitansky, his former professors at Vienna; however, his ideas were strongly attacked by many of the medical leaders in Europe such as Liebig, Silberschmidt, and Scanzoni. This violent opposition caused Semmelweis to leave Vienna. Eventually he felt compelled to publish his findings.[24]

In the introduction to his book, Semmelweis offered an explanation for publishing his doctrines in a completed form at last, so many years after his discovery: "The object of this treatise is to present to the reader an historical account of the observations which I made at this clinic . . . and how I had become skeptical as to the current theory of the origin and nature of childbed fever, how my present conviction had been irresistibly forced upon me. . . . Because of my aversion to controversy, I did not reply to the numerous attacks on my doctrine. . . . To this disinclination for controversy is added an innate aversion to everything in the nature of writing . . . Fate has chosen me as an advocate of the truths which are laid down in this work . . . since my silence has been futile . . ."[25] It must have seemed to Semmelweis that this writing was futile also, for his theories did not receive wide acceptance at that time. Indeed, the correctness of his observations was not generally recognized until some time after his death.

The basis for Holmes's theory of puerperal fever

The 2 historic writings that eventually convinced the medical world of the true nature of puerperal fever have essentially the same message. The 1855 publication by Oliver Wendell Holmes, "The Contagiousness of Puerperal Fever," was a short but eloquent essay. It began with a statement of Holmes's position, followed by comments that had been made by his two major critics, Hodge and Meigs. The introduction, aimed specifically at medical students, stated his reasons for writing the 1843 paper and gave a brief outline of the article. Holmes attacked his critics' views and stated, "There is a point of mental saturation, beyond which argument cannot be forced without breeding impatient, if not harsh, feelings towards those who refuse to be convinced."[26]

[23] *Ibid.*, pp. 395–396.
[24] *Ibid.*, pp. 591, 665, 340.
[25] *Ibid.*, p. 351.
[26] Holmes, *Medical Essays*, p. 129.

Texas Rep Biol Med 33 2-4, 1975

Holmes laid the foundation for his conclusions by first stating that he considered the subject no longer to be a question. He then built a framework of premises:

> 1) Puerperal fever may be carried from one patient to another by medical personnel; 2) the above fact does not have to fit any previous etiological hypotheses; 3) it cannot be assumed that the "alleged laws of contagion deduced from observation in other diseases can be cited to disprove the alleged laws deduced from observation in this"; 4) puerperal fever is an uncommon disease, causing about 3 deaths per 1000 births; 5) if a disease is rampant in a single location and not elsewhere, this is proof that some local cause is active and responsible; 6) if many successive cases occur in one physician's practice and not in that of others, the patients being in approximately the same condition and located in different places, then one may "connect the cause of the disease with the person . . ."; 7) it is impossible that a given physician should have 16 fatalities in one month, given an attendance of 250 births per year, 3 out of 1,000 postpartum deaths due to puerperal fever, and no epidemic being prevalent, due only to chance; 8) cause and effect are related in the instance of a physician's presence and a patient's disease; 9) until there is proof of exactly what about the physician causes the disease, he should withdraw from obstetric practice for at least a month.[27]

Holmes then supported his premises with numerous case descriptions in which a physician attended a patient with puerperal fever, then had fatality after fatality from this disease in his practice, or in which the physician had first performed an autopsy on a victim of puerperal fever, then had fatalities after seeing patients. Case series submitted by physicians from both local areas and elsewhere were quoted, leading Holmes to conclude that "It does appear a singular coincidence that one man or woman should have 10, 20, 30, or 70 cases of this rare disease following his or her footsteps . . . while scores that cross the same paths on the same errands know it only by name."[28]

That the disease could affect males also was shown by the cases in which physicians wounded while performing autopsies became ill and died. The number of these cases following dissection of the bodies of those who perished from puerperal fever was greatly in excess of the number of fatalities following autopsies involving typhus or pneumonia and "from all diseases put together, that the conclusion is irresistible

[27] *Ibid.*, pp. 112–115.
[28] *Ibid.*, p. 157.

that a most fearful morbid poison is often generated in the course of the disease." In support of this, Holmes quoted Rigby, who had used as his source of information the studies done in the lying-in hospital in Vienna. No mention was made of Semmelweis.[29]

At the close of his paper, Holmes cited such authorities as Gordon, John Clarke, and Ramsbotham to support his views and mentioned that "a few Continental writers have adopted similar conclusions." His footnote here referred only to British journals. No German publication was cited as a reference.[30]

Eight suggestions for prophylaxis of the disease concluded the essay. These included change of dress and cleanliness for physicians leaving autopsies, forbidding obstetricians to do autopsies on victims of puerperal fever, and refusal of physicians to practice obstetrics if several cases of the fever occurred consecutively in their patients. A final appendage was an abbreviated list of additional references and cases.[31]

Holmes, moved to great anger by the apparent irresponsibility of his colleagues who reported many cases of puerperal fever, had strong words for them: "Indifference will not do here; our journalists and committees have no right to take up their pages with minute anatomy and tediously detailed cases, while it is a question whether or not the 'black death of childbed' is to be scattered broadcast by the agency of the mother's friend and advisor . . . if there is any voluntary blindness, any interested oversight, any culpable negligence, even in such a matter, and the facts shall reach the ear of the public; the pestilence-carrier of the lying-in chamber must look to God for pardon, for man will never forgive him."[32]

The basis for Semmelweis' theory of puerperal fever

In contrast to Holmes's article, Semmelweis's treatise was lengthy, redundant, and disorganized.[33] He began with an introduction in which he stated his reasons for publication and then listed a table of contents.

First, he described the difference in mortality rates in the two clinics in the Allgemeine Krankenhaus, as shown by a 6-year tabulation. He then proceeded to refute the previously accepted causes of puerperal fever, such as miasma and suppression of uterine discharge, since these

---

[29] *Ibid.*, pp. 162–163.
[30] *Ibid.*, p. 166.
[31] *Ibid.*, p. 168.
[32] *Ibid.*, p. 128.
[33] Guttmacher, "Introduction," p. xxvi.

Texas Rep Biol Med 34:2-4, 1976

would have affected both clinics equally. His conclusions in almost every instance were supported by numerous tables computed from the records of both clinics.[34]

Semmelweis developed his doctrine with the following observations:

1) Documentation by means of statistical tables of the consistent differences in mortality rates between the First and Second Clinics; 2) proof that the above difference could not be due to "atmospheric-cosmis-telluric" influences since the external environment was the same for both clinics; 3) proof that the difference could not be due to overcrowding, as the First Clinic, with the higher mortality rate, was less crowded than the Second Clinic. There were more births in the First Clinic during the 6 years studied because patients were admitted 4 days a week compared to 3 days a week for the Second Clinic. The First Clinic also had more floor space. In fact, the month in which there were fewest patients (November, 1842) showed a higher death rate than the month in which the clinic was most crowded (January, 1846); 4) deduction that puerperal fever is not an epidemic disease since epidemics show periodic intermissions; 5) proof that the difference was not due to treatment, as this was the same in both clinics as were cleanliness factors, linen, and diet; 6) observation that patients in the First Clinic who were in labor for more than 24 hours usually contracted the disease 24 to 36 hours postpartum. This did not happen in the Second Clinic; 7) observation that women giving birth before reaching the hospital became less ill than those admitted; 8) formation of conviction due to the case of Professor Kolletschka, who died from an infected cut received while performing an autopsy. The findings at his autopsy of pleuritis, pericarditis, peritonitis, and meningitis resembled the findings of puerperal fever victims.[35]

Thus, Semmelweis concluded: "There was forced on my mind with irresistible clarity . . . the identity of this disease of which Kolletschka died, with that from which I had seen so many hundred puerperae die . . . the wound produced by the autopsy knife was contaminated by cadaveric material. Not the wound, but the contamination of the wound . . . was the cause of death . . . if Kolletschka's disease and the disease from which I saw so many puerperae die are identical, then in the puerperae, it must be produced by the self-same engendering cause. I must ask myself the question: Did the cadaveric particles

[34] Semmelweis, *Medical Classics*, pp. 356–358.
[35] Guttmacher, "Introduction," pp. xxvii–xxviii.

Texas Rep Biol Med 34:2–4, 1976

make their way into the vascular systems of the individuals whom I had seen die of an identical disease? This question I answered in the affirmative."[36]

Having made this decision, Semmelweis began an experiment himself in 1847 by making attendants wash their hands with chlorinated lime as soon as they entered the labor room. By the end of 1848, the mortality rate in the First Clinic dropped to 1.27%, which was practically equivalent to the 1.33% rate in the Second Clinic. The difference between the two seemed to have been eliminated by Semmelweis' prophylactic routine. Possibly he derived the idea of using chlorinated lime from Robert Collins of England, even though he made no specific reference to him.[37]

The next observation made was that the transferral of the disease could also be caused by "ichorous discharges originating in a living organism." After examining a patient with a medullary carcinoma of the uterus, some practitioners had only used soap and water to cleanse their hands; following this, 11 of the 12 women afterwards delivered became ill and died. Semmelweis also believed that the air could be the "carrier of the decomposed organic matter which engenders puerperal fever." A patient with a diseased knee but healthy genital organs had been admitted to the ward, and the "ichorous exhalations of the various knee-joint were so considerable . . . that childbed fever flared up among the puerperae in the ward."[38]

Semmelweis did not regard puerperal fever as a contagious disease because it could not be carried from every patient with puerperal fever to healthy ones and because a healthy patient could contract the disease from a patient who did not have it. He decided, as Holmes had, that the disease was not limited to women. He concluded the disease was a transmissible kind of pyemia.[39]

Approximately the last 200 pages of Semmelweis' treatise dealt with the current literature for and against his hypotheses. He summoned to his support Skoda and Hebra of Vienna, who were not obstetricians. Michaelis of Kiel, Telanus of Amsterdam, and Carl Haller provided corroborative testimony also. Many bitter words were spent vigorously combating the criticism he had received from Scanzoni, Silberschmidt, and Carl Braun. In doing so, Semmelweis repeated most of the findings documented in the first part of his book.[40]

Like Oliver Wendell Holmes, Semmelweis denounced those who re-

[36] Semmelweis, *Medical Classics*, pp. 391–392.
[37] Guttmacher, "Introduction," p. xxx.
[38] Semmelweis, *Medical Classics*, pp. 396–397.
[39] *Ibid.*, pp. 503–504.
[40] *Ibid.*, pp. 592–773.

Texas Rep Biol Med 34.2-4, 1976

fused to believe the mound of evidence before them, those "men of science (who) so obstinately oppose the truth, men whose vocation is the saving of human life, yet who persist in a stiff-necked adherence to a teaching which condemns to death the patients committed to their care and attack him who would teach them how to save these lives. . . ."[41]

In summary, the author listed at least 4 etiological factors for puerperal fever:

> 1) The contamination of physicians' hands with decomposed material; 2) allowing diseased patients to be delivered in the same room as healthy ones, or placed on the same ward; 3) using the same medical instruments for sick and healthy patients, and 4) lack of ventilation in the wards or private rooms.

Semmelweis also suggested that auto-infection of patients could and did occur, due to retention of the placenta, retention of blood clots in the uterine cavity after hemorrhage, and bruised genital organs following prolonged labor.[42]

Prophylaxis of the disease was as important to Semmelweis as it was to Holmes, and his prescription list echoes that of the Boston physician. For Semmelweis, washing the hands with chlorinated lime after attending a diseased patient or cadaver was absolutely mandatory. For prevention of auto-infection, he recommended proper corrective procedures such as removal of the placenta or blood clot.[43]

To men of intelligence and sensitivity, Semmelweis offered his treatise as "proof of the everlasting truth of this doctrine." He fought his critics bitterly, refuting them sentence by sentence. His work ended on this note, requesting with mocking irony that his opponents take a course in logic. Semmelweis acknowledged his bitterness and even labeled his own work as a polemic; yet he seemed to draw some solace from the conviction that the time would come when he would be vindicated and his work recognized and acclaimed everywhere as the truth.[44] Ultimately this came about, but he did not live to see it.

DISCUSSION

Comparison of the two works by Holmes and Semmelweis provides many clues as to why the Hungarian's work is more renowned. For

41 *Ibid.*, p. 559.
42 *Ibid.*, pp. 551–552.
43 *Ibid.*, pp. 553–557.
44 *Ibid.*, pp. 658, 771–772.

brevity, clarity, and sheer eloquence, Holmes's paper receives the honors. For detailed and documented evidence, the longer treatise is certainly the more outstanding.

Both men were clearly handicapped by the fact that the world of micro-organisms was yet to be discovered by Pasteur. Holmes presented no theories on the nature of the ultimate cause of puerperal fever, but simply reached his conclusions on the basis of deductive reasoning. From a vast volume of case histories, Holmes pieced together cause and effect with impeccable logic. He had no way to test his theories in a controlled experiment. Nevertheless, to him the conclusions were inescapable. Semmelweis, equally convinced, had the good fortune of teaching in a natural experimental situation and the intelligence to take advantage of it. His evidence is statistically compiled, detailed, and overwhelming.

Semmelweis, through observation, deduction, and a vast amount of patience, learned enough facts from patients and autopsy cases to draw some basic conclusions about the etiology of puerperal fever. He made the distinction between "contagious" and "transmissible," which Holmes had not done.[45] He came closer than others had done before to the nature of the agent being transmitted from person to person, although he did not conceive of microscopic organisms. He reached the valid conclusion that the disease was a type of pyemia. Holmes, on the other hand, concentrated on establishing the fact that the disease could be transmitted from one person to another, but did not consider the nature of that process. Both men were greatly concerned about prophylaxis of the disease.

At this time, the Continent was considered the educational center of the world. Semmelweis was, of course, intimately associated with the medical school and teaching facilities at Vienna, the finest medical institution in Europe. Comparatively, Boston, Massachusetts, was little known outside the United States for its contributions to medical knowledge.

Semmelweis was probably completely unacquainted with the work of Holmes. He was bilingual and wrote his papers in both Hungarian and German. He did learn English in 1846–47, with the intention of going to England to study. In his treatise, he referred to the English theory of contagion, but considered it too vague; Semmelweis quoted Continental physicians for support.[46] The Holmes article also had a rather limited circulation, even with the 1855 republication. According

---

[45] Clendening, *The Romance of Medicine*, pp. 330–331.
[46] Guttmacher, "Introduction," xxvii.

to reviews, the work attracted attention in the United States and Great Britain. Semmelweis did not list any American journals as references.

During his education, Holmes had studied French, Italian, and Spanish at Harvard University.[47] Therefore, although Holmes read medical journals from various countries omnivorously, he most likely avoided those written in German. He did not list any German references in his article.

Semmelweis did not publish his book until 1861, although his ideas were mentioned in various medical publications between 1847 and 1855. The evidence seems to indicate, therefore, that neither man was aware of the other's work, or surely they would have used each other's papers as support, if possible, for both were under fairly severe attack for their ideas.[48]

CONCLUSION

Holmes was a man of many accomplishments. He was involved in a thriving general practice, the teaching of anatomy to medical students, and writing prose and poetry. Although he received much criticism for his ideas on puerperal fever, he received widespread acclaim for his other activities. Semmelweis, however, devoted himself to the practice of obstetrics. His writings were limited to several preliminary papers and his book on puerperal fever, the contents of which were ridiculed by his contemporaries.

The short and tormented life of Semmelweis has been compared to the long, varied, and happy life of Holmes many times. This circumstance has been used often to explain the greater notice given to the Hungarian physician's work in discovering the etiology of puerperal fever, but this is not a valid basis for judgment. The detailed, careful compilation of proof of his theories is sufficient to grant him the greater honor. The scope and depth of his treatise, his teaching, and his devotion to the practice of obstetrics have all combined to give Semmelweis an unassailable place in history as the discoverer of the "etiology, concept, and prophylaxis" of puerperal fever. Holmes's work has been granted the recognition it deserves, and is regarded as the most important forerunner of Semmelweis' treatise. The work of these two men has been responsible for saving a countless number of lives. Oliver Wendell Holmes and Ignaz Philipp Semmelweis were great pioneers in the field of medical science. Their contributions to the understand-

[47] Tilton, *Autocrat*, pp. 38–39.
[48] Guttmacher, "Introduction," p. xxi.

Texas Rep Biol Med 34:2-4, 1976

ng of the etiology of puerperal fever will always stand as a major
chievement of their time.

ELECTED BIBLIOGRAPHY

1. Clendening, Logan. *The Romance of Medicine.* New York: Garden City Publishers, 1933.

2. Currier, Thomas Franklin. *A Bibliography of Oliver Wendell Holmes,* Eleanor
   M. Tilton, ed. New York: Russell & Russell, 1953.

3. Guttmacher, Alan F. "Introduction" to *Die Aetiologie, der Begriff und die
   Prophylaxis des Kindbettfiebers* by Ignaz Philipp Semmelweis. New York and
   London: Johnson Reprint Corporation, 1966.

4. Holmes, Oliver Wendell. "The Contagiousness of Puerperal Fever." *Medical
   Essays.* New York: Houghton, Mifflin, and Co. 1883, pp. 103–172.

5. Holmes, Oliver Wendell. "Letter to William Osler." Quoted in "A Cross-Light
   on Doctor Holmes and His Investigation of Childbirth Fever" by J. Morris
   Slemons. *Western Journal of Surgery, Obstetrics, and Gynecology,* LI: 165–
   170, April, 1943.

6. Mani, Nikolaus. "Review of Ignaz Philipp Semmelweis und die Wiener Medizinische Schule" by Erna Lesky. *Bulletin of the History of Medicine,* XL:
   389–390, 1966.

7. Murphy, Frank P. "Ignaz Philipp Semmelweis, An Annotated Bibliography."
   Bulletin of the History of Medicine, XX: 692–703, 1946.

8. Semmelweis, Ignaz Philipp. *Die Aetiologie, der Begriff und die Prophylaxis
   des Kindbettfiebers.* Translated by Frank P. Murphy. *Medical Classics,* V-
   VIII: 339–773, Jan.-April, 1941.

9. Small, Miriam Rossiter. *Oliver Wendell Holmes.* New York: Twayne Publishers, Inc., 1962.

0. Tilton, Eleanor M. *Amiable Autocrat.* New York: Henry Schuman, 1947.

Diagnosing Unnatural Motherhood

Nineteenth-century Physicians and 'Puerperal Insanity'

Nancy Theriot

On December 16, 1878, Elizabeth S., age twenty-seven, was admitted to the Dayton Asylum for the Insane. The cause was "puerperal"; the form was "mania." About three weeks before admission she had given birth, and her insanity appeared a few hours after the child was born. When Elizabeth was admitted to the hospital she was "very noisy and excited, clapping her hands and talking incessantly." She would sometimes tear her clothing and "expose her person." She had a poor appetite, did not sleep at night, and was in poor physical condition. Her physician "insisted" that she take plenty of milk and beef-tea every day, gave her iron three times a day, and thirty-five grains of hydrate of chloral (a sedative) at bed time. Under this treatment Elizabeth remained the same for almost two months, except that she rested at night. Near the end of February, she began to improve. She started to "take an interest in things around her, was more neat in her dress; thought she ought to have something better to wear, and would help do the work." She continued to improve and was removed from the institution by her husband on June 19, 1879.[1]

The case of Elizabeth S. was one of hundreds reported by physicians in nineteenth-century medical journals. Elizabeth's was a case of puerperal mania, the most common type of puerperal insanity. Physicians also described two other forms of the disease which usually had melancholic

0026-3079/89/3002-0069$01.50/0

symptoms: "insanity of pregnancy" and "insanity of lactation." Although doctors described puerperal insanity in various ways and although medical opinion about the nature of the malady changed over the course of the century, most physicians agreed that it was a very common ailment and that it was responsible for at least 10 percent of female asylum admissions. Yet, by World War I the disease had all but disappeared. Except for "postpartum depression," the twentieth-century re-naming of "insanity of lactation," puerperal insanity was cured by the World Wars.

Like other nineteenth-century female diseases that have disappeared or been redefined in the twentieth century, puerperal insanity raises many questions about the relationship between the predominantly male medical profession and women patients. Was puerperal insanity an invention of men? Was it an expression of male physicians' ideas about proper womanly behavior, defining women's anti-maternal feelings and activities as "insane"? Or was puerperal insanity only incidentally a gender issue; could it be understood as a professional struggle between male gynecologists and male alienists (nineteenth-century psychiatrists) over the treatment of insane women? Given the sexual politics involved when women's illness is named and treated by a male medical establishment, can physicians' accounts of puerperal insanity provide valid information about the meaning of the disease for women? If so, was puerperal insanity an indication of dissatisfaction with motherhood, disappointment with marriage or anguish over abandonment or financial problems? In short, was puerperal insanity an expression of sexual ideology, medical professionalization struggles or gender tension?

These questions cannot be answered adequately using either the traditional approaches to the history of insanity or the more critical approaches taken by historians interested in the history of women and madness. Both traditionalists and critics explain nineteenth-century insanity (or specific insanities) from one of three perspectives: that of the disease, the physician/medical institution or the patient. Each vantage point is important, but incomplete.

Although concentrating on the disease itself can provide information essential to interpretation, disease-focused studies deal with the disease either as an idea or as an essence gradually becoming known/named. Treating insanity or insanities as histories of ideas is interesting and useful, but this approach sidesteps questions of power.[2] Understanding how the idea of puerperal insanity changed over time and how it related to other insanities is essential, for example, but this understanding does not begin to answer the questions posed earlier about gender and power. Similarly, it would be a mistake to see puerperal insanity as a "real" disease, misunderstood or misnamed by nineteenth-century physicians, but understood and rightly differentiated by twentieth-century psychiatry.[3] This approach to insanity or insanities ends up begging all the questions of the meaning of

70

insanity: why was this set of symptoms seen in a particular way at this particular time? why was this group of patients seen as "at risk"? why was this disease named one way in 1850 and another way in 1910? Interpreting changing insanities as a change in medical nomenclature leaves all of the important questions not only unanswered, but also unasked.

Interpreting the history of insanity from the perspective of physicians or medical institutions is more fruitful than the disease-centered approach because focusing on the medical establishment demands that insanity be situated within a specific socioeconomic setting. From this point of view the "reality" of the disease is questioned or ignored, as the historian concentrates on the role of professional and institutional politics or individual physicians in the creation of insanity. Perhaps the most well known example of this approach is *Madness and Civilization* in which Michel Foucault argues that medical discourse on insanity helped to define "reason" by medicalizing and silencing an ever-increasing category of "unreason."[4] Similarly, many twentieth-century medical sociologists see insanity as a "label" applied by a powerful medical establishment to society's deviants.[5] Historians writing about nineteenth-century insanity have also noted the role of professional rivalries between alienists and neurologists in defining the nature of insanity, as well as the role of individual physicians (such as Charles Beard and S. Weir Mitchell) in discovering, classifying, and treating insanities.[6] What all of these approaches share is an emphasis on the power of organized medicine to define certain behavior as "insane" or "neurotic."

Many feminist historians and sociologist writing about women's insanity have concentrated on the power of physicians to categorize women's behavior as normal, neurotic or insane, and have pointed out how such categorizations both reflect and help maintain gender stereotypes and the imbalance of power between women and men.[7] While this perspective is superior to a disease-focused approach because it makes visible the sexual politics of medicine, there are problems with the physician-oriented interpretation. A major difficulty with concentrating on the medical establishment as the creator of insanity categories, or as the agent of "Society" in its quest to control deviants, is that patients/the public/women are seen as passive victims of medical definition. Reducing insanity to a behavior pattern defined as "sick" by a powerful profession tells us little about the meaning of that behavior in the lives of the patients.

Since Carroll Smith-Rosenberg's early article on hysteria, some feminist historians have interpreted women's insanity from the point of view of the patient, asking what the symptoms meant to the women afflicted. Like the physician-oriented perspective, concentrating on the meaning of the disease for the patient involves situating insanity in a particular cultural location. Smith-Rosenberg's study, and a later study of anorexia by Joan Jacobs Brumberg, interpret the illness within a specific family dynamic:

71

woman as wife or daughter in a constricted or contradictory life pattern.[8] This patient orientation moves away from the "essence" of the disease and the politics of defining it, and instead asks why a woman might have behaved in a certain way. When trying to understand women's insanity it is absolutely essential to focus on the meaning of the behavior within the context of women's lives, but there are at least two risks involved in relying solely on this perspective. Insane behavior might be misconstrued as heroic, as the only "sane" thing to do when confronted with a particular life situation. And, in concentrating on the family dynamics or the specific gender constraints of the patient, one might miss the medical dynamic and the process of defining/labeling behavior as insane or abnormal.

In order to understand the relationship between gender and insanity in general, and puerperal insanity in particular, we need a method of analysis that will encompass all three perspectives—that of the disease, the physician/medical establishment and the patient—and will describe the three in dynamic interrelationship. We need an interpretation that will be able to offer an explanation of both the meaning of symptoms in the lives of patients and the translation of symptoms into disease categories by medical professionals. What follows is an interpretation of puerperal insanity that divides the symptoms into "illness" and "disease," and sees both as social constructions.[9] The illness of puerperal insanity was a behavior pattern expressing dissatisfaction or even despair over the constraints of womanhood in a particular time; while the disease of puerperal insanity was a definition given by physicians to the illness symptoms, a definition which both legitimized the behavior pattern and played a role in medical specialization. As both illness and disease, puerperal insanity involved relationships: between the woman and her family, between the woman and her doctor, between the husband and the doctor and between different medical specialists. Puerperal insanity can be interpreted as a socially-constructed disease, reflecting both the gender constraints of the nineteenth century and the professional battles accompanying medical specialization. Male physicians and their female patients, together, created puerperal insanity; and that creation both reflected and contributed to sexual ideology and medical specialization.

Before elaborating this interpretation, a more thorough examination of puerperal insanity is in order. As mentioned earlier, most physicians believed puerperal insanity manifested itself differently in the three phases of the reproductive process. Milton Hardy, the medical superintendent of the Utah State Insane Asylum, defined puerperal insanity as a condition developing "during the time of and by the critical functions of gestation, parturition, or lactation, assuming maniacal or melancholic types in general" and characterized by "a rapid sequence of psychic and somatic symptoms which are characteristic not individually, but in their collective groupings."[10] Some physicians preferred to classify puerperal insanity as maniacal, melancholic or depressive, instead of dividing it according to reproductive phase; but in both groups there was consensus as to the type of insanity most associated with pregnancy, parturition and lactation.

Insanity of pregnancy was thought to be the rarest of the three, and usually involved melancholic (and suicidal) symptoms or depressive symptoms. Nineteenth-century physicians described patients as "melancholic" who appeared to be apathetic, hopeless and prone to suicide; while "depressive" patients were those with "low spirits." In cases of insanity of pregnancy, the symptoms sometimes lasted only a few weeks or months, but in other cases the patient was cured only by childbirth. Insanity of pregnancy was thought to occur most often with first pregnancies; however, some women who had developed symptoms once would develop symptoms in subsequent pregnancies. This form of puerperal insanity was rarely fatal.[11]

Lactation insanity was similar to gestation insanity in its symptoms, melancholic and depressive, but was seen as more frequent. Lactation insanity differed from insanity of gestation and parturition in that it seemed to occur most often in women who had several children rather than in women going through their first pregnancies. In some cases of lactation insanity, the melancholy ended in dementia and life-long commitment to an asylum, but most cases recovered in under six months.[12]

Insanity of parturition was considered the most common type of puerperal insanity and was associated with maniacal symptoms. Usually puerperal mania began within fourteen days of childbirth, but some cases started up to six weeks later. Like the insanity of pregnancy and lactation, puerperal mania was rarely fatal and usually lasted only a few months. Of the three forms of puerperal insanity, puerperal mania was the most baffling to medical writers in the nineteenth century. Indeed, most of the medical literature on puerperal insanity was a description of puerperal mania. Characteristic symptoms included: incessant talking, sometimes coherent and sometimes not; an abnormal state of excitement, so that the patient would not sit or lie quietly; inability to sleep, with some patients having little or no sleep for weeks; refusal of food or medicine, so that many patients were fed by force; aversion to the child and/or the husband, sometimes expressed in homicidal attempts; a general meanness toward caretakers; and obscenity in language and sometimes behavior.[13]

Until the end of the century when doctors began to express suspicion about puerperal insanity as a specific illness, there was widespread agreement about its frequency, duration and prognosis. A physician writing in 1875 asserted that puerperal insanity was a "class of cases to be met with in the practice of nearly every physician," others cited asylum records indicating that the disease was responsible for "a very large proportion of the female admissions to hospitals," and still others claimed that puerperal insanity affected anywhere between 1 in 400 or 1 in 1000 pregnant

73

women.[14] Doctors also agreed that most cases of puerperal insanity lasted only a few months, with most recovering completely within six months.[15] Except for those cases with suicidal or homicidal tendencies, the prognosis was good for patients suffering from puerperal insanity, and doctors asserted that most cases could be, and were, treated at home.[16]

Treatment for puerperal insanity remained mostly the same over the course of the century, and the change reflected a more general change in medical therapeutics. In the first part of the century, bleeding was considered the proper treatment, no matter if the symptoms were manic or melancholic. By mid-century, that treatment was no longer recommended, and instead physicians were treating puerperal insanity patients with rest, food, a little purging and sedation. Most physicians also recommended that patients be restrained or watched closely and that family and friends be kept away.[17]

One of the first explanations of puerperal insanity to occur to an historian sensitive to gender as a category of analysis is that the disease represented male physicians' definitions of proper womanly behavior.[18] To nineteenth-century men, a woman who rejected her child, neglected her household duties, expressed no care for her personal appearance and frequently spoke in obscenities had to be "insane." Certainly there is much in the medical literature to support this explanation. Many physicians wrote in very sentimental terms about the mysterious beauty of motherhood being defiled by insanity. Dr. R. M. Wigginton wrote of the special horror of puerperal insanity: "The loving and affectionate mother, who has so recently had charge of her household, has suddenly been deprived of her reason; and instead of being able to throw around her family that halo of former love, she is now a violent maniac, and feared by all."[19] Physicians commented on a woman's "letting herself go" or being "indifferent to cleanliness" as symptoms, and many listed willingness and ability to perform household tasks as evidence of a cure.[20]

By far the most shocking symptoms of puerperal insanity were women's indifference or hostility to children and/or husbands and women's tendency to obscene expressions. The first upset physicians' ideas about women's maternal and wifely devotion, while the second undermined doctors' assumptions about feminine purity. Allan McLane Hamilton described a patient who before her labor was "a loving and devoted wife, but shortly after lost all of her amiability, and treated her husband and mother with marked coldness, and sometimes with decided rudeness."[21] Even more difficult to explain than coldness was a woman's "thrusting the baby from the bed, disclaiming it altogether, striking her husband," a woman who looks at her baby "and then turns away," or a woman who "commenced to abuse it [the newborn child] by pinching it, sticking in pins, etc." So frequent was "hostility or aversion to husband and child" noted in cases of puerperal insanity that this was considered one of the defining character-

74

istics of the disease, and physicians recommended that the woman not be left alone with her infant.[22]

If doctors were horrified at women's treatment of husbands and children, they were equally shocked at women's obscene words and behavior during an attack of puerperal insanity. "The astonishing familiarity of refined women with words and objects and practices of obscene and filthy character, displayed in the ravings of puerperal mania, gives a fearful suggestion of impressions which must have been made upon their minds at some period of life, "wrote George Byrd Harrison, a Washington, D. C. physician. W. D. Haines of Cincinnati described a case in which the woman would repeat one word a dozen or so times "then break forth into a continuous flow of profanity. The subject of venery was discussed by her in a manner that astounded her friends and disgusted the attendants." Another doctor wrote of the typical puerperal mania patient "tearing her clothes, swearing, or pouring out a stream of obscenity so foul that you wonder how in her heart of hearts such phrases ever found lodgment." An Atlanta physician expressed similar puzzlement: "it is odd that women who have been delicately brought up, and chastely educated, should have such rubbish in their minds." And still another physician described this symptom as "a disposition to mingle obscene words with broken sentences ... modest women use words which in health are never permitted to issue from their lips, but in puerperal insanity this is so common an occurrence, and is done in so gross a manner, that it is very characteristic." W. G. Stearns, a Chicago physician, went so far as to note that in "all such cases [puerperal mania] there is a tendency to obscenity of language, indecent exposure, and lascivious conduct."[23]

Clearly, these physicians were shocked and dismayed by their patients' "indecent" behavior and use of language, as well as by their hostility toward husbands and infants, their neglect of household duties and their refusal to pay attention to personal appearance. Even in their empirical reporting of patients' symptoms doctors revealed their disgust and horror over such unwomanly women. In naming their behavior "puerperal insanity," physicians were both reflecting and supporting nineteenth-century sexual ideology.

As authoritative spokesmen for the new scientific view of the nature of humanity, physicians were also helping to *create* sexual ideology in their explanations of puerperal insanity. Many doctors wrote of insanity as a logical by-product of women's reproductive function. George Rohe, a Maryland physician, asserted that "women are especially subject to mental disturbances dependent upon their sexual nature at three different epochs of life: the period of puberty when the menstrual function is established, the childbearing period and the menopause."[24] Dr. Rohe regarded insanity as an ever-present danger to all women throughout their adult lives. Other doctors, however, wrote of pregnancy as a special challenge to women's

75

mental balance, asserting that most women suffer mild forms of mental illness throughout their pregnancies. "In females of nervous temperament, the equilibrium of nerve force existing between these two organs [the brain and the uterus] is of the most delicate nature," wrote a Denver physician. He went on to say that "pregnancy is sufficient to produce insanity."[25] Probably the clearest statement along these lines was made by a professor of gynecology who wrote: "From the very inception of impregnation to the completion of gestation, some women are always insane, who are otherwise perfectly sane." He went on to say that others "manifest defective mental integrity in the form of whimsical longings for the gratification of a supposed depraved appetite."[26]

It would seem that nineteenth-century physicians' views of proper womanly behavior, along with their ideas about the power of the uterus to disrupt women's mental balance influenced their perception and definition of puerperal insanity. It would be a mistake, however, to conclude that puerperal insanity was simply an indication that male doctors reflected their time or that the medical establishment influenced sexual ideology. Focusing too closely on the obvious ideological content of physicians' accounts of puerperal insanity, one might overlook that physicians' guesses about the nature of the disease were very much in keeping with nineteenth-century ideas about insanity in general and that many physicians offered what late-twentieth-century people would call "sociological" explanations for women's behavior. Indeed, much of the medical discourse on puerperal insanity seems to have been influenced very little by male doctors' concepts of femininity, but instead reflected the state of medical knowledge about insanity, on the one hand, and a jurisdictional dispute between alienists and gynecologists over the treatment of insane women, on the other.

For example, throughout the nineteenth century physicians asserted that mental illness in general, not just women's mental illness, reflected a connection between mind and body; if the mind was unbalanced, a brain lesion was responsible, and the "exciting" cause of the brain lesion could be physical or emotional.[27] Indeed, this argument was one of the ways physicians convinced the public that mental illness was a medical problem. From the general assumption of a mind/body link as part of the nature of mental disease, it was logical to conclude that puerperal insanity was in some way caused by the physical state of pregnancy, parturition or lactation. Doctors reasoned that the physical system was taxed by the reproductive process and that this added strain could be an "exciting" cause of insanity. A Pennsylvania physician wrote that "[t]here is no organ or portion of viscera which is not intimately connected with the brain through the sympathetic nervous system," and the Ohio physician who admitted Elizabeth S. to the Dayton Asylum noted more specifically about puerperal insanity: "the physical derangements attendant upon pregnancy, child-bearing and nursing, are the principal causes of the insanity, which would be equally produced by any other physical suffering or constitutional disturbance of the same intensity."[28] Another indication of this line of reasoning was physicians' notation of any physical problem associated with labor as the probable cause of the insanity. If there was infection or a mild fever, if the labor was unusually long or difficult, if the woman required forceps, if her perineum was torn: these were seen as explanations for the puerperal insanity.[29]

Physicians also cited "heredity" as a primary cause of puerperal insanity, especially by the middle of the century. Like the mind/body theme, this too reflected a more general trend in medical ideas about the nature of mental illness. If there was insanity in a woman's family, regardless of how remote a relationship, this was considered a "predisposition" to mental unbalance. In such a case, pregnancy, childbirth or lactation was seen as the stress that pushed the already unstable mind over the edge.[30]

Finally, many physicians argued that puerperal insanity was caused by situation, what the nineteenth-century writer called "moral" factors and what the late-twentieth-century writer would call "sociological" factors. This too was in keeping with nineteenth-century theories about insanity in general. Just as financial problems or job stress were seen as possible causes of insanity in men, women were thought to develop puerperal insanity sometimes because of being abandoned or poorly treated by husbands, being pregnant and unmarried, being overburdened with too many children and household cares or being emotionally drained because of grief or fear. In such cases physicians were very clear that the woman's insanity was brought on by her situation, and that the puerperal state simply lowered the woman's strength so that she could no longer deal with the adverse environmental conditions. Kindness, rest and reassurance was the best treatment.[31]

The mind/body connection and the possibility that physical or moral factors could be the "exciting cause" of puerperal insanity were both stressed throughout the century, but by the 1870s gynecologists began to emphasize the physical causes. The earliest proponent of this point of view, cited later as a man ahead of his time, was Horatio Storer. He argued as early as 1864 that most insanity in women is "reflex" insanity; that is, the primary cause of the insanity is a malfunction of the reproductive organs. For Storer and his post-Civil War followers, this meant that women's insanity could be prevented, treated and cured by medical and/or surgical means.[32] It also meant that a gynecologist should be consulted in any case of female insanity. Medical ideas about the nature, cause and treatment of puerperal insanity were complicated by this professional struggle. Because it was in their best interest to link women's insanity with their reproductive organs, gynecologists "saw" a connection that other physicians saw less clearly. Furthermore, they wrote authoritatively, as the

77

medical "experts" on women, and assumed disagreement was the result of ignorance. Charles Reed, professor at the Cincinnati College of Medicine, expressed surprise to hear any dissent from "the long-recognized doctrine of the genital origin of insanity in the female sex."[33] One Washington, D. C. physician claimed that puerperal insanity could be prevented only by good pre-natal care.[34] These gynecologists directed their arguments to general practitioners and to alienists, who ran asylums. Many, though not all, of the gynecologists' articles about puerperal insanity or about women's insanity in general concluded that asylums should employ gynecologists—a clear expression of the professional struggle influencing medical perceptions of women's insanity.[35]

The medical discourse among gynecologists, alienists and general practitioners about the nature of female insanity affected practice, which in turn affected discourse. From the mid-1870s to the 1890s gynecologists practiced their medical and increasingly surgical techniques on private patients and institutionalized women. Increasingly diseases of the reproductive system were listed as the cause for the insane symptoms of women admitted to asylums.[36] More and more asylums employed gynecologists to examine female patients upon admission, and physicians found a variety of gynecological disorders among the women. Believing that there was a direct connection between these disorders and the women's insanity, the doctors administered medical and surgical cures. In the surgical category, removal of the ovaries was the most popular operation, but more and less extreme operative procedures were also tried, such as hysterectomy and birth repair surgery.[37]

Some physicians reported patients being cured of insanity as a result of a gynecological procedure, and puerperal insanity was said to be especially responsive to physically oriented therapy. However, as gynecologists treated more insane women, in and out of asylums, medical discourse reflected their growing disillusionment with surgical and medical treatment. Even those physicians who supported operative treatment reported disappointing cure rates.[38] By the 1890s there was lively debate over surgical treatment of insane women, with some physicians denouncing "mischievous operative interference" and others asserting that only physical (not mental) symptoms should prompt a surgical response. What made the debate different from the earlier one in which gynecologists successfully fought for the right to treat insane women was that the later debate was based on empirical studies. Having won access to asylum patients, gynecologists generated the numerical evidence against their own case. Two Minnesota physicians working at the state hospital at St. Peter found a large number of women asylum patients with serious pelvic disease in whom "there was not only no apparent relation between the pelvic disease and the mental disturbance, but there was no complaint or evidence of physical discomfort." They called this finding "the most unexpected result

78

of our investigation."[39] Other physicians recorded the effect of surgery on women's insanity and found no significant link between operations and cures. Although they argued that gynecological problems could add to a woman's worry and discomfort and that all women (in and out of asylums) should have those problems treated, most gynecologists by the end of the century no longer claimed that women's diseased reproductive organs caused their insanity.[40]

If the empirical evidence, most of it gathered by gynecologists themselves, would not support a straight physiological explanation of women's insanity, how were physicians to account for puerperal insanity? Gradually, beginning in the 1890s, puerperal insanity was seen as a suspect category, and the emerging specialty of psychiatry emphasized the similarity between puerperal mania and any other mania, between the melancholy some women experienced during pregnancy or lactation and any other melancholy.[41] The particular physiological process was seen as less and less significant, and so the very term "puerperal" insanity was eventually dropped. Just as its appearance and growth was complicated by struggles of medical specialization, the *dis*appearance of puerperal insanity from medical discourse was due to the empirical studies of one specialty and the reconceptualization of insanity that accompanied the rise of a new specialty (psychiatry).

Seen from this angle, puerperal insanity was not simply an expression or creation of sexual ideology by the medical profession. Certainly gynecologists were able to convince other physicians of the physiological basis of women's insanity (and puerperal insanity) because the argument fit common ideas about woman's nature. Physicians "saw" mad women in a particular way because of generally held cultural ideas. That medical discourse was altered by empirical investigation at a time when most Americans, including feminists, believed in a biologically determined "woman's nature" indicates that gender was not a simple factor in the medical debate. Perhaps the most significant way gender affected the medical construction of puerperal insanity is in the absence of women from the professional discourse until the late nineteenth century. There is no way to measure the impact of women's silence, but it is interesting to note that women physicians in the 1880s and 1890s were overrepresented in the group of doctors gathering evidence that separated women's insanity from their reproductive organs and eroded the assumptive framework for puerperal insanity as a specific illness.[42] It is safe to assume that the exclusion of women from medicine in the early and mid-nineteenth century affected the "scientific" view of women's mental (and physical) illness.

But what of the women who were diagnosed as having puerperal insanity? So far we have been concentrating on physicians, and the ideological and professional issues influencing their conception of puerperal insanity. The medical discourse, however, also offers a way to understand

79

the women who were patients. Most medical articles dealing with puerperal insanity included case studies, detailed descriptions of the situation, behavior and treatment of the patients. Of course, what doctors selected as important information and what they recorded and did not record of patients' speech and behavior was subjective. Yet they were attempting "objective" observation. Although we cannot take case studies as the "complete picture" or as an entirely unbiased account, they reveal much about the possible meaning of puerperal insanity to the women who were so diagnosed and they also provide a somewhat blurry snapshot of the doctor/patient dynamic.[43]

On the most literal and superficial level, case studies of puerperal insanity indicate that many women responded with melancholic or maniacal behavior to situations that they found unbearable. Illegitimacy, the fear that often accompanied first pregnancies, a traumatic birth experience or a stillborn infant, infection following birth and extreme cruelty of husbands—were all cited in case studies, sometimes with the doctor attributing the insanity to the situation and other times not. One woman developed maniacal symptoms after her baby was delivered with forceps ("the head was extracted with considerable difficulty") and she suffered physical damage in this her first delivery. Another woman "frail and feeble" developed insane symptoms after her infant died a few days after birth. A woman whose symptoms included disclaiming her infant, striking her husband if he came near and accusing people of trying to kill her was unimproved after five months in an asylum; her baby had died two months earlier and her husband, it turned out, had been continually abusive to her during her pregnancy.[44]

Other situational difficulties also appeared in case studies, such as women having many children in very few years and seemingly overburdened with work and responsibility. One woman, Mrs. S. who was thirty-five and had had five children, three of them within five years, developed "anxiety and slight confusion of ideas" during her last pregnancy. After the child was born she went into a "furious delirium . . . tried to leap from the window to avoid imaginary pursuers." A few days later she was no better; she said she "expects to be tortured soon, remonstrates bitterly." By the tenth day she was a little better: "Talks less and sleeps better. Tries to explain her sickness but cannot."[45] In another case a twenty-two-year-old woman was melancholic after the birth of her fourth child; her husband confined her and abandoned her once she was hospitalized.[46]

Case studies of puerperal insanity almost always included some physical or situational problem that late-twentieth-century readers would see as cause enough for insane behavior, even when the physicians failed to note the connection. But while we may conclude that these women had good reason to act strangely for a few months, the meaning of puerperal insanity is more complicated than this. The symptoms provide a clue to the

80

meaning of the disease for women and also point to the doctor/patient relationship as a key factor in the waxing and waning of puerperal insanity.

Whether on a conscious or unconscious level, women who suffered from puerperal insanity were rebelling against the constraints of gender. The symptoms clearly indicate that rebellion. Case studies document that women refused to act in a maternal fashion by denying their infant nourishment or actively attempting to harm the child. Many women "did not recognize" the child, "ignored" its presence or denied that that child belong to them.[47] Similarly, women refused to act in a wifely fashion; they claimed not to know their husbands, expressed fear that the husband wanted to murder them and sometimes struck out physically at their husbands.[48] Women were refusing the role of wife/mother, a role that most nineteenth-century Americans saw as the essence of "true womanhood."

Moreover women suffering from puerperal insanity were not acting like women at all. They were "apathetic," "irritable," "gloomy" and "violent," instead of tuned in to the needs of those around them. In fact, these women required that others pay attention to them, in their constant talking and pacing the floor and in their refusal to care for themselves in the simplest ways, such as feeding themselves and keeping themselves clean. In a time when modesty was thought to be a defining characteristic of femininity, women with puerperal insanity "laughed immodestly," tore their clothing in the company of men and used obscene language. Rebellion against cultural notions of "true womanhood" was the one thing tying together the various symptoms of puerperal insanity.

Physicians, new to the lying-in chamber, made these rebellious symptoms legitimate by defining them within a medical framework. Doctors responded to women's behavior with a name: puerperal insanity. That naming was the result not only of the general ideas of the culture and the specific professionalization struggles of physicians, but also was related to doctors' new relationship with women patients: as birth attendants. From the late eighteenth century, male physicians had begun to describe pregnancy and childbirth as a traumatic ordeal. Even doctors who did not think of birth as a sickness, but described it as a natural phenomenon, expressed a mixture of amazement, disgust and respect at women's ability to undergo all the physiological changes associated with pregnancy, birth and lactation. The assumptions of nineteenth-century physicians provided a framework both for their acceptance of women's strange behavior as a side-effect of reproduction and their definition of that behavior as, mostly temporary, insanity.

The medicalization of pregnancy, birth and lactation provided a kind of permission for women to express rebellion and desperation in the particular symptoms of puerperal insanity. But if physicians and women patients both participated in the creation of puerperal insanity, the relation-

81

ship was not a straightforward one. Women played out their rebellion against the male physician, and doctors translated that rebellion into an acceptable medical category. But doctors also "cured" the rebellion with their treatment and systematically silenced women in their case study reporting. In both cases, women were unequal partners in the construction of the disease.

Treatment of puerperal insanity consisted of various levels of constraint and intrusion. In what late-twentieth-century readers would judge the mildest, most humane treatment, women were confined to their rooms, denied the company of family and friends and forced to rest by the admission of tranquilizers. If the woman refused to eat, which happened in an overwhelming majority of puerperal insanity cases, she was force-fed. Indeed, the element of force was characteristic of most treatment plans. One physician recorded force-feeding and threatening to cut the patient's hair if she continued to refuse food, and others noted that patients were confined to their rooms or their beds if their behavior did not change quickly enough.[49] In non-surgical cures force-feeding was the most intrusive aspect of the treatment, but surgical cures were penetrating in a more drastic sense. For the doctor, these cures were restoring the unfortunate patient to her rightful and happy role. For the woman? Regardless of how women perceived the cures, and we will never know their perceptions, they certainly gave up their insane behavior usually within a few months. If women were expressing rebellion in puerperal insanity symptoms and male physicians were defining that behavior as medically explainable and therefore legitimate, male physicians were also forcefully putting down the rebellion. In the social construction of puerperal insanity both parties were not equally powerful. A more interesting example of women's subordinate position in the relationship defining puerperal insanity is the judging and editing of women patients in the male-controlled medical discourse. The language physicians used to describe their women patients was often sympathetic, but more often judgmental. One doctor described a woman before her insanity as having a "naturally obstinate and passionate disposition," and another wrote of a suicidal mother who tried to harm her four-month-old infant: "she should be hung."[50] More subtle than judgments of behavior were descriptions in case studies which substituted judgement for information. Physicians recorded "obstinate" and "indelicate" behavior and "immoderate" laughter. In some cases the physician's judgmental words were simply reflections of husbands' accounts of their wives' behavior; but that acceptance of the husbands' point of view was very much a part of the sexual politics involved in puerperal insanity. To many male physicians, the women were to blame for their deviant, unwomanly behavior, and physician case studies recorded the blame.

Although women patients and male physicians constructed puerperal insanity together, the clearest indication that men controlled the discourse

82

146

was the near absence of women's words from the case studies. Over and over again physicians claimed that women suffering from puerperal insanity "talked incessantly," yet no attempt was made to record what the women talked about. Similarly, some women were said to complain of "imaginary wrongs," with no explanation of the content of those complaints. The most glaring omission in the case studies was physicians' refusal to record women's "obscene" language. An overwhelming majority of case studies referred to one or all of these speech acts, yet no content was provided.

If women were silenced partners in the construction of puerperal insanity, what can we conclude about the meaning of the disease for women? Although women's words were not reported, physicians' accounts of women's behavior and situations indicate that puerperal insanity was an unconscious act of rebellion against gender constraints for many women. The particular symptoms of puerperal insanity involved a denial of motherhood and a reversal of many "feminine" traits. Women presented these symptoms and acted out their rebellion; male physicians who for ideological and professional reasons were disposed to define women's behavior as "insanity," legitimized women's rebellion as illness. Yet part of the meaning of puerperal insanity for women must also have been the curing, the silencing. So many of the symptoms were aggressively, willfully expressive: the tireless pacing, the continuous talking, the laughter, the obscenity—all un-listened-to, unrecorded. It is almost as if women usurped the power of language only to find that it held no power at all. The woman cured of puerperal insanity surrendered these self-assertive symptoms and went back to being the "halo of love" in her family, without having been heard. There is no way of knowing whether she saw herself as victorious or defeated.

In spite of the sexual politics inherent in the doctor/patient relationship defining puerperal insanity and in spite of women's silence in the case studies, women's symptoms were taken seriously enough to constitute a disease, at least until the turn of the twentieth century. What did it mean for women that puerperal insanity disappeared? Certainly it can be argued that the constraints of gender were not as tight in the early twentieth as they had been in the nineteenth century. Women were having fewer children, childbirth was less dangerous and less painful, women had wider opportunities in terms of education and work and women's marriage relationships were more companionate. If puerperal insanity was a rebellion against the constraints of nineteenth-century "true womanhood," women may have had less trouble with the twentieth-century variety and therefore ceased to manifest the symptoms of puerperal insanity.

Although changes in women's situation contributed to the demise of puerperal insanity, changes in the relationship between doctors and women patients also played a part. As we saw earlier, empirical studies and the rise of psychiatry altered medical perception of mental illness. Reliance on more "objective," "scientific" studies as the basis of medical discourse meant that there was less tolerance for puerperal insanity as a category. Regardless of how much or little women's situation had changed by the twentieth century, the symptoms of puerperal insanity were no longer a legitimate response to pregnancy, birth or lactation in 1910, as they had been in 1870. Changing medical ideas, which had little to do with women patients, meant that physicians would no longer legitimize puerperal insanity as illness.

Elizabeth S. was admitted to the Dayton Asylum for the insane in 1878. Her illness was the product of several intertwined relationships: her own response to her marriage and motherhood; her physician's response to her story; and her story's resonance in the medical and cultural score of the nineteenth century. The interaction of these layers of relationship defined her condition as puerperal insanity. By the twentieth century, changes in all three layers made the disease obsolete. The creation and demise of puerperal insanity illustrates not only the social construction of illness but also the cultural embeddedness of medical categories.

Notes

Research for this article was made possible by a Summer Faculty Research Award (1987) from the University of Louisville Commission on Academic Excellence and by a Graduate Research Grant for Travel and Equipment (1987) from the University of Louisville, Graduate Programs and Research.

1. J. M. Carr, "Puerperal Insanity," *Cincinnati Lancet-Clinic* 7 (1881), 537-542.
2. I do not mean to imply that studies of the history of ideas about insanity are inappropriate. Such studies as Norman Dain, *Concepts of Insanity in the United States, 1789-1865* (New Brunswick, New Jersey, 1964); and Ellen Dwyer, "A Historical Perspective," in Cathy Spatz Widom, ed. *Sex Roles and Psychopathology* (Bloomington, Indiana, 1984), 19-48 are absolutely essential to our understanding of the history of insanity. In her essay, Dwyer goes beyond a history of ideas approach and attempts to test how ideas about gender and insanity related to actual practice. This relationship between ideas and practice deserves more attention. In another study, Dwyer is particularly interested in comparing ideas and practice: Ellen Dwyer, "The Weaker Vessel: Legal Versus Social Reality in Mental Commitments in Nineteenth-Century new York," in D. Kelly Weisberg, ed. *Women and the Law: A Social Historical Perspective*, II (Cambridge, Massachusetts, 1982), 85-106. A twentieth-century study that compares ideas and practice in that same volume is Robert T. Roth and Judith Lerner, "Sex-based Discrimination in the Mental Institutionalization of Women," 107-139.
3. The approach to insanity taken by Mark S. Micale, "On the 'Disappearance' of Hysteria: A Medical and Historical Perspective," paper read at the annual meeting of the American Association for the History of Medicine, Birmingham, April 1989, I believe is not helpful. Micale explains the disappearance of hysteria as due to more specific medical definitions. The real question, however, is how/why definitions change.
4. Michel Foucault, *Madness and Civilization: A History of Insanity in the Age of Reason*, translated by Richard Howard, (New York, 1965).
5. For discussions of the labeling theory, see: Roy Porter, *A Social History of Madness* (New York, 1987); Agnes Miles, *The Neurotic Woman: The Role of Gender in Psychiatric Illness* (New York, 1988); Elaine Showalter, "Victorian Women and Insanity," in Andrew T. Scull, ed. *Madhouses, Mad-Doctors, and Madmen: The Social History of Psychiatry in the Victorian Era* (Philadelphia, 1981), 313-331; Richard W. Fox, *So Far Disor-*

84

dered in Mind: Insanity in California, 1870-1930 (Berkeley, 1978); Nancy E. Waxler, "Culture and Mental Illness: A Social Labeling Perspective," Journal of Nervous and Mental Disease 159 (1974), 379-395.

6. See for example: Bonnie Ellen Blustein, "'A Hollow Square of Psychological Science': American Neurologists and Psychiatrists in Conflict," in Scull, Madhouses, Mad-doctors, and Madmen, 241-270; and Barbara Sickerman, "The Paradox of Prudence: Mental Health in the Gilded Age," in the same volume, 218-240.

7. For example, Waxler, "Culture and Mental Illness;" Showalter, "Victorian Woman and Insanity," and The Famale Malady: Women, Madness, and English Culture, 1830-1980 (New York, 1987); Miles, The Neurotic Woman; Dwyer, "The Weaker Vessel."

8. Carroll Smith-Rosenberg, "The Hysterical Woman: Sex Roles and Role Conflict in Nineteenth-Century America," Social Research 39 (1972), 562-583; Joan Jacobs Brumberg, Fasting Girls: The Emergence of Anorexia nervosa as a Modern Disease (Cambridge, Massachusetts, 1988).

9. For an explanation of "illness" and "disease," see: Arthur Kleinman, Social Origins of Distress and Disease: Depression, Neurasthenia, and Pain in Modern China (New Haven, Connecticut, 1986); Claudine Herzlich and Janine Pierret, Illness and Self in Society, translated by Elborg Forster (Baltimore, 1987); Arthur Kleinman, Patients and Healers in the Context of Culture (Berkeley, 1980); Peter Conrad and Rochelle Kern, eds., The Sociology of Health and Illness: Critical Perspectives (New York, 1981); Peter Wright and Andrew Treacher, eds., The Problem of Medical Knowledge: Examining the Social Construction of Medicine (Edinburgh, 1982), especially the essays: David Ingleby, "The Social Construction of Mental Illness," 123-141, and Karl Figlio, "How does Illness Mediate Social Relations: Workmen's Compensation and Medico-Legal Practices, 1890-1940," 174-224; Bryan S. Turner, The Body and Society: Explorations in Social Theory (Oxford, 1984).

10. Milton H. Hardy, "Puerperal Insanity," Western Medical Review 3 (1898), 14.

11. W. H. B. Stoddart, "A Clinical Lecture on Insanity in Relation to the Child-bearing State and the Puerperium," The Clinical Journal 14 (1899), 242; Hardy, "Puerperal Insanity," 14; R. M. Wigginton, "Puerperal Insanity," Transactions of the Wisconsin State Medical Society 60 (1975), 40; L.R. Landfear, "Puerperal Insanity," Cincinnati Lancet and Observer 19 (1876), 54; Harry L. K. Shaw, "A Case of Insanity of Gestation," Albany Medical Annals 19 (1898), 459-462; Fleetwood Churchill, "On the Mental Disorders of Pregnancy and Childbed," American Journal of Insanity 7 (1850-1851), 297-317.

12. W. F. Menzies, "Puerperal Insanity: An Analysis of One Hundred and Forty Consecutive Cases," American Journal of Insanity 50 (1893-1894), 147-185; George H. Rohe, "Lactational Insanity," Journal of the American Medical Association 21 (1893), 325-327; W. G. Stearns, "The Psychiatric Aspects of Pregnancy," Obstetrics 3 (1901), 23-26, 32-36; Wigginton, "Puerperal Insanity," 41.

13. These symptoms were listed in numerous nineteenth-century articles. Since we will be dealing with the symptoms in more detail later, I will refrain from citing all of the articles here.

14. Landfear, "Puerperal Insanity," 54; Wigginton, "Puerperal Insanity," 41. See also R. E. Haughton, "Puerperal Mania," Cincinnati Lancet and Observer 9 (1866), 713; B. C. Hirst, "Six Cases of Puerperal Insanity," Journal of the American Medical Association 12 (1889), 29; F. C. Fernald, "Puerperal Insanity," American Journal of Obstetrics 20 (1887), 714; George Byrd Harrison, "Puerperal Insanity," American Journal of Obstetrics 30 (1894), 530. Arthur C. Jelly, "Puerperal Insanity," Boston Medical and Surgical Journal 144 (1901), 271 is the only medical writer I found claiming puerperal insanity was not common.

15. Hirst, "Six Cases of Puerperal Insanity," 29; Landfear, "Puerperal Insanity," 57; Anna Burnet, "Puerperal Insanity: Cause, Symptoms and Treatment," The Woman's Medical Journal 9 (1899), 269; "Abstracts," American Journal of Obstetrics 13 (1880), 641; T. W. Fisher, "Two Cases of Puerperal Insanity," Boston Medical and Surgical Journal 79 (1869), 233-234; Charles E. Ware, "A Case of Puerperal Mania," American Journal of Medical Sciences 26 (1853), 346; Churchill, "On the Mental Disorders of Pregnancy and Childbed," 309.

16. On the generally good prognosis expected of puerperal insanity patients, see: Stearns, "The Psychiatric Aspects of Pregnancy," 24; William Mercer Sprigg, "Puerperal Insanity: Prognosis and Treatment," American Journal of Obstetrics 30 (1894), 537. On home versus hospital treatment, see: Jelly, "Puerperal Insanity," 275; Wigginton, "Puerperal Insanity," 43; Landfear, "Puerperal Insanity," 59; W. W. Godding, "Puerperal Insanity," Boston Medical and Surgical Journal 91 (1874), 318-319.

17. On bleeding as a treatment for puerperal insanity, see: Sprigg, "Puerperal Insanity: Prognosis and Treatment," 540; Landfear, "Puerperal Insanity," 58; Churchill, "On the Mental Disorders of Pregnancy and Childbed," 315; J. A. Wright, "Puerperal Insanity," Cincinnati Lancet-Clinic 23 (1889), 651; Victor H. Coffman, "Puerperal Mania," Nebraska State Medical Association Proceedings 4 (1872), 18. On purging as a treatment see:

85

Haughton, "Puerperal Mania," 729; A. Bryant Clarke, "On the Treatment of Puerperal Mania by Veratrum Viride," *Boston Medical and Surgical Journal* 59 (1859), 237-239; J. MacDonald, "Observations on Puerperal Mania," *New York Medical Journal* 1 and 2 (1831), 279; Thomas Lightfood, "Puerperal Mania; Its Nature and Treatment," *The Medical Times and Gazett* 21 (1850), 274. Many physicians recommended that the patient be removed from family and friends; for example see: J. A. Reagan, "Puerperal Insanity," *Charlotte Medical Journal* 14 (1899), 309; Fernald, "Puerperal Insanity," 720; J. Thompson Dickson, "A Contribution to the Study of the So-Called Puerperal Insanity," *Journal of Mental Sciences* 16 (1870-1871), 390; C. S. May, "Puerperal Insanity, with Statistics Regarding Sixteen Cases," *Proceedings of the Connecticut State Medical Society* 85 (1877), 106; Carr, "Puerperal Insanity," 540; Wigginton, "Puerperal Insanity," 44; Landfear, "Puerperal Insanity, " 59. Nearly every physician who wrote of treatment recommended rest, food, and some form of sedation. For examples not yet cited see: W. S. Armstrong, "Case of Puerperal Mania," *Atlanta Medical and Surgical Journal* 8 (1867), 419; Thomas H. Mayo, "Puerperal Mania," *Southern Medical Record* 4 (1874), 84; J. P. Reynolds, "Puerperal Mania," *Boston Medical and Surgical Journal* 72 (1865), 281; W. A. McPheeters, "Forceps; Puerperal Mania," *New Orleans Medical and Surgical Journal* 16 (1859), 660; Edward Kane, "Puerperal Insanity," *Medical Independent and Monthly Review of Medicine and Surgery* 2 (1856), 156; Horace Palmer, "A Case of Puerperal Mania," *Cincinnati Lancet and Observer* 2 (1859), 5; Horatio Storer, "Puerperal Mania; Recovery," *Boston Medical and Surgical Journal* 55 (1856-1857), 20.

18. See for example the explanation of Elaine Showalter in *The Female Malady*, especially 57-59, 71-72.

19. Wigginton, "Puerperal Insanity," 43.

20. For example, see: W. L. Worcester, "Is Puerperal Insanity a Distinct Clinical Form?" *American Journal of Insanity* 47 (1890-1891), 56; Edward J. Ill, "A Clinical Contribution to Gynecology," *American Journal of Obstetrics* 16 (1883), 264; Rohe, "Lactational Insanity," 325-326.

21. Allan McLane Hamilton, "Two Cases of Peculiar Mental Trouble Following the Puerperal State," *Boston Medical and Surgical Journal* 94 (1896), 680.

22. Lambert Ott, "Puerperal Mania," *The Clinical News* 1 (1880), 337; W. P. Manton, "Puerperal Hysteria (Insanity?)," *Journal of the American Medical Association* 19 (1892), 61; W. I. Richardson, "Puerperal Septicaemia: Puerperal Mania," *Boston Medical and Surgical Journal* 102 (1880), 448. See also: Carr, "Puerperal Insanity," 538; Fernald, "Puerperal Insanity," 717; W. D. Haines, "Insanity in the Puerperal State," *Cincinnati Lancet-Clinic* 23 (1889), 371; Worcester, "Is Puerperal Insanity a Distinct Clinical Form," 55; Burnet, "Puerperal Insanity: Cause, Symptoms and Treatment," 267-269. This is only a sampling of the articles listing these symptoms.

23. Harrison, "Puerperal Insanity," 532; Haines, "Insanity in the Puerperal State," 371; Godding, "Puerperal Insanity," 317; V. H. Taliaferro, "Puerperal Insanity," *Atlanta Medical and Surgical Journal* 15 (1877), 324; Carr, "Puerperal Insanity," 538; Stearns, "The Psychiatric Aspects of Pregnancy," 25. Almost every physician describing symptoms of puerperal insanity listed obscenity. For example see: Stoddart, "A Clinical Lecture," 242; Reagan, "Puerperal Insanity," 308; Menzies, "Puerperal Insanity," 169; Rohe, "Lactational Insanity," 325; Worcester, "Is Puerperal Insanity a Distinct Clinical Form?" 56; May, "Puerperal Insanity," 106; Wigginton, "Puerperal Insanity," 43; MacDonald, "Observations on Puerperal Mania," 268-270; Clarke, "On the Treatment of Puerperal Mania by Veratrum Viride," 238.

24. George H. Rohe, "Some Causes of Insanity in Women," *American Journal of Obstetrics* 34 (1896), 802. See also John Young Brown, "Pelvic Disease in Its Relationship to Insanity in Women," *American Journal of Obstetrics* 30 (1894), 360; Montrose A. Pallen, "Some Suggestions with Regard to the Insanities of Females," *American Journal of Obstetrics* 10 (1877), 207. Carroll Smith-Rosenberg, "Puberty to Menopause: The Cycle of Femininity in Nineteenth-Century America," *Feminist Studies* 1 (1973), 58-72 is a discussion of this attitude.

25. P. V. Carlin, "Insanity of Pregnancy," *The Denver Medical Times* 3 (1883-1884), 233. See also: Churchill, "On the Mental Disorders of Pregnancy and Childbed," 298; C. P. Lee, "Puerperal Mania," *Kansas Medical Index* 2 (1881), 200.

26. Pallen, "Some Suggestions with Regard to the Insanities of Females," 212.

27. For a clear explanation of this point especially with reference to gender, see Dwyer, "A Historical Perspective."

28. C. C. Hersman, "The Relationship between Uterine Disturbance and Some of the Insanities," *Journal of the American Medical Association* 33 (1899), 709; Carr, "Puerperal Insanity," 537. See also: Edward Jarvis, "Causes of Insanity," *Boston Medical and Surgical Journal* 45 (1851), 289-305; Reagan, "Puerperal Insanity," 309; Kane, "Puerperal Insanity," 147.

86

29. For example see: Fernald, "Puerperal Insanity," 716; Landfear, "Puerperal Insanity," 56; Jelly, "Puerperal Insanity," 271-272; G. H. Rohe, "The Influence of Parturient Lesions of the Uterus and Vagina, in the Causation of Puerperal Insanity," *Journal of the American Medical Association* 19 (1892), 59-60.

30. About heredity as a factor in puerperal insanity, see: Churchill, "On the Mental Disorders of Pregnancy and Childbed," 305; Fisher, "Two Cases of Puerperal Insanity," 233; Dickson, "A Contribution to the Study of the So-called Puerperal Insanity," 382; Taliaferro, "Puerperal Insanity," 328; May, "Puerperal Insanity," 106; Landfear, "Puerperal Insanity," 55; Fernald, "Puerperal Insanity," 714; Jelly, "Puerperal Insanity," 272; Reagan, "Puerperal Insanity," 309.

31. This point of view was expressed in many of the articles. See for example: Carr, "Puerperal Insanity," 537; Jelly, "Puerperal Insanity," 272; Wigginton, "Puerperal Insanity," 40; Fernald, "Puerperal Insanity," 715; Wright, "Puerperal Insanity," 648; Harrison, "Puerperal Insanity," 532; Menzies, "Puerperal Insanity: An Analysis of One Hundred and Forty Consecutive Cases," 162; Churchill, "On the Mental Disorders of Pregnancy and Childbed," 299-300; Kane, "Puerperal Insanity," 152.

32. Horatio Robinson Storer, "The Medical Management of Insane Women," *Boston Medical and Surgical Journal* 71 (1864), 210-218; Horatio R. Storer, "Cases Illustrative of Obstetric Disease—Deductions Concerning Insanity in Women," *Boston Medical and Surgical Journal* 70 (1864), 189-200.

33. Charles A. L. Reed, "The Gynecic Element in Psychiatry—with Suggestions for Asylum Reform," *Buffalo Medical and Surgical Journal* 28 (1888-89), 571. See also: Charles F. Folsom, "The Prevalence and Causes of Insanity; Commitments to Asylums," *Boston Medical and Surgical Journal* 103 (1880), 97-100; J. H. McIntyre, "Disease of the Uterus and Adnexa in Relation to Insanity," *Transactions of the Medical Association of Missouri* (1898), 191-195; Pallen, "Some Suggestions with Regard to the Insanities of Females," 207; W. P. Jones, "Insanity Dependent Upon Physical Disease," *Tennessee State Medical Society Transactions* 47 (1880), 97-104.

34. Fernald, "Puerperal Insanity," 719.

35. In addition to Reed, other gynecologists calling for specialists in insane asylums included: Joseph Wiglesworth, "On Uterine Disease and Insanity," *Journal of Mental Sciences* 30 (1884-85), 509-531; I.S. Stone, "Can the Gynecologist Aid the Alienist in Institutions for the Insane," *Journal of the American Medical Association* 16 (1891), 870-873; Ernest Hall, "The Gynecological Treatment of the Insane in Private Practice," *Pacific Medical Journal* 43 (1900), 241-256; Pallen, "Some Suggestions with Regard to the Insanities of Females."

36. Dwyer notes this trend of attributing women's insanity to problems with the female reproductive system in "The Weaker Vessel," "A Historical Perspective," and in her study of two New York asylums, *Homes for the Mad: Life Inside Two Nineteenth-Century Asylums* (New Brunswick, New Jersey, 1987).

37. Physicians who described medical and surgical attention to female asylum inmates include: H. A. Tomlinson and Mary E. Bassett, "Association of Pelvic Diseases and Insanity in Women, And the Influence of Treatment on the Local Disease Upon the Mental Condition," *Journal of the American Medical Association* 33 (1899), 827, 831; W. P. Manton, "The Frequency of Pelvic Disorders in Insane Women," *American Journal of Obstetrics* 39 (1899), 54-57; Eugene G. Carpenter, "Pelvic Disease as a Factor of Cause in Insanity of Females and Surgery as a Factory of Cure," *Journal of the American Medical Association* 35 (1900), 545-551; W. J. Williams, "Nervous and Mental Diseases in Relation to Gynecology," *Transactions of the Eighth Annual Meeting of the Western Surgical and Gynecological Association* (Omaha, December, 1898; published 1899), 49-57; W. O. Henry, "Insanity in Women Associated with Pelvic Diseases," *Annals of Gynecology and Pediatry* 14 (1900-1901), 312-320; W. P. Manton, "Post-Operative Insanity, Especially in Women," *Annals of Gynecology and Pediatry* 10 (1896-97), 714-719; Hall, "The Gynecological Treatment of the Insane in Private Practice."

38. See for example: Henry, "Insanity in Women Associated with Pelvic Diseases"; Manton, "The Frequency of Pelvic Disorders in Insane Women"; Hall, "The Gynecological Treatment of the Insane in Private Practice"; Rohe, "The Influence of Parturient Lesions of the Uterus and Vagina, in the Causation of Puerperal Insanity." I do not mean to imply that all doctors were treating puerperal insanity with surgery. "Rest and restoration" was probably the most popular therapy throughout the century. See Hardy, "Puerperal Insanity."

39. Tomlinson and Bassett, "Association of Pelvic Diseases and Insanity in Women," 827. See also: Brown, "Pelvic Disease in Its Relationship to Insanity in Women"; Carpenter, "Pelvic Disease as a Factor of Cause in Insanity of Females and Surgery as a Factor of Cure"; and Williams, "Nervous and Mental Diseases in Relation to Gynecology" for examples of the argument that doctors should only resort to surgery when there is physical disease.

40. Stone, "Can the Gynecologist Aid the Alienist in Institutions for the Insane"; Manton, "Post-Operative Insanity, Especially in Women"; Clara Barrus, "Gynecological Disorders and Their Relation to Insanity," *American Journal of Insanity* 51 (1894-95), 475-491; Alice May Farnham, "Uterine Disease as a Factor in the Production of Insanity," *Alienist and Neurologist* 8 (1887), 532-547; Adolf Meyer, "On the Diseases of Women as a Cause of Insanity in the Light of Observations in Sixty-nine Autopsies," *Transactions of the Illinois State Medical Society* (1895), 299-311; C. B. Burr, "The Relation of Gynaecology to Psychiatry," *Transactions of the Michigan Medical Society* 18 (1894), 458-464, 478-487. An excellent article about removal of the ovaries in the nineteenth century is Lawrence D. Longo, "The Rise and Fall of Battey's Operation: A Fashion in Surgery," *Bulletin of the History of Medicine* 53 (1979), 244-267.

41. See for example: Helene Kuhlmann, "A Few Cases of Interest in Gynecology in Relation to Insanity," *State Hospital Bulletin* 1 (New York: 1896), 172-179; Mary D. Jones, "Insanity, Its Causes: Is there in Woman a Correlation of the Sexual Function with Insanity and Crime," *Medical Record* 58 (1900), 925-237; Edward B. Lane, "Puerperal Insanity," *Boston Medical and Surgical Journal* 144 (1901), 606-609; Manton, "Puerperal Hysteria."

42. For example: Jones, "Insanity, Its Causes: Is there in Woman a Correlation of the Sexual Function with Insanity and Crime"; Kuhlmann, "A Few Cases of Interest in Gynecology in Relation to Insanity"; Burnet, "Puerperal Insanity: Cause, Symptoms and Treatment"; and the work of Mary Putnam Jacobi. An important study of women physicians working in asylums is Constance M. McGovern, "Doctors or Ladies? Women Physicians in Psychiatric Institutions, 1872-1900," *Bulletin of the History of Medicine* 55 (1981), 88-107.

43. A creative use of case studies to describe the doctor-patient relationship and the doctor-family relationship is Ellen Dwyer, "The Burden of Illness: Families and Epilepsy," paper read at the annual meeting of the American Association for the History of Medicine, Birmingham, April 1989.

44. McPheeters, "Forceps; Puerperal Mania"; Ware, "A Case of Puerperal Mania"; Lambert, "Puerperal Mania." Numerous case studies included information about cruelty, illness, illegitimacy and stillbirth, although often doctors did not connect the situation to the symptoms. For example: W. H. Parish, "Puerperal Insanity," *Transactions of the Obstetrical Society of Philadelphia* 4-7 (1876-79), 50-54.

45. Fisher, "Two Cases of Puerperal Insanity," 233.

46. Harrison, "Puerperal Insanity," 535.

47. Lee, "Puerperal Mania," 205; Lambert, "Puerperal Mania," 337; Denslow Lewis, "Clinical Lecture on Obstetrics and Gynecology—Mental and Nervous Derangements in Obstetric Practice," *Clinical Review* 11 (1899-1900), 181.

48. This theme of women denying their husbands and/or expressing fear or hatred of their husbands was common in the case studies.

49. Dickson, "A Contribution to the Study of the So-Called Puerperal Insanity," 383.

50. Storer, "Puerperal Mania; Recovery," 20; MacDonald, "Observations on Puerperal Mania," 270.

88

UNDER THE SHADOW OF MATERNITY: AMERICAN WOMEN'S RESPONSES TO DEATH AND DEBILITY FEARS IN NINETEENTH-CENTURY CHILDBIRTH

JUDITH WALZER LEAVITT

In 1846 a young woman in Warren, Pennsylvania, gave birth to a son and soon after was taken with "sinking spells." Her female friends and relatives were there to help her; they took encouragement when she appeared better and consoled each other when she fell into a stupor. A woman who was with her during these days wrote to a mutual friend, describing the scene around Mary Ann Ditmer's bed.

Oh my beloved Girl – You may imagine our sorrow, for you too must weep with us – How can I tell you: I cannot realize myself – Mary Ann will soon cease to be among the living – and numbered with the dead. . . . Elizabeth, it was such a scene that is hard to be described – L and I remained until the afternoon. Mrs. Mersel came and relieved us, also Mrs. Whalen came. We took a few hours sleep and returned – She had requested us to remain as long as she lived – there was every indication of a speedy termination of her suffering – Mary had come over – Mrs. N remained to watch. . .all thought she was dying – She was very desirous of living till day light – She thought she might have some hope if she could stand it until morning – She retained her sense perfectly – She begged us to be active and not be discouraged that she might live yet – that life was so sweet – how she clung to it – Elizabeth I would wish you might be spared such a sight – we surrounded her dying bed – Each one diligent to keep life and animation in the form of one they so much loved and who at that very time was kept alive with stimulating medicines and wine – I cannot describe it for o my God the horrors of that night will ever remain in the minds of those who witnessed it – our hearts swelled at the sight.[1]

Mary Ann lingered a few days, during which time she bestowed rings and locks of hair upon her friends so they might remember her; she made her peace with God and provided for her child. Then she died. Her story, both in its recognition of the childbirth-related dangers to women's lives and in its revelations of women

---

Feminist Studies 12, no. 1 (Spring 1986). © by Feminist Studies, Inc.

helping women, represents a reality visited upon countless numbers of American women in the eighteenth and nineteenth centuries, and it is a reality with supreme significance for understanding women's lives.

In this article I will examine the meaning of maternity's influence over women's lives by analyzing specifically the physical dangers of childbearing and women's responses to those childbirth-related risks. During most of American history, women's anticipation of the possibility of dying or of being permanently injured during childbirth influenced their life expectations and experiences. But women's responses to their repeated and dangerous confinements suggest, instead of resignation to their difficulties, an active participation in shaping events in America's birthing rooms.

Feminists reject the notion that biology is destiny and deny that biological constraints themselves determine the course of women's lives. But feminist historians, looking back at women's experiences, are forced to acknowledge that biology has been a significant factor in setting the limits of life's choices for most women. Specifically, the "shadow of maternity," in the words of many nineteenth-century women,[2] provided the material conditions under which the culturally imposed social parameters of women's lives were defined. Most married women, and many unmarried women, had to face the physical and psychological effects of recurring pregnancies, childbirths, and postpartum recoveries, all of which took a toll on their time, energy, dreams, and bodies. The biological act of maternity, which carried with it severe risks, significantly marked women's lives as they made their way from birth to death. My examination of childbirth's biological domination over women's lives focuses on women's fear of the physical dangers of childbirth and examines the extent to which the fears reflected the reality of their life experiences, but I do not mean to suggest that these fears and dangers encompassed the totality of women's childbirth experiences, or that they alone determined the direction of life's choices. Childbirth had many meanings in women's lives, but this article will focus on the physical dimension of the birthing experience and on the female-centered birthing environment women developed to counteract the potentially deleterious nature of confinement.

My conclusions about biology's influence over women do not

connote biological control, inevitableness, or women's passive acceptance of their fate. In contrast to the work of Edward Shorter,[3] which posits that biology held a stranglehold over women such that they could not escape until twentieth-century medical science came to their rescue, my work emphasizes the decisions women made within their confines to break the boundaries that biology seemed to set. My research reveals women in control of many aspects of their lives, including biological aspects, and I think women's culture developed through these biological bonds – even when those bonds were limiting their other activities. Women's biological functions might have led society to try to circumscribe women's nondomestic activities, but women themselves were not bound by their biological functions. Throughout American history, women struggled to overcome their most significant biological limitations – as they perceived them – ofttimes successfully. The very processes of coping with and trying to change and expand available choices created in some cases improved conditions, but more importantly, the processes created a support system for women that opened wider worlds. Women used the strengths and help of other women to face their problems, and in their unity developed coping mechanisms that were illustrative of what I think can be called a feminist impulse embedded within traditional women's experiences. Feminism did not develop when or because modern medicine saved women from their bodies (as Shorter posits), but, rather, feminist inclinations and the collective behavior they fostered developed out of the basic and shared experiences of women's bodies at times when those bodies seemed most confining and difficult. In this sense, feminism, women grasping control and working together to overcome their commonly experienced burdens, can arise out of the very essence of biological femaleness and reside alongside the most traditional part of women's experiences.[4]

The shadow of maternity, under which so many women lived, has had numerous features, only some of which I will be able to discuss here. Underlying the shadow of maternity most significantly were high fertility rates. At the turn of the nineteenth century, American women bore an average of seven children before their fertile years ended. This implies considerably more than seven pregnancies, because many terminated before term. For many groups in the expanding American population, rates remained high throughout the nineteenth century.[5] Although control over fertility is not the subject of this article, we must view women's past life experiences within the context of limited choices over conception. Pregnancy, birth, and postpartum recovery occupied a significant portion of most women's adult lives, and the ensuing motherhood defined a major part of women's identity.

Take, for example, the life of Mary Vial Holyoke, who married into a prominent New England family in 1759. In 1760, after ten months of marriage, she gave birth to her first baby. Two years later, her second was born. In 1765 she was again "brought to bed" of a child. Pregnant immediately again, she bore another child in 1766. The following year she delivered her fifth, and in one more year delivered her sixth. Free from pregnancy and childbirth in 1769, she gave birth again in 1770. During the next twelve years, she bore five more children. The first twenty-three years of Mary Vial Holyoke's married life, the years of her youth and vigor, were spent pregnant or recovering from childbirth. Because only three of her twelve children lived to adulthood, she withstood, also, frequent tragedies. She devoted her body and her life to procreation throughout her reproductive years. Mary Holyoke had more pregnancies and suffered more child deaths than her average contemporary, and she presents a poignant example of the extreme physical trials women endured. Mary Holyoke had little choice in her frequent pregnancies: her life reveals how the biological capacity of women to bear children historically has translated into life's destiny for individual women.[6]

Mary Holyoke's experience became less common in nineteenth-century America, especially among white women, as fertility rates declined. By 1900, white women, showing the ability to cut their fertility in half over the century, averaged 3.56 children. Historians and demographers trying to understand this decline have suggested that as much as 75 percent of the dropping fertility rate can be explained by active fertility control, including abortion and birth control techniques. Some people seem to have succeeded in asserting partial control over the size of their families, but it is important to keep in mind that the fertility declines demographers have identified with nineteenth-century America apply only to white native-born women; immigrant and black women continued to have babies in larger numbers.[7]

Fertility rates explain only part of the impact of childbirth on women's lives. Maternity cast a shadow greater than its frequent repetition alone could have caused. Maternity, the creation of new life, carried with it the ever-present possibility of death. The shadow that followed women through life was the fear of the ultimate physical risk of bearing children. Young women perceived that their bodies, even when healthy and vigorous, could yield up a dead infant or could carry the seeds of their own destruction. As Cotton Mather had warned at the beginning of the eighteenth century, and as American women continued to believe, conception meant "your *Death* has Entered into you." Nine months' gestation could mean nine months to prepare for death. A possible death sentence came with every pregnancy.[8]

Many women spent considerable time worrying and preparing as if they would not survive their confinements. During Nannie Stillwell Jackson's pregnancy in 1890, she wrote in her diary: "I have not felt well today am afraid I am going to be sick I went up to Fannies a little while late this evening & was talking to her, & I told her to see after Lizzie & Sue [other children] if I was to die & not to let me be buried here . . . & I want Lizzie & Sue to have *everything that is mine,* for no one has as good a rite [*sic*] to what I have as they have."[9] A pregnant Clara Clough Lenroot confided in her diary in 1891: "It occurs to me that *possibly* I may not live. . . . I wonder if I should die, and leave a little daughter *behind* me, they would name her 'Clara.' I should like to have them." Three days later she again was worrying. "If I shouldn't live I wonder what they will do with the baby! I should want Mama and Bertha [sister] to have the bringing up of it, but I should want Irvine [husband] to see it every day and love it so much, and I should want it taught to love him better than anyone else in the world." With the successful termination of the birth, Clara's husband wrote in his wife's diary, "Dear Clara, 'mama and Bertha' won't have to take care of your baby, thank God." He continued, "Everything is all right, but at what cost. My poor wife, how you have suffered, and you have been so brave. . . . I have seen the greatest suffering this day that I have ever known or ever imagined."[10]

When her sister Emma experienced a difficult pregnancy in 1872, Ellen Regal came to be with her and found her "so patient and resigned." Ellen wrote to their brother, "It is not strange that she should tremble and shrink at the thought of that Valley of the Shadow of Death which she must so soon enter." In the middle of the nineteenth century, Lizzie Cabot wrote to her sister when she was pregnant with her first child, "I have made my will and divided off all my little things and don't mean to leave undone what I ought to do if I can help it." Sarah Ripley Stearns, returning from church near her time of confinement, wrote in her diary: "Perhaps this is the last time I shall be permitted to join with my earthly friends."[11]

The extent to which these death fears spread to other family members beyond the parturients is evident in the diary of Albina Wight, whose sister living in another state was pregnant and near confinement. In 1870 Albina wrote, "I am so affraid [sic] she won't live through it." Three days later, she continued to think of her sister, "I could not keep Tilda out of my thoughts It has seemed like a funeral all day . . . I fear she is not living."[12]

I could go on with examples of how much some women feared that they might die, but I think the point is made. Young, vigorous, healthy women who should have been anticipating a long life ahead instead faced the very real possibility that their pregnancies would bring their deaths, that in creating a life they would pay with their own.

Women and family members were not the only ones who anticipated maternal death. Many physicians who attended parturients through the fearful hours of labor and delivery also brooded on mortality. In the 1870s, Dr. James S. Bailey of Albany, New York, pondered the sometimes sudden and unexplained deaths of women following childbirth. He wrote: "To see a female, apparently in vigorous health until the period of accouchement, suddenly expire from some unforeseen accident, which is beyond the control of the attending physician, is well calculated to fill the mind with alarm and gloomy forebodings" and make it impossible "while attending a case of confinement, to banish the feeling of uncertainty and dread as to the result of cases which seemingly are terminating favorably."[13] Similarly, Dr. William Lusk, after relating the tragic story of a twenty-three-year-old "very beautiful young woman" who died after delivery, warned his fellow physicians that "the exhausted condition in which the woman is left after childbirth render[s] her an easy prey to the perils of the puerperal state."[14] Fort Wayne, Indiana, physician H.V. Sweringen wrote that "parturition under the most favorable circumstances is attended with great risk."[15] Most physicians and families were well aware of the possibility of death: fears of confinement's dangers permeated society.

The extent to which social fears about maternal deaths reflected a reality of high death rates is almost impossible for historians to determine with any degree of confidence. Graphs of maternal deaths, such as the one below created from New York City data, illustrate that deaths from causes associated with maternity seem to have been declining toward the last part of the nineteenth century. The statistics also show that the maternal death rate leveled out toward the end of the century and continued at a high level (and even increasing) in the twentieth century. But these figures do not tell the whole story. They record the deaths per live births that physicians or other attendants attributed to puerperal causes, but they remain silent on the deaths associated with childbirth, such as from tuberculosis, that physicians did not directly attribute to confinement-related causes. Officials might have recorded that women who died while pregnant or within a month after childbirth died from tuberculosis, which was exacerbated by maternity, when it would be accurate also to have attributed the deaths to maternity-related causes. Even the imperfectly reported maternal deaths and live births are only available for certain parts of the country for certain years in the nineteenth century.[16]

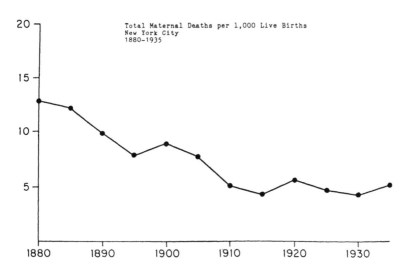

Source: Haven Emerson and Harriet Hughes, Populations, Notifiable Diseases and Deaths Assembled for New York City, New York (New York: Dehamar Institute of Public Health/College of Physicians and Surgeons, 1941).

Perhaps more valuable to our understanding of the reality of
maternal death is the observation that most women seemed to
know or know of other women who had died in childbirth. One
woman, for example, wrote that her friend "died as she has expected to" as a result of childbirth as had six other of their
childhood friends. Early in the twentieth century approximately 1
mother died for each 154 live births. If women delivered, let us
estimate, an average of five live babies, these statistics can mean
that over their reproductive years, one of every thirty women
might be expected to die in childbirth. In another early-twentieth-
century calculation, one of every seventeen men claimed they had
a mother or sister who had died as the immediate results of
childbirth.[17]

Despite the real decline in the number of births women endured,
and a corresponding but smaller decline in the rate of maternal
deaths, women remained fearful of maternity. Women might have
been at risk for puerperal death fewer times during their lifetimes,
but for them the fear of dying during childbirth continued to influence the possible parameters of their lives. Part of this, I
believe, can be explained by the fact that maternal deaths continued at higher than acceptable (that is, preventable) levels.
Physicians and women realized that by the turn of the twentieth
century deaths from many infectious diseases, such as tuberculosis and diphtheria, were declining, but that deaths from
childbirth-related causes remained high. Improvements in living
conditions and in medical knowledge about disease transmission
seemed to lead to improvements in mortality statistics, except for
women in childbirth. Furthermore, maternal mortality statistics
from other countries showed that women elsewhere fared better
than women in the United States did. In 1910, when the United
States recorded that 1 mother died for every 154 babies born alive,
Sweden's record showed that 1 mother was lost for every 430 live
births.[18]

In the past, the shadow of maternity extended beyond the possibility and fear of death. Women knew that if procreation did not
kill them or their babies, it could maim them for life. Postpartum
gynecological problems—some great enough to force women to
bed for the rest of their lives, others causing milder disabilities—hounded the women who did not succumb to their labor and
delivery. For some women, the fears of future debility were more

disturbing than fears of death. Vesicovaginal and rectovaginal fistulas (holes between the vagina and either the bladder or the rectum caused by the violence of childbirth or by instrument damage), which brought incontinence and constant irritation to sufferers; unsutured perineal tears of lesser degree, which may have caused significant daily discomforts; major infections; and general weakness and failure to return to prepregnant physical vigor threatened young women in the prime of life. Newly married women looking forward to life found themselves almost immediately faced with the prospect of permanent physical limitations that could follow their early and repeated confinements.

Chicago physician Henry Newman believed that the "normal process of reproduction [is] a formidable menace to the after-health of the parous woman."[19] Lacerations—tears in the perineal tissues—probably caused the greatest postpartum trouble for women. The worst of these, the fistulas, which led to either urine or feces constantly leaking through the vaginal opening without the possibility of control, were, in the words of one sympathetic doctor, "the saddest of calamities, entailing. . .endless suffering upon the poor patient. . .death would be a welcome visitor."[20] Women who had to live with this condition sat sick and alone as long as they lived unless they were one of the beneficiaries of Dr. J. Marion Sims's operation in the second half of the century. Their incontinence made them unpleasant companions, and even their loved ones found it hard to keep them constant company.[21]

More frequent and less debilitating, but still causing major problems for many women, were tears in the vaginal wall or cervix that might have led to prolapsed uterus, uncomfortable sexual intercourse, or difficulties with future deliveries. One physician noted that "the wide-spread mutilation. . .is so common, indeed, that we scarcely find a normal perineum after childbirth."[22] Most perineal lacerations probably were minor and harmless; but if severe ones were not adequately repaired, women might suffer from significant postpartum discomfort.[23] Women complained most frequently of a prolapsed uterus. This displacement of the womb downwards, sometimes even through the vaginal opening, often resulted from lacerations or postpartum relaxation and consequent elongation of the ligaments. One physician noted that fallen womb is often a temporary condition, but he also found it quite common: "Any woman subject to ill turns, lassitude, and

general debility will tell you that not unfrequently upon these occasions she is sensible of a falling of the womb."[24] The condition
caused misery for women. Albina Wight's sister Eliza, to give just
one example from the 1870s, had a difficult delivery that was
followed by prolapse. Six weeks following one of her sister's confinements, Albina recorded: "Eliza is sick yet can only walk across
the room and that overdoes her. She has falling of the Womb. poor
girl." Eliza's medical treatment by "a calomel doctor" who gave her
"blue pills" did not help. Five months following the delivery she
could only "walk a few steps at a time and cannot sit up all day." A
second doctor predicted that "it will be a long time before she will
get around again."[25]

The typical treatment for this common female ailment was the
use of a pessary, a mechanical support for the uterus inserted into
the vagina and left there as long as necessary (see figure 1).
Pessaries themselves often led to pelvic inflammations and pain
for the women whose conditions they were designed to alleviate.
In the opinion of one physician,

I think it is indisputable that a pessary allowed to remain for a very short
period will invariably produce irritation, and if continued longer, will produce
almost as certainly, ulceration. I have removed many pessaries that have produced ulceration; one in particular, hollow and of silver gilt, was completely
honey combed by corrosion, its interior filled with exuviae of the most horrible offensiveness, the vagina ulcerated through into the bladder, producing a
vesico-vaginal fistula, and into the rectum, producing a recto-vaginal fistula;
the vagina in some portion obliterated by adhesive inflammation and
numerous fistulae made through the labia and around the mons veneris for the
exit of the various discharges.[26]

Uterine displacements puzzled physicians and pained women
throughout the nineteenth century. A midcentury physician noted
that anteflexion, an abnormal forward curvature of the uterus that
seemed not amenable to pessary correction, "is the dread of almost
every physician, and the constant, painful perplexity of many a
patient." He told of his recent case:

In the winter of 1863, I was consulted by a young lady from a distant part of
the State, on account of a disease from which she had suffered for nearly four
years. She had received the advice of many a physician of high and low
degree – had worn the ring pessary – the globe pessary – the horseshoe
pessary – the double S pessary and the intra-uterine stem pessary – and the
common sponge. . . . The patient gave a history of frequent inflammation of
the uterus and ovaries, and there appeared to be quite strong adhesions

FIGURE 1

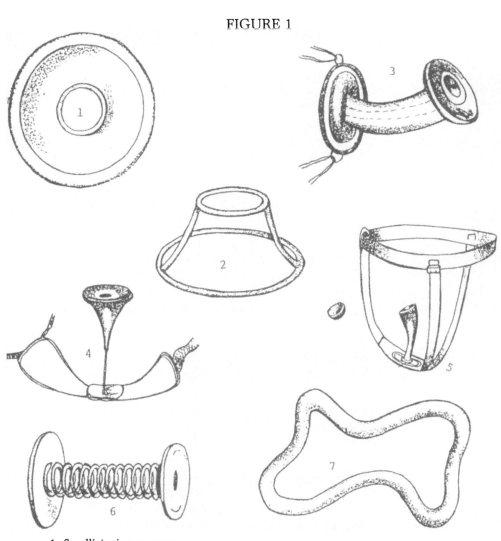

1. Smellie's ring pessary
2. Meig's double ring pessary, of gutta percha
3. Merriam's glass pessary to be fastened externally
4. O'Leary's hard rubber cup, with a screw to regulate its length, resting on a plate secured externally
5. Taft's ball and socket
6. Schaffer's spiral spring
7. Sims' pure, flexible Britannia pessary, capable of being bent in any desired form

SOURCE: Augustus K. Gardner, "On the Use of Pessaries," *Transactions of the American Medical Association* 15 (1865): (109-22).

binding the womb in its assumed place. She had had too frequent menstruation – profuse and intolerably painful – frequent and painful micturition
[urination].

The physician inserted his "modified" ring pessary and reported
that "the patient went to her home after a few weeks entirely
relieved from all bad symptoms,"[27]

In the last half of the nineteenth century, physicians reported increased incidence of perineal and cervical lacerations and their accompanying gynecological problems, attributed by many
observers to increased use of forceps and other interventions in
physician-directed deliveries. If it is true that physicians' interventions caused problems for women in this period (and that is a
question I explore elsewhere), it is also the case that physicians
became increasingly adept at repairing the problems. The medical
journals are filled with case studies of women whose badly
managed deliveries had caused them problems, which could then
be fixed by superior medical care. For example, an Iowa physician, Dr. Nicholas Hard, reported in 1850 a case he salvaged. A
thirty-five-year-old woman "with her first child, having had the
forceps applied at an improper time during her labour, suffered
from inflammation of the vulva, vagina, and contiguous soft parts,
and had a tardy convalescence. . . . The vaginal orifice was perfectly closed. . .she suffered exceedingly from retained catamenial
[menstrual] fluid." The doctor instrumentally reopened the vagina
and happily reported that his patient now "walks to church, visits,
and does house-work."[28]

Women who had already had children were more likely than
first-time mothers to worry about the possible aftereffects of labor
and delivery. They remembered how long it took them the first
time to recover from the birth, they remembered how they had
suffered, and they were particularly loath to repeat the ordeal. As
one woman wrote about her second pregnancy: "I confess I had
dreaded it with a dread that every mother must feel in repeating
the experience of child-bearing. I could only think that another
birth would mean another pitiful struggle of days' duration,
followed by months of weakness, as it had been before."[29]

Apart from their concern about resulting death and physical
debility, women feared pain and suffering during the confinement
itself. They worried about how they would bear up under the pain
and stress, how long the confinement might last, and whether

trusted people would accompany them through the ordeal. The short hours between being a pregnant woman and becoming a mother seemed, in anticipation, to be interminably long, and they occupied the thoughts and defined the worries of multitudes of women. Women's descriptions of their confinement experiences foretold the horrors of the ordeal.

Josephine Preston Peabody wrote in her diary of the "most terrible day of [her] life," when she delivered her firstborn, the "almost inconceivable agony" she lived through during her "day-long battle with a thousand tortures and thunders and ruins." Her second confinement brought "great bodily suffering," and her third, "the nethermost hell of bodily pain and mental blankness. . . . The will-to-live had been massacred out of me, and I couldn't see why I had to."[30] Another woman remembered "stark terror was what I felt most."[31]

"Between oceans of pain," wrote one woman of her third birth in 1885, "there stretched continents of fear; fear of death and dread of suffering beyond bearing."[32] Surviving a childbirth did not allow women to forget its horrors. Lillie M. Jackson, recalling her 1905 confinement, wrote: "While carrying my baby, I was so miserable . . . . I went down to death's door to bring my son into the world, and I've never forgotten. Some folks say one forgets, and can have them right over again, but today I've not forgotten, and that baby is 36 years old."[33] Too many women shared with Hallie Nelson her feelings upon her first birth: "I began to look forward to the event with dread—if not actual horror." Even after Nelson's successful birth, she "did not forget those awful hours spent in labor."[34]

Regardless of the particular fear that women carried along with their swelling uteruses, the end result was similar for all of them. The prospect of often repeated motherhood promised hardship and anxiety. As Hannah Whitall Smith wrote in her diary in 1852:

I am very unhappy now. The trial of my womanhood which to me is so very bitter has come upon me again. When my little Ellie is 2 years old she will have a little sister or brother. And this is the end of all my hopes, my pleasing anticipations, my returning youthful joyousness. Well, it is a woman's lot and I must try to become resigned and bear it in patience and silence and not make my home unhappy because I am so. But oh, how hard it is.[35]

Many women walked with Hannah Smith under the shadow of maternity, experiencing repeated and agonizing births in unrelenting succession with no relief throughout their fertile years.

Many women suffered physical complications through their confinements that stayed with them the rest of their lives. For many women the physical hardships of childbearing determined the parameters of their lives and defined their social destiny. Although it is also true that childbearing and the ensuing motherhood held many happy times for women, it is the difficult part of the experience that created the boundaries within which most women had to construct their lives. The childbirth experience was, of course, heavily influenced by cultural and economic conditions, the particular time and place in which women lived, and their socioeconomic class or ethnic group. But much of the meaning of childbirth for women was determined not by the particulars of the event, but by what women shared with each other by virtue of their common biological experience.

With all the horrors and dangers and worries, women could have easily given up hopes of improving their childbirth experiences or their hard domestic prospects. And no doubt some women did merely resign themselves to lives of invalidism and deprivation. But what comes through the written record much more strongly are the positive aspects of the experience that women chose to emphasize, the caring ways in which they tried to help each other, and the simple fact that women were able to change the childbirth experience for themselves in significant ways throughout the nineteenth century.

Let us examine first the cooperative nature of the labor and delivery experience. Throughout American history up until the twentieth century, when childbirth moved to the hospital, most women gave birth at home with the help of their female friends and relatives. Birth was a women's event, and women eagerly gave their aid when it was needed. Albina Wight, who was unable to attend her sister's confinement, wrote in her diary, "Poor poor girl how I pitty [sic] her. She says the two wimen [sic] that were there were as kind and good as Sisters could be. I am glad of that . . . Oh how I do wish I could be with her."[36] When possible, sisters and cousins and mothers came to help the parturient through the ordeal of labor and delivery, and close friends and neighbors joined them around the birthing bed. One woman who described her 1866 confinement wrote: "A woman that was expecting had to take good care that she had plenty fixed to eat for her neighbors when they got there. There was no telling how long they was in for.

There wasn't no paying these friends so you had to treat them good."[37] To this women's world, husbands, brothers, or fathers could gain only temporary entrance. In an 1836 account, the new father was invited in to see his wife and new daughter, and then: "But Mrs. Warren, who was absolute in this season of female despotism, interposed, and the happy father was compelled, with reluctant steps, to quit the spot."[38]

Most crucial to the support networks women tried to gather around themselves during and following confinement were their own mothers. "If you could but be with me now, what wouldn't I give," wrote Anita McCormick Blaine to her mother, Nettie Fowler McCormick, in 1890 as she prepared for the birth of her first child. "Dearest mother mine – all would be complete if you were here." Nettie returned the sentiment. "Dearie," she wrote, "I wish I were there to thoroughly rub olive oil upon your hips, your groin muscles, your abdominal muscles all throughout – in short all the muscles that are to be called upon to yield, and be elastic at the proper time. See how reasonable it seems that they should be helped to yield, and to do their work if they are kneaded by the strong hand of mother, while olive oil is being freely applied."[39]

Some women could marshal only one or two women to help them, but many accounts list eight or ten women helpers in addition to the midwife or physician who might be attending. Nannie Jackson, in rural Arkansas in 1890, gathered six women to help when she delivered, and her oldest daughter noted at the time that "Mama had a heap of company today."[40] Antebellum southerner Madge Preston gave birth to a child in 1849, which her husband, who waited in another room, reported this way: "At this birth were present Dr. J.H. Briscoe, Mrs. Margaret Carlon, Mrs. Connolly her friend – our servant Mary Miskel, and our Negroes Lucy and Betty. They inform me that Mrs. P. bore her protracted labor, difficulty, pain and anxiety, which endured forty eight hours, with calmness, courage, and fortitude."[41]

Women went to considerable sacrifice to help their birthing relatives and friends, interrupting their lives to travel long distances and frequently staying months before and after delivery to do the household chores. When relatives were not available, neighbors stayed for the labor and delivery and brought food and kept up with washing and other domestic duties. Christiana Holmes Tillson wrote in her journal of her second confinement in 1825: "I

had made the acquaintance of Mrs. Townsend, who was with me
and remained until John was a week old."[42] Ann Bolton recalled
with enormous fondness and gratitude her good friend: "Of thirteen children which I brought into the world, she bore me company with ten of them."[43] Even in the relatively unusual event of a
woman being alone for her delivery, her friends rallied round
afterwards to make sure that she got the rest she needed.[44]
Women who could not summon friends were described as in this
diary entry: "[I] went thence to see Mrs. Ray who has been very ill
in Childbed – Had a little girl which died in a few hours. – She is
much to be pitied having no female relation or intimate friend to
be with her."[45] Another woman pitied herself: "It seemed very
gloomy when I found my time had come, to think that I was, as it
were, destitute of earthly friends. No mother, no husband, and
none of my particular friends that belong to the town; they happening to be out of town."[46]

The women's network that developed at least in part through the
strong attachments formed across the childbirth bed had long-
lasting effects on women's lives. When women had suffered the
agonies of watching their friends die, when they had helped a
friend recover from a difficult delivery, or when they had participated in a successful birthing they developed a closeness that
lasted a lifetime. Surviving life's traumas together made the crises
bearable and produced important bonds that continued to sustain
other parts of women's lives. "It was as if mothers were members
of a sorority and the initiation was to become a mother," Marilyn
Clohessy wrote.[47] Nannie Jackson's female support network offers
one example of the importance of good friends. Her diary, only
one year of which survives, is a litany of friends helping each
other. Her best friend was Fannie, who lived one-half mile away;
Nannie and Fannie visited each other daily, and sometimes, two,
three, and four times a day. Once, during the eighth month of her
third pregnancy, Nannie visited her friend three times in one
evening and her husband got angry. But, Nannie noted, "I just talk
to Fannie & tell her my troubles because it seems to help me to
bear it better when she knows about it. I shall tell her whenever I
feel like it."[48] Indeed, in this diary fragment, there is evidence of
significant rebellion against her husband's wishes and her strong
reliance on her relationship with Fannie. When Nannie was confined, Fannie stayed over with her for four nights. But Fannie is

only the most important in a long list of close friends. Nannie, who was white, visited daily with many other women, both white and black, cooking special things for them, sharing the limited family resources, helping them with sewing projects, sitting up with them when they were sick, helping out at births, arranging funerals. These women, whose economically limited lives left nothing for outside entertainment or expense, found rich resources within their own group.

We see that the psychological dimension of the women's network played a significant role in making the difficult lives of these women bearable. Perhaps more significant to these women, however, was the very real support friends could provide during times of crisis. During labor and delivery, when a woman might not be able to stand up for herself, she could rely on her women friends to do her talking for her. Women influenced almost every aspect of birth procedures by having very important on-the-spot input into birth practices for most of the home birth period, and they made significant changes in birth procedures through their collective behavior.

Not until the last half of the eighteenth century did some urban women begin calling in physicians early in normal labor as the major attendants. Yet even then, and throughout the nineteenth century, most women continued to call their women friends and relatives to help them and relied on the advice of the women alongside or before the advice of the physician. Sometimes the women, who were called first, advised that no medical attendant be called. As one physician realized, "A certain amount of inconvenience is anticipated, and so long as this supposed limit is not passed, the patient contrives, with the advice of her female friends, to dispense with a medical attendant."[49] At other times, the attending women suggested additional help. Many physicians attributed their obstetrics calls to midwives or to neighbor women who were already present at a progressing labor. Dr. John G. Meachem, struggling to establish himself after graduating from medical school, recorded a successful first case: "Mrs. Doolittle was present, and I always thought that she had a good deal to do with engineering this call. At least I gave her the credit."[50]

The collectivity of women gathered around the birthing bed made sure that birth attendants were responsive to their wishes. They made decisions about when and if to call physicians to births that midwives were attending; they gave or withheld permission for physicians' procedures; and they created the atmosphere of female support in a room that might have contained both women and men. The result of women's seeming lack of control over biological imperatives was in fact increased control and the ability to influence events.

Women friends were so common and so active in the birthing room that physicians tried to limit them to one or two in their efforts to gain some control over the birth process. Dr. Edward Henry Dixon, for example, wrote in his popular advice book that physicians "mildly, yet firmly exclud[e] from the room all who are not absolutely necessary as attendants."[51] Until birth moved to the hospital, however, physicians shared their authority with neighbor women, most of whom had had significant birth experience. There were times, of course, when the attending women encouraged physicians' interventions. One of Wisconsin's earliest physicians reported his first forceps operation "in the presence of all the old women of the neighbourhood." He was pleased to note that "all the relatives and friends expressed themselves quite satisfied with my exertions & skills."[52]

Often, however, physicians noted ruefully that they did not control events in the birthing rooms. One reported that "podalic version [turning the fetus before delivery] was again attempted but was forcibly interfered with by friends."[53] Another physician noted: "The officiousness of nurses and friends very often thwarts the best-directed measure of the physician, by an overweening desire to make the patient 'comfortable'. . . . All this should be strictly forbidden. Conversation should be prohibited the patient . . . . Nothing is more common than for the patient's friends to object to [bloodletting], urging as a reason, that 'she has lost blood enough.' Of this they are in no respect suitable judges."[54] Others wrote that they found it difficult to accomplish aseptic conditions because of the interference of the woman's friends. In fact, the record shows that the parturients' friends and family made decisions about the use of forceps, anesthesia, and other interventions usually considered to be within the control of the attending physician. Physicians went along with the women's demands or risked being removed from the case. One doctor related, for example, why he would not try to shave the pubic hair of his parturient patients. "In about three seconds after the doctor has made the first rake with his safety [razor], he will find himself on his back out in the yard with the imprint of a woman's bare foot emblazoned on his manly chest, the window sash around his neck and a revolving vision of all the stars in the firmament presented to him. Tell him not to try to shave 'em."[55] Dr. John Milton Duff of Pittsburgh unhappily recorded that "the obstetrician can not always control the general environment of his patient," and he worried about her "obstreperousness." This physician lamented the "sometimes dangerous interference of ignorant and superstitious neighbors and friends." His colleague, Dr. Joseph Price of Philadelphia, agreed that "very few households will permit the practice of well-organized and disciplined maternity work."[56]

The power that the friends had did not necessarily result in better care for the parturient, but it does indicate a level of support that the birthing woman could count on. Dr. E.L. Larkins of Terre Haute, Indiana, believed that pressures from these other birth attendants led physicians to poor practices. "The sympathy of attending friends, coupled with the usual impatience of the woman from her suffering, will too often incite even the physician, against his better judgment, to resort to means to hasten labor, resulting in disaster which time and patience would have avoided."[57] But from the birthing women's point of view, this network of women supporting each other through this difficult ordeal assisted them in getting through a situation in which they felt so powerless.[58] One woman concluded that "the most important thing is not to be left alone and to know that someone is there who cares and will help you when the going gets rough."[59] Through their social network, women were able to keep control over childbirth despite the presence and authority of male physicians.

I cannot quantify my findings to say what percentage of women found the kind of support that Nannie Jackson and others developed. Nor can I determine to what extent these friendship networks might have worked better among the middle classes. I can say that I have found them across class and ethnic lines, in the rural areas and in the cities, in the beginning of the nineteenth century and at its end. I am not positing a universal experience. I'm sure that there were countless women who underwent their severest suffering virtually alone or accompanied only by their husbands, with whom they may not have been able to share their deepest feelings. I understand that unremitting poverty took its toll on many suffering women who could not develop even the outlines of a support network. I think, also, that some rich women stood outside a meaningful network of friends, isolated perhaps by their status and background. But personal accounts of childbirth by women and birth attendants suggest that the birth experience was crucial in creating the social dimensions of most women's lives distinct from other socioeconomic factors. Anita McCormick Blaine, living an affluent life in Chicago at the end of the nineteenth century, shared in many respects the birth experience of Nannie Jackson, living in impoverished rural Arkansas at the same time. They both needed, sought, and got the help of their close women friends at the crucial time of their confinements. Although it is certainly true that Blaine had more advantages and more choice in the particulars of the birth experience, to both women the female context in which they delivered their babies was crucial to a successful experience. The biological female experience of giving birth provided women with some of their worst moments and some of their best ones, and the good and the bad were experiences that all women could share with each other.

Despite the very real changes in the technical and physical experience of birth during the nineteenth century, women's perceptions of its dangers and methods of dealing with those dangers within a female-centered protective environment remained very much the same during the course of the time that birth remained in women's homes. When birth moved to the hospital for the majority of American women in the twentieth century, women lost their domestic power base and with it lost certain controls that they had traditionally held. This is the change, as I argue elsewhere, that took away women's traditional controls over childbirth and caused a basic transformation in womens' birth experiences.[60]

The silver lining in maternity's shadow that accompanied the crisis of childbirth during the home birth period – women actively helping each other shape their childbirth experiences – enabled women to find each other, to learn to give solace and support, and to receive them back in turn. It is, in fact, in the combination of shadow and light, of despair and of hope, that we can best view women's procreative experiences. Although the fears and dangers of childbirth followed women, the experience itself opened up new vistas and created practical and emotional bonds beyond the family that sustained them throughout the rest of their lives. Participating together in the function of procreation led women to share with each other some other aspects of their lives in close intimacy. This "female world of love and ritual,"[61] as Carroll Smith-Rosenberg so aptly called it, with its strong emotional and psychological supports and its ability to produce real change in women's lives, was in large part created around women's shared biological moments including repeated confinements and procreative death and debility fears. The valley of the shadow of birth gave women the essence of a good life at the same time it contributed to a strict definition of that life's boundaries. In uniting women, it ultimately provided the ability for women to stretch the boundaries of their world.

NOTES

A grant from the University of Wisconsin Graduate School supported parts of the research for this paper. I would like to thank Evelyn Fine for her excellent research help. Nancy Schrom Dye, Susan Friedman, Ann Gordon, Gerda Lerner, Florencia Mallon, Ronald Numbers, Jane Schulenberg, Steve Stern, and Anne Stoler contributed valuable comments on earlier drafts of the paper, and for these I am very grateful. The editors and readers at *Feminist Studies* provided useful suggestions and aid. I presented a shorter version of the paper at the Sixth Berkshire Conference on the History of Women at Smith College on June 3, 1984.

1. Jane Savine (?) of Warren, Pennsylvania, to Elizabeth Gordon of Cleveland, Ohio, 26 Feb. 1846; see also letter of 10 Mar. 1846, in Elizabeth Gordon Correspondence, Wisconsin State Historical Society Archives, Madison, Wisconsin.
2. See, for example, Augustin Caldwell, *The Rich Legacy: Memories of Hannah Tobey Farmer, Wife of Moses Gerrish Farmer* (Boston: Privately Printed, 1890), 97.
3. Edward Shorter, *A History of Women's Bodies* (New York: Basic Books, 1983).
4. I use the phrases "feminist impulse" and "feminist inclinations" to differentiate this analysis from any confusion with a publicly political feminism as manifested by those women who were active in the suffrage movement or in any public advocacy for women's rights and emancipation. In my interpretation of women's activity in the birthing rooms, women consciously acted to keep childbirth within women's power, where it had traditionally been, when that power was being threatened by a medical profession growing in power and ability in the nineteenth and early twentieth centuries. By banding together to retain female traditions and values and to shape the events in their own birthing rooms, women acted in a way that acknowledged a specific women's agenda. I stop short of labeling the women as feminist, and refer instead to impulses and inclinations, because I think their actions were not consciously creating a new world so much as they were supporting an autonomous women's dimension within the existing one. For historians' debates on these issues, see Ellen DuBois, Mari Jo Buhle, Temma Kaplan, Gerda Lerner, and Carroll Smith-Rosenberg, "Politics and Culture in Women's History: A Symposium," *Feminist Studies* 6 (Spring 1980): 28-64.

5. For the history of birth control and fertility patterns in America, consult Linda Gordon, *Woman's Body, Woman's Right: A Social History of Birth Control in America* (New York: Viking, 1976); James Reed, *From Private Vice to Public Virtue: Birth Control in America* (New York: Basic Books, 1978); Robert V. Wells, *Revolutions in Americans' Lives: A Demographic Perspective on the History of Americans, Their Families, and Their Society* (Westport, Conn.: Greenwood Press, 1982). On the history of childbirth, consult Janet C. Bogdan, "Care or Cure? Childbirth Practices in Nineteenth-Century America," *Feminist Studies* 4 (June 1978): 92-99; Nancy Schrom Dye, "History of Childbirth in America: Review Essay," *Signs* 6 (1980): 97-108; Catherine M. Scholten, "'On the Importance of the Obstetrick Art': Changing Customs of Childbirth in America, 1760-1825," *William and Mary Quarterly* 34 (July 1977): 426-45; Richard W. Wertz and Dorothy C. Wertz, *Lying-In: A History of Childbirth in America* (New York: Free Press, 1977); Jane B. Donegan, *Women and Men Midwives: Medicine, Morality, and Misogyny in Early America* (Westport, Conn.: Greenwood Press, 1978); Judy Barrett Litoff, *American Midwives 1860 to the Present* (Westport, Conn.: Greenwood Press, 1978); and Judith Walzer Leavitt and Whitney Walton, "'Down to Death's Door': Women's Perceptions of Childbirth in America," in *Women and Health in America: Historical Readings*, ed. Judith Walzer Leavitt (Madison: University of Wisconsin Press, 1984), 155-65.

6. *The Holyoke Diaries, 1709-1856*, Introduction and annotations by George Francis Dow (Salem, Mass.: Essex Institute, 1911).

7. Warren C. Sanderson, "Quantitative Aspects of Marriage, Fertility, and Family Limitation in Nineteenth-Century America: Another Application of the Coale Specifications," *Demography* 11 (August 1979): 339-58; Ansley J. Coale and Melvin Zelnik, *New Estimates of Fertility and Population in the United States: A Study of Annual White Births from 1855 to 1960 and of Completeness of Enumeration in the Censuses from 1880 to 1960* (Princeton: Princeton University Press, 1963). Significant variations even among white native-born women suggest that fertility control was exceedingly variable. Southern farm women, for example, continued to bear an average of almost six children at the end of the nineteenth century. In Philadelphia in 1880, German- and Irish-born women bore over seven children during their lives. See Stewart E. Tolnay, Stephen N. Graham, and Avery M. Guest, "Own-child Estimates of U.S. White Fertility, 1886-99," *Historical Methods* 15 (Summer 1982): 127-38; Phillips Cutright and Edward Shorter, "The Effects of Health on the Completed Fertility of Nonwhite and White U.S. Women Born between 1867 and 1935," *Journal of Social History* 13 (Winter 1979): 191-217; Michael R. Haines, "Fertility and Marriage in a Nineteenth-Century Industrial City: Philadelphia, 1850-1880," *Journal of Economic History* 40 (March 1980): 151-58.

8. Cotton Mather, chap. 53, "Retired Elizabeth: A Long tho' no very Hard, Chapter for A Woman whose Travail approaches with Remedies to Abate the Sorrows of Childbearing" (1710), in *The Angel of Bethesda* (Barre, Mass.: American Antiquarian Society, 1972), 235-48; quotations from p. 237.

9. Margaret Jones Bolsterli, ed., entry for July 1890, in *Vinegar Pie and Chicken Bread: A Woman's Diary of Life in the Rural South, 1890-1891* (Fayetteville: University of Arkansas Press, 1982), 38.

10. Clara Clough Lenroot, Journals and Diaries, pt. 1, 1891 to 1929, edited by her daughter, Katharine F. Lenroot, typescript (May 1969) in family hands. My thanks to Katherine Vila, who shared copies of this diary with my class at the University of Wisconsin, Madison, "Women and Health in America" during the spring semester 1983.

11. Ellen Regal to Isaac Demmon, 13 May 1872, Regal Family Collection, Michigan Historical Collection, Bentley Historical Library, University of Michigan; quoted in Carl N. Degler, *At Odds: Women and the Family in America from the Revolution to the Present* (New York: Oxford University Press, 1980), 60. Women also wrote of joyful anticipation and looked forward to surviving their pregnancies and enjoying their

children. Fear seemed a common sentiment among those women who detailed their feelings. It should be noted here that many women chose not to talk at all about their feelings during pregnancy, and if these women differed from their more articulate sisters, their sentiments are lost. Also lost to us are the feelings of women who did not leave any written records of their lives.

12. William Wight Papers, Wisconsin State Historical Society; vols. 11-15 are the diaries of William's wife, Albina Wight, 1869-76. Quotations are from vol. 11, entries for 14, 17 Apr. 1870. See also entry for 13 May 1870.

13. James S. Bailey, "Cases Illustrating Some of the Causes of Death Ocurring Soon after Childbirth," *New York State Medical Society Transactions,* 1872, 121-29; quotation from p. 121. For more on physicians' experiences with sudden puerperal death, see James L. Taylor, "What Killed the Woman?" *Journal of the American Medical Association* 14 (14 June 1890): 876-77; Fayette Dunlap, "Sudden Death in Labor and Childbed," *Journal of the American Medical Association* 9 (1887): 330-34; Edward W. Jenks, "The Causes of Sudden Death of Puerperal Women," *Transactions of the American Medical Association* 29 (1878): 373-91.

14. William Thompson Lusk, "On Sudden Death in Labor and Childbed," *Journal of the American Medical Association* 3 (1884): 427-31.

15. H.V. Sweringen, "Laceration of the Female Perineum," *Transactions of the Indiana State Medical Society* 32 (1882): 135. I am grateful to Ann Carmichael for this reference.

16. Haven Emerson and Harriet E. Hughes, *Populations, Notifiable Diseases and Deaths, Assembled for New York City, New York* (New York: DeLamar Institute of Public Health, College of Physicians and Surgeons, 1941) and *Supplement 1936-1953* (January 1955). I would like to thank Gretchen Condran and Morris Vogel, who brought these volumes to my attention, and Evelyn Fine, who decifered the figures and drew the graph. The figures are for New York City and not meant to be representative of the rest of the country, although the trend shown in these figures was probably similar outside the city. Statistics gathered by the Metropolitan Board of Health in New York after 1866 were more complete than those gathered for other cities or states.

17. The use of the figure five births per married woman in the United States is not far off the mark, and may in fact be low, given that the 3.56 recorded average includes only white and mostly native-born women. The Northwestern Mutual Life Insurance Company recorded that of 10,000 applicants for life insurance, "one man in every 17.3 who applied for insurance had a mother or sister or both who died from the immediate effects of childbirth." The May 1920 *Crusader* noted: "It is believed that a considerable percentage of these deaths from childbirth were recorded on the death certificate as being due to tuberculosis, heart disease, etc., and that the applicant for insurance remembered the associated childbirth and not the cause of death given on the death certificate. Our present mortality records do not show the frequency with which childbirth is a contributing cause of death" (5). See also C.W. Earle's comments during a Chicago Medical-Legal Society discussion of J.H. Etheridge, "The Medico-Legal Aspect of Utterances Made in Medical Societies," *Journal of the American Medical Association* 10 (5 May 1888): 570. The quotation is Anne Lesley, in Susan Inches Lesley, *Recollections of My Mother* (Boston: Press of George H. Ellis, 1889), 306.

18. I explore this issue in "'Science' Enters the Birthing Room: Obstetrics in America since the Eighteenth Century," *Journal of American History* 70 (September 1983): 281-304. See also Janet Bogdan, "The Mortality Experience of Nineteenth-Century New York City Women" (Paper presented at the Sixth Annual Berkshire Conference on the History of Women at Smith College, 3 June 1984). International comparisons of maternal mortality can be found in Grace L. Meigs, *Maternal Mortality from All Conditions Connected with Childbirth in the United States and Certain Other Countries,* Children's Bureau Publication no. 6 (Washington, D.C.: GPO, 1917). Women became aware of continuing

high maternal deaths in part from their own experience and in part from articles appearing in popular health journals such as the *Crusader* and in women's journals. See, for example, S. Josephine Baker, "Why Do Our Mothers and Babies Die?" *Ladies' Home Journal* 39 (April 1922): 32, 174.

19. Henry Parker Newman, "Prolapse of the Female Pelvic Organs," *Journal of the American Medical Association* 21 (2 Sept. 1893): 335.

20. S.D. Gross, "Lacerations of the Female Sexual Organs Consequent upon Parturition: Their Causes and Their Prevention," *Journal of the American Medical Association* 3 (1884): 337-38.

21. J. Marion Sims developed the surgical repair of the vesicovaginal fistula through his experiments on slave women in the 1840s; it gathered adherents in the second half of the nineteenth century and relieved many women of their suffering. See, for example, J. Marion Sims, *The Story of My Life* (New York: D. Appleton & Company, 1889); Seale Harris, *Woman's Surgeon: The Life Story of J. Marion Sims* (New York: MacMillan Co., 1950); Irwin H. Kaiser, "Reappraisals of J. Marion Sims," *American Journal of Obstetrics and Gynecology* 132 (15 Dec. 1978): 878-84.

22. J. O. Malsbery, "Advice to the Prospective Mother: Assistance during Her Confinement and Care for a Few Days Following," *Journal of the American Medical Association* 28 (15 May 1897): 932.

23. On postpartum lacerations, see, for example, the following articles in the *Journal of the American Medical Association:* Charles P. Noble, "The Causation of Diseases of Women," vol. 21 (16 Sept. 1893): 410-14; John C. Da Costa, "An Easy Method of Repairing the Perineum," vol. 13 (2 Nov. 1889): 645-47; Henry T. Byford, "The Production and Prevention of Perineal Lacerations during Labor, with Description of an Unrecognized Form," vol. 6 (6 Mar. 1886): 253-57, 271; and H.V. Sweringen, "Laceration of the Female Perineum," vol. 5 (15 Aug. 1885): 173-77. See also the discussion of this last paper in the *Transactions of the Indiana State Medical Society,* 258-264, during which Dr. Woolen of Indianapolis blamed physicians' interventions for the increased rate of perineal tears in women: "The frequent use of forceps is filling the country full of cases for our gynecologists, and it does seem to me that we are making a mistake" (263). Physicians, anxious to clear themselves of possible blame, more frequently named the baby's hard head rather than the hard forceps as the principal agent. Regardless of agent, however, the state of medical knowledge about repairing such damage remained at issue.

24. Augustus K. Gardner, "On the Use of Pessaries," *Transactions of the American Medical Association* 15 (1865): 110.

25. Albina Wight Diary, vol. 11: entries of 20 Aug., 6 and 9 Oct. 1873; 18 Jan. 1874. Gerda Lerner noted that Angelina Grimke suffered from prolapsed uterus and other postpartum complications following the birth of her second child, and the biographies of numerous other famous and not famous women indicate the problem was a common one. Gerda Lerner, *The Grimke Sisters from South Carolina: Pioneers for Woman's Rights and Abolition* (New York: Houghton Mifflin, 1967), 288-92.

26. Gardner, 113.

27. Homer O. Hitchcock, "A Modified Ring Pessary for the Treatment and Cure of Anteflexion and Anteversion of the Uterus," *Transactions of the American Medical Association* 15 (1865): 103-106.

28. Reported in "Midwifery" section, *Transactions of the American Medical Association* 6 (1851): 361. I address the debate concerning physicians' blame for women's postpartum problems in "'Science' Enters the Birthing Room" and in *Brought to Bed: Birthing Women and Their Physicians in America 1750-1950* (Oxford University Press, forthcoming). For some contemporary comment, see Hiram Corson, "On the Statistics of 3,036 Cases of Labor," *Journal of the American Medical Association* 7 (31 July 1886): 138-39.

29. Agnes Just Reid, *Letters of Long Ago* (Caldwell, Idaho: Caxton Printers, 1936), 24.

30. Christina Hopkinson Baker, ed., *Diary and Letters of Josephine Preston Peabody* (Boston: Houghton Mifflin Company, 1925), 214-15, 226-29.

31. Elsa Rosenberg to the author in response to author's query in the *New York Times Book Review*, 30 July 1983.

32. Elizabeth H. Emerson, *Glimpses of a Life* (Burlington, N.C.: J.S. Sargent & Co., 1960), 4-5.

33. Lillie M. Jackson, *Fanning the Embers* (Boston: Christopher Publishing House, 1966), 90-91.

34. Hallie F. Nelson, *South of the Cottonwood Tree* (Broken Bow, Neb.: Purcells, 1977), 173.

35. This diary entry is all the more poignant because it influenced two generations in this family. Hannah Whitall Smith's niece, M. Carey Thomas, found the journal and was so moved by it that she copied it into her own diary in 1878. Marjorie Housepian Dobkin, ed., *The Making of a Feminist: Early Journals and Letters of M. Carey Thomas* (Kent, Ohio: Kent State University Press, 1979). Hannah Smith's diary entry was dated 20 Dec. 1852, and Thomas copied it on 1 Sept. 1878, p. 149.

36. Albina Wight Diary, vol. 11, 14 Apr. 1870.

37. Malinda Jenkins, *Gambler's Wife: The Life of Malinda Jenkins,* as told in conversations to Jessie Lilienthal (Boston: Houghton Mifflin Co., 1933), 48.

38. Elizabeth Elton Smith, *The Three Eras of Woman's Life* (New York: Harper & Brothers, 1836), 85.

39. Anita McCormick Blaine to Nettie Fowler McCormick; Nettie Fowler McCormick to Anita McCormick Blaine, both in August 1890. McCormick Family Papers, series 1E, box 459; series 2B, box 46, Wisconsin State Historical Society.

40. Entries for 15, 16, 17 Aug. 1890, Bolsterli, 60-61.

41. William P. Preston to his daughter, May, on her fifteenth birthday, 19 May 1864, from the collection of the McKeldin Library Archives and Manuscripts, University of Maryland, College Park. I would like to thank Virginia Beauchamp for sending me this reference from her forthcoming book, *The Language of Silence: Madge Preston's Story.*

42. Christiana Holmes Tillson, *A Woman's Story of Pioneer Illinois,* ed. Milo Milton Quaife (Chicago: Lakeside Press, 1919), 128.

43. *The Life of Mrs. Robert Clay, Afterwards Mrs. Robert Bolton (Nee Ann Curtis), 1690-1738* (Philadelphia, 1928), 154.

44. Laura B. Gaye, *Laugh on Friday, Weep on Sunday: One Woman's Reminiscence* (Calabassas, Calif.: Loma Palaga Press, 1968), 55; May Harley, *Whither Shall I Go: A Story of an Itinerant Circuit Rider's Wife* (Southold, N.Y.: Academy Printing Services, 1975), 76.

45. Anna Maria Thornton, Diary of Mrs. William Thornton, 1800-1863, *Records of the Columbia Historical Society* 10 (1907): 100.

46. *Esther Burr's Journal* (Washington, D.C.: Howard University Print, 1903).

47. Marilyn Clohessy to the author, 9 Sept. 1983, in response to author's query in the *New York Times Book Review.*

48. Entry of 27 June 1890, Bolsterli, 35.

49. Fleetwood Churchill, *The Diseases of Females: Including Those of Pregnancy and Childbed,* 4th American ed. (Philadelphia: Lea & Blanchard, 1847), 340.

50. John G. Meachem, Sr., Papers 1823-1896, State Historical Society of Wisconsin, Autobiography, box 1, p. 6. See also Carl Binger, *Revolutionary Doctor: Benjamin Rush, 1746-1813* (New York: W. W. Norton & Co., 1966), 77.

51. Edward Henry Dixon, *Woman and Her Diseases from the Cradle to the Grave,* 10th ed. (Philadelphia: G.G. Evans, 1860), 261.

52. Letter from Dr. Thomas Steel to his father, 12 Dec. 1844, in the Steel Collection at the State Historical Society of Wisconsin. I am grateful to Peter Harstad for calling my

attention to Steel's obstetrical cases. For more of this kind of evidence see Leavitt, "'Science' Enters the Birthing Room."

53. Reported in James A. Harrar, *The Story of the Lying-In Hospital of the City of New York* (New York: Society of the Lying-In Hospital, 1938), 34. On the point of rebellion of women inside the hospital as well as outside, see Nancy Schrom Dye, "Scientific Obstetrics and Working-Class Women: The New York Midwifery Dispensary" (Paper delivered at the American Historical Association, San Francisco, December 1983).

54. Dixon, 262.

55. S.H. Landrum, Altus, Oklahoma, letter to the editor, *Journal of the American Medical Association* 58 (1912): 576. I would like to thank Carolyn Hackler for calling this letter to my attention.

56. John Milton Duff, "Parturition as a Factor in Gynecologic Practice," *Journal of the American Medical Association* 35 (25 Aug. 1900): 465. Price's comment came during the discussion of Duff's paper, p. 467.

57. E.L. Larkins, "Care and Repair of the Female Perineum," *Journal of the American Medical Association* 32 (11 Feb. 1899): 284.

58. See "'Science' Enters the Birthing Room" for more examples of physicians lack of control in home deliveries.

59. Clohessy to the author.

60. Discussed in "Alone among Strangers: Childbirth Moves to the Hospital" (Paper delivered at the American Historical Association Annual Meeting, San Francisco, December 1983); and Leavitt, *Brought to Bed*.

61. Carroll-Smith Rosenberg, "The Female World of Love and Ritual: Relations between Women in Nineteenth-Century America," *Signs* 1 (1975): 1-29.

Medical History, 1991, 35: 89-102.

THE LESSER PESTILENCE: NON-EPIDEMIC PUERPERAL FEVER

by

STANLEY A. SELIGMAN *

Puerperal fever was first described by Hippocrates.[1] However, the epidemic form of the disease does not seem to have existed before the mid-seventeenth century, when "an unknown affection occurred at Leipzig in 1652 and returned again in 1665. It attacked puerperal women and was so deadly that but one in ten escaped".[2] Sporadic outbreaks were recorded over the following century[3] until the winter of 1746, when there was an epidemic at the Hôtel-Dieu in Paris.[4] Thereafter the disease became increasingly prevalent; the first English epidemic was in 1760, at the British Lying-in Hospital.[5]

Virulent epidemics continued together with sporadic cases until 1936 when, associated with the introduction of the sulphonamides, there was a sudden, profound and sustained fall in maternal mortality, which had remained static in England and Wales from the middle of the eighteenth century (when comprehensive reports on deaths in childbirth first became available).[6] The experience of other countries was similar.[7]

* Stanley A. Seligman, MD, FRCS, FRCOG, Luton and Dunstable Hospital, Dunstable Road, Luton, Beds. LU4 0DZ.

I wish to express my gratitude to Anne Cunnington and Drs A. G. and G. A. Pistofidis for invaluable help with translation of foreign papers. Irvine Loudon kindly advised on medical attitudes to the theory of endogenous infection in puerperal sepsis. My colleague at Luton, Trevor Willis, advised on all matters microbiological.

[1] Francis Adams, *The genuine works of Hippocrates: translated from the Greek*, vol. 1, London. The Sydenham Society, 1847, pp. 544-5.

[2] Jean-Antoine-François Ozanam, *Histoire médicale, générale et particulière, des maladies épidémiques*, 2nd ed., Paris, 1835, p. 14. See also: James Hawley Burtenshaw, 'The fever of the puerperium (puerperal infection); a chronological review of the doctrines of its aetiology and of the methods of treatment from the earliest times to the present', *N.Y. med. J. & Phila. med. J.*, 1904, 79: 1073-8, 1134-8, 1189-94, 1234-8; 80: 20-5.

[3] August Hirsch, *Handbook of geographical and historical pathology*, vol. 2, *Chronic infective, toxic, parasitic, septic and constitutional diseases*, London, New Sydenham Society, 1885, p. 422.

[4] Paul Jacques Malouin, 'Histoire des maladies épidémiques de 1746, observées à Paris, en même temps que les différentes températures de l'air', *Mém. Acad. roy. Sci.*, 1746, 160: 151-74. See also: Robert Lee, *Researches on the pathology and treatment of some of the most important diseases of women*, London, S. Highley, 1833, pp. 5-8.

[5] John Leake, *Practical observations on the child-bed fever*, London, Baldwin, 1772, p. 242.

[6] Irvine Loudon, 'Deaths in childbed from the eighteenth century to 1935', *Med. Hist.*, 1986, 30: 1-41.

[7] *Idem*, 'Maternal mortality: 1880-1950. Some regional and international comparisons', *Soc. Hist. Med.*, 1988, 1: 666-9.

89

Puerperal fever may be caused by different organisms; each produces its own characteristic picture.[8] The common type, which can occur in epidemic or sporadic form, is due to the *β-haemolytic streptococcus*. Another common cause is the anaerobic organisms normally resident in the vaginas of healthy women, which only produce disease under certain conditions. A variety of other different organisms, less commonly, also give rise to infection.

It is the intention of this paper to explain why the type of fever due to the *β-haemolytic streptococcus* seems to have existed before the mid-seventeenth century in non-epidemic form only, and to trace the discovery of anaerobic infection as the other important cause of sporadic puerperal sepsis.

SPORADIC AND EPIDEMIC PUERPERAL FEVER

Evidence is lacking for the occurrence of epidemics of puerperal fever before the mid-seventeenth century. "With the eye of faith it is possible to perceive from early authors the existence of puerperal epidemics, but these ideas are too vague, and the relevant texts too obscure for any positive conclusion".[9] Thus an account of a supposed early epidemic from the pseudo-Hippocratic treatise *De morbis mulierum* was quoted by Hirsch,[10] but he omitted that part of the text stating that puerperal women were not the only ones affected; in fact, fewer women than men were attacked.[11]

The onset and spread of epidemics of puerperal fever has been linked with the establishment of maternity hospitals and other institutions for the reception of the lying-in.[12] This is manifestly not so. The first epidemic at the Hôtel-Dieu was in 1664, when a prodigious number of women died after their confinement; infection was attributed to impure air from a ward, filled with wounded, which was situated underneath the lying-in ward.[13] This was a century and a half after the formation of the school of midwifery at the hospital, and there was no further outbreak until 1746. The British Lying-in Hospital had been open 11 years before its first outbreak in 1760, and other hospital beds for lying-in women had existed in London since 1747 without being affected.[14]

Why should a previously endemic condition assume epidemic proportions? It seems likely that this was due to a change in virulence of the *β-haemolytic streptococcus* responsible for the disease. It has been claimed, for example, that it was a sudden decrease in the virulence of the streptococcus in the mid 1930s, coinciding with the arrival of prontosil and sulphanilamide, which was the real cause of the fall in mortality associated with puerperal fever, and that the drugs did not really do what was claimed for them. Leonard Colebrook could find no such change at Queen Charlotte's Hospital, but wrote that on the other side of London, at Hampstead, the

[8] George F. Gibberd, 'Puerperal sepsis, 1930–1965', *J. Obstet. Gynaec. Br. Commonw.*, 1966, 73: 1–10.

[9] E. Hervieux, *Maladies puerpérales*, Paris, Adrien Delahaye, 1870, p. 3.

[10] Op. cit., note 3 above, p. 418.

[11] Adams, op. cit., note 1 above, p. 363.

[12] Hirsch, op. cit., note 3 above, p. 419.

[13] Philippe Peu, *La pratique des accouchemens*, Paris, Boudot, 1694, p. 268.

[14] Stanley A. Seligman, 'The Royal Maternity Charity: the first one hundred years', *Med. Hist.*, 1980, 24: 403–18.

puerperal fever cases in the LCC unit did appear to have been somewhat less severe in 1935 and the early part of 1936 than they had been before that time.[15] Seventeenth- and eighteenth-century accounts of puerperal fever and other diseases often caused by the *β-haemolytic streptococcus*—hospital gangrene, scarlet fever, and erysipelas—do indicate that there was an increase in the severity and contagiousness of such infections during these centuries.

Alexander Gordon, in his classic epidemiological study of an epidemic of puerperal fever in Aberdeen in 1789, stated:

> The disease was new and unknown in Aberdeen ... The only disease supposed by the vulgar to be incident to lying-in women, is a disorder commonly called the weed, which is an ephemera similar to the paroxysm of an intermittent fever, and always terminates without any danger.[16]

"The weed"—a Scottish and Anglo-Irish term—was mainly applied in Scotland, although known in England.[17] The condition, characterized by rigors, lasted between 18 and 36 hours and was not usually life-threatening.

Even after puerperal fever epidemics became established, not all of them were severe. There were no deaths associated with an outbreak in Derbyshire at a time when those in London were accompanied by many deaths.[18]

Hospital gangrene appears to have been a disease of all times and of every part of the habitable globe.[19] However, since wounding of the skin predisposes to infection by a multitude of bacteria, there is no certainty that the streptococcus was responsible for many outbreaks.

The early history of scarlet fever is unclear since it was confused with measles and, as late as the seventeenth century, after it had been clearly described, was still regarded by many physicians as a modification of measles.[20] A malignant as well as a mild form of the disease was first described by Richard Morton in 1694; and there is evidence that in the first half of the eighteenth century sore throats accompanied by scarlatiniform rashes were a serious medical problem.[21]

Erysipelas—an inflammatory reddening of the skin—was described mainly in association with wounds, in ancient and medieval times.[22] A virulent form of epidemic erysipelas was first observed in 1750 at Caillan, on the bay of Saint-

---

[15] Leonard Colebrook, 'The story of puerperal fever—1800 to 1950', *Br. med. J.*, 1956, I: 247–52.

[16] Alexander Gordon, *A treatise on the epidemic puerperal fever of Aberdeen*, London, Robinson, 1795, p. 4.

[17] Alexander Hamilton, *A treatise of midwifery, comprehending the whole management of female complaints, and the treatment of children in early infancy. To which are added prescriptions for women and children*, 2nd ed., Edinburgh, Dickson, Creech & Elliot, 1785, p. 253.

[18] William Butter, *An account of puerperal fevers, as they appear in Derbyshire, and some of the counties adjacent*, London, Payne, 1775, p. 121.

[19] Hirsch, op. cit., note 3 above, p. 476.

[20] Idem, *Handbook of geographical and historical pathology*, vol. 1, *Acute infectious diseases*, London, New Sydenham Society, 1883, p. 171.

[21] Charles Singer and E. Ashworth Underwood, *A short history of medicine*, 2nd ed., Oxford, Clarendon Press, 1962, p. 203.

[22] Hirsch, op. cit., note 3 above, p. 390.

Tropez.[23] A similar type of malignant erysipelas swept the western hemisphere, starting in Nova Scotia in 1822 and growing into a pandemic which did not cease until the beginning of the 1860s.[24]

Laboratory studies have now confirmed that, not only do human historical, social, and economic factors cause variations in the frequency, severity and manifestations of infections due to group A streptococci, but also that these versatile micro-organisms can undergo rapid change.[25] A waxing and waning of the different organisms has been observed with isolates of one serotype predominating and then being replaced by another.[26] There has been a recent relative increase in the number of strains of type 1 group A streptococci isolated in England, these being associated with invasive disease with a high fatality rate,[27] and there have been a number of maternal deaths reported from this form of infection.[28]

It seems likely that variations in the prevalence, toxicity, and infectivity of strains of the streptococcus were important factors in the establishment of an epidemic pattern of puerperal fever in the seventeenth and eighteenth centuries, and that these can explain the apparent absence of such a state before that time.

MEDDLESOME MIDWIFERY

For many centuries puerperal fever was attributed to retention of the menses, with such diverse precipitating factors as "catching cold, errors in diet, or anxiety of the mind".[29] However, it was observed that retention of all or part of the afterbirth could lead to infection. In the seventeenth century, William Harvey commented on midwives being much to blame, "especially the younger and more meddlesome ones . . . by leaving behind portions of the membranes, or even the placenta itself",[30] whilst Mauriceau referred to their "rough handling".[31] Peu[32] and Platter[33] noted the effect of retention of the secundines, and Percival Willughby gave details of six cases

---

[23] M. Darluc, 'Des maladies épidémiques qui ont régné en 1750 & 1751 à Caillan & aux environs', in M. Vandermonde (ed.), *Receuil périodique d'observations de médicine, chirurgie, pharmacie, &c.*, vol. 7, Paris, Didot le jeune, 1757, p. 55.

[24] Hirsch, op. cit., note 3 above, pp. 396–405.

[25] Gene H. Stollerman, 'Changing group A Streptococci. The reappearance of streptococcal "toxic shock"', *Arch. intern. Med.*, 1988, **148**: 1268–70.

[26] Ewa Gaworzewska and G. Colman, 'Changes in the pattern of infection caused by *Streptococcus pyogenes*', *Epidem. Inf.*, 1988, **100**: 257–69.

[27] G. Colman, A. Efstratiou, and E. T. Gaworzawska, 'The pyogenic streptococci', *PHLS Microbiol. Dig.*, 1988, **5**: 7–9. For recent American experience see: Dennis L. Stevens et al., 'Severe group A streptococcal infections associated with a toxic shock-like syndrome and scarlet fever toxin A', *New Eng. J. Med.*, 1989, **321**: 1–7. The original demonstration that different strains of haemolytic streptococci caused different clinical types of infection or could be harmless was given by Rebecca C. Lancefield and Ronald Hare in 'The serological differentiation of pathogenic and non-pathogenic strains of haemolytic streptococci from parturient women', *J. experiment. Med.*, 1935, **61**: 335–49.

[28] G. R. Swingler et al., 'Disseminated intravascular coagulation associated with group A streptococcal infection in pregnancy', *Lancet*, 1988, **I**: 1456–7.

[29] John Leake, *Practical observations on the child-bed fever*, 3rd ed., London, Baldwin & Evans, 1775, p. 41.

[30] William Harvey, *Works. Translated, with a life of the author, by R. Willis*, London, Sydenham Society, 1847, p. 533.

[31] François Mauriceau, *The diseases of women with child and in child-bed*, tranl. Hugh Chamberlen, 3rd ed., London, Bell, 1697, pp. 271–2.

[32] Op. cit., note 13 above, p. 1135.

[33] Felix Platter, *De ventris dolore*, Basel, 1656. See: Burtenshaw, op. cit., note 2 above, p. 1075.

92

of puerperal sepsis, four of whom died, associated with retention of the placenta, trauma, or both.[34] Other, eighteenth-century, authors recorded similar experiences.[35]

The importance of this type of fever following childbirth was put in perspective in 1861 by Semmelweis, who thought that such episodes could not be prevented and attributed them to self-infection.

> The decomposed animal organic material which when absorbed brings on puerperal fever is rare in cases not conveyed to the individual from without but originates within the affected individual owing to the retention of organic material which should have been expelled in child-bed. Before its expulsion decomposition has already begun, and when absorption occurs puerperal fever is produced by Self-infection. These organic materials are the lochia, remnants of decidua, blood coagula which are retained within the cavity of the uterus. Or the decomposed animal organic material is the product of a pathological process, for example, the result of a forcible use of the midwifery forceps causing gangrene of bruised portions of the genital organs and consequent child-bed fever by Self-infection.[36]

As will be described presently, this type of infection is caused by the woman's own bacteriological flora, by anaerobic organisms normally present in the healthy vagina. "Self-infection" is an accurate description of the pathological process. It is ironic that the biographer of Semmelweis, having repeatedly emphasized how much of his work was not accepted because it was taken out of context, or misunderstood, rejected his observations on this type of sepsis as being founded on error.[37]

THE ACCEPTANCE OF ANAEROBES AS A CAUSE OF DISEASE

Modern views on the nature of surgical sepsis started with the work of Robert Koch in the 1870s, work that was continued by Alexander Ogston, assistant surgeon to the Aberdeen Royal Infirmary.[38] Ogston not only distinguished streptococci, which he named, from staphylococci, but also demonstrated that the micrococci that he isolated from abscesses were anaerobic organisms. To understand the difficulties associated with the investigation of the role of anaerobic organisms in the production of infection it is necessary to appreciate concepts of bacteria as a cause of disease

[34] Percival Willughby, *Observations in midwifery*, edited from the original MS by Henry Blenkinsop, 1863, with a new introduction by John L. Thornton, Wakefield, SR Publishers Ltd., 1972, pp. 40, 88, 94, 117, 171, 218, 222.

[35] Guillaume Mauquest de La Motte, *A general treatise of midwifery: illustrated with upwards of four hundred curious observations and reflections concerning that art....* Translated into English by Thomas Tomkyns, London, Waugh, 1746, p. 488; Benjamin Pugh, *A treatise of midwifery, chiefly with regard to the operation. With several improvements in that art*, London, Buckland, 1754, pp. 25, 31; Thomas Kirkland, *A treatise on child-bed fevers, and on the methods of preventing them. Being a supplement to the books lately written on the subject*, London, Baldwin & Dawson, 1767, pp. 64–6; John Clarke, *Practical essays on the mangement of pregnancy and labour; and on the inflammatory and febrile diseases of lying-in women*, London, Johnson, 1793, p. 98.

[36] Ignaz Philipp Semmelweis, *Die Aetiologie, der Begriff und die Prophylaxis des Kindbettfiebers*, Pest, Vienna and Leipzig, C. A. Hartleben, 1861. Translated in, Sir William J. Sinclair, *Semmelweis: his life and doctrine*, Manchester University Press, 1909, p. 205.

[37] Ibid., pp. 208, 367.

[38] Leonard G. Wilson, 'The early recognition of streptococci as causes of disease', *Med. Hist.*, 1987, 31: 403–14.

93

before the present century. Initially, it was not even agreed whether bacteria were the cause or the product of disease.

In 1680, in his 32nd letter to the Royal Society, Anton van Leeuwenhoek described how animacules had developed in a sealed glass tube containing powdered pepper, clear rain water, and a minimal amount of air. Nearly 100 years later Lazzaro Spallanzani, the Italian naturalist who destroyed the doctrine of spontaneous generation, showed that animacules could develop in a high vacuum and live and move for 16 days.[39] These observations were overlooked until the second half of the nineteenth century, when Louis Pasteur undertook his investigations into the manufacture of alcohol from beet. In one experiment he put a drop of fermenting fluid on a slide under a cover slip. On looking down the microscope he saw that, whilst the organisms in the centre of the field were moving actively, the ones at the edge near to the air became sluggish; they seemed to want to move to the centre away from the free oxygen. Pasteur called these organisms *anaérobies*, as distinct from *aérobies*.[40]

It was at first believed that every bacterial species appeared in several morphological and physiological forms which could be changed, the one into the other, by external conditions, this process being called "adaption". The term "pleomorphism" was introduced to describe the supposed change of bacteria from spherical cocci to bacillary rods to spirals. Although bacteriology began to emerge as a definite science towards the end of the 1870s, the doctrine of pleomorphism lingered, with the result that many workers investigating the microbiology of infection were unaware that they were dealing with mixed cultures rather than a single specific agent, particularly where anaerobic agents were involved. From her investigation of war wounds in Flanders, Muriel Robinson concluded that mixed cultures accounted for most of the anomalies.[41] This and similar findings by others were largely ignored and it was only in the 1980s that the importance of mixed microbial populations in infection became generally understood.[42]

A further obstacle to the investigation of anaerobic infection was the difficulty of isolating the organisms. It was not until 1916, when MacIntosh and Fildes published their first paper on the anaerobic jar, that plate cultures could be made easily and consistently.[43] A do-it-yourself approach was prevalent in laboratory practice at that time and the authors suggested the use of a paint tin with a lever-off lid.

Despite all these difficulties the importance of anaerobic infection in non-epidemic puerperal fever had already been established by French and German workers, although it was to be some time before their results were to be rediscovered and accepted in America and England.

[39] William Bulloch, *The history of bacteriology*, London, Oxford University Press, 1938 (repr. 1960), p. 232.

[40] Ibid., p. 232.

[41] Muriel Robertson, 'Notes upon certain anaerobes isolated from wounds', *J. Path. Bact.*, 1915-6, **20**: 327-49.

[42] B. Styrt and S. L. Gorbach, 'Recent developments in the understanding of the pathogenesis and treatment of anaerobic infections', *N. Eng. J. Med.*, 1989, **321**: 240-6, 298-302.

[43] James McIntosh and Paul Fildes, 'A new apparatus for the isolation and cultivation of anaerobic micro-organisms', *Lancet*, 1916, i: 768-70.

ANAEROBIC INFECTION AS A CAUSE OF PUERPERAL FEVER

The first to isolate an anaerobe from a case of puerperal fever was E. Levy, clinical assistant to the Department of Surgery in the University of Strassburg.

> Frau F. . . . following a normal birth in June 1890 developed severe right iliac fossa pain on the third day. Soon after, a large swelling followed, which affected the hip joint . . . The pain got worse so that the patient was confined to bed for five months. She was admitted to hospital at the end of November 1890 . . . The whole of the upper third of the right thigh was very swollen and fluctuant . . . On deep palpation one clearly has a feeling as if pressing a cavity filled with air. Percussion over the abscess produces a light tympanic sound . . . With a little firm pressure one can bring the deep masses above and below Poupart's ligament towards each other as proof that one is dealing with a single large abscess . . .
> On 30 November 1890, operation under chloroform anaesthetic . . . To collect the gas, puncture of the abscess is made on the outside of the thigh near to the trochanter with a boiled trocar. Gas streams out at once . . . the abscess in incised and some of the foul smelling pus taken for bacteriological examination . . .
> After the operation the fever fell at once. On the first change of dressing there was only minimal discharge. After eight days a drain could no longer be introduced and after three weeks the woman was discharged completely cured of her large pelvi-femoral abscess.[44]

Professor Hoppe-Seyler's chemical analysis of the gas showed, by volume, carbon dioxide, 47.845%; hydrogen, 20.134%; nitrogen, 32.021%.

Levy correctly anticipated the presence of a polymicrobial infection, including anaerobes, and so did not use bouillon for culture as advocated by the Paris school, as this would not separate out the different organisms. He used gelatin plates and agar tubes incubated anaerobically. The gelatin plates grew only a few colonies of *Streptococcus pyogenes*. These grew also in the agar tubes in small amounts, but the main colonies, resembling the anthrax bacillus, displayed a fine granular structure surrounded by a tangle of fine, entwined threads. Around each colony a vacuole of gas had formed. Microscopically, the colonies consisted of quite short fine immobile bacteria arranged in long chains and threads of up to 30 or more segments. They stained Gram-positive. Whilst it is impossible to identify this organism with certainty, it was most probably a *Clostridium*, possibly *C. sporogenes* or *C. sordellii*.

The clinical description of the patient's condition is typical of anaerobic pelvic infection, with a chronic course and the presence of profuse stinking pus.

In 1893, M. A. Veillon reported the recovery of an anaerobe from pus from a Bartholin's abscess and described how this organism, either alone or with other bacteria, could produce fetid suppuration.[45] He thought that this *Micrococcus fetidus* was probably the same as that isolated from dental caries by Rosenbach in 1884. Under Veillon's direction at the Faculty of Medicine in Paris, anaerobic infection in

---

[44] E. Levy, 'Ueber einen Fall von Gasabscess', *Dt. Z. Chir.*, 1891, **32**: 248–51.
[45] M. A. Veillon, 'Sur un micrococque anaérobie trouvé dans suppurations fétides', *C. Mém. Soc. biol.*, 1893, **5**: 807–9.

95

man was extensively investigated, including female genital tract[46] and putrid puerperal infections.[47]

In Germany, the microbiology of the female genital tract was further studied by Bernhard Krönig. He had learned the fundamentals of bacteriology from Robert Koch in Berlin. Later, accompanied by his friend and co-worker Carl Menge, he moved to Leipzig as assistant to Paul Zweifel. In his post-doctoral lecture of 1895, Krönig described fever following childbirth as a polymicrobial infection essentially determined by the anaerobes,[48] but German workers were divided in their views as to whether anaerobic organisms could cause disease or were merely commensal. It was Hugo Schottmüller (1867–1936) who finally was able to isolate and culture these organisms before and after death in severe cases of puerperal sepsis.

Schottmüller became director of the Medical Polyclinic in Hamburg-Eppendorf. He was a clinical bacteriologist and introduced a number of techniques still in use today, including blood-culture and the blood-agar plate. He seems to have been unaware of much of the research into anaerobic infection being carried out in Paris.

From 1903 Schottmüller was able to culture anaerobes from blood by incubating it in bouillon. Anaerobic conditions occurred from the blood clotting or settling to the bottom of the tubes. Growth was demonstrable after 24 hours. He also successfully used stab cultures in agar to which he had added a reducing substance.

On 16 November 1909, Schottmüller spoke to the Biological Association of Hamburg on the importance of some of the anaerobic bacteria in medicine, most specifically in puerperal infections. He used the term "puerperal" to mean following pregnancy, rather than following the birth of a child (L. *puer*—child; *parere*—to bring forth) and all his "puerperal" infections were in fact post-abortal infections. Infection following abortion, invariably due to interference with the pregnancy, differs from infection following childbirth. He presented case histories of 16 post-abortal infections as well as nine others with pelvic inflammatory disease, otitis media, lung abscess, pulmonary tuberculosis, and urinary tract infection. Although he included patients infected with tetanus (*Clostridium tetani*) and gas gangrene (*C. perfringens*) organisms, those described were mainly due to anaerobic cocci, which he called *Streptococcus putridus* from the offensive smell. He showed clearly the tendency for these infections to invade the blood stream, with the production of rigors, and proceed to venous thrombosis, which could give rise to septic embolism. The common findings at post-mortem were septic endometritis, septic thrombophlebitis of the pelvic and hypogastric veins, lung abscesses, and splenomegaly. He concluded: "We now know the reason for puerperal sepsis. The only thing that remains is to find the appropriate treatment." By the time the report of the meeting was published, he was

---

[46] J. Hallé, *Recherches sur la bactériologie du canal génital de la femme (état normal et pathologique)*. Thesis, Faculty of Medicine, University of Paris, 1898.

[47] C. Jeannin, *Etiologie et pathogénie des infections puerpérales putrides (recherches cliniques et bactériologiques)*. Thesis, University of Paris, 1899.

[48] H. Spitzbart, 'Zur Geschichte der Anaerobier in der Geburtshilfe', *Zent bl. Gynäk.*, 1986, **108**: 1261–3.

96

able to add details of six cases which followed childbirth as distinct from abortion: five from *S. putridus* and one from *C. perfringens*.[49]

A year after this initial paper, Schottmüller published two more articles, on the aetiology of puerperal fever[50] and on bacteriological investigations and methods therein.[51] In a series of 50 cases of true post-partum infection he found anaerobic infections to be as common as those due to aerobic streptococci. Most of his positive cultures were from the cervix, although he was able to isolate the same organism from the blood on a number of occasions. He noted that an anaerobic infection could be suspected if there was an offensive-smelling vaginal discharge which differed from that produced by infections with other bacteria. He described how anaerobic infections often gave rise to salpingitis and pelvic abscess formation: venous thrombosis was another common complication.[52] He thought that anaerobic infections usually were caused by the passage of the streptococcus, which was commensal in the vagina, into the uterus from intrauterine intervention or operation. He also thought that the infections had a pronounced contagious property with an increase in virulence through transmission from person to person or when the organism entered the blood stream. He was undoubtedly wrong about the infectivity and change in virulence of the normal resident flora, but all of his other findings have since been confirmed. He also had more severe infections and deaths in those infections due to anaerobic streptococci, but this may have been associated with the factors leading to the superadded infection.

By 1923 Schottmüller had collected 231 fatal cases following labour, with anaerobic streptococci isolated from 72, seven of these being polymicrobial. In 41 of the anaerobic infections, death was from peritonitis.[53] Despite all this he seemed optimistic that the problem of puerperal sepsis would be overcome and that, although it would not disappear altogether, the number of deaths in childbirth could be reduced from its still frightening height to a minimal figure.[54] Schottmüller died in 1936, the year when sulphonamides were coming into use and turning his hope into reality.

In America the role of anaerobic streptococci in puerperal infection was investigated by Otto Schwarz and William J. Dieckmann at Washington University School of Medicine. Schottmüller's work was mentioned in at least two of the then-current American textbooks of obstetrics, but it was thought that, although anaerobic streptococci were occasionally found in puerperal infections, Schottmüller

[49] Hugo Schottmüller, 'Zur Bedeutung einiger Anaëroben in der Pathologie, insbesondere bei puerperalen Erkrankungen *(Streptococcus putridus, Bac. phlegm. emphysemat., Bac. tetani.)*', *Mitt. Med. Chir.*, 1910, **21**: 450–90.

[50] *Idem*, 'Aetiologie des febris puerperalis und febris in puerperio', *Münch. med. Wschr.*, 1911, **58**: 557–8.

[51] *Idem*, 'Ueber bakteriologische Untersuchungen und ihre Methoden bei febris puerperalis', ibid., pp. 787–9.

[52] This work was undertaken in Schottmüller's department by Konrad Bingold; 'Putride embolische Lungeninfektionen und Pathologie', *Virchow's Arch.*, 1921, **232**: 22–34.

[53] Hugo Schottmüller, *Leitfaden für die klinisch-bakteriologischen Kulturmethoden*, Berlin, Urban & Schwarzenberg, 1923.

[54] *Idem*, 'Die puerperale Sepsis', *Münch. med. Wschr.*, 1928, **75**: 1580–3, 1634–8.

97

overestimated the frequency of this type of infection.[55] The interest of Schwarz and Dieckmann was stimulated by the repeated negative cultures they obtained in cases that they thought were obviously infected clinically.

In July 1924 the School's Department of Obstetrics took over its own bacteriology work, after which all the uterine and blood cultures were grown both aerobically and anaerobically. It was at this time that Schwarz and Dieckmann became interested in Schottmüller's researches. They could find only one report of serious puerperal infection due to anaerobic streptococci in the American literature, from 1905. They also found a report of the accidental culture of an anaerobic streptococcus in the blood following a death from puerperal infection reported from the Rotunda Hospital, Dublin in 1925.

Schwarz and Dieckmann presented their findings at a meeting of the Section of Obstetrics of the Southern Medical Association in Dallas, Texas, in 1925.[56] They were able to demonstrate that Schottmüller was right about the relative incidence of the various types of puerperal infection, and that their experience confirmed the clinical characteristics of the cases that he had described. Anaerobic streptococci played a considerable role as a causative factor.

Between July 1924 and September 1926 they had a total of 45 puerperal infections with 10 deaths from 1,913 deliveries.[57] Anaerobes were present in eight of the deaths, three of which were associated with thrombophlebitis. They thought that the relatively small number of patients developing thrombophlebitis was due to prompt treatment of the uterine lesion. In any case where there was a profuse foul-smelling discharge they made a point, when they took their uterine culture, of removing retained products or clots digitally or with a blunt curette followed by a 1:4,000 potassium permanganate douche. In cases of thrombophlebitis they had hoped, on account of the saprophytic character of the organism in the non-invasive state, that its virulence might become exhausted; and that by supporting the patient with blood transfusions of 500ml or more, given early and repeated frequently, and keeping up her nutrition with forced feeding, the patient's life might be saved; but of four cases handled in this manner, only one recovered. They thought, from a review of the literature, that in future cases of pelvic thrombophlebitis due to anaerobic organisms they would attempt ligation of all of the pelvic veins, even though the results in Schottmüller's clinic had not been gratifying. Other modes of treatment which they used were intravenous analine dyes (mercurochrome and gentian violet), neoarsphenamine, autogenous vaccine, and anti-streptococcal serum.

A later paper from Washington gave extended experience to 1930, with a further 11 deaths from puerperal sepsis.[58] The conclusion was that anaerobic streptococcal infections would perhaps best be reduced by using some antiseptic preparation in the

---

[55] In a series of 150 cases, described in 1903, in which the temperature rose to 101°F or higher during the first 10 days of the puerperium, unidentified anaerobic bacteria were demonstrated in eight. J. Whitridge Williams, *Obstetrics*, New York and London, D. Appleton, 1903, p. 762.

[56] Otto Schwarz and William J. Dieckmann, 'Anaerobic streptococci: their role in puerperal infection', *South. med. J.*, 1926, **19**: 470–9.

[57] *Ibidem*, 'Puerperal infection due to anaerobic streptococci', *Am. J. Obstet. Gynec.*, 1927, **13**: 467–85.

[58] T. K. Brown, 'The incidence of puerperal infection due to anaerobic streptococci', ibid., 1930, **20**: 300–9.

98

vagina at the beginning of and during labour, although no particular agent could be recommended,[59] and that the subject would command one of the most important investigations in modern obstetrics.

Other American workers, namely John Harris and Howard Brown, from the Johns Hopkins Hospital, also investigated the bacteriology of the genital tract in pregnancy.[60] They collected 113 cases of streptococcal puerperal infection with approximately equal numbers of aerobic and anaerobic organisms, and emphasized the necessity of using anaerobic methods in suspected cases of such infection.

By this time the place of anaerobic infection in puerperal sepsis was being investigated in England, although initially this was in complete ignorance of the work already carried out in Germany and America. The researcher concerned was Leonard Colebrook, bacteriologist to Queen Charlotte's Hospital, London.[61]

Between 1923 and 1928 Colebrook investigated about 230 cases of severe and moderately severe puerperal fever. He isolated pyogenic streptococci from the blood or uterus in about two-thirds of them but was puzzled by cases that he encountered from time to time in which, in spite of frequent rigors and high pyrexia, the blood cultures were always negative. One such patient in 1928 had several weeks of irregular fever with almost daily rigors, but repeatedly negative blood cultures. Finally, by using a strictly anaerobic technique, he succeeded in isolating a gas-forming streptococcus which could not be subcultured aerobically. The woman eventually developed a large abscess with foul-smelling pus, from which he isolated the same organism.

From his experience with this patient Colebrook determined to investigate future cases of puerperal fever more carefully, with a view to detecting these infections if they should occur, and he made anaerobic cultures from the cervix of every case, modifying the routine procedure for blood cultures to favour the growth of strict anaerobes as well as aerobic organisms. He realized that uterine cultures might not give a reliable picture of the bacteria causing the sepsis, but accepted the evidence from blood cultures as indicating true infection.

From October 1928 until June 1930 he was able to investigate 76 cases of puerperal fever, as a result of which he had to change many of his beliefs about the nature of the infection. He reported a negative blood culture in 44 cases and positive in 34.[62] There was a pure growth of a haemolytic streptococcus in 12 with anaerobic cocci in 17, the remaining five positive cultures being different organisms. Of the positive anaerobic cultures, nine gave a pure culture of a single type of streptococcus, the other eight being polymicrobial. Most of the patients developing anaerobic infections had been subjected to some type of intrauterine manipulation, the commonest being manual removal of the placenta. In no case was the infection fulminating. The women were much less ill and the fever less sustained than in women infected with haemolytic

[59] As early as 1896, Charles Jewett had concluded that prophylactic vaginal douching as a routine measure was unnecessary, and even in skilled hands was probably injurious: 'The question of puerperal self-infection', *Am. gynaec. obstet. J.*, 1896, **8**: 417–29.

[60] John W. Harris and J. Howard Brown, 'A clinical and bacteriological study of 113 cases of streptococcal puerperal infection', *Bull. Johns Hopkins Hosp.*, 1929, **44**: 1–31.

[61] Leonard Colebrook, 'Infection by anaerobic streptococci in puerperal fever', *Lancet*, 1930, ii: 134–7.

[62] The figures in the original text do not add up to a correct total.

99

streptococci. They had frequent rigors but their general condition remained good with a slow pulse. When the infection was prolonged severe anaemia developed. Septic thrombus formation was frequent, often giving rise to abscesses from embolism by infected clot.

In September 1930 an isolation block was opened at Queen Charlotte's Hospital for the reception and treatment of cases of puerperal sepsis and five months later the accompanying laboratory began providing a full service. Leonard Colebrook realized that Queen Charlotte's Hospital, still situated in Marylebone at that time, was never likely to provide enough patients to make any study worthwhile. Accordingly, the co-operation was sought of the London County Council and of numerous County, Borough, District, and Town Councils in south-east England and even further afield, as well as general practitioners. All were asked if they would be prepared to send their patients to the Isolation Block to provide ample material for study.[63] Working with R. M. Fry, R. Hare, and Elizabeth Cooper, Colebrook was able to confirm his earlier impression, that infections by anaerobic streptococci were particularly prone to follow upon internal manipulations and exhausting labour.[64] Over the next three years more than 500 cases were admitted to the block, 60 per cent of them from outside the hospital.[65] Of in-patients transferred to the isolation block only 25 per cent were found to be infected with haemolytic streptococci, whilst over half of the district cases were so affected, an observation not in accord with the then-accepted view that the incidence of potentially serious infection was greater among women delivered in hospital than among those delivered in their own homes. It was established beyond doubt that anaerobic cocci were potentially pathogenic organisms.

The most constant pathological condition associated with anaerobic septicaemia was shown to be thrombophlebitis spreading upwards from the pelvic veins.[66] The cases were sporadic, with nothing to suggest epidemic spread.

With this work, the clinical picture of puerperal infection by non-sporing anaerobes normally resident in the woman's own genital tract became complete. The "self-infection" theory of Semmelweis was confirmed, together with the relationship of this type of infection to traumatic delivery and retained products. The question of whether healthy or diseased vaginal secretions could infect the woman had finally been answered.[67] The association between endogenous infection and obstetric intervention in labour also destroyed the view, popular with many doctors, that it was the woman who was to blame for infecting herself, rather than her medical attendants.

[63] Sir John Dewhurst, *Queen Charlotte's. The story of a hospital*, Privately printed, 1989, p. 187. It appears that some of the cases admitted were post-abortal rather than puerperal; a book of records of some of the early cases treated with sulphonamides, in the library of the Royal College of Obstetricians and Gynaecologists, includes one case following abortion out of a total of 23.

[64] Leonard Colebrook, 'Infection by anaerobic streptococci in puerperal fever', *Br. med. J.*, 1931, ii: 777.

[65] L. C. Rivett, Leslie Williams, Leonard Colebrook, and R. M. Fry, 'Puerperal fever—a report upon 533 cases received at the isolation block of Queen Charlotte's Hospital', *Proc. Roy. Soc. Med.*, 1933, 26: 1161–75.

[66] It was R. M. Fry, working in Leonard Colebrook's laboratories in the 1930s, who showed that each of the more common pyogenic organisms tended to produce its own characteristic pathological lesions.

[67] Jewett, op. cit., note 59 above, p. 418.

100

There remained one area in which the work done up to that time was incomplete—full knowledge of the organisms involved. This had to await improvements in the technical methods of culturing, isolating, and identifying non-sporing anaerobic bacteria.[68]

One feature of the septicaemic cases at Queen Charlotte's Hospital was that more than half of them yielded two or more bacterial types on blood culture. Leonard Colebrook, together with Ronald Hare, was able to detect four types, although they thought that one of them might have been a variant of one of the others. Another—type C—produced coal-black colonies on culture.[69] Schwarz and Dieckmann had frequently encountered a similar organism in their researches.[70] They called it an anaerobic streptococcus, and described it as a Gram negative cocco-bacillus which produced a black pigment, probably melanin on blood agar and had haemolytic properties. There seems little doubt that these organisms were not cocci but pigmented *Bacteroides*, now known to be a common infecting agent in pelvic sepsis.

The importance of *Bacteroides* in anaerobic infection was slow to gain recognition. The genus was named in 1919,[71] and isolated and described in 1921.[72] The first review of *Bacteroides* bacteraemia was not published until 1932; the authors could find references to only ten cases in the literature and added two of their own. Only one case, from 1927, was from a puerperal pelvic infection.[73] As late as 1967 Ronald Hare, Colebrook's co-worker and a recognized authority on anaerobic infection, reviewing recent advances, merely mentioned the suggestion by Dr Hildred Baker that synergism with anaerobic Gram negative bacilli, which were frequently present with anaerobic cocci, might be an important factor in the causation of puerperal fever.[74]

Another non-sporing anaerobe which could cause puerperal infection was described by Harris and Brown from the Johns Hopkins Hospital in 1927.[75] They named it *Actinomyces pseudonecrophorus*. In modern terminology, this is a fusobacterium—*F. necrophorum*.

PUERPERAL FEVER TODAY

Fatal puerperal sepsis is rarely seen nowadays in the developed world although, as discussed above, there has been a worrying resurgence of the more toxic species of the

[68] L. V. Holdeman and W. E. C. Moore, *Anaerobic laboratory manual*, Blacksburg, The Virginia Polytechnic Institute Anaerobe Laboratory and State University Anaerobe Laboratory, 1972.

[69] Leonard Colebrook and Ronald Hare, 'The anaerobic streptococci associated with puerperal fever', *J. Obstet. Gynaec. Br. Emp.*, 1933, **40**: 609–29.

[70] Op. cit., note 57 above, p. 471.

[71] A. Castellani and A. J. Chalmers, *Manual of tropical medicine*, London, Baillière Tindall, 1919, pp. 933, 937.

[72] Wade W. Oliver and William B. Wherry, 'Notes on some bacterial parasites of the human mucous membranes', *J. infect. Dis.*, 1921, **28**: 341–4.

[73] Luther Thompson and Donald C. Beaver, 'Bacteremia due to anaerobic gram-negative organisms of the genus *Bacteroides*', *Med. Clinics N. Am.*, 1932, **15**: 1611–26.

[74] Ronald Hare, 'The anaerobic cocci', in A. P. Waterson (ed.), *Recent advances in medical microbiology*, London, J. & A. Churchill, 1967, p. 306.

[75] John W. Harris and J. Howard Brown, 'Description of a new organism that may be a factor in the causation of puerperal infection', *Bull. Johns Hopkins Hosp.*, 1927, **40**: 203–15.

101

group A *β-haemolytic streptococcus* formerly associated with fever epidemics. When it occurs, sepsis is generally due to organisms different from those commonly implicated in the days before the introduction of sulphonamides and such later antimicrobial drugs as metronidazole, effective in the prevention as well as the cure of anaerobic infections. In England and Wales during the years 1982–4, the last period for which we have full information, there was not a single death from puerperal infection.[76]

Sepsis following delivery is still a cause for concern, particularly after Caesarean section, with febrile morbidity in 44 per cent,[77] and wound infection in up to 14 per cent of women.[78] Interest in the harmful effects of anaerobic infection on childbearing has largely switched to the time before delivery, when the presence of anaerobes in the vagina is associated with premature rupture of the membranes, pre-term labour, and amniotic fluid infection.[79]

In the developing world, post-partum infection remains a serious problem, and the availability of a large array of recent and potent antibiotics has not helped to diminish deaths from this cause.[80]

[76] Sir Alexander Turnbull et al., *Report on confidential enquiries into maternal deaths in England and Wales 1982–1984*, London, HMSO, 1989, p. 56.

[77] H. A. Hirsch, 'Prophylactic antibiotics in obstetrics and gynecology', *Am. J. Med.*, 1985, **78** (suppl. 6B): 170–6.

[78] B. R. Moir-Bussy, R. M. Hutton, and J. R. Thompson, 'Wound infection after Caesarean section', *J. hosp. Infect.*, 1984, **5**: 359–70.

[79] M. G. Gravitt et al., 'Independent associations of bacterial vaginosis and *Chlamydia trachomatis* infection with pregnancy outcome', *J. Am. med. Ass.*, 1986, **256**: 1899–1903.

[80] A. A. El Kady et al., 'Obstetric deaths in Menoufia Governorate, Egypt', *Br. J. Obstet. Gynaec.*, 1989, **96**: 9–14.

Other Disorders
and Diseases

Medical History, 1986, **30**: 1-41

DEATHS IN CHILDBED FROM
THE EIGHTEENTH CENTURY TO 1935

by

IRVINE LOUDON*

'A deep, dark and continuous stream of mortality.'[†]

INTRODUCTION

This paper is concerned solely with maternal mortality and not with maternal morbidity, neonatal mortality, or the stillbirth rate. Maternal mortality is expressed as the number of deaths per 1,000 births. "Births" meant "live births" until stillbirth registration was introduced in 1927; thereafter, it meant "total births", i.e. live + still births.

Maternal deaths were traditionally divided into two main groups: (1) associated deaths; (2) puerperal deaths. (They are now known as "indirect" and "direct" obstetric deaths.) (1) Associated deaths were deaths from some incidental illness (for example, phthisis, typhoid, or pneumonia) during pregnancy or the lying-in period. Associated deaths were included in most accounts of maternal deaths before death registration (1838) and in many private reports even in the second half of the nineteenth century. They were also included, at least partially, in some of the early reports of the Registrar General up to 1864. (2) Puerperal deaths were divided into two main groups. (A) Puerperal fever or puerperal sepsis - sometimes described as "metria" or "puerperal pyaemia" in the eighteenth and nineteenth centuries. (B) Accidents of childbirth, which consisted of all other puerperal causes of death. Deaths from haemorrhage (ante- or post-natal) and toxaemia (pre-eclampsia and eclampsia) were the two main groups.

Maternal deaths are deaths occurring in pregnancy, labour, or the lying-in period. The latter was not clearly defined before the mid-nineteenth century and some late deaths were included in early reports. Then it became the convention that the lying-in period was one month from birth: today, for registration purposes, it is six weeks.

For the purpose of this paper, factors which affected the level of maternal mortality are divided broadly into two groups. (1) Clinical factors which include every aspect of obstetric knowledge, education, care (including availability of care provided by midwives and medical practitioners). (2) Social and economic factors operating through their effect on the health of the mother.

*Irvine Loudon, DM, FRCGP, Wellcome Unit for the History of Medicine, 45-47 Banbury Road, Oxford OX2 6PE.

[†]William Farr in *39th report of the Registrar General for 1876*, 1878, p. 242.

THE MATERNAL MORTALITY RATE: AN ANOMALOUS STATISTIC

An examination of the maternal mortality rate from the mid-nineteenth century until 1935 leads to an unexpected conclusion. It is that the risk of a mother dying in childbirth, especially if she lived in the north of Britain rather than the south, remained substantially the same from 1850, and possibly from the early nineteenth century, until 1935. The maternal mortality remained undiminished in spite of changes in medical care and standards of living during this period. The main purpose of this paper is to examine the implications of this finding.

Today, maternal deaths are so rare that risk in obstetrics and standards of care are assessed by reference to the perinatal mortality rate.[1] Until the 1930s, however, the maternal mortality rate was the dominant statistic. The mean rate for the quinquennium 1856-60 was 4.6 per 1,000 births and it was the same not only for 1896-1900 but also for 1930-34. Between the mid-nineteenth century and the mid-1930s, the rate remained generally between four and five deaths per 1,000 births in England and Wales, although there were large regional variations (table 1 and fig. 1). In Scotland between 1850 and 1930, the rate was higher because associated deaths were included. There, the maternal mortality remained level for the first fifty years, but it actually increased from 1900 to 1930 from just under five per 1,000 births to well over six by 1930. This rise occurred within the category "accidents of childbirth"[2] (see fig. 5, p. 30).

The anxiety created by the absence of any improvement in maternal mortality is apparent in a memorable series of reports by William Farr published as letters to the Registrar General in the Registrar General's Reports. In 1875, Farr was moved to ask, "How long is this sacrifice of lives to go on?", and it was he who was chiefly responsible for presenting the facts of maternal mortality to the public and the medical profession not as an unfortunate and unavoidable fact of life, but as a growing scandal.[3] Farr's reports were followed by a long series of publications on maternal mortality, which included those by Williams in 1895-96 and 1904, Cullingworth in 1898, Bonney in 1918-19, Janet Campbell (and her colleagues) in 1924, 1932 and 1935, Munro Kerr in 1933, and Douglas and McKinley in 1935, as well as reports from the Ministry of Health and the Medical Research Council in the 1930s.[4]

---

[1]In 1982, the rates for England and Wales were: maternal mortality 11.9 per 100,000 total births (or 0.119 per thousand) and the perinatal mortality rate (= stillbirths and neonatal deaths) was 11.2 per 1,000 total births. *On the state of the public health. Report of the Chief Medical Officer*, DHSS 1983, London, HMSO. Hereinafter, *On the state of the public health*, although that title was only used for the second and subsequent reports, not the first.

[2]Within this group the main components of the increase were deaths from toxaemia, hyperemesis, and "other accidents of childbirth". There was no significant increase in deaths from haemorrhage or abortion or from associated diseases except for a brief sharp peak in the latter from influenza in 1918–19 accompanied by a corresponding increase in deaths from abortion at the same time. C.A. Douglas and P.L. McKinley, *Report of maternal morbidity and mortality in Scotland,* Edinburgh, Department of Health for Scotland, 1935.

[3]William Farr in *38th Report of the Registrar General for 1875*, 1877, p.234.

[4]W. Williams, 'Puerperal mortality', *Trans. Epidemiol. Soc. Lond.*, 1895–96, **15**: 100–133. *idem, Deaths in childbed*, London, H.K. Lewis, 1904. C.J. Cullingworth, 'On the undiminished mortality from puerperal fever in England and Wales', *Trans. Obstet. Soc. Lond.*, 1898, **39**: 91–114. Victor Bonney, 'The continued high mortality of childbearing', *Proc. R. Soc. Med.*, 1918–19, **12**(3): 75–107. Janet Campbell,

2

TABLE 1. MATERNAL MORTALITY

Deaths per 1000 births: 1847-1980. England and Wales. Quinquennial rates.

5-year period	Puerperal sepsis	Accidents of childbirth	Total
(1847-50)	1·9	3·9	5·8
1851-55	1·5	3·4	4·9
1856-60	1·5	3·0	4·6
1861-65	1·6	3·2	4·8
1866-70	1·5	3·1	4·6
1871-75	2·4	3·0	5·4
1876-80	1·7	2·2	3·9
1881-85	2·8	2·1	4·9
1886-90	2·4	2·1	4·5
1891-95	2·5	2·9	5·4
1896-00	2·0	2·6	4·6
1900-05	1·9	2·3	4·2
1906-10	1·6	2·2	3·8
1911-15	1·5	2·3	3·8
1916-20	1·6	2·3	3·9
1921-25	1·5	2·2	3·7
1926-30	1·8	2·2	4·0
1931-35	1·6	2·7	4·3
1936-40	0·77	2·47	3·24
1941-45	0·36	1·90	2·26
1946-50	0·14	0·95	1·09
1951-55	0·098	0·60	0·702
1956-60	0·06	0·37	0·43
1961-65	0·04	0·28	0·32
1966-70			0·27
1971-75			0·13
1976-80			0·12

Sources: Reports of the Registrar General, and *On The state of the public health;* reports of the Chief Medical Officer of the Ministry of Health and the Department of Health.

All these reports were concerned with the absence of any significant, let alone sustained, improvement in maternal mortality.[5] All were also convinced that many of the deaths could have been prevented.[6] Although there are no national statistics before 1838, data from a number of sources will be considered here which suggest that a similar level of maternal mortality may have prevailed from the early nineteenth century. If that is the case, there was little alteration in maternal mortality

'Maternal mortality', *Reports on public health and medical subjects*, No. 25, London Ministry of Health, 1924. *idem, Maternity services*, London, Faber, 1935. J. Campbell, I. D. Cameron, and D.M. Jones, 'High maternal mortality in certain areas', *Reports of public health and medical subjects*, No.68 London, Ministry of Health, 1932. J.M. Munro Kerr, *Maternal mortality and morbidity*, Edinburgh, E. & S. Livingstone, 1933. Douglas and McKinley, op. cit., note 2 above.

[5]"... in spite of the general and particular advance of the science and art of medicine in its application to childbirth and in spite of efforts made and arrangements designed to reduce this death rate, the mortality remains, on the whole, unimproved." *Interim report of the Departmental Committee on Maternal Mortality and Morbidity*, London, Ministry of Health, HMSO, 1932.

[6]"The death rate persists at the present unsatisfactory level chiefly because the essential factors prejudicial to betterment are permitted to continue - not because we are ignorant of them but because we have not sufficient determination to remove them." Munro Kerr, op. cit., note 4 above.

3

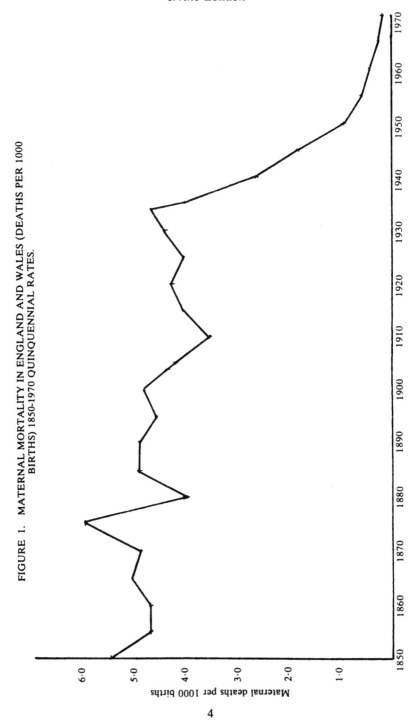

FIGURE 1. MATERNAL MORTALITY IN ENGLAND AND WALES (DEATHS PER 1000 BIRTHS) 1850-1970 QUINQUENNIAL RATES.

4

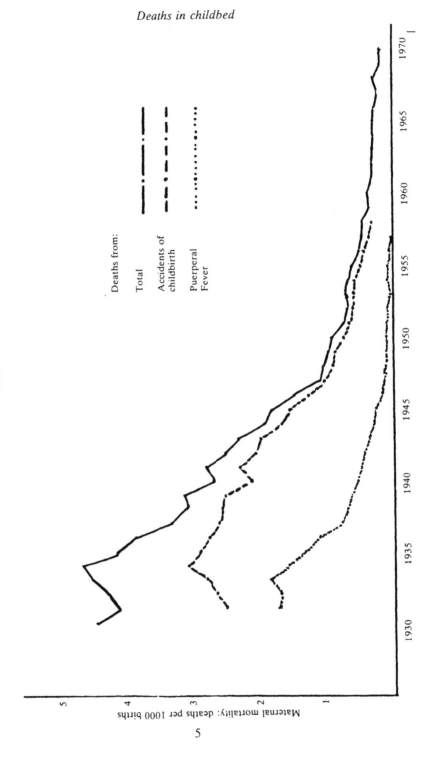

Deaths in childbed

FIGURE 2. MATERNAL MORTALITY ENGLAND AND WALES, 1930-1970 ANNUAL RATES

Deaths from:

Total

Accidents of childbirth

Puerperal Fever

Maternal mortality: deaths per 1000 births

5

199

for more than a century before the mid-1930s. It is not hard to understand why, for so long, the statistics of maternal mortality remained a continual reproach to the practitioners of obstetrics.

It was not until 1936 that maternal mortality rates began to fall.[7] When they did, the fall was sudden, profound, and sustained. There is no more remarkable change in any health statistic during the twentieth century (figs. 1 and 2). There can be little doubt that this change was initiated by the introduction of the sulphonamides,[8] but after the first few years it cannot have been the only factor. The reasons for the fall are discussed very briefly as a postscript to this paper, but a detailed discussion lies outside the scope of the study, which falls into three main sections.

In the first section the distribution of obstetric care between medical men and midwives is examined, and in the second, the position of obstetrics within the medical profession. Both are essential preliminaries to the third and main section in which an examination of the statistics is used as a means of investigating the standards of maternal health and obstetric care between the beginning of the nineteenth century and 1935.

WHO UNDERTOOK THE DELIVERIES?

Before 1730, midwives enjoyed a virtual monopoly of normal midwifery in London and probably an absolute monopoly in the provinces. The traditional view is that man-midwifery was rare or nonexistent before the early eighteenth century.[9] Wilson, however, has shown convincingly that the term "man-midwife" was used in England in the early seventeenth century and that man-midwifery was probably a more or less routine part of surgical practice throughout that century. Nevertheless, the role of the surgeon was almost certainly that of intervention in abnormal labours when instruments were required.[10] The remarkable innovation of the 1730s was the attendance of medical practitioners at normal labours which they had agreed to attend beforehand. Until that period, it is reasonable to assume that most surgeons had little or no experience of normal labours, and, indeed, the mechanism of labour was not understood.[11]

[7]W. Taylor and M. Dauncey, 'Changing pattern of mortality in England and Wales. II. Maternal mortality', *Br. J. prevent. soc. Med.*, 1954, 8, 172–175, concluded that 1937 was "the first year of sustained decline" in maternal mortality. They analysed the falls separately for deaths from puerperal sepsis, haemorrhage, and toxaemia and concluded that the introduction of prontosil was "one of the rare situations which endorse the identification of an agency of major importance as contributory to a statistical trend".

[8]The first sulphonamide to be used in clinical practice (by E. Anselm in 1935) was prontosil. The classic paper on the treatment of puerperal fever with this drug was Leonard Colebrook and Méave Kenny, 'Treatment with prontosil of puerperal infections due to haemolytic streptococci', *Lancet*, 1936, ii: 1319–1322. In this, they showed that treated patients suffered a mortality rate of four per cent compared to twenty per cent for untreated patients. Fortunately, over ninety-five per cent of puerperal infections were sulphonamide-sensitive. Colebrook and Kenny presented their results with commendable caution. See F. Hawking and J. Stewart Lawrence, *The sulphonamides*, London, H.K. Lewis, 1950.

[9]See especially J.H. Aveling, *English midwives*, London, 1872; J. Glaister, *Dr William Smellie and his contemporaries*, Glasgow, 1894; Jean Donnison, *Midwives and medical men*, London, Heinemann, 1977, Herbert R. Spencer, *The history of British midwifery from 1650–1800*, London, John Bale, 1927, and for interesting sidelights on midwifery care there is much scattered information in Sarah Stone, *A complete practice of midwifery*, London, 1737.

[10]Adrian Wilson, 'Childbirth in seventeenth- and eighteenth- century England', University of Sussex, DPhil thesis, 1984.

6

Why this remarkable change should have occurred when it did is debatable. As Wilson points out, "fashion and forceps" is the traditional explanation. In other words, that just as surgeons were becoming more fashionable, forceps were discovered in 1730[12] and conferred great power and prestige on the man-midwife. At the same time, the establishment of lying-in hospitals, dominated by medical men, advertised the place of men in midwifery.[13] According to this view, forceps were the key to understanding the beginning of obstetrics as a branch of medicine. But the explanation is unsatisfactory. An alternative explanation may be the change that was taking place in the rank-and-file practitioners. About 1730, the surgeon-apothecary experienced a substantial rise in status and prosperity as he expanded his activities and looked for new openings in the thriving business of medical practice.[14] Man-midwifery was an additional source of income and an excellent way to acquire and to keep a practice of regular patients. The expansion in the activity of the rank-and-file practitioners was accompanied by a demand for better medical education. Hospital training commenced around the middle of the eighteenth century and it was often combined with attendance at private courses in midwifery. Smellie arrived in London in 1739 and began teaching.[15] One of his pupils was Richard Kay from Lancashire, who attended two courses of midwifery with Smellie in 1744.[16] Kay's account of a course consisting of lectures followed by attendance at labours, first with Smellie and then on his own, must be one of the earliest accounts of a system of training which became routine by the nineteenth century.

Between 1750 and 1800, medical practitioners had established themselves as the proper attendants at all complicated labours and at as many normal ones as women would choose to employ them. While the opportunities for obstetric training increased rapidly for medical students, for midwives it remained with very few exceptions simply a process of "picking up" the art from the older woman.[17] The

---

[11]When the midwife Sarah Stone practised in Bridgewater and Taunton between 1702 and c. 1730, there were no men-midwives, just as there was none during the time of her mother, Mrs Holmes. When, c.1730, she moved to Bristol, she found to her intense disgust that "every young MAN who hath serviced his apprenticeship to a Barber-Surgeon, immediately sets up for a Man-Midwife; although as ignorant, and indeed, much ignoranter than the meanest Woman of the Profession". Sarah Stone was witnessing the incursion of men into "her profession" and thus the start of the medicalization of childbirth. Stone, op. cit., note 9 above.

[12]The time when forceps were first used in England is uncertain. They were invented by the Chamberlens and kept secret for three generations, but there is evidence of their possession, if not their use, by a surgeon in Brentford in Middlesex in the late seventeenth or early eighteenth century. Their design was published in England for the first time in 1730 and thereafter they were widely known and used. (Wilson, op. cit., note 10 above.) However, evidence from Somerset shows they were not known or used by surgeons in Bridgewater as late as 1800. (Jonathan Toogood, 'On the practice of midwifery, with remarks', *Prov. med. sur. J.*, 1844, 103–108.) This suggests that the spread of the use of forceps in provincial England may have been slower than generally realized.

[13]The first lying-in hospital in England was the General Lying-In Hospital, established in 1739. The Lying-In Hospital, Dublin (The Rotunda), was established in 1745, and the first voluntary general hospital to open maternity wards was the Middlesex Hospital in London in 1747.

[14]I. Loudon, 'The nature of provincial medical practice in eighteenth-century England', *Med. Hist.*, 1985, 29: 1–32.

[15]Glaister, op. cit., note 9 above.

[16]W. Brockbank and F. Kenworthy (editors), *The Diary of Richard Kay (1716—51) of Baldingstone, near Bury*, Manchester, Chetham Society, 1968.

[17]In 1806, a medical practitioner in Suffolk wrote to say that three female practitioners had settled in the county "after hearing a course of lectures [on midwifery] in London". They were the first to have done so

7

licensing of midwives by bishops, (which never contributed substantial numbers) ceased during the eighteenth century,[18] and the competence and education of women who adopted the role of midwife varied widely;[19] but the only possible definition of midwives before the Midwives' Act of 1902 - a definition that says nothing about background or training - is that they were women who earned their living partly or entirely by the practice of midwifery and were recognized within their community for the possession of expertise in deliveries.

It is certain that the number of medical men practising midwifery increased rapidly between 1730 and 1800, and that the midwives bitterly resented this invasion of what they believed was their territory. John Blunt was one of a number of laymen and medical men who joined forces with the midwives to attack man-midwifery. In 1793 he complained that "... there are 99 men-midwives for one midwife, and that the male practitioners are still increasing insomuch that five new ones (some men and some boys) have set up in one street near my house, within 200 yards of each other, during the last six months."[20] It is likely that this was a gross exaggeration; but his statement underlines the increase in the involvement of medical practitioners in midwifery.

From the middle of the eighteenth century, therefore, the following options were available to pregnant women: delivery at home by a medical practitioner or by a midwife; delivery as an in-patient in a lying-in hospital; or as an out-patient under the care of a dispensary or lying-in charity; or unattended delivery, meaning that labour took place in the absence of any "professional" (in the widest sense of that term) assistance. Unattended deliveries were still the rule in North Wales,[21] and probably elsewhere in Britain, even at the end of the nineteenth century.

There are, in fact, no accurate data for the distribution of deliveries in each of the above categories, although Munro Kerr in 1933 suggested a simple answer to the question "Who undertook the deliveries from the eighteenth to the twentieth century?". Before 1750, he suggested, midwives predominated. From 1750 to 1900, general practitioners delivered the majority of women, including most of the poor in the industrial areas. From the introduction of the Midwives' Act in 1902, midwives slowly began to regain the majority of deliveries in the urban areas, at least amongst the poor.[22] This version, however, is too simple.

---

and were thus exceptional. (See note 23 below)

[18] Spencer, op. cit., note 9 above.

[19] Aveling, op. cit., note 9 above. D.N. Harley, 'Ignorant midwives - a persistent stereotype', *Bull. Soc. soc. Hist. Med.*, 1981, **28**: 6–9; Adrian Wilson, 'Ignorant midwives, a rejoinder', ibid., June 1983, **32**: 46–49; and Bernice Boss and Jeffrey Boss, 'Ignorant midwives, a further rejoinder', ibid., December 1983, **33**: 71.

[20] John Blunt, *Man-midwifery dissected*, London, S.W. Fores, 1793, pp. 48–49. (John Blunt was the pseudonym of the Piccadilly bookseller S.W. Fores.) See also: Leading article 'Sir Anthony Carlisle and man-midwifery', *Lancet*, 1826–27, 177–179, 456–461; 'Proprietas', *Address to the public on the propriety of midwives instead of surgeons practising midwifery*, London, 1826; Anon. *Observations on the impropriety of men being employed in the business of midwifery*, London, Hunt & Clarke, 1827; M. Adams, *Man-midwifery exposed*, London, S.W. Fores, 1830; John Stevens, *Man-midwifery exposed*, London, 1849; W. Talley, *He, or man-midwifery*, London, 1863; Anon., *The accoucheuse and the accoucheur*, London, Cauldwell, 1864.

[21] *38th Report of the Registrar General for 1875*, 1877, p.234.

[22] Munro Kerr, op. cit., note 4 above, pp. xxiii-xiv.

8

In 1806, for example, a number of reports of practice in the provinces were published, some of which included relative numbers of midwives and medical men.[23] In Nottingham, for instance, there were at the beginning of the nineteenth century "15 surgeon-apothecaries all practising as men-midwives, and 11 midwives all uninstructed". In "the district of Nottinghamshire", however, there were "25 surgeon-apothecaries all undertaking midwifery and 123 midwives, all uninstructed".[24] This report was in general confirmed by accounts from other provincial areas.

Matthew Flinders (1750-1802) of Donington in Lincolnshire, who practised as a surgeon-apothecary, was probably a typical country practitioner of the last quarter of the eighteenth century. He undertook normal midwifery on a routine basis and recorded in his diary his attendance at many normal labours, always noting the time he arrived at the patient's house and the time he left. In 1775, he attended forty-three deliveries, staying at the bedside from the onset of labour until its completion, often for twelve hours or more. In March 1775, he attended two cases in succession and noted that he "had not been in bed or my boots off for 40 hours". All except a few of the cases were described as "easy", "normal", or "excellent" labours, or at worst as "lingering" ones. None died. Although he regarded midwifery as tiring and tedious, and not well paid (half a guinea to one guinea a delivery), he saw it as central to his practice as a country surgeon and feared the competition of local midwives.[25] Nevertheless, medical practitioners in England and Wales as a whole never obtained a monopoly of midwifery.

In 1843, one writer asserted that "A larger proportion of the 500,000 English women who lie in every year *and have any attendance at all* [my italics] are attended by midwives."[26] A report by a committee of the Obstetrical Society of London published in 1870 and 1871 included a description of the relative numbers of poor women attended in labour either by midwives or by medical men.[27] There were large variations. In villages, the number attended routinely by midwives varied from thirty to ninety per cent. In small non-manufacturing towns - i.e., market towns - midwives attended at most ten per cent, nearly all being delivered by medical practitioners. In the large manufacturing towns, attendance by midwives was the rule, amounting to seventy-five to ninety per cent of all deliveries amongst the poor. In a large majority of deliveries amongst the poor in South Wales, especially in the industrial areas, midwives attended; in North Wales deliveries were said to be unattended, or attended only by "ignorant old women".[28] In London, fifty per cent of deliveries in

---

[23]These reports were the published replies to a questionnaire sent out by Dr Edward Harrison of Horncastle, Lincs., in connexion with his plans for medical reform. They were published in *Med. chirurg. Rev.*, 1806, **13**.

[24]Ibid., pp. CI–CIII.

[25]Lincolnshire Archives Office, Lincoln. The diaries of Matthew Flinders, surgeon of Donington, Lincolnshire (1775–1802). His eldest son of the same name was the famous explorer and hydrographer whose name is to be found in Flinders Bay, Flinders River, and Flinders Island in Eastern Australia, as well as Flinders University.

[26]Leading article, 'Deaths in childbirth', *Lond. med. Gaz.*, new series, **1**: 1843–44, 747–749.

[27]'Report of the Infantile Mortality Committee of the Obstetrical Society of London', *Trans. Obstet. Soc. Lond.*, 1870, **12**: 132–149; 1871, **13**: 388–403.

[28]Williams (1904), op. cit., note 4 above, p.33.

9

the East End were attended by midwives, but in the West End, two per cent or less, and in the suburbs - Wimbledon, for example - five per cent or less.

The Report of the Select Committee on Midwives' Registration in 1892, underlined the uncertainty about the number of midwives.[29] The census of 1881 gave 2,646 as the number of women professing to act as midwives. But the committee was presented with estimates of between 10,000 and 20,000 as the true figure, and concluded that as many as 450,000 out of a total of about 800,000 deliveries took place solely under the care of midwives.[30] Mr Haywood, a general practitioner and medical officer of health from Lancashire, said that in his district "scarcely a fifth of the confinements are attended at any stage by a doctor; the work is done by women who practise as midwives".[31] So large were local differences that it is extremely difficult to reconstruct a picture of midwifery for England and Wales as a whole in the nineteenth century. But a very large majority of the medical practitioners who undertook midwifery were general practitioners. The number who could be described in the modern sense as specialists or consultants, although they are prominent in the obstetric literature, were far fewer than consultant physicians and surgeons. Even by the end of the nineteenth century, as Dr Aveling commented in 1892, rarely, if ever, would one find - even in London - private practitioners who depended on midwifery alone. If anyone attempted to do so, he added, "I think it would kill him very soon".[32] Instead, the consultant was a practitioner who, while undertaking a large amount of midwifery, combined it with practice as a physician, surgeon, or general practitioner.

THE MEDICAL CORPORATIONS, THE GENERAL PRACTITIONERS, AND ATTITUDES TO MIDWIFERY

Midwifery cut across the traditional boundaries of the tripartite division of the medical profession. By the end of the eighteenth century, it was practised by a few physicians, some hospital surgeons, and a large majority of surgeon-apothecaries. But midwifery lay outside physic, surgery, and pharmacy and was thus not accepted by any of the medical corporations. The College of Physicians asserted their responsibility for disorders of women before and after labour, but not during it. Intra-partum care was a manual operation, and the essential messiness and immodesty of delivering a baby made it, in the view of the President of the College, unsuitable for a gentleman with a university education.[33] In 1783, the College introduced a licence in the *ars obstetrica*, which it conferred on a few physician

[29]*Select Committee on Midwives' Registration*, PP 1892, **XIV**, p.144.
[30]The estimate — fifty-six per cent of deliveries by midwives— is close to the estimate of Munro Kerr in 1933 of sixty per cent for England: in Scotland the corresponding figure was thirty per cent.
[31]Loc. cit., note 29 above, Q.931. Fifteen years later, it was estimated that fifty per cent of women in England and Wales were delivered by midwives. Examples of regional variation were the following percentages of midwife deliveries: Newcastle upon Tyne 11.2%; London 25%; West Riding, Yorks, 35%; Hertford 39.5%; Lancaster 49.9%; Liverpool 52%; Manchester 60.9%; Derby 62.5%; Salford 76.5%; Gloucester 83.6%; St Helens 93%; Lancashire, urban districts 50.8% - rural districts 30.9%. *Report of the Departmental Committee appointed by the Lord President of the Council to consider the working of the Midwives Act 1902*, PP 1909, **XXXIII**, para. 23.
[32] Loc. cit., note 29 above Q.341.
[33]Select Committee on Medical Education, PP 1834, **XIII**, Q.232.

10

man-midwives before it was discontinued in 1800. This licence, however, was no more than a kind of honorary conferment and implied no responsibility on the part of the College for the teaching of midwifery or the examination of candidates.[34] The Royal College of Surgeons in London, established in 1800, was a new institution intent on creating a small tight élite of London hospital surgeons. They held the practice of both midwifery and pharmacy (the hallmarks of the general practitioner) in contempt. To practise either was to be excluded from office or position within the College. The senior members of the Society of Apothecaries, essentially a City company concerned with the wholesale drug market, had little clinical experience of any kind, least of all in midwifery. In spite of administering the licence held by most general practitioners, the Society was the least suited of the three corporations to take midwifery under its wing.

Responsibility for midwifery fell, therefore, to the general practitioners when they emerged under that name in the second and third decades of the nineteenth century, proclaiming themselves as "general practitioners in physic, surgery, pharmacy *and* midwifery". From 1815, it was customary for most general practitioners to hold the Licence of the Society of Apothecaries and the diploma of Membership of the College of Surgeons. At first, neither qualification included an examination in midwifery, so that it was alone in that "there are no means of ascertaining the qualifications of persons who take it in charge".[35] The history of the education of the general practitioner from 1815 was notable for an ever-increasing emphasis on the biological sciences, physic, surgery, and pathology. Obstetrics had to struggle desperately for a proper place in the curriculum.

In 1827, twelve years after it was introduced, the Licence of the Society of Apothecaries included for the first time the requirement that students should have attended two courses of lectures on midwifery, and the revised regulations in 1835 added "practical instruction" to this requirement. But there was never a separate examination. Instead, from 1827, the examination in the Principles and Practice of Medicine included questions on the pregnant and puerperal woman and diseases of children. The Royal College of Surgeons in London introduced a Diploma in Midwifery in 1852. In 1876, three women - Sophia Jex-Blake, Miss Thorne and Miss Pechey - applied to take the examination, and the examiners resigned rather than examine them. London introduced a separate examination in midwifery for the final MB in 1841, and the conjoint examination of the Colleges of Physicians and Surgeons did the same, but not until 1884.[36]

A.B. Granville established the Obstetrical Society of London in 1825 "to raise to a proper and dignified status, the practitioners in midwifery".[37] (The society faded out

---

[34]Sir George Clark, *A history of the Royal College of Physicians of London*, vol.2, Oxford, Clarendon Press, 1966. See also for a justifiably caustic comment on the Royal College of Physicians. E. Harrison, *Remarks on the ineffective state of the practice of physic*, London, 1806, p.13. In 1804, the College introduced a regulation whereby anyone practising as a physician-accoucheur was barred from election as a Fellow.

[35]A.B. Granville, correspondence, *Lancet*, 1830–31, i: 301–302.

[36]For a detailed account of the regulations of the Licence of the Society of Apothecaries see 'Society of Apothecaries: intelligence', *Med. quart. Rev.*, 1835, 4; 511–518. For the College of Surgeons' Diploma in Midwifery and the Sophia Jex Blake affair, see Sir Zachary Cope, *The Royal College of Surgeons of England, a history*, London, Anthony Blond, 1959, chs. 14 and 15, pp.121–132.

11

and was re-established in 1858.) This, together with the details of examinations given above, simply underlines the low regard for obstetrics which sprang from the rejection of midwifery by the medical corporations. Donnison has described how obstetricians were snubbed in society by people who would consider physicians and surgeons as socially acceptable.[38]

Thus obstetrics was regarded, even at the end of the nineteenth century, as an "extra" not worthy of the time devoted by students to the study of physic, surgery, or the pre-clinical sciences. Dr Elizabeth Garrett Anderson in 1898 saw a direct connexion between the low status of midwifery and the high rate of maternal mortality:

> It is unfortunately true that the puerperal mortality all over England is higher than it ought to be.... The responsibility for this rests in great measure with the examining bodies. When they recognise that a sound and extensive knowledge of practical midwifery is infinitely more important to a practitioner than a minute acquaintance with organic chemistry and with the refinements of physiology there will be a chance of improvement, but not till then . . . . If every medical student were compelled to spend six months in acquiring skill in midwifery, the puerperal mortality all over the country would soon approach that which I think it is at the present moment in the London maternity charities, namely, about 1 in 500.[39]

In spite of its poor rating in medical schools, general practitioners embraced the practice of midwifery. It rapidly became the accepted wisdom that the key to success as a family doctor lay in the successful practice of midwifery. "The successful practice of midwifery... at the outset of life as surely establishes a professional man's reputation as the contrary retards his progress", wrote a Bridgewater practitioner in 1844.[40] Likewise, a maternal death was the most tragic and disturbing event in general practice. Even when such deaths were common, they could ruin a reputation. "The unfortunate termination of a surgical or medical case", wrote a general practitioner in 1809, "will in time be forgotten; but the *unlucky* death of a midwifery patient (and chance has too great an influence in these cases) begets the greatest distrust, and often ruins his reputation and future prospects for ever".[41]

John Greene Crosse of Norwich, well known as a hospital surgeon, spent much of his time attending midwifery cases, both as the normal attendant and through being called in by other practitioners as a consultant. One of the first he attended, just after arriving in Norwich in 1815, happened to die of sepsis through no fault of Crosse's.

---

[37] Augustus Bozzi Granville (1783–1872), the son of the postmaster general in Milan, came to London in 1817 to practise medicine. Sir Walter Farquhar advised him to go to Paris for a year to learn midwifery, and on his return, Granville was appointed physician-accoucheur to the Westminster General Dispensary. He wrote extensively on obstetrics and was the founder of the Obstetrical Society of London. On the latter see *Report of the Select Committee on Medical Education*, PP 1834, **XIII**, evidence of Sir Charles Clark, Q.4179–4220.

[38] Donnison, op. cit., note 9 above, pp.42–43

[39] Elizabeth Garrett Anderson, 'Deaths in childbirth', *Br. med. J.*, 1898, **ii**: 839–840, 927.

[40] Toogood, op. cit., note 12 above. Until recently, it was common for vacant partnerships or assistantships in general practice to include the words "midwifery essential".

[41] 'H' (Letter) *Med. phys. J.*, 1809, **21**: 382–385. Amongst the labouring classes of the nineteenth century there seems to have been a fatalistic acceptance of infant mortality, possibly because of the large families. Thus the statement of a mother, for instance, that she had borne nine children and "lost" five in childhood, was a commonplace. The same fatalism did not apply to maternal deaths. Midwives and medical men tended to be held directly responsible for the tragedy of a dead mother.

12

Unfortunately, through his attendance on this case he was unable to attend a poor woman whom he had promised to deliver free of charge. The latter was therefore delivered by an "ignorant old woman" and came to no harm. This episode so damaged his reputation that it was over three years before he could begin to build what was to become a very large practice in midwifery.[42] The readiness with which the practitioner was blamed was confirmed at the end of the century by Dr Rentoul:

> When a hearse follows us into a street after a confinement it is most likely to ruin our practice in that particular street; for the nurses and others begin saying that puerperal fever has followed us. We are accused first, the nurse next, and after that the house, the sanitary arrangements . . . .. It comes to this that practically every doctor who loses a confinement case receives very great blame, no matter whether he deserves it or not, very serious blame indeed.[43]

Midwifery was essential to retain the patients in general practice, but it was risky, anxious, time-consuming, and, in view of the hours spent, not profitable financially.[44] Moreover, it was undertaken against a background of poor obstetric education. Most who started in general practice had only the dimmest idea of the conduct of normal, let alone complicated, labours, and learnt by hard and often bitter experience. The opinion of Mr Brown, MRCS, LSA, was echoed over and over again by his fellow practitioners: "I have no hesitation in saying, after more than thirty years' experience as student and practitioner that midwifery is the most anxious and trying of all medical work and to be successfully practised calls for more skill, care and presence of mind on the part of the medical man than any other branch of medicine."[45]

The concept of the general practitioner as the family doctor, which grew steadily through the second half of the nineteenth century, was centred around the delivery of the baby.[46] The young family doctor would deliver the baby, and, if it was a girl, attend her through infancy and childhood and inquire tenderly after her progress until she, too, engaged him to deliver the next generation of the family. A general practitioner might loathe the long night vigils and the anxiety of midwifery, but he had to conform. Small wonder, therefore, that general practitioners were so possessive about midwifery. Their opposition to the Midwives' Act is not one of the happier episodes in the history of general practice, but it is easy to understand the roots of their opposition.[47]

MATERNAL MORTALITY BEFORE 1850

There are no reliable estimates of maternal mortality before, at the earliest, the late eighteenth century. Eccles suggested an average rate of twenty-one per 1,000

---

[42]Library of the Wellcome Institute for the History of Medicine. The midwifery notebooks of John Greene Crosse of Norwich. MS. 1916, 1917. Another important account of midwifery in the pre-registration period is the notebook of Richard Paxton of Maldon in Essex for the period 1760–99, in the same library, MS 3820.

[43]Loc. cit., note 29 above, Q.361 and 466.

[44]In the 1890s, however, when midwives' fees were from 2s. 6d. to 10s. per case, doctors amongst the poor would sometimes charge as little as 5s. to 7s. 6d. for a midwifery case, payable by instalments. Ibid., p.415. These fees were substantially lower than those charged by medical practitioners in the late-eighteenth century when half a guinea was the lowest and one guinea was common.

[45]Ibid., Q.1660.

[46]I. Loudon, 'The concept of the family doctor', *Bull. His. Med.*, 1984, **58**: 347–362.

[47]Donnison. op. cit., note 9 above. ch. 6, is a notable account of the opposition to the Midwives' Act.

13

births for London between 1657 and 1700, with wide annual variations.[48] Willmott
Dobbie estimated a rate of between 24.4 and 29.4 per thousand baptisms in three
Somerset parishes between the sixteenth and eighteenth centuries.[49] M.C. Buer
quoted values of 16.7 per 1,000 in 1760 and 15 per 1,000 in 1781 as the maternal
mortality based on the London Bills.[50] Charles White of Manchester believed that
maternal mortality in London was 13.9 per 1,000 from 1737-1772, 12.5 per 1,000 in
Northampton between 1754 and 1772, while in Manchester it fell from 9.6 per 1,000
from 1754-59 to 8.3 per 1,000   for 1759-65 and to only 5.1 per 1,000 in
1771.[51]

TABLE 2. DOMICILIARY MIDWIFERY IN THE NINETEENTH CENTURY.

Reports from private practice showing the author, his status, the period in which the deliveries took place,
the number of deliveries, the forceps rate and the maternal mortality.

Author and date of publication	Professional status	Period in which the deliveries took place	Number of deliveries	Forceps rate	Maternal mortality per 1000 deliveries
1. S. Merriman 1814	Physician accoucheur	—	1800	0·6%	5·0
2. E. Copeman 1841-42	General practitioner Norfolk	1835-41	840	—	2·3
3. J Waddington 1843-44	General practitioner Margate	1788-1844	2159	0·1%	0·9
4. J. Toogood 1844	Physician accoucheur Bridgewater	c. 1810-17	1135	1·3%	7·0
5. C. Earle 1846	Surgeon Norfolk	1800-46	4320	—	3·9
6. Anderson Smith 1859	General practitioner	—	1300	2%	0·8
7. Robert Dunn 1859-60	General practitioner	1831-50	4049	0·5%	6·7
8. Wm. Farr 1870 quoting	Mr Rigden General practitioner Canterbury	1860s	4390	—	2·05
9. Fleetwood Churchill 1872	Consultant obstetrician	1831-70	2547	1·6%	6·6
10. H.W. Bailey 1860	General practitioner Thetford	1808-58	6476	1·7%	2·3

[48]Audrey Eccles, 'Obstetrics in the seventeenth and eighteenth centuries and its implication for
maternal and infant mortality', *Bull. Soc. soc. Hist. Med.*, 1977, **20**: 8–11.
[49]B.M. Willmott Dobbie, 'An attempt to estimate the true rate of maternal mortality, sixteenth to
eighteenth centuries', *Med. Hist.*, 1982, **26**: 79–90.
[50]M.C. Buer, *Health, wealth and population in the early days of the Industrial Revolution*, London,
Routledge, 1926, p.147.
[51]Charles White, *A treatise on the management of pregnant and lying-in women*, London, 1772.

14

Deaths in childbed

Author and date of publication	Professional status	Period in which the deliveries took place	Number of deliveries	Forceps rate	Maternal mortality per 1000 deliveries
11. S. Lawrence 1862-63	General practitioner Montrose	—	1000	—	5·0
12. Dr. Thomson 1867-68	General practitioner Wanbury, Chesire	1850-68	2200	—	0·9
13. Grailly Hewitt 1868	Consultant obstetrician	1846-66	2438	—	10·2
14. W.T. Greene 1878	General practitioner	1869-77	1500	—	8·0
15. E. Copeman* 1874	Consultant obstetrician Norfolk	c. 1850-74	216	2·7%	83·0
16. H.C. Rose** 1876	General practitioner Hampstead	—	1250	0·7%	1·6

* All cases "attended in consultation . . . therefore of an unusually severe or complicated character". None "attended alone as ordinary cases of midwifery". Compare the results achieved by the same author as a young general practitioner: 2, above.

** "The majority of cases amongst the well-to-do people . . . *none* amongst the paupers."

N.B. The results recorded by consultant obstetricians include complicated cases to which the consultant was called either by a midwife, or, more usually, by a general practitioner. They therefore could be expected to show a higher mortality rate than the cases of general practitioners.

Sources:

1. S. Merriman, *A synoposis of the various kinds of difficult kinds of parturition,* London, Callow, 1814.
2. E. Copeman, 'Report on midwifery in private practice', *Prov. med. Surg. J.* 1834, 3.
3. Joshua Waddington, 'Statistics of midwifery', *Lond. Med. Gaz.,* 1843-44, **2**: 144-145.
4. Jonathan Toogood, 'On the practice of midwifery with remarks', *Prov. med. surg. J.,* 1844, 103-108.
5. C. Earle, 'Report on obstetric cases occuring in private practice', ibid., 1846, 261-263
6. Anderson Smith, '1300 midwifery cases attended in private practice', *Lancet,* 1859, **i**: 481.
7. Robert Dunn, 'On the statistics of midwifery from the records of private practice', *Trans. Obstet. Soc. Lond.* 1859-60, **1**: 279-297.
8. W. Farr, *Report of the Registrar General for 1870,* p.410.
9. Fleetwood Churchill, 'Report of private obstetric practice for twenty-nine years', *Dublin J. med. Sci.,* 1872, **53**: 525-540.
10. H.W. Bailey, 'Statistics of midwifery'. *Trans. Obstet. Soc. Lond.,* 1860, **2**: 299-307.
11. S. Lawrence, 'Statistical report of 1000 midwifery cases', *Edinb. med. J.* 1862-63, **8**: 712-724, 800-814.
12. Dr Thomson, 'A few notes on country obstetric practice', *Edinb. med. J.,* 1867-68, **13**: 69-71.
13. Grailly Hewitt, 'On puerperal fever', *Trans. Obstet. Soc. Lond.,* 1868, **10**: 69-92.
14. W.T. Greene, 'A synoposis of one thousand consecutive labours', ibid., 1878, **19**: 204-217.
15. E. Copeman, 'Statistical and practical remarks on consultation midwifery in private practice', ibid., 1874, **16**: 103-110.
16. Henry Cooper Rose, 'A contribution to the statistics of midwifery in private practice', ibid., 1876, **18**: 146-159.

15

TABLE 3. MATERNAL MORTALITY.

Mortality rates, expressed as deaths per 1000 births, recorded at domicilliary deliveries: dispensaries, lying-in (out-patient) charities, and the out-patient divisions of certain lying-in hospitals

Source	Institution	Period of deliveries	No. of deliveries	Forceps rate ‰	Maternal mortality (deaths per 1000 deliveries)
1. Robert Bland (1781)	Westminster General Dispensary	1774-80	1,897	0·2‰	3·7
2. A.B. Granville (1822)	,,	1819	687	0·7‰	5·8
3. A.B. Granville (1860)	,,	1848-59	7,717		2·2
A.B. Granville (1860)	Benevolent Institution	1848-59	4,761		1·6
4. T. H. Bickerton (1936)	Liverpool Ladies Charity	early 1800s	6,101		1·3
5. F.M. Ramsbotham (1829)	E. District of the Royal Maternity Charity*	1828	2,400	0·1‰	3·0
6. F.M. Ramsbotham (1843-44)	,,	1831-43	35,743		4·6
7. J. Hall Davis	W. District of the Royal Maternity Charity*	1842-64	13,783		1·96
8. Select Committee on Midwives Registration (1892)	Royal Maternity Charity*	1867-91	84,467		average 2·5 range 1·5–3·6
9. Select Committee on Midwives Registration (1892)	Out-patient divisions of:				
	City of London Lying-in Hospital	1889			1·3
	Queen Charlotte's Hospital	1889			0·8
	British Lying-in Hospital	1889			1·6
	General Lying-in Hospital	1889			1·8
10. Sir George Newman	Queen's Institute Midwives	1924-33	over 600,000		1·9

*The Royal Maternity Charity covered an area of three miles' radius around St Paul's Cathedral, and was divided into South, East, and West divisions, each under the charge of a physician-accoucheur. In the 1880s, the percentage of deliveries to which a medical practitioner was called lay between three and four per cent. Otherwise, the patients were under the sole care of trained midwives.

Sources:

1. Bland, op. cit., footnote 52.
2. Granville, op. cit., footnote 53.
3. A.B. Granville, 'Phenomena, facts and calculations connected with the power and act of propagation in females of the industrial classes in the metropolis institutions', *Trans. Obstet. Soc. Lond.*, 1860, **2**: 139-196.
4. T.H. Bickerton, *A medical history of Liverpool,* London, John Murray, 1920, p. 216.
5. and 6. F.M. Ramsbotham, 'Table of difficult midwifery cases', *Lond. Med. Gaz.*, 1829, **3**: 284-286; and 'Report on the Royal Maternity Charity', ibid., 1843-44, new series **2**: 142-143 and 619-623.

16

7. J. Hall Davies, *Parturition and its difficulties*, London, Hardwicke, 1865.
8. and 9. *Select Committee on Midwives Registration*, 1892, **XIV**.
10. Sir George Newman, *The building of a nation's health*, London, Macmillan, 1939.

The Dispensaries and Private Practice

How do these values compare to those of midwifery practice in the late eighteenth century and the first half of the nineteenth century? The answers are summarized in tables 2 and 3, which include the statistics of private and dispensary practice respectively. The reports in these tables were chosen with care on the basis of evidence of careful written records kept, in many cases, over a period of several decades. A number of reports where the author depended on his memory, or the number of cases was too small, were rejected. Individually, the reports may be of limited statistical value. Collectively, however, they provide evidence of a remarkably low maternal mortality, especially when compared to the mortality experienced in the twentieth century. Robert Bland's report of the midwifery department of the Westminster General Dispensary, published in 1781, is, as far as I know, the first comprehensive account of an unselected series of deliveries amongst the poor. Carefully compiled and thoughtfully discussed, the report is based on 1,897 deliveries between 1774 and 1780.[52] The maternal mortality rate was 3.7 per 1,000 deliveries amongst a population living in poverty under some of the worst conditions of urban squalor. At this, as at other dispensaries and the out-patient lying-in charities in the eighteenth and nineteenth centuries, midwives were engaged and paid by the institution. They were subject to strict rules and were instructed by the physician- or surgeon-accoucheurs of the charity who attended all complicated cases. Granville published as an appendix to his book an impressively sensible and comprehensive set of instructions for the midwives of the Westminster General Dispensary.[53] Almost certainly, the dispensary midwives, by selection, training, and regulation, provided a higher standard of obstetric care than the private "midwives" of the poor areas who, on many occasions, may have combined midwifery with the treatment of ordinary septic conditions or the laying-out of the dead.[54]

In 1882, Granville published a similar report to Bland's.[55] There were 687 deliveries with a maternal mortality of 5.8 per 1,000 amongst patients living "in the utmost state of wretchedness and want... being confined in small, cold and damp

[52]Robert Bland, 'Midwifery reports of the Westminster General Dispensary', 1781. Full title: 'Some calculations of the number of accidents or deaths which happen in consequence of parturition; and of the proportion of male to female children, as well as of twins, monstrous productions, and children that are dead-born; taken from the midwifery reports of the Westminster General Dispensary: with an attempt to ascertain the chance of life at different periods, from infancy to twenty-six years of age; and likewise the proportion of natives to the rest of the inhabitants of London. In a letter from Robert Bland, MD, Physician-Man-Midwife to the Westminster General Dispensary, to Samuel Foart Simmons, MD FRS', *Phil. Trans. R. Soc. Lond.* 1781, **71**: 155–171.
[53]A.B. Granville, *A report on the practice of midwifery at the Westminster General Dispensary during 1818*, London, 1819, pp.201–220.
[54]Jane Lewis, *The politics of motherhood: child and maternal welfare in England, 1900–1939*, London, Croom Helm, 1980, pp.149–151. Since the handywomen, even in the 1920s, combined the occupations of midwife with laying out the dead, it is a reasonable assumption that this tradition went back at least to the mid-nineteenth century.
[55]A.B. Granville, 'A report of the practice of midwifery at the Westminster General Dispensary during 1819', *Lond. med. phys. J.*, 1822, **47**: 282–288, 374–378.

17

rooms, either in cellars or garrets". Both Bland and Granville presented their results so that we know how many cases were delivered, as Granville put it, "without the slightest interference, by nature alone", and how many, as Bland put it, with "little more than common assistance". From such data we can estimate how many patients might have been expected to survive an unattended labour. The answer from both reports is between 97 and 97.5 per cent; in other words, a mortality rate of twenty-five to thirty per thousand deliveries, and this may well verge on the side of pessimism. Although this is no more than a rough estimate, it does suggest that institutions or obstetricians whose records showed a mortality rate of thirty per 1,000 or more were almost certainly increasing the risks of childbirth, while those achieving a rate of fifteen, or less than ten, were probably providing worthwhile obstetric care. But many of the lying-in charities and dispensaries did a great deal better. The Royal Maternity Charity, for example, which covered a three-mile radius from St. Paul's Cathedral, produced consistently low maternal mortality rates. Even the figure of 4.6 in 1843-44 (table 3, no. 6) is inflated because it contained associated deaths; the puerperal mortality was 3.5. Otherwise, the results speak for themselves.

The data from private practice (table 2), some of which encroach on the second half of the nineteenth century, are more suspect in one respect; they are probably not representative. It is a reasonable assumption that practitioners in the emotive subject of family obstetric practice who obtained poor results (whether they were to blame or not) would not have advertised the fact. Nevertheless, they show that low mortality rates could be achieved by some general practitioners and some consulting practitioners, although the latter would have had the added problem of an excess of complicated cases.

How was it possible for maternal mortality rates as low or lower than the national rates of the 1920s and early 1930s to be achieved before the introduction of anaesthesia, antisepsis, or twentieth-century methods? The answer is probably that the management of normal labour, and of the common complications, although remarkably poor at the beginning of the eighteenth century,[56] was remarkably good, or at least well understood, at the end. Denman's account of the management of normal labour could, with minor amendments, almost stand as a text for today.[57] Deaths in childbed could be substantially reduced much more by simple routine good practice than by highly skilled manoeuvres. Correction of bad practice and unnecessary interference such as manual dilatation of the cervix was as important as the instillation of good practice. The introduction of forceps was a real advance for two reasons. First, because they largely replaced the brutal and dangerous perforator, hook, and crotchet;[58] second, because obstetricians between 1770 and

---

[56] William Clark, *The province of midwives*, Bath, 1751. In this treatise, written for the instruction of midwives, manual dilatation of the cervix in labour and getting the woman to bear down on an undilated cervix was recommended as a routine procedure.

[57] T. Denman, *An essay on natural labours*, London, 1786; and *An introduction to the practice of midwifery*, 5th ed., London, 1805.

[58] Edmund Chapman, *A treatise on the improvement of midwifery*, London, 1759. Chapman blamed the use of the perforator and hook for "The malicious but false Report, that wherever a MAN comes, *the* MOTHER, *or* CHILD, *or* BOTH *must necessarily die.*"

18

about 1860 tended to be very - even excessively - conservative in their use.[59] This can be seen in tables 2 and 3, and David D. Davies (the first professor of midwifery in London) believed that forceps were necessary, at the most, only once in every 250 to 300 cases.[60] Today, the forceps rate in a general practitioner maternity unit is usually about five to seven per cent, and the rate in National Health Service hospitals is about fifteen per cent.[61]

In short, the low maternal mortality achieved by some dispensaries and some practitioners suggests that obstetrics had reached quite a high level in the space of fifty or sixty years following the mid-eighteenth century. That was more than could be said of physic, surgery, or pharmacy during that period. But it was not true of obstetrics in the institutions where surgery was beginning to advance - the hospitals.

The Lying-in Hospitals

It was William Farr who remarked in 1870 that:

> Seeing how destitute of comforts, means, and medical appliances many women are, the thought occurred to some benevolent person that they might be received and delivered in hospitals. It was the extension of the hospital system to midwifery cases, which have some analogy with wounds and injuries for which hospitals had been used from the date of their foundation. Contrary to expectations the advantages these institutions offered were over-balanced by one dread drawback; the mortality of mothers was not diminished; nay it became in some instances excessive; in other instances appalling.[62]

The contrast between the mortality rate of domiciliary practice and the rates of the British Lying-In Hospital are shown here in table 4.[63] Charles White quoted the mortality rates at three unnamed London lying-in hospitals as ranging from 19.5 per 1,000 deliveries to 39 per 1,000 during the eighteenth century. At a fourth hospital it was only 7.5 per 1,000,[64] and when he sought the reason, he was told it was because they avoided the overcrowding that occurred at the other institutions, foreshadowing the remark of Dame Janet Campbell in 1935 that"one of the dangers of maternity hospitals is overcrowding".[65] However, a high hospital mortality rate was not confined to the eighteenth century. The rate at Queen Charlotte's Hospital between 1857 and 1879 was on average 29.6 per 1,000, reaching the spectacular levels of 84.4

[59]See A.W. Edis, 'The forceps in modern midwifery', *Trans. Obstet. Soc. Lond.*, 1878, **19**: 69–92.

[60]J. Waddington, 'Statistics of midwifery in private practice', *Lond. med. Gaz.*, 1843–44, new series **2**: 144–145. See also Robert Lee, 'Clinical reports of difficult cases in midwifery', ibid., 1838–39, n.s. **2**: 827–832.

[61]A. Macfarlane and M. Mugford, *Birth counts: statistics of pregnancy and childbirth*, London, HMSO, 1984, table A.7.32. Forceps rates as percentage of all deliveries rose from 3·7% in 1953 to 5·1% in 1963 and 13·3% in 1978.

[62]*33rd Report of the Registrar General for 1870*, 1872, p.407.

[63]*An account of the British Lying-In Hospital for Married Women in Brownlow Street*, London, 1797. For a very extensive account of data on mortality in lying-in hospitals in various countries see A. Hirsch, *Handbook of geographical and historical pathology*, translated by C. Creighton, London, New Sydenham Society, 1885, pp.416–474, and esp. table, pp.422–431. Hirsch believed that puerperal fever was primarily a disease of lying-in hospitals, but he also produced a list of reports from the eighteenth and nineteenth centuries showing that it could be spread by medical practitioners and underlining the special risk of transmission from cases of erysipelas. For additional information on historical aspects of maternal mortality in various countries in Europe and the USA see E. Shorter, *A history of women's bodies*, London, Allen Lane, 1982, especially the supplementary tables, pp.311–317.

[64]White, op. cit., note 51 above. The lying-in hospital can be identified as the Westminster Lying-In Hospital, later the General Lying-In Hospital, York Road.

[65]Campbell. (1935), op. cit., note 4 above.

19

TABLE 4. THE MATERNAL MORTALITY RATE IN THE BRITISH LYING-IN HOSPITAL IN THE EIGHTEENTH CENTURY AND IN QUEEN CHARLOTTE'S HOSPITAL IN THE NINETEENTH CENTURY.

	The British Lying-in Hospital			*Queen Charlotte's Hospital*	
Period	*Number of deliveries*	*Maternal mortality rate*	*Period*	*Number of deliveries*	*Maternal mortality rate*
1749-58		23·8	1860-64	1746	42·4
1759-68		20·0	1865-69	1918	18·2
1769-78		18·8	1870-74	2228	22·0
1779-88		16·6	1875-79	2201	26·8
1749-96	24,079	16·0	1880-84	3401	10·5
			1885-89	4564	4·2
Worst years:			1890-94	4894	5·9
1760		60·8	1895-99	5638	4·2
1770		59·3	1900-02	3738	4·5

Source: An account of the British Lying-in hospital for married women in Brownlow Street, London, 1797.
Library of the Wellcome Institute for the History of Medicine, London.

Source: Williams (1904), op. cit., footnote 4, table XVIII, p. 42.

TABLE 5. THE CAUSES OF MATERNAL MORTALITY: 1872-76 and 1930

1872-76	*No. of deaths*	*% of total*	1930	*No. of deaths*	*% of total*
Puerperal fever	12,805	55·5%	Puerperal sepsis	1243	43·5%
Accidents of childbirth			Accidents of childbirth		
Flooding	3,524	15·3%	Puerperal nephritis,	467	16·3%
Puerperal convulsions	2,692	11·6%	uraemia, nephritis,		
Placenta praevia	1,308	5·7%	and convulsions		
Miscarriage and abortion	924	4·0%			
Puerperal mania	573	2·5%	Puerperal haemorrhage	348	12·2%
Phlegmasia dolens	456	2·0%	Embolism and sudden death	167	5·8%
Retained placenta	354	1·5%	Ectopic gestation	73	2·6%
Rupture of uterus	181	0·7%	Abortion	65	2·3%
Extra-uterine foetation	54	0·2%	Puerperal insanity	25	0·9%
Other causes (4 categories)	180	0·8%	Others	466	16·3%
Total	23,051	99·9%	Total	2854	99·9%
Deaths from puerperal fever, toxaemia, and haemorrhage		88%	Deaths from sepsis, toxaemia, and haemorrhage		72%

Source: Registrar General's Report for 1876.

Source: On the state of public health, 1930

20

per 1,000 in 1859 and 70.3 per 1,000 in 1860 (see table 5).[66] To quote another example, from 1838 to 1860 the average maternal mortality rate at the General Lying-In Hospital in Dublin (The Rotunda), which had varied between seven and eleven per 1,000 in the eighteenth century, rose in the nineteenth to twenty-four per 1,000 between 1854 and 1861 and thirty-four per 1,000 between 1861 and 1868.[67] In general, it is fair to say that, before about 1880, it was much safer to be delivered at home than in a lying-in hospital. But there are two factors to be considered in regard to the lying-in hospitals. The first is the significant fall in mortality rates after the introduction of antiseptic and aseptic techniques about 1880.[68] At Queen Charlotte's Hospital, the average mortality rate during the twenty-three years 1857-1879 was 29.6 per 1,000 deliveries (table 4). During the twenty-three years from 1880 to 1902, it was 6.0 per 1,000. At the General Lying-In Hospital, maternal mortality fell from a level of 30.8 per 1,000 for 1838-1860 to 6.2 from 1880-87 and 0.5 for 1893-1903.[69] The second factor concerns emergency admissions. Until about the mid-nineteenth century, the population delivered in lying-in hospitals and the population cared for at home by maternity charities were similar, socially and clinically, and there were few transfers from home to hospital in labour. From 1850 onwards, there was a tendency for the lying-in hospitals to admit an increasing number of emergencies from "the district". The emergency cases were often women who had been long in labour, had sometimes been subjected to an unsuccessful forceps delivery, or had bled profusely. Some arrived at hospital in a moribund state. The mortality amongst the emergency admission was very high and influenced the statistics of the hospital.[70] Thus Queen Charlotte's Hospital undertook deliveries at patients' homes as well as in hospital and used the same antiseptic techniques and staff with the same training. The mortality rate of the patients delivered "on the district" was consistently lower, often about one-fifth of the hospital deliveries, and the main reason was the admission of difficult cases as in-patients.[71]

[66]Williams (1904), op. cit., note 4 above, pp.42–45 and tables XVIII–XXXI.

[67]O'Donel T.D. Browne, *The Rotunda Hospital: 1745–1945*, Edinburgh, E & S Livingstone, 1947. A.B. Steele, *Maternity hospitals; their mortality, and what should be done with them.* (London, Churchill, 1874) is a key reference to this subject. In this work the author, a Liverpool obstetrician, shows conclusively that the maternal mortality was unacceptably high in lying-in hospitals throughout Britain. He also shows that a large majority of leading obstetricians of this period knew this and believed without doubt that it was safer for a woman "of the hospital class" to have her baby at home than in a lying-in hospital. "If I read current literature aright the prevalent opinion is, that while Medical and Surgical Hospitals are on their trial, Maternity Hospitals are already condemned." This quotation of Matthews Duncan appears at the opening of this important and valuable pamphlet.

[68]Williams (1904), op. cit., note 4 above, used this as his prime evidence that the failure of the maternal mortality rate to diminish was due to the failure to use antiseptic methods in domiciliary practice.

[69]Ibid. David Hamilton has recently thrown doubt on the belief that the falling rate in deaths after surgery was due to the use of the antiseptic method. He suggests the improvement was probably due to a better-fed and more healthy population of hospital patients. D. Hamilton and M. Lamb, 'Surgeons and surgery', in O. Checkland and M. Lamb (editors), *Health care as social history*, Aberdeen University Press, 1982, pp. 74–85.

[70]Munro Kerr, op. cit., note 4 above, pp.238–241. At the Glasgow Royal Maternity Hospital the mortality rates were: district cases, 2.4 per 1,000 deliveries; transferred to hospital in labour, 46.2 per 1,000. East End Maternity Hospital, London, 1928–31, mortality rate for cases delivered in the district, 0.7 per 1,000, booked cases delivered in hospital, 1.2 per 1,000, emergency admissions, 50 per 1,000. See esp. table 50, p.259, which shows that in some maternity hospitals in 1929–30 emergency admissions outnumbered booked cases.

[71]Williams (1904), op. cit., note 4 above, tables XVIII and XIX, pp.42–43.

21

In the context of England and Wales as a whole, however, the statistics of hospital delivery had very little effect. In 1890, only 2,700 deliveries took place in the voluntary hospital sector, representing 0.3 per cent of all births. One per cent took place in poor law hospitals, and 4.6 per cent under the care of the dispensaries and out-patient lying-in charities.[72] Over ninety per cent were home deliveries attended privately by medical practitioners or midwives, except for the unknown number of unattended births.[73] The pattern of maternal mortality was essentially that of private domiciliary midwifery, the remainder being too few to influence the national statistics to a noticeable extent. Hospital births were still only fifteen per cent of the total in 1927, twenty-four per cent in 1933, and fifty-four per cent in 1946.[74] The hospital deliveries increased rapidly, and home deliveries fell from 33.2 per cent in 1960 to thirteen per cent in 1970 and 1.2 per cent in 1980.[75]

MATERNAL MORTALITY IN THE POST-REGISTRATION PERIOD

Before the reasons for the undiminished maternal mortality in the post-registration period can be considered there are two connected questions that need to be answered. First, what were the components of maternal mortality and did they change significantly during this period? Second, do the national statistics reflect the true level of puerperal mortality or were they so distorted by changes in the classification of disease, and the completeness and accuracy of death certification, that a true fall in mortality was obscured by statistical artefact?

Causes of death in childbirth

Broadly speaking, the relative contribution of various causes to maternal mortality did not change significantly during the period 1850 to 1935 (see table 5). Puerperal sepsis was responsible for about half the total deaths and remained the single most common cause of death until 1937. Ante- and post-natal haemorrhage, and toxaemia were next in importance, accounting in most years for a little over one-quarter of all deaths. Deaths from abortion are considered below, and a variety of other causes accounted for the remainder.

Toxaemia is a difficult cause to assess.[76] It is still a disorder the cause of which is unknown and which cannot be defined precisely. It is primarily a disease of the young primagravida, while post-partum haemorrhage is most common in older mothers who have borne many children. Thus, between 1915 and 1923, toxaemia deaths (recorded as "puerperal convulsions and nephritis") accounted for thirty-nine per

---

[72]Loc. cit., note 29 above. The calculation is based on the data in appendix 4, p.136.

[73]Ibid. From evidence given to this committee it seems that few women were delivered at home by poor law surgeons. Instead, it was insisted that they should go into poor law hospitals. While this is certainly true in some areas, it is impossible to be certain how general this was.

[74]*Maternity in Great Britain. Survey of social and economic aspects of pregnancy and childbirth undertaken by the Joint Committee of the Royal College of Obstetricians and Gynaecologists and the Population Investigation Committee*, Oxford University Press, 1948, p. 48ff.

[75]Macfarlane and Mugford, op. cit., note 61 above, fig.7.4, p.158.

[76]On the epidemiology of toxaemia see esp. T.W. Eden, 'Eclampsia', *J. Obstet. Gynaec. Br. Empire*, 1922, **29** no.3: 386–401; I. McGillivray, 'Some observations on the incidence of pre–eclampsia', ibid., 1958, **65**: 536–539; D. Baird, 'Epidemiological aspects of hypertensive pregnancy', *Clin. Obstet. Gynaec.*, 1977, **4**: 531–547.

22

cent of maternal deaths in the age group 15-20 and 14.8 per cent in the age group 40+; but the respective rates for deaths from post-partum haemorrhage ("haemorrhage other than placenta praevia") were 4.7 per cent for the 15-20 group and eight per cent for the 40+ group.[77] From the late nineteenth century, there were repeated exhortations concerning the early diagnosis and treatment of toxaemia. In fact, there was, and still is, very little that can be done to treat toxaemia apart from induction of labour and delivery.[78] The apparent fall in the incidence of toxaemia is simply a reflection of the increased use and efficiency of induction of labour; the more mothers were allowed to go past the date of expected delivery, the more cases of toxaemia. There is no evidence that the tendency to develop toxaemia was more common in the past, although it may have been more frequent due to a larger number of cases of post-maturity.

It is commonly believed that deaths from obstructed labour (usually a consequence of contracted pelvis associated with rickets) was a common cause of mortality in the nineteenth century.[79] It is certain that contracted pelvis was much more common than it is today, and it reached a high peak in Glasgow in 1870-80 following an "epidemic" of rickets there in the mid-nineteenth century, which led to the extensive employment of caesarean section.[80] But this was exceptional, and caesarean section was rarely employed before the 1930s.

If there was gross cephalo-pelvic disproportion preventing the head from entering the pelvis, death from ruptured uterus or exhaustion was inevitable unless the condition was dealt with. It could be dealt with by caesarean section, but, as seen above, this was so uncommon, except in a few areas, that deaths associated with it can be discounted. The rest would have been relieved either by craniotomy or, in minor degrees of disproportion, by the use of the long forceps. Deaths in these cases could result from injuries or infection associated with these dangerous manoeuvres.

Table 6 is based on the detailed report of the very large number of cases delivered under the care of the Royal Maternity Charity in the 1830s and 1840s. There, if anywhere, deaths from obstructed labour should be obvious. Yet the deaths associated with ruptured uterus, exhaustion, and the use of instruments amounted to eighteen out of 126 deaths compared to fifty-six deaths from haemorrhage and thirty-four from sepsis.[81] Copeman, in 1874, reviewed his cases, which were all attended "in consultation practice, and are therefore of an unusually severe or complicated character and do not include any attended alone as ordinary cases". Out of 216 cases attended as a consultant, eighteen died but only three deaths could be attributed to obstructed labour. Craniotomy was carried out in fourteen cases with only one death; forceps were used in six cases with no deaths, and ruptured uterus

---

[77]Munro Kerr, op. cit., note 4 above, table IV, p.19.

[78]The usual treatment of toxaemia is rest; it was seldom helpful advice for working-class mothers in times of social and economic deprivation.

[79]Rickets could cause not just one but a variety of deformities of the pelvic inlet, all tending to make it difficult or impossible for foetal head to enter the pelivs. See J. Chassar Moir, *Munro Kerr's operative obstetrics*, 6th ed., London, Baillière, Tindall & Cox, 1956,

[80]Derek A. Dow, *The Rotten Row. The history of the Glasgow Royal Maternity Hospital*, Carnforth, Parthenon Press, 1984, ch.5, pp.59–70.

[81]F.H. Ramsbotham, 'Tabular view of the cases admitted to the Eastern District of the Royal Maternity Charity', *Lond. med. Gaz.*, 1843–44, new series **2**: 619–623.

23

occurred on two occasions, both fatal.[82] Robert Dunn, a general practitioner, kept very careful record of his work in the mid-nineteenth century. Out of 4,049 cases there were twenty-seven deaths, two after craniotomy, none after forceps or due to ruptured uterus or exhaustion.[83] Obstetric texts of the nineteenth century and early years of this century dealt at length with obstructed labour because it was a terrifying complication and difficult to deal with, giving the false impression that it was very common. The statistics confirm that obstructed labour often carried a high mortality, but that deaths from this cause were much less common than from the causes noted above. Most cases of puerperal sepsis occurred after normal labours in which no interference had taken place.

TABLE 6.   AN ACCOUNT OF THE STILLBIRTHS AND MATERNAL DEATHS RECORDED BY THE ROYAL MATERNITY CHARITY IN LONDON BETWEEEN 1831 AND 1843.

Total number of deliveries	35,743	
children born living	33,868	
children stillborn	2,263	(6·2‰)
Total maternal deaths	166	(4·6/1000 del.)
associated deaths	40	
puerperal deaths	126	(3·5/1000 del.)
Associated deaths		
phthisis	15	
pneumonia	6	
typhus	6	
Asiatic cholera	4	
other diseases	9	
Puerperal deaths	126	
haemorrhage	56	
peritonitis, hysteritis, pelvic inflammation, and common fever	34	
other	36	
of which all which might have been associated with obstructed labour were:		
deaths due to ruptured uterus	8	
deaths after craniotomy	6	
deaths after forceps	3	
'exhausted under lingering labour'	1	
Total in this group	18	

Source: F.H. Ramsbotham, 'The Eastern District of the Royal Maternity Charity', *Lond. Med. Gaz.,* 1843-44, new series **2**: 619-625.

Maternal mortality statistics: accurate or artefact?

Death certification was voluntary until 1874, and certification of maternal deaths was imperfect until 1881 when Farr introduced an inquiry into all deaths in women of

[82]E. Copeman, 'Statistical and practical remarks on consultation midwifery in private practice', *Trans. Obstet. Soc. Lond.,* 1874, **16**: 103–110. Of the craniotomy case that died, he remarked that she was "almost in articulo mortis when the operation was resorted to as a last resource. There can be but little doubt that craniotomy is generally a safe operation if not too long delayed . . .. I must say a word about the crotchet in order to denounce it as a more or less dangerous instrument, and very often ineffective . . .."

[83]R. Dunn, 'On the statistics of midwifery from the records of private practice', ibid., 1859–60, **1**: 279–297.

24

childbearing age where childbirth was not mentioned, but a puerperal cause was suspected - e.g., deaths from "peritonitis" or "pyaemia". To a certain degree, therefore, under-reporting of puerperal mortality occurred before the 1880s. However, there was a tendency to include associated deaths in the total, especially in private reports, but also in the national figures until 1864, when Farr stated that these should be "referred to the fatal disease in question".[84] Moreover, there was no explicit rule at first on the official length of the "lying-in" period for the purposes of death registration. Some late deaths were included until the convention of using one month (it is now six weeks) was adopted. In 1911, the introduction of the International List of Causes of Death (ILCD) led to deaths in the puerperium due to "nephritis and albuminuria" being included as maternal deaths. This made little difference to the statistics because deaths from eclampsia were already included as "puerperal convulsions".[85] In 1926, puerperal pyrexia was defined as a "fever of 100·4°F over a period of 24 or more hours during the three weeks after childbirth". In 1927, as noted above, stillbirth registration was introduced; since this increased the denominator from "live" to "total" births, this tended to reduce the maternal mortality rate. Taken together, these factors undoubtedly produced some distortion of true puerperal mortality, but only to a slight degree. The question of deaths from abortion, the extent to which these were hidden and the possible effect on puerperal mortality is, however, complicated and a matter for debate.

The influence of abortion deaths on the maternal mortality rate

Deaths from abortion were always included in the national figures and remained approximately the same proportion to the total. In 1929, following the fourth revision of the ILCD, deaths from abortion were divided into two groups (nos. 140 and 141), septic and without sepsis. Spontaneous abortion deaths could be septic but sepsis was more likely to occur after induced or criminal abortion. When the latter was recognized and came before a coroner's jury, the death was recorded amongst deaths from violence and excluded from maternal death rates. Although the number of reported deaths from criminal abortion increased through the first three decades of the twentieth century, they were always a small minority of all such deaths and in total were too few to affect the maternal mortality rate materially even if they had been included.[86] The important question, therefore, concerns the possible large-scale increase in maternal deaths from undetected, or unproven, criminal abortion. Shorter believes they had a major distorting influence on the national statistics from 1880 to 1930. "So overwhelming was the torrent of abortion fatalities [in the 1930s] that many ended up in general 'puerperal sepsis' put there by local doctors anxious to circumvent scandal or to avoid offending the family."[87] He attaches such importance

---

[84]*Registrar General's Report for 1864*, pp.192 and 205. In the report for 1841, there is a long and important account of current views on the contagious nature of puerperal fever, including letters from various practitioners. But the opening section of this account (p.380) seems to show quite clearly that during this period, associated deaths were being included in the statistics of maternal mortality.

[85]Macfarlane and Mugford, op. cit., note 61 above, fig. 10.1, p.197.

[86]They amounted to about two to three per cent of all maternal deaths. See Munro Kerr, op. cit., note 4 above.

[87]Shorter, op. cit., note 63 above, chs. 5, 6, 8. Shorter tends to draw on sources from a number of different countries in order to make general statements on abortion and sepsis in midwifery. The difficulties of such an approach are discussed briefly at the end of this paper.

25

to the scale on which this occurred (an increasing scale from 1880 to the 1930s) that he dismisses the undiminished maternal mortality as a myth, asserting that there was a substantial fall in the full-term maternal mortality rate between 1880 and the 1930s and that the abortion deaths were hidden in "puerperal sepsis". If Shorter is right, the fall in full-term deaths should be evident in "accidents of childbirth" as the standard of obstetrics improved, while puerperal sepsis deaths should have increased to maintain the overall level of maternal mortality. But this did not occur.

PUERPERAL SEPSIS DEATHS AS A PERCENTAGE OF TOTAL MATERNAL DEATHS

1880-85	57%	1906-10	42%	1931	40%
1886-90	53%	1911-15	39%	1932	38%
1891-95	46%	1916-20	41%	1933	40%
1896-1900	43%	1921-25	40%	1934	44%
1901-05	45%	1926-30	45%	1935	41%

But it may be argued that the fall in full-term maternal deaths was confined to puerperal sepsis where, to an increasing extent, deaths from septic abortion replaced full-term deaths from sepsis. To have caused a substantial fall in maternal mortality, this would have required a very large fall indeed in full-term puerperal sepsis. Such a decline would have removed full-term sepsis from its place as the most common cause of death. All the evidence from the 1920s and 1930s contradicts this assertion. For example, when the Medical Research Council in 1929-30 became concerned with the subject of maternal mortality it identified *full-term* puerperal sepsis as much the most important cause of death and directed its research entirely into the cause, prevention, and treatment of this complication.[88]

Shorter does not quantify the extent of the alleged fall in full-term maternal mortality, but alleges it was "substantial" and refers the reader to a figure of twenty-one as the percentage of all *septic* deaths due to induced abortion in Britain in the 1930s.[89] Even if allowance is made for these septic abortion deaths, it makes relatively little difference to total mortality. If deaths from septic abortion are subtracted from the total maternal mortality rate, a rate of 4.6 in the late nineteenth century would be reduced to 4.48 and a rate of 4.6 in the late 1920s or early 1930s would be reduced to 4.21.[90] Thus, allowance for hidden deaths from induced abortion would at most produce a slight fall, not a substantial one. However, the most important reason for rejecting the hypothesis that there was a substantial fall in

[88] *Medical Research Council Annual Reports* from 1929–30, and the archives of the Council, file 2060.

[89] The source of this value of twenty-one per cent as the percentage of septic deaths due to abortion is the *Statistical Review* for 1929 quoted in Munro Kerr, op. cit., note 4 above, pp. 132-133. The annual rates were 1926 20.0%, 1927 21.0%, 1928 18.9%, 1929 20.6%, 1930 24.1%.

[90] This calculation is based on the assumption that twenty-one per cent of total *septic* maternal deaths in the late 1920s and early 1930s were due to abortion when total deaths from sepsis were between forty and forty-five per cent of total maternal mortality. Induced abortion also occurred in the nineteenth century and was also concealed, but I have assumed a value of five per cent for the percentage of puerperal sepsis deaths in the 1880s and 1890s due to abortion when puerperal sepsis accounted for about fifty per cent of all deaths.

26

full-term maternal mortality, hidden by septic abortion deaths, is the view of medical practitioners working in this period.

Janet Campbell and her colleagues in 1924 and 1932,[91] Munro Kerr in 1933,[92] and Douglas and McKinley in 1935[93] were all aware of the problem of fatalities due to induced abortion and to the fact that they were increasing. None, however, believed these deaths disguised a substantial fall in full-term deaths from puerperal sepsis. Munro Kerr in 1933 dealt with this in detail.[94] He concluded that deaths from abortion, including hidden deaths, had not increased to such an extent as to affect seriously the maternal mortality rate as a whole; he believed they might in the future, and had already done so in some countries, notably in Germany; but not in Britain in 1933.

The evidence therefore suggests that, from the mid-nineteenth century until the mid-1930s, there was no substantial or sustained fall in full-term maternal mortality in England and Wales, or in Scotland.

The causes of the undiminished maternal mortality before 1935

A persistent high maternal mortality, or a higher rate in one part of a country than the country as a whole is likely to be due to one or both of two groups of factors. Poor obstetric care, judged by the standards of the time, due to poor education or poor application in practice; or, second, to social and economic deprivation. Social and economic deprivation would operate through its effect on the health of the mother before, during, and immediately after pregnancy and labour. Common sense suggests that poor health due to poor nutrition, housing, and sanitation must lower resistance to most, if not all, the causes of maternal deaths. High maternal mortality, in short, may be due to bad midwives, bad medical practitioners, or unhealthy mothers, and these factors, acting in concert, are often difficult to disentangle. Since the evidence of the relative importance of these factors is sometimes complex, it might be helpful at this stage to anticipate my final conclusion, because it may be regarded as an unexpected one. It is that *maternal mortality appears to have been remarkably resistant to the ill-effects of social and economic deprivation, but remarkably sensitive to the good and the bad effects of medical intervention.* Not all the evidence points this way, but most of it does.

To start with, the pattern of maternal mortality since 1850 is in stark contrast to the pattern of deaths from all causes in women of childbearing age (fig.3); and also to the infant mortality rate (fig.4). The death rate from all causes diminished steadily from 1838, and the infant mortality rate, after remaining level from 1838 to 1900, also fell substantially and steadily until the present. It is generally agreed in both instances that the decline in mortality from 1850 to 1930 had little if anything to do with medical intervention and much to do with rising standards of living. The pattern of maternal mortality for England and Wales as a whole (and also for Scotland)

[91]Campbell *et al.* (1932), op. cit., note 4 above.
[92]Munro Kerr, op. cit., note 4 above.
[93]Douglas and McKinley, op. cit., note 2 above.
[94]Munro Kerr, op. cit., note 4 above. Chapter 5 deals with abortion in careful detail.

27

therefore suggests that changes in the standard of living, which had a marked effect on health in other respects, had little influence on deaths from childbirth.

This, however, appears to be contradicted when regional differences are examined, for there appears to be a correlation between regions of high mortality and regions traditionally associated with deprivation and poverty. Williams observed in the late nineteenth century that if a line was drawn from the Severn to the Humber (fig.6) nearly all the counties to the north and west of the line had a higher than average maternal mortality, nearly all to the south and east a lower than average.[95] What is more, this pattern of regional difference remained largely unaltered from the 1860s until 1935 (table 7). It was surprising how clear-cut this difference remained. In 1926, the maternal mortality in Wales was 4.92 per 1,000 deliveries, 4.75 in the north of England, 3.78 in the midlands, and 3.43 in the south.[96] In 1929, when the mortality for England and Wales was 4.33 it was 11.46 in Radnorshire, 10.33 in Wigan, 8.04 in Bolton, 2.49 in Oxfordshire. In Bootle, strangely, it was 1.80.[97]

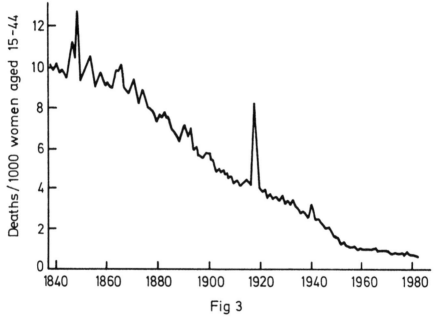

Fig 3

Death rates from all causes in women aged 15-44,
England and Wales, 1838-1982
(source: OPCS Mortality statistics)

[95] Williams (1895–96), op. cit., note 2 above.
[96] Munro Kerr, op. cit., note 4 above, p.12.
[97] *On the State of the Public Health for 1929.* Although it changed in detail, the general picture here described remained remarkably constant year after year, with Wales and the industrial north showing the highest maternal mortality rates.

28

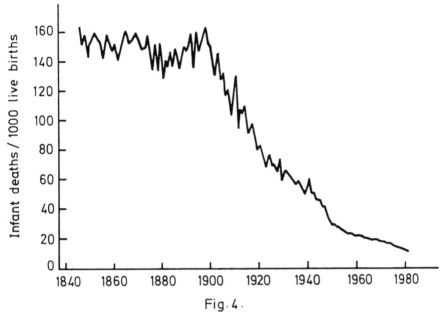

Fig. 4.

Infant mortality rates, England and Wales 1846-1928.
(source: OPCS Mortality statistics)

Dame Janet Campbell, in 1935, assessed this regional difference as one due to a high maternal mortality in heavily industrial and remote rural areas.[98] The feature that these two types of region would seem to have in common is poor socio-economic conditions. Williams, a medical officer of health with a lively appreciation of the effects of poor nutrition and living conditions on health, nevertheless rejected this as the explanation of the persistent high mortality in the Welsh mining valleys. At the beginning of the twentieth century, the miners, he stated, were relatively well off, "wages are high, and nourishing food plentiful".[99] Poor housing might play a part, but the main reason for maternal deaths was that south Wales was cursed with ignorant midwives who spread puerperal fever from house to house.[100] To the observers of regional differences the cause was far from obvious. It might be poverty, overwork, and poor housing that afflicted the poor of the north and west, but equally it might be that these were the least attractive regions for medical practice and they had more than their fair share of inefficient general practitioners and ignorant, dirty midwives. This conclusion was confirmed, at least in part, by Janet Campbell and her colleagues in 1932, when they conducted an examination into causes of maternal

[98]Campbell (1935), op. cit., note 4 above, who pointed out that Holland's good record in obstetrics was associated with an absence of any large heavily industrialized areas and remote rural ones, which had the conspicuously high mortality rates in England and Wales.
[99]Williams (1904), op. cit., note 4 above, p.33.
[100]Ibid.

29

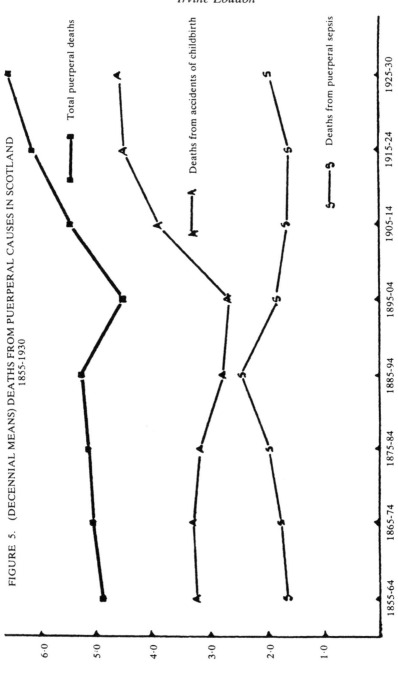

FIGURE 5. (DECENNIAL MEANS) DEATHS FROM PUERPERAL CAUSES IN SCOTLAND 1855-1930

Total puerperal deaths

Deaths from accidents of childbirth

Deaths from puerperal sepsis

Death Rate per 1000 births.

Sources: Douglas and McKinley, op. cit., footnote 2; Munro Kerr, op. cit., footnote 4.

30

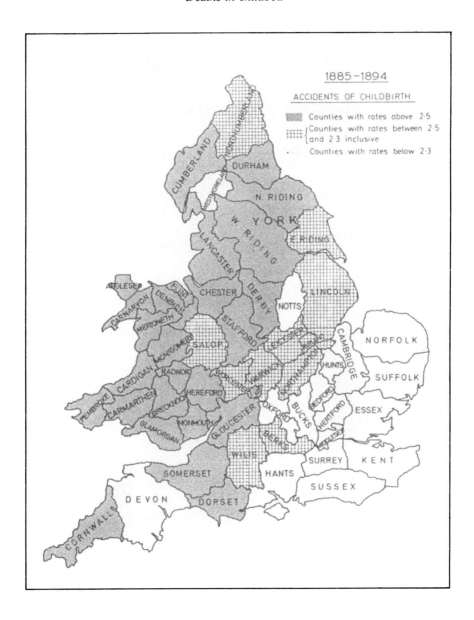

FIGURE 6(a).   ENGLAND AND WALES. DEATHS FROM ACCIDENTS OF CHILDBIRTH
1885-94, EXPRESSED AS DEATHS PER 1000 BIRTHS.

Source: Williams (1895-6), op. cit., footnote 4.

31

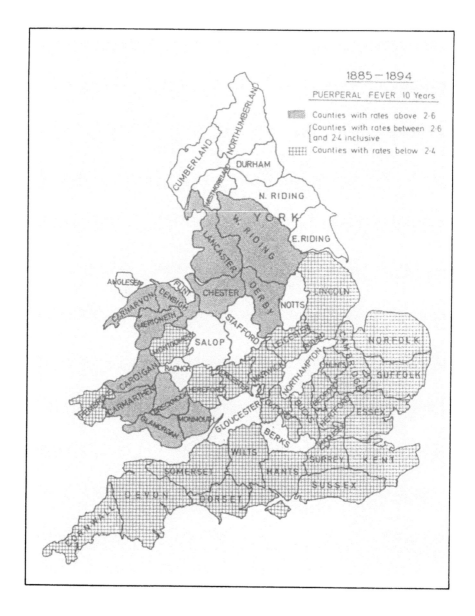

FIGURE 6(b). ENGLAND AND WALES, DEATHS FROM PUERPERAL FEVER 1885-94, EXPRESSED AS DEATHS PER 1000 BIRTHS.

Source: Williams (1895-6), op. cit., footnote 4.

32

TABLE 7.   MATERNAL MORTALITY RATES IN COUNTIES AND COUNTY BOROUGHS IN ENGLAND IN 1923; SELECTED COUNTIES, AND MORTALITY RATES IN CERTAIN SELECTED METROPOLITAN BOROUGHS, 1919-1922.

	Deaths from		
County boroughs and counties with the highest rate	*Puerperal fever*	*Accidents of childbirth*	*Total maternal deaths*
Halifax	2·51	5·31	7·82
Blackpool	2·83	4·72	7·55
Rochdale	1·80	5·25	7·05
Huddersfield	1·61	5·09	6·70
Swansea	2·29	4·30	6·59
County boroughs counties with the lowest rate			
West Ham	0·79	1·24	2·03
Worcester	0·51	1·53	2·04
East Ham	1·35	0·95	2·30
Reading	1·20	1·47	2·67
Northampton	1·40	1·40	2·80
Certain selected metropolitan boroughs			
Bermondsey	1·26	1·64	2·90
Chelsea	1·78	4·01	5·79
Hampstead	1·87	1·31	3·18
Kensington	1·89	2·42	4·31
Poplar	1·15	1·75	2·90
Shoreditch	1·48	1·07	2·55
Stoke Newington	2·91	2·18	5·09
Westminster	1·70	2·49	4·19

Source: Campbell (1924), op. cit., footnote 40.

deaths in two areas of high mortality, Lancashire and Wales.[101] In Wales, it was concluded that poor obstetric facilities were mainly to blame for the excess deaths. In Lancashire, while rickets and other disorders of nutrition played a part, they were not considered factors of first importance. It was difficult to separate the effects of poor nutrition and poor obstetric care, but the latter seemed to be the more important.

More positive evidence of the lack of importance of social and economic factors comes from a finding so unusual that it has been called the "reverse" relationship between social class and maternal mortality, for it shows that social classes I and II often suffered a higher mortality rate than social classes IV and V. This difference was usually confined to deaths from puerperal sepsis. It is interesting that Robert Bland made a similar observation in 1781:

[101]Campbell *et al.* (1932), op. cit., note 4 above.

33

I am inclined to believe that the lower sort of people recover more certainly after parturition than persons in higher stations of life; at least they are less subject to the puerperal fever, which is so fatal if not checked at the first attack; and which, if not caused, is certainly nourished and its malignancy increased by great fires, close rooms, warm septic diet, and costiveness. But the apartments of the poor are generally so crazy, that without opening doors or windows, to which they are sufficiently averse, the air pours in upon them from all sides.[102]

Such a conclusion was not as surprising then as it is today. The naturalistic philosophies of the eighteenth century suggested that the poor were closer to the "noble savage" of nature and therefore efficiently prolific in their breeding, while the effete and pampered rich were prone to barrenness and the complications of childbirth.[103] One might be tempted to dismiss this as impressionistic were it not for subsequent evidence. For example, the mortality rates achieved amongst the poor of London by the dispensaries and out-patient lying-in charities, which were substantially lower than the national rates, suggest that poverty was not an important factor in maternal mortality. But it was Cullingworth who showed in 1898 that if one examined the districts of London in terms of deaths from puerperal sepsis, contrary to expectation, the poorer areas had the lower mortality. Hampstead and Islington had high rates, Rotherhithe and Bermondsey low ones. Kensington and Chelsea had higher rates than Lambeth, Whitechapel, St George's in the East, and Shoreditch.[104] The inference, that high mortality rates were associated with a high percentage of deliveries by medical practitioners, low rates with deliveries by midwives, was suggested but not pursued when it was shown that there was even stronger evidence of such an association for Leeds and Glasgow.[105] In 1930-32, further confirmation of this tendency was shown by analysis of maternal mortality according to social class of husband in England and Wales (table 8). Contrary to so many indices of health, this showed clearly that maternal mortality decreased from social classes I and II to social class V. This was especially noticeable for puerperal sepsis but not for puerperal haemorrhage. The greater risk of sepsis through delivery at home by a general practitioner seems to have been the main but not the only factor in the higher maternal mortality of the higher social classes. What was the explanation?

The likelihood that medical practitioners could carry infection from a fever case to a maternity case had been recognized long before Semmelweis's classical work on the contagious nature of puerperal fever in 1843-46.[106] But the association of a high rate of fever with medical attendance was probably not so much due to case-to-case

[102]Bland, op. cit., note 52 above.

[103]J.S. Lewis, 'Maternal health in the English aristocracy: myths and realities, 1790–1840', *J. soc. Hist.*, 1983, **17**(1): 97–114.

[104]Cullingworth, op. cit., note 4 above.

[105]Munro Kerr, op. cit., note 4 above. In Leeds from 1920 to 1929, the maternal mortality in the city as a whole was 4.49 per 1,000 births. In the middle-class areas it was 5.93 and in the working-class areas 3.01. An investigation in Aberdeen through the 1920s failed to show any association between maternal mortality and poor housing or overcrowding. The worst areas for housing showed no higher rates of maternal mortality than the best. Medical Research Council Archives, file 2060.

[106]See esp. Hirsch, op. cit., note 63 above, chapter on puerperal fever; and A.W.W. Lea, *Puerperal infection*, London, Oxford Medical Publications, 1910. See also William Farr, 'Childbirth fatal by contagion', in the *5th Annual Report of the Registrar General for 1841*, 1843, pp.384–396. J.G. Adami, *Charles White of Manchester (1728—1813) and the arrest of puerperal fever*, London, Hodder & Stoughton, 1922, brings out the advances due to simple cleanliness well before Semmelweis's publications.

34

TABLE 8. MORTALITY OF MARRIED WOMEN ACCORDING TO THE SOCIAL CLASS OF HUSBAND, ENGLAND AND WALES, 1930-32.

Cause of death	All married women	Class I & II professional and managerial	Class III skilled workers	Class IV semi-skilled	Class V unskilled
All causes	4·13	4·44	4·11	4·16	3·89
Total, excluding abortion	3·57	3·94	3·55	3·60	3·32
Puerperal sepsis	1·29	1·45	1·33	1·21	1·16
Puerperal haemorrhage	0·49	0·50	0·44	0·48	0·60
Toxaemia	0·79	0·81	0·81	0·84	0·68

Source: J.M. Munro Kerr, R.W. Johnstone, and M.H. Phillips (editors), *Historical review of British obstetrics and gynaecology 1800-1950*, London, E. & S. Livingstone, 1954, table 9, ch.29.

spread as to the greater tendency of medical men to carry out vaginal examinations, use forceps, and — compared to midwives — be more impatient.[107]

This "reverse" social class/maternal mortality relationship was, by implication, a serious criticism of the standard of care in general-practitioner obstetrics. Milne Murray roundly accused general practitioners of the misuse of anaesthesia and of "the ridiculous parody which, in many practitioners' hands, stands for the use of antisepsis".[108] Unnecessary interference was a recurrent accusation and in some areas at least appears to have been true. Andrew Topping in 1936, whose evidence is considered later, described the conduct of some general-practitioner obstetricians as "nothing short of murder".[109] Dr Cameron of Glasgow informed the Select Committee on Midwives' Registration (1892) that "a chapter of horrors might easily be written upon mismanagement of labour, in which only the mystic letters appended to the operator's name protected him from prosecution".[110] But the most telling evidence comes from a report of deliveries in Wales.[111] In cases in which the midwife was booked to attend — and these were on the whole the poorest sections of the community — the forceps rate was three to five per cent. But in cases in which the general practitioner was retained, an excessively high forceps rate was often recorded, as this table shows:

FORCEPS DELIVERIES AS A PERCENTAGE OF TOTAL DELIVERIES IN CASES "BOOKED" BY A GENERAL PRACTITIONER, WALES, 1929-1931

Breconshire (1929)	5·48%	Bridgend Urban Dist. Council (1931)	42%
Caernarvonshire (1929)	30%	Penybont (1931)	50·7%
Carmarthenshire (1930)	55·8%	Port Talbot (1931)	19·7%
Denbighshire (1931)	32·9%	Neath Borough Council (1930), (1931),	20%
Flintshire (1930)	38·9%	Rhondda Urban D.C. (1920)	7·9%

Source: Jones, op. cit., note 111, table F, p.81.

[107]Loc. cit., note 29 above, Q.327–336, see also Lewis, op. cit., note 54 above, notes 92 and 119. The confidential inquiry into maternal deaths in 1929 showed that in deaths from puerperal fever transmission from one patient to another was uncommon. Most cases were isolated cases. Out of 616 deaths from sepsis, forty-eight per cent followed a normal labour, forty-four per cent followed a complicated labour, and eight per cent followed a forceps delivery in an otherwise normal labour. *Interim Report of Departmental Committee on Maternal Mortality and Morbidity*, London, Ministry of Health, 1930, chapter 2.

35

The author's comment that "forceps are applied unnecessarily often owing to the multiple calls of general practice and the entreaties of the patient" is mild in the face of evidence of such blatantly unnecessary interference. The contrast with the ultra-conservatism of early- and mid-nineteenth-century general practitioners is striking, and it is a nice question whether the inexperience in the use of forceps of the earlier practitioners was more or less dangerous than the unnecessary use of forceps by their more experienced successors in the 1920s and 1930s.

Those who believed that poverty and malnutrition were an important contributory cause of maternal mortality were relatively few compared to those who saw the problem entirely in terms of poor clinical care. Nevertheless, the social and economic dimension was not ignored. Williams in 1904 was sensitive to this aspect, and a fellow medical officer of health, observing the high mortality in Wales, suggested in 1937 that it was more likely to be cured by a herd of cows than a herd of specialists.[112] Janet Campbell, at the Ministry of Health in the 1920s and early 1930s, was especially concerned with the social as well as the medical aspects of the high maternal mortality. One, however, who was convinced that malnutrition was the prime cause was Lady Rhys Williams, the honorary secretary to the Joint Midwives' Council. Selecting the Rhondda because of its high maternal mortality rate, she conducted an experiment in which food supplements were distributed to expectant mothers. She claimed that, as a result, the maternal mortality rate (which included "associated deaths") fell from 11.29 in 1934 to 4.7 in 1935. It looked impressive.[113] Unfortunately, this experiment was seriously flawed in two respects. First, obstetric services in the Rhondda were extensively improved just before food supplements were introduced: second, the food supplements were, to say the least, odd and inadequate, consisting of the distribution to each mother (on average) of 6 x 4 ozs. of Marmite, 6 x 6 ozs. of Brandex Extract of Beef, 6 x 8 ozs. of Ovaltine Egg and Milk Extract, less than one-fifth of a one-lb. tin of Dorella dried milk, and a free pint of milk a day in the last three months of pregnancy. There is no knowing how much of this was given to husbands or children, and even if it was none, "it seems probable", as Lady Williams admitted, "that the malnutrition of these women was not fully overcome". Packed and concentrated foodstuffs of this kind were then much in vogue, but their choice, says the author, was dictated by "the difficulties of administration and distribution of fresh foods". The paper is not convincing.

It is possible to criticize the medical profession and official bodies in the 1920s and 1930s for their relative neglect of social aspects of obstetric care. It is certainly true that most observers blamed poor clinical performance for the high mortality. Neither midwives nor general practitioners escaped blame, for not only were the general

---

[108] Milne Murray quoted in Williams (1904), op. cit., note 4 above, pp.35–36.

[109] Andrew Topping, 'Maternal mortality and public opinion', *Public Hlth*, 1936, **49**: 342–349. "Many cases of maternal deaths were nothing short of murder, and he described several glaring examples" (p.349).

[110] Loc. cit., note 29 above, Q.378.

[111] The report by Dilys Jones in Campbell (1932), op. cit., note 4 above.

[112] Leading article, 'Maternal mortality in Wales', *Med. Officer*, 1937, **57**: 215.

[113] Lady Williams, 'Malnutrition as a cause of maternal mortality', *Public Hlth*, 1936–37, **50**: 11–19.

36

levels of obstetric care provided by each considered to be unacceptably low, but the absence of co-operation between the two, stemming from traditional competition and mutual hostility, was also perceived as an important cause of obstetric disasters.

In 1929 and the early 1930s, the Medical Research Council, at the request of the Ministry of Health, turned its attention to maternal mortality. In 1932, with a frankness and force in the preliminary draft which was muted in the final publication, the committee on maternal mortality listed the sins of omission and commission.[114] The most important were thought to be, perfunctory attention to antiseptic techniques; failure to appreciate the importance of wearing masks; much unnecessary interference in normal labours; inadequate ante-natal care and selection of difficult cases for hospital delivery; midwives harassed by financial anxiety; poor co-operation between midwives and general practitioners in domiciliary midwifery; too few maternity beds; and poor obstetric training of midwives and doctors. Conspicuous by its absence was any suggestion that social and economic factors were important. In a remarkable letter on the hopelessness of persuading general practitioners to read a report on maternal mortality, let alone act on it, the director of the Stationery Office remarked: "The terrible thing about this latest Maternal Mortality Report is the revelation of the lives which might be saved, not by advanced technique, but by the simplest aseptic precautions that one would have expected medical men to observe on their own initiative".[115] We share his sense of horror. Between 1930 and 1933, 10,660 mothers died in childbirth and at least forty per cent of these deaths were considered to have been potentially avoidable.

In 1979-82, the expected maternal deaths from the same number of deliveries would have been 295.

But there was nothing new in most of these conclusions. Through the work of William Farr in the 1870s, Williams in 1904, and a number of authors up to 1932, most of the Council's conclusions had already become established dogma, especially those concerning the failure to adopt antiseptic and aseptic techniques. These did not need to be applied with as much care as was needed in surgery to be effective in midwifery.[116] The statistics of the lying-in hospitals seemed to show how much could be achieved by antisepsis because, as Bonney observed in 1919, "Taking the conduct of labour in general, not much more than a bowl of antiseptic stands between the practice of today and the practice of the [eighteen] sixties".[117] Whether it was the bowl of antiseptic, or the influence of the latter in effecting a new standard of cleanliness, is debatable. Probably it was both. In certain aspects of surgery a fall in

---

[114]Medical Research Council Archives, file 2060/2.

[115]This letter from Mr Scrogie of His Majesty's Stationery Office to Sir Walter Fletcher, Secretary of the Medical Research Council dated 13 October 1932, includes such gems as: "Excepting only the lack of interest shown by farmers in research for their benefit, there is nothing in the Stationery Office experience more disappointing than the lack of interest in the medical profession in the public health"; "In one [medical] man's house there is a stack of Lancets and British Medical Journals all unopened in their wrappers. He is 'much too busy'. He plays bridge five nights a week, belongs to every local club that can possibly attract business and lectures to girl guides on first-aid. Some girl guides are quite pretty. In his spare time he plays golf and reads the Sketch." Medical Research Council, London. Archives MRC 2060/2 G39/1195.

[116]Bonney, op. cit., note 4 above.

[117]Ibid., p.81.

37

the mortality in the 1880s may well have been due to improved nutrition as much as antiseptis.[118] In midwifery, however, antiseptic techniques seem to have been conspicuously successful in hospital and conspicuously absent outside.[119] The root cause was poor training, which can be traced to the traditional hostility towards obstetrics of the teaching hospitals and the examiners, and, as far as midwives were concerned, the hostility of medical practitioners to the Midwives' Act. Donnison and Lewis have written admirable accounts of the obstructions placed in the way of obstetric education.[120] The reports of the Select Committee on Medical Education in 1834, the Select Committee on the Medical Act Amendment Act in 1878-79, and the Select Committee on Midwives' Registration in 1892 provide a wealth of evidence on attitudes to midwifery, on recommendations for increasing the time spent on teaching midwifery and on the stubborn refusal of the examiners to agree to such changes. Even in 1932, when the Joint Education and Examination Committee of the General Medical Council reviewed the teaching of midwifery, the recommendation that students should spend six months in obstetrics and gynaecology and infant hygiene, and that this should include a two months' residency for practical experience in deliveries, was opposed by the teaching bodies, who proposed one month's residency and three months or less in all.[121]

It is not surprising that those concerned with the teaching of obstetrics, seeing what they believed was a low standard in general practice and, at the same time, faced with the opposition of their medical and surgical colleagues in teaching hospitals over the curriculum time for teaching obstetrics, believed the future lay in developing obstetrics as a hospital speciality with the ultimate elimination of the home delivery by the general practitioner.

One of the most uncompromising proponents of hospital delivery was Victor Bonney in 1919. In his opinion, "midwifery is a pure surgical art" since the baby was a "neoplasm" and "labour is a process accompanied by self-inflicting wounds and the puerperium a period of their healing". Hospitals, he said, were safe because: "Although the antiseptic measures employed in lying-in hospitals fall far short of those in use in general surgery, they have sufficed practically to abolish extrinsic infection [in spite of] the collection of a number of patients under one roof." There should be, he said, "large lying-in hospitals all over the country" and outside emergencies could be dealt with by a hospital team travelling by motor-car -the "flying-squad" principle. It was implied that, if general practitioners were to continue to practise obstetrics, it should be within the hospitals.[122]

The ignorance of the nineteenth-century midwives, the Sarah Gamps, was a byword amongst doctors, and since there was so much mutual hostility and most of the evidence about midwives comes from the medical profession, it is difficult to know how bad they were. Farr in 1841 admitted that some were excellent but continued that in many cases "the nurses and old women in attendance... have peculiar views of their own which they lose no opportunity of announcing and

[118]Hamilton, op. cit., note 69 above.
[119]See note 68 above.
[120]Donnison, op. cit., note 9 above; and Lewis, op. cit., note 54 above.
[121]Medical Research Council Archives, file 2060.
[122]Bonney, op. cit., note 4 above.

38

carrying into effect with the best intentions and the worst consequences". To Farr, the need for formal training of midwives was obvious. The time had passed when it could be argued that "midwives were born, not made".[123]

The Midwives' Act of 1902 was expected to lead to a rapid transformation in the standard of midwifery. What had not been anticipated, although it should have been, was the slowness of the transformation. In 1908, seventy-three per cent of midwives still practised without antiseptics and twelve per cent conformed to the drunken stereotype of Sarah Gamp.[124] Because the Act allowed those who had been in active practice before 1902 to continue as "bona fide" midwives (like the "pre-1815" medical practitioners who continued to practise after the introduction of the Apothecaries' Act), it was not until the end of the 1920s that the majority of midwives ceased to be elderly and often unteachable local residents (some could not be taught to read a clinical thermometer) and became younger middle-class professionals.[125] Not only was the "bona fide" group - some able and experienced, others not - active and numerous, especially in the country, but employment of the cheaper "handywomen" continued through the 1920s.[126] For the first three decades of the twentieth century, therefore, the expected dramatic improvement in women employed as midwives occurred only slowly. The evidence that standards of care in midwifery before the Second World War were considered to be unacceptably and unnecessarily low is considerable. The evidence that this had a direct effect on the maternal mortality rate was largely circumstantial until the Rochdale experiment.

When Dr Andrew Topping went to Rochdale as Medical Officer of Health in 1930, it had "the very unenviable distinction of having the highest [maternal] mortality rate in the country over a period of years". The average for the four years 1928-31 was "a fraction less than 9". By 1932, it had been reduced to 1.76; by 1933 to 2.87; a few unusual deaths brought the rate back up to 5.65 in 1934, but in 1935 it fell back to 1.75. This dramatic fall was achieved by simple measures. Propaganda and the help of the press led to a high attendance rate at specially established ante-natal clinics; medical practitioners were made aware that "case reports for the previous years had shown... no ante-natal care... evidence of unnecessary and violent interference [whereby] shock and haemorrhage following a difficult labour was by far the commonest cause of death". Deliberate and effective publicity, the establishment of a genuinely effective and co-operating service of midwives, general practitioners, and a consultant recruited from Manchester, and the opening of a puerperal fever ward, seem to have brought a new optimism and to have been remarkably effective in lowering the mortality rate from childbirth.[127] Although the paper was hailed as a breakthrough at the meeting where it was given, it was soon eclipsed by Colebrook and Kenny's paper on the use of sulphonamides in puerperal fever, published only five months later.[128] Topping's paper is, however, historically important. It would be simple and tempting to attribute the undiminished maternal

[123]*Registrar General's Report*, 1841, pp.380, 1870.
[124]Lewis, op. cit., note 54 above, p.143.
[125]Ibid., p.143.
[126]Ibid., pp.149–151.
[127]Topping, op. cit., note 109 above.
[128]Colebrook and Kenny, op. cit., note 8 above.

39

mortality up to 1935 to the absence of an effective agent for treating puerperal fever, and this view receives apparent confirmation by the steep decline in deaths after 1935. Yet, this was only part of the story. As many authors had suggested since the 1870s, the continuing high maternal death rate was not so much due to some extraordinary and insurmountable factor but rather to the summation of a whole series of relatively slight and rather dull defects in education and sins of omission. Remedies were known and at hand but not applied. The Rochdale experiment provided vivid confirmation of this thesis. But it did more than that. When Oxley, Phillips, and Young reviewed the Rochdale experiment, they remarked:

> It is significant that the analysis of the individual death records failed to reveal any evidence for the view that the high death rate of Rochdale could be attributed to factors arising out of the economic disabilities from which, as a highly industrialised community, this borough, in common with its neighbours, was naturally suffering during the years of the investigation. In other words, the investigation showed, in the majority of the cases, the existence of obstetrical factors which in many instances were capable, with considerable justification, of being regarded as preventable.[129]

CONCLUSION

It seems that the absence of any significant fall in the maternal mortality rate in Britain between the mid-nineteenth century (and possibly earlier) and 1935 was due to the absence of any significant improvement in the standard of domiciliary care by midwives and general practitioners during this period. Delivery at home by Denman or Granville in the early nineteenth century may have been as safe as delivery by the average midwife or general practitioner in Rochdale or Doncaster in 1930. The apparent absence of any relation between the maternal mortality rate and changing standards of living is surprising. While it suggests that social and economic factors were generally much less important than clinical factors, it would be a mistake to conclude that poverty and malnutrition can never affect maternal mortality. That would be an absurd proposition, and the explanation for the absence of any clear historical evidence of a connexion between malnutrition and maternal mortality within the period considered here may be due to a tacit assumption. That assumption is that the relationship is linear — that mild, moderate, and severe malnutrition respectively would produce a proportionate increase in mortality. The actual relationship may be quite different. It is possible that the physiological processes of childbirth are little affected by moderate or even quite severe degrees of malnutrition until, at some point of great severity, those processes break down and maternal mortality increases both suddenly and greatly. The imagined graph, instead of being a straight line, may be a very gentle slope turning suddenly into a steep ascent. Current studies from the Third World may throw light on this proposition. Indeed, answers might be sought on this and other problems of maternal mortality from a study of maternal mortality in other countries in the past two centuries. It was tempting to include such data during the preparation of this paper, but it became increasingly clear that comparative statistics would have no meaning unless they were presented within the context of all aspects of obstetric care in each country considered. In other words, it would be necessary to compare not only the statistics,

[129]W.H.F. Oxley, Miles H. Phillips, and James Young, 'Maternal mortality in Rochdale. An achievement in a black area', *Br. med. J.*, 1935, i: 304–307.

40

but also the development of obstetric care, the relative amount of care provided at home or in hospital, the distribution between midwives and medical practitioners, the development of obstetric training and attitudes to obstetrics, and other factors which are known to affect mortality rates. This would have to be done for every country whose statistics were compared to those of Britain. While this would undoubtedly be an important contribution to the history of obstetric care, it was clearly impossible to contemplate within the confines of this paper.

POSTSCRIPT

This study terminated with the introduction of the sulphonamides. But a brief discussion of maternal mortality after 1936 has a bearing on the earlier period. The fall in maternal mortality from 1936 was, in the first few years, almost entirely due to the decrease in deaths from puerperal fever (fig.2). It can be attributed with confidence to the sulphonamides, and later the antibiotics. The fall in deaths from the "accidents of childbirth", which was largely unaffected by antibiotic treatment, started about 1939 and then followed a steep downward path in parallel with the fall in deaths from puerperal fever. Why? The suggested reasons for the overall reduction in mortality, are first the antibiotics and blood transfusion, and second, better clinical care, better education of medical students and midwives, greater co-operation between general practitioners and midwives and consultants, the increasing application of ante-natal care, and better nutrition with iron and vitamin supplements. All these changes were introduced on a very wide scale as a result of the wartime organization of food and maternity services.[130] Once introduced, they were extended during the post-war period. Thus the changes which led to the dramatic fall in the deaths from "accidents of childbirth" were those which were conspicuous by their absence in the first third of the twentieth century. The reasons suggested for the undiminished mortality up to 1935 are consistent with those suggested for the subsequent sharp and sustained fall in childbirth deaths. The story as a whole can be seen to be consistent.

ACKNOWLEDGEMENTS

This work was undertaken during the tenure of a Wellcome Research Fellowship, and the author wishes to express his gratitude to the Wellcome Trust. Dr C. Redman, Obstetric Physician to the John Radcliffe Hospital in Oxford, kindly advised the author on current views on toxaemia. Charles Webster, Jonathan Barry, and David Hamilton of the Wellcome Unit for the History of Medicine in Oxford provided invaluable advice in the preparation of the manuscript, and Adrian Wilson gave kind permission to quote from his thesis on midwifery during the seventeenth and eighteenth centuries. Two secondary sources have been of very great value in understanding the complexities of medical men, midwives, and maternal care. They are Jean Donnison, *Midwives and medical men*, 1977, and Jane Lewis, *The politics of motherhood: child and maternal welfare in England, 1900-1939*, 1980, and the author would like to acknowledge their importance to his work. The author is grateful to Dr Alison Macfarlane for permission to reproduce figs. 3 and 4.

[130]For a review of the maternity services during the second world war, see *On the state of the public health, 1939—45*, Ministry of Health, section IV, 'Maternity and child welfare.' For the effect of wartime measures and other factors in the reduction of maternal mortality see W.Gilliat, 'A discussion on maternal mortality' in A.W.Bourne and W.C.W.Nixon, (editors), *XIIth British Congress of Obstetrics and Gynaecology*, London, Austral Press, 1949.

41

CASES

OF

PUERPERAL CONVULSIONS,

WITH REMARKS.

BY JOHN C. W. LEVER, M.D.

T HE following Fourteen Cases of Puerperal Convulsions, out of Seven thousand four hundred and four women attended by the Pupils attached to the Lying-in-Charity of Guy's Hospital, have occurred between the years 1834 and 1843.

The symptoms which marked their course, and the principles which guided their treatment, present no new or extraordinary feature ; but the coincidence of an albuminous condition of the urine, in nine out of ten cases in which that secretion was examined, is a fact which, so far as my investigations and inquiries have extended, has not been previously remarked.

CASE 1.

Fifth Confinement—Anæmic Convulsion from Loss of Blood—
Mother recovered—Child born alive.

ELIZA H——, aged 36, in labour with her fifth child. When seven months pregnant, she had a discharge of blood ; and about a week previous to her labour, whilst rising from her chair, about half-a-pint again passed from her, unattended by pain or effort: this discharge continued, in greater or less quantities, up to the time of her labour. She was much depressed in spirits, and complained of feeling weak : her pulse was feeble, 80. She had been living in a state of most abject penury for two or three months, subsisting for days on a single meal of bread and tea. Her face and body were covered with cachectic sores. Mr. Tweedie, who was called to Mr. Champion's assistance, made an examination. The os uteri scarcely admitted the point of his finger, and the disturbance brought back a return of the bleeding. She was ordered,

Ol. Ricini ʒvi. Tinct. Opii. ʒſs. s. s.
Infus. Rosæ C. c̄ Acid. Sulph. dilut. pro potione.
A little sago, flavoured with wine.

On the 28th, and morning of the 29th, she was better: the discharge was not so great, but of a more offensive character. At 10 P.M.

L L 2

Mr. Tweedie was summoned: he was informed, that since 2 o'clock she had had several fits resembling those of epilepsy, followed by stertorous breathing, and insensibility: her pulse was 72, feeble; pupils variable: on being roused, she said she had a most severe headache.   During Mr. Tweedie's visit, she was seized with a rigor, followed by paroxysms of convulsion, alternating with stertorous breathing.   Towards the conclusion of these fits, there seemed to be a certain degree of uterine contraction; and, on examination, the os uteri was found fully dilated, the child's head presenting at the brim of the pelvis.   Her hair was removed from her head; but the pulse would not admit of the least depletion.   From this time the convulsions increased in force and frequency until 1 A.M., when the child was suddenly expelled during a fit;—a female, living, but very small, and apparently but seven months advanced.   The placenta was readily removed.   There was no unusual hæmorrhage, and the perinæum had not been injured.   After the birth of the child, she lay insensible, and could not be made to swallow either medicine or sustenance: the pulse remained exceedingly feeble, and 72: the convulsions continued to recur, though less powerfully than before; and as depletion was contra-indicated, abundant dashing of cold water over the face was the only remedy which circumstances permitted to make use of.   A full dose of æther, liq. opii sed., and ammonia, was with difficulty administered.   The convulsions continued all night, with scarcely any abatement, interrupted only by intervals of coma: pulse 72, weak: pupils contracted: conjunctiva clear: she passed her urine in the bed.

In consequence of the abject destitution of her home, she was removed into Guy's Hospital, and placed, under Dr. Ashwell's care, in the Obstetric Ward.   During the removal she had a convulsion, and reached the ward nearly lifeless.

> Lot. Spirit. cap. raso.   Hyd. Chlorid. gr. xij. stat.
> Enema Colocynth. postea.
> To have sago, flavoured with wine.

She remained in this critical state for some days; but then gradually and slowly recovered, and left the ward in a state of convalescence.

Case 2.

Primipara—Unmarried—Mother recovered—Child born alive.

Ellen B——, unmarried, and 21 years of age, was taken in labour on Monday evening, April 21st.   The membrane ruptured when the os uteri was of the size of a dollar, firm, and resisting.   After complaining of considerable pain in the head, and vomiting violently, she was attacked with convulsions.   Mr. Chabot, her attendant, bled her, cut off her hair, applied cold to her head, and administered a dose of calomel. Mr. Chabot requesting my assistance, I visited her. The head was then pressing on the perinæum: her pulse was full, bounding, 72: her pupils contracted. The fits occurred three times. Blood was again drawn. The fits continued to occur until the birth of the child and secundines, which was effected in about four hours. From this period she had no more fits, but was insensible for a long time. As she was in great distress, being with her mother, a poor widow, she was removed into the Obstetric Ward of Guy's Hospital, where she speedily convalesced.

CASE 3.

Primipara—Anæmic Convulsions—Child born alive—
Mother recovered.

M. S——, aged 21, a thin delicate young woman, was taken in labour on April 5th. The membranes ruptured early, before the dilatation of the os uteri; and by the time the head had advanced into the pelvic cavity she was extremely exhausted. As the head was pressing in the perinæum, she was attacked with a convulsion: the pulse was 130, scarcely to be felt: the extremities cold; and the head hot. Warmth was applied to the extremities, cold to the head; and so soon as she could swallow, some stimulus was poured into the stomach. Three fits occurred before, and one after the expulsion of the child. Both mother and child recovered.

CASE 4.

Convulsions before delivery—9th Confinement—Mother recovered—
Child born alive.

LOUISA M—— was seized with a very severe convulsive fit six weeks before her confinement: this was speedily followed by a second. Venesection, mercurial purgatives, tartar emetic, purgative enemata, cold applications to the head, were ordered, and with relief. Four weeks after, or two weeks before her labour, she was again attacked, and similarly treated. As she complained of a constant pain in her head, noise in the ears, dimness of vision, &c., a seton was passed through the nape of the neck: this afforded her great relief. The labour was natural, although some considerable hæmorrhage followed the expulsion of the placenta. The child was born alive.

CASE 5.

Primipara—Version—Urine highly albuminous—Mother recovered
—Child still-born.

ELLEN D——, aged 23, a very large muscular Irishwoman, who had been married nine months, sent for Mr. Woolnough at half-past 3 o'clock P.M., October 20th. He was told that at 3 P.M. she began to talk at random. At 5 o'clock she was attacked with a very severe convulsion: during its continuance, her pupils alternately contracted and dilated in quick succession: her pulse varied, ranging from 100 to 160 beats in a minute. He bled her from the arm to ℥xl.; her head was shaved; cold evaporating lotions were kept constantly on the scalp; mustard-poultices were applied to the feet; a turpentine injection administered; and ten grains of calomel were placed upon the tongue. At 8 o'clock P.M. another severe convulsion occurred, when ℥xij. more blood were abstracted from the arm. At 10 o'clock, Dr. Lever found, upon examination, the os uteri was dilated to the size of a half-crown, the membranes protruding, and the head presenting: and as the convulsions recurred very frequently; and as their strength by no means diminished, he thought it advisable to perform the operation of version: this was accomplished, and a still-born female child expelled: the uterus contracted firmly, and in ten minutes expelled the placenta. After her delivery, the convulsions recurred; and as the pulse maintained its firmness and tone, blood was again abstracted, by opening the temporal artery and by cupping. At 2 A.M., October 29th, her fits continued, at intervals of about twenty minutes: her pupils were dilated: she was insensible: her pulse was full, 110. She was ordered hyd. chlorid. gr. iv. 3tis horis. At 10 A.M. she had another convulsion: her pulse was full and hard, 100. ℥xx. more blood were taken from the arm: and this last quantity of blood was found to be *very much buffed and cupped*, although *none* of the blood abstracted *previously* presented these appearances. At the suggestion of Dr. Ashwell, she took ant. pot. tart. gr. ¼ every quarter of an hour; and remained nearly an hour without being convulsed. At 1 o'clock she had a very violent fit; and was ordered to continue the ant. pot. tart. At half-past 10 P.M. her pulse was 110; and there were some symptoms of returning consciousness.

Oct. 30. Much the same: rather more sensible: the bowels have been relieved: she was ordered hyd. chlorid. gr. i. cret. prep. gr. ij. 4tis horis.

Oct. 31. As she was in great distress, living in a very low lodging-house, she was brought into Petersham Ward, Guy's Hospital, and continued there upwards of five weeks. The mercury produced considerable irritation of the mouth and bowels; to relieve which, various remedies were resorted to. She suffered also very considerably from a vaginal abscess, accompanied with ulceration of the sphincter.

Her urine, which was daily abstracted by the catheter, was subjected to the usual tests; and was found, at first, *to be highly charged with albumen*. This gradually decreased until November 3, when it lost all traces of that substance.

Three weeks previous to this woman's confinement, her legs and thighs were considerably swollen: and so œdematous were the eye-lids in the morning, that she could scarcely see. She presented the appearance offered by patients labouring under the Morbus Brightii, to such a degree, that my late colleague Mr. Tweedie, Dr. Gull, and myself, who saw her at distinct times, were equally impressed with the idea that she was affected with that disease; and it was this im-pression that led us to investigate the nature and character of her urine.

Case 6.

Anæmic Convulsions — Married — 4th Confinement — Partial Pla-cental Presentation—Mother recovered—Child still-born.

C. W——, a female of moderate stature, with light hair, 23 years of age, and who had never borne a living child, sent for Mr. Wool-nough, November 19th. There had been some considerable hæmor-rhage (a pint), and the pains were short and frequent. On examination, the os uteri was dilated to the size of a crown-piece; the soft parts were relaxed, the placenta partially presenting; posteriorly, the mem-branes were entire. As the bleeding continued, Mr. Woolnough ruptured the membranes: the feet of the child and a large coil of funis presented: the pains continued, and in about half-an-hour the child was expelled. It was still-born, and to all appearance had been dead for some days.

This patient progressed favourably until November 22d, at mid-night, when Mr. Woolnough found her in convulsions: her pulse was slow and feeble, 55: the pupils were dilated. The *urine drawn from the bladder* gave abundant evidence of albumen, upon the appli-cation of the proper tests. I ordered her,

> Jul. Am. Sesq. c̄ Sp. A. Aromat. m xij. 4tis horis.
> Ol. Ricin. ʒi. cras primo mane sum.

At noon, the bowels had been freely opened; the pulse was feeble, 65; the tongue clean: no return of convulsions: the *traces of albu-men in the urine are very faint.*

Nov. 27. In every respect improved.

Dec. 1. Convalescent. *All traces of albumen lost.*

Case 7.

Primipara — Unmarried — Child expelled by the natural efforts — Urine coagulable—Mother recovered—Child born alive.

Elizabeth G——, aged 19, a short girl, unmarried, with light hair and of fair complexion, was taken in labour at 9 P.M. on Monday, February 7th. The labour progressed slowly, but naturally, until Tuesday at 3 P.M., when the os uteri was dilated to the size of a crown-piece, the labour-pains recurring with vigour: the head soon descended to the outlet; but the parts offered great resistance, from their rigidity. At half-past 5 she began to talk incoherently; and suddenly a convulsive paroxysm supervened, rapidly followed by a second; and during the fit the child was expelled. The uterus contracted firmly. In a short time a third convulsion took place, and the placenta was then expelled. She was bled to ℥xvi. Hyd. chlorid. gr. x. were placed upon the tongue. The head was shaved; and ice, in a bladder, kept continually applied. The pulse was slow and labouring. Hirudines xxiv. were ordered to the temples; but during their application she was attacked with a convulsion much more violent than the preceding fits; and she lay in a state of coma for three-quarters of an hour. At 12 o'clock, another convulsion took place. The ant. pot. tart. was administered, in half-grain doses, every two hours; but as the fits recurred more frequently, it was administered every hour, for three hours; and as nausea was produced, the dose was diminished to ¼ of a grain. After two o'clock she had no more convulsions; but as the calomel had not operated, 15 grains of jalap were given, followed in an hour by the enema saponis. This had the effect of producing copious very offensive dejections. During the course of the evening the urine was abstracted from the bladder by the catheter; and when subjected to a boiling heat, it *became like gruel;* and a subsequent examination, with nitric acid, shewed that it contained a *considerable quantity of albumen.* As this girl was in great distress, she was removed into Petersham Ward. For several days she continued the ant. pot. tart.; with occasional doses of aperients, as her bowels were naturally torpid. She left the hospital perfectly recovered.

It appeared, on inquiry, that for some time previous to her confinement she was troubled *with puffiness of the eyelids* and *with œdema of the legs.*

CASE 8.

*Primipara; delivered by the Forceps—Urine albuminous—
Child born alive—Mother recovered.*

Reported by Mr. SPONG.

" ANN M —, aged 19, a married woman, of small stature, of leuco-
" phlegmatic temperament; has been in good health during her gesta-
" tion. For several days previous to the commencement of labour
" she was annoyed with spurious pains referred to the back and sto-
" mach. On Friday night, uterine efforts commenced: these continued
" throughout Saturday, until 3 o'clock on Sunday afternoon, when Dr.
" Lever was called to see her. The head was partly in the cavity; the
" membranes ruptured; the pelvis of small size, and the perinæum thick
" and rigid. At half-past 4 she had a convulsion: she was bled to
" 26 ounces; a castor-oil injection was administered, and the mist.

" antim. pot. tart. was given every half hour. *The urine, drawn from*
" *the bladder by the catheter, became cloudy both upon the application*
" *of heat and nitric acid.* During the convulsion the head descended
" a little; but made no further progress until 8 o'clock, when she was
" attacked with another fit. She was again bled from the arm; and
" as the external parts had become relaxed, Dr. Lever delivered her of
" a living child, by the forceps. *The urine continued albuminous for*
" *twenty-four hours* after the first attack of convulsions; but there
" was no return of fits after her delivery. She rapidly convalesced."

Upon inquiry, I could not ascertain that this patient had suffered
from any œdematous swellings before her confinement; but for two
or three days she had complained of pain in the head, accompanied
with some torpor, and unusual obtuseness of intellect.

CASE 9.

Second Confinement—Convulsions after Delivery—Urine Albuminous
—Mother recovered—Child born alive.

ELLEN D ——, who was attacked with convulsions in her first confinement (see Case 5), was delivered, on the 25th October 1842, of
a living male child, by Mr. Woolnough. He left her at 1 P.M. conscious: her pulse 75. At 4 P.M. he was called to her, and found
that in the intervening three hours she had had several convulsions.
Her pulse was 110, full: she was totally insensible. She was bled
to 20 ounces, and took the mist. ant. pot. tart. (gr. $\frac{1}{4}$), every half hour.
The head was kept cool by an evaporating lotion, and mustard cata
plasms were applied to the feet. *The urine, which had been drawn*
by the catheter, became milky, both upon the application of heat and
nitric acid. From this period the convulsions ceased, and she convalesced; her recovery being retarded by a distressing cough.
The urine did not entirely lose the albumen until November 3.

CASE 10.

Ninth Pregnancy—Child Still-born—Mother died—Inflammation
of the Membranes of the Brain.

C. A ——, aged 32, married, and has borne eight children; of intem-
perate habits; sanguineous temperament, and very corpulent. On
the morning of January 5th, her attendant, Mr. Cotton, was sent for.
She had been out on the previous evening to make some purchases,
and had indulged rather freely in drinking: she was found sitting on
her bed, rather excited, but sensible: she gave rational answers to the
questions put to her. She complained of violent pain in the head,
which had been troublesome for a week; and her pulse was much
accelerated. To relieve the headache, she had the previous day
applied a blister to the nape of the neck; and on the morning of the

day on which she was seen, three leeches to her temple. There were
no labour-pains; neither were there any symptoms of labour apparent
to Mr. Cotton; but as she stated she had lost a considerable quantity of blood, he fetched me from the hospital, to see her. When
we entered her room, we found her lying on the bed, comatose;
her pupils dilated: her head was hot: in a very few minutes she was
attacked with an epileptic convulsion, marked by the usual symptoms. The hair was removed, and cold affusion employed. She was
bled to ℥xxx: a glyster was thrown into the rectum, but not retained.
About half-a-pint of urine was abstracted by the catheter: this, when
examined by heat and nitric acid, afforded no traces of albumen. On
vaginal examination, the os uteri was found opened to the size of a
half-crown-piece, and very dilatable: the head presented. It was
deemed advisable to complete the labour by the operation of turning;
and the patient being placed in the usual position, version was readily
accomplished, but the proper remedies, diligently employed, failed to
resuscitate the child. The uterus contracted well, and expelled the
placenta in twenty minutes: this organ was flabby; more dry than
usual; and in it there were many deposits, giving it the appearance of
hobnailed liver. For two hours the convulsions recurred, with increasing intensity, and the intervals between these attacks were shorter.
As the patient was in a dreadfully destitute condition, it was deemed
advisable to remove her to the hospital. At half-past 2, when admitted, the heat of the head was increased; the pupils were inobedient,
dilated; the left larger than the right: respiration stertorous; pulse
small, and thready; extremities warm. In about a quarter of an
hour after her admission, she had another slight fit: the mouth was
drawn to the right side: she took two deep inspirations, and suddenly
and quietly expired.

POST-MORTEM EXAMINATION.—The body was examined twenty-four
hours after death, by Mr. King. "The arachnoïd above was opaque,
tumid, and yellowish, being raised by a large quantity of turbid water
in the pia mater. The dura mater on the right hemisphere was lined
by a soft pale red tumid arachnoïd; that of the left side incipiently so.
The disease of all the membranes was most visible on the right side.
The base was similarly affected. The brain was pale: there were four
or five drachms of milky fluid in the ventricles: the lumbar arachnoïd
was slightly clouded: the heart was flabby; the right side contained
large dark coagula: the liver was pale, soft, of clear texture, seeming
(only) fatty: the spleen was tumid, and much softened: the kidneys
gave out much blood, but were not dark; their texture coarse and
flabby: the uterus was larger than a child's head, white and pudding-
like: the left end of the stomach was digested, and ecchymosed."

This woman was talking to a friend in her room five minutes before she was attacked with the convulsion which left her in that comatose state in which she was found by Mr. Cotton and myself, and from which state of insensibility she never rallied. When did the cerebral effusion take place? Was there any effusion before the convulsion? Did all these evidences of cerebral disease display themselves in three hours?

CASE 11.

Primipara—Convulsions—Delivered by Forceps—Emphysema—
Death—Child alive—Urine albuminous.

To JULIA C——, a short stout Irishwoman, of sanguine temperament, plethoric habits, married, and about eight months advanced in pregnancy, Mr. Hewitt was suddenly called, on June 23d. The account he received from the mother was, that for some days the patient's bowels had been constipated; that for 48 hours she had complained of considerable pain in the head, and her face had been alternately flushed and pale. At 4 A.M. she had taken a dose of salts and senna, but soon vomited it: at 9 A.M. she was seized with a convulsion: her lips were livid: eyes fixed; mouth distorted, and covered with foam. Although much alarmed, her friends did not send for Mr. Hewitt for three hours; during which time she had several returns of the fits, and had been perfectly insensible during the intervals. Mr. Hewitt found her comatose: her skin was cool; her countenance placid; breathing tranquil; the pupils slightly dilated, but obedient to light: the pulse was 100, full, and bounding: she was perfectly unconscious, all attempts to rouse her being ineffectual. V. S. ad ℥xxv. was practised, when the pulse became rapid and fluttering. As the arm was being tied up, she had another most violent fit, during which the pupils became dilated. The hair was removed from the scalp; an aperient glyster immediately administered; and liq. ant. pot. tart. ʒi. was given every half hour. On vaginal examination, the os uteri was found dilated to the size of a shilling, with a thin sharp edge; and the head presenting. From this time until half-past 2 P.M. the fits continued at intervals of about half-an-hour. Twenty ounces more blood were abstracted from the arm, and she continued the tartar emetic. The os uteri became soft and dilated; and labour was evidently progressing. Between the fits, the patient rolled about the bed and moaned: this was apparently caused by the uterine efforts. At half-past 3 the fits still recurred, and more frequently: ℥viij. of blood were taken from the temporal artery. At 5 o'clock P.M. I delivered her with the short forceps; but previous to their introduction, the bladder was emptied by the catheter: the urine, when examined, proved to be *highly albuminous*, of the sp. grav. 1010. The uterus contracted well, and soon expelled the placenta. Very soon after delivery, the patient had a fit, again repeated in half-an-hour: at the termination of the latter, the heart's movements and respiration were completely suspended for several actions, and were but very slowly re-established. At 8 P.M., finding the pulse full and rapid, and the fits as violent and more frequent, I ordered,

V. S. ad ℥xxiv.

Ant. Pot. Tart. gr.fs. omni horâ ; et Hyd. Chlorid. gr. x. stat.

Ice was kept constantly applied to the head ; and the antimony was given every hour, until 4 A.M. on Friday morning, when the convulsions ceased altogether : there having been twenty fits after delivery, and about seventeen before. The antimony was continued at intervals of three hours. The calomel produced several stools ; which, together with the urine, were passed involuntarily : the pulse was 130, small and compressible. A blister was ordered to the nape of the neck, and sinapisms to the soles of the feet. At 6 P.M. she was exceedingly restless ; and so violent, that it was deemed necessary to confine her arms and legs : half-a-pint of urine was drawn by the catheter, which, tested by heat and nitric acid, *did not coagulate.* Two grains of calomel were given, with the quarter of a grain of tartar emetic ; and as the blister had been rubbed off, another was applied to the nape of the neck. At 1 A.M., Saturday, she suddenly exclaimed, "Give me a drink of water !" At 10 o'clock she was quite conscious, and able to recognise every one in the room : complained of pain in the forehead : her pupils were natural : respiration tranquil : pulse 130 : the right cheek, and right side of the neck, were emphysematous.

Hyd. Chlorid. gr. fs. 4tis horis superbibendo.

Liq. Ant. Pot. Tart. m xxv. Sp. Æth. Nit. ℥ fs. ex Julep. Ammon.
Acet. et Mist. Camph. āā ℥fs.

She was ordered sago ; and the refrigeration of the head was maintained by the ice.

At 11 P.M. the emphysema had considerably increased : the breathing was oppressed. Incisions were made on each clavicle, and a roller was placed around the chest.

Sunday, 9 A.M. The breathing much more tranquil ; the bowels have been opened three times ; the gums swollen and tender.

Omit. Hyd. Chlorid. et Liq. Ant. Pot. Tart.

Monday, the bandage was removed, and the chest examined. The whole of the lungs were very resonant on percussion, anteriorly ; puerile respiration at both apices ; at other parts, great deficiency of respiration ; and the inspiration, especially posteriorly, accompanied with a wheeze : no decided *craquement.* On listening over the anterior mediastinum, and causing the patient to hold her breath, a crackling was heard synchronously with the heart's systole. The patient continued in about the same state until Friday. The skin was tolerably cool; the tongue moist; the bowels open; but there was an almost constant contraction of the flexors of the thumb. Beef-tea and arrow-root were ordered. On Friday evening, diarrhœa supervened, accompanied with considerable tenesmus: the skin was hot, the face flushed; and the pulse became rapid, but readily compressed. A starch enema, with syrup of poppies, subdued the tenesmus, and the bowels were controlled by the mist. cret. comp. On Monday she was decidedly worse (her relations having given her kidneys and porter); her face was flushed; the surface of the body hot, and harsh; the conjunctivæ injected; and the edges of the eyelids were covered with viscid secretion: the pupils were contracted; the eyebrows knitted; the gums tender; the tongue red and dry; bowels opened twice in twelve hours; the pulse rapid and feeble.

Liq. Ant. Pot. Tart. ʒiv. Jul. Am. Acet.. Mist. Camph. āā ʒiv. ft. mist. cujus cap. coch. ij. amp. 4tis horis.

On Tuesday she was reported to have coughed frequently, without expectoration; the surface of the body still very hot; conjunctivæ as before. From this time she sank gradually, and died on Saturday, at 4 A.M.

No post-mortem examination was permitted.

CASE 12.

*Unmarried—Primipara—Convulsions supervening after delivery—
Child living—Mother recovered—Urine albuminous.*

Reported by Mr. HARDY.

M. S——, aged 18, of middle stature, stout, but pale, unmarried, was taken in her first labour at 1 A.M. of September 12th. At half-past 2 P.M. the os uteri was dilated to the size of a shilling. For the next four hours the pains were neither strong nor frequent. At half-past 8, their strength and frequency returned, and continued until half-past 10, when a living child was expelled; followed, in a quarter of an hour, by the secundines. In half-an-hour after delivery this female was suddenly seized with a convulsive paroxysm, followed quickly by a second and third.

V.S. ad ʒ xl.

Cap. abrad.; et Lot. Evap. Spirit. const. applic.

Hyd. Chlorid. gr. x. statim; et Mist. Ant. Pot. Tart. ʒi. omni 2dâ horâ.

In two hours, the pupils, which had been dilated, obeyed the stimulus of light. Her bowels were loaded with fæces, and the enema terebinth. was administered. The urine, which was drawn from the bladder by the catheter, was acid and *highly albuminous*, of the sp. gravity of 1005.

From this time she had no more convulsions; although she complained for several days of heaviness and pain across the forehead, which was relieved by the local abstraction of blood. Her gums were swollen; her breath fetid; and her tongue covered with vesicles, although but 10 grains of calomel were administered, and these at one dose at the commencement.

The urine, drawn twelve hours after her delivery, was high-coloured, sp. gravity 1020; and contained *albumen*, although its quantity was less, compared with that abstracted at the period of the fits. This secretion was rigidly examined from time to time; and evidence of its containing albumen became fainter and fainter, until it entirely ceased, thirty-six hours after her delivery.

For three or four months previous to her confinement, this girl was in the habit of taking considerable quantities of ardent spirits.

CASE 13.

Primipara—Convulsions—Twins—Forceps—Turning—-Urine albuminous—Mother recovered—Children alive.

H. R ——, aged 33, a strong healthy young woman, unmarried, sent for her medical attendant at 8 P.M. on Nov. 13. He found she had been suffering from spurious irregular pains since the Thursday previous. Upon examination, the os uteri was found high in the vagina, of the size of a sixpence : its edge sharp and cutting, but dilatable. At 2 A.M. on Nov. 14th, examination was again instituted. The mouth of the womb had dilated considerably: the head presented, and the pains continued strong and vigorous. At half-past 3 their duration was lessened: they recurred at irregular intervals; and between the periods of their occurrence the patient dosed. At 5 A.M. the head was engaged in the pelvic cavity: the perinæum was not distended, but was rather thick and unyielding. At half-past 6 the pains entirely ceased; when the patient suddenly became unconscious; her eyes fixed and staring; the pupils alternately dilated and contracted; and the pulse was strong and labouring. Her attendant, Mr. Cotton, bled her to ℥viij.; and when this quantity of blood was abstracted, she complained of faintness. Having been sent for, I had scarcely entered the apartment when she was attacked with a severe convulsion: her features were distorted; the head was thrown back; the limbs stretched and rigid, and the eyes fixed and staring: the vein was again opened, and about a pint of blood was drawn, in a full stream, until the pulse became small, soft, and compressible. The catheter was introduced, and a pint of urine was drawn off. By means of the forceps, I succeeded in delivering the first child. After waiting for half-an-hour, without any effort at expulsion becoming manifest, I determined to perform the operation of version: this was accomplished with facility. The uterus contracted well, and the secundines were expelled naturally. When she was left, at half-past 9, she was conscious; complained of a weight on the forehead, and of the loss of her sight. Pulv. jalap c̄. hyd. Ɖi. was ordered, immediately to be followed by an enema. At 11 she had another convulsive fit, during which a severe wound was inflicted on the tongue. Twelve leeches were ordered to the temples; the head to be shaved; and a cold refrigerating lotion kept constantly applied. The liq. ant. pot. tart. was ordered, in half-drachm doses, every four hours. At 4 P. M. Mr. Cotton was called to this patient, who was attacked with another convulsion more violent than either of the preceding: he found her in a semi-comatose state: the leeches, which had not been applied, were immediately placed upon the temples; her pulse was 92. At 7 P. M., about a pint and a half of turbid urine was drawn off: at this time she answered questions rationally, and could both see and hear distinctly. The bowels not having been relieved, the enema terebinth. was immediately administered.

Nov. 15, half-past 7 A. M. Has passed a good night: the pain in the head lessened: the urine, drawn by the catheter, has the well-known odour communicated by the turpentine administered on the previous evening. Pulse 80, soft. From this time she gradually recovered; and the report on the 30th is, " Quite convalescent."

The following particulars, shewing the character and quantity of urine, are interesting :—

	Sp.G.	Effect of Heat.	Nit. Acid.
Water taken away before the delivery of the first child } turbid,	1017	milky,	very coag., acid.
6 hours after delivery, cloudy,	1022	flocculent,	coag., acid.
24 . . . . clear,	1010	turbid,	turbid, very acid.
36 . . . . clear,	1004	none,	none, acid.
72 . . . . dark col.	1007	none,	none, very acid.

QUANTITY OF URINE.

Nov. 14th. Before delivery of the first child, one pint was drawn off.
At 7 P.M. . . . . one pint and a half.
15th. At half-past 7 A.M. . . . . one pint and a half.
At 1 P.M. . . . . two pints.

Thus, in twenty-eight or twenty-nine hours six pints of urine were abstracted.

CASE 14.

Second Confinement—Forceps—Mother recovered—Child born dead.

M. F——, a short stout woman of light complexion, was delivered of a six-months' child in October 1841. At 2 A.M. October 4th, 1842, Mr. Rubidge was summoned to her in her second labour: the pains had commenced at 10 o'clock on the previous evening, but during the last hour had greatly increased in severity: at the same time, their duration had augumented. On examination, the os uteri was found to be about one inch in diameter, and rigid. She complained of head-ache, and vomited frequently. Pulse 95, full and hard. The pains continued severe and frequent; but the os uteri dilated but slowly. At half-past 5 A.M. she was suddenly seized with a violent convulsion, and the fits continued to recur with but little intermission until 7 o'clock. During this time, ℥xxx. of blood were abstracted from the arm, and a tea-spoonful of the liq. ant. pot. tart. administered every quarter of an hour. The os uteri became relaxed, but the pains were feeble. At half-past 7, Dr. Oldham delivered with the forceps. The child was still born, and the cord was empty and contracted. Cold evaporating lotion was continually applied to the head. At 1 P.M. she complained of severe headache, and some abdominal tender-ness. Pulse 140, and jerking: pupils dilated. Enema ol. ricini stat. injiciend.

5th. She was reported to have slept well; there had been no return of convulsions; her bowels had been freely opened: pulse 90. From this time she rapidly convalesced, and went into the country on the 14th.

Her urine, which was abstracted by the catheter at the time of her delivery, was of sp. gr. 1010, slightly acid : it became *very flocculent* upon the application of heat, and when nitric acid was added. This coagulability of the urine disappeared gradually ; and on October 8th the appearance and character of the excretion were perfectly normal. This patient had suffered from slight puffiness of the eyelids, and œdema of the legs and feet, previous to her delivery.

Ratio of Mortality.—(1. To Mother.)   From these Reports it will be seen, that out of fourteen cases of Puerperal Convulsions two only were fatal.   Drs. Hunter, Lowder, &c. former Teachers of Midwifery, were accustomed to state, in their Lectures, that this disease proved fatal in more than half of the cases attacked.   Dr. Parr, in his Medical Dictionary, gives even a worse picture than this.   But the results of the disease may be gathered from the following Table :—

	Cases of Convulsions.	Mothers Lost.	Prop. Per Cent.
Dr. Bland	2	0	—
Mr. Perfect	14	5	35·7
Mr. Gifford	4	2	50·
Dr. John Clarke	19	6	31·5
Dr. Smellie	8	2	25·
Dr. Merriman	36	8	22·2
Dr. Ramsbotham	26	10	38·4
Dr. Maunsell	4	2	50·
Dr. Collins	30	5	16·6
Dr. Beatty	1	—	—
Dr. Churchill	2	—	—
Mr. Mantell	6	2	33·3
Dr. Lever (Guy's)	14	2	14·2
Total	166	44	26·5

Thus it will be seen, that out of 166 cases of convulsions, 44 women died, or 26·5 per cent.   If the fourteen cases recorded in this Paper be omitted, the number of cases will be 152, and the number of deaths 42, or 27·6 per cent.; while the cases attended at the Lying-in-Charity of Guy's Hospital have proved fatal only in the proportion of one in seven, or 14·2 per cent.

(2. To Children.)   The fourteen women gave birth to fifteen children; eleven of whom were born alive, and four still-born.   Of the four still-born, two were delivered by the operation of turning; one by the employment of the forceps; and the other was a case of partial presentation of the placenta, in which the child descended with the feet forwards.

Cases of Labour, and Method of Delivery.—In seven cases the children were born by the natural efforts; in three, the forceps were employed; in two, the operation of turning was resorted to: in one case there were twins, the first of whom

Vol. I.   M M

was delivered by the forceps, the second by the operation of version; and in the last there was a partial presentation of the placenta.

Nine of the women were married, and five unmarried. Of the fourteen women, eight were primiparæ, and six had been previously confined.

Dr. Ramsbottom, sen., is of opinion that "women with large families are equally or perhaps more liable to be assailed;" but of twenty-one cases of convulsions recorded by him, in which the number of the pregnancies is stated, there are only two cases in which the pregnancy is not the first, with the exception of those instances in which the children were born prematurely at the sixth or seventh month. In five cases out of twenty-six, he has omitted to mention whether or no they were first pregnancies. Of nineteen cases recorded by Dr. Clarke, sixteen were first children; twenty-eight out of thirty-six, recorded by Dr. Merriman, were first children; and of thirty related by Dr. Collins, twenty-nine were first children.

In two of the cases, convulsions supervened before labour was established; in ten, they occurred during the progress of the labour; and in two, they did not exhibit themselves until after the birth of the child and the expulsion of the secundines.

Some writers, as Drs. Smellie and Denman, have imagined that this disease is, in a great measure, influenced by atmospheric causes. Andral is of opinion that the disease is probably connected with an electrical condition of the atmosphere, acting primarily on the nervous system, and producing cerebral excitement.

Through the kindness of Mr. Roberton, Assistant Librarian of the Royal Society, I have been enabled to insert the following Table, shewing the state of the weather upon the days each of the fourteen cases of convulsions was attacked.

CASE	9 A.M.		3 P.M.		EXT. THERMOMETER.				DIRECTION OF WIND.	STATE OF WEATHER.
	Barom.	Att. Therm	Barom.	Att. Therm.	Fahrenheit.		Self. Regis.			
					9 a.m.	3 p.m.	9 a.m.	3 p.m.		
1.	29·677	46	29·336	49	47	52	41	53	S. W.	Cloudy ; high wind.
2.	29·814	55	29·855	58	53	61	47	61	S. W.	Cloudy ; light wind.
3.	29·688	40	29·710	42	38	43	35	44	N. E.	Light clouds ; wind.
4.	30·304	79	30·278	61	51	57	44	64	N. W.	Light clouds ; wind.
5.	29·372	27	29·378	28	26	28	24	26	N.	Overcast ; light rain, freezing in falling.
6.	29·642	49	29·732	50	46	47	47	50	N.	Wind and rain.
7.	29·462	40	29·252	41	43	46	34	44	S. E.	Wind and rain.
8.	29·940	50	30·086	51	46	51	43	56	W.	Cloudy ; brisk wind.
9.	30·018	69	29·934	71	66	76	59	76	S.	Cloudy ; light wind.
10.	29·896	77	29·882	69	62	68	53	78	W.	Fine ; light clouds and breeze.
11.	29·844	61	29·882	63	60	63	56	65	N. W.	Fine, but windy.
12.	30·096	52	30·098	53	50	54	45	59	N. N. W.	Fine.
13.	30·312	52	30·286	53	51	54	49	54	W.	Wind.
14.	29·720	50	29·804	51	47	47	46	55	W.	Fog and wind.

M M 2

Condition of the Urine.—In the first four cases here recorded no mention is made of the condition of the urine, for our attention was not at that time directed to the investigation of this secretion. In the fifth case, Mr. Woolnough, my late colleague Mr. Tweedie, Dr. Gull, as well as myself, particularly noticed the great similarity that presented in her appearance and that of ·patients labouring under anasarca with the Morbus Brightii; and it was with this view that we proceeded to examine the condition of her urine.

At first, I was induced to believe that it was merely a case of pregnancy occurring in a woman affected with granular degeneration of the kidney; but as the traces of albumen became daily more faint, until they entirely disappeared on November 3, I was led to suppose that the albuminous condition of the urine depended upon some transient cause probably connected with the state of gestation itself.

To settle this point, I have carefully examined the urine in every case of puerperal convulsions that has since come under my notice, both in the Lying-in-Charity of Guy's Hospital and in private practice; and in *every case, but one,* the urine has been found to be *albuminous* at the time of the convulsions. In the case (10) in which the albumen was wanting, inflammation of the membranes of the brain, with considerable effusion, was detected after death. I further have investigated the condition of the urine in upwards of fifty women, from whom the secretion has been drawn, during labour, by the catheter; great care being taken that none of the vaginal discharges were mixed with the fluid: and the result has been, *that in* NO *cases have I detected albumen, except in those in which there have been convulsions, or in which symptoms have presented themselves, and which are readily recognised as the precursors of puerperal fits.*

Several obstetric writers have remarked that œdema of the face and extremities predispose to convulsions. M. Dugés, at p. 238, says, " On l'observe plus particulièrement chez les femmes enceintes qui sont affectées d'une anarsaque considérable des membres inférieurs, surtout si l'infiltration se propage aux membres supérieurs et à la face." I. T. Osiander considers a swollen condition of the face and hands as premonitory of the attacks. Velpeau, at p. 51 of his Treatise

" Des Convulsions chez les Femmes," says, " L'infiltration des membres pelviens surtout est une autre cause d'éclampsie:" and again, " J'ai la conviction, que les femmes infiltrées sont fortement exposées aux convulsions." Dr. Montgomery, at p. 6 of his " Signs and Symptoms of Pregnancy," after relating the case of a lady, in whom, " about the middle of the eighth month of pregnancy, the feet and legs began to swell," says, " when this latter form of œdema takes place, it ought to claim our most serious attention, as it is connected with a state of the vascular system, which, if active depleting measures be not previously adopted, will probably give rise to convulsions at the time of labour:" and of which the case of this lady was a well-marked instance.

In reply to a Letter I addressed to the Doctor, he states, that " it had never occurred to him to investigate the condition of the urine in these cases; but from the state of the system, under the circumstances, he thinks such a condition of the urine extremely probable." Dr. James Reid also, in his Report of Parochial Lying-in Cases, extending from June 1840 to February 1842, and published in the London Medical Gazette, after detailing a case of convulsions occurring in a strong robust woman, in whom " the legs were very œdematous, and the labia also very much enlarged," says, " I have known this state of the system to precede an attack of puerperal convulsions, in several cases." From what I have seen in public and private practice, I am led to the conclusion, that cases of convulsions complicated with an albuminous condition of the urine are divisible into two forms : in the one, the urine is *albuminous during pregnancy ;* and there are external evidences, as shewn in the œdema of the face, eyelids, hands, &c. In such cases, the convulsions will be more violent, and will last for a longer time after delivery. The urine also retains its albuminous properties for a longer period than in the second form, or that in which the urine becomes *albuminous during the labour.* In this variety, the urine contains less albumen ; the fits are less violent ; seldom re-appear after delivery has been completed ; and if they do, it is in a milder form, unless complicated with some lesion of the brain. The urine, in this form, very speedily loses all traces of albumen after labour is completed. Mr. Robinson,

in his Monograph *, has satisfactorily proved, that causes
which induce congestion of the kidney by preventing or
obstructing the return of blood through its veins, as abdominal tumors, &c., will produce renal congestion and albuminous urine : and I am of opinion, that the gravid condition of the uterus, by its pressure, prevents the return of the
blood through the emulgent veins; and hence is the cause of
the renal congestion, and the consequent albuminous condition of the urine. This opinion is supported by the facts
I have already adverted to; viz. that the urine was found to
be albuminous only in those women who were affected by, or
who had the premonitory symptoms of convulsions. The
pressure of the gravid uterus is by no means uniform, as
stated by some writers: this may be remarked in the difference in size and figure that females present in their
several pregnancies. In some, the uterus is distended more
at its posterior and lateral parts than at its anterior, and
vice versâ; and yet, in both, the contents of the uterus may
be equally great.

In these cases, the congestion will take place and the
urine become albuminous towards the close of pregnancy :
but this untoward pressure may not be excited until the
onset of labour; and as this progresses, the congestion may
be increased, and consequently the albuminous condition of
the urine be caused. Thus, in my opinion, we have the
same cause producing this condition of the urine both during
pregnancy and parturition. The great similitude that exists in
the appearances presented by females attacked with eclampsia,
and those observed in persons affected with albuminuria,
must have been oftentimes noticed by those who had atten-
tively regarded both. In neither case do the convulsions
strictly deserve the term "epileptic." Epilepsy is a chronic
disease; while puerperal convulsions, and the convulsions
which attend the progress of the Morbus Brightii, are of a
clonic character.

Condition of the Blood.—In but one case (No. 13) was the
blood submitted to analysis, but without detecting urea.

---

* An Inquiry into the Nature and Pathology of Granular Disease of the
Kidney, and its mode of action in producing Albuminous Urine.

If this case be referred to, it will be seen that the congestion took place during the labour; and although the congestion in the emulgent vessels may have been sufficient to have produced the albumen in the urine, yet there may not have been time for the blood to have become so impregnated with the urea as to permit its detection by the usual tests.

Treatment.—General Remarks.—It is not my intention to enter at length into the question of treatment in puerperal convulsions, but merely to make a few general remarks on the principal means of relief employed in the foregoing cases.

The cases are divisible into two kinds — anæmic and sthenic. Cases 1, 3, and 6, are examples of the anæmic variety; the remainder are of the sthenic form. In the treatment of the latter variety, our objects are, to cut short the paroxysm, remove the coma, and guard against another fit: these are to be accomplished by allaying the vascular excitement and congestion of the cerebral vessels; and by putting an end to the gestation, and thus removing the prime cause of congestion and irritation.

In the accomplishment of the first object, active depletion is essential. Moderate bleedings will be of no service, either in relaxing the uterus or in preventing effusion. The quantity of blood abstracted must depend entirely upon the urgency of the case, and the effects which the loss produces. In Case 5, one hundred and twenty-two ounces of blood were abstracted topically and generally in the course of seventeen hours. This large depletion is but seldom required; a more moderate loss of blood, in quantities sufficient to relax the uterus and prevent effusion, is all that is demanded, especially if the depletion be followed up by the prompt and regular exhibition of

Tartar Emetic.—By the use of this medicine the abstraction of blood in large quantities is rendered unnecessary, although its beneficial effects are seen to more advantage after some depletion has been practised. It possesses the power of lowering arterial excitement, and, at the same time, of relaxing those structures through which the child has to pass. In all cases of sthenic convulsions, it should be exhibited in doses sufficient to put the system under its nauseating influence, so that, by its agency, the return of the fits will be prevented, or, if not prevented, their force and frequency will be diminished. It is sometimes necessary to combine this medicine with a small proportion of opium, to prevent irritation of the mucous lining of the bowels, and consequent diarrhœa. If its exhibition be persevered with for some time, it may give rise to an erythematous eruption.

Purgatives.—Purging is of great importance in puerperal convulsions. In cases where the presence of deglutition is impeded or lost, a dose of calomel, from ten to fifteen grains, mixed up with butter, should be placed upon the tongue, and this followed by a drop or two of croton-oil: at the same time, the action of the bowels should be promoted by an enema of soap, colocynth, or turpentine. It is no unusual thing to find large quantities of hard scybala evacuated, even though the bowels may have been daily relieved.

Mercury.—This medicine I now only employ as a purgative in combination with other aperients; and even when exhibited with this view, great caution must be exercised, as the system is very readily affected by mercury in puerperal convulsions attended with albuminous urine; and if once it be allowed to display its effects, the diarrhœa, insalivation, and consequent debility, are extremely distressing, as well as difficult to remedy.

Question of Delivery.—The facts stated in this Paper lead me to the conclusion, that where convulsions occur during parturition before the birth of the child, and are complicated with an albuminous state of the urine, it is advisable to complete the delivery as soon as consistent with the state of the patient herself and the condition of the parts through which the child has to pass.

And thus, while, on the one hand, I deprecate artificial dilatation of the os uteri (which may induce a convulsion)—while I am no advocate for rupturing the membranes, and the induction of premature labour—while I declare myself altogether opposed to incisions in the vaginal portion of the os uteri, as recommended by Velpeau—I do most strongly recommend that delivery be resorted to so soon as the state of the parts will permit its accomplishment.

If the membranes be unbroken—if the os uteri be soft and dilatable—if the external parts be lax and moist—then version may be readily performed : but unless there are circumstances of great moment, calling for the immediate delivery of the woman, I would rather wait until the head of the child can be grasped by the forceps or vectis, and the delivery be, by their aid, accomplished.

THE MEDICAL HERALD.

VOL. VIII.   APRIL, 1875.   No. 10.

Original Communications.

PUERPERAL ECLAMPSIA.

By J. H. VAN EMAN, M. D., Tonganoxie, Kansas.

On the 9th of December, 1873, at 8:15' P. M., I saw, in consultation, Mrs. ——, æt. 20, of medium height, heavily built, and previous to this a healthy woman. I received the following history of the case:

Pregnant, between five and six months, six weeks before had taken a long ride over a rough road in a common lumber wagon, to the effects of which her friends ascribed her present trouble; had headache very severe for the last few weeks, and vulva very much swollen; in the last eight hours has had three convulsions, at intervals of exactly two hours. It is just one hour and fifteen minutes since last convulsion; patient lies on her back with lower limbs as widely separated as possible, face dark and with but little expression; unable to give intelligent replies to questions; in fact, is almost comatose. Little, if anything, has been done to avert the evidently impending fit. With the concurrence of attending physician tied up arm and drew 20 ℥ blood. This changed the pulse from being slow, full and hard to a quick and rather soft condition, and the face, instead of being congested, became pale;

breathing also became easier and more regular. I also punctured both vulva at a depending point to permit the serum to drain away. At 12 M. I left the patient, after giving a full saline cathartic. The understanding being that I was to take charge of the case.

December 10th, 2 P. M.—Again saw patient; has had no more convulsions or symptoms of any; intelligence has returned; knows her relatives, but has no knowledge of anything that has taken place within the last twenty-four hours; cathartic has acted pretty freely; pulse about 100; vulva reduced in size fully one half; no headache; has urinated freely. She says she has not felt any *movement* for more than one week. Persistent auscultation fails to detect any evidence of fœtal life. To repeat saline cathartic and give the following:

℞. Potassii bromidi, . .
    Chloral hydrate, . . āā grs. x;
    Aquæ, ... ℥ j.
M.

Every three hours.

December 11th, 11 A. M.—Patient decidedly better; quite cheerful; rested well last night; intelligence perfect; vulva reduced to normal size, so that she can lie in any position; pulse about 80; some appetite. Directed a restricted diet; bromide and chloral three times a day; bowels to be kept acting with mag. sulph.

December 19th.—Labor set in and terminated in four hours by the expulsion of a dead fœtus; labor normal in every

261

respect. Convalescence rapid, complete and satisfactory.

———

March 10*th*, 1874.—Called out in the night (3 A. M.) to see Mrs. B., æt. 26, supposed to be eight months pregnant; is a full sized, compactly built woman; general health has been better during pregnancy than for a long time previous; no œdema of limbs or genitals. Her husband reports that she has complained terribly of headache for the last forty-eight hours, and that she wakened him by the noise she was making, and that he found her in a fit; also that she has had two more. She can answer questions, but looks very wild; pulse strong and full, but not quick. While I was getting the history of the case she again went into a convulsion, which proved to be a very hard one. As soon as it was over tied up arm and drew 24 oz. blood. Had another convulsion within an hour; unbound arm and drew six more oz. of blood; also sent for croton oil mixture, strength five drops to teaspoonful; commenced giving teaspoonful doses olei tiglii mixt. every hour at 7 A. M. At 11 A. M. had another spasm. Soon after this bowels moved freely several times. I then commenced giving the following:

R. Potassii bromidi   .   .
   Chloral hydrate, .   . āā grs. x;
   Aquæ, ...   ℨ j.
M.
Every three hours.

No more convulsions, though the symptoms tended strongly in that direction for the next eighteen hours.

March 11*th*, 8 A. M.—Patient rational and comparatively comfortable, excepting great muscular soreness. She only recollects having a severe headache on the morning of the 10th, nothing since. Directed bromide and chloral mixture three times a day, bowels to be kept open.

March 18*th*.—Delivered patient of an average sized, well nourished female child. Labor lasted ten hours. No abnormal symptoms or accidents. Convalescence normal.

———

January 10, 1875.—Was called out at 12:30 A. M. to see Mrs. ——, a young married woman, æt. 19. Messenger reported that she had some kind of a fit. Coming to the residence of the patient, I received the following history:

Patient about eight months pregnant with her second child; miscarried at seven months with first; has had good general health until within a week or two; has since that time been troubled with diarrhœa. On the 9th inst. they checked the bowels; headache rather worse; a little before midnight waked her husband by her complaints of pain in her head; the night being cold, he asked her to pull the clothes over his shoulders; her movements in attempting to carry out his request convinced him that something more than usual was wrong; he got up and commenced starting a fire; before he had succeeded she had a convulsion, and he at once sent for me. I was at the house within one hour, arriving just after she had her third spasm. While examining into the case she had her fourth attack. Found her speechless; pupils not sensitive; eyes more or less fixed; breathing hard and slow; pulse 60, full and hard; heart stroke very powerful. Gave her fifteen drops tinct. veratrum viride as an arterial sedative, and, still fearing irreparable brain injury, tied up arm and drew off thirty-two ounces blood. This had the effect of increasing the frequency of the pulse to 115 per minute, and also moderating the force. At 3 A. M. repeated veratrum and sent for chloroform, as she had two more convulsions, and her general condition is getting worse. I now made a vaginal examination. Found the ostium vagina and all other parts moist and relaxed; os uteri dilatable, and can get the tips of index and second fingers within it.

4 A. M.—Has had two more convulsions, and they are evidently getting more severe. Informed the friends that, in my judgment, the only thing that would save the patient would be to deliver the child, also that it was practicable. (Sent for my forceps at the same time I did for chloroform.) I also suggested that they send for counsel. They replied that they were willing to trust me and did not desire counsel.

5 A. M.—Another convulsion. Gave ten drops more veratrum. Oiling my hand thoroughly, I introduced two fingers into the vagina; passed first my second and afterward my index finger within the os, and gently, but forcibly, commenced the dilating process, in the meanwhile steadying the uterus with my other hand. By steady work I gradually introduced my whole hand into the vagina, and in time passed in my third finger beside the other two. In all this I attempted to imitate nature, by giving periods of rest between the efforts to dilate. After dilating the mouth of uterus to about half the necessary size and rupturing the membranes, I ascertained that it was a presentation of the breech. This effort occupied two hours' time, during which she had two more convulsions. I waited for one hour hoping that labor might set in. During this time I was able to prevent, or at least she did not have convulsions, by giving chloroform as soon as I saw the least twitching of the face.

At 9 A. M. examined and found everything as at 8 o'clock. I now determined to deliver at once. Introducing my hand I soon succeeded in dilating the os; hooked first one and then two fingers over the child's thigh, and keeping in my mind the curve of carus, I commenced traction. I again imitated nature in periods of action followed by rest. In thirty minutes succeed in delivering her of a living child, and ten minutes later removed the secundines. The uterus contracted well, and but little blood was lost. Neglected to say that I gave her two doses of emulsion olei tiglii, each dose containing five drops of the oil. This did not act till about 1 P. M. Sitting down by patient, chloroform bottle in hand, I watched for the slightest evidence of the commencement of a convulsive seizure, and at once smothered it down. Twice I succeeded, and the spasm was very slight. The third time it in some way got the start of me and she had a very hard eclamptic seizure, which proved to be the last. I kept her more or less under the influence of the anæsthetic for the next six hours. I drew off the urine soon after delivering the child, and once in six or eight hours for the following twenty-four hours. After which time she passed it in the bed as she had the feces from the beginning. I might as well say here that the child lived four days, and died convulsed. From this time up to January 20th, she lived like a child a few days old. Anything that touched her lips she would try to swallow; drank greedily any liquid put in her mouth. For the first five days did not make any articulate sound. During this time her respirations ran up as high as 40 per minute and pulse 160. Heart's action very tumultuous at this time, shaking her body at each stroke. On placing my ear to her chest could hear a loud, whining sound over the heart, arch of aorta, and in both carotids by using stethescope. This bruit continued for over a month, and was always strongest when the heart's action was hurried. At about the sixth day she began to speak. There was no connection in anything she said, and she could not speak certain words at all—that is, correctly. Any word in which it was necessary to finish with the tongue pressed against the upper front teeth or back of the teeth she could not say—e. g., grass for grand, driss for drink, etc., etc.

By the 25th of January she knew what was said to her; was sensible of the calls of nature; had a fair appetite; could hear the whistle of the locomotive and tell what it was; no improvement in articulation or vision; still stone blind. It was now evident that in the right side of the face all power of expression was gone, but *not of motion.* The same condition obtained in the whole right side as well as could be ascertained; e. g., she was at that date eating crackers while bolstered up in bed—put a cracker in her left hand and she had no trouble in feeding herself, put it in her right hand and she did not know anything about it. Yet she moved the arm readily, but could not tell at any time where it was.

January 27th.—Patient still more intelligent; begins to connect ideas; connecting the whistle of the train with the idea of getting letters from absent friends; is able to tell me for the first time who she is, but using her maiden name instead of her husbands, but when corrected sees her mistake; still labors under the difficulty of being unable to recollect the names of things; often uses one word when she is meaning to speak another; again, cannot recall the word she wishes to use at all; pulse respirations and all other nutritive functions normal.

March 20th.—Her general health is good; is not very strong yet; can tell night from day, and distinguish colors, particularly red and green; has no knowledge of her past condition; still has some hesitation of speech and connects ideas slowly.

A word as to treatment: Morphia, opium or Dovers powders at night, or when necessary to give rest; iodide and bromide of potassium as nervous sedatives, and sorbefacients, digitalis (tinct.) on the theory of its being a heart tonic. At the time her pulse ran up to 160, viz: the fifth day, I brought it down below 100 by the cautious exhibition of tinct. veratrum, and kept it there for four days by a continuation of the same line of treatment. She was kept on full supporting treatment almost from the beginning, by giving brandy; milk, eggnog, beef tea, quail broth, and later tinct. of iron and quinine. In fact, I endeavored to meet each indication as it arose. At no time did any abdominal or pelvic tenderness exist. I do not write this as being a model case as to treatment. It was one that caused me much trouble and thought. I prescribed certain things with fear and trembling; for instance, tinct. veratrum when the pulse rose to 160 per minute. The result, however, seemed to justify the experiment, for such it was. Also as to the venesection under similar circumstances, with the amount of light I now have, I should feel in duty bound to adopt the same procedure; and yet the question arises in my mind, and like Banquo's ghost, "will not down," Was not that abnormal heart sound a murmur produced by excessive depletion.

These three are the only cases I ever saw; and, although I perhaps managed them reasonably well, I am not at all anxious to see any more like them. I regret that I neglected to make an analysis of urine in these cases; but at the time I was not looking at them from an etiological stand-point. The two first were primipraa. I should be glad if this paper should bring out the views of my professional brethren. I would like a larger amount of knowledge on the subject of Puerperal Eclampsia than I have been able to obtain from the text books in my possession.

THE

Journal of Obstetrics & Gynaecology
of the British Empire

| VOL. 58, No. 6 | *NEW SERIES* | DECEMBER 1951 |

THE PRINCESS CHARLOTTE OF WALES: A TRIPLE OBSTETRIC TRAGEDY*

BY

SIR EARDLEY HOLLAND

THE news of Princess Charlotte's death in childbirth on 6th November, 1817, after she had given birth to a stillborn Prince, struck Britain like a thunderbolt. The state of grief and consternation was indescribable. For many days the nation presented the picture of one united family in deep mourning.

"Her death produced throughout the kingdom the feelings of the deepest sorrow and most bitter disappointment. It is scarcely possible to exaggerate, and it is difficult for persons not living at the time to believe, how universal and how genuine those feelings were. It really was as if every household throughout Great Britain had lost a favourite child."—(Brougham).

Lord Holland records that on his return to England, three days after her death, everyone he met on the road between Dover and London, including postboys and turn-pikemen, bore signs of mourning on their persons. Byron from Venice, where he was writing the fourth Canto of *Childe Harold* (into which he inserted six verses on the tragedy), wrote: "The death of the Princess Charlotte has been a shock even here and must have been an earthquake at home."

One has only to see the number of memorial books and pamphlets, the torrent of poems, the sermons from almost every pulpit, the commemorative pictures and engravings, the medals and china, the variety of other memorial objects that were made to suit the pockets of both rich and poor, and to read the newspapers of those days, and the many diaries and memoirs of the Regency period, to appreciate the feelings of the people.

The sustained and, one might say, inordinate grief began to strike fear into the expectant mothers and fathers of the nation, as was expressed in a letter to *The Times* of 18th November, in which the writer asked if the most direful results might not be expected if the minds of interesting females were allowed continually to dwell on so distressing a subject. "The daily papers," he went on, "the shops, the public handbills, in fact everything on which we can cast our eyes, brings the great loss the nation has suffered continually to mind."

I have said that the grief was inordinate, and the impression is indeed given that the public reaction was greater even than that which would be expected normally to result

---

* The William Meredith Fletcher Shaw Memorial Lecture delivered at the Royal College of Obstetricians and Gynaecologists, 28th September, 1951.

from the death in such circumstances of the heiress to the Throne and an infant prince.

There were indeed associated circumstances that heightened the tragedy, and I must remind you of the history of Charlotte and her background before I come to the medical side.

She was only 21 when she died. Captain Gronow describes her when she was 18, at a fête at Carlton House, her first public appearance: "She was a young lady of more than ordinary personal attractions; her features were regular and her complexion fair, with the rich bloom of youthful beauty; her eyes were blue and very expressive, and her hair was abundant, and of that peculiar light brown which merges into the golden. . . . In figure her R.H. was somewhat over the ordinary height of women, but finely proportioned and well developed. She created universal admiration, and I may say a feeling of national pride amongst all who attended the ball." Such was the impression of a young guardsman.

Fanny Burney records her a year later, at a Drawing Room at the Queen's Palace: "The Princess Charlotte looked quite beautiful. It was impossible not to be struck with her personal attractions, her youth and splendour."

Evidently, she had radiant vitality, but no one can begin to understand her behaviour, her moods, and her few minor maladies, without realizing that her whole life was spent in a state of emotional stress that originated in the bitter and intractable quarrel between her father and mother.

Her father, the Prince of Wales, had made a disastrous marriage with Princess Caroline of Brunswick. She was chosen by the King, and the Prince never set eyes on her until just before the marriage ceremony. His debts amounted to £500,000, and it was to get this huge sum paid off by Parliament that he consented to a royal marriage. He was already married, secretly, to Mrs. Fitzherbert, a virtuous widow of good Roman Catholic family, with whom he was deeply in love. But this union was easily annulled because the Prince had broken the Royal Marriage Act under which, until he was 25 years old, he could not marry without the King's leave. Moreover, under the Act of Settlement he had forfeited his rights to the Crown by marrying a Roman Catholic.

To a Prince who had been surrounded by the most cultured and wealthy aristocracy in the world, and had enjoyed for many years the favours of women remarkable for beauty and elegance, this poor young Princess, brought up in a minor German court, where both manners and morals were coarse, could not fail to be unattractive and even repulsive. She was quite pretty but was hoydenish, ill mannered, voluble, badly dressed. Directly the Prince saw her he demanded brandy, and it is said he never shared her bed after the first night. Three months after Charlotte's birth they parted company for ever.

Charlotte had, in consequence, from infancy been more or less kept apart from her mother, whom she loved. For her father it is unlikely that she felt much affection or respect; he seems to have taken only a spasmodic interest in her, was jealous of the nation's affection, and though not without a father's fondness, was sometimes unkind. As a result she was lonely and secluded, dependent on governesses and tutors, with no real family life, and deprived of parental love. Being a high-spirited, impulsive, warm-hearted girl, she demanded affection but never got it until that year and a half of indescribably happy marriage with Prince Leopold.

When she was nine, an event occurred that led to complete separation from her mother. Caroline was accused of the terrible and treasonable crime of having an illegitimate baby. Though declared innocent by the so-called "Delicate Investigation", she was never granted the full reward of innocence. As Charlotte grew up, the breach between her father and mother widened, her mother's conduct became even more recklessly undignified, indiscreet and suspect, and the daughter's confidence in her mother must have been shaken. When she "came of age" at 18, her mother appealed for a closer association, but without success, and in 1814 the wretched and persecuted woman left England to live on the Continent.

But sentiment governs the world, and the people, especially when they were mourning for Charlotte, were roused to exasperation by the persecution of her mother. The unpopularity of the Regent was at its height; he was pelted on his way to the Houses of Parliament and on another occasion a man put his head in at the carriage window and cried, "Prince, where's your wife?"

But the height of the nation's tragedy was that with her seemed to die the direct succession to the Crown.

"... in the dust
The fair-haired daughter of the Isles is laid,
The love of millions, how we did intrust
Futurity to her ..."

In those lines Byron summarizes the two-fold theme—how the people loved her and how their hopes for the succession were destroyed.

We must remember that her grandfather, George III, although he had seven sons and five daughters, had only one legitimate grandchild—Charlotte. There was scant likelihood of more offspring from the Regent; he was 59, excessively corpulent and otherwise decayed and, besides, even if Caroline did oblige by dying it was doubtful if any other Princess could be found with the inclination or courage to marry him. As for Charlotte's six uncles, the prospect also seemed bleak.

The Duke of York had had 26 years of childless marriage and was 54. The Duke of Clarence, later William IV, was by no means childless; the ten little Fitzclarences lived at Bushey Park with their handsome mother, Mrs. Jordan, a devoted mistress and mother. The Duke of Kent had had 27 years of domestic bliss with Madame St. Laurent. The Duke of Cumberland, said to be the most unpopular man in England, had been two years married to his cousin, a Princess of 40 years and doubtful virtue; everyone hoped that their marriage would remain childless. The Duke of Sussex, the only uncle who took Charlotte's part against her father, had married a commoner when he was 20, and when she died, 37 years later, defied the Marriage Act a second time by marrying another. The Duke of Cambridge, the youngest, was only 43, irreproachable and unattached, and in him there seemed to lie some hope.

Of the daughters of George III, whom the Marriage Act hit far harder than it did their brothers, two were married and childless, two were secretly married but not childless, and one was unmarried and 49.

One wonders if ever there could have been, maritally, so tragic a family. It is clear that the Marriage Act, as applied so rigidly and exclusively by the King, had all but brought the Royal Family to disaster.

It is easy to see how the regrets of the nation at the loss of Charlotte were enhanced by the prospect of the importation of a foreign monarch. Failing offspring from the elderly uncles and aunts the crown would ultimately pass to the Duke of Brunswick, then a boy of 13 and mentally weak. What did happen was that the Royal Dukes discarded their mistresses and scrambled for German brides and handsome grants from Parliament, with the result that two children were born.

The Duke and Duchess of Cambridge had a son, whose succession, however, was set aside two months later by the birth of the Princess Victoria to the wife of the elder brother, the Duke of Kent.

MEDICAL HISTORY

The Old Sources of Information

Anyone who has tried to discover anything new about Charlotte's confinement has had to give up in despair. The authentic sources of information are scanty and already well explored, whilst the larger amount of material has, heretofore, been found only in sources which, to a medical historian, are suspect but which, nevertheless, have proved most tempting to Charlotte's many biographers. It is refreshing to see a medical appendix, revised by obstetric experts, in the recently published biography by Miss D. M. Stuart.

The only reliable information is that which was given by the four doctors concerned; Sir Richard Croft, the accoucheur, Dr. John Sims, the consulting accoucheur, Dr. Matthew Baillie, the Royal Physician, and Sir Everard Home, Sergeant Surgeon to the King, who examined and embalmed the bodies of Charlotte and her baby.

A few words about the doctors. Croft, Baillie and Home make a compact little family group. Home was a brother-in-law of the Hunters, Baillie was their nephew, and Baillie and Croft were brothers-in-law, having married the twin daughters of Dr. Thomas Denman, who dominated London midwifery in the Regency period.

The mystery man of the confinement was Dr. Sims. The *D.N.B.* describes him as a botanist and physician, and that is the right order of his activities. He was 69, and from 1801 to 1826 was editor of the celebrated Curtis's *Botanical Magazine*, which made great demands on his time and energy (Dopson, 1950). He was physician to the Surrey Dispensary and Charity for delivering Poor Women in their own houses, and was consulting physician to the Royal Ear Dispensary. Sims published many important papers on botany. The Mexican genus of compositae is named *Simsia* after him. He was an original member of the Linnaean Society and his herbarium is (or was) at Kew. One wonders how much time Sims had left for midwifery or if he really was a " celebrated accoucheur ". It seems astonishing that he was chosen as the consultant when there were in London such active and skilful men as David Davis, Merriman and John Ramsbotham. He was scarcely of the calibre to help Croft in his anxious duties. Another odd thing was that when Sims arrived at Claremont he did not see Charlotte, and never entered the lying-in chamber until she was on the point of death.

The Authentic Documents

The only authentic documents, and they have long been known, are the following:

1. The reports published three weeks after the events in the two chief London medical journals. There can be no doubt that these were written in collaboration with the doctors and should be regarded as authentic. Their aim was to satisfy public opinion and end rumours.

2. The statement written at the time " for the satisfaction of the Royal Family." It was in general terms and was a private document, kept in the archives at Windsor, and unknown to the public until 1926, when a copy appeared among the Hunter-Baillie papers deposited in the library of the Royal College of Surgeons. The R.C.S. copy is in the handwriting of Mrs. Baillie and is headed " Dr. Baillie's account of Princess

Charlotte's labour". There are other reasons too that lead me to believe that Croft took no hand in drawing up this statement. To begin with, try and picture to yourselves what his state must have been—utterly exhausted and heartbroken, and in no fit condition to draw up statements. Moreover, in an unpublished letter to Croft, dated 9th November, Baillie writes: "I thought it proper to leave a copy of the general statement with the Queen and I enclose another which you should carry to Carlton House to the Prince Regent."

3. A long letter written by Sims on 15th November, 1817, to Dr. Joseph Clarke, of Dublin, which appeared, for no particular reason, in 1849 in the *British Record of Obstetric Medicine and Surgery*. It was republished in 1872 in the *Medical Times and Gazette* by Dr. W. S. Playfair, with copious comments. It is of interest in confirming certain points.

No amount of search into all sorts of likely and unlikely sources has brought anything more to light. Then, two years ago, having almost abandoned hope, I had the good fortune to be introduced to a great-great-grandson of Sir Richard, the present Lord Croft, who, I found, was as much interested in the association between Charlotte and his ancestor as I was. He had just found some important letters. A little later I was fortunate enough to meet also Major Richard Croft, another great-great-grandson, who had just discovered some even more important documents, and into whose possession all the letters and documents have now passed.

Both Lord Croft and Major Croft are here this afternoon and I am sure you would like to join me in thanking them for the honour they have done your lecturer in entrusting him with the precious information these documents contain and for permitting him to give it to the College.

But before dealing with the new material I wish to run through the story as it was known at the time and up to now, and particularly the way it was put across to the public.

HOW AND WHAT THE PUBLIC WERE TOLD

It is remarkable how little the doctors told; on the other hand, it was a family bereavement, though on a National scale, and as such was a private affair.

Apart from the three bulletins and the notice in the *London Gazette** the public had to rely on second-hand newspaper reports and on the semi-medical "letters from Claremont" undoubtedly sent to the Press by a gentleman called the "Court news man" (we should nowadays call him a "Press representative"), which were printed by most of the newspapers but seldom by *The Times*. An extra bulletin printed in *The Times* for 6th November, amongst the three official bulletins, is guarded by the description, "Also a bulletin of less authority than the preceding, from the Court news man." *The Times* of those days evidently had the same high standard of journalistic integrity as it has today.

It was the manner in which the story was slowly, imperfectly and inaccurately unfolded that gave rise to the outburst of public anger at the time and to the confusion and misrepresentation that has gone on ever since.

The Pregnancy

Early in July the newspapers announced that the accouchement was expected in October.

In a letter dated 19th October from Claremont, from Croft to his sister, he writes, "This is the first day I could by

---

* *v. infra.*

reason expect H.R.H. to be put to bed." In one of the new Croft letters, dated 14th March, Charlotte tells Croft that "the 2nd period is now safely past over a week." She seems to have been well throughout; even the critical Stockmar records that "the Princess passed through the whole of her pregnancy without any drawbacks". Prenatal care was still primitive, but we have now, in the new Croft papers, a copy of his simple directions. She was to rise at 9 and take breakfast before 10; to eat a little cold meat, or some fruit and bread at lunch about 2; to take food plainly cooked and easy of digestion at dinner; to take exercise, both walking and on horseback every day that the weather was fine, but the exercise should not be violent; to use the shower bath every other day and to begin with the water tepid, and to have the loins sponged with cold water daily.

Charlotte was sometimes bled during pregnancy. In a letter of 10th August to Croft, she writes, "I am certainly much the better for the bleeding." In "a letter from Claremont" that appeared in the newspapers on 22nd October, no doubt from the Court news man, we read that she had occasionally suffered a little from headache, for which it had been necessary at different times to extract blood. The letter goes on to state that on one occasion four incisions were made in the arm without effect from the veins being deeply buried, and that after a consultation the blood was ordered to be withdrawn from a vein at the back of the hand, "where the operation has several times been successfully performed by Mr. Neville, with great relief to H.R.H." This is the sort of unauthentic stuff that I find hard to believe. (Mr. Neville was the surgeon and apothecary attached to Claremont.)

As the public were becoming anxious, expecting hourly the accouchement to take place, the newspapers on 21st October were told that Charlotte was very well and continued to take daily exercise. From that date daily reports were sent out. Mrs. Griffiths, the nurse, had arrived at Claremont on 1st October, and Sir Richard resided at Claremont for three weeks waiting for labour to begin.

Labour

On Tuesday, 4th November, a letter, evidently from the Court news man, announced that labour had started the previous evening.

The next day (Wednesday, 5th November) three brief bulletins were sent out from Claremont over the names of Baillie, Sims and Croft. The first, at 8 a.m., stated that labour was going on slowly but favourably. The next, at 5.30 p.m., stated that labour had considerably advanced during the last three or four hours and would, it was hoped, within a few hours be happily completed. At 10 p.m., a third bulletin announced that Charlotte had been delivered of a stillborn male child and was "doing extremely well".

After that not another word from the doctors; a curtain came down. The news of her death reached the public about midday on Thursday, 6th November, in a special issue of the *London Gazette*, the gist of which was that about three and a half hours after delivery H.R.H. was seized with great difficulty of breathing, restlessness and exhaustion, "which alarming symptoms increased until half past two in the morning when she expired. . . ." The morning papers had gone to press too early to include the fatal news, but the next day they startled the public with their heavy black borders. They also printed two "letters written from Claremont" timed at 6 o'clock and 9 o'clock on the morning of the 6th, containing what were called "painfully interesting details". They must have been written by our friend the Court news man. They stated that labour began on Monday night; that during Tuesday the labour advanced slowly, and Dr. Sims was sent for. On Wednesday morning labour advanced more quickly and at 9 p.m. the child was born. At about a quarter past twelve the medical gentlemen retired to their bedrooms; for they considered she wanted no more assistance than Mrs. Griffiths, the nurse, could render her, and that during the remainder of the night she should be kept as quiet as possible. She took some gruel, but found a difficulty in swallowing it. She then complained of severe chilliness and a pain at her stomach. Mrs. Griffiths instantly called up the doctors, but human assistance was of no avail and Charlotte expired about half past two in a severe attack of spasm.

It is not easy to realize that in this great national disaster that was all the public and the profession were allowed to know—a second-hand medley of truth, half-truth and supposition. If only they had been told that after the baby's birth there were complications that led to haemorrhage and that in spite of all that could be done the haemorrhage would not stop and she died from its effects—or something like that—how different would have been the subsequent course of events. Even today, in spite of modern technique, about 20 per cent of women who die in childbirth die from postpartum haemorrhage and shock. Surely, in those days of, relatively, primitive practice, no leading accoucheur need have been ashamed of losing a postpartum patient.

But the public, almost hysterical with grief, became alarmed. They believed that the truth was being hidden. Rumours were quickly afloat, a campaign was started; letters and paragraphs appeared in the newspapers and there was much talk and gossip at all levels. The doctors were accused of ignorance, mismanagement, neglect. Poor Croft had to bear the force of the storm. He was accused of lowering Charlotte in pregnancy by excessive bleeding and a low diet; of starving her for the 50 hours of labour; of not allowing Sims to come into the room until the final moments, and of going to bed and leaving her in charge of the nurse, only to be called up to find her dying. For none of these charges is there a jot of reliable evidence.

The medical attack was led by Jesse Foot in a letter to the *Sun Newspaper*, on 13th November, entitled " On the necessity of a Public Inquiry into the cause of the death of Princess Charlotte and her Infant ". Foot was a well-known surgeon with a great belief in his own merits. He tried to surpass John Hunter in fame, and failing that did all he could to defame him. His *Life of Hunter* shows jealousy on every page. His letter protested that the public could not remain satisfied with what they got from the newspapers and asked if it were really true that Croft and the others had gone to bed and left Charlotte with the nurse. As to what were called "spasms" in the letter from Claremont, he considered this a meaningless term purely to belong to the late John Hunter and to the lecture rooms in Windmill Street. He demanded a public inquiry.

Three weeks later the sensible thing was done and reports came out in the leading London medical journals. The Editors of the *London Medical Repository* began by stating that, being aware that the profession expected some account of the case, and having learnt that the physicians in attendance did not mean to publish any statement, they strenuously tried to get all possible information from dependable sources. Their exertions had been successful and their report could be regarded as strictly authentic.

Emphasis was laid on the irregular and

weak action of the uterus; Dr. Sims had concurred that the use of instruments was never indicated. The third stage complications were revealed for the first time. Half an hour after the delivery there was haemorrhage and Dr. Sims had agreed that manual removal of the placenta was necessary, which was done by Sir Richard Croft.

In describing Charlotte's final symptoms the Editors stated that the respiratory organs were evidently under the influence of spasm and continued in that state until she breathed her last. The report also gave a complete enough account of the postmortem findings, the most important of which was that a considerable amount of blood was found in the uterus. Two ounces of blood-stained fluid were in the pericardium.

In commenting on the immediate cause of death the Editors made two remarkable suggestions. Although it must have been obvious that death was due to the effects of haemorrhage, the Editors, nevertheless, drew two red herrings across the path of truth. One was that the fluid in the pericardium, however it came to be there, might have obstructed the due action of the heart. The other was their emphasis on the so-called " respiratory spasms ". " We have been informed," they wrote, " that the whole of the Royal Family are liable to spasms of a violent description; and to this hereditary disposition and the increased excitability of the amiable sufferer, owing to the tedious nature of the labour, are we led to ascribe an event which . . .", and so on.

The speciousness of all this was easy to discern and the redoubtable Jesse Foot lost no time. In a second letter he mocked at the spasms—these were but the last symptoms of exhaustion from haemorrhage. Why did Home measure the fluid in the pericardium and stomach but not the blood in the uterus? Why was Baillie—our

leading morbid anatomist—not present in the dissecting chamber? He could understand a community of sentiment between the Princess's doctors; for were they not all mostly related?—another tilt at Hunter, which marred an otherwise able letter.

There were other letters and pamphlets, some for and some against the doctors, and the controversy slowly faded out.

The New Croft Papers

These come under three headings:

(1) A number of letters written by Croft in 1790 from Paris, when he was an aspiring young accoucheur of 28, in attendance on Georginiana, Duchess of Devonshire, for her third confinement—when " the bachelor Duke " was born. The letters are of great interest in relation to later events because they suggest that Croft had not the degree of resolute self-confidence that is a desirable temperamental endowment of a Royal accoucheur and for which no amount of skill, experience and professional integrity can compensate at the critical moment.

(2) Nine letters written by Charlotte to Croft and Baillie during pregnancy. That they are, unfortunately, an incomplete series is known because on the paper band securing them is written, "Some of these have been destroyed " initialled by Croft's two executors, his brothers-in-law, T. Denman (the future Lord Chief Justice) and M. Baillie. Some are undated. Two have been referred to—the one dating a last menstruation and the one about blooding.

(3) This group is the important one and comprises four documents: (a) Croft's personal record of the labour. For the first time we are told the duration of the first and second stages, and can follow the progress of the first stage from four vaginal examinations, and of the second stage from the time when perineal pressure began. There

are full notes of the conduct of the third stage. (*b*) His reflections on the general course of labour and his views on the cause of death. (*c*) His prenatal instructions on diet and exercise. (*d*) A copy of the post-mortem report.

I shall now describe the labour, making use of all the authentic material, old and new.

The Labour—The Full Story

About 7 o'clock in the evening of Monday, 3rd November, 42 weeks and 1 day from Charlotte's last "recovery", there was an escape of liquor amnii and labour pains soon followed.

At 11 p.m., Croft examined and found the os uteri the size of a halfpenny. The pains were coming every 8 or 10 minutes, but very weak.

On Tuesday, 4th November, at 3 a.m., Charlotte was seized with a violent attack of retching and Croft, thinking that this might hasten labour, sent for the Officers of State and Matthew Baillie. The Archbishop of Canterbury, the Bishop of London, the Lord Chancellor, the Home Secretary, the Chancellor of the Exchequer, the Secretary for War, and Baillie all arrived, in their coaches-and-four, before 8 a.m.

The lying-in chamber, Charlotte's bedroom, was a corner room with large windows on two sides. Fortunately the room was at the back of the house, but she must have heard the clattering and rumbling of the coaches. Two doors opened into the room, one into Prince Leopold's dressing room, occupied by Sir Richard Croft, and the other into the "breakfast room", where the Archbishop and Ministers sat, awaiting the event; this room led into the big gallery and other principal rooms. We cannot doubt that everything was done to give Charlotte peace and quiet during the 40 hours the Archbishop and Ministers kept their vigil. But there must

have been a lot of coming and going and talking, and the conditions cannot have been ideal for labour.

From whatever cause, the pains continued insufficient; in general, during the first 24 hours, though weak, they were sharp, acute and distressing, at intervals of about 8 minutes and but little advancing the labour.

Nevertheless, labour progressed, and at 11 a.m., after 16 hours, the os uteri was found the size of a crown piece with thin margins. At this point it would seem that Croft began to be worried, finding that the uterus was acting irregularly, and that unless the pains improved in the course of the next 12 or 18 hours, some assistance might be necessary or some circumstances might arise to make consultation desirable. Moreover, he felt, it would be improper to use instruments without a consultation. It had been settled before that Dr. Sims was to be the consulting man in case such should be required. He therefore wrote a note to Sims, though he held back sending it till later, probably because the pains began to improve.

Croft made another examination at 6 p.m. (Tuesday, 4th November) and found that the os had gone back over the head except just under the symphysis pubis. The labour continued progressive and at 9 p.m. he found that the os uteri had perfectly retired and for the first time an ear of the child could be felt.

Croft must now have had a feeling of great relief. In spite of poor pains, the first stage had lasted only 26 hours, the head was low, Charlotte was well. Nevertheless, as the pains continued unusually feeble he sent his note to Sims summoning his immediate attendance. What made him feel over-anxious? It was, I think, that the uterus was still acting inertly and irregularly, and he knew what the later consequences might be.

Sims arrived at 2 a.m. on 5th November, after the second stage had then been going of for five hours. Croft told him the details and proposed that he should be presented to Charlotte; but both Baillie and Sims considered this unnecessary and she was not told of his arrival. He remained in the next room, where he was told regularly of the state and progress of the labour and was at hand to see Charlotte whenever it might be thought necessary. Labour by then was advancing more favourably, though progress was very slow. It was allowed to continue naturally; the patient was in good spirits, the pulse calm. Instruments were in readiness " but the employment of them never became a question."

From about midday on Wednesday, 5th November—that is, after the second stage had lasted for 15 hours—the uterine discharge became of a dark green colour, which made the medical attendants suspect that the child might be dead or be born in a state of suspended animation.

At between 3 and 4 p.m., the second stage having lasted for 18 hours, the child's head began to press on the external parts; and at 9 p.m. the child was born, by the action of Charlotte's pains only.

The child, a 9-pound boy, was dead, and had evidently been dead for some hours, for the navel-string was very small and of a dark green or black colour. Nevertheless, every known method was made by Sims to reanimate it.

To sum up, the labour up to the time of delivery had lasted 50 hours, comprising 26 hours of first-stage and 24 hours of second-stage, including 5 to 6 hours of perineal pressure. The second-stage pains had been no more efficient than those of the first.

Croft states that Charlotte showed no signs of deficient strength during labour. She had taken some repose in bed during part of the nights of 3rd and 4th November, but was generally up and frequently walking about the rooms during the daytime and remained up until a short time before delivery.

The Third Stage

About 10 minutes after the birth of the child, Croft found that the uterus was still acting irregularly. He informed Sims that he suspected hourglass contraction with the placenta in the upper part, for he could not feel the placenta and the uterus continued high. They agreed that nothing should be done unless haemorrhage came on. In another 20 minutes haemorrhage did come on and Sims agreed that the placenta should be taken away. This was done before much blood had been lost. In passing his hand, Croft met with some blood but with no difficulty till he got to the contracted part of the uterus; and though it was contracted so as to admit only the points of three fingers, and had a portion of the placenta embraced by it, it readily gave way, so as to allow his hand to pass with tolerable ease, and he peeled off the near two-thirds of the adhering placenta without difficulty, and before much blood appeared to be lost.

Immediately on its being separated Charlotte complained of violent pain (" the strongest pain of the whole labour "), and the upper part of the uterus contracting on his hand, Croft grasped the placenta and gradually brought it down into the vagina. Leaving it there he went again to Sims and the Council and reported what he had done. On returning, he found Charlotte complaining of pains which recurred at intervals, and when these had continued to 10 o'clock, or about 25 minutes from the time the placenta was left in the vagina, as she complained of it giving her great inconvenience and that it was considerably protruding, he took it away, and this was followed by a very moderate discharge of either fluid blood or coagulum. At this time, as well as he could determine by feeling the abdomen through the bandage, the uterus appeared moderately contracted.

Charlotte appeared quite as well as women commonly do after so tedious a labour, and much better than they often do under such circumstances, and for the next two hours Croft felt no apprehension, as she took plenty of nourishment, made few complaints and had a pulse not exceeding 100.

But at about a quarter to twelve there was a change. She became a little sick and complained of a singing noise in her head, so he gave her a little camphor mixture which she shortly afterwards brought up. After this she took a cup of tea and seemed to sleep for about half and hour, when finding her becoming irritable and restless and speaking too much, he gave her 20 drops of laudanum in wine and water.

About a quarter to one (6th November) she complained of great uneasiness in her chest and great difficulty of breathing. Her pulse became rapid, feeble and irregular. She became extremely restless, not being able to remain a single moment in the same posture. The most active support by cordials, nourishment, antispasmodic and opiate medicines was given. This very alarming state continued and kept increasing until, at half past two in the morning, Charlotte died.

It was then the custom of the Sergeant Surgeon to embalm members of the Royal Family. As, during the process, every organ, including the brain, was removed and treated separately, it amounted to a complete postmortem examination. On 7th November Sir Everard Home went to Claremont for the purpose. The uterus was found to contain a considerable quantity of blood and extended as high as the navel, and the hourglass contraction was still very apparent (Croft gives the amount of blood as "about a pound," but he was not there). The pericardium contained two ounces of red-coloured fluid. The child was well formed, and every part of its internal structure was quite sound.

Croft comments as follows: " The cause of H.R.H.'s death, as it was quite unexpected until half past twelve, so it is still somewhat obscure. The symptoms were such as precede death from haemorrhage; but the quantity of blood lost was scarcely sufficient to create any alarm, being less than usual on such occasions, yet, added to about a pound of blood found in the cavity of the uterus, might have been enough to produce the unfavourable symptoms in so excitable a constitution. It is most possible that the two ounces of fluid found in the pericardium were poured out during the violence of the spasmodic affection of the chest, and if so it must have had very great influence in preventing the heart from recovering its regular and vigorous action, and it is possible it might have been deposited earlier and thus have produced all the distressing symptoms, and have had more to do with the fatal issue than has been imagined."

The Labour in the Light of Contemporary Practice

The management of Charlotte's labour must be judged in the light of the midwifery practice of the day. The chief criticism is that Croft allowed labour to go on so long without using the forceps. But, by the principles and rules of contemporary practice, he was not wrong. To realize the astonishing degree of conservatism that prevailed at that time one must read the standard textbooks.

It seems that after Smellie had retired from practice, about the year 1760, the forceps began to be used too freely, often by unskilful men, and much damage resulted. This period of abuse reached into the time of William Hunter (who died in 1783), Osborne and Denman, all of London, with the result that they reacted—indeed over-reacted—strongly, and an ultraconservative phase of midwifery practice began.

This retrograde phase in the evolution of obstetrics will be found discussed in the Transactions of the Obstetrical Society of London for 1879, when Robert Barnes opened a discussion which spread over three meetings. As Barnes well said: " These illustrious men thought it right to exert all their authority in discouraging the use of instruments, and in inculcating blind faith in nature as the better way. So earnest was their zeal, so commanding their authority, that men were driven into the opposite extreme of supine inaction . . . Rules were laid down, and widely obeyed, which too often allowed parturient women to drift into danger, injury and death."

This was the system into which Croft was born. He was trained by the renowned Denman, whose assistant he became, whose daughter he married and whose practice he inherited. It was natural that he should be a faithful adherent of the Denman system. Denman's famous book *An Introduction to the Practice of Midwifery*, first published in 1788, was a sort of obstetrical bible. As edition succeeded edition, Denman's doctrines were not modified—if anything, they were fortified. I will take from the first edition a few excerpts pertinent to Charlotte's labour.

On the use of forceps he writes: " The use of the forceps ought not to be allowed from any motives of eligibility (i.e. of choice, election or expediency). Consider the possible mistakes and lack of skill in younger practitioners, and the instances of presumption of those who by their experience have acquired dexterity." . . .

" When it is proposed to deliver with the forceps the intention is to supply the total want or deficiency of the natural pains of labour; to extract the head of a child that cannot be expelled by the efforts of the mother. But so long as those efforts continue with any degree of vigour, there is always reason to hope that they will ultimately expel the child. We are, moreover, to recollect that in long labours there will often be an abatement or a temporary cessation of the pains without any apparent reason, but that cessation of the pains, which is the consequence of long continued fruitless action, and of great debility is to be considered as the only justification of the use of the forceps."

Another rule: " A practical rule has been formed, that the head of the child shall have rested for six hours as low as the perineum before the forceps are applied, though the pains should have ceased during that time." (II, 128–133). This was known as " Denman's Law." But Denman must be credited also with the following aphorism: "Care is also to be taken that we do not, through an aversion to the use of instruments, too long delay that assistance we have the power of affording them."

The last edition of the book published in Denman's lifetime (1816) has the very significant sentence: " But if we compare the general good done with instruments, however cautiously used, with the evils arising from their unnecessary and improper use, we might doubt whether it would not have been happier for the world if no instrument of any kind had ever been contrived for, or recommended in, the practice of midwifery."

Under the third stage he writes: " For many years I have made it a rule to leave the placenta, whether naturally or artificially separated, to abide in the vagina for one hour after it was voided out of the cavity of the uterus."

Under concealed postpartum haemorrhage (after the placenta is out) he writes: "Sometimes the size of the uterus, though contracted, shows that there are large coagula in its cavity. These coagula are supposed to keep up a distension of the uterus and cause a haemorrhage; and it is recommended to introduce the hand to dilate the cervix and clear them out from the uterus . . . This is not necessary and I have never practised it; nor even troubled myself with the state of the uterus unless it was inverted after the placenta was brought away; but have left whatever coagula it contained to be expelled by its own action."

If we put these quotations beside the main incidents of Charlotte's labour we have to admit that Croft acted strictly according to Denman. It is of interest that in the edition of Denman's *Aphorisms* published the year of Charlotte's death (and two years after his own) the title page is adorned with the apt quotation from the Book of Hebrews: "He being dead, yet speaketh."

Comments on the Labour

It seems hardly possible to doubt that Charlotte died of postpartum haemorrhage. Four haemorrhages are recorded, the first before the placenta was removed, the second during its removal, the third when it was taken from the vagina, and the fourth, the concealed haemorrhage in the uterus found after death. None was severe but their cumulative effect must have been considerable. Charlotte's symptoms, from near midnight until her death 2½ hours later, were typical of blood loss, slowly mounting, the lethal phase being a slow leak into the uterus.

I have told you of Denman's emphatic teaching, obeyed by Croft. But not all the accoucheurs of the day obeyed Denman. Merriman (1820), writing on "Haemorrhage after delivery cured by removing coagula from the uterus", describes a case he saw in consultation on 29th November, 1817. Some time after a normal labour the patient became faint and much alarmed at her situation, which she thought similar to that of an "illustrious Lady" who had recently died after delivery (Charlotte had died about 3 weeks before. She became cold and blanched, with rapid pulse. Merriman saw her 6 hours after labour. The uterus was larger than it should be, and therefore he passed his hand and brought away about 14 ounces of clot, upon which the uterus contracted and the patient recovered.

One must try and put oneself in Croft's place. His responsibility was enormous, unique. He was attending the accouchement of the, dynastically, most important young woman in the world—the Princess who was to be the Queen of the country that then stood supreme among the nations. The eyes of Britain, of Europe, of the world were fixed on Claremont, on what was about to happen there, and on the two leading figures—both, in the end, so tragic —Charlotte and her accoucheur.

I have already given my view that Croft was a diffident, sensitive man without much self-confidence despite his skill and experience. He was not the sort of man to deviate from his rules of practice by doing something unconventional and perhaps risky. There is evidence that from the start he was over-anxious. He sent for the Archbishop and Privy Councillors far too soon, just because there was an attack of retching; he wrote a note to Sims hours before he sent it. He was a lonely man in the lying-in chamber. Sims was no good to him. Sims would not go into the room.

We may say that both Charlotte and

Croft were the victims of a system. That was what, in as many words, was said by Dr. Stockmar who knew nothing of practical midwifery, but was an uncommonly clever man. "It is impossible," wrote Stockmar, "to resist the conviction that the Princess was sacrificed to professional theories." But the Princess and her accoucheur were not only the victims of a system. There was something far worse. They were caught in the toils of a most difficult and dangerous labour.

Why was the second stage so long? On and on it went for 24 hours in spite of uterine contractions. We can rule out disproportion and the occipito-posterior positions. Croft knew all about these and would not have omitted to mention them in his detailed record. To account for the long delay we are left with uterine inertia—the hypotonic variety, and the hypertonic variety that may go on to the formation of a constriction ring. For those who believe in the psychologic aetiology of this condition, there is the life-long emotional stress from which Charlotte suffered. There was, besides, for her, a feeling of great personal responsibility, knowing that her accouchement was critical for the monarchy and the nation, a feeling not lessened by the presence of the high officers of State.

It is odd that though Smellie so well described delay in birth "due to contraction of the uterus below the shoulders of the child," some of his successors, including Denman, left it out of their books. Denman knew about irregular and asymmetrical uterine action and described it well, and of course he knew all about hourglass contraction in the placental stage.

Croft found Charlotte's uterus contracting inertly and irregularly throughout most of the time, and the pains were sharp, acute and distressing without advancing labour very much; in the placental stage he had to dilate an hourglass contraction

to take the placenta away, and after death the ring was still there. It is justifiable, I think, to suggest that the remarkably long second stage was due to a constriction ring that in the end proved slowly reversible. If so, how fortunate that Croft did not attempt forceps delivery. We must leave it at that. It is unlikely there will ever be more exact data for finality.

I hold no special brief for Croft; but I cannot imagine an obstetrician who suffered more cruel misfortune, more undeserved criticism nor more false accusations. "May God grant that you nor any connected with you may suffer what I do at this moment," he wrote next day to Stockmar.

The new documents, as well as a close study of the old, have, to my mind, shown that if he erred it was only by sticking too closely to accepted rules and principles. And, in such circumstances and with such a patient, who would have acted differently?

Three months later Croft shot himself whilst attending a patient, the balance of his mind disturbed with depression and despair at the blame cast upon him, and that is why I name my lecture "A Triple Obstetric Tragedy" — mother, baby, accoucheur, all dead, all victims, most likely, of a mistaken system, a bad patch, a veritable craze of midwifery practice.

LIST OF AUTHORITIES

General

Aspinall, Dr. A., *The Letters of the Princess Charlotte* (1811–1817), 1849, London, and *The Letters of King George IV* (1812–1830), 1938, Cambridge University Press; Brougham, Lord, *Life and Times of Henry, Lord Brougham*, 1871; Byron, Lord, *Childe Harold*, Canto IV, 167–172, and *Letters*; Creevy, T., *The Creevy Papers*, Sir. H. Maxwell, 1903; Croker, J. W., *Croker's Correspondence and Diaries*, J. L. Jennings, 1885; D'Arblay (Fanny Burney), *Diary and Letters of*

Madame d'Arblay, 1854; Dormer, Creston, *The Regent and his Daughter*, 1932; *Faringdon Diary*, 1827; Fulford, Roger, *Royal Dukes*, 1935, and *George the Fourth*, 1949; Gronow, Capt., *Reminiscences and Recollections*, 1889; Green, T., *Memoirs of H.R.H. Princess Charlotte*, 1818; Holland, Lord, *Further Memoirs of the Whig Party*, 1905; Huish, R., *Memoirs of Princess Charlotte*, 1817; Jones, Mrs. Herbert, *An Illustrated Monograph, etc.*, 1885; Layard, G. S., *Sir T. Lawrence's Letter-bag*, 1906; Stockmar, Baron, *Memoirs*, edited by his son E. von Stockmar, trans. by G. A. M., 1872; Stuart, D. M., *Daughter of England*; Weigall, Lady R., *A Brief Memoir of Princess Charlotte*, 1847; *The Times*, and other contemporary newspapers.

Medical

Barnes, R. (1879): *Trans. obstet. Soc., Lond.*, 21, 121.

British Record of Obstetric Medicine and Surgery (1849), 2, 110.

Burns, J. (1814): *The Principles of Midwifery*, 3rd edition, London.

Croft, Sir R.: *The New Croft Papers* (not yet published).

Denman, T. (1817): *Aphorisms on the Application and use of the Forceps*, 6th edition.

Denman, T.: *An Introduction to the Practice of Midwifery* (1788), Vol. I, 1st edition; (1798), Vol. II, 2nd edition; (1830), last edition. Edited by C. Waller. London.

Dopson, L. (1950): *Practitioner, 164*, 156.

Foot, Jesse (1817): *A letter on the necessity of a public enquiry into the cause of death of the Pss Charlotte*. Nov. 18th, 1817 (pamphlet). A second letter, same title (pamphlet), Dec. 3rd, 1817.

Hunter-Baillie papers in Library of the Royal College of Surgeons of England.

London Medical Repository (1817): 8, 534.

London Practice of Midwifery (1823): 5th edition.

Merriman, S. (1820): *A Synopsis of the Various kinds of Difficult Parturition*. 3rd edition. p. 261.

Sims, John: see (1) *Dictionary of National Biography*; (2) *Medical Times and Gazette*, 1872, Dec. 7th, p. 636 (W. S. Playfair); (3) L. Dopson (1950): *Practitioner, 164*, 156.

Smellie, W. (1779): *A treatise on theory and practice of midwifery*. London. Vol. I, pp. 208, 209; Vol. II, pp. 296–299.

Spencer, H. R. (1927): *The History of British Midwifery, 1650–1800*. London. Bale, Sons and Danielsson.

LATENT GONORRHEA, ESPECIALLY WITH REGARD TO ITS INFLUENCE ON FERTILITY IN WOMEN.

BY EMIL NOEGGERATH, M. D.,

New York.

In the year 1872 I published in the German language a monograph on Latent Gonorrhea, which was not received very favorably by the medical press. The suggestions laid down were so new, and so contrary to the theories prevalent at that time, that the book was looked upon with distrust.

I now find, however, the subject of latent gonorrhea gradually making its way into most of the gynecological handbooks and treatises of recent date, both here and abroad. This has encouraged me to bring the subject, at least the most important part of it, that concerning its connection with fecundity, before this meeting ; the more so, since my experience has been enlarged, and my views have become clearer and better defined, in more than one direction.

The attempt to demonstrate the existence of what I call latent gonorrhea, is surrounded by difficulties hard to overcome, to such a degree, that I waited ten years after its discovery before I dared to put the matter into shape for publication. For, with all the advance in the physical sciences, I have been unable to bring forth a direct proof of its existence. In my work, published four years ago, I expressed the hope, that the key to solve the question might be found in the presence of a fungus peculiar to the secretion of women affected with latent gonorrhea, of which my researches up to that time had given much encouragement. I have, however, not followed them up, for several reasons, principally owing to the fact, that I found the same fungus in discharges from very young children, in cases where I was unable to trace all the points in the etiology of the case, that would be necessary to establish the value attributable to the presence of this growth.

Another difficulty, which is connected with the history of latent gonorrhea, consists in the fact, that the symptoms of the disease vary in almost every instance ; and although it is possible to give a description of typical cases as I occasionally encounter them, they are met with rarely, one or another, or even the majority of signs not being present, or the disease so hidden by other uterine affections, more apparent to the senses, that its recognition is often a matter of difficulty and doubt. Furthermore, certain peri-uterine alterations, the result of latent gonorrhea, are so apt to escape detection by the most experienced of us, that a majority of the cases fail to receive as yet their true appreciation.

Again, our branch of the medical sciences being of recent development, the views entertained by its most eminent representatives, as to the clinical importance of the several diseases of the uterus, show such a discrepancy, that it will be very difficult to convince followers of one or the other school that, in a case, for instance, of anteflexion and latent gonorrhea combined, the former is not the origin of all the disturbance in the functions of the organs affected, as well as of the system in general. I will now endeavor to give you a description of a typical case of latent gonorrhea.

Mr. M., a merchant of this city, formerly a commercial traveler for a large manufacturing firm in Europe, like almost every one of his tribe, acquires a gonorrhea. The treatment recommended by a renowned specialist is at once carefully followed, and the affection cured in two months.

Two years later this gentleman returns to Europe and marries a healthy, robust young lady from B., a village in the province of Westphalia, Germany.

Three months later, the woman begins to complain of backache and general malaise ; it becomes difficult for her to attend to the common household affairs ; the usual promenade, instead of being a pleasure, becomes fatiguing. Men-

283

struation, which appeared hitherto without giving any pre-
paratory notice, is now connected with backache, more
profuse than usual, and followed by a white discharge. By
and by the desire to urinate becomes more frequent, and is
occasionally accompanied by a sensation of burning at the
meatus. The white discharge gradually extends from one
period to the other. About eight weeks later a pain is felt
in the left side of the abdomen, which suddenly increases
upon an unusually severe exertion, to such an extent that
the patient has to take to her bed. At the same time the
dysuria is considerably increased, the discharge becomes profuse and of a greenish-yellow color, like matter. The physician attending her recognizes an acute attack of perimetritis. A year after this she consults me for sterility. I
find her suffering from general weakness, backache, pain in
the left side, increased before the now scanty menstruation,
and a muco-purulent discharge. On examination, the uterus
is found in right lateroversion, and anteflected ; the left
vaginal roof, or parts above, hardened and contracted ; the
uterus soft, succulent, very tender on being gently pushed
into its normal position, great tenderness of posterior cul-de-
sac, neck of a high color, os surrounded by a thin rim of
eroded tissue, discharging a tenacious yellow mucus. Both
outlets of Cowper's glands eroded to some distance, and
painful to the touch.

Now, Mr. President, this combination and development of
symptoms, physical as well as rational, you never will encounter in women who are married to husbands that have
not exposed themselves to the danger of venereal affections.
I say, advisedly, never! and if any one has a right to speak
thus positively, I claim this privilege.

In the history of this patient we find no trace of the existence of acute gonorrhea, either before or after marriage;
but a condition very like, if not truly gonorrhea, is being
developed during the acute attack of perimetritis.

You will now begin to understand why I have chosen the
term " latent gonorrhea." The patient has never been infected in the accepted meaning of the word, but she grad-

ually develops a condition, which we usually observe as the result of an attack of acute gonorrhea. And still the husband is apparently cured, not only according to his own opinion, but by that of his physician.

Now, if all this I am treating of is not simply a delusion, to what conclusion does it lead ? First, that the husband is diseased, all appearances to the contrary notwithstanding ; second, that the infection with gonorrheic poison does not only take place in the ordinary way by producing an acute gonorrhea, and afterwards gleet, but that under certain circumstances, the gleety state, if I may be permitted to call it so, is the primary, or only state of gonorrheal manifestation, occasionally followed by an outbreak of acute gonorrhea. To my mind, this latter *modus propagandi* is true beyond all doubt, and only fails to be recognized by the profession at large, because specialists or general physicians see the wives of their former patients, only in case they are affected soon after marriage by an acute manifestation of the disease, — in cases, for instance, where the husband has been allowed to marry with an apparently insignificant gleet. It was from the wives of men entering marriage with gleet that the first glimpses of the true state of affairs were obtained by me. I had followed up about five cases where women married men with *chronic* gonorrhea. These patients had no attacks of true gonorrhea, but they all began to be ailing in a similar manner, remained sterile, slowly developed chronic or sub-acute disease — in two cases attacks of acute perimetritis with ovaritis, and a muco-purulent catarrh, which yielded to energetic treatment, to relapse under the most trifling provocation. But this same state of things I find to exist also in women coupled with men who have had gonorrhea months or years before marriage.

In my treatise on this subject I expressed the opinion that gonorrhea in the male gradually pervaded the entire tract of mucous membrane, from the meatus to the ejaculatory ducts and down through the vasa deferentia to the epididymis, just as it does in the majority of cases pass from the external os of the vagina through the uterus and tubes to the fimbriated extremities ; the affection is cured, in the male, wherever the urine — loaded with, or even without the antidotes — comes in contact, and sweeps away the newly formed secretion, while beyond this point the disease often persists for life in a milder form.

Later observations, which I shall present in the course of this paper, have modified my views in this matter, or at least rendered that explanation unnecessary for many cases.   I will say this much now, that in many instances the male, although cured to all appearance, can be proven, by examination, to be suffering, unknown to himself, from the effects of a gonorrhea which he contracted years ago.

I have chosen the term latent gonorrhea instead of chronic gonorrhea, first, for the reason alleged above, that the patient is being gradually infected without any apparent symptoms of disease developing themselves in the beginning.   I have chosen this name better to define the truly imperceptible manner by which the disease works its slow progress in the organs affected up to the first more or less severe attack, when it passes from the latent into the active state ; and secondly, because the disease in the female, although she be discharged, cured to all appearances, after an attack, say of gonorrheal ovaritis, keeps within her, at least up to the time of menopause, the germ of similar more or less severe relapses.   The gonorrhea, after an acute attack, has simply returned to its state of latency to rest there, for months or years, the patient meanwhile being always in danger of a renewed outbreak, on proper provocation.

Admitting the persistence of gleet in the male after its outward disappearance, the question remains, how does it affect the female ?

The course of the disease is only in comparatively few instances so well defined as in the case related above.   We can, however, point out four different and clinically distinct groups of manifestations of the gradual infection of the woman by the repeated contact with minute quantities of the poison.   It appears, —

1st, as *Acute Perimetritis.*

2d, as *Recurrent Perimetritis.*

3d, as *Chronic Perimetritis.*

4th, as *Ovaritis.*

All of these affections are accompanied with a *catarrh* of several sections of the mucous membrane. Often this catarrh is the only symptom present. Among one hundred and five cases, of which I have written notes, I found —

10 patients suffering from acute and subacute perimetritis.

8 patients suffering from recurrent perimetritis.

38 patients suffering from chronic perimetritis.

17 patients suffering from chronic ovaritis.

32 patients suffering from catarrh of the uterus, apparently uncomplicated.

In looking over this statement, it will strike you at once that there is one characteristic feature apparent, namely, the prevalence of peri-uterine affections.

I have noted, among all of these, only five cases of so-called chronic metritis. The occurrence of acute, subacute, recurrent, and chronic perimetritis to such a large extent, is observed in another class of female patients, namely, those who lead the lives of prostitutes.

We find the position of the uterus entirely in accordance with this view. It is now generally admitted, that forward and lateral dislocations of the uterus involving the whole of its axis, when acquired during life, have their origin in contractions of one or more of the ligaments from inflammatory or other irritation.

It is, therefore, not surprising that among one hundred and five cases of latent gonorrhea, where the position of the uterus was noted, forward and lateral dislocations of the entire uterine axis were observed in fifty-one instances, while backward dislocations occurred only six times. Among the former, lateroversion in thirty-six; and anteversion, with or without lateroversion, in fifteeen instances, which proves that lateroversion, with a marked tendency to tilt toward the right side, is the most commonly observed dislocation among women suffering from latent gonorrhea.

18

Normal position	27
Right lateroversion	31
Left lateroversion	5
Lateroversion and anteversion	3
Lateroversion and anteflexion	4
Anteversion	8
Anteflexion	17
Retroversion	6
Retroflexion	5
	105

Acute perimetritis, symptomatic of gonorrhea, occurs in the puerperal, as well as in the non-pregnant state of the uterus. It would take too long a time to discuss before you, Mr. President, all the several interesting points connected with the clinical history of acute and subacute perimetritis as it occurs, in consequence of latent gonorrhea ; and I must, therefore, refer you to the more detailed account in my work on the subject. I there stated that one form of puerperal fever was owing to a sudden transition of gonorrheal catarrh of the womb existing in a so-called chronic or gleety state during pregnancy, into its acute form after confinement. I had found that women impregnated from men, having suffered either at the time of conception, or previously, from gleet or gonorrhea, were subject to attacks of puerperal endometritis, accompanied, as a rule, with perimetritis, often recurring at every subsequent confinement. I am happy to say that my observations in this direction have been confirmed, among others, by *Angus McDonald*, of Edinburgh, *Amman*, of Munich, and *Hennig*, of Leipzig. As a rule, the puerperal inflammation is of perimetritic, and not of parametritic origin ; the non-puerperal is always perimetritic, with the exception of those cases where a lesion of the mucous membrane has been produced with or without intention.

An attack of non-puerperal perimetritis, symptomatic of latent gonorrhea, is either the consequence of exposure to wet and cold, of protracted exertion, or of a violent shock, physical or mental. I have seen it follow a fright ; the act of cohabitation after prolonged absence of the husband ; introduction of the sound by an experienced surgeon, application of a non-cauterizing medicine into the uterus in its mildest form, in the shape of a salve ; wearing of an intrauterine pessary ; incision of the os externum ; discission of the neck ; dilatation of the womb by compressed sponge ; appearance of menstruation ; application of leeches to the neck ; examination of the internal genital organs by the double touch.

It therefore appears that no kind of manipulation of the uterus, or of its lining membrane, is not, under certain circumstances, liable to start an acute perimetritis. The fact that grave accidents do occasionally follow trifling operations on the neck of the womb, as, for instance, acute peritonitis of a dangerous type, after the application of leeches, is thus sufficiently explained by the local predisposition. It has impressed itself on the minds of gynecologists sufficiently, so that all of us have been trying to find an explanation of the fact, and to avoid the danger resulting therefrom. By many they were, and are now, ascribed to careless after-treatment, to rough and indiscriminate use of sound, pessaries, knife, etc. The advice strongly insisted upon by advocates of this theory, to keep patients in bed for at least five days, up to as many weeks, according to the gravity of the proceeding, must be accepted thankfully by all of us, and has certainly saved many precious lives. Still, numerous cases are on record where, with the best care in public as well as in private hospitals, perimetritis has been the immediate consequence of the interference. I do not speak of those cases where, from a deep incision into the vulnerable supervaginal tissue of the womb, the patients die in consequence of lymphangitis, or shock ; but of those where simple incision of the neck is the immediate cause of inflammatory explosion inside the pelvic cavity. Wherever I have had occasion to examine post-mortem under these circumstances, I have found the existence of salpingitis ; and in those cases which could be carefully investigated during life, the history of gonorrhea, either in the patient herself, or in the husband, has rarely been absent. In this way a sufficient, and probably the only simple and acceptable explanation has been given. There exists a catarrh of the uterus and the tubes to so slight a degree as not to raise any suspicion as to its presence. The cut in the neck is followed by a congestion of the blood-vessels of the uterus and appendages, the catarrhal secretion is consequently increased and *altered* in its character ; one drop of it overflowing into the peritoneal cavity calls forth its inflammation.

We have been taught by experience that it is not safe to perform an operation on the womb while symptoms of perimetritis exist. The precaution thus shaped is insufficient, for two reasons ; first, because the larger number of cases of chronic perimetritis is so very little characterized by physical signs, that its presence is very often not suspected ; and secondly, because salpingitis, not to be diagnosed during life, may be present, yet no signs of chronic perimetritis.

If, therefore, we are enabled to recognize the existence of latent gonorrhea in a case where the question of an operation is at issue, we shall be even more successful in detecting the cases which give the best chance of success.

Acute perimetritis does, however, occur when symptomatic of latent gonorrhea, independently of any exciting cause, in its idiopathic form, and most frequently in cases where the husband has cohabited with his wife very soon after the gonorrheal affection has run its course.

Permit me to give you, in illustration, the history of a case.

Mrs. L., born in one of the Southern States, a rather weakly, spare woman, has been married for two years to a healthy gentleman, born in Germany. She has a baby thirteen months old.

The summer of 1871 she spent with her parents in Missouri, while her husband was forced to stay in the city, being an insurance agent. During that time he contracted gonorrhea. He was attended by Dr. Livingstone of this city, and the discharge was cured after two months' treatment.

His wife having meanwhile returned to the city, Mr. L. asked and received permission from his physician to cohabit with his wife, no trace of the disease being left. This occurred in the beginning of September, at the interval between two menstrual periods ; five days before the expected menstruation, Mrs. L. noticed for the first time in her life a pretty profuse discharge, accompanied with pain in her back and stomach. The ensuing menstrual flow was more free, and lasted longer than usual. Immediately after its cessation the abdominal pains increased, and were accompanied by fever.

I saw the patient for the first time on September 24th, 1871, about a week after the menses had ceased. The pulse was 100 in the minute during the day, 120 in the evening. The abdomen was tympanitic, painful on pressure in both sides ; the uterus was very tender, succulent, in lateroversion, the right vaginal roof shortened, very painful on being touched ; there was profuse purulent discharge from the vagina.

Under treatment the acute symptoms rapidly disappeared, and she was able to call at my office on the 6th of October. She complained still of back and stomach ache. On examining, I found the whole of Douglas's cul-de-sac filled with a mass of lymph about the size of a large fist, and the uterus pushed forward. The discharge was very profuse, the vaginal mucous membrane inflamed, a superficial erosion around os, and there was catarrh of the ducts of Cowper's glands.

On October 30th, the greatest part of the exudation had disappeared ; a mass of the size of a pigeon's egg could be felt behind and towards the left of the uterus.

The discharge existed for at least a year after I first saw the patient, notwithstanding it was attacked by very energetic remedies.

Now, Mr. President, a case of this kind can only be understood, if looked at in the proper light. Suppose I had not been acquainted with and convinced of the truth of this doctrine of latent gonorrhea, I should have examined my patient, should have recognized the acute perimetritis, should *never* have inquired into her husband's condition, and probably ascribed the whole trouble to the long railroad journey, combined with exposure to wet and cold during the same.

But I have seen such cases before, numerous cases, where there was no jolting in the cars, no possible exposure to any injurious influence, but always a gonorrhea preceding, at a more or less remote period, the explosion in the female pelvis ; and those of the gentlemen present who feel interested enough in the matter, will find a number of similar instances recorded on page 15 and following, of my monograph. If Mrs. L. had stayed away from her husband say a year or two, she would probably have been taken with chronic instead of acute perimetritis.

Perimetritis from this cause is apt to recur ; not so perimetritis following other causes. For instance, if a compressed sponge be inserted for diagnostic purposes, and its use followed by septic endometritis and salpingitis, the one patient, who has never come in contact with a man that has suffered from gonorrhea, will be through with this one attack, while another, with latent gonorrhea, will probably have one or many more attacks of acute perimetritis after this first one.

In about half the number of cases of *recurrent perimetritis* which I have observed, the first attack was one of puerperal endometritis and perimetritis, the others following a more or less severe manipulation of the uterus ; the first attack in the other half was produced without any traceable cause whatever. For instance, Mrs. F. is married in one of the Western cities in 1861. She has never known before what sickness was. Her husband is treated for gonorrhea by a medical gentleman, a friend of mine, to whose kindness I owe the facts of her former history. The disease is very obstinate but yields at last, and the patient is permitted to get married three months after all the symptoms have disappeared. Six weeks later Mrs. F. begins to complain of pains in the left side, which gradually increase, and the doctor finds her suffering from acute perimetritis. She is confined to bed for two months. The next attack she has in April, 1867, immediately after confinement ; the third severe attack in March, 1872, six months after the second labor.

In one instance, a patient, after a first attack of acute peri-metritis without appreciable cause, had six more attacks during ten years ; the second after cohabitation, the others without any cause. In another instance, the first attack was produced by the application of a pessary ; the second, by the use of the sound ; the third, by intra-uterine application of a salve ; the two following, without any cause whatever.

Usually, the first attack is of the greatest intensity, the second not much less severe, the third and fourth are of a milder character, and the last ones take place without pro-ducing much reaction.

With regard to recurrent perimetritis, I venture to state that every single case has its remote origin in gonorrhea. I have seen a large number of cases of this variety of perime-tritis, but I have to see the first one, where the husband has not been afflicted with gonorrhea, and usually with an ob-stinate affection followed by protracted gleet.

I now pass over to the consideration of the important subject of *chronic perimetritis;* important, on account of its frequency ; important, on account of its effect on the general health, and the difficulty of diagnosis ; and I shall endeavor to be as concise as possible. It is of importance, for the views which I intend to develop, to show that the etiology of perimetritis is not sufficiently cleared up. The two writers who have dealt more especially with this ques-tion of causation are Matthews Duncan and E. Bernutz. The former, in his " Practical Treatise on Perimetritis and Parametritis," sums up his dissertation to the effect that both parametritis and perimetritis are, almost without ex-ception, the direct results of metritis, while, occasionally, diseases of the ovary and the Fallopian tubes are the start-ing points ; and he goes on to state that they are most fre-quently the result of endometritis. He, therefore, assumes that the inflammatory process originating in the mucous membrane of the uterus passes through the tissue of the uterus to the peritoneum. Duncan is right in his view as to the endometritic origin of the affection, wrong as regards the manner of propagation. If we should accept his explanation we should have to give up the now well established fact, that metritis is a disease of extremely rare occurrence; just as rare as inflammation of the penis, an organ very similar in its construction to the upper section of the womb.

Dr. Bernutz has published a tabulated statement of ninety-nine cases of perimetritis, with especial regard to the cause of the disease. Of these, forty-three were of puerperal, twenty-eight of blennorrhagic, twenty of menstrual origin, and eight the result of traumatic causes. If we look closely at this division, we find coördinate as causes, the puerperal state, blennorrhea, menstruation, and mechanical injuries. Now, while puerperal and menstrual can only signify the peculiar physiological condition during which the female was attacked, the latter, and blennorrhea especially, expresses the morbific agent that caused the disease, while, traumatic means an irritation, which either produced the attack in a hitherto healthy organ, or caused an acute paroxysm of a disease already present in its chronic state.

Thus, according to Bernutz's statistics, the only ones existing at the present time, we have, as causes of perimetritis, blennorrhea in twenty-eight cases out of ninety-nine, syphilis in two, and six cases of truly mechanical origin.

Since we cannot admit that labor, the puerperal state, or menstruation, per se and alone, constitute a cause of perimetritis, we conclude with our author that perimetritis is, in the majority of cases, owing to the presence of gonorrheic endometritis and salpingitis. Bernutz is, as you are all aware, our earliest and still our best authority in this matter. My experience goes to confirm his views to their fullest extent. I have examined quite a number of cases of perimetritis post-mortem, and I have yet to see the first instance — the presence of fibroid, cancerous, tubercular disease and hemorrhagic perimetritis, excepted — where it was not associated with catarrh of the Fallopian tubes, and I except, also, the very few instances where the ovary has been the primary seat of inflammation. This refers to the non-puerperal state *only*.

Now, gonorrhea in the female is, as a rule, followed by tubal catarrh. It is, as I have stated already, a peculiarity of gonorrhea to affect the entire tract of the female genital organs, to disappear in some portions of it, to remain for life in others, in the tube among the latter. And, since the majority of females who are married to husbands who have had gonorrhea, are, as a rule, in the same condition as if they had gone through an attack of gonorrhea themselves, you find that chronic perimetritis, the effect of salpingitis, is one of the most frequent results of latent gonorrhea.

Under these circumstances, the affection presents itself in two different forms : first, the inflammatory or adhesive ; and, second, the congestive form of perimetritis. The former is well known to you, being characterized by the presence of large clots or small bands of lymph. The latter is not quite as often seen, and is recognized more readily during life than after death. On this occasion, I will remind you of those cases published in our department of literature, and of those described in my work, where death has occurred from perimetritis in non-puerperal, even nulliparous, women, and where the most careful post-mortem examination has failed to find anything but a few drops of secretion from the Fallopian tubes in the abdominal cavity, and a highly congested peritoneum, with well marked and dilated blood-vessels. Not in every woman, however, is the pelvic cavity vulnerable enough to allow the shock from the presence of a few drops of tubal secretion to cause death, or is the secretion, in most patients, acrid enough to excite such serious trouble. In by far the larger number of cases, the contact with the secretion of the overflowing tubes is just enough to either produce a few thin films of exudation, or merely a chronic congestion, kept up by intermittent discharges, periodical or not, from the abdominal ostium of the tubes, the sphincters of which have been relaxed, either by influence from the nervous system or by pressure from suddenly increased secretion.

I have met with and diagnosticated in my gynecological practice as the most frequent disease treated, catarrh of the womb, and after that, chronic perimetritis, especially that of the latter class, where the palpable results of inflammation are almost none. These cases are recognized during life : —

1. By the inadequately large amount of suffering of the patient, when compared with the physical changes existing in the genital organs, as far as accessible by examination.

2. By the presence of a right, rarely a left, lateroversion or an anteversion of the uterus.

3. By more or less decreased mobility and great tenderness of the womb when it is gently pushed upwards, or the attempt is made to rectify its position.

4. By tenderness and rigidity in the posterior cul-de-sac.

If no other affection of the uterus complicates the disease, it is comparatively easy to recognize, but if chronic metritis, other dislocations, or idiopathic diseases of the ovary exist at the same time, it is very often impossible to form an opinion about the true state of affairs.

My views as to the frequency of chronic perimetritis will, in the near future, be endorsed but by a very few of my colleagues, for two reasons : —

First. Because the doctrine of the importance of displacements and of purely inflammatory diseases of the womb itself, predominates as yet so much, that I cannot expect a revolution to take place at once.

Second. Because the diagnosis of chronic perimetritis, in this its obscure form, is beset with difficulties only to be overcome by protracted, careful study in this direction.

The fourth class of cases is that where signs of affection of one or both *ovaries* prevail ; but although in many instances rational as well as physical symptoms clearly point to a diseased condition of these organs exclusively, we must consider ovaritis, when occurring in consequence of gonorrhea, as a part and the result of perimetritis, the affection starting from the lining membrane, which is almost always covered with web-like exudations, and developing towards the centre of the parenchyma.

During life we can recognize two varieties, or rather, different degrees of ovaritis, occasionally both in the same patient ; first, the stage of exudation, when the ovary becomes rounded, enlarged, and softened ; second, that of sclerosis, accompanied by hardening of tissue, and shrinking of all its diameters beyond the normal size.

Now, ovaritis, as well as perimetritis, is always accompanied by a catarrh of several sections of the mucous tract covering the genital organs ; this catarrh, however, is occasionally the only symptom which can be recognized during life, either on account of the small degree of alteration produced in the peritoneal portion, or because the disease has not yet reached its final development.

The nature of this secretion, as far as we see it by the aid of a speculum, has nothing of a specific character in regard to its physical quality, yet it varies very much indeed in the duration of its existence, and the degree of virulence that it possesses at the moment of observation. However, in the majority of cases, the secretion is what we may call muco-purulent, of a grayish-green color, part of it liquid, part tenacious, and adherent to the mouth of the womb, which is surrounded by a circular, highly colored erosion, not more than a line or two in width. Another peculiarity connected with it is the fact that it changes very much in quantity as well as quality in the same patient, becoming reduced at times without treatment even to a scanty, pellucid mucus, and again increased and altered, as above described, and assuming the nature of a true purulent discharge in case the patient be subject to attacks of acute perimetritis. This catarrh extends upwards to the fundus, and always into the Fallopian tubes. The vaginal mucous membrane is often intact, while that covering the vulva is, as a rule, involved to some extent. The orifice of the urethra does not show any signs of disease in cases of long standing, and it would be very difficult to make the diagnosis of the true character of a catarrh, when unaccompanied by affections of the peritoneum, if there were not one sign, which, almost always present, is eminently characteristic of the nature of the disease.

It is catarrh and erosion of and around the orifices of the ducts of the vulvo-vaginal glands. It usually exists in both outlets, occasionally only in one.

Let me mention one other characteristic of this catarrh. It resists treatment very obstinately, and is often incurable because fed from the tubes all the time with new elements of infection. Is there one of the gentlemen present who has not treated, to his own and his patient's satisfaction, an ulceration and an obstinate discharge, and found, after two or three months' intermission of treatment, that things were exactly in statu quo ante? At best, you succeed in altering the character and amount of the cervical secretion to a certain degree ; you will seldom be able to restore the normal condition.

To sum up, let me state again by what means we may distinguish a catarrh of gonorrheal origin from a simple leucorrhea. It is very rare that the discharge itself is of such a character as to enable us to recognize its nature by its quality alone. Just as gonorrhea in the male in its gleety state, has often all the characters of a harmless, bland discharge, the secretion in the female looks, in the great majority of cases, exactly like that of a simple cervical endometritis. No means of examination, not even the microscope, under these circumstances, will add to our knowledge. Only exceptionally, in cases that have been allowed to go on from bad to worse, without cleansing injections or other hygienic measures, the secretion itself reveals its nature at once. Whenever you find the upper part of the vagina filled with a copious, glairy, greenish-yellow glue, which adheres to the cervix tenaciously on the attempt to remove it, you may rest assured that you have to deal with gonorrhea. But where the discharge is scanty, pellucid, white, or of a pale straw color, you have to look for circumstancial evidence to pronounce about its nature. It is of gonorrheal origin, if you find the following combination, —

1. A red, eroded, narrow rim around the os.

2. Signs of existing or previous pelvi-peritonitis, such as tenderness of the parts above the roof of the vagina, con-

tracted utero-sacral or broad ligaments, lateroversion of the uterus, swollen and dislocated ovaries.

3. Catarrh of the whole or part of the vulva, the latter confined to the outlets of the vulvo-vaginal and peri-urethral glands ; occasionally the presence of condylomatous excrescences of small size in the fourchette, or around the urethral orifice.

4. The absolute, or almost absolute, incurability of the discharge.

5. The fact that it began to develop in a healthy woman during and soon after a mere physiological change in the function of the sexual organs, namely, after marriage, without the intervention of any other recognized morbific cause.

If you find all, or the majority of these circumstances present, your diagnosis admits of no doubt.

I have taxed your patience, Mr. President, already too long, I am afraid, and therefore hurry on to the consideration of the last and most important question, that of the influence of latent gonorrhea upon fecundity in women.

It was this chapter of sterility in connection with latent gonorrhea which called forth the most — let me say — passionate criticism, here, as well as in Europe. This year I have to lay before you more statistics, which will not materially alter those published four years ago.

In 1872 I had taken notes of eighty-one patients with latent gonorrhea ; of these, thirty-one became pregnant, twenty-three were delivered at the end of the full term, three were delivered prematurely, and five had miscarriages. Consequently, not every third woman had a full-born child.

Among the twenty-three women who carried to the end, —

> 12 had only 1 child,
> 6 had 2 children,
> 4 had 3 children (1 twin birth),
> 1 had 4 children.

Or, to state the matter in a different way : —

Eighty-one women had altogether thirty-nine children. Forty-nine were absolutely sterile, eleven were not impreg-

nated within three to eighteen years after the first child ;
we therefore count sixty sterile women among eighty-one.

I am able to add on this occasion sixty-six cases, with the
following result : Of these twenty became pregnant, thirteen
were delivered at the end of the full term, seven had miscarriages. Consequently only one out of five patients had a
full-born child.

Among the thirteen women who carried to the full term, —

> 10 had only 1 child,
> 1 had 2 children,
> 1 had 4 children,
> 1 had 6 children.

Or, sixty-six women had altogether twenty-two children,
forty-six were absolutely sterile, ten were not impregnated a
second time ; we therefore count fifty-six sterile among
sixty-six women.

Thus you will perceive that the statistics, few as they are,
collected at different times, yield about the same result.

100 women among the former have given birth to 48 children.
100 women among the latter have given birth to 33 children.

It is especially this class of patients suffering under the
bane of sterility, which is met with in the consulting rooms
of our prominent gynecologists ; they are found to make the
rounds among our specialists, applying to one after another
for relief. Let us be candid, and confess that the reason
why the statistics of our treatment of sterility are not coming forth, is simply due to the scarcity of results obtained
by our present means. And of all the several varieties of
sterility, this one, except that caused by congenital malformation, resists treatment most obstinately. Long before the
views represented in this paper had developed themselves in
my mind to their present state of completeness and conviction, I was struck by the fact, that of two patients who came
under treatment with apparently the same affection, say
anteversion with catarrh and cervical erosion, who exhibited
no difference either in their constitution or external circumstances, — one was rapidly cured, while the same remedies

procured only temporary relief with the other. The former becomes pregnant after the cure of the ulceration, while the latter remains sterile. In the last class, you will find only one in fifty who is married to a husband that has not suffered from gonorrhea at one time or another of his life.

The question now arises, which is the cause of this want of fecundation, husband or wife. Prima facie evidence points to the latter; diseased ovaries, tubes filled with an overflow of secretion, the cervical canal blocked up with an acrid, tenacious mucus, — how many obstacles for the admission of spermatozoa to the body of the uterus, how many dangers for the integrity of the ovum.

Now, from my inquiries into this matter, it has become evident that the spermatozoa, when they are thrown into the vagina, are already either all dead or of a very low degree of vitality; and again, in a great many instances, these vital elements are entirely wanting in the seminal fluid. I have examined up to the present time the semen of fourteen husbands of women suffering from sterility in consequence of latent gonorrhea. The semen was obtained in all cases in the same manner and at the same time of the day. The men had connection between seven and eight o'clock, A. M., the semen was collected in a condom, and the latter with its contents thrown into a bottle and kept warm until I examined it, either at the house of the patient, or at my office, usually by nine o'clock.

I found, 1st, in three cases, a semen with a large number of living spermatozoa.

2d. In one case few animalcules, and among them but few living.

3d. In two cases a great many spermatozoa, most of them without motion, a few only living.

4th. In one case hardly any animalcules, and the few present all dead.

5th. In seven cases no spermatozoa at all.

The gentlemen from whom these last-mentioned specimens were obtained were to all appearance healthy men, some of them unusually large and vigorous, their sexual functions unimpaired. The cases were not picked, and could not be, because I had no guide by which to choose them, and the number is large enough not to call it an accident, that fifty per cent. should be found without a trace of spermatozoa. In about one third of this last class, epididymitis had existed during or after the existence of gonorrhea; it had not occurred in the rest. In many of these cases the gonorrhea had not lasted longer than its usual course of six weeks. Not believing my own eyes in cases where the men were unusually robust, and the sexual organs very well developed in every respect, I asked Dr. Zinsser to repeat the microscopical investigation, and his report confirmed what I had found before.

The question now arises, what destroys the spermatozoa under these circumstances? In those cases where they were found dead, or only part of them alive, we may account for it by the persistence of morbid secretion in some part of the urethra or vasa deferentia, which, being mixed with the semen at the time of ejaculation, acts as a direct poison on the spermatozoa.

But for that more frequent condition, where no spermatozoa are formed, we must look to another explanation; and this will not be difficult if we apply the facts characteristic of the nature and development of gonorrhea in females to that in the male. Among the former, as we have seen, the whole length and depth of the mucous membrane, from the vulva to the peritoneum, is apt to become involved after an attack of gonorrhea, and this also probably takes place in the male. The only author whose anatomical researches in this direction have become known to me is *Littré.* As far back as 1711, Littré proved by his examinations (post mortem) on gonorrhea, published in the "Mémoires de l'Académie Royale des Sciences," that all of the ducts and vesiculæ for the retention and emission of semen became diseased after an attack of gonorrhea, and occasionally even exulcerated, while the orifices of the seminal ducts, where they enter into the urethra, were reddened in every single instance.

Thus the analogy with the course which the disease takes in the female, is complete. The inflammation passes through the whole of the mucous tract. That it does not each time, or even very often, affect the epididymis in an acute form, does not prove anything against this explanation, since acute ovaritis in the female is also seen in a comparatively limited number of cases, although salpingitis — and perimetritis to a slight degree — is usually present.

It requires, however, more extended researches by a very experienced pathologist, and probably experiments in animals, to decide finally at what stage of the gonorrheal infection, and in what section of the glands and ducts the animalculæ are destroyed.

My observations with regard to this affection, called azoöspermia, have been made unaided by any literary research, a large number having been published as far back as 1872. Since the publication, however, of Dr. H. Curshman's article on the functional diseases of the genital organs in the male in 1875, I find that both Gosselin and Liegois have made similar observations. The latter has demonstrated that of eighty-three cases of bilateral epididymitis, only eight had afterwards spermatozoa in the semen.

Azoöspermia, in consequence of gonorrhea, finds its natural explanation in an obliteration of the vasa deferentia or epididymis, and is now generally accepted. But I have no doubt that occasionally the testis itself is the seat of the affection. In two instances I have found bodies, which in refraction of light, relation of outside membrane to contents, much resembled the spermatozoa, but had no tails, and looked in one instance like very much enlarged and distorted heads ; while in the other they were smaller than the normal corpuscle and rounded off, a condition which we may properly call dyszoöspermia.

Thus, the question of sterility in women assumes a different aspect from the manner in which we were used to look at it, and a great many things may be explained that have, up to the present time, appeared mysterious. The large amount of labor wasted on our side in the attempt to cure

19

sterility is explained. You will be forced to do what I have been in the habit of doing for the last fifteen years, *i. e.*, to inquire into the history of the husband of every woman that calls upon you to be treated ; and if advice be asked for the cure of sterility, the semen of the husband must be examined first.

You will now understand that it is of no use to conduct these examinations in the manner Dr. Sims has performed them, and laid before the profession in his pamphlet on the treatment of sterility. The first thing to be done is to ascertain the presence and viability of the spermatozoa before they get into the vagina. The fact that live spermatozoa are found in the vagina, and dead ones in the cervix, or vice versa, does not prove anything as regards the noxious effect of the discharges on the semen ; I have seen all kinds of varieties, as to the relative proportion of living and dead spermatozoa, before they ever reached the vagina.

I now come to the question, in what manner does a husband infect his wife in case he has had gonorrhea, say from three months to three or more years before his marriage ? It seems impossible that a disease which is apparently cured, should, years after its disappearance, suddenly develop again the germ of infection ; and still the facts are there, they cannot be denied.

I have before me a record of nineteen examinations of men, the wives of whom I attended for latent gonorrhea. Except two, all professed to have lost all trace of any disease about them for a number of years. At the first few attempts to examine with the ordinary elastic or steel bougies, I was not able to detect any abnormal condition of the urethra. But since I have become acquainted with the use of the French olive-pointed bougie, I have been enabled, in all of these nineteen cases, with the exception of two, to find the existence of disease in a more or less marked degree. In most of these cases (17) I found one to three semicircular strictures, not much elevated above the surface, located in the membranous portion of the urethra. If the bougie was passed beyond this place, and then drawn back again, so as to grate the surface of tissue just behind the stricture, it was found to be covered with a drop of muco-pus, or a tenacious mucus slightly tinged with a yellowish matter.

In 9 cases, all signs of disease had disappeared in from 1 to 3 years.
In 4 cases, from 4 to 5 years.
In 2 cases, from 6 to 7 years.
In 4 cases, from 10 to 14 years.

In all of these, the secretion of one or the other portion of the urethra was abnormal in the manner described. In the one exception, mentioned above, the stricture was situated about half an inch behind the urethral orifice, and the patient had what is usually called gleet. The other sixteen patients had gleet too, but the secretion was not profuse enough to accumulate between two acts of micturition along the entire length of the urethra, and make its appearance at the orifice. Whatever small amount was carried this side of the stricture, was removed with the next current of urine that swept over it. Now, it is very probable that during the act of coition, when the member as well as its lining membrane is stretched to its fullest extent, that the groove behind the stricture becomes flattened, and all of the secretion accumulated for the time is carried along with the semen, and deposited again and again near or into the cervical canal. In illustration, I will give a short account of the last case which I examined.

At the beginning of February, a lady of this city called at my office to be treated for dysmenorrhea and sterility. She is a short, well built, healthy looking woman of Jewish descent. She does not recollect having been ill until after her marriage, which took place in the fall of 1874, when her menses were preceded by abdominal pains, and followed by a white discharge. On examination I found a uterus in normal anteflexion, somewhat swollen and softened, the os and upper part of the vagina bathed in a greenish, thick mucus ; the mucous membrane of both lips eroded, both the outlets of the vulvar glands reddened. The fact that this woman, who appeared to belong to an unusually healthy family, had acquired for the first time in her life, signs of illness immediately after marriage, and the nature of the discharge from her womb, made me inquire into the history of her husband. He appeared to be equally healthy, and professed not to have anything the matter with him now, but that he had been treated for gonorrhea seven months before his marriage, and declared cured by a well-known physician of New York, who enjoys the confidence of the public in ailments of this nature. On the 13th of February, of this year, I examined Mr. C. in the manner described, and when I withdrew the bougie from behind a stricture, distant about five inches from the meatus, its button was covered with a thick, yellowish glue. Now, here was a case of true gleet, which infected the wife, and the presence of which could only be suspected by circumstantial evidence, since it gave no sign of its presence except by its effect on another person. As I expected, the discharge of Mrs. C. was very obstinate to treat, yielding rapidly at first, to return after treatment was less energetically applied, or temporarily stopped. This condition of things explains : —

1. Why so many healthy, blooming, young girls, begin to suffer and fail as soon as they enter the bonds of marriage.

2. Why so many apparently healthy young women remain sterile.

3. Why the patient labor of our best physicians is so often thwarted in the attempt to cure certain affections of the female genital organs. It explains to some extent the prevalence of uterine diseases in large cities, and their increase during the last twenty-five years.

The time is too short for me to speak of the treatment applicable to these affections, the result of latent gonorrhea. I will make only one remark. I have found that an obstinate catarrh of the womb, which would not be influenced by remedies, yields pretty rapidly when the husband of the patient is also taken care of, especially where the signs of stricture and muco-purulent discharge have been very evident.

To conclude, I will sum up the result of these considerations in the following manner : —

1. Gonorrhea in the male, as well as in the female, persists for life in certain sections of the organs of generation, notwithstanding its apparent cure in a great many instances.

2. There is a form of gonorrhea which may be called latent gonorrhea, in the male, as well as in the female.

3. Latent gonorrhea in the male, as well as in the female, may infect a healthy person either with acute gonorrhea or gleet.

4. Latent gonorrhea in the female, either the consequence of an acute gonorrheal invasion or not, if it pass from the latent into the apparent condition, manifests itself as acute, chronic, recurrent perimetritis, or ovaritis, or as catarrh of certain sections of the genital organs.

5. Latent gonorrhea, in becoming apparent in the male does so by attacks of gleet or epididymitis.

6. About ninety per cent. of sterile women are married to husbands who have suffered from gonorrhea either previous to, or during married life.

DISCUSSION.

THE PRESIDENT. — The well known character of Dr. Noeggerath, as a conscientious and scrupulously careful observer, must inspire great respect for him in the minds of all, but he must anticipate that such views as are set forth in his paper, so startling in the present state of the morals in society, will receive the most careful scrutiny. If these views are true, a modification of this paper should be found in every Sabbath-school library throughout the land. I know not whom to call upon to take part in discussing this subject, and therefore shall ask for the expression of opinions from such members of the Society as are familiar with the phenomena mentioned in the paper.

DR. TRENHOLME, of Montreal. — On behalf of one half of this continent, at least as far as area is concerned, I feel that I should call for protection from the doctrines of this paper. We, upon our side of the line, look upon it as rather a reproach not to have a large family; and if our Canadian ladies found out that their sterility was dependent upon the former condition of their husbands, I do not know what would take place.

With regard to the gonorrheal germ and its effect before marriage, there is probably something of value in the paper, but that the disease is continuous in its effects, and does a perpetual work, I am not ready to believe.

DR. ENGELMANN. — Dr. Noeggerath's paper has explained some facts which I have repeatedly seen in post-mortem examinations, but have not understood. I allude to the frequent occurrence of salpingitis. I have noticed an enlargement, a thickening and cystic formation in the tubes, especially in cases where disease had existed in the husband at a previous time. That fact, as the doctor has already stated, would explain the facility with which this disease is at any time, and by any manipulation, carried to the peritoneum or peritoneal covering of the uterus. So much in support of the paper, perhaps. But I must be allowed to say that I have known of a number of cases where the gentlemen have been under treatment for gonorrhea, and yet, having subsequently married, their wives have had healthy children, and there has been no sign of disease either in the father or mother.

DR. CHADWICK. — I have had no experience which will enable me to bring forward a series of facts and cases bearing upon the doctrines enunciated by Dr. Noeggerath; but when I received the title of his paper, I hunted up his former pamphlet in my library, and glanced it over. There are, I think, decided flaws in the train of argument which he gives there, and I myself should not be willing to accept the cases presented in the book as clearly proven cases of perimetritis or sterility, dependent upon gonorrhea. I will take up the first seven cases, as grouped together in the first chapter under the sub-head of Acute Perimetritis, giving them in abstract only.

CASE I.[1] Mrs. L., married for two years, had a child thirteen months old. The business of the husband kept him from home during the summer of 1871, when he contracted a gonorrhea that was supposed, both by him and his physician, to have been cured at the end of two months. He returned home midway between his wife's catamenia; eight to nine days after cohabitation, the

[1] E. Noeggerath, *Die Latente Gonorrhoe im Weiblichen Geschlecht,* Bonn, 1872, pp. 15-20.

wife, for the first time in her life, had quite a profuse vaginal discharge, accompanied by pains in the abdomen and sacrum. The catamenia then set in more abundantly than usual; immediately after their cessation the pains were augmented and attended by considerable fever. Examination five weeks later revealed a peritonitic effusion in Douglas's Pouch, an injected vagina, a cervix superficially eroded, a profuse discharge, catarrh of the ducts of Cowper's glands, etc., etc.

This case I have no hesitation in accepting as one of perimetritis, due to a gonorrhea acquired from the husband a few days after his supposed cure from an acute attack.

CASE II. Mrs. N., two and a half years ago married a German, who, eight months before his marriage, had had gonorrhea, followed by gleet, which was cured only three months before the wedding, and has not since reappeared. Soon after marriage the wife had, for the first time, a slight discharge, which caused no inconvenience, did not affect micturition, or give rise to burning or itching of the genitals. Two months later, Mrs. N. had a severe attack of abdominal inflammation. Subsequent examination revealed a partially absorbed peritonitic effusion in the region of the right ovary, and a profuse muco-purulent discharge from the vagina.

The history of this case supplies no evidence, satisfactory to my mind, of the infection of the wife, or of the dependence of the peritonitic attack, in any way, upon the gonorrhea of the husband. Surely a slight leucorrhea in the early months of marriage is not an uncommon occurrence, and, even if followed by a localized attack of pelvi-peritonitis, allows of many explanations more natural than that adduced by the writer.

CASE III. Mrs. E. R., known to be healthy as a girl, married a German who had been treated and cured of the residue of a former gonorrhea three months before. She at once became aware, in the first weeks of marriage, of a discharge, which was soon accompanied by pain; she took to her bed immediately, and had an attack of acute perimetritis. . . . . Examination revealed induration in the direction of the left cul-de-sac of the vagina, a very profuse muco-purulent discharge, and catarrh of both Cowper's glands. . . . .

This case surely allows of doubt, although there is some reason for suspecting the gonorrheal origin of the leucorrhea and perimetritis. The attack, in the woman, does not appear to have

had a sudden origin, as is common when gonorrhea is communicated. The train of symptoms will admit of more than the one
explanation.

Case IV. In 1867, a brewer, B., was treated by Dr. N. for
gonorrhea, complicated with orchitis ; after two months of treatment he was discharged, all traces of the gonorrhea having vanished. Two years later he married a healthy girl from the country, who soon began to fail in health. The catamenia became
more profuse, and were attended by so much pain, that at the
fifth month after marriage, the woman was confined to her bed
for eight days. Several weeks later a perimetric effusion was
found to the left of the uterus. Although the patient did not
seem to be aware of any vaginal discharge, a muco-purulent secretion, far exceeding the normal, was found. and a red erosion
around the external os. Two years later she applied for the
relief of sterility. There was then a very small erosion on the
os, a little transparent, viscid secretion, and some slight remains
of the peritoneal exudation.

In this case there was no one of the symptoms which are commonly believed to accompany an acute vaginitis, such as is
caused by gonorrheal infection. We must modify our present
pathological views, and accept the theory that gleet, of gonorrheal origin, will, by contagion, produce a chronic vaginitis of so
mild a type as not to attract the attention of the individual infected. It is certainly not uncommon for a young married woman, brought from the healthy air and life of the country to a
crowded city like New York, to fail in health, and to develop
symptoms of uterine congestion, and ultimately inflammation,
under the influence of the excessive indulgence in the marital
pleasures that occurs during the early months of married life.

Case V. Mr. M. had had gonorrhea of two months' duration
one year before marriage. His wife, in perfect health as a girl,
began to fail soon after marriage, remained sterile, began to have
pains preceding the catamenia, and, as never before, slight fluor
albus. At the end of a year the cervix uteri was incised by Dr.
Sims to facilitate conception. A very profuse hemorrhage occurred at the time, requiring tamponade of the vagina. A severe
attack of acute perimetritis followed, confining her to bed for two
or three months, since which time she has never had a "well day."
The uterus was found to be anteverted, and not freely movable ;
the ovaries were very tender to the touch ; and evidence of an

310

antecedent peritonitis was present. The whole vagina was red, and covered with a muco-purulent discharge. . . . .

I fail to see by what right the attack of perimetritis in this woman can be attributed to the gonorrhea that existed in the husband years before ; on the other hand, it was directly and indisputably caused by the incision of the cervix, being one of the recognized dangers which attend that operation.

CASE VI. Mr. R. had had gonorrhea, two and a half years before marriage, which was completely cured in eight weeks. His wife began to fail in health from the day of marriage, complaining chiefly of abdominal pains, which gradually increased in intensity, until, at the end of three months, she was obliged to take to her bed, where she lay for eight weeks with inflammation of the womb, she said. She remained sterile, and a great sufferer. The catamenia were regular, and there was very slight leucorrhea. The right ovary was found prolapsed, and very tender. Catarrh of Cowper's glands was present, and a little creamy discharge in the vagina.

Here again I fail to detect any symptoms of gonorrhea in the wife.

CASE VII. (Communicated by Dr. Simrock.) Mr. S. had gonorrhea, of a month's duration, six months before marriage. Four days after the wedding he had a white discharge, of viscid character, from the urethra, which yielded to treatment by astringent injections in eight days. During this period no cohabitation took place. About six weeks later Mrs. S. was attacked with feverish symptoms, and severe abdominal pains, after having had leucorrhea for eight days before. Acute perimetritis was diagnosticated.

I am not disposed to cavil at the connection traced between the gonorrhea in the man, if such it was, and the illness of the wife in this instance, although the evidence is far from satisfactory.

To sum up: In one case (I.) the connection between the gonorrhea in the husband, and the ill health, perimetritis, and sterility of the wife, is satisfactorily established ; in two cases (III., VII.) it is assumed with some reason ; and in the other four it is not only unproven, but highly improbable. I have not studied critically the remaining cases adduced in the pamphlet, but if these may be taken as samples, I would affirm that the facts on which Dr. Noeggerath has based his theory do not warrant his deductions.

I will now turn to the chapter on the "Relative Fecundity in Latent Gonorrhea," and beg your attention to a comparison that is instituted in the third paragraph. After stating that the eighty-one women whose cases had been recorded had only thirty-nine children, this rate of fecundity is demonstrated to be far below the normal by comparing it with the average number of four children that are born to other women in the course of the whole period of wedlock. The fact is entirely overlooked that none of Dr. Noeggerath's patients had passed the period of child-bearing; or, to put it more correctly, the great error is made of comparing the fertility of women who have been married from one to five or more years, with what has been shown to be the average fertility of women in their whole child-bearing period of about thirty years.

It is impossible to adduce a sufficient array of cases to offset those given by Dr. Noeggerath in proof of his theory, but I think that I have indicated the untrustworthiness of enough of his data, and the fallaciousness of some of his reasoning, to justify my withholding assent to his views. I do not believe them to be true.

The President. — Dr. Noeggerath, in his paper, gives a certain class of phenomena, which he assumes to be characteristic proof of an infection coming from special cause. It is therefore proper that we should take the supplemental paper now read in connection with the paper previously published. I am sure that Dr. Noeggerath is willing to have his paper thoroughly criticised.

Dr. Johnson, of Washington, D. C. — I wish to call attention to the fact that, if the views of Dr. Noeggerath were correct, it seems as though the mere instinct of man ought to restrain him from so brutal an act as becoming married to a pure woman, when aware of the consequences. I know that there is a large number of such cases, and I think that, in view of such positive statements as have been made by Dr. N., counter-statements should be made covering this point. I may state that in conversation with twenty different physicians, who acknowledged having had gonorrhea in early life, in no single case had any such symptoms, as have been referred to, been developed in their wives, and all have had quite large families of children. These cases would seem to contradict the positive declarations made by Dr. Noeggerath.

Dr. Taliaferro, of Georgia, remarked that he agreed entirely with the Secretary in reference to the published cases mentioned and the cases given this morning. He regarded leucorrhea as a natural condition, and one almost universally present after marriage, occurring as the result of more than the usual amount of coition.

DR. CHADWICK added two cases to those mentioned by Dr. Johnson, in which gonorrhea had been present before marriage, but one had had a family of four children in four years, and the other one child in eighteen months of married life.

DR. NOEGGERATH. — I perceive that the contradictions which have been raised, are based upon a few single facts. The theory which I propose requires careful study and a great deal of experience for its recognition.

I have mentioned cases where not only two, but six children were born of previously infected men. I only state, if I examine fourteen men who have had gonorrhea, and whose wives are sterile, and find seven out of the fourteen without spermatozoa, it is evident the cause of sterility is with the husband and not with the wife. These are facts which cannot be denied. There is no direct proof for or against my theory in one or in seven cases, but if you look over the fifty cases published in my work on latent gonorrhea, you will find a certain combination of diseases which are only seen to such an extent in women who are married to men who have had gonorrhea. Among these I have pointed to the prevalence of chronic perimetritis, an affection characterized as obscure, regarding symptoms both rational and physical. And if I make the diagnosis of chronic perimetritis in a given case, there will be probably but few to coincide with my view in the matter for reasons enumerated in this paper.

The leucorrhea which sets in after marriage under ordinary circumstances is bland, of no consequence, and remains so ; but the woman who is married to a man who has had gonorrhea, will have only a slight leucorrhea at first, but it will gradually begin to irritate the mucous membrane of the vulva, creep up into the uterus, and subsequently develop salpingitis, perimetritis, ovaritis, etc.

The fact that I can demonstrate the existence of gleet in those men is stronger evidence *for* the theory than can be adduced *against* it. The gleet in the male exists, although not in a degree to make its appearance at the orifice of the urethra.

With regard to the question, whether a medical man who once

has had gonorrhea has a right to get married, that is a personal affair with which I have not to deal.

After the gentlemen have given five years or more of careful study to this question, I shall expect to hear more approval than I have done to-day.

FIVE CASES OF EXTRA-UTERINE PREGNANCY OPERATED UPON AT THE TIME OF RUPTURE.

By LAWSON TAIT, F.R.C.S.Ed. & Eng.,
Surgeon to the Birmingham and Midland Hospital for Women.

PENDING the discussion on the pathology and treatment of extra-uterine pregnancy, which is to take place at Belfast, I desire to place on record this, the first series, as I believe, of cases of extra-uterine pregnancy operated upon at the time of rupture; that is, from the tenth to the thirteenth weeks. Most of us are familiar with such dramatic incidents as that of the actress in the Bois de Boulogne, where sudden or very rapid death has occurred from hæmorrhage due to the tear of a venous sinus in the rupture of an early Fallopian pregnancy. I have been unfortunate enough to see a large number of them, five or six and twenty, and of late I have been encouraged by my success in other abdominal diseases to try what surgery could do in these cases.

For this treatment, of course the difficulty was the diagnosis, but as I have now completely adopted the principle of always opening the abdomen when I find a patient in danger with abdominal symptoms, this barrier no longer exists. The diagnosis is, however, not so very difficult after all, for in many cases the existence of pregnancy has been suspected before the rupture occurred. It may be in the majority, however, that this misleading feature is present; the patient has never been pregnant, or has not been so for many years, and then the arrest of menstruation attracts no particular attention. If, however, it be found that the patient has been eight weeks or more without a period, that there is a pelvic mass fixing the uterus and on one side of it, and that sudden and severe symptoms of pelvic trouble and hæmorrhage came on, the rupture of a tubal pregnancy may be at once suspected, and if an operation is to be done—and it clearly ought to be done—it must be done without delay. Early interference is clearly a chief element of success in modern abdominal surgery.

The first case to which I was called after I had made up my mind as to the line to be adopted in such cases, occurred on January 17th, 1883, in the practice of Mr. Spackman of Wolverhampton. He had already made the diagnosis, and I was of opinion that he was perfectly correct. The patient had not had a child for many years; menstruation had been arrested for eleven weeks, and symptoms of rupture had occurred. When I saw her she was blanched from hæmorrhage, and her skin had the peculiar staining which is characteristic of the extravasation of blood into the peritoneum. The contents of the pelvis were fixed, and there was a distinct mass on the left side. The abdomen was distended, and the patient in a good deal of pain.

Though I feared that interference might have come too late, still I advised operation, and immediately proceeded to carry it out. I opened the abdomen, and found a quantity of clot derived from a ruptured Fallopian pregnancy on the left side. As well as I could, I stitched the edges of the rent to the abdominal wound, but every touch caused hæmorrhage, so that I had to desist without doing much save removing the fœtus and some of the placenta. The patient never regained consciousness, and died shortly after being removed from the operating table.

On March 1st, 1883, I saw, with Dr. Page of Solihull, a patient who had not been pregnant for many years, in whom there was a fixed mass in the pelvis, and whose menstruation had been arrested for about three months. She had a high pulse and an exalted temperature and great pain. I advised abdominal section, and found the abdomen full of clot. The right Fallopian tube was ruptured, and from it a placenta was protruding. I tied the tube and removed it. I searched for, but could not find the fœtus, and I suppose it got amongst the folds of intestine and there was absorbed. Certainly it has not since been seen. The patient made a very protracted convalescence, but she is now perfectly well.

On April 9th, 1884, I opened the abdomen in the case of a patient whom I had seen a few days previously with Dr. J. W. Taylor, of Moseley, Birmingham. She had symptoms of acute pelvic inflammation, the organs being fixed, and there was a mass behind and to the right of the uterus. She also had not been pregnant for many years. I admitted her to my private hospital; and during the removal, doubtless, the rupture occurred. At the operation, I found the abdomen filled by a quantity of blood-serum and free clot. The left tube was distended by a placenta, which protruded through a rupture. I tied and removed the tube, but I could not find the fœtus. She made an easy recovery, and now has almost completed her convalescence.

On May 25th, I operated upon a patient in the Hospital for Women, aged 27, who had had two children, the last having been born three years ago. She had menstruated regularly till three months previously. Pelvic pain had been in existence for some weeks, and had become steadily worse. I found the uterus fixed, and a larger tender mass on the left side; and I diagnosed the case as possibly one of pyosalpinx. At the operation, I found the left Fallopian tube had burst, and that there was a quantity of loose clot in the pelvis. The fœtus was lying in the pelvis, attached to the placenta, which remained in the tube. The tube was adherent to surrounding structures, but was easily detached, tied, and removed. She made an easy recovery; the wound has completely healed, and she has left the hospital.

. The fifth case has just occurred, an illustration of the curious sequence of exceptional cases often seen in practice.

A. M., aged 34, married fifteen years, has had four children, the last having been born six years and a half ago. Her last menstruation was early in April. Late in May she had an attack of intense abdominal pain, which increased in intensity till June 3rd. I found the uterus fixed, and a boggy swelling to the left. The abdomen was swollen, and peritonitis was clearly beginning, the pulse and temperature being both high, intense pain occurring occasionally, and the patient's expression being anxious. I opened the abdomen on June 5th, and found the pelvic contents matted together with recent lymph and blood-clot. I found the left tube torn almost in two, and occupied by a placenta, apparently of about the tenth week. I could not find the fœtus. I tied and removed the tube, drained the pelvis, and the patient has made an easy recovery.

These cases all confirm the view of the pathology of extra-uterine pregnancy, which I advanced many years ago, that in origin it is always tubal, and that its varieties depend merely on the direction in which rupture occurs. These results also confirm the soundness of the policy of interfering early in such cases, for four out of the five have been easily and completely cured of one of the most formidable conditions of pregnancy. The first and only fatal case might have had a better ending if Mr. Spackman had seen her sooner, for it is only just to him that I should say he recognised the nature and gravity of the case at once, and sent for me immediately.

317

Infantile Syphilis as an Example of Nineteenth Century Belief in the Inheritance of Acquired Characteristics

ELIZABETH LOMAX

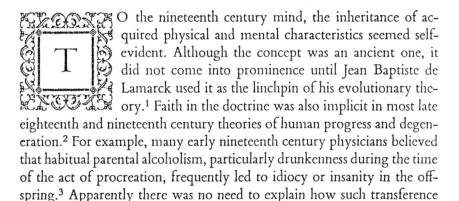O the nineteenth century mind, the inheritance of acquired physical and mental characteristics seemed self-evident. Although the concept was an ancient one, it did not come into prominence until Jean Baptiste de Lamarck used it as the linchpin of his evolutionary theory.[1] Faith in the doctrine was also implicit in most late eighteenth and nineteenth century theories of human progress and degeneration.[2] For example, many early nineteenth century physicians believed that habitual parental alcoholism, particularly drunkenness during the time of the act of procreation, frequently led to idiocy or insanity in the offspring.[3] Apparently there was no need to explain how such transference

1. Conway Zirkle, 'The early history of the idea of the inheritance of acquired characters and of pangenesis,' *Trans. Am. phil. Soc.*, 1946, *2nd ser. 35*, 91–151. The phrase 'Lamarckian inheritance' will be used occasionally in this paper as a synonym for 'the inheritance of acquired characteristics' to avoid undue repetition.

2. For discussion of the social consequences of nineteenth century belief in the inheritance of acquired characteristics, see Charles E. Rosenberg, 'The bitter-fruit: heredity, disease and social thought in nineteenth century America,' *Persp. Am. Hist.*, 1974, *8*, 189–235, reprinted in Charles E. Rosenberg, *No other gods: on science and American social thought* (Baltimore, 1976), pp. 25–53. The use of the doctrine to explain biological and medical phenomena is discussed in Frederick B. Churchill, 'Rudolf Virchow and the pathologist's criteria for the inheritance of acquired characteristics,' *J. Hist. Med.*, 1976, *31*, 115–148.

3. Amy A. Pruit, 'Approaches to alcoholism in mid-Victorian England,' *Clio Med.*, 1974, *9*, 93–101; William Bynum, 'Chronic alcoholism in the first half of the nineteenth century,' *Bull. Hist. Med.*, 1968, *42*, 160–185. Alcoholism as a cause of family degeneration was discussed at length by Benedict A. Morel, *Traité des dégénérescences physiques, intellectuelles et morales de l'espèce humaine* (Paris, 1857), pp. 79–140. Morel only made casual mention of syphilis as a cause of human degeneration. In view of current research interest in the fetal alcohol syndrome, it should perhaps be noted that Joseph Adams, *A treatise on the supposed hereditary properties of diseases* (London, 1814), p. 62, remarked 'that women who are habitual drunkards, generally produce immature or ideot [*sic*] children.' In Adams's opinion such effects were transmitted *in utero* and were uncommon since 'female ebriety, especially at the age of conception, is very rare.'

Supported in part by NIH Grant LM 02429 from the National Library of Medicine, Bethesda, Maryland.

might occur until the end of the century when August Weismann challenged supporters of Lamarckian inheritance to supply evidence for their theory. During the first decades of the twentieth century, the inheritance of acquired characteristics was much debated, only to pall, as a question of biological importance, as evidence for evolutionary change through gene mutation became overwhelming.

Nineteenth century theories on the causes of infantile syphilis reflected the acceptance that acquired characteristics could be inherited. Then, as now, it was recognized that acquired parental syphilis could lead to abortion, stillbirth, disease of the newborn, or even disorders appearing later in infancy or childhood.[4] Today intrauterine infection is held responsible for all manifestations of infantile syphilis. The treponema or spirochaete is believed to cross the placental barrier during the later months of pregnancy. But in the nineteenth century, physicians commonly thought that syphilis could be a truly hereditary disease, that is, it might be due to a vitiated sperm or ovum.[5] Some physicians insisted further that parental syphilis could lead to progressive degeneration of the offspring without their inheriting the disease itself. Children might be born with a defective constitution which, unless remedied, would be transmitted to the next generation until either cure or family extinction supervened. Early in the twentieth century, this tenet was to serve as ammunition for biologists who defended the reality of Lamarckian inheritance. In contrast, during the same period clinicians clarified the etiology of infantile syphilis without paying much attention to current biological arguments about the susceptibility of the resting germ plasm to external somatic influences.

Not until the nineteenth century was the term *hereditary* used with any consistency to denote characteristics acquired only at conception.[6] Previously the word *hereditary* usually included characteristics thought to have been acquired during gestation, a meaning which from the early nine-

---

4. For details of modern views about congenital syphilis, plus a chapter on its history, see David Nabarro, *Congenital syphilis* (London, 1954). For the history of ideas about the causes of infantile syphilis see, P. Diday, *A treatise on syphilis in new-born children and infants at the breast*, trans. G Whitley from the 1854 French ed. (London, 1859); E. Lancereaux, *Traité historique et pratique de la syphilis* (Paris, 1866); and E. Jeanselme, *Histoire de la syphilis* (Paris, 1931).

5. In the nineteenth century there was general agreement that a mother could transmit the disease before birth but no consensus as to how, *per ovum* or *per utero*. Many physicians thought it impossible for the syphilitic virus to be transferred during gestation since there was no direct exchange of blood between mother and fetus. For discussions on this subject see Diday, *Treatise on syphilis* (n. 4), pp. 22–32; Lancereaux, *Traité . . . de la syphilis* (n. 4), p. 657; and Abner Post, 'Intra-uterine infection of syphilis,' *Boston med. surg. J.*, 1896, *135*, 77–81.

6. For the introduction of the term *heredity* as distinct from the adjective *hereditary*, see Ruth Schwartz Cowan, 'Francis Galton's contributions to genetics,' *J. Hist. Biol.*, 1972, *5*, 389–412.

teenth century onwards began to be subsumed under the term *congenital*.[7] Terminological change bore some relation to changing ideas about the process of generation. In the sixteenth century, when the Aristotelian view that the male provided the active principle of fertilization while the female contributed matter for further development was commonly accepted, gestation might reasonably be regarded as a period during which maternal influences could act. Later, when preformationism was at its height, it was essential to assume the transmission of characteristics during pregnancy, if only to explain resemblances between progenitors and offspring.[8] The term *hereditary* began to develop its modern connotations in the nineteenth century as more natural scientists became persuaded that both parents contributed to formation of the conceptus. Yet caution must be used in interpreting nineteenth century texts for, as Charles Rosenberg has noted, the majority of physicians and the laity still 'assumed that heredity was a dynamic process beginning with conception and extending through weaning.'[9] Most students of syphilis, although not all, were more precise because of their special interest in differentiating various possible prenatal, natal, and postnatal causes of the disease.

Descriptions, albeit brief, of infantile syphilis date from the early sixteenth century when, according to both contemporary and modern historians, the disease was raging in acute and epidemic form in western Europe. The rapid, telescoped course of illness in the sixteenth century provided unusual opportunity for the recognition of infantile syphilis. According to Jacques de Bethencourt writing in 1527, 'sick parents give birth only to sick children. In consequence there is nothing astonishing in that children can receive this evil as a heritage from their ascendants.'[10] Soon, probably beginning in the second half of the sixteenth century, adult syphilis was to become a more chronic affliction, characterized by long periods of latency or apparent cure. Were it not for observations made during the era of extreme virulence, infantile syphilis might not have been recognized as a consequence of adult venereal disease. Instead, this relation was established early, although detailed descriptions date mainly from the late eighteenth century, stimulated by the establishment in 1781 of the Hospice de

7. *Oxford English Dictionary*, s.v. 'Congenital,' provides a quotation from the year 1796 as the first known occurrence of the word.

8. See Joseph Needham, *A history of embryology* (New York, 1959), pp. 215–216; and Jacques Roger, *Les sciences de la vie dans la pensée Française du XVIIIe siècle* (Paris, 1963), pp. 187–188, 398–418.

9. Rosenberg, *No other gods* (n. 2), pp. 26–27.

10. Jacques de Bethencourt, *Nouveau Carême de pénitence . . . à l'usage des malades effectés du mal Français*, trans. Alfred Fournier from the 1527 Latin ed. (Paris, 1871), p. 35.

Vaurigard in Paris for the reception of pregnant syphilitic women and for the care of their offspring.[11] Such descriptions, however, also illustrated the prevailing inability to distinguish between syphilis and gonorrhea. For ophthalmia was considered one of the most frequent symptoms of infantile syphilis, a fact which suggests that many of the babies were actually suffering from gonorrhea, or from both disorders.[12]

Most of the early commentators assumed that an infant acquired syphilis through suckling, either from a breast lesion or from the milk. Paracelsus, however, stated that the disease on occasion could be hereditary, transmitted from father to son.[13] A few decades later, the surgeon Ambroise Paré asserted that he had never observed instances of this kind of transmission; in his opinion the mother's womb was the most likely site of infection.[14] The seventeenth century French accoucheur François Mauriçeau taught that if skin lesions were present at birth then the disease was acquired *in utero*, while signs appearing postnatally indicated infection at the breast.[15] Some notable eighteenth century students of venereal disease, including Hermann Boerhaave, Jean Astruc, and François Swediaur, mentioned the possibility of hereditary transmission as well as transference by contact.[16] But while Boerhaave and Astruc did not specify quite what they meant by *hereditary*, Swediaur was most explicit. In his words, 'children, therefore, receive the syphilitic infection, 1st. By the semen of their father, or during their existence in utero; this constitutes the hereditary syphilis. Hence, as asserted by some writers, new born children sometimes come into the world bearing the marks of this disease.'[17]

Most eighteenth century physicians would probably have agreed with

11. Physicians attending the Hospice de Vaurigard seem to have initiated the writing of monographs on infantile syphilis, for example P. A. O. Mahon, *Recherches importantes sur l'existence, la nature et la communication des maladies syphilitiques dans les femmes enceintes, dans les enfants nouveau-nés et dans les nourrices* (Paris, 1804) and R. J. H. Bertin, *Traité de la maladie vénérienne chez les enfants nouveau-nés, les femmes enceintes et les nourrices* (Paris, 1810).

12. Nabarro, *Congenital syphilis* (n. 4), p. 11, points out that Bertin and his contemporaries regarded pus around the eyes as a common early symptom of infantile syphilis.

13. Theophrastus Paracelsus, *Werke*, ed. Will-Erich Peuckert, 5 vols. (Basle, 1965–68), II, 367. Paracelsus suggested that the child could receive the venereal poison during conception, or from its mother's body, or externally from her milk. See also Jeanselme, *Histoire de la syphilis* (n. 4), p. 180.

14. Ambroise Paré remarked that 'infants oft-times conceive the seeds of this disease in the wombs of their mothers,' or might 'chance to catch the disease after they are born by sucking from an infected nurse'; Ambroise Paré, *Collected Works*, trans. Thomas Johnson (London, 1634), p. 754.

15. François Mauriçeau, *Les maladies des femmes grosses et accouchées* (Paris, 1668), pp. 520–521.

16. *Boerhaave's Aphorisms*, trans. J. Delacoste (London, 1715), p. 392; J. Astruc, *A treatise of the venereal disease*, trans. W. Barrowby, 2 vols. (London, 1737), I, 138.

17. F. Swediaur, *A complete treatise on the symptoms, effects, nature and treatment of syphilis*, trans. T. T. Hewson from the 4th French ed. (Philadelphia, 1815), p. 329.

Swediaur's definitions, but not quite all. As early as 1749, the Parisian surgeon Antoine Louis had analysed this problem of biological semantics in a dissertation attempting to prove that hereditary diseases could not exist. Louis defined his understanding of such diseases as follows:

> I would not give, as do some authors, this name to certain diseases that children bear at birth and of which the parents are actually afflicted. If a woman, for example, infected by the venereal virus gives birth to a child showing signs of this illness produced by debauchery; can one say that in this child the pox is a hereditary disease? No without doubt: it is an acquired illness; it is an illness that has been communicated to the infant: the liquors of the mother and child are in mutual communication; the vice in the mother's humors must necessarily influence the health of the child.[18]

Louis noted further that advocates of hereditary disease constantly supported their opinion with the example of a syphilitic child born to a luetic mother, while he insisted that any illness communicated after fecundation must be classified as an acquired one.

Preformation theory required the inclusion of gestation in the period during which hereditary transmission could occur, for the doctrine postulated that all parts of an organism existed preformed in every particular, in miniature, within either the male or the female germ. Development of the embryo was merely an enlargement of preexisting parts, as opposed to the epigenetic belief that a new being was created by interaction between material derived from each parent. Extreme preformation led to the theory of emboîtement, postulating that all the individuals of a species ever to be born were enfolded within each other, rather like the parts of a Chinese puzzle, within the egg or sperm of the first individual created. When this theory was ascendant it was extremely difficult to explain the production of a malformed fetus. As Louis pointed out, in such instances ill-formed seeds must have been implanted by the Creator, hardly an acceptable hypothesis.[19] To get around this impasse in accounting for obvious resemblances between parents and children, and the occurrence of fetal abnormalities, both ovists and spermists postulated influences acting via the maternal organism during pregnancy.

Louis did not believe preformation theory likely. He supposed that the germ or seed of a new organism was formed in the male parent by some process of organization (pangenesis). Given this conviction he could argue

18. Antoine Louis, *Dissertation sur la question . . . Comment se fait la transmission des maladies hérédi-taires?* (Paris, 1749), pp. 12–13.
19. *Ibid.,* p. 24.

that no disease could be transmitted beyond one generation and that hereditary or familial disease could not be a reality. Having further noted that men with syphilis did not necessarily transmit the illness to their offspring, he seems to have concluded that morbid parental dispositions did not become incorporated in any new germ or seed. Louis consequently believed neither in inherited disease nor in the inheritance of acquired disease characteristics for even one generation.

With the decline of preformation theory toward the end of the eighteenth century, Louis's criteria for hereditary disease became more general. Now also an increasing number of venereologists claimed that syphilis could be hereditary, that is, derived from the diseased germ of either the father or the mother, on the grounds that healthy women could give birth to syphilitic babies. In such instances the male parent must have been responsible and, by analogy, it was assumed that the female could transmit the disease *per ovum* as well as *per utero*. The British physician Jonathan Hutchinson described the change in opinion that had taken place by 1856 as follows:

When cases of congenital syphilis first came to be observed it was customary, I believe, misled by the circumstance that such infants are usually born remarkably healthy, and do not show symptoms of the disease until a week or more afterwards, for Surgeons to hold that the disease had been contracted by the foetus from its mother during delivery. Close upon this doctrine followed the observation that mothers suffering from constitutional syphilis brought forth children liable to the same disease. For long it was held that the father could only communicate the disease to his offspring by first giving it to his wife. Numerous cases, not to be so explained, at length led to the doctrine, now almost universally held, that a father begets children liable to his own diseases and constitutional taints, and that, consequently, a child may be born of a healthy mother, which shall, in virtue of a morbid predisposition derived from its father, suffer from hereditary syphilis.[20]

John Hunter had claimed that infantile syphilis was acquired during delivery. Hunter probably came to this erroneous conclusion because he was mainly seeing cases of neonatal gonorrhea which neither he, nor most of his contemporaries, distinguished from infantile syphilis.[21] Swediaur, for example, also thought that children were most commonly infected during their passage through the vagina, but without excluding other possibili-

20. Jonathan Hutchinson, 'On the communication of syphilis from the foetus to its mother,' *Med. Times & Gaz.*, 1856, ii, 615–617, p. 615.
    21. See n. 12.

ties.[22] Hunter appeared more categorical. Actually he did not express his meaning clearly, but most syphilologists interpreted Hunter as absolutely denying the possibility of intrauterine transmission. The passage in question ran thus:

It is also supposed, that a foetus, in the womb of a pocky mother may be infected by her. This I should doubt very much, both from what may be observed of the secretions, and from finding that even the matter from such constitutional inflammation is not capable of communicating the disease. However, one can conceive the bare possibility of a child being affected in the womb of a pocky mother, not indeed from the disease of the mother, but from a part of the same matter which contaminated the mother, and was absorbed by her; and whether irritating her solids to action or not, may possibly be conveyed to the child, pure as absorbed; and if so it may affect the child exactly in the same way it did or might have done the mother.[23]

Because Hunter wielded so much influence, even after death, subsequent writers with different interpretations usually felt obliged to refute his allegations. By 1856, when Hutchinson was reviewing the situation, gonorrhea and syphilis were becoming recognized as two distinct venereal diseases, mainly through the efforts of Philippe Ricord.[24]

Hutchinson's next proposition was that a fetus with syphilis inherited from its father could communicate the disease to its mother *in utero*. As one piece of evidence, Hutchinson offered the following:

Although abundant instances are recorded in which syphilitic infants having sore mouths have infected the nipples of wet-nurses who have suckled them, yet not a single one, as far as my knowledge goes, has occurred in which the child's own mother was so contaminated. It was Abraham Colles of Dublin who first drew attention to this startling fact, and his experience has been confirmed by subsequent statements by M. Baumès, Mr. Egan and M. Diday. Now as mothers suckle their own infants in a proportion vastly greater than wet-nurses, they ought, were their liability equal, to furnish a larger number of instances of the disease spreading by this mode. Whence their immunity? Excepting we admit

22. Swediaur, *Treatise on . . . syphilis* (n. 17), p. 329.

23. J. Hunter, A *treatise on the venereal disease*, ed. Joseph Adams (London, 1818), pp. 398–399. Adams appended the following editorial comment: 'it is worth remarking how generally the error has prevailed, that Mr. Hunter denied that the fetus in utero could be infected: yet in this passage we see him not only admitting such a possibility, but explaining how it might take place.'

24. The two venereal diseases were variously confounded long before John Hunter performed his memorable self-inoculation experiment; in this context and for a discussion of Ricord's contributions, see Kenneth M. Flegel, 'Changing concepts of the nosology of gonorrhea and syphilis,' *Bull. Hist. Med.*, 1974, *48*, 571–588.

that they have already received the disease to the extent to which the foetus could convey it, I know not of any explanation which can possibly be suggested.[25]

Colles, writing in 1837, had drawn no such conclusion. He had merely stated that he had never observed, 'nor ever heard of an instance in which a child deriving the infection of syphilis from its parents had caused an ulceration in the breast of its mother.'[26] Later Colles reiterated the point: 'One fact well deserving our attention is this: that a child born of a mother who is without any obvious venereal symptoms, and which . . . shows this disease when a few weeks old; this child will infect the most healthy nurse . . . and yet this child is never known to infect its own mother.'[27]

A few years later Baumès, and then Diday, asserted that in such instances the child was infected through the father's semen and passed the disease, in a mild form, on to its mother *in utero* so that she became immune to later primary infection at the breast.[28] This set of propositions, to be known as Colles's law, was most useful, quite apart from its implications, for it justified persuading a mother to suckle her syphilitic infant without fear of medico-legal complications.[29] It had long been recognized that breast feeding offered the best chance of survival for many reasons, including the possibility of administering toxic mercurial remedies to the child indirectly. The drugs would be taken by the nurse or mother in the hopes that she would be protected and some effect passed on to the infant via her milk. Following Colles's findings, it became less justifiable than ever to recommend a wet nurse to relieve a mother from suckling.[30] The Dublin surgeon, who died in 1843, would have approved this turn of events al-

25. Jonathan Hutchinson, 'On the communication of syphilis from the fetus to its mother,' (cont.), *Med. Times & Gaz.*, 1857, i, 31–34, p. 32.

26. Abraham Colles, *Selections from the works of Abraham Colles*, ed. Robert McDonnell (London, 1881), p. 271.

27. *Ibid.*, p. 287.

28. Prosper Baumès, *Précis théorique et pratique sur les maladies vénériennes*, 2 vols. (Paris, 1840), I, 180–181, made the following statements: 'Madame B . . . , who suckled her five children, never contracted anything from any of her infants. This is in accordance with the observation that a mother, having carried in her womb a syphilitic child, who acquired the infection from the semen of his father, does not usually contract syphilis from suckling her own child, as would a strange nurse.' Diday, *Treatise on syphilis* (n. 4), pp. 176–177, cited both Colles and Baumès then added that if the infant had received congenital syphilis from its father, 'then the infecting influence of the foetus upon its mother finds, in the inaccessibility of the latter to contagion from suckling her child, one of the most powerful arguments that could be desired.'

29. French authors sometimes called it 'la loi Colles-Baumès,' since Baumès was responsible for the rider about paternal inheritance. They also referred to the implied communication of syphilis from fetus to mother as 'la theórie du choc en retour.'

30. Diday, *Treatise on syphilis* (n. 4), pp. 187–203, has a fascinating chapter on the medico-legal aspects of congenital syphilis.

though he might have been indignant that his expressly empirical state-ment was later endowed with such positive meaning. For the next hundred years Colles was almost persistently misquoted. For example, the Amer-ican syphilologist John H. Stokes in 1934 gave the following definition: 'Colles' law states that a nonsyphilitic mother may bear a syphilitic child and that she may nurse her own child with impunity, although others may be infected by it.'[31] This common interpretation was to confuse the issue of the etiology of congenital syphilis well into the twentieth century.

Most nineteenth century syphilologists interpreted Colles's findings as suggested by Baumès and Diday to account for the fact that the mother was, and apparently always had been, symptom free.[32] They argued that she could not have received the disease through coitus because primary or secondary lesions would have been inevitable. Instead she must have ac-quired an attenuated form via the placenta from an already infected fetus. In effect, latent syphilis could easily escape detection prior to the introduc-tion of the Wassermann test in 1906, and even afterwards. In the nine-teenth century, general standards of modesty further muddled the issue by preventing a surgeon from insisting upon the complete examination of a patient unless she was a prostitute. The physician usually accepted a pa-tient's statement that she had never suffered from a chancre or disseminated rash.[33] Since respectable women simply did not confess to venereal disease, the concept of paternal transmission was strengthened further. Men ap-parently had no such inhibitions, frequently requesting medical examina-tion before marriage to ensure that a previous infection was well cured.

If most nineteenth century physicians accepted that the syphilitic virus, lodged in the parental sperm or ovum, could cause active disease in the offspring, a few also regarded syphilis as hereditary under more general terms. According to this group, the disease could not only be transmitted

---

31. John H. Stokes, *Modern clinical syphilology* (Philadelphia, 1934), p. 1215.

32. A small minority of nineteenth century clinicians refused to admit the possibility of paternal transmission. Jeanselme, *Histoire de la syphilis* (n. 4), pp. 368–369, gives Adam Oewre of Christiania and Edmund Langlebert of Paris as proponents of the theory that congenital syphilis was always de-rived from a contaminated mother. For further examples see A. Cullerier, 'De l'hérédité de la syphilis, *Mém. Soc. de chir. de Par.*, 1857, *4*, 230–264; A. Charrier, 'De l'hérédité syphilitique,' *Archs. gén. Méd.*, 1862, 5th ser. *20*, 324–330; and A. H. Notta, 'Mémoire sur l'hérédité de la syphilis,' *Archs. gén. Méd.*, 1860, 5th ser. *15*, 272–284.

33. A mid-nineteenth century reviewer made the point that a surgeon 'should, before hazarding an opinion, insist upon a *careful scrutiny of the woman's person*, in order to see if she may not have a pri-mary syphilitic ulcer, or the vestiges of it. Nothing less than this can be satisfactory;' 'Bibliographical notices: *Syphilitic diseases; their pathology, diagnosis, and treatment*, by John C. Egan, London, 1853,' *Am. J. med. Sci.*, 1853, 2nd ser. *26*, 417–424, p. 422. Egan's case histories suggested that he eliminated the possibility of venereal disease on the basis of 'good character' alone.

as obvious syphilis, but also as a predisposition to a host of other disorders including scrofula, tuberculosis, rickets, general underdevelopment, and idiocy. Furthermore, the inherited defective constitution would be transmitted from generation to generation until it led to family extinction, unless combatted by effective remedies. French clinicians were to label this condition, *l'hérédité syphilitique*, in contradistinction to *la syphilis héréditaire*, or transmission of active disease.[34]

By the late eighteenth century, some physicians had suggested that parental syphilis could be translated into other disorders in the offspring. This was one way of explaining the development of conditions such as scrofula, rickets, and scurvy in babies who had seemed quite healthy at birth, and for some months afterwards.[35] Acute diseases, for example smallpox and measles, were attributed to a contagious virus, but it was not so easy to suggest an etiology for the chronic wasting disorders of late infancy that did not spread from one victim to another. So it was argued that although the immediate cause was probably some external agent (toxic food, lack or excess of food, exposure to cold, impurity in the atmosphere, and so on), such an agent could act only on a constitution already predisposed to the illness. Thus the sporadic nature of chronic illness in early childhood, and its tendency to occur in siblings, was rationalized. Theorists who sought a unitary origin to disease—quite a common outlook in the late eighteenth century—regarded syphilis as a likely cause of inherited liability to illness. Here was a disorder known to be originally spread by contact and also to be transmissible from one generation to the next. To the systematic mind it was tempting to conclude that the syphilitic virus could become modified or degenerate leading to debility or the so-called *syphilitic constitution* in the offspring. Astruc, for example, taught that one sign of parental syphilis was: 'Sickly constitution of the children, who being strumous, ricketty, gibbous, hectical, lean, die miserably before their time; or if they live, are short, broken-back'd, large headed, crooked, bandy-legged, vari-

34. Unfortunately, terminology was not consistent either in the French or in the English language The distinction drawn in this paper is based on usage in Paul-Louis Gastou, *Rapport sur la syphili héréditaire et l'hérédité syphilitique* (Corbeil, 1906), a report presented to the fifteenth International Congress of Medicine at Lisbon, April 1906. Synonyms for *l'hérédité syphilitique* (a term sometimes used to embrace all forms of syphilitic inheritance) were *l'hérédo-syphilis*, and *syphilis héréditaire larvée*; in English, *syphilitic heredity* or *occult syphilis*. The realization late in the nineteenth century that 'true' congenital syphilis could remain symptomless for years after birth, helped further to confuse terminology.

35. For further discussion of a degenerated syphilitic 'virus' as a primary cause of scrofula see Elizabeth Lomax, 'Hereditary or acquired disease? Early nineteenth century debates on the causes of infantile scrofula and tuberculosis,' *J. Hist. Med.*, 1977, *32*, 356–374.

ously distorted, and thick jointed.'[36] Astruc's descriptions were vague and, therefore could mislead, but congenital syphilis can cause specific damage to all systems of the body.

In the first decade of the nineteenth century, the French physician Antoine Portal further elaborated this theme. He reported that he could cure infantile rickets with antiscrofular or with antisyphilitic remedies.[37] If one failed, he tried the other. From this and other evidence, mainly family case histories, Portal concluded that many developmental diseases of infancy were essentially due to hereditary scrofula, and that a scrofular taint was often itself derived from a degenerate venereal virus. Consequently, syphilis, scrofula, and perhaps scurvy (Portal was none too consistent about his disease entities) were leading to the physical degeneration of whole families, particularly in cities such as Paris and London, which would become depopulated were it not for the constant influx of healthy men and women from the country. 'A good choice in marriages contributes not a little to attenuate hereditary taints,' Portal reflected.[38] But his main message was the advocacy of special remedies, mercurials combined with antiscorbutics and bitters, for underdeveloped or sickly children.

Belief in the inheritance of acquired characteristics, while encouraging the elaboration of pessimistic theories of racial degeneration, rendered rational the use of relatively simple external means of reversing the degenerative process. Syphilis, for example, was curable through the liberal application or intake of mercury, or so it was thought in the nineteenth century. Extreme eugenic measures were not seriously contemplated. As far as I am aware, no nineteenth century syphilologist suggested that patients should be sterilized for the protection of the innocent. Nor was this restraint prompted by squeamishness, for surgeons occasionally performed vasectomies and even orchidectomies in cases of persistent masturbation.[39] Syphilitics were more fortunate. Not only was their illness deemed sensitive to drug therapy, but it was acquired during normal sexual relations, while masturbation invited all the sanctions accorded to a perversion. Further-

36. Astruc, *Venereal disease* (n. 16), II, 56.

37. Antoine Portal, 'Considerations on the nature and treatment of some hereditary or family disease,' *Lond. med. phys. J.*, 1809, *21*, 229–239, 281–296.

38. *Ibid.*, p. 294.

39. See, for example, T. Haynes, 'Surgical treatment of hopeless cases of masturbation and nocturnal emissions,' *Boston med. surg. J.*, 1883, *109*, 130; and J. H. Marshall, 'Insanity cured by castration,' *Med. surg. Reptr.*, 1865, *13*, 363–364. For analyses of nineteenth century attitudes about masturbation, see E. H. Hare, 'Masturbatory insanity: the history of an idea,' *J. mental Sci.*, 1962, *108*, 1–25; and H. Tristram Engelhardt, Jr., 'The disease of masturbation: values and the concept of disease,' *Bull. Hist. Med.*, 1974, *48*, 234–248.

more, syphilitics came from all walks of life and many a surgeon may have been restrained from even considering drastic intervention by the thought that but for the grace of God he too might be a patient.

Although society extended a blanket of tolerance over venereal disease in the male, the same was not true for the female victim. The natural target was the prostitute, seen as responsible for introducing disease into respectable households. She was, of course, the most vulnerable link in the chain of contacts involved in the spread of syphilis. During the nineteenth century some French and German cities and states attempted to control venereal disease by legislating for the registration and medical inspection of prostitutes.[40] At the 1899 International Conference for the Prophylaxis of Syphilis, the president of the French delegation, Professor Alfred Fournier, pleaded passionately for stricter public regulation on the grounds that the hereditary consequences of syphilis represented the main social dangers of the disease.[41] The few American and British delegates present disagreed on the principle that registration did not work when tried in their own countries.[42] They argued further that the control of prostitution was an infringement of individual liberty and encouraged immorality by giving it the appearance of safety from disease.

Alfred Fournier was very friendly with Sir Jonathan Hutchinson. The two men dominated syphilology in their respective countries during the second half of the nineteenth century.[43] They both taught that a father could transmit syphilis to his offspring, that is, they both believed in *la syphilis héréditaire*. But on the question of *l'hérédité syphilitique* they differed profoundly. Fournier upheld, and effectively extended, the very general French presumption that syphilis could be transmitted from generation to generation in the form of a predisposition to all kinds of other diseases and malformations. He also regarded the transmission of active syphilis to a third generation as a possibility, although one difficult to demonstrate. (In this belief he is supported by present opinion. Third generation syphilis is theoretically possible but cannot be proven.) Hutchinson simplified the

40. For an account of nineteenth century efforts at regulation, see Vern L. Bullough, *The history of prostitution* (New Hyde Park, N.Y., 1964), pp. 166–172; the early twentieth century situation is described by Abraham Flexner, *Prostitution in Europe* (New York, 1914).

41. A. Fournier, 'Danger social de la syphilis,' *Conférence internationale pour la prophylaxie de la syphilis et des maladies vénériennes*, 2 vols. (Brussels, 1899), I, 1–45.

42. *Ibid.*, II, 85–125, 351–354, 367–370. For details of an American experiment in regulation, see John C. Burnham, 'Medical inspection of prostitutes in the nineteenth century: the St. Louis experiment and its sequel,' *Bull. Hist. Med.*, 1971, 45, 203–218.

43. For a biography of Fournier from the British perspective, see M. A. Waugh, 'Alfred Fournier, 1832–1914: his influence on venereology,' *Brit. J. vener. Dis.*, 1974, 50, 232–236.

issue by stating that he had never seen a convincing case of third-generation syphilis and by dismissing the phenomenon of occult syphilis as most unlikely. On the latter question, for example, he made the following statement: 'My argument, if I have made it plain, has pointed to the conclusion that no minified transmission of syphilis is possible, that the child gets either nothing at all or the germs of the disease, and that in the latter case they will, subject to the laws of idiosyncrasy, develope [*sic*] equally in all cases.'[44] On third generation syphilis he was equally incisive. According to David Nabarro, 'The opinion of English authorities at the turn of the century was largely influenced by that of Jonathan Hutchinson who, in the last edition of his work "Syphilis" (1909), says he is "absolutely incredulous as to the inheritance in the third generation." '[45] Indeed, British syphilologists rarely discussed the degenerative aspects of syphilis in their writings, while the contrary was true of French authors.

By the early twentieth century, doubts were growing as to the reality of hereditary syphilis in either form. In so far as clinicians were concerned, such doubts were mainly inspired by new methods of investigating venereal disease, and only indirectly by biological research findings that challenged the likelihood of Lamarckian-type inheritance. Among biologists, on the other hand, August Weismann's germ plasm theory was fast becoming one of the most provocative issues of the era. According to Weismann, during fertilization only nuclear material from the spermatozoon and ovum combined to form the germ plasm destined to develop into a new individual. The only continuity between generations was that provided by the germ cells. Weismann maintained 'that somatogenic characters [characters originating in the cells and tissues of the body] are not transmitted, or rather, that those who asserted that they can be transmitted must furnish the requisite proof.'[46]

As Frederick Churchill has indicated, this challenge was taken up not only by biologists but also by physicians specializing in pathology.[47] Contemporary literature of venereal disease also suggested that pathologists, but not clinicians, began to question whether the known circumstances of syphilitic intergenerational transmission really did support the doctrine of inheritance of acquired characteristics. By the early twentieth century most biologists and pathologists were agreed that even if syphilis were trans-

44. Jonathan Hutchinson, *The pedigree of disease* (London, 1884), p. 91.
45. Nabarro, *Congenital syphilis* (n. 4), p. 383.
46. A. Weismann, *On heredity*, trans. Poulton, Schönland and Shipley (Oxford, 1889), p. 413, quoted by J. Adami, *Medical contributions to the study of evolution* (London, 1918), p. 134.
47. Churchill (n. 2), p. 119.

mitted via microbial infection of the sperm or ovum, such transmission was irrelevant to the debate. For in such instances, the actual exciting cause of disease was the element being transferred rather than acquired somatic modifications. However, if occult hereditary syphilis, namely, transmission of syphilitic constitutional weakness through one or more generations, were a reality, as maintained by much of the French clinical school, such transmission would be evidence for Lamarckian inheritance. In 1901 the British pathologist John Adami expressed this view:

Hence, while syphilis as such is not inherited, the toxines of the disease must be regarded as prone to set up molecular disturbances in the germinal idioplasm, and the offspring may show, not syphilitic lesions, but parasyphilitic lesions— various forms of arrested and imperfect development of different tissues due to the intoxication, and therewith modification of the germ plasm while still a portion of the parental organism.[48]

The concept of *parasyphilis* had been developed by Alfred Fournier. In the 1870s he had proposed that locomotor ataxia, a syndrome described by Duchenne de Boulogne in 1858, was due to syphilis.[49] At about the same time Fournier published evidence favoring the hypothesis, first proposed by Esmarch and Jessen in 1857, that syphilis was a cause of general paralysis of the insane. He suggested the term *parasyphilis* to designate such late manifestations as were not, he thought, caused directly by the syphilitic virus since they were resistant to treatment with mercury.[50] In Fournier's words:

[Syphilis] is an illness that, by the action it exerts on the organism, can lead to lesions other than its own specific ones. For example, it may undermine what is commonly called 'health,' lessen vital resistance, influence development, create organic defects and morbid predispositions, in other words, lead to a class of lesions that are no longer syphilis proper, but its indirect derivatives, and to which I propose to assign the name of *parasyphilis*.[51]

Here Fournier seems to have equated occult syphilis in the child with parasyphilis in the adult.

48. Adami, *Medical contributions* (n. 46), p. 155.

49. Jeanselme, *Histoire de la syphilis* (n. 4), pp. 360–364; Waugh (n. 43).

50. At the turn of the century, general paralysis of the insane, tabes dorsalis, and primary optic atrophy were generally considered as parasyphilitic lesions.

51. A. Fournier, *L'hérédité syphilitique: leçons cliniques, recueillies et rédigées par le Dr. P. Portalier* (Paris 1891), p. 18. Parasyphilitic lesions in the offspring, according to Fournier, pp. 15–24, included: 1) a macerated fetus or stillbirth, 2) various forms of development retardation, 3) congenital malformations including hare lip, cleft palate and spina bifida, and 4) predisposition to affections such as tuberculosis and rickets.

The concept of parasyphilis suffered a severe setback in 1913 when Hideyo Noguchi and J. W. Moore demonstrated the presence of spirochaetes in the brain of patients dying of general paresis. But at the turn of the century when Adami was writing, it was a popular concept. A similar opinion was expressed in 1908 by the zoologist J. Arthur Thomson:

Syphilis—As this disease appears to be due to a specific microbe, its reappearance in the offspring of syphilitic parents is not strictly a fact of inheritance. . . . But the chances are so many that a patently syphilitic father will have syphilitic or in some way deteriorated children, that the marriage of a patently syphilitic subject can only be called a crime—the more heinous since the disease in ·the offspring is often more serious than in the parent. It seems, furthermore, certain in the case of this disease that, apart from the specific antenatal infection of off-spring, the toxins produced by the microbes in the body of the parent or parents may induce general disturbance or debility of constitution in the germ-cells, and thus result in inferior offspring.[52]

Biologists lost interest in the possibility of the inheritance of acquired characteristics at about the same time as clinicians were dismissing the probability of syphilitic inheritance, roughly during the third decade of the twentieth century. By 1934, according to John H. Stokes, most observers accepted 'the maternal transmission of syphilis by the diaplacental route as the usual if not the invariable mechanism.'[53] Notable exceptions were some French clinicians who continued to believe in paternal transmission of infection and in the inheritance of occult syphilis. Stokes summed up the French position as follows: 'The conception of *syphilis héréditaire larvée* or occult syphilis, has the ardent support of most French pediatricians, including especially Martelli, Pinard, Marsan, Hutinel, Lemaire, and others. According to this group the incidence of syphilis in France, including generations beyond the second, ranges from 19 per cent (Lemaire and David) up to 40 per cent (Hutinel) of the population.'[54]

Elsewhere occult syphilis was no longer taken very seriously, nor was paternal inheritance, because by the 1930s most evidence favored transmission during pregnancy.[55] A series of laboratory discoveries, including the isolation in 1905 of the spirochaete responsible for syphilis (later to be

---

52. J. Arthur Thomson, *Heredity* (New York, 1908), pp. 286–287.
53. Stokes, *Modern clinical syphilology* (n. 31), p. 1216.
54. *Ibid.*, p. 1271.
55. For a German viewpoint see *Handbuch der Haut- und Geschlechtskrankheiten*, ed. J. Jadassohn, 24 vols. (Berlin, 1927–37), XIX, *Kongenitale Syphilis*, particularly the articles by H. Rietschel and C. Hochsinger; also H. Rietschel, 'Die angeborene Syphilis in ihrer klinischen Bewertung in Frankreich,' *Med. Klin.*, 1931, 27, 1287–1291.

called treponema), Wassermann's elaboration of the complement fixation test in 1906, and Ehrlich's introduction of salvarsan as a spirochaetocidal agent in 1910, threw new light on the mode of transmission of syphilis. The treponema was of larger volume than the head of the human spermatozoon, rendering it inconceivable that a sperm cell invaded by a spirochaete could ever give rise to anything resembling a fetus. As put by a French skeptic, 'To imagine such an event we would have to believe that we are dealing with an ancient, tired, but good natured treponema, in a period of latency, and reluctant to interfere with germination.'[56] Other studies revealed that from 70% to 90% of mothers with syphilitic children had positive Wassermann reactions, while fewer fathers, about 50%, so reacted.[57]

The small proportion of women showing neither clinical nor serological evidence of disease, the so-called *Colles mothers*, still posed a problem, but now began a revision of the nineteenth century interpretation of Colles's law.[58] Such women must have syphilis since they could feed their babies with impunity. Whereas previously the masking of symptoms was interpreted as due to fetal transmission, now it was attributed to the suppressive immunological effects of pregnancy in a woman with recent or latent venereal disease.

To this day the problem of third generation syphilis has not been resolved. An untreated or maltreated congenitally syphilitic female could conceivably transmit the disease to her offspring during pregnancy. Nor are suggestive family case histories lacking. The difficulty lies in establishing beyond doubt that the second generation mother has never suffered a reinfection. The concept of the hereditary transmission of occult syphilis, however, has faded away. Observations that led to this theory, such as the tendency of syphilitic parents to have debilitated children, are now explained on socio-economic principles. Because venereal disease can lead to both ill health and unemployment, the children of the marriage are liable to suffer from the worst disadvantages of poverty. Such explanations were offered in the nineteenth century but then did not carry enough conviction to exclude the hereditary hypothesis.

---

56. M. Carle, 'Les conceptions modernes sur la transmission héréditaires de la syphilis,' *Ann. Derm. Syph.*, 1933, *7th ser. 4*, 106–110, p. 110.

57. Stokes, *Modern clinical syphilology* (n. 31), p. 1213.

58. One of the most closely argued theses against paternal transmission and for the reinterpretation of Colles's law was provided by Rudolf Matzenauer in 1903, R. Matzenauer, 'Die Vererbung der Syphilis. 1st eine paterne Vererbung erwiesen?' *Wien. klin. Wschr.*, 1903, *16*, 175–181; discussions of this presentation follow pp. 229–236, 263–267, 292–296, 325–330, 361–368, and 392–398.

Syphilologists dismissed nineteenth century theories of inheritance on clinical evidence without paying much attention to the concurrent biological debate regarding the possibility of Lamarckian inheritance. Adami accounted for the indifference of most physicians, not just venereologists, to biological interpretations of the process of inheritance, by suggesting that physicians did not understand the terms of the argument. Too few, he thought, received a sound biological training. 'As a consequence the medical world in general has to depend upon the biologist proper . . . for its views upon heredity, and the pure and simple biologists have run riot in their lucubrations upon this subject.'[59] Such were the difficulties engendered by increasing specialization. Yet among pathologists were some with the knowledge to understand both the biological and the medical aspects of heredity. The disinterest of syphilologists in basic theory may have been fortuitous in that, by the second decade of the twentieth century, they had sufficiently novel methods of inquiry of their own not to require biological theory for clarification of clinical problems of inheritance. By the 1930s a majority in each discipline had reached complementary conclusions: most venereologists discounted the possibility of hereditary syphilis, while Lamarckism was a dead question for most biologists. Some French syphilologists and pediatricians may have continued to insist on the reality and widespread nature of hereditary occult syphilis well into the twentieth century because they had been trained in the Lamarckian rather than the Darwinian viewpoint. This might offer some explanation of their persistence in treating as hereditary what almost everyone else now interpreted as having an environmental origin.

Division of Medical History
Department of Anatomy, and
Department of Pediatrics
UCLA School of Medicine

59. Adami, *Medical contributions* (n. 46), p. 133.

THE SIGNIFICANCE OF SYPHILIS IN PRENATAL CARE AND IN THE CAUSATION OF FŒTAL DEATH[1]

By J. Whitridge Williams

I think that it may safely be said that the propaganda for the development and extension of prenatal care, which has been conducted during the past few years in this country, constitutes one of the most important advances in practical obstetrics; as it has taught us to appreciate the unnecessary wastage of fœtal life which has occurred in the past and to consider seriously how it may be diminished.

Unfortunately, this movement is not of medical origin, except in so far as the efforts of the pediatricians to popularize maternal suckling had led to some supervision over pregnant women. Years ago Budin instituted consultations for pregnant women in Paris, and Ballantyne of Edinburgh did important pioneer work concerning the production of fœtal abnormalities and insisted upon the benefits which might follow intelligent antenatal care, yet real interest in the prophylactic supervision of pregnant women originated with laymen. Indeed, I do not think that I shall go far wrong when I state that the greatest credit in this respect belongs to Mrs. William Lowell Putnam, who some years ago organized at her own expense in Boston a small service in which women could be

supervised during the latter half of pregnancy for the purpose of instruction in the rudiments of the hygiene of pregnancy, of seeing that they were properly nourished and not over-worked, of teaching the importance of suckling their children when born, and particularly of preventing the occurrence of eclampsia by the early recognition and treatment of the toxæmias of pregnancy.

One of the most important agencies in bringing about the reform in this country has been The Association for the Prevention of Infantile Mortality—now the American Child Hygiene Association; for at its meetings each year philanthropic laymen, social workers and trained nurses, as well as occasional medical men, read papers upon the subject and gradually aroused popular interest in it, and it was not until after the movement had attained considerable momentum that obstetricians became generally concerned with it, and even at present many of them still treat the subject in a luke-warm manner.

In its broadest sense, prenatal care may be defined as such supervision of the pregnant woman as will enable her to go through pregnancy safely, to bring forth a normal living child with minimal danger, and to be discharged in such good physical condition as to be able to care for her child

[1] Read before the Section on Obstetrics and Gynecology of the Medical Society of the state of New York, March 25, 1920.

efficiently and to suckle it for at least the first months of its life. This means that the women must be under medical supervision from the earliest possible period of pregnancy, so its various abnormalities may be recognized at their inception and treated prophylactically. It also means the application of the best methods of obstetrical diagnosis during the weeks immediately preceding labor, so that abnormal presentations, disproportion due to contracted pelves, as well as other complications may be recognized, and corrected if possible before its onset. It further means the proper conduct of labor, and such supervision during the weeks immediately following it, that the woman may be discharged in such physical condition as to be able to carry on her usual avocations efficiently, and to give her child the necessary care. Finally, it implies medical supervision of the child during the first year of life, so that the effort expended during pregnancy and at the time of labor be not wasted; as it should be realized that the object of pregnancy is to secure a child which will have a reasonable prospect of reaching adult life, and that every preventable fœtal or infantile death means biological and economic waste.

It is evident that such a program requires not only first-rate obstetrical care, but such supervision of the patient before and after delivery by trained nurses and social workers as will make it possible for her to realize the importance of following closely the various regulations laid down for her guidance. In other words, efficient prenatal care must be regarded in great part as a campaign of education for physician and patient, in which both must be taught to realize that ideal obstetrics implies not merely intelligent care at the time of labor, but that it has a much wider scope and should begin as soon as the woman realizes that she is pregnant and continue until she is discharged in ideal physical condition and suckling a normal child. As the majority of hospital patients belong to the less intelligent classes, it is only by means of education through prenatal workers that they can be induced to make the necessary visits to the dispensary before and after delivery, and consequently I have become convinced that efficient prenatal and postnatal care cannot be carried out by physicians alone, and is feasible only when the requisite number of trained nurses and social workers are available.

In the earlier work, attention was principally concentrated upon three points: (1) The recognition and earliest possible treatment of the toxæmias of pregnancy in the hope of preventing the development of eclampsia; (2) supervision of the general physical and material condition of the patient with the object of diminishing the chances of premature labor; and (3) such instruction during the latter part of pregnancy that the mother will be prepared to suckle her child after it is born. When, however, the subject was taken up by obstetricians, it became apparent that the best results could not be obtained unless the scope of the work were materially widened so as to include everything which is implied by good obstetrics, plus the supervision and instruction derived from nurses and social workers.

Soon after taking up this work, I realized that the recognition and treatment of syphilis early in pregnancy constituted an important and fruitful field for a radical reduction in fœtal mortality, and in my presidential address—" Upon the Limitations and Possibilities of Prenatal Care "—before the American Association for the Prevention of Infantile Mortality in 1915, I developed the idea that more lives could be saved along such lines than by any other single method. That address was based upon the critical study of 500 fœtal deaths occurring in 10,000 consecutive deliveries in the Obstetrical Service of The Johns Hopkins Hospital, and included not merely the deaths at the time of labor, but also those occurring during the last ten or twelve weeks of pregnancy, as well as those during the two weeks immediately following delivery. Upon analyzing the causes of death, it was found that syphilis was responsible for 26 per cent of the entire number, and that it caused more deaths than any other single factor, and very many more than the toxæmias of pregnancy, which up to that time had been considered the greatest field for prophylactic effort. Consequently, I concluded that if syphilis could be eliminated from among the causes of fœtal death, greater progress in prenatal care would be made than by any other means at present available.

In the 700 cases under consideration the diagnosis was made by the recognition of congenital syphilis in the living child, or from the presence of certain histological changes in the placenta which we had learned to associate with the disease, while in only a relatively small proportion of the cases was it made at autopsy. With the discovery of the Wassermann reaction and the demonstration that the spirochete is the cause of syphilis, our knowledge concerning the disease became greatly widened, so that we were able to diagnosticate it in many mothers and infants in whom it had formerly been overlooked, as well as to demonstrate the syphilitic nature of certain lesions which had previously not been considered as having any relation with that disease.

While preparing my article in 1915, I became convinced that the only way in which the problem could be approached with any hope of effective solution was by determining the Wassermann reaction in every pregnant woman who registered in the Dispensary, and subjecting her to intensive anti-syphilitic treatment whenever it was positive.

This work was begun in April, 1916, and the present paper is based upon the critical study of 302 fœtal deaths occurring in 4000 consecutive deliveries between that period and December 31, 1919. In this series every effort was made to elicit a possible history of syphilitic infection and to detect the presence of the clinical signs of the disease; moreover, a Wassermann test was made at the first visit of the patient, and, if a positive result were obtained, she was subjected to proper treatment in the Syphilis Clinic, provided sufficient time was available before delivery. At the conclusion of labor a Wassermann was likewise taken from the fœtal blood obtained from the maternal end of the umbilical cord. Every placenta was preserved and examined histologically, and finally, if the child was born dead or died after delivery, every effort was made to obtain an autopsy in order to determine accurately the cause of death, particular attention being given to the recognition of syphilitic lesions and to the demonstration of the presence of spirochetes. Consequently, in each of these 4000 cases we have a careful clinical history of the patient, as well as a record of the maternal Wassermann, of the fœtal Wassermann at the time of birth, of the microscopical examination of the placenta, and in case of death of the child a complete autopsy, so that it is apparent that few cases of syphilis could escape recognition. Furthermore, all patients who presented a positive Wassermann were followed up by our social workers, and every effort was made to see that they were appropriately treated. At present we are endeavoring to get back as many patients as possible, who at any time presented signs of syphilis, for the purpose of ascertaining what has happened to them and their children. Unfortunately, however, this information will not be available for incorporation into this paper, which is based more particularly upon the critical study of the fœtal deaths occurring in this series of cases, while the conclusions to be drawn from the Wassermann reaction will be considered in a report to be made to the American Gynecological Society in May.

I think it only fair to preface our study by saying that our material differs from that which may be collected in many other cities by the fact that somewhat more than one-half of our patients were blacks. Thus, in the 4000 cases under consideration, there were 1839 white and 2161 black women, in whom a positive Wassermann reaction was present in 2.48 and 16.29 per cent, respectively. In other words once in every fortieth white, and once in every sixth colored woman. It should, however, be borne in mind that this incidence does not exhaust the possibilities of syphilis, as there were 105 additional women in the series in whom the Wassermann reaction was negative, but in whose histories some mention was made of syphilis. Forty-four of these had presented a positive Wassermann in a previous pregnancy, which had later become negative following efficient treatment, with the result that the present pregnancy ended in the birth of a normal child. On the other hand, in the remaining 61 women, autopsy revealed characteristic lesions and the presence of spirochetes in the fœtal tissues, or the live child presented clinical evidence of hereditary syphilis, or the placenta showed characteristic histological lesions.

Of the 302 dead babies 212 came to autopsy. In the former are included not only those dying at the time of labor or during the two weeks immediately following it, but also those dying during pregnancy from the time of viability onward: namely, children weighing between 1500 and 2500 grammes or measuring between 35 and 45 cm. in length. Of the 302 deaths, 99 occurred in white and 203 in black infants, an incidence of 5.4 and 9.4 per cent, respectively; while 157 occurred at the time of labor or during the first two weeks of the puerperium, and 145 were in premature children.

Syphilis was noted in 104 cases, in 89 of which the diagnosis was confirmed by autopsy with the demonstration of spirochetes in the fœtal tissues; while in the remainder it was

made from the presence of syphilitic lesions in the placenta, associated with a positive Wassermann on the part of the mother. Upon analyzing the causes of death, we obtained the following figures:

	Cases	Percentage
Syphilis	104	34.44
Dystocia	46	15.20
Toxæmia	35	11.55
Prematurity	32	10.59
Cause unknown	26	8.61
Placenta prævia and premature separation	16	5.28
Deformity	11	3.64
Eleven other causes	32	10.69
	302	100.00

Before considering these figures critically, it may be well to say a few words as to how the classification was established, it being understood that the cause of death was determined partly from the autopsy findings and partly from careful study of the clinical history of each case. Thus, in 89 of the 104 syphilitic cases, the cause of death was determined by autopsy, while in the remaining 15 it was based upon clinical findings in the child, or upon the presence of syphilitic lesions in the placenta associated with a positive maternal Wassermann.

Under dystocia are included all deaths resulting from mechanical difficulty or undue delay at the time of labor; as for example, craniotomy, decapitation, birth injuries following operative delivery, prolapse of the cord, undue delay during the second stage incident to disproportion between the size of the child and the pelvis, etc. A certain proportion of such deaths must be attributed to error in judgment on the part of those conducting the delivery, while others were unavoidable. Under the deaths attributed to toxæmia are included not only the children which were born dead during an eclamptic attack, but also the premature live children, which were born spontaneously, or as the result of the induction of labor, and could not be raised.

In the category of prematurity, we have included only children whose imperfect state of development appeared to be the sole cause of death. In such cases, no lesions were found at autopsy, and the children appeared to be normal except for their small size. Of course it is possible that a more intensive search for spirochetes might have led to a positive result in a certain number of these cases, particularly when the maternal Wassermann was positive, but, as they were not found, the cause of death was set down as prematurity. Moreover, it should be understood that we have not included in this category premature children born of mothers suffering from toxæmia, placenta prævia or acute infectious diseases, etc., as under such circumstances death was attributed to the underlying disease, and not to the imperfect development of the child.

Great interest attaches to the 26 cases for which no cause of death could be ascertained. In none of the 14 babies included in this group which came to autopsy could definite lesions be demonstrated; while in the other 12 careful study of the clinical course of labor did not enable us to formulate a satisfactory explanation for the fatal outcome. In several of the autopsy cases, syphilitic lesions could not be demonstrated in the fœtal organs nor spirochetes be found, despite the fact that the mothers presented a positive Wassermann or the placenta showed specific changes, so that death could not be attributed to syphilis, no matter what the presumption might be. This group of deaths is of great interest as it affords striking evidence of how little we really know of antenatal pathology, and suggests important possibilities for future research.

It is not necessary to consider in any detail the deaths associated with placenta prævia or with premature separation of the normally implanted placenta, as they are clearly the result of the underlying abnormality. Likewise, in the category of deformity, which includes examples of hydrocephalus, anencephalus, spina bifida, atresia of the intestinal tract, developmental abnormalities of the heart, etc., the condition originated in the earliest periods of embryonic life, and could not have been prevented by any means at our disposal.

Finally, in the last group are collected 32 deaths, which were attributable to one of eleven different causes, including atalectasis, about which we know nothing, acute infectious diseases of the mother, accidental suffocation, fœtal bacteræmia, hæmorrhagic disease, etc. Many of these were clearly unpreventable, while in others our knowledge concerning the underlying cause is so hazy as to make any positive statement inadvisable.

Upon analyzing the figures in the summary given above, it is seen that 89.3 per cent of the deaths are attributable to seven groups of causes, of which syphilis is the most important, as it accounts for 34.44 per cent of the total number, which is almost as high as the mortality for the next three groups combined, as dystocia, toxæmia and prematurity were responsible for 37.34 per cent, or only 3 per cent more than syphilis. Consequently, it is apparent that if it were possible to eradicate syphilis from our material, we should effect as great a reduction in fœtal mortality as by doing away with all fœtal deaths due to the various accidents at the time of labor, toxæmia, and prematurity combined. This, however, is manifestly out of the question.

As large as these figures seem, they do not entirely represent the ravages of syphilis, since we have already pointed out that it is quite possible that more careful search might have revealed the presence of spirochetes in the tissues of a considerable fraction of the autopsies in which the cause of death was attributed to prematurity, as well as in a certain number included in the unknown group. Moreover, these figures do not include the cases of congenital syphilis which appeared in babies which were discharged alive, or in whom the disease developed later.

It must be admitted that this unusually large incidence of syphilis can only apply to hospital services with a large black clientele, such as ours, and will not be noted in private practice or in hospitals in communities in which the majority of the inhabitants are white, or in which the colored people are more intelligent than here. Nevertheless, even if we consider only our white patients, syphilis still continues to be a very important cause of fœtal death, and this we know by experience can be in great part eliminated. As was indicated above, there were 99 white and 203 black infant deaths in our material, and in them syphilis was the etiological factor in 12.12 and 45.23 per cent, respectively. In other words, one out of every eight of our white babies died from syphilis as compared with every other black baby.

Upon comparing this 12 per cent mortality from syphilis in white infants with the other causes of death, it is seen that it exceeds all other causes except dystocia, and is nearly as great as for that. In other words, while 15.2 per cent of our children died from the various accidents of labor, 12.12 per cent of the white children died from syphilis, so that it is apparent that even in the white race syphilis represents one of the most important causes of fœtal death, and is responsible for a greater mortality than toxæmia. Consequently, we should avail ourselves of every method to recognize its existence as early as possible, and then to treat it energetically. This means that all obstetrical patients should be encouraged to register not later than the third or fourth month of pregnancy, that a routine Wassermann should be made at the first visit, and in case the result is positive, intensive treatment should be started immediately. In the case of the ignorant patient, mere advice to return at stated dates for treatment will not suffice, and it will be necessary for the social worker to follow her to her home and insist upon the necessity of following all directions implicitly. This frequently requires numerous visits, but only in this way can ideal results be obtained. Of course this means the expenditure of a large amount of time on the part of the workers, as well as a considerable financial outlay.

I had hoped to be able to give figures showing a marked contrast between the results obtained in the past when the Wassermann was made only when indicated by the history of the patient and those obtained in the present series in which it constituted a routine procedure. Unfortunately, so many elements enter into such a comparison that the tabulations are not convincing, but the following figures will give a graphic idea of what may be accomplished. Of the 4000 women under consideration, 421 presented a positive Wassermann reaction, but unfortunately all of them did not receive ideal treatment. In many instances they registered too late to receive any treatment, while others returned so irregularly that they were imperfectly treated, as for some time we had too few prenatal workers to supervise the patients efficiently, with the result that only a relatively small proportion received ideal treatment. With this in mind, we have divided the 421 patients into three groups, namely:

a. No treatment.

b. Inefficient treatment. The patients who received only two or three injections of salvarsan and no after treatment.

c. Satisfactory treatment. The patients received from four to six injections of salvarsan followed by a course of mercurial treatment, with the result that the Wassermann became negative and remained so.

In the three categories there were 157, 103, and 163 patients, respectively, and the results of treatment are graphically showed by the fact that in group *a* 52 per cent of the children were born dead or presented some evidence of syphilis, as compared with 37 per cent in group *b*, and only 7.4 per cent in group *c*. In other words, the evidence at our disposal shows that if syphilis is recognized early in the pregnant woman, and is intensively and appropriately treated, almost ideal results may be obtained so far as the child is concerned. Consequently, there is every reason to hope that in the future syphilis may be practically eradicated as the cause of fœtal death in all properly conducted clinics in which the women register prior to the middle of pregnancy.

On the other hand, it must be realized that even with the most perfect mechanism, ideal results will never be obtained, inasmuch as our investigations show that the disease will escape recognition in a certain proportion of pregnant women for the reason that the women frequently exhibit no clinical manifestations and occasionally present a negative Wassermann as well, so that the existence of the disease is not suspected until a macerated child is born and is shown to be syphilitic at autopsy. This, however, should not discourage us, for such occurrences are comparatively rare, and if the course of procedure here outlined is faithfully followed, syphilis can be reduced from the most important cause of fœtal death to one of the least frequent.

I hope that you will not think I have been one-sided in presenting the subject as I have, or that my judgment has been warped by our experience in Baltimore. I am well aware that syphilis represents only one of the causes of fœtal death, and that all the others must be taken into consideration in a broad program for the reduction of fœtal mortality, but at the present time syphilis appears to offer the most promising field for immediate results. A little thought will make it clear that a considerable proportion of the deaths from dystocia are unavoidable, and until our knowledge concerning the mode of production of eclampsia has become further extended, we must consider that its prophylaxis has almost reached its limit. Likewise, there is no immediate prospect of reducing the mortality from prematurity, as we are almost entirely ignorant concerning the causation of spontaneous premature termination of pregnancy, except when syphilis, toxæmia or gross over-exertion is the underlying factor. Moreover, it must be acknowledged that the fœtal death-rate associated with placenta prævia and premature separation of the placenta is susceptible of only very gradual improvement while that due to congenital deformity is at present altogether beyond our control.

Abnormalities in offspring related to maternal rubella during pregnancy

Anatole Dekaban, M.D., James O'Rourke, M.D. and
Tillye Cornman, M.D.

In 1941 Gregg[1] made the original observation that rubella during the early stages of pregnancy can cause damage to the fetus. Subsequently, a number of other authors[4-6] reported similar cases. The chief abnormality encountered in the newborn infant consists of congenital lesions involving various body organs. It has been suggested that the type of anomaly may depend on the stage of gestation when the rubella infection took place.

We are reporting a patient who showed almost all abnormalities ever described in association with maternal rubella. The eye findings, results of surgical excisions of cataracts at a widely separated interval, and his general state warrant more detailed consideration. In addition, on the basis of 108 cases selected from the literature, an attempt is made to correlate and analyze more closely the occurrence of various lesions in different organs with the stage of gestation when rubella complicated the pregnancy.

CASE REPORT

An eight year old boy was a first child born to young parents. His mother developed severe rubella at the end of the fourth week of gestation and had to be confined to bed for one week. She suffered from sore throat, general malaise, enlargement of the glands in the back of her neck and in the axillae, and also a reddish rash involving her face and trunk. Several cases of rubella occurred about the same time in the immediate neighborhood. The family physician who diagnosed the disease was not aware that she was pregnant. A few weeks later this became obvious and the age of gestation was estimated. Apparently, the risk of possible damage to the fetus was realized. She had routine prenatal care and the course of her pregnancy was uneventful. Delivery took place at term under general anesthesia. No difficulty was encountered with the infant's

breathing, but his head was noted to be small, he had bilateral cataracts, and there was a blowing systolic murmur in the pulmonic area. At the age of five months extraction of the cataract from the right eye was performed. The final result of this operation was not satisfactory, however.

The development of the patient was retarded from his first months of life. He was not able to lift his head up in prone position until several months old. He began to roll over at the age of about 15 months. With marked sagging of his back and dropping down of his head, he first sat up when three years of age. At the age of seven years he began to pull himself up to a standing position on his toes. He never showed an appropriate response to auditory or visual stimuli. Psychologic examination at the age of one year and three months gave him the mental age of about three months. In his second year of life he was confined to the District Training School in Laurel, Maryland.

The authors examined him at the age of seven and a half years. His height and state of nourishment were normal. He spent most of his time lying down, although he could sit without support with sagging of his back for about half an hour. No abnormality was detected in the lungs and abdomen. The heart was slightly enlarged in the transverse diameter. The pulse was regular, 86 per minute. There was a grade III, harsh systolic murmur best heard left of the sternum. The head was small and rounded, its circumference being 48.5 cm. (normal for his age is 53 cm.). Both external ears were formed defectively. Generally he was quiet and cheerful and appreciated any attention given to him by means of tactile stimulation. He laughed aloud to himself or when handled; otherwise, apart from an occasional shrill noise, he had no vocalizations. When supported he would stand briefly on his tiptoes and attempt a few steps (figure 1). He manipulated toys and showed some persistence in tactile exploration of his surroundings. Clean habits were not acquired and he had to be fed. Because of auditory and

From the National Institute of Neurological Diseases and Blindness, National Institutes of Health, Public Health Service, Bethesda, Maryland.

visual deprivation, it was felt useless to apply any formal psychologic testing. However, it was obvious that he functioned below the level of a 12 month old infant.

Special senses. Vision. The right eye showed buphthalmos associated with secondary glaucoma, the cornea being grossly enlarged and opaque. The left eye showed a slight reduction in the diameter of the cornea (9 mm.), but a normal anterior chamber, clarity, and depth. Generally it was a microphthalmic eye. On ophthalmoscopic examination the cornea appeared clear and showed free margins, but the lens was completely occluded by a white opaque cataract of undetermined thickness which prevented funduscopic examination. There seemed to be just a trace of visual perception in this eye, for he lifted the left upper lid maximally and turned his head upward and to the left when a strong source of light was presented. However, there was no indication that he could see any objects.

Hearing. Drums were intact. Hearing was grossly defective in both ears. No response was obtained to loud ringing of a bell from a distance of one meter. Ringing close to either ear would make him cease his activity momentarily.

Caloric test. The response to irrigation with cold and hot water was delayed and the duration of nystagmus shortened; it lasted one minute and ten seconds in the right ear and one minute and five seconds in the left ear, as estimated from the onset of stimulation.

Taste. He differentiated well between salt and sugar and between pleasant and disagreeable substances.

Smell. He accepted coffee and clover but inconstantly rejected asafoetida.

Cranial nerves. Eyeballs could be moved in all directions. Their relative position was as symmetric as might be expected in a blind person. Remainder of the cranial nerves were normal.

Motor system. He had contractures of Achilles tendons and his feet were in an equinovarus position. Active movements in all joints could be performed, but the muscle power was generally decreased. When supported, he could stand for several minutes in an awkward position; then the hip and knee joints buckled and he slipped to the ground. He rolled and crept actively.

Coordination. No routine tests could be applied because of the lack of cooperation. During spontaneous and induced movements there was no tremor or decomposition of movements.

Sensation. He readily responded to the stimuli of light touch, pain, and temperature throughout his body; other modalities could not be tested.

Reflexes. All tendon reflexes were brisk and equal, except for ankle jerks which were hypoactive because of tendon contractures. Plantar response was flexor on both sides.

Laboratory tests. Urinalysis, Kahn test, cerebrospinal fluid, and blood studies were all within normal limits. Tests for toxoplasmosis and phenyl-

pyruvic acid were negative. Radiologic examination of the skull revealed its smallness in all dimensions (figure 2) but no other pathology. Maturation of bones was normal for his age. Electroencephalogram showed fairly well developed alpha activity in the range of 7 to 9 cycles per second. In addition, there were infrequent slower rhythms recorded diffusely. The tracing was interpreted as borderline normal. Pneumoencephalogram disclosed a symmetric and normal size ventricular system and symmetric distribution of air in the subarachnoid space (figure 2). The electrocardiogram was consistent with left axis deviation and sinus arrhythmia.

Clinical diagnosis. Microcephaly, deafness, congenital cataracts, secondary glaucoma with buphthalmus of the right eye, congenital heart disease (probably interventricular defect), and marked mental retardation, all related to maternal rubella during the early stage of gestation. The severe degree of mental deficiency was probably due to combined causes: effects of rubella, together with deprivation of eyesight and hearing. It was felt that removal of the cataract in the left eye could benefit the patient's vision.

A linear extraction of the cataract in the left eye was attempted under general anesthesia. With keratome section of the superior limbus, the point of the blade was allowed to penetrate the cataract surface. At this stage it was discovered that the opacity consisted of a tense, white membrane without cortical content. As the membrane edges retracted, an opening was established which was equal to two-thirds of the total pupillary area. Particles of lens debris were removed by irrigation and the wound was closed.

A fundus examination made through the new opening revealed the following findings: the vitreous was clear and the nerve head was definitely pale, particularly at its temporal margin; in addition, there was peripheral narrowing of the arterioles and a granular pigmentation scattered throughout the posterior fundus, mainly in the paramacular area (figure 4). The pigment was of granular type and did not appear to have any configuration similar to that of an established retinitis pigmentosa. The macular reflex was diminished and the foveal reflex abolished.

The patient was rechecked eight months later at the age of eight years. In general, his motor ability progressed very little. However, he was able to walk for a longer distance when led, perhaps up to 20 feet, and would pull himself up to the standing position on the radiator in order to get stronger visual stimulus from the light coming through the window. Ophthalmologic examination gave findings essentially similar to those seen immediately following the operation (figure 3). Electroretinogram at this time was normal.

DISCUSSION

The most common abnormalities encountered in the offspring of mothers who had ru-

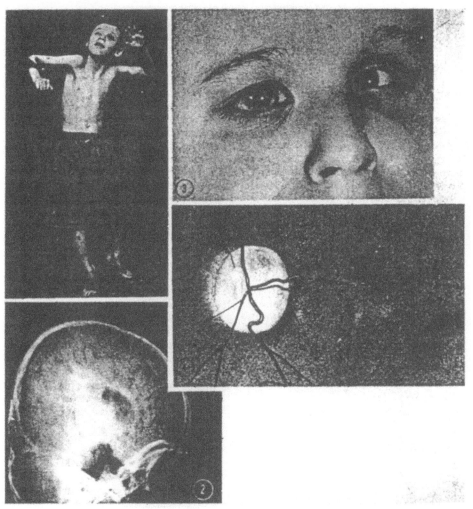

Fig. 1. At the age of eight years the patient was able to stand and walk for a short distance on his tiptoes when supported.

Fig. 2. Pneumoencephalogram, brow-up lateral projection. Smallness of skull in the anteroposterior dimension is apparent. The ventricular system and subarachnoid space are within normal limits.

Fig. 3. The right eye shows buphthalmos and corneal opacity. The left eye after excision of the cataract at eight years of age.

Fig. 4. Left optic fundus. The optic nerve is pale. The retina is thin and contains fine granular pigment, predominantly in the paramacular area.

bella during early gestation include congenital cataracts, congenital heart disease, perception deafness, microcephaly, and coexistent mental deficiency. Less frequently seen are other conditions such as microphthalmos, buphthalmos, retinal lesions, talipes equinovarus, syndactyly, hypospadiasis, generalized muscular weakness, cerebral diplegia, and cleft palate. Dental ab-

normalities are probably quite common, although they are seldom looked for. The affected infants generally show various combinations of several of these conditions and it is uncommon to find only one single lesion.

In the patient reported here the association of two particular features is of interest. The first is the very profound disturbance of embryonic development which resulted in as many as 11 out of the total of 15 pathologic lesions recorded in the literature. The second feature relates to the unusually severe course of the rubella which complicated pregnancy very early, that is before the end of the fourth week of gestation. The occurrence of more severe abnormalities during the earliest stages of pregnancy and the substantial decline of incidence of malformations after two to three months of gestation were stressed by Swan,[2] Gregg and co-workers,[3] and others. It appeared important to us to analyze the frequency with which the abnormalities in various organs are encountered relevant to different stages of gestation. For this purpose the available literature was surveyed, but only those cases were accepted in which there were adequate data regarding the medical condition of the patient and the stage of pregnancy when rubella occurred. These criteria were met by 108 cases selected from reported series.[2,3,5–14] To make the analysis easier the data obtained from this material were plotted in a form of a graph (figure 5). It is apparent that the highest incidence of three major abnormalities in offspring, namely cataracts, congenital heart disease, and deafness, occurred when rubella complicated the first four weeks of pregnancy. However, the embryos which were exposed to maternal infection with rubella virus between the fifth and tenth weeks of gestation still showed quite frequent occur-

rence of these malformations. There was a rapid decline of fetal susceptibility to the effects of maternal rubella from the tenth week of gestation and it came to a very low figure at 14 weeks of pregnancy; no instances of fetal abnormality were encountered past 20 weeks of gestation.

It is known from experimental studies that the most easily damaged are those regions of the embryo in which cell proliferation is particularly active at the time of exposure to a noxious factor. By the end of the fifth gestation week differentiation of the three primary layers into organs is completed and from then on the organs undergo independent growth and organization. The highest incidence of malformations coincides with this earliest stage of primary formation of organs. It is likely that a greater intensity of teratogenic agents is necessary to induce similar malformations in later stages of gestation. This would explain the reduced occurrence of abnormalities in infants whose mothers had rubella between six and 12 weeks of pregnancy. Another interesting question relates to the fact that more profound damage probably results from exposure to a greater severity of the rubella infection, even during the earliest stages of gestation. This conceivably may account for the variability in the clinical picture of the affected infants, as well as for the fact that not all products of pregnancy complicated by rubella, even during the earliest stage, develop congenital lesions. However, the incidence of non-affected infants could not be estimated from this material.

In general, the frequency with which cataracts, congenital heart disease, and deafness occurred during the first ten weeks of gestation was quite congruous. However, no instance of cataract was encountered in association with maternal rubella past ten weeks of gestation. Also, the numerical incidence of deafness during the first four weeks of pregnancy was less than that of cataracts and congenital heart disease. This may be related to the fact that milder forms of deafness are more difficult to detect on routine clinical examination than, for example, cataract or heart murmur. The most frequent type of congenital heart disease was patent ductus arteriosus and persisting foramen ovale. Microcephaly and mental de-

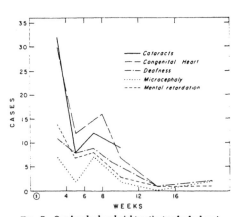

FIG. 5. One hundred and eight patients who had various congenital abnormalities associated with maternal rubella during pregnancy are plotted in relation to the stage of gestation when damage occurred.

ficiency showed considerably lower incidence than cataracts and congential heart disease. In our opinion this is unlikely to be a true state. A proportion of patients included in this analysis were very young infants in whom the examining physician would not be confronted with evidence of milder forms of mental retardation. Similarly, unless of a severe degree, smallness of the head would be easily missed on routine examination.

The mechanism and detailed pathology of the described lesions are poorly understood. No comprehensive postmortem examinations of the central nervous system are available to allow the formation of reasonably objective concepts. Experimental evidence from another type of diffuse damage to the fetus[13] suggests the possibility of selective damage to proliferating cells of the particularly sensitive structures during early embryonal life. Simple arrest or delay of development during a particular phase in organ differentiation is less likely.

Considered in terms of vision restored, the results of congenital cataract surgery are less pleasing than those which follow removal of the senile lens. There appear to be two main reasons for this state: 1) a not uncommon association with other congenital abnormalities involving the retinae, optic nerves, or eyeball, and 2) a relatively frequent postoperative complication, such as secondary glaucoma, pupillary occlusion, and retinal detachment.[16] Falls[17] and Costenbader and associates[18] are of the opinion that linear extraction technic with removal of the contents of the lens in toto lessens the danger of complications.

The membranous cataract encountered in the present case is uncommon and represents complete intrauterine absorption of intracapsular lens parenchyma so that the remaining capsule forms a thin, dense, white sheet. More typical of the postrubellar lens is a cataract of the zonular variety whose dense, central opacity completely fills the pupillary opening; when examined with the pupils dilated, the central whiteness is seen enclosed by a thin zone of gray opacified cortex, peripheral to which the cortex is clear. When macular changes are not severe, an early operation will permit normal development of fixation reflexes, thus offsetting the occurrence of ocular nystagmus. The type and size of the opacity in postrubellar cataract depend largely on the state of lens development at the time of damage.[19] Surgery is not indicated in all cases of congenital cataracts, the decision depending mainly on the degree of vision permitted by the opacity. When mydriasis materially improves visual acuity, an optical iridectomy will often suffice and cause fewer complications.[18]

Following surgery on the left eye, the ophthalmoscopic examination revealed pallor of the optic disk and a dispersion of fine, pigmented spots in the retina, with predominant involvement of the macular region. Dispersion of pigment of this type on the postrubellar fundus has been named pseudoretinitis pigmentosa.[20] The distinguishing feature of the true retinitis pigmentosa is the presence of arteriolar narrowing and perivascular collection of pigment.

From the practical viewpoint, early management of the affected infants is important. A considerable proportion of these patients are born with lowered intellectual capacity (usually of mild degree) which can conceivably be related to primary dysfunction of the brain. Gross impairment of vision and hearing, if present, will further handicap development and may lead to a very severe degree of mental deficiency amounting to idiocy. Comprehensive and timely medical assessment during infancy, removal of cataracts, provision of a hearing aid whenever indicated, and institution of appropriate devices will increase the patient's chance to remain in the family and even may allow him to attend a regular school.

SUMMARY

A patient is described who suffered multiple congenital abnormalities as a result of maternal rubella during the fourth week of gestation. The results of various laboratory tests are outlined. Operation on the right congenital cataract at the age of five months was unsuccessful. The left cataract was removed at eight years of age and clear eye media were obtained; this, however, did not result in a significant increase of the functional vision. The need for early treatment of children suffering from a similar condition is stressed.

One hundred and eight patients with evidence of damage from maternal rubella were selected from the literature and their condition analyzed in respect to the stage of gestation when rubella infection took place. It was found that the highest incidence of the three most important congenital anomalies (cataracts, deafness, and congenital heart disease) occurred when rubella complicated pregnancy

during the first five weeks of gestation. The occurrence of malformations in later stages of pregnancy was analyzed. The most common types of cataracts encountered in this condition, as well as general management of the affected infants, were discussed.

REFERENCES

1. Gregg, N. M.: Congenital cataract following german measles in the mother. Tr. Ophth. Soc. Australia 3:35, 1941.
2. Swan, C.: Study of three infants dying from congenital defects following maternal rubella in early stages of pregnancy. J. Path. & Bact. 56:289, 1944.
3. Gregg, N. M., Beavis, W. R., Heseltine, M., Machin, A. E., Vickery, D., and Meyers, E.: The occurrence of congenital defects in children following maternal rubella during pregnancy. M. J. Australia 2:122, 1945.
4. Caruthers, D. G.: Congenital deaf-mutism as sequela of a rubella-like maternal infection during pregnancy. M. J. Australia 1:315, 1945.
5. Beswick, R. C., Warner, R., and Warkany, J.: Congenital anomalies following maternal rubella. Am. J. Dis. Child. 78:334, 1949.
6. Swan, C., Tostevin, A. L., Moore, B., Mayo, H., and Black, G. H. B.: Congenital defects in infants following infectious diseases during pregnancy, with special reference to relationship between German measles and cataract, deaf-mutism, heart disease and microcephaly, and to period of pregnancy in which occurrence of rubella is followed by congenital abnormalities. M. J. Australia 2:201, 1943.
7. Gregg, N. M.: (Further observations) congenital defects in infants following maternal rubella. Tr. Ophth. Soc. Australia 4:119, (1944) '46.
8. Evans, M. W.: Congenital dental defects in infants subsequent to maternal rubella during pregnancy. M. J. Australia 2:225, 1944.
9. Erickson, C. A.: Rubella early in pregnancy causing congenital malformations of eyes and heart. J. Pediat. 25:281, 1944.

10. Reese, A. B.: Congenital cataract and other anomalies following German measles in mother. Am. J. Ophth. 27:483, 1944.
11. Albaugh, C. H.: Congenital anomalies following maternal rubella in early weeks of pregnancy, with special emphasis on congenital cataracts. J.A.M.A. 129: 719, 1945.
12. Watson, J. R. H.: Hepatosplenomegaly as a complication of maternal rubella: A Report of 2 cases. M. J. Australia 1:516, 1952.
13. Lindsay, J. R., Caruthers, D. G., Hemenway, W. G., and Harrison, M. S.: Inner ear pathology following maternal rubella. Ann. Otol. Rhin. & Laryng. 62:1201, 1953.
14. Kirman, B. H.: Rubella as a cause of mental deficiency. Lancet 269:1113, 1955.
15. Hicks, S. P.: Developmental brain metabolism; effects of cortisone, anoxia, fluoroacetate, radiation, insulin and other inhibitors on embryo, newborn and adult. Arch. Path. 55:302, 1953.
16. Cordes, F. C.: Failure in congenital cataract surgery. Am. J. Ophth. 43:1, 1957.
17. Falls, H. F.: Developmental cataracts; results of surgical treatment of 131 cases. Arch. Ophth. 29:210, 1943.
18. Costenbader, F. D., and Albert, D. G.: Conservatism in the management of congenital cataract. Arch. Ophth. 48:426, 1957.
19. Swan, C.: Section II in A. Sorsby: Systemic Ophthalmology. Mosby, St. Louis, 1951, p. 34-44.
20. Franceschetti, A., and Bourquin, J. B.: Rubéole pendant la grossesse et malformations congénitales de l'enfant. Ann. d'ocul. 179:623, 1946.

EMOTIONS OF PREGNANCY

NILES NEWTON, Ph.D.

From the Department of Obstetrics and Gynecology, The University of Mississippi School of Medicine, Jackson, Mississippi

THE IMPORTANCE OF EMOTIONS IN PREGNANCY was emphasized by the psychoanalytic writers of the 1920's, 1930's, and 1940's, and their insight has borne rich scientific fruit in recent years. Eight years ago, in reviewing the literature on emotions of pregnancy, the present author wrote: "The average American woman spends more than two years of her life being pregnant. Considering the prevalence of the pregnant state, there have been remarkably few objective, well-controlled psychological studies on pregnancy. However, there is a rapidly growing interest in the field which should greatly increase our knowledge in the next few years This prediction has come true. The year 1963 is a good time to survey what has been learned about the emotions of pregnancy.

THE DESIRE FOR A BABY

For most women, the initial impact of pregnancy on the emotions comes about the time of the first missed menstrual period. Not only does the missed period lead the woman to believe she is pregnant, but changing hormonal balance at this time lays the foundation for changing emotional patterns. Whether the reaction to the idea of having a baby is predominantly one of joy or of dislike depends on a number of sociologic and psychologic variables that have been studied statistically.

Sociologic Factors Related to Rejection

Women with no children are more likely to be pleased with the idea of the coming baby. A questionnaire given by Winokur and Werboff, to Air Force wives late in pregnancy, found a highly significant correlation ($r = .45$) between the number of children the pregnant woman had and her initial dislike of the pregnancy. A study of 379 New England women by Sears *et al.* found a statistically significant difference in remembered

The author wishes to acknowledge the very helpful editorial advice of her husband, Michael Newton, M.D., and the suggestions of Virginia Larsen, M.D. and Carolyn Rawlins, M.D.

reaction to pregnancy: almost twice as many women recalled being "delighted" at first pregnancy as compared with later pregnancies.

Space between children also appears to influence the emotions with which a new pregnancy is greeted. Sears *et al.* found a steady increase in remembered acceptance of pregnancy as the space between children lengthened. Only 9 per cent of the mothers whose children were born less than 21 months apart were "delighted" at the new pregnancy, as compared with 28 per cent with children spaced 22 to 31 months apart, 42 per cent with children spaced at 32-to-54-month intervals, and 52 per cent of those with children coming 55 or more months after the last.

"Planned babies," however, are not always accepted babies, once the mother faces the reality of pregnancy; nor are "unplanned babies" always unwelcome. L. J. Thompson, using psychiatric interview technique, found that strong rejection developed in 12 per cent of women with planned pregnancies and 20 per cent of those with unplanned pregnancies. The majority of women with unplanned pregnancies had mixed feelings about the pregnancy, but 23 per cent found the idea of pregnancy totally acceptable.

Babies conceived out of wedlock are not always unwelcome. It depends on the social class and type of culture. In England, in a study of 278 primigravidas in social classes 4 and 5, 29 per cent had prenuptial pregnancies, as contrasted with only 2 per cent of primigravidas in social classes 1 and 2. Scott, Illsley, and Biles conclude that at some social levels prenuptial conceptions are "so common they can scarcely be regarded as unconventional." More "unwanted" pregnancies occurred among the young, among those of lower social class, and among those unmarried at the time of conception. However, in the opinion of the authors, the "unwantedness" of the pregnancies usually did not involve extreme resentment.

Another indication that illegitimacy does not always cause strong negative feelings toward the baby comes from the study by Gebhard *et al.* of the Negro female with less than an eighth-grade education. Only 19 per cent resorted to induced abortion when there was a premarital conception. This rate is only about twice as high as that of married women in the same social group. This figure compares with an induced abortion rate of over 80 per cent in unmarried college-educated women, both Negro and white, when they found themselves pregnant.

OTHER FACTORS RELATED TO REJECTION

There have been a number of speculations about the deeper psychologic factors which may determine initial reaction to the idea of the baby, but little objective, statistical work has been done in the field. One study has been done on a woman's career attitudes versus reaction to the idea of a coming child. In the study by Sears *et al.* on New England women, it was found that work attitudes made little difference to the acceptance of pregnancy in working class mothers. However, among the upper-middle socio-economic groups, delight in pregnancy was shown more often by women who enjoyed some things about their careers than by those who were indifferent about work, and by women who were eager to start having a family than by those so intense about their job that they did not want to give it up to have children. The authors suggest that women's enjoyment of their jobs does not necessarily interfere with their acceptance of the maternal role. The woman who enjoys work may also enjoy motherhood, because this is her characteristic "style" of dealing with all of life's situations.

That health is another factor involved in reactions to pregnancy is indicated by the work of Coppen. Among a control group of 50 healthy English mothers, about half planned and desired the child, about a quarter did not plan but accepted the idea of the child from the start, and about a quarter did not plan on the baby but gradually accepted the idea. None continued in complete rejection. Among 50 pretoxemic women, 11 continued to express unmitigated dislike even as pregnancy proceeded. Another 4 were so upset they showed extreme hostility toward the baby or made attempts at adoption or abortion. These differences in attitude were highly significant statistically.

Extreme Rejection: Induced Abortion

Extreme resentment and dislike of pregnancy to the point of induced abortion appears to be very common in our culture (Table 1). Gebhard *et al.* interviewed at length a national sample of over 5000 women. They found that about 1 out of every 6 conceptions in married women terminated in induced abortion. The fate of 89 per cent of all pregnancies in white single non-prison American women interviewed was induced abortion. Those married during pregnancy tended to act like those married before pregnancy in regard to induced abortion.

Since few women who plan induced abortion seek prenatal care of any kind, the ratio of 1 induced abortion to 1 spontaneous abortion, or 1 induced abortion to every 4 live births in married women may be surprising. The negative feelings toward pregnancy that obstetricians see in their offices have already had the most extreme elements eliminated by abortion. It is usually the ones whose hatred of the baby is mitigated somewhat by social and emotional considerations who find their way into reputable medical hands.

The high rate of successfully induced abortion probably indicates that many women also unsuccessfully try to get rid of the fetus—with resulting emotional repercussions. Hall and Mohr found that out of 66 expectant mothers skillfully interviewed in a prenatal clinic 10 said that some unsuccessful steps had been taken to terminate the pregnancy. Such women *do* find their way into physicians' offices for prenatal care, possibly feeling considerable unconfessed uneasiness about their attempts to induce abortion. Verbalized fears for the normalcy of the baby and for their own health might be the logical way to express such uneasiness in a socially acceptable way.

Table 1. Incidence of Extreme Rejection: Abortion[*]

Marital status and number of women	Induced abortion	Spontaneous abortion	Live birth
Women single at conception, remained single (355)	89%	5%	6%
Women single at conception, married during pregnancy (60)	18%	7%	75%
Women married at conception, remained married (3575)	17%	18%	65%

[*] Adapted from data on white non-prison U. S. Females from Gebhard *et al.*[25]

The probability of extreme negative feelings at the idea of having a baby appears to be deeply rooted in human beings—a price they pay for foresight and the possession of knowledge of how to diagnose pregnancy. Taboos against abortion are widespread among primitive peoples indicating, according to Ford's monograph, that there is a desire to induce abortion. It is not necessary to develop taboos unless there is an inclination to act in the tabooed direction. Many primitive peoples have also been interested enough in abortion to develop efficient abortion techniques. Some kill the fetus by pounding on the abdomen, but others rely on the use of effective abortifacients.

The type and source of negative emotions involved in abortion can more freely be studied in countries where induced abortion is legal for social reasons. In a recent study by Milosevic and Prica, 1000 women in Yugoslavia who asked for abortions were compared with another thousand women. The findings suggest that the majority of applications for induced abortion were made for social and economic reasons and a smaller number for psychologic and psychopathologic reasons.

Shifts in Feelings Toward Pregnancy

As pregnancy progresses, there is a tendency for the prospective mother to express more and more acceptance. In the Winokur and Werboff study, for instance, of 30 army wives who reported not wanting the baby at the time they became pregnant only 2 indicated they did not want the child in the third trimester of pregnancy. This finding is in accord with an earlier finding of Hall and Mohr, who observed that a few pregnant women fully accepted the idea of having the baby immediately, and a few continued to reject the idea of having the baby. Almost two-thirds of the women first had a negative reaction and then became reconciled to the pregnancy.

In view of this evidence that most mothers in our culture appear to learn to adapt to the idea of the coming child during the middle months of pregnancy, it is of interest that recent Russian research by Nemtsova et al. suggests that the middle period portion of pregnancy is the time of "maximum adaptation." The Russian work was done on both dogs and rats, using the stability of conditioned reflexes as a measure of adaptation.

The *initial* reaction to pregnancy, unless it leads to abortion and to such neglect of health that the fetus is injured, is probably not as important as the ability of the mother to adjust to the situation. For instance, Klein et al. found in their exploratory study that women with considerable negative feelings toward pregnancy were just as likely to have comfortable pregnancies as difficult ones. However, the personality structure of the mothers was important. Of the 16 patients they studied who had easy pregnancies, all but 2 were "reasonably mature, stable individuals"; while of 11 who had difficult pregnancies, 8 were categorized as "unstable and had poorly organized personality structures."

EMOTIONAL CHANGES IN PREGNANCY

Fears and anxieties tend to increase in pregnancy and decrease after delivery. Poor clinic women were studied during pregnancy and then again after delivery by Hirst and Strousse. Their chief worry seemed to center around their economic situation. Yet after delivery, a follow-up interview indicated that 40 of the 50 women now had a general lowering of the level of anxiety, although their economic situation had not improved. More recently, Davids *et al.* found a suggestive drop in the level of anxiety after delivery as measured by Taylor's Manifest Anxiety Scale. However, Eron found no meaningful difference between pregnant and nonpregnant women in regard to fantasies stimulated by ambiguous pictures.

Cramond approached anxiety in pregnant women from another angle. He considered that a pregnant woman showed excessive anxiety when, (a) she slept so badly she required a sedative, or (b) where there was a history of dreams with a strong anxiety content. About one-third of a group of patients who went on to have normal deliveries showed this degree of restlessness. About half the mothers dreamed, and most of the dreams reported were unpleasant. However, a few dreamed about the baby safe in their arms and all being well.

Frequent Types of Worries

Folklore probably influences pregnancy fears to a far greater extent than is commonly realized, particularly among the less well-educated portions of the population. For instance, a study by Estes of 50 expectant Negro mothers in an Alabama hospital clinic revealed that 86 per cent believed that the mother's actions before birth can determine if the cord encircles the baby's neck, and 82 per cent believed the mother can mark the unborn baby. Twenty-eight per cent believed some people have the power to "cast a spell" over the expectant mother and her unborn baby.

The type of fears and worries to which married primiparous New York City clinic women are particularly subject has been catalogued in a study by Pleshette *et al.* Answers to standardized questions were obtained prenatally in private interviews, with the following results:

Dominant Fears and Problems
(*expressed by over 50 per cent of patients*)

Baby unplanned
Pregnancy accidental
Worried about getting too fat
Frightened by doctors about getting too fat
Afraid pain will be bad
Afraid of being cut or torn at birth
Afraid fall will hurt baby
Difficulty sleeping

Important Fears and Problems
(expressed by 20 to 49 per cent of patients)

Frightened by baby's movements
Dislike of certain foods
Worry about figure changing
Shortness of breath
No sexual desire
Fear sex will hurt baby
Fear sex might lead to loss of baby
Husband thinks sex will lead to baby loss
Has not asked doctor about sex during pregnancy
Afraid baby might die before birth
Afraid baby will not be normal
Afraid of bleeding during pregnancy
Frightened by bleeding during pregnancy
Frightened by someone about having a baby
Husband not living at home this pregnancy
Worried that doctors might not be friendly

The type of fear in private patients, who represent a more educated group, might tend to differ in some ways from the above listing. For instance, Hamilton found in an exploratory study that women who had previously valued intellectual pursuits were sometimes bothered by a slowing down in intellectual life.

Previous Childbirth as a Cause of Fear

The experience of childbirth in our culture appears to frighten some women to an extent that it causes apprehension in the next pregnancy. One would expect that familiarity with childbirth would lessen fears. However, Winokur and Werboff found that slightly *more* multiparas than primiparas expressed apprehension about having the baby.

Jeffcoate has pointed out the fear-producing effect of previous labors. He comments: "The harrowing experience of labor complicated by severe inertia and incoordinate action is a serious deterrent to further childbearing, and about one-third of the women or their husbands deliberately avoid further pregnancies."

Lack of memory of the birth experience does not necessarily mean that it is not a cause of anxiety. For instance, Kartchner cites a case history of a woman who was frequently awakened by nightmares filled with unremembered terrifying content. While partly anesthesized during the birth of her second child she screamed, "There they are! The lights! The people! They said they wouldn't hurt but they did! I just didn't remember!" As a primipara she had had painful manipulations in labor and a forceps delivery.

Medically Induced Anxieties

The existence of doctor-induced anxieties has been mentioned by D. F. Lawson, an Australian physician. He comments: ". . . Doctors do tell patients that they are 'small made' or that the womb is twisted and that they will either not become pregnant or are likely to miscarry if they do. . . . The overcautious doctor . . . is inclined to see every pregnancy as a miscarriage. . . . He scares his patient into a state in which she spends her life in a frightened existence precariously hanging on to her pregnancy."

Another area of doctor-induced anxieties may come from the way weight gain is sometimes handled. Pleshette *et al.* describes a routine observed in one clinic: "On arriving in the morning the patient was immediately weighed by the nurse in charge. At this point some comment was usually made about the change in weight. The tone of the entire staff was either punitive or approving, depending on the increment of gain. Thus the patient had either been a good or bad girl. On examination, the doctor would note the weight on the chart and make additional remarks to the patient and perhaps suggest salt and dietary restriction. . . . The final touch came from the receptionist, who took it upon herself to comment about the weight as she gave the next appointment." Strangely enough, signs of pretoxemia, edema, and blood-pressure rise are usually not treated in the same anxiety-producing manner, but as matter-of-fact physical symptoms.

ANXIETY IN PRIMITIVE PEOPLES

Although the routines and habits prevalent in our culture may serve to heighten some types of fears and worries in pregnancy, it is probable that in most cultures anxieties do surround pregnancy to some extent. The development of a brain that can generalize means that a pregnant woman sees some similarity between her condition and the death and pain of her unfortunate sister or neighbor who was also pregnant. The ability to use language also makes the experiences of other pregnant women not directly observed a source of identification, with possible frightening effects. Primitive cultures, like industrial ones, have elaborate rituals and routines surrounding pregnancy that may serve as a method of decreasing anxicty about pregnancy. Ford's study of a large sample of primitive peoples revealed evidence of pregnancy dietary rules in 38 cultures as opposed to only 4 who definitely had no such customs. Rituals and customs believed to avoid painful delivery had developed in 35 cultures as opposed to only 3 cultures that lacked such ideas.

Some of the primitive customs and rituals catalogued by Ford, like some of our own, may actually have some somatic effect on the body as well as serve as anxiety-lessening devices. A common rule is to encourage pregnant women to have as much exercise as possible. For instance, the Ainu is urged to exercise so her baby will be small and her labor short. The Hopi expectant mother is urged to rise early and not sit around all day. In the area of food regulations many primitive societies urge mothers to eat moderately so the baby will not grow too large before birth. Some primitive peoples duplicate the efforts of the more nutrition-conscious physicians in our own culture. The Jivaro woman, for instance, as soon as she believes herself to be pregnant, starts abstaining from salt and sweet things; these items are believed to make the fetus big and delivery difficult.

In many cultures both the father and mother of the unborn child are required to avoid and/or do certain things to help insure a healthy baby, according to Ford. For instance, the Malekulan's father is not allowed to leave the house as the delivery date draws near for fear he might do something to hurt the child. The Tongan woman is not allowed to cut anything with a knife for fear of deforming the child.

The existence of this type of custom among primitive cultures highlights the fact that pregnancy causes anxiety even in non-industrial societies. Ford emphasizes that customs for preventing difficult labors and assuring normal babies do not occur unless the fear exists.

Craving for Certain Foods

Excessive and peculiar cravings are another way anxiety can show itself. Food cravings are probably much more widely spread and much more bothersome problems than is commonly realized. For instance, a brief mention of the food cravings of pregnancy was made on a radio program in England. An invitation for listeners to write in their experiences resulted in 514 letters, which the broadcasting company considered a strikingly large number in view of the competing program on the airwaves at the time and also because of the casual way the invitation was made to listeners. The replies were in general agreement about the seriousness of the cravings during pregnancy, although the cravings seemed humorous to some women afterwards. The craving tended to be associated with the early part of pregnancy when adjustment problems are at their height. Many women felt such shame about their cravings that they reported going to great lengths to keep them secret, even from their husbands. Some women reported cravings so strong that they were tempted to steal.

A mild degree of craving may almost be a characteristic of the majority of women in pregnancy. When Tobin administered a questionnaire to 1000 pregnant patients, 64 per cent answered, "Yes," when asked, "Did you have any peculiar food cravings in pregnancy?" It is possible that the "yes" answer came because the women were culturally conditioned to believe "yes" was the right answer. However, food craving occurs in other cultures as well. Ford reports 13 primitive cultures where there was information on this point. Twelve reported the existence of food cravings in pregnancy and in only one was it absent.

Changes in Sexual Feelings

Pregnancy was associated with a decrease in sexual desire in women, according to studies by Landis. Twenty-seven per cent of the women reported decreased desire in the first trimester, 43 per cent in the second trimester, and 79 per cent in the third trimester. Pleshette et al. had similar findings. Only 16 per cent of the pregnant clinic women stated that they had an increase of desire in pregnancy, while 24 per cent stated that they had no desire. Only half felt their desire had stayed the same.

There is a tendency to cease coitus as the pregnancy approaches term. A study by Pugh and Fernandez on 500 women indicated that the median time for stopping coitus was about 28 days before delivery. Many patients stopped coitus considerably before this, but others continued to within a few days of term with no significant increase in obstetrical complications.

This variation in behavior in regard to coitus during pregnancy is paralleled by the various ways primitive peoples handle the problem. In a few societies, Ford reports, the husband is enjoined to continue cohabiting with his wife to insure the growth of the fetus. A few tribes forbid coitus during the greater part of pregnancy, while quite a number have taboos against intercourse during the last month or two.

Intercourse during pregnancy, to the extent practiced by industrial and non-industrial man, appears to be characteristically human and possibly dependent somewhat on the invention of marriage. Hummer, of the Veterinary Sciences Department of the Aerospace Medical Division of Brooks Air Force Base, reports that intercourse during the early stages of pregnancy in monkeys has been known to occur. Evidently, however, it is not common. Riopelle, of the Yerkes Laboratories of Primate Biology, reports that male chimpanzees rarely make sexual advances to pregnant females, since the females seldom solicit male attention, nor do they exhibit the perineal swelling that seems to attract the male. In man, the relationship between marriage and pregnancy coitus was found by Pugh and Fernandez to be quite marked. Unmarried pregnant women stopped intercourse on the average of 26 days before married women.

Mood Changes

Women having difficulty getting used to the idea of the coming of a new baby to care for and women plagued by increased fears and worries about future events might be expected to show greater irritability and depression. Recent studies indicate that this appears to be true of women in pregnancy.

Tobin gave questionnaires about moods in pregnancy to Toronto women and compared their answers with the answers of control cases chosen at random from the practices of a gynecologist, surgeon, internist, and general practitioner. He found that crying spells, feelings of depression, and irritability were reported by the large majority of pregnant patients, but by only a minority of the nonpregnant controls (Table 2).

Table 2. Negative Moods in Women°

	Pregnant women (1000 subjects)	Nonpregnant women (500 subjects)
Crying spells for no apparent reason	68%	5%
The blues, lasting over 30 minutes or coming more than once a week	84%	26%
Extreme irritability as judged by patient herself	61%	18%

* Adapted from data given by Tobin.[65]

These findings tend to be confirmed by Bushnell and by Klein *et al.* Bushnell administered a mood-elevating drug to every woman who seemed to need it in the second lunar month of pregnancy. Out of 55 consecutive cases, he found only 8 who did not show signs of fatigue and depression sufficient to merit medication on his program. Klein *et al.*, studying 27 primiparous pregnant clinic patients in detail, observed absence of mood changes in only 3. It was the feeling of these investigators that it was women who had previously showed moodiness, acute irritability, or poor capacity to tolerate frustration who were more likely to show exaggerated mood changes in pregnancy. They observed that only an occasional woman felt quieter and more genial, but none showed joyous feelings commonly believed to occur during pregnancy.

These mood changes appear to be uniquely human. Riopelle reports that the chimpanzee, one of man's nearest living relatives, does not experience mood changes in pregnancy in the same way human beings appear to do. He comments: "We do not see any increased irritability or aggressiveness during pregnancy, although there may be a little preoccupation during the period of labor."

Severe Emotional Disturbances

Moderately severe psychologic disorders of childbearing were carefully studied by a British general practitioner, Ryle. His criterion of the diagnosis of "psychologic disturbance" is that the disturbance should have necessitated 3 consultations with a physician in the course of 1 year. He found his rate of psychologic disturbances was lower in his childbearing patients than in his women patients of similar age who were not reproducing. When emotional disturbances did occur, they were more likely to occur after the birth of the child rather than before. Out of 313 full-term deliveries, there were 8 psychologic disturbances in pregnancy, 10 in the 3 months following delivery, and 5 occurring 3–12 months after delivery. In the case of miscarriages, however, the ratio was reversed. Three women showed psychologic disorders before the miscarriage to only 1 who showed it afterwards. Of the 11 disorders which did occur during pregnancy, 10 were clearly reactive disorders and 1 was uncertain. In contrast to this, disorders diagnosed as endogenous depressions occurred in the postdelivery or post-miscarriage phase.

The problem of forecasting which obstetric patient will actually develop a severe emotional disturbance in childbearing has recently been investigated using controls. Gordon and Gordon (1957) found the following factors related to emotional problems in childbearing: (1) having come from broken homes; (2) history of emotional disorder in self, parents, or immediate family; (3) history of previous severe physical illness or physical complications of pregnancy; (4) complications in marriage, such as differences in religion or great differences in age; (5) rising or falling in the economic or social ladder; (6) recent move to suburbs; (7) older parents; (8) unplanned pregnancy or a female child; (9) acute strains in period of childbearing, like change of residence, husband being away from home, or no outside help from family or practical nurse. Tetlow's work, also done with adequate controls, suggests that another stress factor that may be added to the Gordons' list is illicit pregnancy— i.e., pregnancy in single women or by a man who was not the husband.

Markham found a striking difference in attitude toward the mother figure. Ten of 11 women hospitalized for emotional problems during childbearing showed "oral dependence on the mother figure." None of her 11 controls showed this trait.

Gordon and Gordon (1959) also report some objective statistical evidence as to the type of psychotherapy most helpful to emotionally upset childbearing patients. Until 1955 a psychiatrist ordinarily gave "passive dynamic psychotherapy" to maternity patients. Then he changed methods. He more actively pointed out and encouraged his patients to deal with present-day social forces as well as deeper psychodynamics. The therapy became markedly more successful to a statistically significant extent, as measured in several ways. The subjectively evaluated success rate jumped from 26 per cent to 82 per cent. Although the total number of sessions required fell sharply, patients accepted treatment more readily. Only 14 per cent stopped the new method of therapy after the first visit or two, as compared with 44 per cent who previously stopped passive dynamic therapy after 1 or 2 visits. The need for hospitalization of patients was also eliminated, whereas formerly 43 per cent had been hospitalized.

These findings strongly suggest that discussion of the stresses of everyday life can be of real aid to obstetric patients. The following social therapeutic principles suggested by the Gordons (1959) can be encouraged by the obstetrician as well as the psychiatrist: (1) Arrange for help from women experienced in the care of infants while the mother is confused and physically weak. This involves good relationships with loving female friends or relatives or substitutes. (2) Encourage emotional support and practical assistance from a loving husband. Assistance should be given if need be in regard to good sexual adjustment. Sometimes when the husband is away from home for very long periods due to such factors as night work or study a less strenuous program for him should be considered. (3) Schedule leisure-time activities involving time outside of the home, and social life with husband and friends. (4) Establish confidence in a trusted physician who will give regular examinations and support in emergencies. This relieves anxiety during and after pregnancy. (5) Insist on recognition of limitations and avoidance of excess strain. For instance, care of aged relatives should be shared; and moving in later pregnancy, or soon after delivery, should be avoided. (6) Encourage discussion of plans, fears, hopes, problems with others—husband, relatives, friends, physician. Discussion yields information and encourages planning and foresight.

Group instruction is also effective in helping middle-class patients to adopt these sociotherapeutic principles. The Gordons (1960) demonstrated that parents instructed in these principles in the course of antenatal training showed significant changes of behavior in the suggested direction and went on to need significantly less psychiatric care than a control group selected from routine antenatal classes.

Physical Causes of Pregnancy Emotions

It is easy for the psychosomaticist, in view of the adjustment difficulties of pregnancy, to assume that all signs of emotional stress are due to conflict, and thus be tempted to treat it only on this level. However, it is quite possible that nutritional and other physical factors play an important part in the etiology of these pregnancy emotions. The pregnant woman is under both physiologic and psychologic stress. In vitamin B-complex deficiency, behavior changes (reviewed by Bell) consist of depression, apprehension, irritability and insomnia. In line with this reasoning a nutrition study done in Alabama by Edwards et al. on women who ate clay or cornstarch during pregnancy is pertinent. Fifty-four per cent of the clay-eaters and 32 per cent of the cornstarch-eaters were classified as having "poor" diets as compared with only 14 per cent of the controls. The search for extra nutritional elements, as well as "anxiety" may well be involved in such patterns of behavior.

PSYCHOSOMATIC DISORDERS

Any stress situation is, ipso facto, a situation which produces both physical and emotional reactions. Hormones affect feelings as well as physiology. It is not surprising that pregnancy, which is a social, nutritional, and physical stress to most women in our culture, should produce many psychosomatic symptoms.

General Complaints

General feelings of ill health and minor complaints during pregnancy may often have emotional as well as physical concomitants. For instance, the monograph by Klein *et al.* reports almost half of 27 primiparas had increased perspiration in the third trimester, often waking up wringing wet at night. Constipation was reported by the majority and about a quarter of the group were slightly incontinent during the last trimester. The majority found they got easily winded, and 6 described "palpitations." Sleep disorders were also extremely common. More than two-thirds of the women had difficulty sleeping in the third trimester, and more than half reported going through another period when they were sleepier than usual or seemed to require more sleep. Pleshette *et al.* found a similarly high incidence of sleep disorders and problems of being easily winded among a larger sample of clinic mothers.

The incidence of psychosomatic disorders seems to vary considerably with social class, being more common in those with lower incomes. Rosengren and DeVault found that women who believed in many superstitions were more likely to view pregnancy as an illness and to have many psychosomatic complaints. Those writers emphasize the importance of social class in influencing these relationships. Newton found a suggestive relationship between higher social class and fewer complaints about pregnancy.

The importance of controlling social class in any study of the psychosomatic phenomena of pregnancy is indicated by the work of Destounis, who reports on 10 Nova Scotia women followed through pregnancy. Psychotherapy sessions began between the second and third months of pregnancy and continued at weekly intervals throughout pregnancy. These women were compared with a control group of 52 women seen only by their family physicians. Only 20 per cent of the group receiving intensive psychotherapy developed complications of pregnancy, as opposed to 82 per cent of the control group. However, the control group was of a significantly lower level in regard to social class, so that the only conclusion that can be drawn from the data is that "sociopsychologic" factors were significantly and highly related to the appearance of pregnancy disorders.

Rejection of the female biologic role may also be involved in feeling "well" or "ill" during pregnancy. Newton compared women who had unpleasant things to say about how they felt during pregnancy ("sick all the time," "not good at all," "all right, but—," "not too good,") with women who expressed more positive feelings ("pretty good," "no trouble," "real well,"). The women who expressed more negative feelings toward the period of pregnancy significantly more often expressed the wish to be reborn men. Further suggestive findings (10 per cent or 20 per cent probability of occurring by chance alone) were that those who said complaining things about their pregnancies tended to (a) dislike looking after their babies in the hospital, (b) be completely unreconciled to the sex of the baby and, (c) say fewer children in the family was the "ideal" situation.

Nausea and Vomiting

The incidence of nausea and vomiting is very sensitive to cultural influences, as was recently discussed by Mead and Newton. Other mammals, who have no cultural traditions, do not have nausea and vomiting in pregnancy. Most primitive peoples do have patterns of nausea and vomiting of pregnancy. However, the Omaha Indians of North America and the Arapesh of Northwest New Guinea do not recognize its existence. A study done by a physician[42] at the Navaho Medical Center on 475 pregnant Indians indicated that only 14 per cent had morning sickness. Almost all of the group who had nausea and vomiting were among those who had sufficient contact with American culture to speak English.

Rejection of the female biologic role, as manifested by dislike of sexual intercourse, appears to be much involved in the occurrence of nausea and vomiting in pregnancy. Robertson, studying a hundred pregnancies in his general practice in England, found that the most marked factor that differentiated those with nausea and vomiting from those without was undesired sexual intercourse. Only 9 per cent of those with no nausea or vomiting had disturbed sexual function as compared to 58 per cent of the minor cases, 76 per cent of the moderate cases, and 100 per cent of the severe cases.

These early findings of Robertson have been reconfirmed by the work of Harvey and Sherfey, who had the same psychiatrist spend 5 to 6 hours interviewing each of 20 New York women hospitalized for severe vomiting, along with their relatives. A control group was used. These authors feel that the most striking finding of their study was the relation of vomiting to sexual disorders. Every one of the patients studied expressed strong conscious aversion to coitus. Half of the total group reported pain on intercourse, and half reported vomiting provoked by coitus and at times by the anticipation of it. All reported coitus made them "upset" and "very nervous and tense." One told of vomiting when her husband came home at night, saying, "I can't stand looking at him." In contrast to this, none of the 14 control patients had experienced coital nausea and none had an aversion to intercourse during the pregnancy being investigated.

It is the conflict in regard to intercourse, rather than "the frigid personality" that may be the underlying factor in this problem. Robertson observed a number of cases of severe vomiting in wives of ex-servicemen who had come back after 2 or more years away. Such husbands insisted on more intercourse than their war-weary wives were able to accept easily. Previous pregnancy in many of these wives had involved no sickness. Robertson also cites the following informative case history. A completely frigid woman had nausea and vomiting with 7 pregnancies. Her husband became an alcoholic, unfaithful, and contracted syphilis, whereupon they separated after pregnancy 7. Pregnancies 8, 9, 10, and 11 resulted in his breaking into the house only once, according to the testimony of a neighbor as well as that of the woman. In these pregnancies the woman had no nausea and vomiting.

Conflict over acceptance of motherhood, another aspect of the female biologic role, may be involved in vomiting. Chertok et al.[9] did a well-controlled study on French primiparas exhibiting the type of vomiting seen in ordinary obstetric practice. None had severe enough vomiting to be hospitalized. They found that the peak incidence of vomiting came in women ambivalent about pregnancy. Eighty-two per cent of those expressing both joy and resentment of pregnancy vomited, as compared with 60 per cent of those expressing only joy, and 47 per cent of those expressing only resentment. The finding of Chertok et al. that ambivalence rather than clear rejection of the pregnancy appears to be related to vomiting is in line with earlier findings reviewed by them. In one study, out of 85 women who sought abortion, not a single one reported vomiting. It has also been observed that unmarried mothers, who presumably tend to reject the baby, tend to have a low incidence of vomiting of pregnancy.

Conflict over the acceptance of other aspects of the adult female biologic role may also be involved in pregnancy vomiting. Harvey and Sherfey found that almost all of their severe vomiters had severe dysmenorrhea, and almost half reported that nausea and vomiting occurred at the time of menstruation. None of the control series reported experiencing vomiting or nausea during menses, but 2 of them reported some dysmenorrhea which was associated with anorexia.

Immaturity is another aspect of the personality which also appears to be involved in the occurrence of nausea and vomiting. Harvey and Sherfey state, "A strikingly impressive and consistent finding was the general psychological immaturity which all these women present." Seventeen out of the 20 showed "passive and compliantly dependent use of other persons, particularly of mothers and mother figures." This fits in well with the findings of Robertson, who noted that vomiting women tended to consult their mothers on every decision of importance. Nine per cent of the control group showed their dependence, as compared with 19 per cent of the minor group, 47 per cent of the moderate group, and 66 per cent of the severe group.

Again the conflict aspects of the situation are underlined by Robertson who observed that when the mothers of these dependent vomiters were removed the vomiting did not tend to recur. For instance, one woman was devoted to her mother, whom she nursed during pernicious anemia. The mother died after pregnancy 5. Pregnancy 6 was the only one without any nausea and vomiting, which had been extreme for the previous 5 pregnancies.

That conflict, rather than personality per se, is involved in vomiting is also suggested by the findings of Harvey and Sherfey. They comment on how quickly vomiting cleared up on hospitalization. Some patients had no vomiting after admission, and only a few continued to vomit for more than 3 days. A difference in the type of vomiting was clinically observed. Anxiousness and depression led to severe acute attacks. When general immaturity and inadequacy were the most prominent feature desultory vomiting occurred over longer periods. Attempts by Harvey and Sherfey and by Bernstein to study the psychodynamic factors of vomiting by projective tests were not particularly fruitful, possibly because the tests were invented for measuring different types of problems.

Psychologic factors appear to act as a trigger mechanism that sets off vomiting when there is a physical tendency to vomit, which seems to occur in normal pregnancy. The role of normal pregnancy physiology can be seen by the striking inverse relationship between abortion and vomiting. Medalie found in a study of 100 Israeli women that about half the group reported no nausea or only mild nausea and vomiting. Of these, 22.9 per cent had complete abortions and 22.9 per cent had threatened abortions. However, of the women having moderate or severe nausea and vomiting, none went on to have complete abortions and only 1.9 per cent had a threatened abortion.

Emotional Aspects of Preeclampsia

Physical and emotional factors also appear to be closely interwoven in the occurrence of preeclampsia. An English study by Coppen compared 50 preeclamptics with 50 control cases matched for age, parity, and time in pregnancy examined, but otherwise chosen at random from the same clinic population that furnished the preeclamptics. All were given a psychiatric interview to rate them on a 5-point scale on various aspects of family relationships, attitudes concerning female biologic role, experience in regard to school and work and housing, and on certain psychiatric and psychosomatic symptoms. In addition, a personality questionnaire was given and certain anthropometric measurements obtained.

The preeclamptics differed from the controls to a statistically significant extent in the following ways:

1. More disturbed emotional relationships with brothers and sisters. Histories of quarrels and jealousy existing for years appeared to be the main difference between the test and control groups.

2. Increase in psychiatric symptoms during pregnancy. The onset of these was so early they seemed important prodromal symptoms of preeclampsia. The preeclamptic group was not only much more intensely disturbed by the usual worries of pregnancy, they showed intense mood swings, irritability, and sensitivity and unreasonable fears about the husband's faithfulness. Insomnia characterized by early waking rather than difficulty in going to sleep occurred. Very severe depressions, lasting a few hours or several days, were part of the pattern.

3. Scores on personality tests indicated more neurotic tendencies. More tendency to introversion was also present, but this did not quite reach the level of statistical significance.

4. More emotionally disturbing events during pregnancy. The cause of these disturbances differed widely and included illness or death or quarrels with relatives or friends, financial worries, illegitimacy, problems with husband's employment. The patient was only rated as disturbed if the event disturbed her. For instance, premarital conception was not rated as emotionally disturbing to some patients, but in others it was very disturbing. Only 36 per cent of the toxemic group were rated totally free from such emotional disturbances in pregnancy, as compared with 88 per cent of the controls.

5. Less welcoming attitudes toward the child. Extreme continued rejection of a type not voiced by the control group was quite common in the preeclamptic group.

6. Vomiting during the day and heartburn. The preeclamptic group had histories of more of the type of vomiting that goes on throughout the day rather than of the type that occurs in the early morning alone. Heartburn occurred about equally frequently in both groups, but the severity was reported as much greater in the preeclamptic groups even before other signs of preeclampsia became apparent.

7. Difficulties in the area of acceptance of the female biologic role. Most of the control group accepted or welcomed menarche, whereas the preeclamptic group often reacted with resentment, fear, shame, or horror. Premenstrual tension, to the extent of interfering with normal life, was

significantly more common in the preeclamptic group. There were marked differences in sexual response, with 78 per cent of the preeclamptic group rated as frigid as compared with 32 per cent of the control group.

8. Heavier and more masculine body build. The preeclamptic group had considerably higher prepregnancy weight. They also had discriminant androgyny scores and chest diameters indicating strong masculine tendencies.

Other studies on preeclampsia and eclampsia, although not as extensive, tend to validate the findings of Coppen when their fields coincide. Soichet found indications of emotional problems in the area of pregnancy and acceptance of the baby in toxemic patients as compared with nontoxemic patients. Weidorn, in a statistically sophisticated study, found an association between toxemia and later developing schizophrenia. Caldwell found that her more introverted, "unhappy" patients tended to be admitted to hospital for toxemia treatment about three times as frequently as her "well-adjusted" patients.

As in the case of vomiting, physical factors working with emotional factors appear to be involved. Coppen's finding of more masculine body build suggests this, as does the well-known fact that preeclampsia and nutrition are strongly related. The magnitude and pervasiveness of this relationship is indicated in a study of Woodhill et al., who found that women with very poor diet ratings had a 35 per cent incidence of preeclampsia, as compared with only a 4 per cent incidence in women with good or excellent diet ratings. It is probable that the nutrition influenced the pathologic process, but it is also probable that the emotions of preeclampsia influenced the mother's food choice.

Emotional Aspects of Abortion

Abortion is another area in which emotional factors and physical factors interact. The team studies done in Halifax by Tupper et al. present a comprehensive approach to the problem. Patients with habitual and threatened abortion were examined by a psychiatrist and an obstetrician and through laboratory tests. When estrogen, pregnanediol, and chorionic gonadotrophin levels were normal, 68 per cent of the patients carried to term, as opposed to only 29 per cent when these hormone levels were low. However, the investigator gained the impression that there was a relationship between the emotional and hormonal factors. Emotional difficulties appeared to cause a lowering in the blood levels of the sex hormones, which would rise to normal again after a psychiatric consultation.

These investigators also interviewed women undergoing normal pregnancy, which enabled them to develop a clear impression of the contrasting personality characteristics of the women who aborted or who threatened to abort. They classified their 100 aborters and threatened aborters into: (a) The inadequate reserved group—44 per cent of the cases. Such women were overly dependent, anxious in their relation to others, confused about their sex roles, with unhappy relationships with their parents and generally immature. (b) Independent, frustrated group —also 44 per cent of the total. Physically they seemed quite healthy, of higher intellectual level and better adjusted socially than the other group, and were usually married to understanding husbands. They were independent women who had often been career women with special interests that they had been reluctant to give up in marriage. They had mixed feelings about their feminine role and had often gotten pregnant just to satisfy their husbands. (c) Mixed group—12 per cent.

The existence of an immature, dependent personality among habitual aborters has also been found by Mann and Grimm. Grimm used the TAT (Thematic Apperception Test) and Rorschach test on a middle-class group of habitual aborters, as well as on a comparison group. She found some significant differences in test scores, which were interpreted to indicate that the aborters had greater immaturity, poorer emotional control, stronger dependence, conventionality and guilt. Mann found evidence of immaturity and dependence in about half of 145 clinic patients evaluated psychosomatically. His most surprising finding was that about one-third of this large group had histories of premarital pregnancy followed by criminal abortion. He also noted the presence of anniversary aborters—one woman repetitively aborted on the date of her criminal abortion and another recurrently miscarried on Mother's Day.

Cole studied not only habitual aborters but their husbands in regard to 65 aspects of their personality. In general, the tests used revealed few differences between test- and control-group wives and test- and control-group husbands. However, there was a possible indication of a more stressful marriage because the aborting couples differed more from each other in personality than did the control couples. Cole suggests that habitually aborting women may not differ in emotionality per se, but only in reaction to stress.

Women having 3 or more abortions can be helped to retain their pregnancies by psychotherapy. Mann found that 85 per cent of the habitual aborters who had a history of premarital pregnancy and criminal abortion had successful pregnancies when they were able to face and accept the unresolved feelings of guilt. Weil and Tupper cite a similar finding, in that 15 out of 18 who had already aborted 3 times, successfully carried to term with the aid of psychotherapy. Grimm found statistically significant changes in the direction of the comparison group in total scores in 18 habitual aborters who had term pregnancies following psychotherapy.

Relation of Pregnancy Psychology to Labor

Pregnancy culminates in a final psychosomatic act—labor. Recent studies have shed considerable light on the relation of emotions to the physical aspects of labor. The relationships are not simple but quite complex and unexpected. Klein *et al.* point out in their exploratory monograph that some women who were cooperative and uncomplaining during pregnancy were tense, noisy, and uncooperative in labor, and vice versa. Furthermore, some women who seemed to want the child reacted poorly in labor, while others who had not wanted the child reacted favorably.

Attempts to relate behavior in labor to neuroticism and maladjustment have not been very fruitful. Eysenck found in a study of 200 women that neuroticism as measured by a personality inventory was not related to either behavior in labor or attitude to labor. Scott and Thompson, in a study of 276 primigravidas, found that patients who were judged emotionally well-adjusted by a psychologist and also had low neuroticism scores on a personality test did have a low incidence of difficult labor. However, patients judged both maladjusted and having high neuroticism scores tended to do better in labor than those presenting an intermediate or less clear personality pattern. Eilenberg studied 22 pregnant women who were under psychiatric treatment in pregnancy. He found they did not have a higher incidence of labor abnormalities than others, and only 3 of them were rated as having "difficult behavior" in labor. Tetlow found that even women whose emotional abnormality was indicated by child-bearing psychoses did not have more complications of labor than controls.

On the other hand, the anxious introverted woman rather than the measurably maladjusted tends to have more difficult labor. Davids *et al.* compared pregnant women who went on to have complicated deliveries with those who experienced no abnormalities. They found that women who had difficulty had significantly (a) higher anxiety as measured by Taylor's Manifest Anxiety Test, (b) more alienated personalities as measured by a sentence completion test, (c) rated themselves as less happy, on a self-rating test.

Rosengren and DeVault found that longer labor time was significantly related to belief in superstitions, regard for self as "ill," and psychosomatic complaints. This observation tends to validate the earlier findings of

Caldwell, who found admissions for false labor occurred 3 times as frequently among the patients she categorized as "introverted, passive, quiet, hypochondriacal" than among those she categorized as "well adjusted or extremely emotional." Winokur and Werboff found significant relationship between apprehension about having the baby and tolerance of labor. Women who expressed more worry about having a baby tended later to be rated by their obstetricians as being less tolerant of labor—i.e., noisier, less cooperative, asking for pain relief oftener or sooner, showing more signs of fear.

The tendency for the anxious personality to have difficulty is emphasized by studies on uterine dysfunction or excessively prolonged labor. Cramond, in Scotland, compared 50 cases of major uterine dysfunction with a control group matched for age, height, and social class. All the dysfunction cases had labors lasting more than 24 hours, and in most more than 48 hours. He found that 54 per cent of the dysfunction cases, as compared with 12 per cent of the controls, had a "dysfunction temperament" characterized by reserve, suspiciousness, difficulty in talking about themselves and their problems, and greater than average conventionality. Specifically the dysfunction group differed to a statistically significant extent from the control group in that (a) they were much less likely to report tremor and sweating as a method of discharging tension; (b) they showed more tension during interview, tending to look ill at ease; and (c) they had higher lie scores on the Minnesota Multiphasic Personality Inventory, which indicates a strong need to place one's self in a conventional and socially acceptable light. In addition, there was a higher incidence of peptic ulcers or peptic ulcer-like symptoms. The dysfunction group had an 18 per cent incidence, as compared with a 4 per cent incidence in the control group. This difference has a probability of just over .05.

Watson interviewed 25 patients who had prolonged labor. He gained a strong clinical impression that these were women who inhibited the expression of their feelings. He comments, "Our series of cases should draw attention to the necessity of paying closer heed to the 'overly good' patient. These women may be suffering at least as acutely as the more vocal ones and we should actively discourage their 'goodness.'" The danger of overlooking the suffering of the normal introvert is also emphasized by Eysenck's finding that, although their labors are just as long as that of the extroverts, they complain less about severe pain.

Acceptance of the female biologic role appears to be an important factor in labor as well as in other psychosomatic aspects of childbearing. Davids and DeVault found significant tendencies for pregnant women who later had abnormalities connected with deliveries to shut out the idea of pregnancy and femininity. When shown an ambiguous picture which is frequently perceived as a pregnant woman, 60 per cent of women who went on to normal deliveries interpreted the picture as a pregnant woman. Only 21 per cent of the group of pregnant women who later went on to have difficulties "saw" the pregnancy. When asked to draw a picture, 84 per cent of the women who went on to have normal deliveries drew a female figure, as opposed to only 57 per cent in the abnormal delivery group.

Chertok et al.,[10] in Paris, found that feelings in the area of femininity correlated ($r = 0.49$) with behavior in labor. Their data suggest that rejection of femininity may influence behavior in the first stage of labor more than in the second stage of labor. Overall negative feelings toward all areas of life were found to be significantly correlated with poor reactions to labor ($r = 0.46$). The woman with a more accepting attitude toward her female biologic role and toward life in general appears to have a more emotionally controlled and comfortable labor.

EFFECT OF PREGNANCY EMOTIONS ON THE FAMILY

The emotions of pregnancy are not only of significance to the woman herself, but also appear to be very much involved with the health and welfare of the whole family unit. The emotions of the mother are experienced directly by the fetus, and indirectly by the infant after it is born and by the husband and other children.

Effect on Fetus

Sontag reëxamined old wives' tales that the mother's emotions can affect the fetus. He pointed out that the fetal and maternal endocrine systems form an endocrine pool, and that thus hormones involved in the mother's stress reactions also affect the baby. The mothers showing the most signs of emotion in the form of rapid respiration, high skin conductivity, and rapid heart beat appear to have fetuses that are more active.

These variations from fetus to fetus are tremendous—levels of activity varying as much as 1000 per cent in the last 3 months of pregnancy. Fetuses that have been very active during the last 2 months of pregnancy due to maternal emotional distress, fatigue, or other causes tend to show a minimum amount of fat storage and to be light in weight in relation to their length.

Furthermore, Sontag observed fetuses of mothers with sharp emotional distress had a large increase in their sharp irritative movements in utero. After birth such babies continued to be irritable and hyperactive. They cried a great deal, slept for short periods only. They tended to regurgitate their food and had loose stools. It took 2 to 4 months for these babies to become physically more normal.

Stott noticed a relation between stress in pregnancy and ill health in infancy. When mothers of mentally retarded children reported no pregnancy illness or stress, only 29 per cent of the children had non-epidemic illness in the first 3 years of life. This illness rate of the retarded children jumped to 76 per cent when they were born of mothers who experienced illness or emotional stress in pregnancy. In the pregnancies that gave rise to 102 retarded children there were 24 cases of maternal illness, of which half were toxemia. There were 38 instances of harassment or distress in the expectant mother. The author concluded, "It will be seen that psychosomatic influences predominate and the fact that these have been largely ignored in previous studies may account for the failure hitherto to relate congenital malformations in man to pregnancy factors in the same way as malformations in animals have been related to stress."

Relation to Mother-Baby Interaction

Although maternal emotions in pregnancy seem to influence the behavior of the infant, maternal desire for the baby is by no means so closely related to the later mother-baby relationship. Contradictory but statistically significant findings have been reported by several authors. Sears *et al.* found a low correlation between remembered attitude toward the pregnancy and warmth toward the child. Mothers scoring either very high *or* very low on a rejection of pregnancy test more frequently have babies who acted in a deviant way in the hospital nursery, according to Ferreira. Contradictory results were also found by Wallin and Riley, who noted a relationship between pregnancy adjustment and infant adjustment in two-child mothers but not in one-child mothers. Still further complexity is indicated by the finding of Zemlick and Watson that mothers who appeared to show the greatest dislike of pregnancy were particularly indulgent and solicitous toward the infant. However, Newton and Newton (1962) found no significant relationship between feelings about pregnancy and reactions to the first sight of the baby.

Maternal personality does, however, influence the baby through the breast feeding relationship. That women who wholeheartedly want to breast feed lactate more successfully was demonstrated by Newton and Newton (1950), and confirmed by Niles Newton. Acceptance of other aspects of the female biologic role appears to be involved in acceptance of breast feeding. Newton found that women who expressed positive feelings about breast feeding felt women's lot in life was as satisfying as men's, and tended to think childbirth was easy. Primiparas who wanted to breast feed actually had quicker labors than primiparas who wanted to bottle feed, which is particularly interesting since oxytocin is involved in both processes. Further suggestive findings indicate that women who liked breast feeding also tended to like looking after their babies in the hospital, and showed their acceptance of their own sex by wanting girl babies more often than boys.

These early findings of Newton have now been confirmed and broadened by a number of other investigators. Potter and Klein, like Newton, found indications that maternal interest is related to breast feedings. Brown *et al.* (1960) emphasized that the pregnant woman who wants to breast feed appears to be more infant centered, whereas those planning to bottle feed stress narcissistic reasons for their feeding choice. Sears *et al.* found that mothers who accepted breast feeding were also significantly more accepting of sexual matters in the area of modesty, masturbation, and social sex play.

In a carefully controlled study by Adams, pregnant women who stated a preference for breast feeding were significantly more independent, more accepting of the coming child and more satisfied with their sex role. The Blacky test given by Adams tended in most ways to confirm her interview findings, while the Rorschach findings of Brown *et al.* (1961) point strongly to the fact that breast feeding attitudes are closely related to personality factors influenced by social class.

Relation to Father and Other Children

Not only the baby but also the other children may be influenced by the mother's emotions in pregnancy. Baldwin used ratings of maternal behavior before, during and after pregnancy. He found that a mother undertakes less activity in the home and makes fewer suggestions to her other children, but increases in her understanding of her other children during pregnancy.

Husbands also feel the indirect effect of pregnancy and its emotions. The difficulty some men have accepting the idea of a baby and the emotional changes in their wives has recently been emphasized by Towne, and by Curtis, in their studies of the psychiatric problems of fatherhood.

SUMMARY

A scientific body of knowledge now exists concerning the emotions of pregnancy and their relation to health and behavior. This has been reviewed. Factors which influence the acceptance of pregnancy and the desire for the child have been discussed. Data have been presented in regard to the type and extent of anxieties, cravings, fears, desires, and moods in pregnancy. The relation of the emotions and personality of pregnant women to their psychosomatic complaints, and particularly to vomiting, preeclampsia, abortion, and abnormal labor have been discussed. Finally, the relation of pregnancy emotions and personality to the health and welfare of the infant and the rest of the family has been surveyed.

REFERENCES

1. ADAMS, A. B. Choice of infant feeding technique as a function of maternal personality. *J. Consult. Psychol. 23:*143, 1959.
2. BALDWIN, A. L. Changes in parent behavior during pregnancy: An experiment in longitudinal analysis. *Child Develop. 18:*29, 1947.
3. BELL, E. C. Nutritional deficiencies and emotional disturbances. *J. Psychol. 45:*47, 1958.
4. BERNSTEIN, I. C. An investigation into the etiology of nausea and vomiting of pregnancy. *Minnesota Med. 35:*34, 1952.
5. BROWN, F., LIEBERMAN, J., and WINSON, J. Studies in choice of infant feeding by primiparas: 1. Attitudinal factors and extraneous influences. *Psychosom. Med. 22:*421, 1960.
6. BROWN, F., CHASE, J., and WINSON, J. Studies in infant feeding choices of primiparae. *J. Project. Techn. 25:*412, 1961.
7. BUSHNELL, L. F. First trimester depression: A suggested treatment. *Obst. & Gynec. 18:*281, 1961.
8. CALDWELL, J. Personality in pregnancy and labor. *South. M. J. 51:*1026, 1958.
9. CHERTOK, L., MONDZAIN, M. L., and BONNAUD, M. Vomiting and the wish to have a child. *Psychosom. Med. 25:*13, 1963.
10. CHERTOK, L., DONNET, J. L., BONNAUD, M., and VINCENT-BORELLI, M. Éléments psychologiques du prognostic de l'accouchement. *Proc. First Int. Congr. Psychosom. Med. & Childbirth, 1962.* Gauthier-Villars, Paris, in press.
11. COLE, D. A. *Some Emotional Factors in Couples Presenting a Pattern of Habitual Abortion.* Ph.D. dissertation, Syracuse University, Syracuse, New York, 1959. (University Microfilms, Inc. Ann Arbor, Michigan. Microfilm Mic. 59-2659)
12. COPPEN, A. J. Psychosomatic aspects of preeclamptic toxaemia. *J. Psychosom. Res. 2:*241, 1958.
13. CRAMOND, W. A. Psychological aspects of uterine dysfunction. *Lancet 2:*1241, 1954.
14. CURTIS, J. A. A psychiatric study of 55 expectant fathers. *U.S. Armed Forces M. J. 6:*937, 1955.

15. DAVIDS, A., and DeVAULT, S. Use of the TAT and human figure drawings in research on personality, pregnancy and perception. *J. Project. Techn.* 24:362, 1960.

16. DAVIDS, A., DeVAULT, S., and TALMADGE, M. Psychological study of emotional factors in pregnancy. *Psychosom. Med.* 23:93, 1961.

17. DESTOUNIS, N. Psychotherapy in newly married pregnant women, a psychosomatic approach. *Proc. First Int. Congr. Psychosom. Med. & Childbirth, 1962.* Gauthier-Villars, Paris, in press.

18. EDWARDS, C. H., McDONALD, S., MITCHELL, J. R., JONES, L., MASON, L., KEMP, A. M., LAING, D., and TRIGG, L. Clay-and-cornstarch-eating women. *J. Am. Diet. Ass.* 35:810, 1959.

19. EILENBERG, M. D. A prognostic study of neurotic pregnant patients. Preliminary communication. *J. Ment. Sci.* 106:1099, 1960.

20. ERON, L. D. Responses of women to the thematic appreciation test. *J. Consult. Psychol.* 17:269, 1953.

21. ESTES, M. M. *A Survey of the Folklore That Could Influence the Antepartum Care of the Negro Clinic Patient in the Out-Patient Department of a Selected Hospital.* M.S. thesis, University of Alabama, University, Alabama, 1962.

22. EYSENCK, S. B. G. Personality and pain assessment in childbirth of married and unmarried mothers. *J. Ment. Sci.* 107:417, 1961.

23. FERREIRA, A. J. The pregnant woman's emotional attitude and its reflection on the newborn. *Am. J. Orthopsychiat.* 30:553, 1960.

24. FORD, C. S. *A Comparative Study of Human Reproduction.* Yale University Publications in Anthropology No. 32. Yale University Press, New Haven, 1945.

25. GEBHARD, P. H., POMEROY, W. B., MARTIN, C. E., and CHRISTENSON, C. V. *Pregnancy, Birth and Abortion.* Harper, New York, 1958.

26. GORDON, R. E., and GORDON, K. K. Social factors in prevention of postpartum emotional problems. *Obst. & Gynec.* 15:433, 1960.

27. GORDON, R. E., and GORDON, K. K. Social factors in the prediction and treatment of emotional disorders of pregnancy. *Am. J. Obst. & Gynec.* 77:1074, 1959.

28. GORDON, R. E., and GORDON, K. K. Some social-psychiatric aspects of pregnancy and childbearing. *J. M. Soc. New Jersey* 54:569, 1957.

29. GRIMM, E. R. Psychological investigation of habitual abortion. *Psychosom. Med.* 24:369, 1962.

30. HALL, D. E., and MOHR, G. J. Prenatal attitudes of primiparae. *Ment. Hyg.* 17:226, 1933.

31. HAMILTON, E. *Emotional Aspects of Pregnancy: An Intensive Study of Fourteen Normal Primiparae.* Ph.D. Dissertation, Columbia University, New York, 1955. *Dis. Abst.* 15:1115, 1955.

32. HARVEY, W. A., and SHERFEY, M. J. Vomiting in pregnancy: A psychiatric study. *Psychosom. Med.* 16:1, 1954.

33. HIRST, J. C., and STROUSSE, F. The origin of emotional factors in normal pregnant women. *Am. J. Med. Sci.* 196:95, 1938.

376

34. HUMMER, R. L.   Personal communication, 1962.

35. JEFFCOATE, T. N. A.   Inco-ordinate uterine action in labor. *Tr. Edinburgh Obst. Soc. 101:23*, 1949.

36. KARTCHNER, F. D.   Study of the emotional reactions during labor. *Am. J. Obst. & Gynec. 60:19*, 1950.

37. KLEIN, H. R., POTTER, H. W., and DYK, R. B.   *Anxiety in Pregnancy and Childbirth*. Hoeber, New York, 1950.

38. LANDIS, J. T., POFFENBERGER, T., and POFFENBERGER, S.   The effects of first pregnancy upon the sexual adjustment of 212 couples. *Am. Sociol. Rev. 15:767*, 1950.

39. LAWSON, D. F.   The anxieties of pregnancy. *M. J. Aust. 2:161*, 1960.

40. MANN, E. C.   Habitual abortion. *Am. J. Obst. & Gynec. 77:706*, 1959.

41. MARKHAM, SYLVIA.   A comparative evaluation of psychotic and non-psychotic reactions to childbirth. *Am. J. Orthopsychiat. 31:565*, 1961.

42. McCAMMON, C. C.   A study of four hundred seventy-five pregnancies in American Indian women. *Am. J. Obst. & Gynec. 61:1159*, 1951.

43. MEDALIE, J. H.   Relationship between nausea or vomiting in early pregnancy and abortion. *Lancet 2:117*, 1957.

44. MEAD, M., and NEWTON, N.   Conception, pregnancy, labor and the puerperium in cultural perspective. *Proc. First Int. Congr. Psychosom. Med. & Childbirth, 1962*. Gauthier-Villars, Paris, in press.

45. MILOSEVIC, B., and PRICA, R.   Influence of social and psychological factors on maternity. *Proc. First Int. Congr. Psychosom. Med. & Childbirth, 1962*. Gauthier-Villars, Paris, in press.

46. NEMTSOVA, O. L., MORACHEVSKAIA, E. V., and ANDREEVA, E. I.   Dinamika uslovnore flektornoi deiatel 'nosti pri bere'nennosti u zhivotnykh (Dynamics of conditioned-reflex activity during pregnancy in animals). *Zh. Vyssh. Nerv. Deiat. Pavlov. 8:234*, 1955. Abstract in *Psychol. Abstr. 33:309*, 1959.

47. NEWTON, N.   *Maternal Emotions*. Hoeber, New York, 1955.

48. NEWTON, N., and NEWTON, M.   Mothers' reactions to their newborn babies. *J.A.M.A. 181:206*, 1962.

49. NEWTON, N., and NEWTON, M.   Relationship of ability to breast feed and maternal attitudes toward breast feeding. *Pediatrics 5:869*, 1950.

50. PLESHETTE, N., ASCH, S. S., and CHASE, J.   A study of anxieties during pregnancy, labor, the early and late puerperium. *Bull. N. Y. Acad. Med. 32:436*, 1956.

51. POTTER, H. W., and KLEIN, H. R.   On nursing behavior. *Psychiatry 20:39*, 1957.

52. PUGH, W. E., and FERNANDEZ, F. L.   Coitus in late pregnancy. *Obst. & Gynec. 2:636*, 1953.

53. RIOPELLE, A. J.   Personal communication, 1962.

54. ROBERTSON, G. G.   Nausea and vomiting in pregnancy. *Lancet 251:336*, 1946.

55. ROSENGREN, R., and DeVAULT, S.   Psychosomatic complaints, attitudes toward pregnancy, birth superstitions and subsequent labor time. *Proc.*

First Int. Congr. Psychosom. Med. & Childbirth, 1962. Gauthier-Villars, Paris, in press.

56. RYLE, A.   Psychological disturbances associated with 345 pregnancies and 137 women. *J. Ment. Sci. 107:279,* 1961.

57. SCOTT, E. M., and THOMSON, A. M.   A psychological investigation of primigravidae. IV. Psychological factors and the clinical phenomena of labour. *J. Obst. & Gynaec. Brit. Emp. 63:502,* 1956.

58. SCOTT, E. M., ILLSLEY, R., and BILES, M. E.   A psychological investigation of primigravidae. III. Some aspects of maternal behaviour. *J. Obst. & Gynaec. Brit. Emp. 63:494,* 1956.

59. SEARS, R. R., MACCOBY, E. E., and LEVIN, H.   *Patterns of Child Rearing.* Row, Peterson, Evanston, Ill., 1957.

60. SOICHET, S.   Emotional factors in toxemia of pregnancy. *Am. J. Obst. & Gynec. 77:1065,* 1959.

61. SONTAG, L. W.   Difference in modifiability of fetal behavior and physiology. *Psychosom. Med. 6:151,* 1944.

62. STOTT, D. H.   Physical and mental handicaps following a disturbed pregnancy. *Lancet 1:1006,* 1957.

63. TETLOW, C.   Psychoses of childbearing. *J. Ment. Sci. 101:629,* 1955.

64. THOMPSON, L. J.   Attitudes of primiparae as observed in a prenatal clinic. *Ment. Hyg. 26:243,* 1942.

65. TOBIN, S. M.   Emotional depression during pregnancy. *Obst. & Gynec. 10:677,* 1957.

66. TOWNE, R. D., and AFTERMAN, J.   Psychosis in males related to parenthood. *Bull. Menninger Clin. 19:19,* 1955.

67. TUPPER, CARL, MOYA, F., STEWART, L. C., WEIL, R. J., and GRAY, J. D.   The problem of spontaneous abortion. 1. A combined approach. *Am. J. Obst. & Gynec. 73:313,* 1957.

68. WALLIN, P., and RILEY, R. P.   Reactions of mothers to pregnancy and adjustment of offspring in infancy. *Am. J. Orthopsychiat. 20:616,* 1950.

69. WATSON, A. S.   A psychiatric study of idiopathic prolonged labor. *Obst. & Gynec. 13:598,* 1959.

70. WEIL, R. J., and TUPPER, CARL.   Personality, life situation, and communication: A study of habitual abortion. *Psychosom. Med. 22:448,* 1960.

71. WEIDORN, W. S.   Toxemia of pregnancy and schizophrenia. *J. Nerv. Ment. Dis. 120:1,* 1954.

72. WINOKUR, K. G., and WERBOFF, J.   The relationship of conscious maternal attitudes to certain aspects of pregnancy. *Psychiat. Quart. Suppl. 30:61,* 1956.

73. WOODHILL, J. M., VAN DEN BERG, A. S., BURKE, B. S., and STARE, F. J.   Nutrition studies of pregnant Australian women. Part 1. Maternal nutrition in relation to toxemia of pregnancy and physical condition of infant at birth. *Am. J. Obst. & Gynec. 70:987,* 1955.

74. ZEMLICK, M. J., and WATSON, R. I.   Maternal attitudes of acceptance and rejection during and after pregnancy. *Am. J. Orthopsychiat. 23:570,* 1953.

The Rh Problem Through a Retrospectroscope

Philip Levine Award Presentation

LOUIS K. DIAMOND, M.D.

Department of Pediatrics, University of California—San Francisco Medical Center, San Francisco, California 94143

THE HIGH HONOR of being the recipient of this award has special meaning for me. More than 30 years ago, in 1941, Dr. Philip Levine first told me about his discovery—that a previously unknown blood factor was the basis for a disease I had been much concerned with and had described in 1932 as "erythroblastosis fetalis" (E.F.).[7] With his usual generosity, he gave me some of his precious diagnostic serum. By testing our earlier patients, I was able quickly to confirm that Dr. Levine's explanation of why and how this disease of the fetus and newborn developed was indeed true. Shortly, we were able to repay with interest his gift of serum, since we had several sensitized mothers as willing donors.

A moment's reflection reveals what Dr. Levine's discovery has meant since then, to medicine, and to the health of millions all over the world. We learned how to save the lives of, and prevent serious sequelae in, thousands of infants with E.F. Transfusion therapy became much safer and is now an important adjunct to our armamentarium in every branch of medicine. The development of new testing methods in immunology has led to great advances in tissue and organ transplantation and to the understanding and control of many diseases with an immunological basis.

Received April 8, 1974; accepted for publication April 26, 1974.

(Key words: *Philip Levine Award*; Rh; Erythroblastosis fetalis; Blood group serology.)

All this from one man's scientific curiosity and careful analysis of an unusual transfusion reaction in 1939!! Since I have been closely involved with the study of Rh problems and E.F., this award named for Philip Levine has particular significance for me and I accept it with gratitude and humility, and special thanks to this Society.

On hearing that I was to be the recipient, I promptly reviewed the addresses to this Society of the previous winners. As the vaudevillians used to say: "That's a hard act to follow,"—and especially since I had not one, but four big ones preceding me. To match their scientific contributions seemed a truly formidable task. I, therefore, decided to take a different path and present a historical review—personalized and maybe slightly biased, but strictly factual—of the course and development of the knowledge of the Rh factor, including a few interesting stories—some untold, some forgotten—to illustrate certain points. If you wondered about the title, a retrospectroscope is a very useful though imaginary instrument that permits a clear look backward, avoiding magnification or diminution of past events. It requires, therefore, a cool and experienced hand to focus it.

To begin with, Levine and Stetson, in 1939,[21] in their epoch-making paper describing a severe hemolytic transfusion reaction in a woman who had recently delivered an infant, reported the discovery of a new and unusual blood-group antibody. This, they perspicaciously surmised, could have been related to the stillbirth of her infant suffering from E.F.

The momentous discovery of this new blood type reawakened an interest in the long dormant field of blood group serology, thought to be sterile by 1930, and stimulated much new research in the specialty of immunohematology. This reached undreamed of heights, leading eventually to the discovery of more than 100 new blood factors. Many proved of considerable clinical importance, and all have had value in the field of genetics. Of course, at first this new blood factor and its possible effects threw a scare into many young women who learned they were Rh negative and feared for future pregnancies. Their reaction is cartooned in Figure 1. But we reassured them that, statistically, other incompatibilities between man and wife were more troublesome than Rh incompatibility.

In addition to fetal problems involving the Rh factor, astute analyses of intragroup transfusion reactions by A. S. Wiener in 1940 and 1941[30,32] allowed many thousands of blood transfusions which previously might have had unfavorable and even dangerous results to be administered year after year thereafter.

The name "Rhesus," or Rh, was first given by Landsteiner and Wiener in 1940[15] to the factor detected by guineapig and rabbit sera following injection of Rhesus monkey blood. When they compared their results with those found by Levine with his original human antiserum, the animal reagents produced the same statistical separation of human red cells, that is, 85% positive and 15% negative reactions.[16] Thereupon, they also named the human blood factor "Rh." Years later, in 1961,[19] it became clear that the two sera were not identical and that the animal serum detected a "D-like" antigen in the Rhesus blood. By then, the large accumulation of literature made it impractical to change the name of the human antibody from "anti-Rh." The

suggestion of Levine[20] that the animal serum be called "anti-LW" in honor of Landsteiner and Wiener has been favorably received. However, the name "Rhesus factor" in human blood probably should never be dropped, if only to remind us that we are not too far removed from this animal ancestry. This, unfortunately, becomes apparent all too often in other ways.

Even before the beginning or "genesis" chapter in our Rh bible, when Levine first brought light into this dark field, we had a good lead, back in 1936, which I failed to follow through. A 3-day-old infant, with what was then called "anemia of the newborn" and "icterus gravis," was admitted and given a transfusion of his father's blood. Although this was apparently compatible, it was rapidly destroyed in the child's circulation. With recurring anemia, the baby needed three more transfusions in the following week, all provided by his father, each helping him only briefly but also making him more jaundiced. When a fifth blood transfusion seemed desirable before discharge, his mother offered to give the needed 3 ounces. Her group O blood, cross-matched in the usual way, was used. To our consternation, the infant rapidly became more anemic and much more jaundiced. Review of the cross-matching, using the usual 2% suspension of red cells in saline, showed no agglutination in the test tube of maternal serum vs. the infant's cells, but a hastily-prepared thicker red cell suspension, examined on a slide, seemed to have agglutinates. The tests were repeated with great care by a consultant working in the medical school, who was a recognized expert in blood grouping. He used the usual 1–2% saline-diluted red cells and found no suspicious clumps. When shown my questionable agglutinates in a thicker smear, he criticized such sloppy technic and advised against pursuing the matter any further. He could not explain the infant's obvious transfusion reaction ex-

LOUIS K. DIAMOND, M.D.

cept to recall he had seen one before from the use of blood from a postpartum donor and he said, "Women, especially during pregnancy, do queer things." Incidentally, he was a confirmed bachelor.

"Sic transit opportunitas gloriae" (which loosely translated means, there went my chance for fame and fortune). I did re-test this mother's serum, as well as that of another woman who had had a number of infants with E.F., but they could produce no agglutination against 2% saline-suspended red cells. Only years later did we prove that they both had high-titered incomplete Rh antibodies. How fortunate that Dr. Levine's first patient had some

IgM antibodies, the type which are active in saline! Dr. Landsteiner's meticulous technic, using saline-suspended red cells, obviously had unforeseen drawbacks.

To complete my story, the last infant did receive another large transfusion and made a good recovery. The donor was his maternal uncle. Years later we were able to prove him Rh-negative, as was the mother. Even in 1948, she had high-titered incomplete anti-Rh antibodies.

In 1945 we returned to the puzzle of why the sera of so many women who had infants with E.F. failed to agglutinate Rh positive cells. Dr. Neva Abelson of Philadelphia,[5] who was working with me, proved they had Rh antibodies that quickly clumped a thick drop of Rh-positive cells on a warmed slide. This simple slide test soon proved invaluable as a ready diagnostic measure. Shortly thereafter, Dr. Ronald Denton of Montreal,[8] then studying in our laboratory, showed that a suspension medium of plasma or, still better, easily standardized bovine albumin, yielded clear agglutination which was not produced in saline dilutions of red cells. These tests, plus the imaginative and most useful Coombs' test, opened up still wider the field of immunohematology and led to the tremendous discoveries and developments we now know so well.

In considering the chronological steps in the management of Rh problems, the progress can be divided into four stages. The first, beginning about five or six years after the discovery of the Rh factor, was the exciting revelation of its increasing complexity as to subtypes, and the advent of more accurate methods of detecting the Rh antibodies, terminated with the life-saving development of exchange transfusion via the umbilical vein.

The second advance consisted of the development of a method of measuring the progression in the fetus of hemolysis resulting from the maternal anti-Rh and prognosticating the risk of stillbirth through measurement of pigment in the amniotic fluid obtained by amniocentesis. This provided more accurate indication for the preterm delivery of an infant at risk. Later, the imaginative therapy of intrauterine transfusion helped to save the severely anemic fetus affected early in gestation.

The third and most important, truly a giant step forward was the prevention of sensitization in Rh-negative women carrying Rh-positive infants. In another generation, this may make the problems of Rh-incompatibility and E.F. truly of historical interest only.

Finally, a fourth advance is vitally important to the present generation of already sensitized persons who produce anti-Rh gamma-globulins. How can these potentially dangerous antibodies be neutralized or eradicated? Of that, I will say more anon—though not much more, I'm afraid.

I now wish to elaborate on each of these steps. Having learned how more accurately to identify Rh sensitization by slide test, albumin test, and the Coombs' test, it soon dawned on us, and several others at about the same time, that the antibody-damaged Rh-positive cells of the newborn had to be replaced by normal cells. For this, Rh-negative blood not susceptible to maternal antibody was obviously the ideal. Complete replacement or large exchange of blood, rather than small amounts of additional red cells, seemed logical. But how to do this? Had we consulted the older literature we would have learned that exchange transfusion was not a new idea. In fact, it had been done successfully by Hart in Canada in 1925.[13] It had even been attempted, though with less than happy results, several hundred years earlier. Even at that point in time the idea of replacing the bad blood of a sick person with good blood of a healthy donor seemed logical, although the latter was an animal since antibodies and species specificity had not yet been discovered. Figure 2 shows a drawing of an exchange transfusion in 1693.

In 1946, however, by a method somewhat similar to this, that is, blood-letting via a cutdown of the radial artery in a newborn while injecting Rh-negative blood into an antecubital vein, several successful exchange transfusions were performed by Wiener on infants with E.F.[31] Also in 1946, Wallerstein[29] accomplished the same results by his replacement transfusion, using the longitudinal sinus under the open fontanelle of a newborn. This was a somewhat hazardous

FIG. 1. The "Rh devil threatens pregnancy." Cartoon by Dr. C. Merrill Leister (1944).

route because of the danger of bleeding into brain structures and was soon abandoned. Our own approach was via the readily accessible umbilical vein, which seemed novel to us. Here, again, perusal of the literature would have revealed that, as early as 1919, Dr. Sidbury of Wilmington,[26] North Carolina, had shown that one could easily give blood to newborns through this large vessel.

In 1945, when Dr. Fred H. Allen, my associate in the Blood Grouping Labora-tory, and I initially tried exchange transfu-sion via the umbilical vein, we encoun-tered discouraging difficulties. We first used long steel needles, which were obvi-ously too inflexible to thread into this unpredictably meandering blood vessel. We then turned to rubber catheters but, with these, blood clotting proved to be an early problem, and systemic heparinization introduced another handicap. Fortu-nately, at about that time, our pediatric neurosurgeon, the late Dr. Franc In-

FIG. 2. Exchange transfusion, 1693, as pictured by Scultetus from G. Keynes: History of Blood Transfusion, Brit. J. Surg. V.31:1943.

graham, demonstrated, in his newly devised bypass treatment of congenital hydrocephalus, that a special polyethylene catheter implanted for months into the brain and veins of human patients as well as experimental animals was completely nontoxic and nonirritating. He was kind enough to allow us to try the plastic catheter for umbilical vein exchange transfusion and, when it proved completely satisfactory, he generously gave us several hundred feet. In fact, our good store of tested plastic catheter allowed us to distribute it among interested neonatologists for the next several years. We were thereafter truly "in business." From October 1946, Dr. Allen and I[6] had considerably less sleep but much gratification as we noted the rapidly improving survival results in liveborn infants with

E.F., not only in our own institution but everywhere.

The practical advantage of having this new tool, a nonwettable, clot-retarding plastic catheter, made the procedure of exchange transfusion fairly safe and easily learned, as its worldwide acceptance quickly proved. The performance soon became so simple that it was the handed-down task of the younger resident on the newborn service instead of the privileged operation of the consultant hematologist, or specially-trained pediatrician. Figure 3 shows the equipment as originally used.

A review of the changing mortality for E.F., from about 1942 to 1946, showed that treatment with one or more small transfusions of Rh-negative blood for developing anemia yielded about 50% recovery. With the introduction of exchange

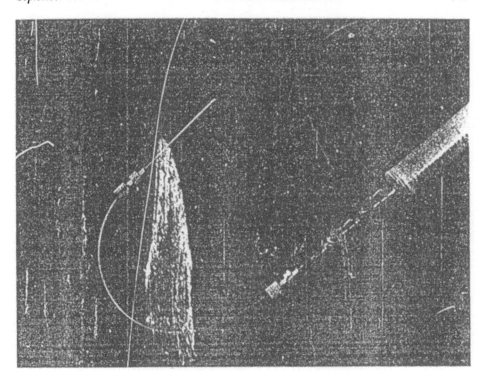

FIG. 3. Original exchange transfusion equipment using plastic catheter in umbilical vein: method of Allen and Diamond, 1946.

transfusion, at first only one per patient, the recovery rate in the following 2-1/2 years rose beyond 76% and the death rate fell from 18 to 13%. But there were still 33% E.F. infants with hyperbilirubinemia and about 10% who became the victims of kernicterus. In 1949,[1] the prevention of this dread catastrophe was achieved through the practice of multiple exchange transfusions. Through our ability to measure serum bilirubin in capillary blood samples by the method developed by David Hsia,[14] we could avoid the dangerous levels of indirect bilirubin. Series of curves were constructed that called attention to the levels of hyperbilirubinemia that usually causes brain damage, and which might indicate the need for prompt exchange transfusion. The statistical results soon supported the conclusion that

kernicterus was a preventable complication of E.F. or of any other cause of hyperbilirubinemia. The mortality for liveborn infants with E.F. now has been reduced to about 2.5%. These are mostly the edematous, severely-affected infants in heart failure at birth. Kernicterus still occurs, very occasionally, as a result of laboratory error in bilirubin measurement or unfortunate delays in treatment, but it should be entirely preventable. Figure 4 shows the changing mortality rates from 1945 to 1964.

Although the curves we prepared for unconjugated bilirubin accumulation still are generally valid, and the danger level is about 20 mg. per 100 ml. for full-term otherwise healthy infants and somewhat lower for premature or small sickly babies, it has been recognized that other factors may influence the toxicity of free bilirubin. Some of these act adversely by displacing bilirubin from its carrier albumin, thereby permitting more free bilirubin to circulate and to reach and enter nerve cells and produce toxic damage. In this category are certain drugs, steroids, and fatty acids. Other factors such as acidosis, hypoglycemia, and anoxia may alter membrane permeability or affect cell metabolism so as to allow bilirubin entry at lower levels. These various conditions are more likely to be found in the presence of infection, as well as in association with immaturity and small birth weight. Therefore, levels must be measured and followed carefully in such hyperbilirubinemic newborn infants. The level at which exchange transfusion is indicated must be lowered in the face of any of these noxious influences. A diagrammatic presentation of the pathways and factors in bilirubin metabolism and kernicterus is shown in Figure 5.

It is necessary to mention here the use of phototherapy to help reduce the levels of unconjugated bilirubin in infants with E.F. This mode of therapy has proven safe and effective in controlling the slowly increasing amounts of free bilirubin. In the face of active hemolysis, however, the rate of bilirubin degradation to a nontoxic form produced by phototherapy may be too slow to protect against a rapid rise to a dangerous level. Therefore, regular monitoring of the serum bilirubin level is necessary, even when phototherapy is used, and especially in an infant who has not had a large percentage of the Rh-positive red cells removed by an exchange transfusion.

The second challenge faced earlier by clinicians who dealt with the Rh problem was that of trying to prevent the infants exposed to potent maternal anti-Rh from succumbing to severe hemolytic disease early in pregnancy. Curiously, this does not occur much before the fifth month of

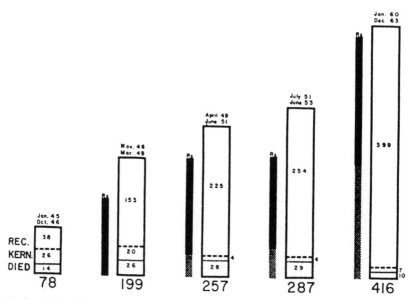

FIG. 4. Results in 1,159 liveborn erythroblastotic infants. Changing mortality rates for liveborn infants with E.F. 1945 to 1964. REC = recovery; KERN = kernicterus. Black bar = single exchange transfusion. Hatched bar = multiple exchange transfusions.

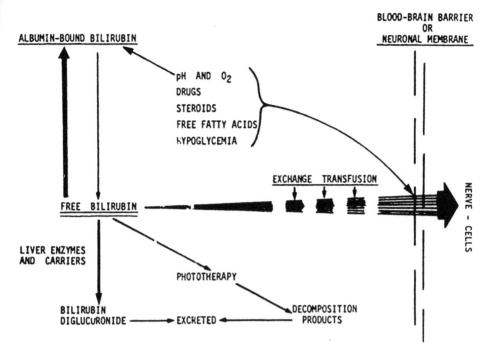

FIG. 5. Bilirubin and kernicterus: diagrammatic presentation of bilirubin metabolism and factors influencing its levels.

gestation, although the Rh-positive fetus produces red cells having Rh-antigen as early as the 8th week. But, worldwide statistics revealed that 20 to 25% of Rh-positive infants of Rh-sensitized women were likely to be stillborn in the last trimester.

The first step in attempting to salvage such infants with severe hemolytic disease was early delivery to avoid exposure to high-titered, noxious antibodies any longer than was absolutely necessary, and then the use of immediate postnatal exchange transfusion to protect the infant from further damage by the antibody. It became customary to schedule delivery at least 1 or 2 weeks before term. Maternal antibody titers were measured every week or two during the last month or more of gestation; if there was a high level or a significant rise, delivery might be advised

in the 35th to 37th week of gestation. This undoubtedly rescued some infants.

However, there were some disturbing features to this procedure. Occasionally, the titration would show little or no change, yet the infant would die *in utero* or would be seriously ill at birth. The reverse was likewise found. A marked rise in maternal antibody titer might dictate that we proceed with early delivery of a small infant, only to find very little hemolytic disease. Rarely, even an Rh-negative baby would be born, and one could only surmise there had been a nonspecific anamnestic rise in maternal antibodies. In both instances, early delivery based on antibody titers imposed the hazards of immaturity, and unnecessary premature delivery was a worrisome problem. Some better index than anti-Rh titer measurement was sorely needed.

Fortunately for E.F. babies and the continuation of our story, a solution soon appeared. In 1950, Dr. Bevis of Manchester,[2] England, had begun to study the changes in amniotic fluid and suggested that measurements of the nonhematinic iron and urobilinogen content were better prognostic indices than serum levels of maternal anti-Rh titer. In later analyses,[3] he included measurements of bilirubin pigments. In 1960, Dr. Liley[22] of New Zealand focused attention on a photospectrometric analysis of bilirubinoid pigment in the amniotic fluid and showed that this was an accurate index of the fetal hemolytic process. The peaks produced in measurements of the optical density at 450 μ were of diagnostic and prognostic value. The next year, by examination of fluids obtained by serial amniocentesis, he proved that pregnancy complicated by Rh sensitization could be managed much more precisely than ever before, as shown in Figure 6. In the effort to guide obstetricians in interpretations of amniotic fluid pigment measurements, another chart was developed by us. This suggests exactly what should be done as serial amniocenteses yield changing results, as shown in Figure 7. This complicated-looking chart probably exemplifies someone's law which holds that "simple charts, with each step in clarification, increase in complexity."

The use of intrauterine transfusion as a replacement and supportive treatment must have occurred to a number of perinatologists as they wondered how to overcome the 20% stillbirth rate in pregnancies of Rh-sensitized women. For the infant *in utero* suffering from the results of increasing hemolytic anemia beyond the capacity to compensate even by hyperactive fetal erythropoiesis, Rh-negative blood injection seemed the only logical solution. But how could this be done? As one trial, hysterotomy with extraction of a fetal limb and exchange transfusion through a delicate leg vein was done, but it proved to be technically difficult.[23] It also precipitated premature labor, and that ended that.

The older pediatricians should have had the answer, for, more than 50 years ago, before the days of sharp, fine i.v. needles, a fairly standard method of transfusing infants and small children easily was via the intraperitoneal route. In fact, the first such transfusion I witnessed was in 1926, when, as a medical student, I helped with the admission of a severely anemic post-tonsillectomy 3-year-old bleeder. Since the surface veins of this child in shock could not be entered, he was given 150 ml of freshly-drawn whole blood intraperitoneally. His recovery was prompt and uneventful. My pediatric preceptor at the time was Dr. Charles F. McKhann, one of our great teachers at the Boston Children's Hospital. He advised me to read an article on intraperitoneal transfusions he had written that year. In the midst of my busy ward service, I failed to do this and promptly forgot that experience and what I should have learned from it.

Recently, I did look up Dr. McKhann's report[24] in the old *Boston Medical and Surgical Journal*, now the *New England Journal of Medicine*, and two additional comprehensive papers on intraperitoneal transfusions by Dr. Siperstein of Minneapolis.[27] They were most interesting and informative, but now a bit too late to help me.

Even had I remembered about the old-fashioned intraperitoneal transfusion of blood, it is doubtful that I would have had the courage to try this approach to the fetus *in utero*—not being an obstetrician who is accustomed to working in the dark and depending chiefly on tactile guidance. But Liley, with his skill and vision, his knowledge of abdominal lymphatic drainage, and with a keen desire to improve the chances of the precious 10% of the most severely affected infants,

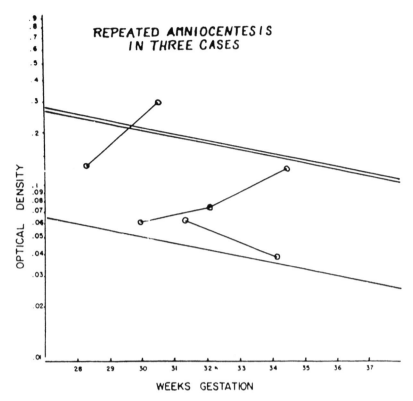

FIG. 6. Bilirubin pigment measurements charted according to method devised by W. Liley. Values below lower single line or above but decreasing with weeks of gestation indicate no danger of E.F.; values approaching upper double line suggest increasingly dangerous E.F.; values above upper double line indicate serious E.F. requiring intrauterine transfusion if earlier than 34 weeks' gestation or early delivery if after 34 weeks.

usually doomed to be stillborn, decided to try intrauterine transfusions. In 1963, Liley[10] showed how this new procedure could save seriously ill victims of E.F. Now, more than 60% of the recurrent catastrophe of stillbirth is prevented.

The third and most important part of the Rh problem can now be reviewed. The basic scientific observation, on which was eventually built one method of preventing Rh sensitization, had been described years earlier. In 1943, Levine[18] had suggested that ABO-incompatibility between the blood groups of husband and wife and between mother and infant

protected the majority of such Rh-negative mothers from Rh sensitization. He proved this beyond doubt in a statistical analysis published in 1958.[17] Speculating on this naturally-occurring protection, Finn and associates,[9] of Liverpool, in 1960 considered the possibility of mimicking it by injection of serum containing anti-Rh antibodies and proved it was effective in 1965.

At about the same time, a similar but more efficient procedure was independently developed in New York. It had been shown experimentally by Theobald Smith,[28] way back in 1909, that the pres-

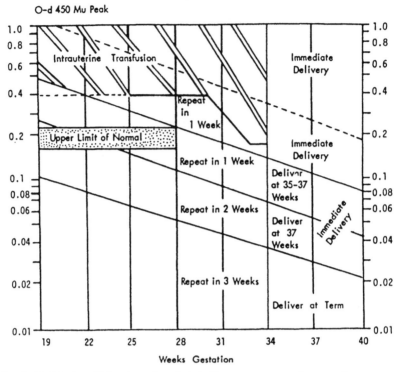

FIG. 7. Modification of Liley chart of amniotic fluid measurements and suggested management based on changes in bilirubin pigment concentration.

ence of passive antibodies prevented an antigen from immunizing an animal. Not until 1960 was this principle put to clinical use in the Rh problem by Drs. Freda, Gorman, and Pollack,[11] to protect unsensitized Rh-negative women who bore Rh-positive infants. They made this a simple and effective operation by using the gamma-globulin concentrate of dilute Rh antiserum. Their method was adopted quickly and enthusiastically by the whole world. In the past ten years, by this application of a basic immunologic principle, several million Rh-negative women have been protected against the development of Rh antibodies after bearing Rh-positive infants.

Earlier in this talk, the subject of Rh was divided into four rather than the historical and famous three parts of Caesar's Gaul. It now seems appropriate to present briefly the fourth category of problems posed by E.F. This deals with the possibility of neutralizing, or inactivating, or stopping the production of, Rh antibodies in the already sensitized women. At present there seems to be no way in which this can be done short of destroying all antibody-producing tissues, a dangerous procedure in our germ-laden, hostile environment. But such great strides have been made in the fields of immunology and immunohematology in the last decade, I feel optimistic that this goal will be reached in the not-too-distant future. There are at least three promising leads that might be pursued. In a chapter on selective immunosuppression, Dr. Robert Schwartz of Boston[25] recently described animal experiments in which the combination of a cytotoxic compound with a specific antigen could be so manipulated that antibodies to that antigen were not produced thereafter. The possibility of this being extended to pre-existent specific antibodies is challenging. A second new approach described a few months ago by Drs. Ha. Waksman, and Treffers,[12] of New Haven, was the identification of a "thymic suppressor cell," a subpopulation of thymocytes that can inhibit specific antibody production. Maybe these could be directed to act against the Rh antibody. A third possibility that cropped up years ago, then appeared to die, might be revived by modern and more sophisticated biochemical techniques. Bettina Carter,[4] of Pittsburgh, in 1956 thought she could obtain a specific extract of Rh-positive cells which, on repeated injection into sensitized Rh-negative women during pregnancy, would modify the fetal hemolytic process. Unfortunately, the material was not chemically pure, and after considerable trial, proved ineffective in a number of patients. Is it not possible, with newer methodology, that a relatively pure soluble extract of Rh-positive red cells could be obtained and used for specific neutralization of the anti-Rh antibody? Obviously, the answer to our fourth problem is not immediately at hand. Table 1 shows a summary chart of E.F. and its problems.

The moral of my stories—and I use the word in the old-fashioned sense of a lesson to be learned from past experience—might be stated as follows: First delve into history and the literature. What you are thinking of doing today may have been tried before, and you may save time and effort by continuing it,

Table 1. Summary of Problems in Hemolytic Disease of the Fetus and Newborn (Erythroblastosis Fetalis)

---

1. *Treatment of newborn:*
   a) Early delivery when indicated
   b) Exchange transfusion: R_x of acidosis, anoxia, etc.; repeat as indicated
   c) Prevent "dangerous" hyperbilirubinemia by (1) repeat ex. tx. A/O (2) phototherapy

2. *Diagnosis and treatment of fetus:*
   a) Amniocentesis: prognostic amniotic fluid pigment levels
   b) Intrauterine transfusion

3. *Prevention of blood group sensitization of mother:*
   a) From transfusion
   b) From fetal R.B.C.

4. *Neutralization of specific blood group antibodies:*
   ??? ??? ??? ???

---

more efficiently possibly, instead of having to learn anew by trial and error. As was once said: "He that would know what shall be, must consider what hath been." Next, remember that old methods may limit your horizons and fail to yield the answers you seek. Be prepared to try new approaches in order to find new solutions.

In closing, I sincerely hope that, having been present at the early recognition of the Rh problem and its relation to E.F. and having been involved to some extent in its elaboration, I will be so fortunate as to see all Rh problems finally resolved in the near future.

References

1. Allen FH, Diamond LK, Vaughan VC: Erythroblastosis fetalis. VI. Prevention of kernicterus. Am J Dis Child 80:779–791, 1950
2. Bevis DCA: Composition of liquor amnii in haemolytic disease of newborn. Lancet 443, 1950
3. Bevis DCA: Blood pigments in haemolytic disease of the newborn. J Obstet Gynaecol Br Commonw 63:68–75, 1956
4. Carter BB, Williamson AC, Loughrey J, et al: Evaluation of Rh hapten. Am J Obstet Gynecol 72:655–659, 1956
5. Diamond LK, Abelson NM: The demonstration of anti-Rh agglutinins, an accurate and rapid slide test. J Lab Clin Med 30:204–212, 1945
6. Diamond LK, Allen FH, Thomas WO: Erythroblastosis fetalis. VII. Treatment with exchange transfusion. N Engl J Med 244:39–49, 1951

7. Diamond LK, Blackfan KD, Baty JM: Erythroblastosis fetalis and its association with universal edema of the fetus, icterus gravis neonatorum, and anemia of newborn. J Pediatr 1:269–309, 132

8. Diamond LK, Denton RL: Rh agglutination in various media with particular reference to the value of albumin. J Lab Clin Med 30:821–830, 1945

9. Finn R, Clarke CA, Donohoe WTA, et al: Experimental studies on the prevention of Rh haemolytic disease. Br Med J 2:1486–1490, 1961

10. Freda VJ, Adamsons K: Exchange transfusion in utero. Am J Obstet Gynecol 89:817–821, 1964

11. Freda VJ, Gorman JG, Pollack W: Successful prevention of sensitization with an experimental anti-Rh gamma globulin. Transfusion 4:26–32, 1964

12. Ha T-Y, Waksman BH, Treffers HP: The thymic suppressor cell. J Exp Med 139:13–22, 1974

13. Hart AP: Familial icterus gravis of the new-born and its treatment. Canad Med Assoc J 15:1008–1011, 1925

14. Hsia DY, Hsia HH: Determination of concentration of bilirubin in serum. A rapid micromethod. Pediatrics 18:433–437, 1956

15. Landsteiner K, Wiener AS: An agglutinable factor in human blood recognized by immune sera for rhesus blood. Soc Exp Biol Med 43:223, 1940

16. Landsteiner K, Wiener AS: Studies on an agglutinogen (Rh) in human blood reacting with anti-rhesus sera and with human isoantibodies. J Exp Med 74:309–320, 1941

17. Levine P: Serological factors as possible causes in spontaneous abortions. J Hered 34:71–80, 1943

18. Levine P: The influence of the ABO system on Rh hemolytic disease. Hum Biol 30:14–28, 1958

19. Levine P, Celano M, Fenichel R, et al: A "D-like" antigen in rhesus monkey, human Rh positive and human Rh negative red blood cells. J Immunol 87:747–752, 1961

20. Levine P, Celano M, Wallace J, et al: A human "D-like" antibody. Nature 198:596, 1963

21. Levine P, Stetson RE: An unusual case of intra-group agglutination. JAMA 113:126–127, 1939

22. Liley AW: Liquor amnii analysis in the management of the pregnancy complicated by Rh sensitization. Am J. Obstet Gynecol 82:1359–1370, 1961

23. Liley AW: Intrauterine transfusion of foetus in haemolytic disease. Br Med J 4:1107–1109, 1963

24. McKhann CF: Intraperitoneal transfusion of citrated blood in acute intestinal intoxications of infancy. Boston Med Surg J 195:1241–1244, 1926

25. Schwartz RS: Immunosuppression: The challenge of selectivity, Immunobiology. Edited by RA Good, DW Fisher. Stamford, Conn., Sinauer Associates, 1973, chapter 24, pp 240–247

26. Sidbury JB: Transfusion through the umbilical vein in hemorrhage of the new-born. Am J Dis Child 25:290–296, 1923

27. Siperstein DM: Intraperitoneal transfusion with citrated blood. Am J Dis Child 25:202–221, 1923

28. Smith T: Active immunity produced by so-called balanced or neutral mixtures of diphtheria toxin and antitoxin. J Exp Med 11:241–256, 1909

29. Wallerstein H: Treatment of severe erythroblastosis by simultaneous removal and replacement of the blood of the newborn. Science 103:583, 1946

30. Wiener AS: Hemolytic reactions following transfusions of blood of the homologous group. Further observations. Arch Pathol 32:227–250, 1941

31. Wiener AS: The use of heparin when performing exchange transfusions in newborn infants. J Lab Clin Med 31:1016, 1945

32. Wiener AS, Peters HR: Hemolytic reactions following transfusions of blood of the homologous group. Ann Intern Med 13:2306–2322, 1940

Drugs of Abuse during Pregnancy: Effects upon Offspring Structure and Function

Joan C. Martin

Two percent of live-born infants suffer major birth defects. A far larger percentage develops minor defects and behavioral (functional) deficits that go unrecognized at the time of birth. Neel has estimated that genetic factors were responsible for 20 percent of all malformations, chromosomal aberrations for another 10 percent, leaving 70 percent of all birth defects attributable to viral agents, drugs, and other environmental stresses.[1] It is with this last and large proportion that we will be concerned, inasmuch as they are determined by the abuse of drugs during pregnancy.

A drug is any substance other than food or water that alters the functions of the body when it is absorbed. Any drug can be abused if enough of it is ingested. My discussion will be limited to widely used nonprescription drugs of abuse, and specifically, to nicotine, a central nervous system activator; a group of opiates, heroin, morphine, and methadone; and a central nervous system depressant, alcohol.

The extent of drug *use* during pregnancy has been estimated in two recent studies. A Scottish study found that 82 percent of an unselected sample of pregnant women were on some type of prescribed medication, and that 65 percent of them self-medicated.[2] When queried, 57 percent admitted to being smokers and 45 percent to using alcohol regularly. A

The preparation of this paper was supported through grants to the author from the National Institutes of Health (no. HD 07895-01), and the National Foundation March of Dimes.

1. J. V. Neel, "Some Genetic Aspects of Congenital Defects," in *First International Congress on Congenital Defects,* ed. M. Fishbein (Philadelphia: J. P. Lippincott Co., 1961).

2. J. O. Forfar and M. M. Nelson, "Epidemiology of Drugs Taken by Pregnant Women: Drugs That May Affect the Fetus Adversely," *Clinical Pharmacology and Therapy* 14 (1973): 632–42.

[*Signs: Journal of Women in Culture and Society* 1976, vol. 2, no. 2] nationwide U.S. study found that 54 percent of the Caucasians and 42 percent of blacks smoked during pregnancy.[3] Another U.S. study found that the average number of drugs taken during pregnancy was 10.3, with the range being from a low of 3 to a high of 29.[4] Obviously, many of those are necessary or useful for the health and well-being of the mother, but just as certainly, many more are not. Still another study found that 14 percent of the sample were taking appetite suppressants during pregnancy, usually one of the amphetamines.[5] Two other major U.S. studies in 1963 and 1965 found that 60–63 percent of U.S. women were drinkers and that 42 percent of these were light-moderate or heavy rather than infrequent drinkers.[6] In a sample of pregnant women whose ages ranged from fifteen to forty-nine, one study in progress classified roughly 54 percent as light to heavy drinkers, with "heavy" defined as consumption of a least one ounce of absolute alcohol daily.[7] It seems clear, then, that drug use during pregnancy is the norm, rather than the exception, at least in the United States and Europe.

Drugs and the Placenta

At the outset, it should be understood that maternal drug administration does not affect the fetus unless the placental barrier is crossed. However, "barrier" is a misnomer. One clinician has suggested that "sieve" would be a more accurate term. Almost all molecules do cross the placenta, and the rate of flow increases with placental and fetal age. A vital parameter is rate, since the agent must have a high enough concentration in maternal blood and cross rapidly enough to maintain that critical amount in the fetus or embryo that will cause defects. Factors which tend to reduce the concentration in maternal blood (such as detoxification, excretion, and tissue storage) and factors which affect placental crossing (such as electrical charge, molecular size, metabolism by the placenta, and lipid solubility) all play a role in determining the

3. K. R. Niswander and M. Gordon, "Cigarette Smoking," in *The Women and Their Pregnancies: The Collaborative Perinatal Study of NINDS* (Philadelphia: W. B. Saunders Co., 1972).

4. M. G. Horning, C. M. Butler, J. Nowlin, and R. M. Hill, "Drug Metabolism in the Human Neonate," *Life Sciences* 16 (1975): 651–72.

5. J. J. Nora, A. H. Nora, R. J. Sommerville, R. M. Hill, and D. G. McNamara, "Maternal Exposure to Potential Teratogens," *Journal of the American Medical Association* 202 (1967): 1065–69.

6. H. A. Mulford, "Drinking and Deviant Drinking, U.S.A., 1963," *Quarterly Journal for the Study of Alcoholism* 25 (1964): 634–50; and D. Cahalan, I. H. Cisin, and H. M. Crossley, *American Drinking Practices: A National Study of Drinking Behavior and Attitudes,* Monograph no. 6 (New Brunswick, N.J.: Rutgers Center for Alcohol Studies, 1969).

7. A. P. Streissguth, personal communication.

concentration of the drug which is available to fetus.[8] Some of the drugs which cross the placenta easily and which have demonstrable effects upon the fetus include nicotine, alcohol, caffeine, amphetamine, LSD, phenobarbitol, morphine, heroin, methadone, and the antihistamines. Among the prescription drugs with these qualities are androgens, estrogens, corticosteroids, cortisone, progestins, reserpine, streptomycin, sulfonamide, and the no-longer prescribed thalidomide.

Limitations of Clinical Research

Before we can consider the results of several studies which indicate the extent and kind of damage resulting from abuse of drugs, we must take into account some limitations of clinical research.

1. *Self-selection.*—As with all studies which utilize patient populations, there is no way to separate the effects of the drug from the individual taking it. For example, there is no method of determining if an affected child functions at a lower level because his mother took drugs during pregnancy or because the type of woman who takes drugs is more likely to have a poorly functioning child. Critics of the studies of smoking during pregnancy have argued that smoking does not result in prematurity and small-for-dates babies, but that women who smoke would have had small babies in any case, due to their physical and biochemical makeup.[9]

2. *Prenatal and postnatal factors.*—There is, furthermore, the impossibility of separating pre- from postnatal factors. Does an unhealthy intrauterine experience result in a poorly functioning child, or is it the poor postnatal care that such a child is likely to receive from its mother that is responsible for its lower level of functioning? Since neurological and behavioral assessments taken at birth correlate very poorly with preschool and later age behaviors, accurate prediction at birth is not possible at this time, except in the case of severe malfunction such as cerebral palsy. In animal studies, the cross-fostering technique, in which offspring from some of the treated mothers are given to control mothers and vice-versa, has been used to separate prenatal from postnatal effects. But this is usually neither legally nor morally justifiable with humans, and when an infant has been adopted it is often not possible to follow the progress of the child. Although it may be stated for an individual case that a mother took a drug during pregnancy and that her

8. S. J. Yaffe, "Fetal and Neonatal Toxicity of Drugs," *Canadian Medical Association Journal* 98 (1968): 301–6.

9. J. Yerushalmy, "Infants with Low Birth Weight Born before Their Mothers Started to Smoke Cigarettes," *American Journal of Obstetrics and Gynecology* 112 (1972): 277–84.

child is retarded or has behavioral problems, it cannot be stated that the problem was caused by the drug.

3. *Prospective human studies.*—The best possible design for human studies is the controlled clinical trial in which individuals are assigned to receive either treatment or nontreatment on a random (objective) basis. But this is legally and ethically impossible with potentially harmful agents. The selection of the control (nondrug) group becomes crucial, therefore. Ideally, one would select pregnant women who are identical to the drug group on all parameters except that they do not take the drug in question. Since it is not possible to match for all variables or, indeed, even to specify them since the group size would become unwieldy, one selects variables known to have an effect on birth outcome. Some of these maternal variables which have been shown to influence the viability, development, and later behavior of the infant include socioeconomic class, race, age, parity (number of prior pregnancies), educational level, height, and weight. The study sample is selected as early in pregnancy as practicable and followed until birth and beyond. But even with this design it cannot be said: (1) when the damage was done, since drug users have usually taken the drug prior to pregnancy as well as during it and following birth; (2) whether poor health and performance in infancy and childhood is due to drug administration, to poor maternal care, or to some interaction; (3) to what extent the drug, rather than poor antenatal habits and nutrition, contributes to the result; and (4) whether the self-selected women constitute a different population. In that case any difference between their children and those of non–drug users could be attributable to different biochemical, physiological, and psychological components and not to the drug itself.

Principles of Teratology

Teratology, from the Greek *teras, teratos* (monster), is the science of the adverse effects of environment on developing organisms, whether germ cells, embryos, fetuses, or neonates. There have been hundreds of empirical studies from this field which allow us to determine the variables relevant to the effects of drug abuse.

1. Susceptibility to an agent varies with the *gene structure* of the conceptus, and the manner in which this structure interacts with the environment. Exposure to an agent may, therefore, affect one unborn child but not another. For example, only 20 percent of the pregnant women who took thalidomide delivered a malformed child.

2. Susceptibility to an agent varies with the *stage of fetal development.* Structures which are undergoing cell differentiation and development are disproportionately affected by an agent; the most critical period for damage occurs during early fetal life, and the least critical during late

fetal life. In mammals, structural defects, such as failure of limbs to develop, cranial deficiencies, small heads or eyes, spinal deformities, etc., occur between the second and eighth weeks, when the major organ systems are developing. A later section of this paper will discuss the major defects that occur in human fetuses during this period. The subtler consequences of behavioral and growth retardation which may result when an agent is applied during the last trimester of pregnancy or when smaller amounts are taken throughout gestation are more difficult to quantify, but nonetheless exert real and lasting effects.

3. Deviant manifestations are positively correlated with *increased dosage*—that is, the higher the dose, the greater the likelihood that damage will result. For example, the recently discovered "fetal alcohol syndrome" in newborns has to date only appeared in the offspring of alcoholic women, not in those of moderate drinkers.[10] With a very high dose, death may result; with smaller doses, not death but malformation, mutation, growth retardation, and, lastly, functional (behavioral) deficits may occur. Pasamanick and his colleagues have proposed a "continuum of reproductive casuality," which hypothesizes a similar behavioral continuum.[11] Events during gestation may produce sublethal effects graded as to severity from cerebral palsy, epilepsy, and mental deficiency to emotional disorders and minor behavior problems.

4. Since *physical agents* such as X-irradiation tend to be partially screened out by maternal tissue, they tend to pose less of a threat to the health of the fetus than do chemical agents, such as heroin and nicotine, which are transported in maternal blood across the placenta with no such screening.

Human Developmental Periods

The following brief discussion of the embryology of development will set the stage for a description of selected drugs of abuse and their effects upon human intrauterine development.

1. *Preimplantation.*—This lasts from conception to six and one-half days of age. If implantation fails to occur at this time, the only visible result is a later menstrual period.

2. *Period of major organogenesis.*—This extends from the end of the second week to the end of the eighth week. It is also called the embryonic

10. K. L. Jones, D. W. Smith, C. N. Ulleland, and A. P. Streissguth, "Pattern of Malformation in Offspring of Alcoholic Mothers," *Lancet* 1 (1973): 1267–71.

11. B. Pasamanick and A. M. Lilienfeld, "Association of Maternal and Fetal Factors with the Development of Mental Deficiency. I. Abnormalities in the Prenatal and Paranatal Periods," *Journal of the American Medical Association* 159 (1955): 155–60; and B. Pasamanick, M. E. Rogers, and A. M. Lilienfeld, "Pregnancy Experience and the Development of Behavior Disorders in Children," *American Journal of Psychiatry* 112 (1956): 613–18.

period. The arm and leg buds are fully formed by days 35–37, the eyes are pigmented by day 40, sexual differentiation of the gonads has begun by day 46, and the earliest reflexes have begun by day 41. All the major anomalies which can occur happen during this period, including limb deformities, facial deformities, spinal anomalies, skeletal defects, and neural defects such as hydrocephaly (fluid accumulation in the cranium) and anencephaly (missing cerebral hemispheres and cranial vault). This is the period in which major structural damage can occur if the organism is stressed. The most vulnerable part of the embryo is that which is undergoing rapid development at the time the agent is taken. Since a woman may not suspect she is pregnant until the sixth to eighth week, particularly if her menstrual periods are irregular, the embryo is most at risk when there is the least chance of the woman's being aware of it. For example, a recent study of 19,000 women found a significant increase in the number of anomalies in human infants whose mothers had taken some of the tranquilizers (meprobamate and chlordiazepoxide) during the first six weeks of pregnancy.[12] When they began taking the same drugs later in gestation, no increase in anomalies was found.

3. *Fetal period.*—This period includes the end of the eighth week until the fortieth week, when the major organ systems have developed. The nervous system, which continues to develop during this period (as well as postnatally), is still very sensitive and may be adversely affected. By the ninth week the cerebellum is a large ball of neuroblasts. Fissures form in the midline of the cerebellum by the fourteenth week, and the first fissures of the cerebral cortex appear at five months, at which time myelination of the spinal cord begins as well. At six months of prenatal life, myelination of fiber tracts within the brain begins. Irradiation of the mother during this period has resulted in mentally retarded children with smaller than average head circumferences.[13]

Drugs of Abuse and Offspring Function

Now that we have considered some of the variables and some of the problems in this type of research, we can look more closely at three drugs of abuse and their known effects on offspring function.

1. *Nicotine and smoking.*—Nicotine, a contact poison in cigarettes, is a central nervous system activator which causes rapid increases in heart rate, blood pressure, and respiration in the smoker. It constricts the

12. L. Milkovich and B. J. Van den Berg, "Effects of Prenatal Meprobamate and Chlordiazepoxide Hydrochloride on Human Embryonic and Fetal Development," *New England Journal of Medicine* 291 (1974): 1268–71.

13. Atomic Bomb Casualty Commission, "Mental Retardation in Children Exposed in Utero to the Atomic Bomb: Hiroshima and Nagasaki," Atomic Bomb Casualty Commission Report TR no. 10-66 (Hiroshima: ABCC, 1966), pp. 1–13.

blood vessels and causes a release of adrenalin; it stimulates and then blocks chemical, thermal, and pain receptors. The effect of nicotine upon the unborn child is partially due to anoxia, because blood flow across the placenta is reduced.[14] More specifically, smoking one or two packs of cigarettes per day results in lighter weight babies,[15] an increased probability of premature births,[16] spontaneous abortions,[17] and an increase in the number of stillbirths and neonatal deaths.[18] A British study has also implicated cigarette smoking, particularly after the fourth month of pregnancy, in the offspring's retardation on reading, mathematics, and general ability tests at ages seven and eleven.[19] A much smaller U.S. study failed to find deficits in intellectual functioning at age seven, although children of smokers were growth retarded in utero and shorter in stature at one year of age.[20]

It should be emphasized that, except for the two studies described above, no long-term effects of nicotine on human offspring have been reported in the literature. Growth retardation at birth and prematurity following maternal smoking during pregnancy have been universally found in studies around the world. Since increases in neonatal deaths and continuing growth retardation and poorer intellectual functioning have been found by only one team of investigators, these results have to be considered as tentative at this time. Smoking has also been implicated in menstrual irregularities and decreased fertility, and, apparently, all risks noted above are increased if the pregnant woman is black.[21]

2. *Narcotics: heroin, morphine, and methadone.*—The narcotics and opiates cause a marked insensibility to pain without excessive drowsiness, muscular weakness, or loss of consciousness. In the central nervous system they deplete norepinephrine stores, thus allowing serotonin to

14. E. W. Wilson, "Effect of Smoking in Pregnancy on the Placental Coefficient," *New Zealand Medical Journal* 74 (1972): 384–85.

15. J. B. Hardy and E. D. Mellits, "Does Maternal Smoking during Pregnancy Have a Long-Term Effect upon the Child?" *Lancet* 2 (1972): 1332–36; and B. MacMahon, B. Albert, and E. J. Salber, "Infant Weight and Parental Smoking Habits," *American Journal of Epidemiology* 82 (1966): 247–61.

16. G. C. Downing and W. E. Chapman, "Smoking and Pregnancy: A Statistical Study of 5,659 Patients," *California Medicine* 104 (1966): 187; and H. J. Heron, "The Effects of Smoking during Pregnancy: A Review with a Preview," *New Zealand Medical Journal* 61 (1962): 545–48.

17. L. Vertes, "Schadliche Wirkungen vom Rauchen auf die Gestation" [Harmful effects of cigarette smoking on gestation], *Zentralblatt für Gynakologie* 92 (1970): 1395–98.

18. N. R. Butler, "Problems of Low Birth Weight and Early Delivery," *Journal of Obstetrics and Gynecology of the British Commonwealth* 72 (1965): 101–3; and G. W. Comstock and F. E. Lundin, Jr., "Parental Smoking and Perinatal Mortality," *American Journal of Obstetrics and Gynecology* 98 (1967): 708–18.

19. N. R. Butler and H. Goldstein, "Smoking in Pregnancy and Subsequent Child Development," *British Medical Journal* 4 (1973): 573–75.

20. Hardy and Mellits (n. 15 above).

21. M. L. E. Lubs, "Racial Differences in Maternal Smoking Effects on the Newborn Infant," *American Journal of Obstetrics and Gynecology* 115 (1973): 66–76.

exert a more pronounced effect; respiratory centers in the brain stem are depressed and death may result from an overdose. Morphine and heroin (a synthetic derivative of morphine) have similar behavioral effects. Methadone is a synthetic narcotic analgesic which is primarily used clinically in heroin detoxification or methadone maintenance programs. All cause a pharmacological blockade of the hypothalamus in chronic users. Because of its low molecular weight, heroin crosses the placental barrier and appears in fetal blood and tissue within an hour after the pregnant woman takes it.[22]

There have been a number of retrospective studies on babies born to heroin addicts.[23] Women constitute 25–50 percent of the heroin addicts in the United States, and 80 percent are of childbearing age.[24] In addition to a high prematurity and stillbirth rate, between 55 and 90 percent of all offspring develop withdrawal symptoms within twenty-four hours after birth. These include evidence of central nervous system irritability with restlessness, shrill crying, cyanosis, vomiting, diarrhea, and convulsions. The mortality rate for untreated infants who develop these symptoms is high. It should be noted that heroin addicts average less than one prenatal visit during pregnancy and have both a poor nutritional history and frequent medical problems. These factors alone would result in a poor neonatal prognosis, although not in withdrawal symptoms per se.

Studies on pregnant ex-heroin addicts being maintained and/or detoxified in methadone tratment programs are relatively recent. At least one investigator has found more severe withdrawal symptoms in the newborn infants of mothers on these programs than those on heroin.[25] Harper and others found that 94 percent of newborns whose mothers were on a methadone treatment program developed withdrawal symptoms; however, there was no increase in mortality since all of the babies were treated for withdrawal.[26] Methadone is also excreted in breast milk. Despite improved prenatal care, 86 percent of the babies

22. E. C. Gaulden, D. C. Littlefield, O. E. Putoff, and A. L. Seivert, "Menstrual Abnormalities Associated with Heroin Addiction," *American Journal of Obstetrics and Gynecology* 90 (1964): 155–60.

23. M. J. Goodfriend, I. A. Shey, and M. D. Klein, "Effects of Maternal Narcotic Addiction in the Newborn," *American Journal of Obstetrics and Gynecology* 71 (1956): 29–36; R. M. Hill and M. M. Desmond, "Management of the Narcotic Withdrawal Syndrome in the Neonate," *Pediatrics Clinics of North America* 10 (1963): 67–86; R. Stern, "The Pregnant Addict," *American Journal of Obstetrics and Gynecology* 90 (1964): 155–60; and J. F. Perlmutter, "Drug Addiction in Pregnant Women," *American Journal of Obstetrics and Gynecology* 99 (1967): 569–72.

24. J. F. Perlmutter, "Heroin Addiction and Pregnancy," *Obstetrics and Gynecology Survey* 29 (1974): 439–46.

25. C. Zelson and Lee Sook Ja, "Neonatal Narcotic Addiction: Exposure to Heroin and Methadone," *Pediatric Research* 7 (1973): 289–91.

26. R. G. Harper, G. I. Solish, H. M. Puron, E. Sang, and W. C. Panepinto, "Effect of a Methadone Treatment Program upon Pregnant Heroin Addicts and Their Newborn Infants," *Pediatrics* 54 (1974): 545–48.

were small-for-dates (weighed less than 3,000 grams). In the only study we have which examined behavior, Kron examined the sucking rates and pressures in newborns of heroin addicts and women maintained on methadone, and found that methadone offspring sucked more poorly than heroin infants.[27]

It should be remembered when comparing heroin addicts and women on methadone that women on methadone were originally heroin addicts, and thus suffered from the same lack of prenatal care. It is not clear why methadone should have a more deleterious effect than does heroin, but the studies are so incomplete at this point in time that the difference may not be a real one or, alternately, may be a function of self-selection by the sample.

3. *Depressants: alcohol.*—Alcohol is a physiological depressant which operates on the central nervous system somewhat like the barbiturates. The effects are euphoric at low doses due to disruption of the inhibitory centers in the central nervous system. With increased doses the excitatory centers are depressed as well, first in the cortex and then downward to the brain stem. Alcohol is the most abused drug in the United States, and an estimated nine million Americans are alcohol abusers as defined by the Department of Health, Education, and Welfare.[28] The government, using a quantity/frequency index, defines a heavy drinker as one who consumes at least one-half ounce of alcohol nearly every day with five or more drinks per occasion at least once in a while. In addition, an abuser experiences difficulty economically, personally, socially, or medically as a result of drinking.

A recent series of studies at the University of Washington has detailed a pattern of altered growth, morphogenesis, and mental retardation in human infants and children whose mothers were alcoholics or heavy alcohol abusers during pregnancy.[29] These children of all races were undergrown, exhibited a failure to thrive, and tended to score in the retarded range on developmental and motor tests. Some of the morphological defects included small eyes, hip dislocations, aberrant creases on the palms, and heart defects.[30] However, as yet, nothing is

27. R. E. Kron, M. Litt, and L. P. Finnegan, "Behavior of Infants Born to Narcotic-addicted Mothers," *Pediatric Research* 292 (1973): 64.

28. Department of Health, Education, and Welfare, *Alcohol and Health: First Special Report to the U.S. Congress*, DHEW Pub. no. (HSM) 72-9099 (Washington, D. C.: Government Printing Office, 1971).

29. K. L. Jones and D. W. Smith, "Recognition of the Fetal Alcohol Syndrome in Early Infancy," *Lancet* 2 (1973): 999–1001; K. L. Jones, D. W. Smith, A. P. Streissguth, and N. C. Myrianthopoulos, "Outcome of Offspring of Chronic Alcoholic Women," *Lancet* 1 (1974): 1076–78; and C. N. Ulleland, "The Offspring of Alcoholic Mothers," *Annals of the New York Academy of Science* 172 (1972): 167–71.

30. A similar study in France on 127 such births was described earlier, but apparently received little attention at that time (P. Lemoine, H. Harousseau, J.-P. Borteyro, and J.-C. Menuet, "Les Enfants de parents alcooliques: Anomalies observees, a propos de 127 cas," *Ouest Medical* 25 [1968]: 476–82).

known about the effects on offspring growth and function of women who are social drinkers before becoming pregnant and who continue to drink during their pregnancy.

Additional Questions

In addition to the numerous questions that have already been raised, there are three areas which have not been discussed and which require future investigation.

1. *Animal studies.* —The burgeoning literature on fetal anomalies in animals has barely been touched upon in this discussion. However, the majority of such studies has administered doses well above the human clinical level in order to determine the pattern of fetal anomalies which were caused by the agent. The studies which have administered doses at levels low enough to result in growth retardation or functional deficits are far fewer in number, and the types of behaviors studied have not been very applicable to human problems. The value of such research on subhuman organisms is that genetic factors can be controlled and pre- and postnatal factors can be separated if cross-fostering techniques are utilized. Perceptual deficits, problem-solving ability, ability to delay a response, timing parameters, responses to stressful stimuli, and longitudinal studies over the life span are areas which need to be examined. With a body of literature thus generated from subhuman studies, one would be better able to utilize the more poorly controlled human data and to examine the children of drug abusers for possible behavioral deficits. Studies using animals, however, obviously cannot answer all the questions which are relevant to humans.

2. *Paternal effects.*—Another virtually unexamined area is that of the effects of the father upon fetal outcome. Although many agents, including alcohol, pass into seminal fluid, few investigations on children of male smokers and alcohol users or abusers have found paternal effects once the maternal effects are omitted.[31] However, one recent German retrospective study on 5,000 males found an increase in prenatal mortality and facial deformities in newborns whose fathers smoked more than ten cigarettes daily.[32] It is to be hoped that this study will act as an impetus to more research in the area.

3. *Sex ratio changes.*—Another poorly researched area, perhaps because it is controversial, is the effect of drug abuse on the sex of the

31. T. Mann, "Effects of Pharmacological Agents on Male Sexual Functions," *Journal of Reproductive Fertility Supplement* 4 (1968): 101–14.

32. G. Mau and P. Netter, "Die Auswirkugen des vaterlichen Zigarettenkonsums auf die perinatale Sterblichkeit und die Missbildungshaufigkeit," *Deutsch Medizinische Wochenschrift* 99 (1974): 1113–18.

child.[33] An interesting Canadian study found that pregnant teenage multiple drug users delivered significantly more live-born female infants than did the teenage control group which was not on drugs. Non–drug users delivered 1.2 males to every female born, which is close to the usual U.S. ratio for normal births. The drug users, on the other hand, delivered two-thirds more females than males (sixty females and thirty-nine males). This could have been due to a number of factors, including a higher miscarriage rate for male fetuses, or a lessened probability of implantation of male blastocysts. It has been demonstrated that there is an increased risk of maternal toxemia with a male fetus, possibly due to histoincompatibility of the fetus and mother.[34] An additional stress such as excessive drug use might then be more likely to trigger an involuntary miscarriage in the case of a male fetus. This additional stress would not be present with a female fetus. Aside from this study, many provocative accounts have appeared in the literature during the past ten to fifteen years which have implicated a variety of agents: LSD,[35] oral contraceptives,[36] irradiation,[37] and methadone.[38] Although the differences do not always reach a level of acceptable statistical significance, they demonstrate a decreased number of male births. Unfortunately, in the majority of these studies, the sex ratio shift was an ancillary result in the data analysis, not the major purpose of the study. If the results above are replicable, the most parsimonious explanation is that certain agents serve to shift the probabilities very slightly in favor of fewer viable male offspring. The area is one which needs research, but until a definitive method for sex selection in utero is developed, the area will probably continue to be neglected.

Conclusion

Taken as a whole, the effects of maternal drug ingestion upon developmental, perceptual, emotional, and intellective functions of the

33. B. J. Poland, L. Wogan, and J. Calvin, "Teenagers, Illicit Drugs, and Pregnancy," *Canadian Medical Association Journal* 107 (1972): 955–58.

34. P. Toivanen and T. Hirvonen, "Sex Ratio of Newborns: Preponderance of Males in Toxemia of Pregnancy," *Science* 170 (1970): 187–88.

35. J. M. Aase, "Children of Mothers Who Took LSD in Pregnancy," *Lancet* 1 (1970): 100–101.

36. J. S. Crawford, "Prepregnancy Oral Contraceptives and Respiratory Distress Syndrome," *Lancet* 1 (1973): 858–60; and T. L. Keseru, A. Maraz, and J. Szabo, "Oral Contraception and Sex Ratio at Birth," *Lancet* 1 (1974): 369.

37. W. J. Schull, J. V. Neel, and A. Hashizume, "Some Further Observations on the Sex Ratio of Infants Born to Survivors of the Atomic Bombings of Hiroshima and Nagasaki," *American Journal of Human Genetics* 18 (1966): 328–38.

38. Harper et al. (n. 26 above).

offspring, as opposed to structural and physiological functions, have hardly been examined. This neglect has been due to a variety of factors, including the time and expense involved in such studies, the difficulties of defining a study population, and the tendency to see as normal an infant who is not structurally deformed. Since the major period of embryonic vulnerability is past before a woman discovers that she is pregnant, it is of crucial importance that agents which have detrimental effects upon infant structure and function be identified. Women of childbearing age need to be given sufficient information to enable them to make an informed decision about their drug intake.

Department of Psychiatry and Behavioral Sciences
University of Washington

Environmental pollution and pregnancy: Risks and uncertainties for the fetus and infant

LAWRENCE D. LONGO, M.D.

Loma Linda, California

Numerous environmental contaminants can affect the developing embryo, fetus, or infant. This essay explores such questions as these: What is the importance in mutagenesis and teratogenesis of macroenvironmental pollutants such as the heavy metals, dioxin derivatives, polychlorinated diphenyl compounds, and pesticides? What is the significance of microenvironmental pollutants (or social environmental factors) such as tobacco smoke, alcohol, and pharmacologic agents over which exposed individuals have considerable control? What are some of the ethical and legal implications of these toxins of which clinicians should be aware? (AM. J. OBSTET. GYNECOL. 137:162, 1980.)

INCREASINGLY we are besieged with news of environmental contaminants which threaten human health and welfare. On occasion the massive release of some heavy metal, herbicide, pesticide, or other toxin results in a virtual pandemic, affecting the lives of thousands of individuals. More frequently, perhaps, the news reports yet another chemical or food additive which is said to add to the body's burden of mutation or carcinogenesis. Some perils of the macroenvironment affect the lives of only a relatively few workers in a particular industry or chemical plant. Others place essentially everyone at risk. Still others, such as smoking, excessive alcohol consumption, or drug ingestion, are problems of the social environment and a function of individual behavioral patterns.

It is apparent that we have struck a Faustian bargain with nature. On one hand, we desire the exhilaration of technological innovation and manipulation of the environment. However, we must recognize that the technological revolution poses a sinister threat; because of the

From the Division of Perinatal Biology, Departments of Obstetrics and Gynecology and Physiology, School of Medicine, Loma Linda University.

Supported by United States Public Health Service Grant HD-03807.

The Memorial Foundation Award Thesis, presented by invitation at the Forty-sixth Annual Meeting of the Pacific Coast Obstetrical and Gynecological Society, Palm Springs, California, September 25-30, 1979.

Reprint requests: Dr. Lawrence D. Longo, Division of Perinatal Biology, Department of Obstetrics and Gynecology, School of Medicine, Loma Linda University, Loma Linda, California 92350.

associated risks and consequences, in the end we may "lose our own souls."

This long-term poisoning of America involves risk not only to the populace in general but especially to the pregnant woman, the fetus, and the newborn infant. For the clinician numerous questions arise as to the nature and extent of these risks. Specific questions for consideration include the following: (1) What are the specific pollutants of most concern? (2) What problems do these agents pose to reproductive outcome and fetal and infant growth and development? (3) How can the presence and distribution of mutagenic or teratogenic agents be most effectively monitored in pregnancy? (4) What are the threshold levels of various agents, above which there is cause for concern? (5) What are the areas of uncertainty regarding exposure limits and effects? (6) What are some of the legal issues in these matters? (7) What are some of the ethical issues? (8) To what extent should the individual obstetrician, pediatrician, or the professional societies participate in the decision-making process whereby public policy is formulated? (9) What should professional groups or individual clinicians be doing to inform patients and the public of the issues and problems involved? This essay will explore some of these issues.

General considerations

Environmental intoxicants can affect many aspects of the reproductive process in man and animals. Table I lists the spectrum of sequelae associated with exposure to various toxins. These effects include abnormalities of maternal or paternal germ cells with decreased fer-

0002-9378/80/100162+12$01.20/0 © 1980 The C. V. Mosby Co.

tility, carcinogenic, mutagenic, and teratogenic effects, subtle effects on childhood behavioral or intellectual ability, the possibility of development of malignancy, and decreased reproductive capacity. Other authors[16] have pointed out the difficulties of recognizing some late-emerging effects which may not become manifest until long after the precipitating events. Only long-term studies involving large numbers of individuals can detect such effects. Thus, one cannot conclude that if such changes are being produced they will presently be evident.

Almost any biologically active substance can behave as a pollutant. For the pregnant woman these substances act as for any other individual; however, the fetus may be more sensitive to such effects. Because the placenta is permeable to essentially everything taken into the maternal organism, the fetus is exposed despite its apparent sequestered locus within the uterus. In some instances the fetus may even concentrate toxins. The infant may acquire these hostile elements by placental transmission, from the mother's milk, by breathing, and by ingestion of contaminated foods. Pollutants can be classified in several ways. Table II presents some of the alternative ways of classifying these diverse materials.

The number of chemicals which pose a threat to the fetus or infant is staggering. As of 1977, the Chemical Abstract Service of the American Chemical Society contained over 4 million entries. Roughly 100,000 chemicals are in relatively common use and 1,000 or so new compounds are being introduced each year. The toxicity, mutagenicity, carcinogenicity, or teratogenicity of only a fraction of these substances has been investigated. To give some perspective to this problem, Table III classifies some of the most important compounds from the standpoint of the embryo, fetus, and infant, according to whether they are macroenvironmental or microenvironmental pollutants. Granted this distinction is somewhat arbitrary. However, I have tried to distinguish those contaminants of the biosphere over which individuals can exert little control from those social environmental problems over which the individual can exert control. For instance, environmental pandemics can result from massive, often accidental release of laboratory-created xenobiotics (molecules foreign to life) or radiation. In contrast, pollutants such as tobacco smoke, alcohol, drugs, etc., are usually inhaled or ingested willfully, albeit by large numbers of individuals.

Both groups of pollutants may cause problems through exposure to relatively high concentrations for short periods of time or to comparatively low concen-

Table I. Reproductive outcomes associated with parental exposure

Altered fertility pattern
Spontaneous abortion
Chromosomal abnormalities
Nonchromosomal congenital defects
Altered sex ratio
Late fetal death
Neonatal death
Low birth weight
Developmental disabilities
Behavioral disorders
Childhood malignancies
Childhood death

Modified from Sullivan, F. M., and Barlow, S. M.: Congenital malformations and other reproductive hazards from environmental chemicals, Proc. R. Soc. Lond. (Biol.) 205:91, 1979.

Table II. Classification of environmental pollutants

By scale: macroenvironmental, microenvironmental
By nature: chemical composition, physical state
By properties: solubility, dispersion rates, biodegradability
By sectors of the environment: air, fresh water, marine, land
By source: fuel combustion, industrial origin, agricultural use, domestic use, military activities
By patterns of use: industry, agriculture, home, transport, "defense"
By target: humans, livestock, nondomestic animals, crops
By effects: mutagens, teratogens, carcinogens

Modified from Holdgate, M. W.: A Perspective of Environmental Pollution, Cambridge, 1979, Cambridge University Press.

Table III. Environmental pollutants

Macroenvironmental:
  Heavy metals: mercury, lead, cadmium, nickel
  Chlorinated dibenzo-p-dioxins: TCDD
  Polychlorinated and polybrominated biphenyls: PCB, PBB
  Organochlorine pesticides
  Polycyclic aromatic hydrocarbons
  Air pollutants: carbon monoxide, ozone
  Radiation
Microenvironmental (social environmental):
  Tobacco smoke: carbon monoxide, nicotine, polycyclic aromatic hydrocarbons
  Alcohol
  Drugs: opiates, barbiturates, anesthetics, sex steroids
  Food additives

trations over long durations. In fact, this latter condition of long-term exposure to low concentrations of various compounds probably poses the greatest threat to the pregnant mother and her fetus.

Heavy metals: Mercury, lead, cadmium

Although it is generally believed that most heavy metals cause embryotoxicity, only mercury, lead, cadmium, and possibly nickel and selenium have been implicated in this regard. Perhaps one of the earliest

May 15, 1980
Am. J. Obstet. Gynecol.

instances of massive, unplanned exposure of a localized population to an environmental intoxicant occurred in 1953, in and around Minamata, a town located on a bay in southern Japan. Strange neurological manifestations, including mental confusion, convulsions, and coma, began afflicting villagers. About 38% of affected individuals died.[44] From 1953 to 1971, almost 700 cases were reported, including children, and many infants were born with brain damage (for review see reference 48). During the 4 years commencing in 1955, 6% of the children born in this area developed cerebral palsy. Other neurological symptoms included chorea, ataxia, tremors, seizures, and mental retardation. Most of the mothers lacked the typical symptoms of Minamata disease. The fact that these infants had not ingested contaminated fish suggests mercury transmission to the fetus across the placenta, perhaps augmented by breast-feeding following delivery.

Local animals and waterfowl were also affected, and experiments showed that the condition could be produced by feeding fish or shellfish from the bay to animals. The marine creatures were discovered to contain high concentrations of methyl mercury. Eventually the source of the mercury was traced to the effluent discharged from a local plastics factory into Minamata Bay. In 1964, an epidemic similar to that in Minamata occurred in Niigata, Japan.[76, 92] As in the Minamata outbreak, the source of methyl mercury was traced to fish contaminated from industrial discharge.

A massive methyl mercury disaster occurred in Iraq during the winter of 1971 and 1972 with over 6,000 victims and almost 500 deaths. Barley and wheat grain treated with methyl mercury as a fungicide had been purchased from Mexico. The grain sacks carried a written warning—in Spanish. In addition to planting the grain, many Iraqi farmers used it for making bread. During this epidemic, 31 pregnant women were hospitalized with mercury poisoning and almost half of them died. The mercury concentration in the infants' blood and mothers' milk paralleled concentrations in the maternal blood. Infants born prior to the epidemic but breast-fed during the outbreak had mercury concentrations less than or equal to maternal values. Infants born during the epidemic had blood mercury concentrations generally greater than those of the mother. A number of infants in both groups showed evidence of cerebral palsy, blindness, and severe brain damage. Similar outbreaks on a smaller scale have also occurred in Russia, Sweden, and elsewhere.[48]

Mercury presents a particular hazard to the fetus, as it is concentrated in fetal blood and in brain tissue. For instance, methyl mercury concentrations in the fetal brain are twice those in the maternal brain under steady-state conditions.[72]

Lead toxicity has long been known to be associated with abortion and menstrual disorders.[78, 85] Evidence as to whether lead is teratogenic is conflicting; some authors report a correlation between atmospheric lead levels and congenital malformations,[33] while others deny these associations.[18] In sheep, prenatal lead exposure has also been shown to affect the offspring's learning ability.[14, 93] Lead is also secreted in breast milk, resulting in paralysis and other neurological deficits in animals so exposed.[64] A lethal lead poisoning epidemic in Thailand, in 1977, was traced to the use of slag from a battery plant as road fill and as schoolyard surfacing.

Several other heavy metals probably affect the fetus and infant. Cadmium, for example, is discharged into sewage systems by the electroplating industry and into air by deterioration of rubber tires. As a constituent of tobacco smoke, cadmium has long been a known cause of developmental malformation in rodents.[26] Exposure of mice to low concentrations of this element (10 to 40 parts per million) results in varying degrees of growth retardation.[96] This may be one of the factors resulting in infants who are small for gestational age born to mothers who smoke.

Cadmium, which appears to have a particular affinity for the placenta,[73] is also associated with destruction of the fetal portions in rats and fetal death. Also, in rats, nickel in low doses without apparent effect on the mother causes embryotoxicity,[88] and even exposure for a few minutes early in gestation can produce eye malformations in the progeny.[87] Selenium is also a suspected teratogen.[77]

The placenta has been proposed as a readily available tissue which might reflect integrated exposure to environmental heavy metals over a period of several months. For instance, placental mercury concentrations correlate fairly well with both maternal and fetal blood concentrations in humans[7] and rats.[39] Placental lead concentrations tend to be higher in those pregnancies associated with increased perinatal deaths.[98] To what extent placental function is altered by these elements and whether the placenta can truly serve as a marker organ, reflecting long-term exposure, remains to be determined.

Chlorinated dioxin derivatives

Serious health hazards have also been caused by toxic trace impurities present in widely used commercial chemicals. For instance, the chlorinated dibenzo-p-dioxins (particularly 2,3,7,8-tetrachlorodibenzo-p-dioxin or TCDD), which are among the most toxic substances known, occur as contaminants in many substances, including herbicides and the wood preservative pentachlorophenol.

Following widespread spraying of the countryside in Vietnam with the herbicide Agent Orange (a combination of 2,4-D and 2,4,5-T), reports of an increased incidence of abortion, stillbirth, and malformation appeared.[66] Recently many Vietnam veterans have claimed that they have developed cancer or sired children with birth defects as a result of their own exposure to this chemical.[34] In Seveso, Italy, in 1976, an explosion at a chemical factory dispersed TCDD over a wide area, especially the villages downwind, with a total population of about 100,000 individuals. The extent to which abortions and malformations increased as a result of this incident remains controversial.

During the early part of this decade large quantities of 2,4,5-T were sprayed in parts of Oregon to increase the productivity in commercial forests. In the town of Alsea eight women, after comparing notes in 1978, reported to the Environmental Protection Agency that among them they had suffered 13 spontaneous abortions during the previous 5 years. A subsequent EPA study, completed early in 1979, not only demonstrated an increased abortion rate throughout the spraying area but also showed that most of these miscarriages had occurred in the months of June and July, just after the peak spraying period of March and April.[23] Breast milk of women in Alsea and the surrounding area also contained significant dioxin concentrations.

Dioxin derivatives are potent teratogens in experimental animals,[22, 69] including primates. Rhesus monkeys 20 to 40 days pregnant (total gestation about 167 days) exposed to TCDD at levels resulting in placental and fetal concentrations measured in parts per trillion showed a marked increase in the rate of abortion[56] and birth defects, particularly cleft palate and kidney abnormalities.[94] Other studies demonstrate a significant concentration of these compounds in the fat of beef grazed on dioxin-sprayed rangelands. Unfortunately, almost nothing is known about the biochemical basis for the toxicity of these agents, nor have safe or "threshold" levels been established.

Polychlorinated and polybrominated biphenyls

Polychlorinated biphenyls (PCBs), used as plasticizers and heat-exchange fluids, comprise another group of chemicals endangering health. In Kyushu, Japan, in 1968, ingestion by pregnant and nursing women of cooking oil contaminated with PCBs resulted in small-for-gestational age infants with dark, cola-colored skin, eye defects, and other abnormalities.[13, 49, 81, 81a]

Some affected infants later displayed premature tooth eruption and gingival hypertrophy.[79] Some breast-fed infants developed hypotonia and apathy and appeared "sullen and expressionless."[63] Subsequent studies in humans suggest that transfer of PCBs via breast milk is probably more important than placental transfer.[1, 61, 99]

Polybrominated biphenyl (PBB), produced commercially as a fire-retardant, is a bromine analogue of PCB. In Michigan, in 1973 and 1974 PBBs were packed in bags mistakenly identified as a component of cattle feed.[13, 28] This led to the death or forced slaughter of over 30,000 cattle, along with large numbers of sheep, swine, and poultry. Although contamination of meat, milk, and eggs was demonstrated and the incidence of stillbirth increased among cattle which had consumed contaminated feed,[11, 62] adverse effects on human pregnancy have not been reported. However, the final word is not in. Because public health authorities were long unaware of the danger and persistence of PBBs, carcasses of contaminated cattle were used as pig food, and manure containing the substances was used as fertilizer. What began as a relatively localized outbreak confined to several hundred farms rapidly became a pandemic affecting the health of the entire state.

Pesticides

According to the EPA about one third of the 1,500 active ingredients of registered pesticides are toxic and one quarter are mutagenic and carcinogenic.[82] Although the agency has established limits on the amounts of pesticide residues in food, it has restricted the use of only five: heptachlor, Chlordane, DDT, Mirex, and DBCP. Once into the food chain these pesticides are almost impossible to eliminate. They may result in sterility and birth defects, and toxaphrene, one of the most widely used chlorinated insecticides, is highly mutagenic.[36] The effect of exposure to low concentrations of these toxins not only is unknown but also is difficult to investigate because of the problem of finding pesticide-free control populations. Chlorinated hydrocarbons such as benzene hexachloride are transmitted readily in breast milk.[8, 100]

Some of these agents act as esterase (i.e., acetylcholinesterase) inhibitors. Despite literally mountains of evidence that these substances produce manifold problems, little work is being carried out on the less obvious effects on the developing organism. For instance, even a single exposure to some common organophosphate pesticides (such as malathion, parathion, Mipofax) can alter brain electrical activity for years.[23] One must wonder at the effects of long-term exposure to esterase inhibitors on the developing brain. Some preliminary studies suggest altered learning patterns and behavior.

Air pollutants

Chemicals which commonly pollute the atmosphere include sulfur dioxide, the oxides of nitrogen, carbon monoxide, unburned hydrocarbons, ozone, lead, and cadmium. Of this group carbon monoxide is the pollutant of most importance during pregnancy, but several others have been implicated. Because maternal smoking unquestionably presents the greatest exposure of the developing organism to carbon monoxide and polycyclic aromatic hydrocarbons, these substances will be considered at greater length in the section on smoking (see below).

Carbon monoxide. Carbon monoxide constitutes a growing menace to the human organism because of air pollution resulting from industry and vehicular traffic. Ambient carbon monoxide concentrations in major urban areas and near some industrial plants not uncommonly reach 50 parts per million (ppm), as compared with "mean" urban concentrations of 3 to 10 ppm and "fresh air" concentrations of 0.1 to 0.5 ppm. These highest urban carbon monoxide levels can produce blood carboxyhemoglobin concentrations of 4% to 6%, concentrations equivalent to smoking one pack of cigarettes per day. Because carboxyhemoglobin concentrations of 4% to 5% are associated with alterations in mental, visual, and other functions (for review see reference 19), these levels can no longer be considered innocuous for the developing fetus, particularly when one remembers that under steady-state conditions, the fetal carboxyhemoglobin concentration exceeds that of the mother by 10% to 15% and that the oxygen tensions of fetal arterial blood are much lower than corresponding levels in the adult.[51]

A contemporary development which gives cause for concern is the possible excessive exposure to carbon monoxide of individuals waiting in "gas lines" while the engines in nearby cars continue to run. Several cases of acute carbon monoxide poisoning under such circumstances have occurred in the Los Angeles area, and for the pregnant mother and fetus, such exposure is particularly hazardous.[51]

Ozone. A bluish gas which comprises part of the atmospheric mantle between 10,000 and 50,000 m above the earth (and absorbs considerable ultraviolet radiation), ozone (O_3) is a powerful oxidizer. Continued human exposure to concentrations greater than 1 ppm is considered hazardous, and irritation of the respiratory tract and eyes and other symptoms can follow smaller dosages.

The peak ozone concentrations allowed for industrial workers by the Occupational Safety and Health Administration is 0.3 ppm for up to 2 hours. In some areas (such as Los Angeles) ozone concentrations greater than 0.1 ppm result in several stages of "alerts" for susceptible population groups. During recent years, with increasing long-range jet flights at high altitudes, aircraft crews and passengers have been reporting severe symptoms traceable to ozone concentrations as high as 1.2 ppm, four times the peak level set by OSHA. Ozone is a mutagen known to cause biochemical alterations in the blood of exposed individuals. Some flight attendants have claimed that their higher rate of spontaneous abortion and birth defects results from ozone exposure.

Other chemicals

Numerous chemicals of a diverse nature are known mutagens or have demonstrated such potential.[3] Because of limited space only a few will be considered. Vinyl chloride, a potent mutagen acting through the male partner, may be responsible for excessive perinatal deaths and congenital malformations among the wives of workers exposed to this chemical.[40] Hexaclorophene is well known for its ability to produce short-term, reversible neurotoxic effects in newborn infants cleansed with this agent. More recently the topical use of hexachlorophene by pregnant women has been implicated as a cause of birth defects,[16] although there is some dispute regarding the exact risk. Nitrosamines are widely distributed mutagens and carcinogens. A study sponsored by the National Science Foundation reports the presence of N-nitrosodimethylamine (NDMA) in six of seven Scotch whiskeys and in 18 brands of beer. Because the concentration of this substance is somewhat higher in beer than in Scotch, and most individuals drink more of the former than the latter, beer probably constitutes the greatest hazard to the pregnant woman from this mutagen. (Of course, this does not consider the problem of the amount of ethanol ingested [see below].) Numerous other substances, including analine, benzene, carbon disulfide, nitrobenzene, toluene, and turpentine, are considered hazardous during pregnancy.[86] Although any pregnant woman may come in contact with these compounds, the greatest hazard occurs from occupational exposure. In addition, the usually accepted allowable concentrations should not be considered safe for the pregnant worker,[6] as the threshold limit values usually set by industrial hygienists do not consider the reproductive hazard. A recent publication, "Guidelines on Pregnancy and Work," published by the American College of Obstetricians and Gynecologists,[2] considers the reproductive effects of chemical hazards on the pregnant woman.

Radiation

The effects of radiation on fertility, embryogenesis, and fetal development are well documented.[13, 45, 83] For instance, large doses can produce mutations in germ cells and microcephaly and mental retardation in the fetus. An absorbed dose of 10 rads by the fetus at any time during gestation is considered a practical threshold for the induction of congenital defects.[13] The National Council of Radiation Protection and Measurement has recommended a maximal dose equivalent to 0.5 rem to the fetus from occupational exposure of pregnant women.[74] The absorption of normally occurring background radiation is not believed to be a factor in the "normal occurring" incidence of congenital malformations, growth retardation, or fetal death.[13]

Following the series of atmospheric nuclear tests during the 1950s and 1960s, a relationship between such tests and infant death was surmised.[84] During the ensuing controversy over this relationship the difficulty of confirming or refuting the hypothesis of this effect became evident, and many authorities regarded these background radiation effects as of little concern. Recently, however, it has been discovered that radiation levels may be abnormally high in some localities. For instance, in Sweden, concrete made from alum shale has been found to contain radium and other radionuclides. Houses built of this concrete, or on the shale itself, contain relatively high levels of radon, and this is aggravated by lower than normal ventilation rates since the energy crisis.[9] In parts of Colorado, uranium slag has been used for building roads and house foundations. For the past 25 years the Tennessee Valley Authority has been selling radioactive slag to companies for fabricating cinder blocks used to construct homes and schools throughout the South, East, and Midwest. In Colorado, Utah, New Mexico, and other states, some drinking water contains radioactive elements leached by the rains from uranium mine tailings, exposing those who drink this water to excessive radiation doses.[80] Although most health experts are concerned about the number of individuals who will develop cancer from this excessive radiation exposure, the possibility of embryonic and fetal effects must not be overlooked.

Tobacco smoke

During the past decade considerable evidence strongly corroborates findings of the 1960s that cigarette smoking during pregnancy has a significant and adverse effect upon the well-being of the fetus and the newborn infant and on the subsequent development of the child (for review see reference 31). Adverse effects on pregnancy include increased rates of spontaneous abortion, bleeding disorders during pregnancy, and spontaneous rupture of the membranes. Fetal deaths, preterm births, and neonatal deaths have increased significantly. In addition, retardation in fetal growth is evident in birth measurements of lower mean body weight, shortened body length, and smaller head circumference as well as evidence of pathologic changes in the placenta. Also there is an increase in the number of problems of adaptation during the neonatal period and in sudden infant death syndrome. Finally, there is suggestive evidence of long-term impairment in physical growth, diminished intellectual function, and deficiency in behavioral development for those babies who survive the first 4 weeks of life. The children of smoking mothers apparently do not catch up with the offspring of nonsmoking mothers in the various phases of development.[31]

Tobacco smoke contains several thousand compounds, including carbon monoxide, oxides of nitrogen, ammonia, polycyclic aromatic hydrocarbons, hydrogen cyanide, vinyl chloride, and nicotine. For the pregnant woman and fetus the most important of these probably are nicotine, carbon monoxide, and the polycyclic aromatic hydrocarbons.[63]

Nicotine. Nicotine is similar to acetylcholine in its effect on both sympathetic and parasympathetic ganglia and on skeletal muscles, as well as on the central nervous system. At all three sites it first stimulates, then depresses. Minute doses of nicotine stimulate the chemoreceptors of the carotid and aortic bodies, causing reflex hypertension. Nicotine also releases epinephrine from the adrenal medulla, thereby producing cardiovascular changes. Thus, it can produce widely differing effects, depending upon the dosage and the particular site that is most sensitive to stimulation.

Studies demonstrate that repeated injections of nicotine into pregnant rats result in decreased fetal weight[10] and prolonged gestation.[39] Nicotine rapidly crosses the placenta[90] to affect the fetus. In some respects its main effects are on the vascular system. In chronically catheterized pregnant sheep, administration of pharmacologic doses of nicotine resulted in a 44% decrease in uterine blood flow and a 200% increase in uterine vascular resistance associated with a doubling of plasma epinephrine and norepinephrine concentrations.[76] Relatively mature rhesus monkey fetuses respond to nicotine infusion with a rise in blood pressure, bradycardia, acidosis, hypercarbia, and hypoxia.[59] Maternal nicotine administration in rats also has been shown to affect the fetal central nervous system and its response to electrical stimulation during the newborn period.[38, 60]

Carbon monoxide

As noted above, blood carboxyhemoglobin concentrations of 4% to 5% are associated with numerous physiologic alterations in adults.[19] Cigarette smoking raises the blood carboxyhemoglobin concentration 4% to 5% per pack smoked per day. Although carbon monoxide diffuses across the placenta relatively slowly (the half time equals 1.5 to 2 hours[34]), fetal carboxyhemoglobin concentrations reflect those of the mother and under steady-state conditions are 10% to 15% higher than maternal levels.[51] Elevated carboxyhemoglobin concentrations in the fetus are associated with decreased fetal blood oxygen tensions. For instance, at carboxyhemoglobin concentrations of 10%, the oxygen tension of the fetal descending aorta decreases to about 16 torr from a control value of 21 torr.[52] These decreased oxygen tensions are associated with a redistribution of fetal blood flow to the brain, heart, and adrenal glands, as during hypoxia from low oxygen mixtures.[53]

Exposure of rabbits[5] and rats[27] to carbon monoxide during gestation resulted in decreased fetal weights and increased perinatal mortality rates. Such animals exposed to carbon monoxide showed less activity[27] as well as decreased lung weights and decreased concentrations of brain protein, deoxyribonucleic acid, and the neurotransmitters norepinephrine and serotonin.[30]

The effects of nicotine on the fetus occur rather rapidly, whereas those of carbon monoxide are slower in onset but probably persist longer. The final common pathway of carbon monoxide insult to the developing fetus is cellular hypoxia.

Polycyclic aromatic hydrocarbons

Other widely distributed mutagens and carcinogens are the polycyclic aromatic hydrocarbons (PAH) such as benzo(a)pyrene. These substances, which are produced by incomplete combustion of organic material, are ubiquitous in the atmosphere, presumably as a result of forest fires. They are also important constituents of tobacco smoke and are produced during the cooking of some food (such as barbecuing meat). Exposure of cells to PAH induces the enzyme aryl-hydrocarbon hydroxylase which, as its name implies, hydroxylates polycyclic aromatic hydrocarbons following exposure to these compounds. The inducibility of this enzyme

system has been used by some workers to demonstrate indirectly that benzo(a)pyrene and other polycyclic hydrocarbons reach the placenta and fetus.

The placental concentration of benzo(a)pyrene is highly correlated with the amount which a pregnant woman smokes.[67, 75] In pregnant rats exposed to this substance higher doses were required to induce enzyme activity in the fetus as compared with the dose required to stimulate placental enzyme activity,[97] suggesting that the placenta may protect the fetus from these substances. However, the placenta is not impermeable to benzo(a)pyrene.[79] The placenta is involved in complex hormonal interrelations between mother and fetus, and oxidative enzyme pathways in the placenta are important in maintaining hormonal and nutrient balance for normal fetal development. The hydroxylation of polycyclic hydrocarbons and the active transport of various compounds by trophoblast cells may share common enzyme systems. Thus, the induction of various enzymes by polycyclic hydrocarbons may interfere with normal transport systems.

An additional consideration is the effect of maternal administration of these agents as a carcinogenic risk for progeny. The offspring of mice that had been injected with benzo(a)pyrene late in gestation showed a high incidence of neoplasms of the lungs, liver, and mammary glands.[71]

Alcohol

Although the teratologic effects of alcohol have been suspected for many years, only during the past decade has a distinct dysmorphic condition been associated with maternal alcoholism during pregnancy.[42, 50] The "fetal alcohol syndrome" phenotype is characterized by a wide spectrum of abnormalities that affect the infant for life. These can be grouped into several categories.[17] The central nervous system dysfunctions include mental retardation, hypotonia, irritability in infancy, hyperactivity in childhood, short attention span, and microcephaly. Growth deficiencies include more than two standard deviations below normal for length and weight and diminished adipose tissue. Characteristic facial abnormalities include small eyes, short palpebral fissures, short upturned nose, hypoplastic philtrum, hypoplastic maxilla, thinned upper lip vermillion, and micrognathia.[17] Although the frequency of this condition is not known, and probably varies among different groups, it is estimated at between one and two per 1,000 live births, with the frequency of partial expressions between three and five per 1,000 live births. Fetal alcohol syndrome is the third most common recognizable cause of mental deficiency.[17]

Physiologic studies indicate that alcohol infusion into

the maternal rhesus monkey results in fetal hypotension, tachycardia, and acidosis.[37] This acidosis is associated with a shift in the oxyhemoglobin saturation curve with decreased oxygen available for transport[38] and alterations in fetal brain electrical activity.[37]

Yet to be determined is the risk to a woman, given a specific drinking history, of producing an infant with fetal alcohol syndrome. Some other problems to be explored include the risks of binge drinking as opposed to daily alcohol consumption in producing the phenotype; the dose-response relations; the interactions with smoking, coffee drinking, or drug ingestion in altering or potentiating the effects of alcohol; and the exact mechanisms whereby alcohol or its metabolites produce their effects on the embryo or fetus.

Pharmacologic agents

With the 1960 to 1961 epidemic of congenital malformations traced to the use of thalidomide, it became apparent that agents other than radiation, rubella virus, and some potent chemicals could be teratogenic. Since then a whole science of teratoepidemiology[46] has developed. Despite initial hopes that most congenital disorders could be accounted for on a drug basis, few such drugs have been implicated (for review see reference 46). Folate antagonists are highly embryotoxic and can cause numerous structural and functional disorders. Maternal ingestion of steroid hormones with androgenic activity induces virilization in female infants, and diethylstilbesterol use can result in vaginal or cervical adenocarcinoma in mature offspring.[32] Anticonvulsant agents such as phenytoin and phenobarbitol are teratogenic and may act synergistically. Anesthetic gases have been implicated as a cause of infertility, spontaneous abortion, and congenital malformation in operating room personnel.[4, 20, 47] In fact, a study by the American Society of Anesthesiologists concluded that the problem was serious enough to warrant exclusion of all pregnant women from operating rooms.[21] Other studies suggest "strong associations" between certain analgesics and anesthetics given during labor and delivery and developmental problems in children.[12] For instance, it is suggested that medications used routinely in many obstetrics units result in subtle intellectual and behavioral alterations. The opiates heroin and methadone have been widely indicted as being teratogens, but this question remains unsettled. Finally, a number of drugs may be behavioral teratogens.[45]

Future problems for consideration

To a great extent pollution of the air we breathe, the water we drink, and the food we eat results from technological innovation. The elimination of this contamination can come only as a result of further technological progress. However, we cannot deceive ourselves that continued industrial development and advancement of civilization will not bring with it a whole new set of complicating problems which, in turn, will require still further solutions. This portends an endless cycle.

The amelioration of pollution of the macroenvironment appears beyond the power of any individual health worker and to a certain extent must be left to legislators, environmental engineers, and economists. In contrast, the elimination of the microenvironmental pollutants such as smoking and alcohol and drug consumption can be sought by individual physicians, nurses, or other health professionals. Obviously, however, such effort requires a favorable set of circumstances, including access to information on the magnitude and seriousness of the problem, personal conviction of the risks posed, and willingness to educate individual patients and the public as to the relevant facts and their meaning.

In addition to technology or education, a number of transtechnical or metaphysical problems require consideration. Several examples of the issues which I have in mind are presented below. These questions will necessitate considerable thought by wise individuals of broad expertise and hopefully will stimulate the dialogue required for their solution.

The New Jersey Supreme Court recognized the right of a woman to sue her obstetrician for failure to inform her of the availability of amniocentesis to evaluate the risks of bearing an infant with Down's syndrome and thus for "wrongful birth."[11] What is the liability of a physician who fails to warn a patient of the hazards which tobacco, alcohol, or drugs present to her unborn child? Will it be long before the courts decide that, indeed, providing such information constitutes the standard of medical practice? Might a fetus so damaged but born alive sue for "wrongful life"?

Under the abortion laws set forth by the Supreme Court the fetus is not regarded as a "person" and, therefore, has no rights. However, some states are beginning to carve out exceptions to this ruling, based on the concept that for purposes of confirming wrongful death the fetus is a "person." In addition, several groups are seeking to strike down the present abortion laws and give the fetus status as a sentient being with personal rights. If this in fact does become more commonly accepted, might not counsel, acting for the fetus, sue for wrongful death in instances of abortion, or could not the fetus sue for death resulting from any of the aforementioned hazards?

A case for perhaps more immediate concern is the

individual who develops hyperkinesis or mental retardation from maternal smoking, drinking, or ingesting some drug. A "fetus" who later becomes a person may seek redress. Thus, what are the risks to the pregnant woman of suit from her own child for actions which she has taken that caused harm to that child? Although few would object to a woman's taking risks for herself, has she the right to make the choice for her fetus?

In Massachusetts an unwed father attempted to prevent the mother of his unborn child from undergoing therapeutic abortion. This action failed because of the Supreme Court decision as to the rights of a woman to exercise control over her own body. However, this raises questions concerning the role of a father in preventing injury by maternal actions to his child in utero. For instance, can a father obtain an injunction to enjoin a mother not to smoke, drink, or ingest drugs during gestation?

And what about the state? For those individuals born with severe mental retardation, cerebral palsy, or other disorders, the state must provide prolonged, often continuous, support either at the patient's domicile or in an institution. In an era of increasing state regulation of individual liberties, is it too heretical to consider a time when the state might decree against (or even incarcerate) a recalcitrant mother to prevent purported injury to a fetus, so that it would not have to incur the liability of a lifetime of maintenance and institutionalization for that child?

What of the industries which manufacture products potentially harmful to the fetus or newborn infant? A group of women who developed vaginal adenocarcinoma as a consequence of their mothers' having taken diethylstilbesterol sued several pharmaceutical companies which manufactured that drug. Ultimately the case was dismissed from the courts because the women could not establish that any particular company produced the compound which their mothers took. Nonetheless, the question remains: To what extent does an individual harmed by "wrongful death" or maimed for life have the right to bring suit against tobacco companies, distilleries, or drug companies for injuries inflicted by their products?

Recent ruling requires that cigarettes and their advertising carry warnings to the effect that smoking may be dangerous to the individual user's health. Legislation is pending for similar warnings on alcoholic beverages. In view of the risks involved, is it not reasonable to extend these warnings to the pregnant woman and the child she carries?

And what of the female industrial worker who may be exposed to chemicals particularly toxic to a developing fetus? At a Willow Island, West Virginia, chemical factory a group of young women voluntarily underwent surgical sterilization to eliminate permanently their child-bearing potential. They did this so that they could hold jobs requiring exposure to lead dust, which of course presented risks not only to themselves but to an unborn child. With increasing opportunities to hold jobs previously open only to men, women face the dilemma of "equal rights" versus the potential risks to an early gestation. Thus, some women are opting to eliminate their child-bearing potential to meet the demands of industry and governmental regulations as well as the demands of their own conscience. Is there no other course for them to take?

In addition, I wonder why it is that many women's groups, while showing legitimate concern for the individual rights of women, have demonstrated so little concern for their health and responsibilities to themselves (avoiding injurious practices) or, more particularly, to the well-being of the children they bear?

Finally, what about physicians, nurses, and other health professionals? Although smoking by men and physicians has decreased somewhat, it has increased among women and nurses (among both male and female teenagers it has increased alarmingly).

What is the role of health professionals in informing and adjuring the public and, in particular, pregnant women of the risks of smoking, drinking, drugs, etc.? What is the role of professional societies in developing effective means to set forth the facts objectively for consideration by the public? Indeed, should professional societies take a stand on these issues?

Obstetricians, pediatricians, other clinicians, and health professionals may believe that concern with such matters lies outside their purview or that the problems are simply too overwhelming for any individual to deal with. To such may I recall the words of the *Talmud*: "It is not for you to complete the task, but neither have you the right to desist from it" (Aboth 2:16).

REFERENCES

1. Allen, J. R., Barsotti, D. A.: The effect of transplacental and mammary movement of PCB's on infant rhesus monkey, Toxicology **6:**331, 1976

2. The American College of Obstetricians and Gynecologists: Guidelines on Pregnancy and Work, Chicago, 1977, United States Department of Health, Education, and Welfare.

3. Ames, B. N.: Identifying environmental chemicals caus-ing mutations and cancer, Science 204:587, 1979.
4. Askrog, V. F., and Harvald, B.: Teratogenic effect of inha-lation anaesthetics, Nord. Med. 83:498, 1970.
5. Astrup, P., Olsen, H. M., Trolle, D., and Kjeldsen, K.: Effect of moderate carbon-monoxide exposure on fetal development, Lancet 2:1220, 1972.
6. Baetjer, A. M.: Women in industry, Philadelphia, 1946, W. B. Saunders Company.
7. Bagland, R. J., Brill, A. B., Schulert, A., Wilson, D., Lar-sen, K., Dyer, N., Mansour, M., Schaffner, W., Hoffman, L., and Davies, J.: Utility of placental tissue as an indi-cator of trace element exposure to adult and fetus, Envi-ron. Res. 8:64, 1974
8. Bakken, A. F., and Seip, M.: Insecticides in human breast milk, Acta Paediatr. Scand. 65:535, 1976.
9. Barnaby, W.: Very high radiation levels found in Swedish houses, Nature 281:6, 1979.
10. Becker, R. F., Little, C. R. D., and King, J. E.: Experi-mental studies on nicotine absorption in rats during pregnancy. III. Effect of subcutaneous injection of small chronic doses upon mother, fetus and neonate, Am. J. Obstet. Gynecol. 100:957, 1968.
11. Berman vs. Allan, New Jersey Supreme Court, 1979.
12. Brackbill, Y., and Broman, S. H.: Obstetrical medication and development in the first year of life. Unpublished data.
13. Brent, R. L.: Environmental factors. Radiation, in Brent and Harris, editors: Prevention of Embryonic, Fetal and Perinatal Disease, Fogarty International Center Series on Preventive Medicine, DHEW Publication No. (NIH) 76-853. Bethesda, 1976, vol. 3, National Library of Medicine, pp. 179-197.
14. Carson, T. L., Van Gelder, G. A., Karas, G. C., and Buck, W. B.: Slowed learning in lambs prenatally exposed to lead, Arch. Environ. Health 29:154, 1974.
15. Carter, L. J.: Michigan's PBB incident: chemical mix-up leads to disaster, Science 192:240, 1976.
16. Check, W.: New study shows hexachlorophene is terato-genic in humans, J. A. M. A. 240:513, 1978.
17. Clarren, S. K., and Smith, D. W.: The fetal alcohol syn-drome, N. Engl. J. Med. 298:1063, 1978.
18. Clayton, B. E.: Lead: the relation of environment and experimental work, Br. Med. Bull. 31:236, 1975.
19. Coburn, R. F.: Carbon Monoxide, Washington, D. C., 1977, National Academy of Sciences, National Research Council, Division of Medical Sciences, pp. 83-104.
20. Cohen, E. M., Belville, J. W., and Brown, B. W., Jr.: Anes-thesia, pregnancy and miscarriage: a study of operating room nurses and anesthetists, Anesthesiology 35:343, 1971.
21. Cohen, E. N., Brown, B. W., Jr., Bruce, D. L., Cascorbi, H. F., Corbett, T. H., Jones, T. W., and Whitcher, C. E.: Occupational disease among operating room personnel: a national study, Anesthesiology 41:317, 1974.
22. Courtney, K. D., and Moore, J. A.: Teratology studies with 2,4,5-trichlorophenoxyacetic acid and 2,3,7,8-tetra-chlorodibenzo-p-dioxin, Toxicol. Appl. Pharmacol. 20:396, 1971.
23. Duffy, F. H., Burchfiel, J. L., Bartels, P. H., Gaon, M., and Sim, V. M.: Long-term effects of an organophos-phate upon the human electroencephalogram, Toxicol. Appl. Pharmacol. 47:161, 1979.
24. Eisenbud, M.: Environment, technology, and health, in Human Ecology in Historical Perspective, New York, 1978, New York University Press.
25. Environmental Protection Agency: 2,4,5,-T and Silvex, Fed. Register 44:15, 874, 1979.
26. Ferm, V. H.: Developmental malformations induced by cadmium. A study of timed injections during em-bryogenesis, Biol. Neonate 19:101, 1971.

27. Fechter, L. D., and Annau, Z.: Toxicity of mild prenatal carbon monoxide exposure, Science 197:680, 1977.
28. Finberg, L.: PBBs: the ladies' milk is not for burning, J. Pediatr. 90:511, 1977.
29. Fraumeni, J. F.: Chemicals in human teratogenesis and transplacental carcinogenesis, Pediatrics (Suppl.) 53:807, 1974.
30. Garvey, D. J., and Longo, L. D.: Chronic low level mater-nal carbon monoxide exposure and fetal growth and de-velopment, Biol. Reprod. 19:8, 1978.
31. Hasselmeyer, E. G., Meyer, M. B., Catz, C., and Longo, L. D.: Pregnancy and infant health, in Smoking and Health: A Report of the Surgeon General, Publication No. (PHS) 79-50066 DHEW, Washington, D. C., 1979, United States Department of Health, Education, and Welfare, Public Health Service, pp. 8-1 to 8-93.
32. Herbst, A. L., Cole, P., Colton, T., Robboy, S. J., and Scully, R. E.: Age-incidence and risk of diethylstilbes-terol-related clear cell adenocarcinoma of the vagina and cervix, Am. J. Obstet. Gynecol. 128:43, 1977.
33. Hickey, R. J.: Ecological statistical studies concerning en-vironmental pollution and chronic disease, in Digest of Technical Papers, Second International Geological Sci-ence Electronics Symposium, Washington, D. C., April 14-17, 1970, p. 13.
34. Holden, C.: Agent Orange furor continues to build, Sci-ence 205:770, 1979.
35. Holdgate, M. W.: A Perspective of Environmental Pollu-tion, Cambridge, 1979, Cambridge University Press.
36. Hooper, N. K., Ames B. N., Saleh, M. A., and Casida, J. E.: Toxaphene, a complex mixture of polychloroter-penes and a major insecticide, is mutagenic, Science 205:591, 1979.
37. Horiguchi, T., Suzuki, K., Comas-Urrutia, A. C., Mueller-Heubach, E., Boyer-Milic, A. M., Baratz, R. A., Morishima, H. O., James, L. S., and Adamsons, K.: Effect of ethanol upon uterine activity and fetal acid-base state of the rhesus monkey, Am. J. Obstet. Gynecol. 109:910, 1971.
38. Hudson, D. B., Meisami, E., and Timiras, P. S.: Brain development in offspring of rats treated with nicotine during pregnancy, Experientia 29:286, 1973.
39. Hudson, D. B., and Timiras, P. S.: Nicotine injection dur-ing gestation: Impairment of reproduction, fetal viability, and development, Biol. Reprod. 7:247, 1972.
40. Infante, P. F., Wagoner, J. K., McMichael, A. J., Wax-weiler, R. J., and Falk, H.: Genetic risks of vinyl chloride, Lancet 1:734, 1976.
41. Jackson, T. F., and Halbert, F. L.: A toxic syndrome as-sociated with the feeding of polybrominated biphenyl-contaminated protein concentrate to dairy cattle, J. Am. Vet. Med. Assoc. 165:437, 1974.
42. Jones, K. L., Smith, D. W., Ulleland, C. N., and Streissguth, A. P.: Pattern of malformation in offspring of chronic alcoholic mothers, Lancet 1:1267, 1973.
43. Katsuki, S.: Reports of the study groups for "Yusho" (chlorobiphenyls poisoning), Fukuoka Acta Med. 60:496, 1969.
44. Katsuma, M.: Minamata Disease. Kumamoto, Japan, 1969, Kumamoto University Press.
45. Kitabatake, T., Watanabe, T., and Sato, T.: Sterility in Japanese radiological technicians, Tohoku J. Exp. Med. 112:209, 1974.
46. Klingberg, M. A., and Papier, C. M.: Environmental teratogens: their significance and epidemiologic methods of detection, Contrib. Epidemiol. Biostat. 1:1, 1979.
47. Knill-Jones, R. P., Moir, D. D., Rodrigues, L. V., and Spence, A. A.: Anesthetic practice and pregnancy: con-trolled survey of women anesthetists in the United King-dom, Lancet 1:1326, 1972.
48. Koos, B. J., and Longo, L. D.: Mercury toxicity in the

pregnant woman, fetus, and newborn infant: A review, AM. J. OBSTET. GYNECOL. **126:**390, 1976.

49. Kuratsune, M., Yoshimura, T., Matsuzaka, J., and Yamaguchi, A.: Epidemiologic study on Yusho, a poisoning caused by ingestion of rice oil contaminated with commercial brand of polychlorinated biphenyls, Environ. Health Perspect. **1:**119, 1972.

50. Lemoine, P., Harousseau, H., Borteyru, J. P., and Menuet, J. C.: Les enfants de parents alcooliques: anomalies observées, Ouest. Med. **25:**476, 1968.

51. Longo, L. D.: The biological effects of carbon monoxide on the pregnant woman, fetus, and newborn infant, AM. J. OBSTET. GYNECOL. **129:**69, 1977.

52. Longo, L. D.: Carbon monoxide: effects on oxygenation of the fetus in utero, Science **194:**523, 1976.

53. Longo, L. D.: Carbon monoxide in the pregnant mother and fetus and its exchange across the placenta, Ann. N. Y. Acad. Sci. **174:**313, 1970.

54. Longo, L. D., Power, G. G., and Forster, R. E., II: Respiratory function of the placenta as determined with carbon monoxide in sheep and dogs, J. Clin. Invest. **46:**812, 1967.

55. Longo, L. D., Wyatt, J. F., Hewitt, C. W., and Gilbert, R. D.: A comparison of circulatory responses to hypoxic hypoxia and carbon monoxide hypoxia in fetal blood flow and oxygenation, in Longo, L. D., and Reneau, D. D., editors: Fetal and Newborn Cardiovascular Physiology: Fetal and Newborn Circulation, New York, 1978, vol. 2, STPM Press, pp. 259-287.

56. McNulty, W. P.: 2,3,7,8-Tetrachlorodibenzo-p-dioxin: abortions in rhesus macaques. In press.

57. Mann, L. I., Bhakthavathsalan, A., Liu, M., and Makowski, P.: Effect of alcohol on fetal cerebral function and metabolism, AM. J. OBSTET. GYNECOL. **122:**845, 1975.

58. Mann, L. I., Bhakthavathsalan, A., Liu, M., and Makowski, P.: Placental transport of alcohol and its effect on maternal and fetal acid-base balance, AM. J. OBSTET. GYNECOL. **122:**837, 1975.

59. Mansour, M., Dyer, N., Hoffman, L., Schulert, A., and Brill, A.: Maternal-fetal transfer of organic and inorganic mercury via placenta and milk, Environ. Res. **6:**479, 1973.

60. Martin, J. C., and Becker, R. F.: The effects of maternal nicotine absorption of hypoxic episodes upon appetitive behaviour of rat offspring, Dev. Psychobiol. **4:**133, 1971.

61. Masuda, Y., Kagawa, R., Kuroki, H., Kuratsune, M., Yoshimura, T., Taki, I., Kusuda, M., Yamashita, F., and Hayashi, M.: Transfer of polychlorinated biphenyls from mothers to foetuses and infants, Food Cosmet. Toxicol. **16:**543, 1978.

62. Mercer, H. D., Teske, R. H., Condon, R. J., Furr, A., Meerdink, G., Buck, W., and Fries, G.: Herd health status of animals exposed to polybrominated biphenyls (PBB), J. Toxicol. Environ. Health **2:**335, 1976.

63. Miller, R. W.: Pollutants in breast milk, J. Pediatr. **90:**510, 1977.

64. National Academy of Sciences: Lead: airborne lead in perspective, Washington, D. C., 1972, National Academy of Sciences, National Research Council, p. 162.

65. National Cancer Institute: Constituents of tobacco smoke, in Smoking and Health: a Report of the Surgeon General, DHEW Publication No. (PHS) 79-50066, Washington, D. C., 1979, United States Government Printing Office, pp. 14-1 to 14-119.

66. National Research Council: The effects of herbicides in South Vietnam. Part A. Summary and conclusions prepared for Department of Defense, Washington, D. C., 1974, National Research Council.

67. Nebert, D. W., Winker, J., and Gelboin, H. V.: Aryl hydrocarbon hydroxylase activity in human placenta from cigarette smoking and nonsmoking women, Cancer Res. **29:**1763, 1969.

68. Nelson, N.: Hazards of mercury. Special report to the Secretary's pesticide advisory committee. Department of Health, Education, and Welfare, Environ. Res. **4:**1, 1971.

69. Neubert, D., and Dillman, L.: Embryotoxic effects in mice treated with 2,4,5-trichlorophenoxyacetic acid and 2,3,7,8-tetrachlorodibenzo-p-dioxin, Naunyn Schmeidebergs Arch. Pharmacol. **272:**243, 1972.

70. Niigata Report. Report on the cases of mercury poisoning in Niigata, Tokyo, Japan, 1967, Ministry of Health and Welfare.

71. Nikonova, T. V.: Transplacental action of benzo(a)pyrene and pyrene, Bull. Exp. Biol. Med. **84:**1025, 1977.

72. Null, D., Gartside, P., and Wei, E.: Methylmercury accumulation in brains of pregnant, non-pregnant and fetal rats, Life Sci. **12:**65, 1973.

73. Parizek, J.: Vascular changes at sites of oestrogen biosynthesis produced by parenteral injection of cadmium salts: the destruction of placenta by cadmium salts, J. Reprod. Fertil. **7:**263, 1964.

74. Parker, H. M., and Taylor, L. S.: Basic radiation protection criteria, Washington, D. C., 1971, National Council on Radiation Protection and Measurements, Report No. 39.

75. Pelkonen, O., Jouppila, P., and Karki, N. T.: Effect of maternal cigarette smoking on 3,4-benzpyrene and n-methylaniline metabolism in human fetal liver and placenta, Toxicol. Appl. Pharmacol. **23:**399, 1972.

76. Resnik, R., Brink, G. W., and Wilkes, M.: Catecholamine-mediated reduction in uterine blood flow after nicotine infusion in the pregnant ewe, J. Clin. Invest. **63:**1133, 1979.

77. Robertson, D. S. E.: Selenium—a possible teratogen? Lancet **1:**518, 1970.

78. Rom, W. N.: Effect of lead on the female and reproduction: a review, Mt. Sinai J. Med. **43:**542, 1976.

79. Schlede, E., and Merker, H. J.: Effect of benzo(a)pyrene treatment on the benzo(a)pyrene hydroxylase activity in maternal liver, placenta, and fetus of the rat during day 13 to day 18 of gestation, Naunyn Schmiedeberg Arch. Pharmacol. **272:**89, 1972.

80. Shaw, G.: Radiation: a deadly fact of everyday life, Los Angeles Times, Sept. 17, 1979.

81. Smith, J.: EPA halts most use of herbicide 2,4,5-T, Science **203:**1090, 1979.

82. Smith, R. J.: U. S. beginning to act on banned pesticides, Science **204:**1391, 1979.

83. Sternberg, J.: Irradiation and radiocontamination during pregnancy, AM. J. OBSTET. GYNECOL. **108:**490, 1970.

84. Sternglass, E. J.: Infant mortality and nuclear tests, Bull. Atomic Sci. **25:**29, 1969.

85. Stofen, D., and Waldron, H. A.: Sub-clinical lead poisoning, New York, 1974, Academic Press, Inc.

86. Sullivan, F. M., and Barlow, S. M.: Congenital malformations and other reproductive hazards from environmental chemicals, Proc. R. Soc. Lond. (Biol.) **205:**91, 1979.

87. Sunderman, F. W., Jr., Allpass, P. R., Mitchell, J. M., Baselt, R. C., and Albert, D. M.: Eye malformations in rats: induction by prenatal exposure to nickel cabonyl, Science **203:**550, 1979.

88. Sunderman, F. W., Jr., Shen, S. K., Mitchell, J. M., Allpass, P. R., and Damjanov, I.: Embryotoxicity and fetal toxicity of nickel in rats, Toxicol. Appl. Pharmacol. **43:**381, 1978.

89. Suzuki, K., Horiguchi, T., Comas-Urrutia, A. C., Mueller-Heubach, E., Morishima, H. O., and Adamsons, K.: Pharmacologic effects of nicotine upon the fetus and mother in the rhesus monkey, AM. J. OBSTET. GYNECOL. **111:**1092, 1971.

90. Suzuki, K., Horiguchi, T., Comas-Urrutia, A. C., Mueller-Heubach, E., Morishima, H. O., and Adamsons, K.: Placental transfer and distribution of nicotine in the

pregnant rhesus monkey, AM. J. OBSTET. GYNECOL. 119:253, 1974.

91. Taki, I., Hisanaga, S., and Amagase, Y.: Report on Yusho (chlorobiphenyls poisoning): pregnant women and their fetuses, Fukuoka Igaku Zasshi 60:47, 1969.

91a. Nishimura and Tanimura: Clinical Aspects of the Teratogenicity of Drugs, Amsterdam, 1976, Excerpta Medica Foundation.

92. Takizawa, Y.: Studies on the Niigata episode of Minamata disease outbreak, Acta Med. Biol. (Niigata) 17:293, 1970.

93. Van Gelder, G. A., Carson, T., Smith, R. M., and Buck, W. B.: Behavioral toxicologic assessment of the neurologic effect of lead in sheep, Clin. Toxicol. 6:405, 1973.

94. Van Miller, J. P., Mailar, R. J., and Allen, J. R.: Tissue distribution and excretion of tritiated tetracholorodibenzo-p-dioxin in non-human primates and rats, Food Cosmet. Toxicol. 14:3114, 1976.

95. Vorhees, C. V., Brunner, R. L., and Butcher, R. E.: Psychotropic drugs as behavioral teratogens, Science 205: 1220, 1979.

96. Webster, W. S.: Cadmium-induced fetal growth retardation in the mouse, Arch. Environ. Health 33:36, 1978.

97. Welch, R. M., Gommi, B., Alvares, A. P., and Conney, A. H.: Effect of enzyme induction on the metabolism of benzo(a)pyrene and 3-methyl-4-mono-methylaminoazabenzene in the pregnant and fetal rat, Cancer Res. 32:973, 1972.

98. Wibberley, D. G., Khera, A. K., Edwards, J. H., and Rushton, D. I.: Lead levels in human placentae from normal and malformed births, J. Med. Genet. 14:339, 1977.

99. Yakushiji, T., Watanabe, I., Kuwabara, K., Yoshida, S., Koyama, K., Hara, I., and Kunita, N.: Long-term studies of the excretion of polychlorinated biphenyls (PCBs) through the mother's milk of an occupationally exposed worker, Arch. Environ. Contam. Toxicol. 7:493, 1978.

100. Yeh, C. Y., Kuo, P. H., Tsai, S. T., Wang, G. Y., and Wang, Y. T.: A study of pesticide residues in umbilical cord blood and maternal milk, J. Formosan Med. Assoc. 75:463, 1976.

PHYSIOLOGICAL REVIEWS

Published by

THE AMERICAN PHYSIOLOGICAL SOCIETY

| VOLUME 28 | JANUARY 1948 | NUMBER 1 |

INTERNAL SECRETIONS AND TOXEMIA OF LATE PREGNANCY

GEORGE VAN S. SMITH AND O. WATKINS SMITH

From the Fearing Research Laboratory, Free Hospital for Women

BROOKLINE, MASSACHUSETTS

CRITICAL, COMPREHENSIVE PUBLICATIONS concerning the toxemias of pregnancy have been written by Berkeley (15), Holland (76), Hinselmann (73), Stander (174), Herrmann (71), Kosmak (83), McIlroy (102), Dieckmann (44), Dexter and Weiss (43) and Browne (26). These authors have made exhaustive studies of the literature on this subject and included their own investigations. The present review was prompted by the increased knowledge of internal secretions in relation to this diseased state, chiefly as regards the hormones elaborated by the placenta. Unfortunately, detailed morphologic studies of the glands of internal secretion in toxemia as well as in normal pregnancy are lacking (43), with the exception of the placenta and only recently has this organ been receiving more thorough histologic attention (*v.i.* under Placental Hormones).

Anterior lobe of the hypophysis. Gonadotropic hormones. No follicular activity was found in the ovaries of hypophysectomized rats following the injection of sera from patients with toxemia (5, 140). The effect noted was the same as that produced both by sera from normally pregnant women and by an extract of human placenta (140). The results supported Philipp's (112) demonstration that the hypophyses of pregnant women are gonadotropically inactive, so far as the ovaries of rodents are concerned, and indicated further that patients with toxemia do not differ in this respect from normal. The anatomical studies reviewed by Dieckmann (44) did not suggest that the anterior lobe is primarily at fault in eclampsia.

Thyrotropic hormone. Bonilla and Kramann (19) extracted a substance with properties similar to those of the thyrotropic hormone from the urine of patients with eclampsia. They did not obtain it from the urine of normal pregnant women.

Adrenotropic hormones. Fauvet and Münzner (58) reported subnormal corticotropic hormone levels in seven of eight women with severe toxemia.

Posterior lobe of the hypophysis. From a perusal of the literature and their own studies, Dieckmann (44), Dexter and Weiss (43) and Browne (26) concluded that the secretions of this gland are not implicated etiologically in pre-eclampsia and eclampsia. Their conclusion holds for pressor as well as antidiuretic activity. Krieger and Kilvington (85) have more recently surveyed the conflicting literature concerning the antidiuretic property of blood and toxemia and tested the blood of 303 women. They found blood antidiuretic activity in 29 to 41 per cent of the groups of patients studied and that the activity in both normal and toxemic cases was related to labor and the early puerperium. Therefore they suggested that the contradictory results in the literature might be explained if considered in relation to the onset of labor.

Antidiuretic substance in the urine. Concentrates prepared from the urine of patients with toxemia were discovered to exert a marked antidiuretic effect which was not obtained with similar extracts from normal women in late pregnancy (18, 43, 67, 84, 125, 183). According to some authors, this effect was not due to pitressin (67, 125). Furthermore, a principle resembling the urinary substance was found in larger amounts in the placentas of toxemic women than in those of normal pregnancy (67).

Melanophore-expanding principle. Küstner and Dietel (87) reported a substance with this property in the blood and placentas of patients with eclampsia. Ehrhardt (51) confirmed this. Others have demonstrated this effect in the blood of toxemic women (6, 104).

Effects of administered posterior pituitary extracts. Chipman (192), Dieckmann and Michel (45) and Hofbauer (74) stated that the use of pituitary extracts in toxemia occasionally precipitates convulsions; Stander (174), referring to reports in which eclampsia appeared to ensue or become aggravated upon the injection of pituitrin, was of the opinion that the routine use of pituitary extracts in many clinics, without appreciably increased incidence of eclampsia, indicated that such observations were coincidental. In this connection, a number of patients with diabetes insipidus have been treated throughout pregnancy with posterior-lobe extracts (44, 121, 138) without any alarming developments. The following is quoted from Dexter and Weiss (43): "Because patients with diabetes insipidus are especially sensitive to the antidiuretic effect of the posterior pituitary hormone, it is worth noting here that usually such patients show no striking improvement during pregnancy and that there have even been instances in which diabetes insipidus appeared during pregnancy and disappeared after delivery."

Dieckmann and Michel (45), however, and others (25, 88, 104, 128, 187, 208) demonstrated an increased susceptibility of toxemic individuals to posterior pituitary extracts, a much higher and longer-lasting rise of blood pressure resulting. Moreover, Browne (25), using the cold pressor test and injecting tonephrin (pitressin), noted that the hypersensitivity of pre-eclamptic women to this hormone persists during the puerperium, being found as late as the two hundred thirty-fifth day. He also noted a similar cold pressor test hypersensitivity to pitressin in normal puerperal women as late as the twentieth day. From further studies he concluded (26) that the high reaction to pressor substances in pre-eclamptic toxemia is not due to predisposition but to something acquired during pregnancy and seemingly after the third month.

Inactivating power of the blood of pregnant women upon pitocin and pitressin.

Fekete and others (59, 195–197) found that posterior-lobe hormones were inactivated when mixed with serum from pregnant women. Woodbury *et al.* (208) confirmed this and noted, moreover, that the hypersensitivity of patients with toxemia to these hormones (pitressin and pitocin) was not associated with a diminished ability of their blood to inactivate them. Plasma pitocinase studies were made by Page (105). After establishing a curve of values through normal pregnancy, he found the enzyme within normal range in only 3 of 16 women with toxemia; in 7 the values were high, in 6, low. There was no correlation between the amount of enzyme and the severity of the disease.

THE THYROID GLAND. Anselmino and Hoffmann (75) presented evidence which they interpreted as demonstrating increased thyroid hormone, or a material with the same action, in the blood in normal pregnancy, the amount being enormously increased in eclampsia. No toxemia occurred in Davis' (41) eight patients with hyperthyroidism complicated by pregnancy, but five of Kibel's (82) nine similar cases developed pre-eclampsia.

It has been suggested that hypothyroidism may play a part in the production of toxemia of pregnancy (37, 38, 78, 109). Since, according to Dexter and Weiss (43), the clinical picture does not indicate hypothyroidism, the basal metabolic rate in this condition is not at myxedematous levels, and the protein content of the edema fluid is extremely low, hypofunction of the thyroid gland cannot play a significant rôle in its causation.

THE PARATHYROID GLANDS. "Many studies have been made of serum calcium in toxemic patients, but the consensus of opinion is that there are no significant changes in the total calcium or in any of its fractions in eclampsia or any of the other toxemias" (44). Patients with eclampsia and pre-eclampsia have been treated with parathyroid extracts (23, 24, 91) but without results sufficiently impressive to indicate any specificity of the therapy.

PANCREAS. *Diabetes.* The incidence of toxemia is greatly increased in diabetic patients (17, 44, 61, 63, 89, 199, 204). No one has elucidated the significance of this.

THE ADRENAL GLANDS. Fauvet and Münzer (58) found the adrenals small in six women who died of eclampsia, the weight of the two glands being less than 10.0 grams in all. In normal pregnancy the adrenal cortex is markedly increased, due to an increase in size and in fat content of the cells of the zona fasciculata, so that the adrenals are larger than in non-pregnant individuals, in whom these glands weigh 12 to 15.5 grams (8).

The adrenal medulla. The injection of epinephrin into patients with toxemia was found to cause a reversal of the usual blood pressure response, *viz.*, a drop instead of a rise (33, 92). Macchiarulo (95) recorded that an excess of epinephrin in the blood was usually present in eclamptic women and to this he attributed in part convulsions, vascular contractions and hypertension.

The adrenal cortex. The results of research on the adrenal have been reviewed by Swingle and Remington (176) but little has been done on any possible relation between adrenal function and toxemia of pregnancy. Over-activity of the adrenals has been considered (26, 43, 181). Taylor *et al.* (181) found in two cases of toxemia after delivery "a pronounced divergence of the sodium and potassium lines which might indicate a return to normal from a previous condition of relatively low potassium and high sodium storage." "This could on theoretical grounds have been produced by hyperactivity of the adrenal cortex." Against this view, however, they pointed out their observation of potassium as well as sodium retention in toxemia, whereas lowered serum potassium and a high excretion rate are characteristic of adrenal hyperactivity. Interesting in this connection are reports concerning two patients with Addison's disease complicated by pregnancy (127, 211) who went through essentially uneventful gestations while under treatment with sodium chloride and cortical extract.

Although urinary corticoids and ketosteroids have been determined during normal pregnancy (188, which includes references to the work of others on ketosteroid excretion in pregnancy), they have not been studied in relation to toxemia.

THE OVARIES. Toxemia has not been stated to have occurred in patients whose pregnancies continued after the early removal of the corpus luteum or of both ovaries (2, 4, 8, 22, 28, 44, 49, 50, 79, 118, 123, 167, 177, 191). This may not be interpreted to mean that toxemia has never developed in such patients. On the other hand, since a fairly large number of such cases has been reported, it may be significant.

In presenting their case of eclampsia associated with ovarian pregnancy, Pride and Rucker (117) stated that it was the seventh recorded instance of toxemia in patients with pregnancies outside of the uterus.

THE PLACENTA. For decades authors have ascribed toxemia of pregnancy to abnormal placental function. The literature concerning this organ has been thoroughly covered by the writers referred to in the first paragraph of this review. Knowledge of the placental hormones, however, was only beginning to be acquired during the period they reviewed. The following statements made by Dexter and Weiss (43) summarize their own conclusions and those of others on the probable significance of findings published before 1940. "The main histological changes in toxemia are found in the placenta, liver, kidneys and retina. The placental changes consist of a premature degeneration of the syncytium. These lesions develop early and may precede even the appearance of albuminuria. The present evidence points to the placenta as the 'intrauterine factor' responsible for toxemia of pregnancy. Although the mechanism by which toxemia is produced is not known in its details, a chemical (hormonal) mechanism . . . may be suspected with some justification. The clinical predisposing factors . . . disturb the placental circulation, causing secondary degenerative changes (premature ageing). The observations reported by us and others regarding the origin of the edema of pregnancy indicate that . . . the abnormalities in water metabolism during pregnancy are not due to causes usually found in the non-pregnant state. A consideration of the various possible explanations . . . suggests specific factors which retain fluid in cells and tissue spaces. By exclusion, endocrine factors such as exist in premenstrual edema and Cushing's syndrome can be suspected. It is possible that the placenta produces a water-retaining hormone and also a vasoconstrictor substance. . . . "

PLACENTAL HORMONES. *Chorionic gonadotropin.* A gonadotropic factor in the urine of pregnant women was discovered by Ascheim and Zondek (7). That it differs from gonadotropic hormones of anterior pituitary origin was demonstrated by Evans *et al.* (56, 57). By tissue culture technic, Gey *et al.* (62, 81) showed it to be a placental product, probably from the cytotrophoblast. The histochemical studies of Wislocki and Bennett (206) also indicated that the cytotrophoblast of the chorionic villi is responsible for its secretion. These latter investigators also pointed out that the growth and activity of the cytotrophoblast are roughly in accord with the previosuly established curves of gonadotropic content in blood and urine throughout gestation (27, 55, 134, 142, 161, 209). Chorionic gonadotropin, or CG, is now the generally accepted appellation for the hormone.

Ehrhardt (52) reported positive tests for gonadotropic hormone in the cerebrospinal fluid of eclamptic and pre-eclamptic women, but normal titers in their blood and urine, and concluded therefrom that the gonadotropic activity of the anterior pituitary was high in toxemia of late pregnancy. Excessive gonadotropic hormone in the blood and urine of patients with toxemia was first reported by Smith and Smith (137–139), who demonstrated also that the placentas of of toxemic patients contained more than could be recovered from those of normal pregnancy and that the high gonadotropic titer of blood and placenta in toxemia was not accountable to pituitary gonadotropes (140). High CG in the blood and urine of women with toxemia has been confirmed (5, 21, 70, 119, 134, 185), as well as the evidence for its placental origin (5). It has been shown, however, not to be demonstrable in all cases, not to bear any direct relation to the severity of the disease and to be associated also with stillbirth and premature delivery in the absence of toxic signs (120, 145, 148, 171, 193). Browne, Henry and Venning (29) could make no correlation between elevated CG and late pregnancy toxemia. Taylor and Scadron (180) and Cohen, Wilson and Brenan (34) found only a slight correlation. The latter investigators studied 119 pregnancies and based their conclusion on the fact that, although 44 per cent of toxemic patients had high serum CG, elevated levels were also present in 15 per cent of normal deliveries. Other studies (120, 148, 161, 171) have indicated that elevation of CG during the last month before labor is a normal phenomenon. This may explain the high values in normal late pregnancy which disturbed Taylor and Scadron and Cohen *et al.*

Smith and Smith, in 1934 (138), noted a marked rise of serum CG early in the third trimester in a woman who later developed pre-eclampsia. They have since performed repeated analyses for serum CG upon 117 women during the last trimester to determine whether or not accidents of late pregnancy could be predicted by an abnormal rise in this factor (139, 144–146, 148, 161, 171). (Since the incidence of late pregnancy accidents was known to be high in patients with diabetes, 68 of the above number were chosen for study because they had diabetes.) In all of 42 women whose pregnancies progressed and terminated normally, serum CG was at a low and uniform level between the twenty-fourth and thirty-sixth weeks, any rise after the thirty-sixth week being considered normal. Of 56 patients in whom a progressive elevation of CG was observed prior to the thirty-sixth week, 45 developed toxemia, eight delivered prematurely and three had their babies die *in utero*. On the other hand, 19 patients in whom no abnormal elevation of serum CG was detected developed late pregnancy complications. Nine had stillbirth or premature delivery and 10 developed toxemia. They concluded that, although an abnormal rise of this hormone in the blood prior to the last month of pregnancy warrants the prediction of later trouble, it gives no indication of the type or severity of the accident and, furthermore, that accidents may occur without any warning so far as a rise of CG is concerned.

High serum CG prior to the appearance of toxic signs was reported by Rakoff (119) in two of three patients. White *et al.* (200–203) performed repeated analyses for serum CG as a prognostic test in patients with diabetes complicated by pregnancy. In 1945 she (200) summarized results concerning 181 such women. The studies on the first 33 of her patients were performed by Smith and Smith (144, 145, 161); therefore these cases were included with the 117 just analysed (*v.s.*). Her results agreed with the Smiths' in that an abnormal rise of serum CG was always followed by clinical abnormalities and the level of hormone was consistently low in uncomplicated pregnancies. She failed to confirm, however, the fairly high incidence of late pregnancy accidents observed by the Smiths in patients whose serum CG did not become abnormally elevated. Only one of her 52 patients with normal CG levels developed toxemia, none delivered prematurely and only 2 lost their babies. Rubin, Dorfman and Miller (120) followed serum CG during the last trimester in 5 diabetic patients, one of whom had normal CG levels and an uncomplicated pregnancy, 2 of whom developed toxemia, 1 with and 1 without high CG, and 2 of whom had fetal death, 1 with and 1 without elevated CG.

Progesterone. Progestational activity has been repeatedly detected in extracts of human placenta (1, 53, 54, 65, 101, 152). Since histochemical studies (42, 206) indicate that the chorionic syncytium elaborates steroïds, progesterone is probably secreted by these cells. The demonstration that pregnanediol glucuronidate is an excretory product of progesterone (190) and the development of a method of quantification (189) led to extensive studies concerning the urinary excretion of this compound in normal and toxemic pregnancy. In normal pregnancy the amount increases from around 10.0 mgm. daily at one month to between 60.0 and 130.0 mgm. daily shortly before term and practically disappears within 24 hours of delivery (10, 12, 28–30, 32, 66, 80, 144, 146–148). The corpus luteum has been removed in pregnancy without more than slight and temporary alteration in the excretion of pregnanediol (28, 79). Browne and his associates (30) noted peaking of pregnanediol excretion at approximately four-week intervals during pregnancy. This was also observed by Smith and Smith (146), who found in individual curves the final and highest peak about two weeks before term, this being followed by decreasing values before and during labor (147). A prepartum drop in pregnanediol was also noted by others (10, 12, 13, 66). Studies by Stover and Pratt on 5 patients (175), by Wilson, Randall and Osterberg on 1 patient (205) and by Bachman on 6 women (9) failed to reveal any decline of pregnanediol before labor, but Lyon (94), reporting results on 68 patients whose labors were spontaneous, determined a peak of pregnanediol excretion about two weeks before delivery, followed by decreasing values and then a precipitous drop for five to seven days prepartum, regardless of whether labor was premature, at term or postmature.

Smith and Smith (135, 136), in their earliest studies of estrogen and progesterone metabolism, discovered that progesterone decreased the destruction of both administered and secreted estrogen. Their finding of low estrogens in toxemia (*v.i.*) led them to suspect, therefore, that progesterone might also be deficient (139, 161). Smith and Kennard (152) attempted to compare the progesterone content of normal and toxemic placentas. Although there was evidence of deficient progesterone in half of the placentas from untreated toxemic patients, the method used was not sufficiently accurate to warrant definite conclusions. In 1938 three groups of investigators, working independently, reported low values for urinary pregnanediol in toxemia of late pregnancy (29, 144, 194). This has been confirmed (11, 13, 146, 148, 180). There is general agreement, however, that the abnormality is revealed only by comparing the averages of normal with those of toxemic pregnancy. Cope (39, 40) did not find it in 10 women with late pregnancy toxemia and Hain (66) observed excessively high urinary pregnanediol in 1 patient with severe pre-eclampsia.

Smith and Smith (148) pointed out the wide range of normal values and concluded that the curve of pregnanediol excretion as pregnancy advances is more inportant than the actual level at any given time. In 14 normal pregnancies they found progressively increasing values, with minor fluctuations, between the twenty-eighth and thirty-sixth weeks; whereas, in 21 patients with toxemia the values steadily decreased during this time, with one exception, in a patient whose toxemia became self-corrected during the period of observation. In two women studied prior to the onset of toxic signs, urinary pregnanediol progressively diminished for four weeks before any clinical abnormality was apparent. These investigators have studied the relationship between progesterone and the urinary excretion of estrogen metabolites (*v.i.* Metabolism of the estrogens) and believe that measurement of the latter, though more laborious, provides more information concerning secreted progesterone than does the determination of urinary pregnanediol. In all of 50 patients studied by them prior to the development of toxemia, premature delivery or intrauterine death, evidence for a progressive deficiency of progesterone before as well as during the clinical abnormality was acquired (144, 146, 148, 149, 171, 172). White and Hunt (202) utilized pregnanediol determinations as a prognostic test in 60 diabetic women of whom 43 were receiving therapy with estrogen and progesterone. Of the untreated patients, 12 had normal curves of pregnanediol excretion and normal pregnancies with live births, though two of the babies died after delivery. Of the five untreated women whose pregnanediol excretion was decreasing between the twenty-fifth and thirty-sixth weeks, three developed toxemia, one delivered prematurely and the fifth showed no clinical abnormality before being delivered by cesarean section in the thirty-fourth week. Rubin, Dorfman and Miller (120) noted diminished excretion of pregnanediol prior to toxemia in two of their diabetic patients but failed to find this abnormality in two others whose babies died, one in utero and the other after delivery.

The estrogens. Estrogenic substance was first demonstrated in the human placenta by Fellner (60). This has been adequately confirmed (3). In 1927, Ascheim and Zondek (7) discovered the great concentration of estrogenic material in the urine of pregnant women, and Margaret Smith (157) found increasing amounts of it in the blood throughout human pregnancy. Removal of the corpus luteum or of all ovarian tissue as early as the sixth to eighth week of pregnancy has been shown not to interrupt gestation (2, 4, 8, 22, 28, 49, 50, 79, 118, 123, 167, 177, 191) or the continued elaboration of estrogen (2, 4, 22, 118, 123, 167, 191). The concentration of estrogens in the placenta, their continued excretion after ovariectomy, and the prompt cessation of excretion after delivery contribute to the generally accepted tenet that the placenta forms estrogens; the site of formation being likely in the syncytial cells of the chorionic villi (42, 206).

Estrogenic activity in the serum is relatively low until after the second month of normal pregnancy. It increases rapidly thereafter, the highest values being acquired during the last month (138, 139, 157, 161). Quantification of blood estrogen is not satisfactory because of still unsolved technical difficulties. The discovery that all but a small part of urinary estrogen is in combined forms, relatively inactive biologically and insoluble in water-immiscible organic solvents (20, 35, 90, 141, 210) made earlier studies of estrogen excretion only roughly significant. Subsequent investigations, in which hydrolysis and improved methods of extraction were used, yielded more accurate and significant results and established that the total estrogenic potency of the urine rises before the first missed period (100, 142), increases gradually and then markedly during pregnancy, reaching a peak in the last month, and diminishes rapidly prior to the onset of labor, becoming negligible within three days after delivery (9, 27, 29, 36, 46, 66, 93, 98, 134, 144, 146–148, 154, 161).

Low levels of estrogen in the blood, urine and placentas of most patients with toxemia of late pregnancy were first reported by Smith and Smith (137–140, 161). This finding, as regards the urine, has been confirmed by nearly all investigators (29, 93, 119, 120, 124, 134, 144, 146, 148, 149, 170, 171, 180, 193). There is, however, general agreement that in individual cases values within or even above the normal range often are obtained. Heim (70) reported high and Hain (66), in one case, very high urinary estrogen in toxemia, and normal blood values have been described (16). Shute (129–133), using antiproteolytic power of serum as a gauge of its estrogen content, claimed both high and low estrogen in toxemia. As with urinary pregnanediol, the curve of excretion in each individual is thought by the Smiths to be more important than the actual level at any one time. This is apparent in their curves for total estrogen of blood and urine in diabetic and non-diabetic women (161). Seven who developed toxemia or had premature delivery failed to show the marked increase of estrogen in blood and urine between the sixth and eighth months that characterized the 17 normal curves. In their later studies, in which urinary estrogen was separated into estradiol, estrone and estriol and the values converted from rat units into milligrams, a progressive decrease of total estrogen was demonstrated before and during toxemia, premature delivery and intrauterine death in all of 50 patients studied (144, 146, 148, 149, 171, 172).

That decreasing excretion of estrogens and pregnanediol before labor and late pregnancy toxemia actually reflects decreasing secretion of placental steroids is indicated by histological and histochemical studies of human placentas. The syncytial degeneration which characterizes normal term placentas involves an almost complete disappearance of the lipoidal droplets associated with secretion of steroid hormones (42, 206, 207). In 1936, Tenney (184) discovered that syncytial degeneration similar to but more pronounced than that of term placentas is of consistent occurrence in toxemic placentas. He and Parker later (186), from an examination of 100 toxemic placentas, correlated the amount of syncytial degeneration with the severity of the disease and concluded that "placenta damage begins before clinical signs of the condition appear." Wislocki and Dempsey (207) confirmed these observations in two toxemic placentas delivered in the fifth month, finding histochemical, syncytial changes typical of the organ at term. (They also noted a decrease of cytoplasmic basophilia and a premature increase of phosphatases suggesting a possible disturbance of nucleoprotein metabolism in this disease.) Histological and histochemical evidence, therefore, substantiates the above hormonal evidence, pointing to a premature aging of the placenta in toxemia and therefrom a premature deficiency in the secretion of progesterone and estrogen. An actual deficiency, then, of estrogen and progesterone, rather than any renal retention or change in conjugation to account for the low urinary levels, appears to be well established. The theory introduced by a number of workers (12, 29, 66, 179, 180, 182) that toxic signs, particularly changes in electrolyte balance and water retention, are due to high levels of these steroid hormones must, therefore, be discarded.

Smith and Smith (145) in summarizing and evaluating their findings on CG in the blood and urine during normal and toxemic pregnancy, postulated utilization of this hormone in the placenta for the production of estrogen and progesterone. They had noted that the precipitous decrease in CG of blood and urine at around the twelfth week of normal pregnancy was accompanied by a marked increase in estrogen excretion (142) and that the prepartum decrease in estrogen excretion coincided with a rise in serum CG (154, 161). This same reciprocal relationship between CG and estrogens had been observed in late pregnancy toxemia (144, 161), suggesting to them that an abnormal elevation of serum CG in this condition and at term reflected failing utilization. To explain the absence of elevated serum CG in some patients with toxemia, they postulated an actual decrease in the secretion of this factor from placental damage. In support of these hypotheses is the following more recent evidence. The cytotrophoblast and its more differentiated derivatives, the cells of Langhans, are the likely source of CG (81, 206). It is well known that the Langhans cells become fewer in number as pregnancy advances and are practically absent in term placentas. There is no increase of cytotrophoblast in toxemic placentas (72, 207). And, finally, in two such placentas delivered in the second trimester Wislocki and Dempsey (207) found premature regression of the Langhans cells as well as the syncytium. As pregnancy continues, therefore, whether normal or abnormal, there is no proliferation of the cells which probably secrete CG to account for high values at term and in toxemia but rather, if anything, a degeneration. In view of the histochemical and hormonal findings pointing to decreased sex steroid production at term and in toxemia, then, it seems possible that failing utilization of CG accounts for the larger amounts of it in the circulation at these times and that decreased elaboration as well as failing utilization account for the normal serum values sometimes acquired. This concept was further corroborated recently (168) by a comparison of hormonal values and placental pathology in the same patients.

Metabolism of the estrogens. Certain changes in the partition of urinary estrogens and in the excretion of what appear to be estrogen metabolites have been found to precede and accompany the onset of labor and of late pregnancy toxemia. In order to evaluate the significance of these, a brief review on the subject of estrogen metabolism is in order.

Three estrogens have been identified in the urine of pregnant women: estrone (31, 48), estriol (47, 96) and α estradiol (77, 153). Of these, α estradiol is commonly regarded as the primary estrogen in humans from which the others are derived. Marrian (97) suggested that estriol may also be secreted by the human placenta. In 1937 Pincus and Zahl (116) injected the three estrogens separately into rabbits under varying conditions and determined their subsequent urinary excretion by separation and colorimetric assay. They concluded, as had been previously demonstrated both in rabbits and women (135, 136) that progesterone increases the amount of estrogen excreted, probably by inhibiting destruction. Moreover, their results indicated the following scheme of conversion within the animal body: α estradiol $\rightleftharpoons$ estrone $\rightarrow$ estriol, the estrone to estriol reaction being facilitated by the presence of progesterone. That the same metabolic relationships pertain in women seems likely from the studies of Smith and Smith and their associates (144, 146–149, 155, 156, 170, 173) and those of Pincus and his associates (113–115). These conclusions are based entirely upon colorimetric (Pincus) and biological (Smith and Smith) assay of the three estrogens separated by admittedly imperfect methods. Chemical confirmation of them in man, however, was at least partially acquired by the isolation of α estradiol and estriol in the urine following estrone administration (110, 111) and of estrone after the administration of α estradiol (68, 69).

All investigators have been impressed by the small percentage of injected estrogen recoverable in the urine under any conditions. Numerous attempts have been made to isolate compounds in human urine which could be identified as products of the endogenous inactivation of the estrogens but none of them has been successful. Smith and Smith (143) evolved a method of Zn-HCl hydrolysis of human urine which results in much more estrogenic activity than can be accounted for by the known estrogens present. The additional activity appears to be derived from reduction into active forms of estrogenically inactive oxidation products of the estrogens.   Since the precursors of this additional potency have not yet been identified, this deduction is based largely upon circumstantial evidence.   The procedure, however, seems to provide a gauge of the rate of oxidation of estrogens within the body (155, 156, 162, 173).   Using this method in conjunction with the separate assay of estradiol, estrone and estriol fractions, they strengthened the evidence that progesterone decreases the rate of estrogen inactivation, by facilitating the conversion of estrone, which is rapidly inactivated *in vivo*, to estriol, which is much less readily destroyed, according to recovery experiments (126, 156).   Their results also indicated that the destructive mechanism inhibited by progesterone is an oxidative one related largely to the reversible estradiol to estrone reaction.   Thus in the presence of adequate progesterone:

$$\text{estradiol} \rightleftharpoons \text{estrone} \longrightarrow \text{estriol}$$
$$\downarrow$$
$$\text{oxidation products;}$$

whereas, when progesterone is deficient,

$$\text{estradiol} \rightleftharpoons \text{estrone} \dashrightarrow \text{estriol}$$
$$\downarrow$$
$$\text{oxidation products.}$$

In applying these methods to the study of estrogen and progesterone metabolism in both pregnant and non-pregnant women, they were led to the concept that estrogenically inactive oxidation products of the reversible estradiol to estrone reaction, rather than estrogens *per se*, stimulate the production of estrogen and progesterone, this being accomplished in the non-pregnant woman through release of pituitary gonadotropes and in pregnancy through increased utilization of CG (147, 148, 150, 156, 166, 171, 173).   This concept was strengthened by the experimental demonstration, 1, that a lactone produced from crystalline estrone by oxidative inactivation (198) causes release of pituitary gonadotropes; whereas, estrone has this property only under conditions involving rapid inactivation *in vivo* (158-160); 2, that diethylstilbestrol behaves like the estrone-lactone (163) and, 3, causes increased excretion of pregnanediol together with a drop in serum CG in pregnant women (168, 172).

In 38 untreated pregnancies the Smiths performed repeated urinalyses for estradiol, estrone, estriol and the additional estrogenic potency recoverable after Zn-HCl hydrolysis (148, 150, 171).   Biological assay was used and the Zn-HCl activity interpreted as a gauge of the rate of oxidative inactivation of the estrogens *in vivo*.   All of these women were studied from early in the third trimester to delivery.   Of the 23 (see second paragraph below) who developed pre-eclampsia or eclampsia or had intrauterine death or premature delivery during the period of observation, three had been followed during the second trimester also.   In 6 of the 15 normal pregnancies analyses were performed from the twelfth week to term.   In normal pregnancy the percentage of total estrogens accountable to estriol was found to increase steadily, with minor fluctuations, reaching a peak at approximately two weeks before term.   At this time estrone was also high, whereas the proportion of activity accountable to estradiol was low, and the Zn-HCl values indicated the lowest rate of oxidative inactivation found at any time of pregnancy.   These findings, together with the thirty-eighth-week peak in pregnanediol excretion were interpreted as reflecting a maximum rate of conversion of estradiol to estrone to estriol and a minimum rate of oxidative inactivation of the estrogens due to a high and balanced rate of secretion of estrogens and progesterone.   The subsequent prepartum drop in estriol and estrone accompanied by an increase in estradiol and in the rate of estrogen oxidation was interpreted as reflecting decreased conversion and increased destruction of the estrogens due to progesterone withdrawal as well as reduced secretion of estrogen.   According to their concept, *the syncytial degeneration of the placenta during these last weeks with decreasing secretion of steroids has its incipience at the time of the peak of estrogen and progesterone production and is due to the deficiency at that time of oxidation products of the estrogens and hence a deficient utilization of CG.*   Once syncytial degeneration is under way, they believe, the process cannot be reversed, despite the increasing rate of estrogen inactivation (150, 168).

Bachman (9), using colorimetric assay, is the only other investigator who separately measured estradiol, estrone and estriol in the urines of pregnant women.   No one has performed Zn-HCl hydrolysis in conjunction with such studies, and Bachman's investigations were limited to six normal pregnancies followed during the last trimester.   His findings agree with the Smiths' as regards estradiol and estriol, but he failed to observe any prepartum drop in estrone.

Changes in estradiol, estrone and estriol and in the rate of estrogen inactivation similar to those during the last two weeks of normal pregnancy were consistently found by the Smiths to precede and accompany late pregnancy toxemia and associated accidents in the 23 abnormal cases studied during the last trimester the only difference being that when they take place prematurely they progress over a longer period and become exaggerated to a degree normally attained only after labor is well advanced.   In the three patients followed from earlier in pregnancy there was urinary evidence of a premature peak in estrogen and progesterone secretion around the twenty-eighth week and a comparative *deficiency of estrogen oxidation products throughout the second trimester.*   These patients were diabetic and, as pointed out, the earlier hormonal abnormality may not precede the premature degenerative changes in the placental syncytium in all cases of late pregnancy toxemia.   Such a deficiency of oxidation products during the second trimester, however, may be the predisposing factor in a certain percentage of patients just as, according to their concept, a similar situation during the last weeks of normal pregnancy is responsible for failing utilization of CG and the prepartum withdrawal of placental steroids.

THEORIES OF ETIOLOGY AND ATTEMPTS AT TREATMENT.   *The thyroid gland.* On the theory that hypothyroidism accompanied by hypercholesteremia produces placental arterial disease predisposing to thrombosis, infarcts and degeneation with resultant absorption of toxins from degenerated placental tissue, Patterson *et al.* (109) administered thyroid as a preventive measure. The clinical results reported by them and others (38, 64, 78, 86) with thyroid or iodine have not indicated specificity of therapy. As stated above, Dexter and Weiss (43) concluded that hypofunction of this gland cannot play a significant rôle in the causation of late pregnancy toxemia.

The adrenal glands. Parks (106, 107), assuming that the upset of sodium and potassium in toxemia is due to excessive hormones from the fetal adrenal glands, reported the control of edema by potassium in patients who had not responded to a low intake of sodium chloride.

Progesterone. Robson and Paterson (108, 122), from experiments with rabbits, concluded that the toxic condition from the uterus might be due to a failure of placental nutrition following removal of luteal secretion and described encouraging clinical results from small amounts of progesterone given early in the disease. These were not consistently achieved by others (14, 99, 103).

Estrogens. Shute (129–133), on the basis of a blood estrogen test devised by himself, classified toxemic patients into two groups, those with low estrogen (true pre-eclampsia and eclampsia) and those with high estrogen. The former he treated with estrogen and the latter with vitamin E, with satisfactory control of both. There are not reports in the literature of attempts to confirm the specificity of his test or his therapeutic results.

Testing their hypothesis that oxidation products of the estrogens cause utilization of CG for the placental secretion of its steroids, Smith and Smith (168, 172) investigated the effect of preventive treatment with diethylstilbestrol, this drug being employed because oxidation products such as estrone-lactone (*v.s.*) were not available in sufficient amounts and because experiments (163) had indicated a superiority of diethylstilbestrol for this purpose. Two diabetic patients with bad obstetrical histories were studied both during treatment and control periods and the placenta of one examined histologically. From the results, utilization of CG was enhanced and a premature aging of the placenta in steroid secretion, as well as late pregnancy complications, were averted. They (168) demonstrated that, once toxemia is evident, therapy with diethylstilbestrol is not likely to stimulate secretion of placental steroids or have any clearly favorable effect on the disease, since an excess of endogenous oxidation products pertains by this time and is unable itself to bring on renewed secretory activity in the already degenerate syncytium.[1]

[1] Since this paper went to press, Davis and Fugo (DAVIS, M. E., AND N. W. FUGO. Proc. Soc. Exper. Biol. and Med. **65**:283, 1947) have reported experiments in which 50 to 200 mgm. of diethylstilbestrol were administered daily by mouth starting at the fourth to tenth week of pregnancy and continued for 6 to 8 weeks. This dosage is greatly in excess of the amounts recommended by Smith and Smith for early pregnancy (168, 172). In normal untreated pregnancy pregnanediol excretion increases steadily as pregnancy progresses; whereas the results presented by Davis and Fugo show no increase during the period of stilbestrol administration. It seems possible that such large doses early in pregnancy might inhibit progesterone secretion through depressing the utilization of CG, just as the prolonged administration of large doses to the non-pregnant woman are known to inhibit ovarian secretion through depressing pituitary gonadotropic activity.

Progesterone and estrogen. On the basis of their evidence for a progressive deficiency of these two hormones before and during late pregnancy toxemia and associated accidents, the clinical and hormonological effect of replacement therapy was investigated by Smith and Smith (144, 146, 149, 170). As a preventive measure in patients in whom studies of blood and urine warranted the prediction of later trouble, the therapy was considered promising but impractical. The first 10 trials of preventive therapy with estrogen and progesterone in diabetic patients at the George F. Baker Clinic of the New England Deaconess Hospital were carried out by the Smiths and reported by them (144, 146), as well as by White and her associates (200-203). The latter continued with this form of therapy and described good results in 91 patients, particularly as regards reduction of fetal mortality (200). There are no other publications concerning the use of such therapy prophylactically in either diabetic or non-diabetic patients, probably because of the expense involved. The prophylactic stimulation of placental secretion of sex steroids by diethylstilbestrol administration starting prior to any evidence of hormonal deficiency, now being investigated by Smith and Smith, would appear to offer a more physiological and practical approach.

Definitive therapy of toxemia with estrogen and progesterone has been disappointing even when seemingly large amounts were given (144, 146, 149, 170 179). Taylor (179) considered this to be evidence against steroid deficiency as solely responsible for the disease. Smith and Smith (149) demonstrated some temporary alleviation of pre-eclampsia with estrogen and progesterone, but their hormonal findings indicated that once toxic signs appear there is a rapid increase in the rate of destruction of administered as well as secreted hormones. This phenomenon, as well as decreased secretion, they believe, contributes to the low levels in toxemia. With Taylor they consider the deficiency of estrogen and progesterone not to be the final precipitating cause of the toxemic syndrome. Its universal occurrence in all cases, however, as shown by hormonal and histological studies (*v.s.*) and the evidence that it precedes toxic signs implicate it as an intermediary and contributory factor.

Menstruation and toxemia. In the publications covered in this review, the Smiths repeatedly referred to similarities between the phenomenon of menstruation and toxemia of late pregnancy, the analogy having been suggested to them primarily because of their evidence from urinalysis for a hormonal situation before and during menstruation entirely like that before and during late pregnancy accidents. The similarity between premenstrual changes and toxemia were observed clinically by Dexter and Weiss (43), who stated further that so far as types of edema and symptoms are concerned there is a certain similarity in menstruation, normal pregnancy and toxemia. The Smiths (150) recently summarized their evidence that withdrawal of hormonal support from the pregnant as from the non-pregnant uterus results in the formation and release of a toxic metabolite of tissue catabolism like the toxin they found in the menstruating endometrium. The pathological effects of this toxin upon experimental animals are such as to warrant the assumption that it is directly responsible for the local changes resulting in menstruation and for the similar but generalized damage of late pregnancy toxemia. This hypothesis is strengthened by their evidence for certain properties in the circulating blood of women with toxemia similar to those of menstrual discharge, *viz.*, pyrogenic and fibrinolytic activity,[2] precipitation by anti-canine necrosin rabbit serum and a pseudoglobulin fraction capable of prolonging the survival time of rats given a lethal dose of the toxic euglobulin fraction of menstrual discharge (151, 165, 169), these properties being absent in normal pregnancy except during prolonged labor. According to their theory, the maternal portion of the placenta, *i.e.*, the decidua, being endometrium, should be the source of the toxin. (As such it could also be the cause of postpartum eclampsia.) A limited number of tests with specimens of decidua removed at the time of cesarean section have revealed marked toxicity in those from pre-eclamptic and eclamptic patients (150). In their publications, they have emphasized the extreme lability of the menstrual toxin (169). Failure to consider this possibility may explain the failures of the past to demonstrate any specific or consistent toxicity in placentas from toxemic women. Hertig (72) finds decidual necrosis and vascular thrombosis in relation to delivery and toxemia.

Certain known interrelationships between vascular supply, hormone production and tissue metabolism suggest that various conditions would bring about a menstrual-like phenomenon in the pregnant uterus. In the section on the metabolism of the estrogens (*v.s.*) the Smiths' data, suggesting that a deficiency of estrogen oxidation products during the second trimester might lead to premature syncytial degeneration was reviewed. Decidual, like endometrial, catabolism would be expected to result from the consequent withdrawal of estrogen and progesterone, with the production of toxin. The toxin in turn, to judge from its action in experimental animals, would be expected to augment degeneration of the syncytium and even cause degeneration of the Langhans cells and cytotrophoblast, thus disturbing hormone production even further.

Page (105-A) pointed out the possible rôle of placental ischemia in the pathogenesis of toxemia. An adequate vascular supply to the placenta is contingent upon an adequate production of estrogen and progesterone. Conversely, the Smiths (147) showed that decreased blood supply to the placenta through uterine contractions depresses the secretion of the steroid hormones. Decreased blood-supply to the uterine contents, such as might result from local mechanical conditions or generalized vascular situations, would be expected to result in degeneration not only of the syncytium but also of the decidua. Furthermore, since the pathological effect of menstrual toxin reflects vasoconstriction (151, 169), its release would in itself interfere with vascular supply.

In the course of their studies, the Smiths (151, 164, 169) deduced that types of injury not related to withdrawal of hormonal support cause the release of a similar if not identical toxin and acquired evidence for its presence in human exudative material and in the circulating blood of women with damaged tissues.

---

[2] Fibrinolytic activity in the circulating blood of patients with late pregnancy toxemia has been confirmed (203-A).

On this basis, damage of the chorionic epithelium might contribute to the production of toxin.

Any one of a number of processes, therefore, might be primarily responsible for setting off a chain of events leading to an overwhelming production of toxin and to toxemia of late pregnancy, unless delivery of the uterine contents intervened. Whatever the primary etiology, the final syndrome would be the same, a vicious circle in which decrease of vascular supply, hormonal deficiency and toxin formation were augmenting one another.

Even in cases wherein a deficiency of oxidation products of the estrogens does not pertain during the second trimester, the prophylactic use of adequate dosages of stilbestrol, now being investigated by Smith and Smith may prove effective through increasing uterine vascularity, both *per se* and by stimulating steroid secretion in the placenta. Once the disease is clinically manifest, according to their findings, the vicious circle of the final syndrome is already established and the best hope of cutting in upon it, aside from delivery of the products of conception, lies in neutralization of the toxin. To investigate this possibility, they (168) studied a few cases of pre-eclampsia to whom a crude preparation of their protective pseudoglobulin was experimentally administered. Clinically the results could be considered no more than promising. Their principal interest lies in the theoretical implications which appear to uphold the above concepts.

The presence of a toxin in toxemia has always offered attractive possibilities for explaining the clinical syndrome. Complete studies on the effects of menstrual toxin remain to be performed but experiments reported show that it causes edema and vasoconstriction and indicate that it produces damage of capillary endothelium as well as of tissues in general and has an antidiuretic effect (169). Dexter and Weiss (9) offered evidence for the existence of generalized damage of the capillary endothelial system in toxemia. That the toxin may be responsible for the hypertension and proteinuria of toxemia remains to be investigated. Damage of the renal glomerular capillaries would explain the proteinuria. The hypertension may be the consequence of a number of effects of the toxin, renal, suprarenal, cerebral and direct upon blood vessels. The antidiuretic substance in the placentas of toxemic patients (67) may be the toxin working directly or through pituitary stimulation (*v.i.*) in the experimental animal. The same explanation may apply as regards the melanophore-expanding principle in the blood and placentas of patients with toxemia (87). That patients with toxemia are hypersensitive to injected posterior-lobe hormones (*v.s.* Effects of Administered Posterior Pituitary Extracts) suggests an effect superimposed on that of the toxin. Smith and Smith (169) showed in rats that menstrual toxin causes the release of pituitary gonadotropic and adrenotropic hormones and believe that it produces an "alarm" reaction involving quite possibly the release of other pituitary hormones. Epinephrinemia in eclampsia (95) may reflect such an "alarm" reaction, and pituitary stimulation may explain a number of observations made in pre-eclamptic and eclamptic patients, *viz.*, urinary thyrotropic hormone (19), possibly the urinary antidiuretic substance (*v.s.* Antidiuretic substance in the urine), thyroid hormone (75) and, particularly, the possibility considered by some of over-activity of the adrenal cortex (26, 43, 181). None of these abnormalities has been demonstrated prior to the clinical onset of the disease.

SUMMARY

From the above it is apparent that the primary etiology of toxemia of late pregnancy has yet to be determined, that no definitive treatment has been rewarded with spectacular cure, such as usually occurs following delivery of the products of conception, and that prevention of the disease by the administration of hormones has yet to be proven. Certain aberrations from the normal in hormonal or hormonal-like findings and in placental morphology appear to be established in women with pre-eclampsia and eclampsia: 1, excessive antidiuretic substance in urine and placenta; 2, a melanophore-expanding principle in the blood and placenta; 3, a hypersensitivity to the injection of posterior pituitary secretions; 4, high titers of chorionic gonadotropin in a large percentage of cases; 5, decreased excretion of estrogens and pregnanediol, and 6, histological and histochemical changes in the placenta similar to but more marked than those of the normal placenta at term and primarily involving degeneration of the syncytial cells which probably secrete the steroid hormones. Of these established abnormalities, the last three are underway prior to clinical manifestations and occur normally at term.

Synthesis. That the primary etiology of toxemia may consist of a number of causes is suggested by the already familiar predisposing factors such as essential hypertension, diabetes, primigravidity, hydatidiform mole, twins and hydramnios. The evidence at hand appears to establish premature senility of the placental syncytium and premature withdrawal of the placental steroid hormones as the final intermediary pathology. This disturbance, which occurs normally at term, must be brought about prematurely by the working of the primary etiology, which probably involves either an intrinsic metabolic abnormality affecting the placenta or a decrease in blood supply to the placenta or both. Since the syncytial-steroid aberration from the normal characterizes all cases, it may logically be assumed to be contributory factor to the development of toxemia in all cases. From the above discussion (*v.s. Theories of etiology and attempts at treatment*), however, it cannot be assigned the rôle of the sole precipitating cause of the toxemic syndrome. Recent incomplete work suggests, 1, that withdrawal of hormonal support from the pregnant as from the non-pregnant uterus may result in the formation of a menstrual-like toxin in the placenta (? maternal portion, *i.e.*, decidua); 2, that the primary etiology may, in conjunction with the steroid deprivation it causes, do the same thing, and 3, that release of this toxin may prove to be the final cause of toxemia of late pregnancy.

REFERENCES

(1) ADLER, A. A., P. FREMERY AND M TAUSK. Nature **133**: 293, 1934.

(2) ALLAN, H. AND E. C. DODDS. Biochem. J. **29**: 285, 1935.

(3) ALLEN, E. Sex and internal secretions. Williams & Wilkins Co., Baltimore, 1939.

(4) AMATI, J. Zentralbl. f. Gynäk. **52**: 2639, 1928.

(5) ANSELMINO, K. J. AND F. HOFFMANN. Ztschr. f. Geburtsch. ü. Gynäk. **114**: 52, 1936.

(6) ANSELMINO, K. J., F. HOFFMANN AND W. P. KENNEDY. Edinburgh Med. J. **39**: 376, 1932.

(7) ASCHEIM, S. AND B. ZONDEK.   Klin. Wchnschr. **6:** 1322, 1927.

(8) ASK-UPMARK, M. E.   Acta Obst. and Gynec. Scand. **5:** 211, 1926.

(9) BACHMAN, C.   Am. J. Obst. and Gynec. **42:** 599, 1941.

(10) BACHMAN, C., D. LEEKLEY AND H. HIRSCHMANN.   J. Clin. Investigation **19:** 801, 1940.

(11) BACHMAN, C., D. LEEKLEY AND H. HIRSCHMANN.   Am. J. Med. Sci. **201:** 311, 1941.

(12) BACHMAN, C., D. LEEKLEY AND H. HIRSCHMANN.   J. Clin. Endocrinology **1:** 206, 1941.

(13) BACHMAN, C., D. LEEKLEY AND B. WINTER.   J. Clin. Endocrinology **1:** 142, 1941.

(14) BENNETT, F. O.   New Zealand Med. J. **38:** 11, 1939.

(15) BERKELEY, C.   J. Obst. and Gynaec. Brit. Emp. **5:** 40, 1904.

(16) BICHENBACH, W. AND H. FROMME.   Klin. Wchnschr. **14:** 496, 1935.

(17) BILL, A. H. AND F. M. POSEY, JR.   Am. J. Obst. and Gynec. **48:** 405, 1944.

(18) BLAZSO, S. AND V. DUBRAUSZKY.   Arch. f. Gynäk. **170:** 651, 1940.

(19) BONILLA, F. AND H. KRAMANN.   ˉMonatschr. f. Geburtsch. u. Gynäk. **105:** 8, 1937.

(20) BORCHARDT, H., E. DINGEMANSE AND E. LAQUER.   Naturwiss. **190:** 1934.

(21) BOURG, R. AND G. LE GRAND.   Arch. Internat. de Méd. Expér. **10:** 551, 1935.

(22) BRINDEAU, A., H. HINGLAIS AND M. HINGLAIS.   Compt. rend. Soc. de Biol. **115:** 1509, 1934.

(23) BROUGHER, J. C.   Northwest Med. **43:** 198, 1944.

(24) BROUGHER, J. C.   Am. J. Obst. and Gynec. **43:** 710, 1942.

(25) BROWNE, F. J.   J. Obst. and Gynaec. Brit. Emp. **50:** 254, 1943.

(26) BROWNE, F. J.   J. Obst. and Gynaec. Brit. Emp. **51:** 438, 1944.

(27) BROWNE, J. S. L. AND E. H. VENNING.   Am. J. Physiol. **116:** 18, 1936.

(28) BROWNE, J. S. L., J. S. HENRY AND E. H. VENNING.   J. Clin. Investigation **16:** 678, 1937.

(29) BROWNE, J. S. L., J. S. HENRY AND E. H. VENNING.   J. Clin. Investigation **17:** 503, 1938.

(30) BROWNE, J. S. L., J. S. HENRY AND E. H. VENNING.   Am. J. Obst. and Gynec. **38:** 927, 1939.

(31) BUTENANDT, A.   Deutsche med. Wchnschr. **55:** 2171, 1929.

(32) CANTOR, M. M., J. R. VANT, L. C. CONN AND M. J. HUSTON.   Canad. M. A. J. **47:** 12, 1942.

(33) CARR, J. L.   Proc. Soc. Exper. Biol. and Med. **30:** 1061, 1933.

(34) COHEN, H. M., D. A. WILSON AND W. F. BRENNAN.   Pennsylvania Med. J. **46:** 1282, 1943.

(35) COHEN, S. L. AND G. F. MARRIAN.   Biochem. J. **28:** 1603, 1934.

(36) COHEN, S. L., G. F. MARRIAN AND M. WATSON.   Lancet **1:** 674, 1935.

(37) COLVIN, E. D. AND R. A. BARTHOLOMEW.   Am. J. Obst. and Gynec. **37:** 584, 1939.

(38) COLVIN, E. D., R. A. BARTHOLOMEW AND W. H. GRIMES.   Am. J. Obst. and Gynec. **43:** 183, 1942.

(39) COPE, C. L.   Lancet **2:** 158, 1940.

(40) COPE, C. L.   Brit. Med. J. **2:** 545, 1940.

(41) DAVIS, G. H.   Bull. School Med. Univ. Maryland **29:** 1, 1944.

(42) DEMPSEY, E. W. AND G. B. WISLOCKI.   Endocrinology **35:** 409, 1944.

(43) DEXTER, L. AND S. WEISS.   Preeclamptic and eclamptic toxemia of pregnancy. Little, Brown & Co., Boston, 1941.

(44) DIECKMANN, W. J.   The toxemias of pregnancy.   C. V. Mosby Co., St. Louis, 1941.

(45) DIECKMANN, W. J. AND H. L. MICHEL.   Am. J. Obst. and Gynec. **33:** 131, 1937.

(46) DINGEMANSE, E., E. LUQUEUR AND O. MUHLBACK.   Monatschr. f. Geburtsch. u. Gynäk. **109:** 37, 1939.

(47) DOISY, E. A.   J. Biol. Chem. **86:** 499, 1930.

(48) DOISY, E. A., C. D. VELER AND S. THAYER.   Proc. XIII Internat. Physiol. Cong., Am. J. Physiol. **90:** 329, 1929.

(49) DOUGLASS, M.   Surg., Gynec. and Obst. **52:** 52, 1931.

(50) DUYVENE DE WIT, J. J. AND V. M. OPPERS.   Nederl. tijdschr. f. geneesk. **83:** 4001, 1939.

(51) EHRHARDT, K. Klin. Wchnschr. **8**: 2330, 1929.

(52) EHRHARDT, K. Arch. f. Gynäk. **148**: 265, 1932.

(53) EHRHARDT, K. Münch. Med. Wchnschr. **81**: 869, 1934.

(54) EHRHARDT, C. AND H. FISCHER-WASELS. Zentralbl. f. Gynäk. **60**: 787, 1936.

(55) EVANS, H. M., C. L. KOHLS AND D. H. WONDER. J.A.M.A. **108**: 287, 1937.

(56) EVANS, H. M., K. MEYER AND M. E. SIMPSON. Am. J. Physiol. **100**: 141, 1932.

(57) EVANS, H. M. AND M. E. SIMPSON. Am. J. Physiol. **89**: 381, 1929.

(58) FAUVET, E. AND L. MÜNZNER. Klin. Wchnschr. **16**: 675, 1937.

(59) FEKETE, K. Endocrinology **19**: 231, 1935.

(60) FELLNER, O. O. Arch. f. Gynäk. **100**: 64, 1913.

(61) GASPAR, J. L. West. J. Surg. **53**: 21, 1945.

(62) GEY, G. O., G. E. SEEGAR AND L. M. HELLMAN. Science **88**: 306, 1938.

(63) GRIMES, O. R. J. M. A. Alabama **15**: 35, 1945.

(64) GROSSI, G. Ann. Ostetricia Ginecol. **8**: 1019, 1929.

(65) HAFFNER, J. Acta Obst. and Gynec. Scand. **18**: 125, 1938.

(66) HAIN, A. M. J. Endocrinology **2**: 104, 1940.

(67) HAM, G. C. AND E. M. LANDIS. J. Clin. Investigation **21**: 455, 1942.

(68) HEARD, R. D. H., W. S. BAULD AND M. M. HOFFMAN. J. Biol. Chem. **141**: 709, 1941.

(69) HEARD, R. D. H. AND M. M. HOFFMAN. J. Biol. Chem. **141**: 329, 1941.

(70) HEIM, K. Klin. Wchnschr. **13**: 1614, 1934.

(71) HERRMANN, E. Die Eklampsie und ihre Prophylaxe. vol. 7. Urban & Schwarzenberg, Berlin, 1929.

(72) HERTIG, A. T. Personal communication.

(73) HINSELMANN, H. Die Eklampsie. F. Cohen, Bonn, 1924.

(74) HOFBAUER, J. Am. J. Obst. and Gynec. **36**: 522, 1938.

(75) HOFFMANN, F. AND K. J. ANSELMINO. Arch. f. Gynäk. **147**: 597, 645, 1931.

(76) HOLLAND, E. J. Obst. and Gynaec. Brit. Emp. **16**: 255, 325, 384, 1909.

(77) HUFFMAN, M. N., D. W. MACCORQUODALE, S. A. THAYER, E. A. DOISY, O. W. SMITH AND G. V. SMITH. J. Biol. Chem. **134**: 591, 1940.

(78) HUGHES, E. C. Am. J. Obst. and Gynec. **40**: 48, 1940.

(79) JONES, H. W. AND P. G. WEIL. J. A. M. A. **111**: 518, 1938.

(80) JONES, G. E. S., E. DELFS AND H. M. STRAIN. Bull. Johns Hopkins Hosp. **75**:359, 1944.

(81) JONES, G. E. S., G. O. GEY AND M. K. GEY. Bull. Johns Hopkins Hosp. **72**: 26, 1943.

(82) KIBEL, I. Am. J. Obst. and Gynec. **48**: 553, 1944.

(83) KOSMAK, G. W. Toxemias of pregnancy. ed. 2. D. Appleton-Century Co., New York, 1931.

(84) KRIEGER, V. T. AND T. B. KILVINGTON. Med. J. Australia **1**: 575, 1940.

(85) KRIEGER, V. T. AND T. B. KILVINGTON. J. Clin. Endocrinology **6**: 320, 1946.

(86) KÜSTNER, H. Klin. Wchnschr. **9**: 21, 1930.

(87) KÜSTNER, H. AND H. DIETEL. Arch. f. Gynäk. **131**: 274, 1927.

(88) LAMBILLON, J. Rev. Belge Sci. Méd. **10**: 1, 1938.

(89) LAVIETES, P. H., D. C. LEARY, A. W. WINKLER AND J. P. PETERS. Yale J. Biol. and Med. **16**: 151, 1943.

(90) LIPSCHÜTZ, A. AND E. POCH. Compt. rend. Soc. de Biol. **111**: 856, 1932.

(91) LOPEZ, R. E. Surg., Gynec and Obst. **49**: 689, 1929.

(92) VON LOUROS, N. Zentralbl. f. Gynäk. **47**: 1667, 1923.

(93) LU, CH'ING-SHEN. Chinese Med. J. **59**: 131, 1941.

(94) LYON, R. Am. J. Obst. and Gynec. **51**: 403, 1946.

(95) MACCHIARULO, O. Arch. f. Gynäk. **159**: 555, 1935.

(96) MARRIAN, G. F. J. Soc. Chem. Ind. **49**: 515, 1930.

(97) MARRIAN, G. F. Endeavor **5**: Jan., 1947.

(98) MARRIAN, G. F., S. L. COHEN AND M. WATSON. J. Biol. Chem. **59**: 109, 1935.

(99) MARSDEN, G. B. Brit. Med. J. **2**: 1221, 1937.

(100) Mazer, C. and J. Hoffman. J.A.M.A. **96:** 19, 1931.

(101) McGinty, D. A., W. B. McCullough and J. G. Wolter. Proc. Soc Exper. Biol. and Med. **34:** 176, 1936.

(102) McIlroy, L. The toxemias of pregnancy. E. Arnold & Co., London, 1936.

(103) McMann, W. Virginia Med. Monthly **65:** 676, 1938.

(104) Murkherjee, C. J. Obst. and Gynaec. Brit. Emp. **48:** 586, 1941.

(105) Page, E. W. Am. J. Obst. and Gynec. **52:** 1014, 1946.

(105-A) Page, E. W. Am. J. Obst. and Gynec. **37:** 291, 1939.

(106) Parks, T. J. J. Clin. Endocrinology **1:** 784, 1941.

(107) Parks, T. J. Med. Record **156:** 355, 1943.

(108) Paterson, S. J. Trans. Edin. Obst. Soc., 49, 1938–1939.

(109) Patterson, W. B., R. E. Nicodemus and H. F. Hunt. Penna. Med. J. **41:** 983, 1938.

(110) Pearlman, W. H. and G. Pincus. J. Biol. Chem. **144:** 569, 1942.

(111) Pearlman, W. H. and G. Pincus. J. Biol. Chem. **147:** 379, 1943.

(112) Philipp, E. Zentralbl. f. Gynäk. **8:** 450, 1930.

(113) Pincus, G. and M. Graubard. Endocrinology **26:** 427, 1940.

(114) Pincus, G. and W. H. Pearlman. Cancer Research **1:** 970, 1941.

(115) Pincus, G. and W. H. Pearlman. Endocrinology **31:** 507, 1942.

(116) Pincus, G. and P. A. Zahl. J. Gen. Physiol. **20:** 879, 1937.

(117) Pride, C. B. and M. P. Rucker. Am. J. Obst. and Gynec. **44:** 575, 1942.

(118) Probstner, A. Endokrinologie **8:** 161, 1931.

(119) Rakoff, A. E. Am. J. Obst. and Gynec. **38:** 371, 1939.

(120) Rubin, B. L., R. I. Dorfman and M. Miller. J. Clin. Endocrinology **6:** 347, 1946.

(121) Ruch, W. A. Memphis Med. J. **16:** 65, 1941.

(122) Robson, J. M. and S. J. Paterson. Brit. Med. J. **1:** 311, 1937.

(123) Saidl, J. Endokrinologie **12:** 147, 1933.

(124) Savage, J. E., H. B. Wylie and L. H. Douglass. Am. J. Obst. and Gynec. **36:** 39, 1938.

(125) Schaffer, N. K., J. P. Codden and H. J. Stander. Endocrinology **28:** 701, 1941.

(126) Schiller, J. and G. Pincus. Arch. Biochem. **2:** 317, 1943.

(127) Sheldon, D. E. Am. J. Obst. and Gynec. **49:** 269, 1945.

(128) Shockaert, J. A. and J. Lambillon. Brux. Médical **17:** 1468, 1937.

(129) Shute, E. Surg., Gynec. and Obst. **65:** 480, 1937.

(130) Shute, E. Endocrinology **21:** 594, 1937.

(131) Shute, E. Am. J. Surg. **49:** 478, 1943.

(132) Shute, E. Am. J. Surg. **71:** 470, 1946.

(133) Shute, E. and M. M. O. Barrie. Am. J. Obst. and Gynec. **40:** 1003, 1940.

(134) Siegler, S. L. J. Lab. Clin. Med. **24:** 1277, 1939.

(135) Smith, G. V. and O. W. Smith. Am. J. Physiol. **98:** 578, 1931.

(136) Smith, G. V. and O. W. Smith. Am. J. Physiol. **100:** 553, 1932.

(137) Smith, G. V. and O. W. Smith. Proc. Soc. Exper. Biol. and Med. **30:** 918, 1933.

(138) Smith, G. V. and O. W. Smith. Am. J. Physiol. **107:** 128, 1934.

(139) Smith, G. V. and O. W. Smith. Surg., Gynec. and Obst. **61:** 27, 1935.

(140) Smith, G. V. and O. W. Smith. Surg., Gynec. and Obst. **61:** 175, 1935.

(141) Smith, G. V. and O. W. Smith. Am. J. Physiol. **112:** 340, 1935.

(142) Smith, G. V. and O. W. Smith. New Eng. J. Med. **215:** 908, 1936.

(143) Smith, G. V. and O. W. Smith. Proc. Soc. Exper. Biol. and Med. **36:** 460, 1937.

(144) Smith, G. V. and O. W. Smith. Am. J. Obst. and Gynec. **36:** 769, 1938.

(145) Smith, G. V. and O. W. Smith. Am. J. Obst. and Gynec. **38:** 618, 1939.

(146) Smith, G. V. and O. W. Smith. Am. J. Obst. and Gynec. **39:** 405, 1940.

(147) Smith, G. V. and O. W. Smith. J. Clin. Endocrinology **1:** 461, 1941.

(148) Smith, G. V. and O. W. Smith. J. Clin. Endocrinology **1:** 470, 1941.

(149) Smith, G. V. and O. W. Smith. J. Clin. Endocrinology **1:** 477, 1941.

(150) Smith, G. V. and O. W. Smith. West. J. Surg., Obst. and Gynec. **55:** 288, 1947.

(151) SMITH, G. V. AND O. W. SMITH. Am. J. Obst. and Gynec., in press.
(152) SMITH, G. V. AND J. H. KENNARD. Proc. Soc. Exper. Biol. and Med. **36:** 508, 1937.
(153) SMITH, G. V., O. W. SMITH, M. N. HUFFMAN, S. A. THAYER, D. W. MacCORQUODALE AND E. A. DOISY. J. Biol. Chem. **130:** 431, 1939.
(154) SMITH, G. V., O. W. SMITH AND G. PINCUS. Am. J. Physiol. **121:** 98, 1938.
(155) SMITH, G. V., O. W. SMITH AND S. SCHILLER. Am. J. Obst. and Gynec. **44:** 455, 1942.
(156) SMITH, G. V., O. W. SMITH AND S. SCHILLER. Am. J. Obst. and Gynec. **44:** 606, 1942.
(157) SMITH, M. G. Bull. Johns Hopkins Hosp. **41:** 62, 1927.
(158) SMITH, O. W. Endocrinology **35:** 146, 1944.
(159) SMITH, O. W. Proc. Soc. Exper. Biol. and Med. **59:** 242, 1945.
(160) SMITH, O. W. Endocrinology **40:** 116, 1947.
(161) SMITH, O. W. AND G. V. SMITH. Am. J. Obst. and Gynec. **33:** 365, 1937.
(162) SMITH, O. W. AND G. V. SMITH. Endocrinology **28:** 740, 1941.
(163) SMITH, O. W. AND G. V. SMITH. Proc. Soc. Exper. Biol. and Med. **57:** 198, 1944.
(164) SMITH, O. W. AND G. V. SMITH. Proc. Soc. Exper. Biol. and Med. **59:** 116, 1945.
(165) SMITH, O. W. AND G. V. SMITH. Proc. Soc. Exper. Biol. and Med. **59:** 119, 1945.
(166) SMITH, O. W. AND G. V. SMITH. J. Clin. Endocrinology **6:** 483, 1946.
(167) SMITH, O. W. AND G. V. SMITH. Unpublished data.
(168) SMITH, O. W. AND G. V. SMITH. West. J. Surg., Obst. and Gynec. **55:** 313, 1947.
(169) SMITH, O. W. AND G. V. SMITH. Am. J. Obst. and Gynec., in press.
(170) SMITH, O. W., G. V. SMITH AND A. G. GAULD. Am. J. Obst. and Gynec. **45:** 23,1943.
(171) SMITH, O. W., G. V. SMITH AND D. HURWITZ. Am. J. Med. Sci. **208:** 25, 1944.
(172) SMITH, O. W., G. V. SMITH AND D. HURWITZ. Am. J. Obst. and Gynec. **51:** 411, 1946.
(173) SMITH, O. W., G. V. SMITH AND S. SCHILLER. Am. J. Obst. and Gynec. **45:** 15, 1943.
(174) STANDER, H. J. The toxemias of pregnancy. Medicine Monographs. vol. 15. Williams & Wilkins Co., Baltimore, 1929.
(175) STOVER, R. F. AND J. P. PRATT. Endocrinology **24:** 29, 1939.
(176) SWINGLE, W. W. AND J. W. REMINGTON. Physiol. Rev. **24:** 89, 1944.
(177) SZARKA, S. Zentralbl. f. Gynäk. **54:** 2211, 1930.
(179) TAYLOR, H. C., JR. J.A.M.A. **120:** 595, 1942.
(180) TAYLOR, H. C., JR. AND E. N. SCADRON. Am. J. Obst. and Gynec. **37:** 963, 1939.
(181) TAYLOR, H. C., JR., R. C. WARNER AND C. A. WELSH. Am. J. Obst. and Gynec. **38:** 748, 1939.
(182) TAYLOR, H. C., JR., R. C. WARNER AND C. A. WELSH. Am. J. Obst. and Gynec. **45:** 547, 1943.
(183) TEEL, H. M. AND D. E. REID. Endocrinology **24:** 297, 1939.
(184) TENNEY, B. Am. J. Obst. and Gynec. **31:** 1024, 1936.
(185) TENNEY, B. AND F. PARKER. Endocrinology **21:** 687, 1937.
(186) TENNEY, B. AND F. PARKER. Am. J. Obst. and Gynec. **39:** 1000, 1940.
(187) DE VALERA, E. AND R. S. KELLAR. J. Obst. and Gynaec. Brit. Emp. **45:** 815, 1938.
(188) VENNING, E. H. Endocrinology **39:** 203, 1946.
(189) VENNING, E. H. J. Biol. Chem. **119:** 473, 1937.
(190) VENNING, E. H., J. S. HENRY AND J. S. L. BROWNE. Canad. M. A. J. **36:** 83, 1937.
(191) WALDSTEIN, E. Ztschr. Gyn. **53:** 1305, 1929.
(192) WARD, G. G., E. C. LYON, JR. AND G. G. BEMIS. Am. J. Obst. and Gynec. **16:** 655, 1928.
(193) WATTS, R. M. AND F. L. ADAIR. Am. J. Obst. and Gynec. **46:** 183, 1943.
(194) WEIL, P. G. Science **87:** 72, 1938. '
(195) WERLE, E. AND G. EFFKEMANN. Arch. f. Gynäk. **171:** 286, 1941.
(196) WERLE, E., A. HEVELKE AND K. BUTHMANN. Biochem. Ztschr. **309:** 270, 1941.
(197) WERLE, E. AND A. KALVELAGE. Biochem. Ztschr. **308:** 405, 1941.
(198) WESTERFELD, W. W. J. Biol. Chem. **143:** 177, 1942.
(199) WHITE, P. Surg., Gynec. and Obst. **61:** 324, 1935.
(200) WHITE, P. J.A.M.A. **128:** 181, 1945.

(201) WHITE, P. AND H. HUNT. J.A.M.A. 115: 2039, 1940.

(202) WHITE, P. AND H. HUNT. J. Clin. Endocrinology 3: 500, 1943.

(203) WHITE, P., R. S. TITUS, E. P. JOSLIN AND H. HUNT. Am. J. Med. Sci. 198: 482, 1939.

(203-A) WILLSON, J. R. AND E. R. MUNNELL. Proc. Soc. Exper. Biol. and Med. 62: 277, 1946.

(204) WILSON, R. B. Med. Clin. No. Am., 1477, 1945.

(205) WILSON, R. B., L. M. RANDALL AND A. F. OSTERBERG. Am. J. Obst. and Gynec. 37 59, 1939.

(206) WISLOCKI, G. B. AND H. S. BENNETT. Am. J. Anat. 73: 335, 1943.

(207) WISLOCKI, G. B. AND E. W. DEMPSEY. Endocrinology 38: 90, 1946.

(208) WOODBURY, R. A., R. P. AHLQUIST, B. AHREAN, R. TORPIN AND W. G. WATSON. J. Pharmacol. and Exper. Therapy 86: 359, 1946.

(209) ZONDEK, B. Klin. Wchnschr. 7: 1404, 1928.

(210) ZONDEK, B. Nature 133: 209, 1934.

(211) VAN ZWANENBERG, D. St. Bartholomew's Hosp. J. 49: 31, 1945.

Doing Harm: The DES Tragedy and Modern American Medicine

RICHARD GILLAM AND BARTON J. BERNSTEIN

"Everyone acted in good faith [on DES], with the best of intentions, and within the established norms of medical procedures of the day. Thus the consequences seem unavoidable."

Roberta Apfel and Susan Fisher

"If my history be judged useful by those inquirers who desire an exact knowledge of the past as an aid to the interpretation of the future, which in the course of human things must resemble if it does not reflect it, I shall be content."

Thucydides[1]

MEDICAL TRAGEDIES resulting from the use of therapeutic drugs or devices are neither rare nor exclusively American problems. Consider

Our interest in DES grew out of a 1978–81 Stanford research project funded by the National Science Foundation. We are indebted to Larry Molton for sharing his own research on DES; to Pat Cody and DES Action for several items; to Arthur Herbst and Howard Bern for recent statistics on DES daughters; to Lincoln Moses for advice on statistics; to Beth Jay for some legal sources; and to groups at the History of Medicine Meeting in San Francisco in 1983 and the Institute of Health Policy seminar at UCSF in 1986, which considered our analysis of DES. We also thank the Stanford Department of History and the Values, Technology, Science, and Society (VTSS) Program for typing aid, and various Stanford colleagues who commented on an earlier version of this essay, especially Estelle Freedman and Margo Horn.

1. Roberta Apfel and Susan Fisher, *To Do No Harm:* DES and the Dilemmas of Modern Medicine (New Haven: Yale University Press, 1984), 131, 1.

57

The Public Historian, Vol. 9, No. 1 (Winter 1987)
© 1987 by the Regents of the University of California

thalidomide, the German drug that deformed thousands of babies in Europe, or the Dalkon shield, an American intrauterine device that killed some women and maimed thousands more both in the United States and elsewhere.[2] Another representative case, now demanding careful re-examination, involves the synthetic estrogen DES (diethylstilbestrol), which, for about three decades, was used widely in this country, and less widely abroad, to prevent miscarriages and is today held responsible for over 300 cases of cancer among "DES daughters" exposed to the drug *in utero*.[3]

A recent book by psychiatrists Roberta Apfel and Susan Fisher, *To Do No Harm: DES and the Dilemmas of Modern Medicine* argues, unlike most previous analyses [4] that no one can be blamed for the DES tragedy. This new interpretation raises larger questions about the structure and culture of medicine itself. Was the DES episode, to pose the issue starkly, inevitable or preventable? If preventable, who erred, what mistakes were made, and how could damage have been avoided? If inevitable, are similar outbreaks of iatrogenic illness—as, presumably, the "cost" of medical progress—likewise inescapable in the future? Is it truly the lot of modern medicine to do repeated harm while trying to do good? To address such questions effectively, it is first necessary to review the medical and human disaster that Apfel and Fisher have attempted to explain.

The Cancer Connection

The dramatic part of the DES story came to light in April 1971. That month, three physicians at Boston's Massachusetts General Hospital reported in the *New England Journal of Medicine,* based on cases dis-

2. Morton Mintz, *The Therapeutic Nightmare* (Boston: Houghton Mifflin, 1965), 248–64; and Mintz, *At Any Cost* (New York: Pantheon, 1985).

3. Of the 522 cases of adenocarcinoma, only about 60 percent (314) were *definitely* daughters exposed in utero to DES or a similar drug, and in about 5 percent (27) of the cases, analysts are "unsure of the maternal exposure history due to lack of information." About 3 per cent (13) of the 522 had been exposed to a progesterone or/and an estrogen, about 9 percent (49) were exposed to other hormones (often thyroid) or some unidentified drug, and in about a quarter (119) no evidence of maternal hormone usage was uncovered. (Arthur Herbst to Bernstein, June 2, 1986) Perhaps some of these other cases can be explained by the mother's or daughter's exposure to DES through the food chain, including meat from DES-fed animals (poultry and beef).

4. Barbara Seaman and Gideon Seaman, *Women and the Crisis in Sex Hormones* (New York: Rawson, 1977), 1–74; Cynthia Orenberg, *DES: The Complete Story* (New York: St. Martin's, 1981); Stephen Fenichell and Lawrence Charfoos, *Daughters At Risk: A Personal DES History* (Garden City: Doubleday, 1981); and Robert Myers, *DES: The Bitter Pill* (New York: Seaview/Putnam, 1983). On cattlefeed and DES, see Nicholas Wade, "DES: A Case Study of Abdicating Regulation," *Science* 177 (July 28, 1972), 353 ff; and *Wall Street Journal,* July 15, 1980, p. 46.

covered in 1966–1969, that DES was "associated"[5] with a rare form of cancer found in some daughters of women who had used the drug while pregnant.[6] This was the first time that a drug taken prenatally by women had been linked to cancer in their children, or that a transplacental effect had shown up so many years after birth.

The three physicians had hit, somewhat by accident, upon their alarming discovery. In 1966, one of them had found a case of clear-cell adenocarcinoma of the vagina in a fifteen-year-old girl. Such a malignancy was rare in women and virtually unknown in such a young girl. Nevertheless, over the next few years seven additional cases came to the attention of Massachusetts General doctors—more than had been reported in the world's medical literature up to that time. In their subsequent search for an explanation of these cancers, the three hospital investigators eliminated such possible factors as sexual activity and the use of birth control pills, douches, tampons, and the like. One of the patient's mothers then suggested that the culprit might be a drug, DES, that she had taken when pregnant with her daughter. This proved to be the crucial clue, implicating DES in at least seven of the cases.

Since 1971, when the *New England Journal* article appeared, further research has suggested that somewhere between 1.4 per thousand and 1.4 per ten thousand of the approximately 1 to 2.4 million American women exposed to DES *in utero* may develop this kind of cancer.[7] About a fifth of the known victims have died. In addition, many DES daughters suffer from other DES-associated problems—changes in vaginal tissue, deformed or altered reproductive organs, and probably a higher than normal incidence of premature births and unsuccessful pregnancies. Recent evidence also suggests that DES sons have their

5. "Association" remains the preferred medical-scientific term, since many experts still avoid speaking of DES as *the* sole or proven "cause" of adenocarcinoma in DES daughters. See Arthur Herbst, *et al.*, "Risk Factors For the Development of Diethylstilbestrol-Associated Clear Cell Adenocarcinoma: A Case-Control Study," *American Journal of Obstetrics and Gynecology* (hereafter, *AJOG*) 154 (April 1986), 814–22.

6. Arthur L. Herbst, Howard Ulfelder, and David C. Poskanzer, "Adenocarcinoma of the Vagina: Association of Maternal Stilbestrol Therapy with Tumor Appearance in Young Women," *New England Journal of Medicine* (hereafter *NEJM*) 284 (April 22, 1971), 878–81; and Peter Greenwald, Joseph J. Barlow, Philip C. Nasca, and William Burnett, "Vaginal Cancer After Maternal Treatment with Synthetic Estrogens," *NEJM* 285 (August 12, 1971), 390–92. For a narrow, methodological critique of these two 1971 studies—a critique that oddly ignores animal and historical evidence suggesting a DES-adenocarcinoma association—see Michael J. McFarlane, Alvan R. Feinstein, and Ralph I. Horwitz, "Diethylstilbestrol and Clear Cell Vaginal Carcinoma: Reappraisal of the Epidemiological Evidence," *American Journal of Medicine* 81 (November 1986), 855–63. For an oblique rejoinder to such arguments, see Arthur Herbst, *et al.*, "Risk Factors for the Development of Diethylstilbestrol-Associated Clear Cell Adenocarcinoma," *AJOG* 154 (April 1986), 814–22, esp. 814 and 819–20.

7. The high estimate is drawn from a DES Action-National analysis, which, in the judgment of researcher Howard Bern, seems reasonable (Bernstein conversation with Bern). Pat Cody of DES Action provided the organizaton's written analysis.

own reproductive and related difficulties, and one study has shown a small, but statistically significant increase in some cancers among mothers who took the drug while pregnant.[8] Most of these victims came from the white middle or upper class, since, ironically, this group had privileged access to a drug once deemed the best and most advanced prenatal therapy available.

DES daughters—and to a lesser extent, mothers and sons—also confront a variety of other medical, emotional, financial, and legal problems. For those born, roughly speaking, between 1940 and 1974, simply determining in utero DES exposure can itself be difficult, since their mothers often do not know or remember what pregnancy drugs they took years if not decades before. Those physicians who have not died are often unwilling, perhaps out of fear of recriminations and litigation, to engage in a time-consuming review of past records in order to identify and then to notify patients who received DES prenatally. Many potential victims are therefore uncertain or unaware that they have been placed at risk. Those who know, or simply suspect, that they are DES children often react with anger—sometimes at their mothers, who themselves feel guilty, or at physicians, drug companies, and government regulators. Although many healthy DES daughters are advised to undergo frequent medical checkups for preventive purposes, they have no effective legal claim to compensation for such medical costs or for psychological suffering. In order to sue, those who do develop cancer or another DES-related illness must either prove which company produced the DES their mothers took (which is often impossible) assert (under theories of "concerted action" or "alternative liability") that a number of drug firms should be held jointly liable for damages, or rely upon a new legal doctrine, adopted initially in California, which apportions financial responsibility among manufacturers based upon their share of the DES market at the time of injury. In some states, courts have held that the statute of limitations bars legal action for past DES injury even though the evidence of such injury could not possibly have been discovered until after the period for filing suit had run out.[9]

---

8. Herbst and Bern, eds., *Developmental Effects of Diethystilbestrol (DES) in Pregnancy* (New York: Thieme-Stratton, 1981), *passim;* Gene R. Conley, *et al.,* "Seminoma and Epididymal Cysts in a Young Man With Known Diethylstilbestrol Exposure in Utero," *Journal of the American Medical Association* (hereafter, *JAMA*) 249 (March 11, 1983), 1325–26; E.R. Greenbert, *et al.,* "Breast Cancer in Mothers Given Diethylstilbestrol in Pregnancy," *NEJM* 311 (November 29, 1984), 1393–98. For further evidence suggestive of the DES association for sons, see Retha Newbold, Bill Bullock, and John McLachlan, "Lesions of the Rete Testis in Mice Exposed Prenatally to Diethylstilbestrol," *Cancer Research* 45 (October 1985), 5145–50.

9. See, *Sindell v. Abbott Laboratories* (1980) 26 Cal. 3d 588 on market-share responsibility, and for other tightened standards possibly harmful to DES plaintiffs, *Brown v. Superior Court* (1986) 182 Cal App 3d 1125. For a discussion of pertinent legal theories, see Naomi Sheiner, "DES and a Proposed Theory of Enterprise Liability," *Fordham Law Review* 46 (1977–78), 963–1007.

Differing Interpretations

Not surprisingly, the story of DES and of its toll in human suffering has attracted considerable critical attention. The first books on this subject, some of high quality, came exclusively from those who were not medical experts—journalists, lawyers, health activists, and DES mothers and daughters. All implicitly or explicitly contended that the DES tragedy resulted from such factors as poor or inept medicine, lax drug regulation, physician insensitivity to women, and deceptive drug company marketing and advertising practices. In effect, this body of literature offered a lay, or "democratic" (and often feminist) critique of crucial elite decisions, holding plausibly—but without providing enough analytical detail to convince skeptics—that the approval and widespread use of DES in pregnancy both could and should have been avoided. From such a perspective, this iatrogenic episode simply did not have to occur.[10]

By contrast, Roberta Apfel and Susan Fisher now offer a very different argument. Much of their book, and by far the best part, explores the psychological trauma of DES victims as they deal with their real or potential injuries, their families, and their doctors. Here there is often much to praise. In addition to this, however, Apfel and Fisher work through the history of DES, attempting to explain how and why the drug became accepted as a prenatal therapy in the 1940s and then remained in use even after later studies showed it to be ineffective in preventing miscarriage. Apfel and Fisher's resulting historical analysis sharply challenges past interpretations of DES.

Unlike earlier lay critics, Apfel and Fisher issue no controversial indictments, identify no responsibility, apportion little blame. They take special care to exonerate their own medical community: "Everyone acted in good faith, with the best of intentions, and within the established norms of medical procedures of the day. Thus the consequences seem unavoidable" (p. 130). Indeed, Apfel and Fisher describe the DES episode as an essentially inevitable "tragedy," the product of large, irresistible forces "intrinsic to the very *structure* of modern medicine" (p. 8, emphasis added). No wonder that one physician, clearly uncomfortable with the alternative lay critique of medicine, has warmly welcomed (in a jacket puff) this exculpatory analysis as "*not* a piece of feminist propaganda, *not* an indictment of the medical profession or a condemnation of the drug industry."[11]

To Do No Harm, while critical of a few insensitive physicians who

10. These include Seaman and Seaman, *Women and the Crisis in Sex Hormones;* Fenichell and Charfoos, *Daughters at Risk;* Orenberg, *DES;* Meyers, *D.E.S.;* and Joyce Bichler, *DES Daughter* (New York: Avon, 1981).

11. E. James Anthony, professor of child psychiatry and director of the Edison Child Development Research Center, Washington University School of Medicine (St. Louis). Also see Monica Starkman, "Hippocrates Unbound," *New Republic* 195 (July 14 and 21, 1986), 40–41.

treat DES daughters, will thus appeal to most biomedical professionals, whose authority and competence it unmistakably endorses. Yet this book's bold claims, which reach beyond the narrow world of expertise, may trouble many others. The thesis of inevitability is a case in point. For if the DES tragedy could not in fact have been prevented—and if the courts agree—then victims in most states cannot hope to sue successfully for damages. At this point, the interpretation of DES history takes on larger public as well as scholarly significance. It becomes crucial to ask, accordingly, whether Apfel and Fisher are right to stress inevitability and determinism to the neglect of expert, elite, and corporate responsibility.

They are not. In the first place, their argument is analytically and conceptually confused. The authors embrace a remarkably ill-defined concept of the "structure of medicine," which appears to encompass such diverse factors as a heroic professional belief in new therapies and pills, a desire among doctors and patients to save babies, and a general cultural faith in medical technology and interventionism. But curiously, Apfel and Fisher also acknowledge that "mistakes were made, that procedures were not adequate, and that the range of available scientific research resources was not fully utilized" (p. 9). For them, there is no contradiction, not even a tension, between their "structure of medicine" argument and their "mistakes [and] not fully utilized" argument, in part because the authors believe that such mistakes, including the disregard of scientific evidence, were and are inherent in the structure of modern medicine. This comfortable reconciliation of potentially conflicting interpretations is facile, unpersuasive, and—as will become apparent—historically untenable.

The authors in fact fail most seriously in their effort to do public history. Their work rests upon shaky, inadequate research, reflects ignorance of archival sources, neglects the role of the FDA, presents a confused and confusing analysis of the drug industry, and asserts conclusions at odds with the book's own evidence. A number of their facts are simply wrong. In addition, the authors' vague and superficial conception of "the structure of medicine"—to which they attribute undue explanatory power—deflects attention from key problems and events, thereby blocking effective historical analysis.

The Hidden DES Story

To a point, Apfel and Fisher offer a standard account of DES developments already described by others.[12] The drug was first synthesized in

12. The indispensable account of the drug's early history is Susan Bell, "The Synthetic Compound Diethylstilbestrol (DES), 1938–1941: The Social Construction of a Medical Treatment" (Ph.D. diss., Brandeis University, 1980). Also see Seaman and Seaman, *Women and the Crisis in Sex Hormones;* Orenberg, *DES;* Fenichell and Charfoos, *Daughters at Risk;* and Meyers, *D.E.S.;* cf. Bell, review of *To Do No Harm,* in *Disability Studies Quarterly,* copy in Bell to Bernstein, August 9, 1986.

England in 1938. Because it was developed under a British government grant, it was not patented there or elsewhere. The new synthetic hormone, like the far more expensive natural estrogens, seemed to promise special help to women in menopause. In the United States, a dozen drug companies banded together in 1941, mounted an unusual collaborative effort, overcame some medical dissent, and gained FDA approval for use of the drug in four specific conditions, including those of menopause. Occasional experimentation during the 1940s led some researchers to conclude that DES could also help women avoid miscarriages. In 1947, the FDA quickly responded to some company applications and approved DES for prenatal use. Despite seemingly persuasive studies in the early 1950s that challenged the efficacy of DES in pregnancy, the drug was widely prescribed to prevent miscarriages until at least the early 1970s, when its association with cancer was reported.

This much is well known and not in dispute. Beneath such bare-bones facts, however, lies a richer, more complex story that Apfel and Fisher often do not grasp and never adequately explain. To begin with, early researchers had reported—well before the FDA's first 1941 approval of DES—serious negative reactions in women who had used the drug. These included nausea, vomiting, diarrhea, dizziness, premature sexual development in girls, and suspected liver and kidney damage. Some laboratory scientists found that DES, like the natural estrogens, was carcinogenic in animals; that it killed embryos in such test animals as rabbits, guinea pigs, and rats; and that it crossed the placenta and distorted the sexual development of animal offspring. One study, published in May 1939, revealed that male rats exposed to DES *in utero* developed female rather than male genitalia, that females likewise had altered sex organs, and that a few animals approached a state of true intersexuality, or hermaphroditism.[13]

13. For a comprehensive survey on DES side-effects, see Charles H. McKenzie, "Diethystilbestrol: A Review of Literature," *The Journal-Lancet* 61 (March 1941), 94–100. For some specifics, see Ephraim Shorr, Frank H. Robinson, and George N. Papanicolaou, "A Clinical Study of the Synthetic Estrogen Stilbestrol," *JAMA* 113 (December 23, 1939), 2312–18; U.J. Salmon, S.H. Geist, and R. I. Walter, "Evaluation of Stilbestrol as a Therapeutic Estrogen," *AJOG* 40 (August 1940), 143–250; R. W. Scarff and C.P. Smith, "Proliferative Mastitis in Stilbestrol Workers; 2 Cases," *British Journal of Surgery* 29 (April 1942), 393–96; Charles W. Dunn, "Stilbestrol-Induced Gynecomastia," *JAMA* 115 (December 28, 1940), 2263–64; "Synthetic Female Hormone Pills Considered Potential Danger," *Science Newsletter* 37 (January 13, 1940), 31, and S.D. Soule and A.R. Bortnick, "Stilbestrol," *Journal of Clinical Endocrinology* 1 (January 1941), 53–57. For data on the carcinogenicity of DES in animals, see, for example, Antoine Lacassagne, "The Appearance of Mammary Adenocarcinoma in Male Rats Treated by Synthetic Estrogenic Substance," (title translated), *Comptes Rendus des Seance de la Societe de Biologie* 129 (November 19, 1938), 641–43; Charles F. Geschickter, "Mammary Carcinoma in the Rat with Metastasis Induced by Estrogen," *Science* 89 (January 13, 1939), 35–37; and the series of articles co-authored by Michael B. Shimkin and Hugh Grady, including "Mammary Carcinomas in Mice Following Oral Administration of Stilbestrol," *Proceedings of the Society for Experimental Biology and Medicine* 45 (October 1940), 246–48 and "Carcinogenic

In December 1939, the influential Council on Pharmacy and Chemistry of the American Medical Association, noticing some of this research, warned in the *Journal of the American Medical Association* that DES "may be carcinogenic under certain conditions" in humans and that it seemed to produce toxic reactions. "Because the product is so potent and because the possibility of harm must be recognized," the Council judged, "its use by the general medical profession should not be undertaken until further studies have led to a better understanding of such drugs."[14]

This warning virtually forced the FDA, initially, to view DES with caution. Under its newly granted authority to judge the safety (although not specifically the efficacy) of drugs before they could be marketed, the agency thus refused, in 1939 and 1940, to approve the first pharmaceutical company applications for DES. The FDA announced its impending denials of applications beforehand, so that applications could be withdrawn "without prejudice" and then resubmitted, often repeatedly, later on.[15] At the same time, key FDA officials maintained close ties with pharmaceutical interests and shared the widespread medical optimism about the potential therapeutic benefits of DES. In fact, agency regulators, never doubting the drug's efficacy, clearly *wanted* to approve DES if the explosive safety issue could somehow be defused. By late 1940, perhaps responding to industry suggestions, FDA officials had hatched a plan to do precisely this. They then asked interested companies not to act separately, as was usual, but, rather, to submit pooled drug data in the form of a collective "Master File." It was hoped that this procedure—never before used in the case of a "life-enhancing" as opposed to a "life-saving" drug—would yield the necessary proof of safety. In addition, the agency relied heavily upon a lobbyist for the American Drug Manufactur-

Potency of Stilbestrol and Estrone in C3H Mice," *Journal of the American Cancer Institute* 1 (August 1940), 119–28; and Charles Geschickter to E.H. Volwiler, October 7, 1939, in stenographic record of depositions in *Gail Abel et al. v. Eli Lilly* (hereafter, *Abel*), II, p. 422B, Wayne County Michigan Circuit Court, No. 74-030-070-NP (partial copy from DES Action). For effects on sexual development, see R. R. Greene, M. W. Burrill, and A. C. Ivy, "Experimental Intersexuality: Modification of Sexual Development of the White Rat with a Synthetic Estrogen," *Proceedings of the Society for Experimental Biology and Medicine* 41 (May 1939), 169–70; Albert Raynaud, "Feminization of Male Embryos of Mice by Injection of Diethystilbestrol into Mother During Pregnancy," (title translated), *Compt. Rend. Soc. de. Biol.* 131 (May 13, 1939), 218–22; E. Wolff, "Action of Diethystilbestrol of Genital Organs of Chick Embryo," (title translated), *Compt. rend. Acad. d. sc.* 208 (May 8, 1939), 1532–34; W. Hackmeister, "Death of Fetus and Organic Changes due to Synthetic Estrogen Substance," (title translated), *Zentralblatt fuer Gynaekologie* 63 (December 16, 1939), 2657–62. The basic medical reference index of the time, the *Index Medicus*, cited all the foregoing foreign-language articles in English. For a later critique of animal studies, see Paul Quirk, "Food and Drug Administration, in James Q. Wilson, ed., *The Politics of Regulation* (New York: Basic Books, 1980), 203.

14. Council on Pharmacy and Chemistry, "Stilbestrol: Preliminary Report of the Council," *JAMA* 113 (December 23, 1939), 2312.

15. Theodore Klumpp to Geist, November 14, 1940, and Durrett to Eli Lilly, November 20, 1939, in NDA 1221-20 file; and Durrett to King, August 3, 1939, "Memorandum of Phone Conversation," in NDA 713 file, FDA Records, FDA Headquarters, Rockville, Md.

ers Association who worked, virtually as a member of the FDA staff, to engineer approval of the drug.[16]

This cozy arrangement enabled drug companies, aided by their lobbyist and supported by the FDA, to construct a highly selective case for DES approval. Thus, a group of industry representatives, called the "small committee," both controlled and defined the contents of the Master File. One consequence was a degree of pro-DES bias in many "testimonial" letters from physicians who had gotten free "research samples" of DES from industry and who, in communicating with the "small committee," expressed both gratitude for such samples and the hope of getting more.[17] Most crucially, the committee also confined Master File data to *clinical* experience with *human* subjects, and thus effectively excluded unnerving evidence (carcinogenicity, fetal toxicity, and transplacental effects on sexual development) based upon *laboratory* work with *animals*. As a result, a number of risks simply disappeared from sight.[18] This strategy left only the troubling reports, admittedly by a small group of university-based researchers, of toxicity in humans. Such warnings were largely brushed aside when another expert—trained at Harvard, then teaching at the University of Wisconsin, and specifically enlisted by industry to counter critics—argued that smaller dosages would eliminate the problem.[19]

Apfel and Fisher contend of this initial 1941 approval that "there was no way the review of DES could have come out differently" (p. 19). But this suggestion of impersonal determinism neglects the conscious alliance of the FDA with industry, the key role of the lobbyist and of the "small committee," the bias of the Master File, and even, as one motivating factor, the lure of corporate profits as well as of therapeutic benefits.[20] Had the FDA wanted to avoid approving DES, it possessed the statutory authority to do so. Had the agency wished to resist the

16. Klumpp Deposition, pp. 202b–246b; Deposition of Don Carlos Hines, pp. 252b–319b; Frailey to Anderson, December 30, 1940, Appendix 4; and, in general, Appendices 4 to 10—all in *Abel*.

17. Hines (for the Small Committee) to Administrator, May 19, 1941 plus accompanying Master File documents, FDA Records; Hines to Herwick, April 23, 1941, Appendix 20 in *Abel*, Klumpp Deposition in *ibid.*, p. 229b; "X" to McCartney (of Sharpe & Dohme), October 23, 1939, in NDA 1948 file (later resubmitted as NDA 3068); and N.R.K. to Scott (Upjohn), February 26, 1941, Master File, FDA Records.

18. See key Small Committee questionnaire in Master File, FDA Records.

19. On dissidents, see Klumpp, Herwick, and Kennedy, "Memorandum of Interview," March 25, 1941, Appendix 16; Hines report, March 28, 1941 of "Meeting . . . March 24, 1941, and . . . March 25, 1941"; Appendix 17 and Appendix 18—in *Abel*. For rebuttal, see Sevringhaus to Durrett, January 4, 1941 and Sevringhaus to Hines, January 6, 1941 in Master File, FDA Records.

20. Although Apfel and Fisher relied upon Bell's rich doctoral thesis for their treatment of the 1938–1941 events, they apparently *chose not* to use much of its material and analysis which were quite critical of the FDA and the industry. Bell did not gain access directly to FDA files but she did obtain copies of some key archival materials from attorneys engaged in DES litigation. Beginning in 1981, however, we gained access to FDA Records on DES under the F.O.I.A.

pressures for approval, it could always have delayed (it had done so before), rejected the Master File tactic (which was highly unusual), stressed the unsettling animal data, and given dissident experts a serious hearing. Put bluntly, FDA officials were predisposed, even eager, to approve the drug for human use, and such approval required a special effort—by no means inevitable—to accomplish this intended purpose.

The FDA's 1941 approval was specifically limited to therapy in four medical conditions—vaginitis, gonorrhea, suppression of lactation, and some symptoms of menopause. DES was to be made available in tablet sizes, or dosages, of no more than 5 milligrams (mg.) and sold by prescription only with a label warning: "This is a potent drug." The required physician literature, approved by the FDA, also warned of DES side-effects and listed such patient contraindications as a personal or familial history of cancer.[21]

In approving DES, the agency, although not explicitly empowered to judge drug efficacy, had been forced to do precisely this. The FDA, as one high official explained, would not approve a drug with serious side-effects (DES was such a drug) if the therapeutic value were "insignificant." "In a broad sense," this regulator wrote, "we may say that a drug is safe when the expected therapeutic gain justifies the risk entailed in using it."[22] The FDA's finding of safety in 1941 thus necessarily meant that DES was also assumed to be effective in the four approved conditions in which, alone, benefits could be said to outweigh risks.

The FDA clearly expected that DES would be used prudently and with caution. It was not. Instead, the routine, even "promiscuous" use of the drug for menopausal and other problems expanded rapidly in the 1940s. "I am expecting daily," one anxious endocrinologist said in 1945, "to hear a radio announcer say, 'Get estrogens at your neighborhood drug store, they are great for your hot flashes or any other ills peculiar to the female sex'."[23] Despite such expanded usage, the FDA, in a little-noticed action, yielded to drug company requests in 1945 and allowed the elimination of the once-mandatory DES label warning, "This is a potent drug."[24] By then, and even earlier, drug companies

21. Apfel and Fisher state, wrongly, that "[a] warning was placed on the physician instruction sheet not to use the drug for amenorrhea" (p. 18). There was no such warning. Instead, the FDA simply asked or, in one case, "suggested" that "all representations concerning the treatment of dysmenorrhea and amenorrhea be *deleted* from the physician literature (emphasis added). Lilly's physician brochure, "Stilbestrol," nevertheless implied that DES might be used to treat "primary amenorrhea" under certain special circumstances. See Kennedy to Lakeside Laboratories, September 26, 1941, NDA 4160, and the Lilly brochure, 14–15, plus other literature and correspondence in NDA 4038, FDA Records.

22. Theodore G. Klumpp, "The Influence of the Food, Drug and Cosmetic Act on the Marketing of Drugs," *Connecticut State Medical Journal* 6 (January 1942), 4–5.

23. Edward Allen, "Discussion," in Lewis, Scheffey, *et al.*, "The Role of Injudicious Endocrine Therapy," *JAMA* 127 (January 13, 1945), 79.

24. Dunbar to Abbott Labs, October 20, 1945, NDA 4047-50, FDA Records.

were pushing DES for various unapproved purposes, including prevention of miscarriages.

The Discovery and Approval of Prenatal DES

Since 1939, a bold Houston physician, Dr. Karl John Karnaky, had been experimenting with the use of DES in pregnant women. "The drug companies," he recalled years later, "came to Houston, . . . fed me and dined me . . . and I started using it." His first test animals died "like flies," but Karnaky persisted, got better results, moved on to humans, tried some hit-or-miss tactics,[25] and concluded ("much to our surprise," he reported) that DES prevented miscarriage. This challenged the then current belief that estrogens, including DES, would cause uterine contractions and, as in some test animals, even kill the fetus. In a careless, vague article, published in 1942, Karnaky described results involving no control group patients and showing high failure rates (up to 60 percent) in some series. His conclusions were nevertheless wildly optimistic. Karnaky insisted—in the absence of firm supporting evidence—that the use of DES prenatally would save babies and that it was safe to give the drug in unlimited amounts.[26] Privately he even offered to finance the funeral costs "up to $1,000" of anyone who died from an excessive dose. In 1947, Karnaky boasted that he had not yet had to pay.[27]

Eventually, the work of other researchers—Dr. Priscilla White, an endocrinologist at the George Baker Clinic in Boston; and Dr. George Smith, head of the Department of Gynecology at Harvard, and his wife, Dr. Olive Smith, a biochemist—encouraged the assumption that DES, in specific circumstances, might help to prevent miscarriages. Yet these new studies, like Karnaky's before, actually offered little in the way of substance. White's work, limited exclusively to diabetics, had involved the prenatal use of various hormones and combinations of hormones, including (in some unspecified number of cases) DES and progesterone together. The data from her poorly-controlled and much-criticized study, when reported in 1943 and 1945, did not even indicate how many diabetic women had been given the DES/progesterone combination and with what results.[28] The Smiths, in a key 1946 article published (with a

25. Meyers, *DES*, 50–55.
26. Karl J. Karnaky, "The Use of Stilbestrol for the Treatment of Threatened and Habitual Abortion and Premature Labor: A Preliminary Report," *Southern Medical Journal* 35 (September 1942), 838–47, and quote on p. 839.
27. Karnaky to King, June 3, 1947, Karnaky File, FDA Records.
28. Priscilla White, "Pregnancy Complicating Diabetes," *JAMA* 128 (May 19, 1945), 181–82; and White and Hazel Hunt, "Pregnancy Complicating Diabetes," *Journal of Clinical Endocrinology* (henceforth *J. Clin End*) 3 (September 1943), 500–11. For criticisms of White, see David Hurwitz and Katherine Kuder, "Fetal and Neo-natal Mortality in Pregnancy Complicated by Diabetes Mellitus," *JAMA* 124 (January 29, 1944), 271–75, esp. 274; and the comments of William Dieckmann in White, "Pregnancy Complicating Diabetes," *JAMA* 128 (May 19, 1945), 182.

colleague) in the *American Journal of Obstetrics and Gynecology,* likewise provided no hard data on efficacy or safety. Instead, they offered a "hypothesis," based partly on animal experiments, justifying a test of prenatal DES therapy in humans. They then described the experience of but a single woman—again a diabetic—who had been treated with various experimental dosages of DES from weeks 17 through 35 of pregnancy. On this basis, they boldly proposed specific dosage schedules (starting either with 5 mg. of DES daily in the seventh week, or with 30 mg. daily in the sixteenth week, and increasing by small dosages through the thirty-fifth week) to prevent accidents of late *and* of early pregnancy—even though their one reported case did not involve early pregnancy. The Smiths, acknowledging the preliminary and often speculative nature of their work, made it clear that only further human experimentation could yield statistically significant results.[29]

None of this early research—even judged by the loose standards of the time—proved, or came close to proving, that prenatal DES worked and was not harmful. Yet the Smiths' study in particular identified the prestige of Harvard, and of the influential *American Journal of Obstetrics and Gynecology,* with the use of DES in pregnancy. Amid the widespread enthusiasm for children in those babyboom years, the Smiths' work undoubtedly helped to shift medical opinion toward acceptance of an unproven, but highly desired new therapy. Many physicians and laypeople found it comforting to think that a simple regimen of pills, or injections, could now result in saving babies.

In the spring of 1947, several drug companies independently submitted "supplemental" applications asking the FDA to approve both the use of DES to prevent miscarriages and the production of larger, 25 mg. dosages intended for the prenatal indication.[30] These manufacturers all cited, as required supporting evidence, the Karnaky, White, and Smith and Smith studies—then the only ones on DES specifically in the literature.[31] Yet, in addition to obvious defects, these cited studies be-

29. O. Watkins Smith, George Van S. Smith, and David Hurwitz, "Increased Excretion of Pregnanediol in Pregnancy with Diethylstilbestrol With Special Reference to the Prevention of Late Pregnancy Accidents," *AJOG* 51 (March 1946), 411–15. Olive Smith's first substantial study of prenatal DES efficacy appeared in late 1948—more than a year *after* the FDA had approved DES for use in pregnancy. (O. Watkins Smith, "Diethystilbestrol in the Prevention and Treatment of Complications of Pregnancy," *AJOG* 56 [November 1948], 821–34.) The 1946 article actually confuses the matter of doses either by miscounting or through a typographical error (p. 414).

30. See Eli Lilly supplemental documents in NDA 4041 file, including Lilly to FDA, April 15, 1947; Abbott documents in NDA 4047 file, especially Carter to King, June 18, 1947 and Nelson to Carter, July 1, 1947; Squibb documents in NDA 4056 file, especially Newcomer to Herwick, April 28, 1947; and E.S. Miller Laboratories, Inc. documents in NDA 6194 file, especially April 2, 1947 application and King to Miller Laboratories, May 20, 1947, FDA Records. For Apfel and Fisher's confusion about what companies filed and what data were submitted, see *To Do No Harm,* pp. 29–30 and p. 135, n. 13.

31. Squibb also submitted a five-page paper by the Smiths, "Results Reported to Feb. 1, 1947 on the Use of Stilbestrol For the Prevention of Accidents in Pregnancy," which

trayed serious, troubling inconsistencies. Each advocated different regimens of DES to be administered, variously, by injection, pill, or both. Karnaky stated that the drug was safe in unlimited amounts, but the Smiths warned against "excessive therapy." White advocated the use of DES in combination with progesterone, while Karnaky and the Smiths used DES alone. Karnaky claimed that DES prevented miscarriages in progress, and yet the Smiths argued that it worked only as a prophylactic therapy. White and the Smiths had limited their work to troubled pregnancies in diabetics, while only Karnaky had reported on its routine use in others.[32]

These studies, plus some additional evidence, also hinted at potential risks. White alluded to the carcinogenic dangers of prolonged therapy and noted that the babies of some patients showed "abnormalities" (which she attributed, perhaps rightly, to diabetes and not to DES). More tellingly, Karnaky had reported such transplacental DES effects on infants as discoloration of the breasts and genitals.[33] In line with this last finding, an animal researcher had warned, in 1944, that sex hormones known (as DES was) to alter the in utero development of animal

---

summarized pregnancy results in sixty-five prenatal DES cases, as reported to the Smiths by eight different physicians. Their data, broken down by treatment category, were as follows: (1) two of three women treated for "hypertension" in pregnancy had living babies; (2) two of two women treated for diabetes had living babies, one of them premature; (3) four of six women treated for threatened or habitual premature labor had living babies; (4) seven of ten women treated for habitual miscarriage or sterility delivered babies "normally"; and (5) twenty-four of forty-four women treated for threatened miscarriage had "normal" infants, representing a salvage rate of only 60 percent. These numbers, resulting from loose, ad hoc experimentation by several different physicians, were either ambiguous or disappointing (as with the low salvage rate of 60 percent), or too small to be significant. See NDA 4056, FDA Records. The Smiths' paper included results of twenty-seven cases reported by Dr. Robert S. Millen of Westbury, New York. In fact, Millen's work was deeply flawed, uncontrolled, and showed a high failure rate of 30 percent to 40 percent. An account of his research, having first apparently been rejected by the AJOG, was published in September 1947 shortly after the first prenatal applications had been approved: Robert S. Millen and Kenneth Schenck, "Case Reports Covering the Usage of Diethylstilbestrol for the Treatment and Prevention of Accidents in Pregnancy," Medical Times 75 (September 1947), 252–55. The Lilly and Abbott applications also cited a brief "Discussion" by Dr. A.R. Abarbanel, in G.H. Gardner, "Female Infertility," JAMA 128 (May 26, 1945), which contains an undocumented assertion "that large doses of diethylstilbestrol will effectively maintain gestation . . . with no side effects." Another study of prenatal DES efficacy, cited in some later applications, was, like Millen's, published only after the FDA had approved the first 1947 applications: Gordon Rosenblum and Eugene Melinkoff, "Preservation of the Threatened Pregnancy With Particular Reference to the Use of Diethylstilbestrol," Western Journal of Surgery, Obstetrics, and Gynecology 55 (November 1947), 597–603.

32. White, "Pregnancy Complicating Diabetes," JAMA (1945), 182; White and Hunt, "Pregnancy Complicating Diabetes," J. Clin. End. (1943), 506; Smith et. al., "Increased Excretion," AJOG (March 1946), 411–14; Karnaky, "Use of Stilbestrol," So. Med. J. (1942), 839 ff.; and Karnaky, "Prolonged Administration of Diethylstilbestrol," J. Clin. End., 1 (July-August 1945), 280.

33. White and Hunt, "Pregnancy Complicating Diabetes," J. Clin. End. (1943), 506, 504, 507–508; Karnaky, "Use of Stilbestrol," So. Med. J. (1942), 846–47; and Karnaky, "Prolonged Administration of Diethylstilbestrol," J. Clin. End., 280.

embryos probably did so in humans too.[34] Several experts, when contacted by the FDA, opposed any endorsement of prenatal DES on safety grounds.[35]

Thus, the FDA could easily have rejected these 1947 applications for a variety of reasons, including weak (almost nonexistent) data, potential fetal and maternal risks, and expert doubts.[36] Instead, the agency swept past all difficulties and quickly approved DES for use in habitual and threatened miscarriages, premature labor, and pregnancy problems complicated by diabetes. At the same time, an agency official privately acknowledged that prenatal DES therapy for even such approved conditions remained "decidedly in the experimental stage."[37] Here, in effect, the FDA had simply gambled that the new therapy worked and *would be* proven safe in use. Curiously, the agency also advised the manufacturer of a non-prenatal DES preparation to *delete* a proposed literature statement warning against its use in pregnancy.[38]

Challenges to Prenatal DES

Meanwhile, even some DES partisans worried about the possibility of fetal damage and of cancer. Two researchers, in a November 1947 article later cited by a few drug companies in prenatal applications, posed troubling questions about such safety issues. Were large doses of DES carcinogenic in pregnant women, these physicians asked, and would the drug cause "pituitary or other glandular disturbance" in later life? Could DES "in any way affect the glandular balance of the child in utero?" Having suggested a potential time-bomb effect, these particular experts then offered just the uneasy reassurance that so far, in "six to eight

---

34. R.R. Greene, "Embryology of Sexual Structure and Hermaphroditism," *J. Clin. End.* 4 (July 1944), 335–48, esp. 342 ff. In 1959, a clinician described a case of male "pseudohermaphroditism" in an infant exposed to DES *in utero*, and cited Greene's 1944 essay as having anticipated this effect in humans: Norman M. Kaplan, "Male Pseudohermaphroditism: Report of a Case, With Observations on Pathogenesis," *NEJM* 261 (September 24, 1959), 642–43.

35. Robert B. Greenblatt (University of Georgia School of Medicine) to Granger, April 23, 1947; E. Perry McCullagh (Cleveland Clinic) to Granger, April 15, 1947; and M. Edward Davis (Chicago Lying-In Hospital, University of Chicago) to Granger, April 22, 1947, all in NDA 6195, FDA Records.

36. On politics, budgets, and the FDA at this time, see House Subcommittee of Committee on Appropriations, *Department of Labor-Federal Security Agency Appropriations Bill for 1948*, Pt. 2, 80th Congress, 1st Sess., pp. 65–74; Senate Subcommittee of the Committee on Appropriations, *Labor-Federal Security Appropriations Bill for 1947*, 79th Cong., 2nd Sess., pp. 151–52; and Series 39.14A, Bureau of the Budget Papers, National Archives (N.A.).

37. King to Lilly, May 26, 1947, and Nelson to Abbott Laboratories (attention Edgar B. Carter), July 1, 1947. On human experimentation, also see Hines Deposition in *Abel*, pp. 308b–309b.

38. Nelson to Forbes Laboratories, June 25, 1947, and "Forbestrin" literature draft, p. 2, in NDA 5622, FDA Records.

years" of human experimentation, "none of these ill-effects [has] been reported."[39]

During the late 1940s, doubts persisted and sometimes grew. One researcher, who opposed the use of DES in patients with family histories of cancer, stressed "the possibility of some latent effects on the reproductive and endocrine system of the infant . . . as indicated by . . . work . . . in experimental animals."[40] In 1949, an editor of the *Journal of the American Medical Association,* responding to a physician's question about the use of DES for the prevention of miscarriages, noted that the research on efficacy was inconclusive and also warned: "One must not lose sight of the fact that there is a possibility that large doses of female sex hormones [like DES] may affect a male fetus adversely."[41] By mid-1949, the editor of a prominent yearbook in obstetrics and gynecology—once, briefly, an advocate of prenatal DES—had decided, because of conflicting research, to back away from this "hotly debated" and possibly harmful therapy. "I shall withhold diethylstilbestrol from patients with threatened and habitual abortion," he informed his physician readers, "until the various investigators come to some agreement."[42]

Although the Smiths in particular continued to publish glowing reports about prenatal DES from 1948 on,[43] their work met with growing criticism, both methodological and substantive in nature.[44] The use of control groups, placebos, and single "blinding" to correct for chance results or bias in clinical experiments had been known, and sometimes practiced, for years.[45] As early as 1941, the same researcher (David Hurwitz) who later collaborated with the Smiths on their influential 1946 article had insisted that studies could not confirm the efficacy of prenatal DES in humans unless patients were assigned, alternately, to a

39. Rosenblum and Melinkoff, "Preservation of the Threatened Pregnancy," *West. J. Surg.* (1947), 601–603.

40. Bernard Lapan, "Diethylstilbestrol in the Treatment of Idiopathic Repeated Abortion," *New York State Journal of Medicine* 48 (December 1, 1948), 2614.

41. *JAMA* 139 (January 8, 1949), 130.

42. J. P. Greenhill, ed., *The 1949 Year Book of Obstetrics and Gynecology* (Chicago: Year Book Publishers, 1949), 40. Also see Greenhill, *Principles and Practice of Obstetrics* (Philadelphia; Saunders, 1951), 10th ed., 398, iii, and 483 and Greenhill's identical remarks in *JAMA* 150 (December 6, 1952), 1444.

43. O. Watkins Smith, "Diethylstilbestrol in the Prevention and Treatment of Complications of Pregnancy," *AJOG* 56 (November 1948), 821–34; and Smith and Smith, "The Influence of Diethylstilbestrol on the Progress and Outcome of Pregnancy Based On a Comparison of Treated With Untreated Primigravidas," *AJOG* 58 (November 1949), 994–1004.

44. See, for example, comments by Dieckmann, Page, and Allen in *ibid.*, 1005–1009.

45. See, for brief overviews, Stuart J. Pocock, *Clinical Trials: A Practical Approach* (New York: John Wiley & Sons, 1983), 14–18; and J.P. Bull, "The Historical Development of Clinical Therapeutic Trials," *J. Chron. Dis.* 10 (September 1949), 218–48. For an early controlled and blinded study, also see J. Burns Amberson, Jr., B.T. McMahon, and Max Pinner, "A Clinical Trial of Sanocrysin in Pulmonary Tuberculosis," *American Review of Tuberculosis* 24 (October 1931), 401–35.

treatment and to a control group, so that results could be compared.[46] Yet the Smiths did not use placebos in their 1940s work, nor, curiously, did Olive Smith, in one 1948 study (involving 632 cases gathered by 117 different physicians) use any controls, much less the alternate controls Hurwitz had advocated in 1941.[47] For some, the Smiths' loose and varying research procedures invalidated their conclusions. After roughly 1948–1950, moreover, advanced clinicians increasingly promoted even tougher standards.[48] Within a few years, most agreed upon the need for larger numbers of cases in research, comparison of randomly-selected as well as equivalent control and treatment groups, and the use of "double-blinding," so that neither the subjects *nor* the researchers would know which group was which.[49]

At no time, then or later, did a well-designed and acceptably executed study confirm the efficacy of DES in pregnancy. After 1950, by contrast, several methodologically advanced investigations showed that the drug was no more effective than a placebo or bedrest in troubled or initially normal pregnancies. Sometimes DES was even less effective.[50] In November 1953, a team of University of Chicago researchers, headed by William Dieckmann, chair of the university's obstetrics and gynecology department, published in the *American Journal of Obstetrics and Gynecology* what was then, and remains, the largest and most complete

46. David Hurwitz, "Pregnancy Accidents in Diabetes," *JAMA* 116 (February 15, 1941), 645.

47. O. Smith, "Diethylstilbestrol in the Prevention," *AJOG* (1948).

48. For an influential study, begun in 1946, which promoted better research methodology, see Medical Research Council, "Streptomycin Treatment of Pulmonary Tuberculosis," *British Medical Journal* 2 (October 30, 1948), 769–82. Also: E.D. Colvin, *et al.*, "Salvage Possibilities in Threatened Abortion," *AJOG* 59 (June 1950), 1208–24; and Dieckmann, Page, and Allen in Smith, "The Influence of Diethylstilbestrol," *AJOG* (1949), 1005–1009.

49. For example, see Arthur G. King, "Threatened and Repeated Abortion," *Obstetrics and Gynecology* 1 (January 1953), 104–14; James Henry Ferguson, "The Importance of Controls in a Clinical Experiment," *Obst. and Gyn.* 3 (April 1954), 452–57; and, for a devastating summary, Joseph W. Goldzieher and Benedict B. Benigno, "The Treatment of Threatened and Recurrent Abortion: A Critical Review," *AJOG* 75 (June 1958), 1202–14.

50. R.E. Crowder, E.S. Bills, and J.S. Broadbent, "The Management of Threatened Abortion: A Study of 100 Cases," *AJOG* 60 (October 1950), 896–99, found DES *less* effective but may have slightly miscalculated (p. 897) their own data by including twenty-eight patients treated partly with progesterone. Two other studies challenged the Smiths' contention that DES accelerated the production of hormones during pregnancy, thus preserving pregnancies: Edward Davis and Nicholas W. Fugo, "Steroids in the Treatment of Early Pregnancy Complications," *JAMA* 142 (March 18, 1950), 778–85; and I.F. Somerville, G.F. Marrian, B.E. Clayton, "Effect of Diethylstilbestrol on Urinary Excretion of Pregnanediol and Endogenous Estrogens During Pregnancy," *Lancet* 256 (April 23, 1949), 680–82. A fourth study denied the effectiveness of prenatal DES in pregnant diabetic women: Ralph A. Reis, Edwin J. DeCosta, M. David Allweiss, "The Management of the Pregnant Diabetic Woman and Her Newborn Infant," *AJOG* 60 (November 1950), 1023–42, esp. pp. 1032, 1039, 1042. Thomas Chalmers, "The Impact of Clinical Controls on the Practice of Medicine," *Mt. Sinai Journal of Medicine* 41 (November-December 1974) 753–58, incorrectly classified the mixed or negative Davis-Fugo study as supporting the use of prenatal DES, as it clearly does not, and Apfel and Fisher (p. 136, n. 15) uncritically follow Chalmers.

double-blind study of prenatal DES. Data from 1,646 cases indicated that the drug was not effective in preventing miscarriages among first-time pregnant women (primigravadas) or others, in either seemingly normal or troubled pregnancies. Not only did DES not work, some slivers of evidence actually suggested that it was worse than a placebo.[51]

The Smiths resisted these findings, clung to their own results, kept endorsing DES, and argued, unfairly, that the Dieckmann study had erred in not dealing with first-time, normal pregnancies, as some (but not all) of the Smiths' own work did. In fact, the Chicago research did yield substantial data on primigravadas, and on normal (*as well as* troubled) pregnancies.[52]

The Dieckmann group's conclusions received strong support from other new research, including a contemporaneous, double-blind 1953 British study of 460 patients that effectively demolished many of the Smiths' claims.[53] The influential editor of the aforementioned yearbook in obstetrics and gynecology also welcomed the Dieckmann study as both convincing and of special value to those many critical physicians—already disinclined to prescribe prenatal DES—who had found it necessary to "do a great deal of explaining to patients and their husbands if they do not give shots' or other forms of 'specific' hormone treatment when a woman has a threatened [miscarriage]." "Perhaps citing this important paper by Dieckmann and his associates," the editor wrote, would make it easier to withhold such therapy in the future. He also mentioned a disturbing clinical report, supported by subsequent research in rats, indicating that large doses of prenatal DES might actually induce miscarriage.[54]

Still, many physicians, ignoring or defying this anti-DES research,

51. W.J. Dieckmann et al., "Does the Administration of Diethylstilbestrol During Pregnancy Have Therapeutic Value?" *AJOG* 66 (November 1953), 1062–75. Also see D. Robinson and L.B. Shettles, "The Use of Diethylstilbestrol in Threatened Abortion," *AJOG* 63 (June 1952), 1330–33; and J. H. Ferguson, "Effect of Stilbestrol on Pregnancy compared to the Effect of a Placebo," *AJOG* 65 (March 1953), 592–601. On slivers, see Yvonne Brackbill and Heinz W. Berendes, "Dangers of Diethylstilbestrol: Review of a 1953 Paper," *Lancet* 2 (September 2, 1978), 520. For considerable confusion about the total number involved, and the number who were not first-time pregnancies, in the Dieckmann study, see *To Do No Harm*, p. 22.

52. See George Smith's comments in *AJOG* 66 (November 1953), pp. 1075–76. Karnaky continues to believe that prenatal DES is effective and that it has not contributed to cancer. (Karnaky to Bernstein, March 1986).

53. G. I. M. Swyer and R. G. Law, "An Evaluation of the Prophylactic Ante-Natal Use of Stilbestrol. Preliminary Report," *Proceedings of the Society for Endocrinology in Journal of Endocrinology* 10 (1953–54), vi–vii. Another British study in 1955, using DES and EES (ethisterone), in a double-blind investigation, concluded that the placebo and the drug combination had about the same effect in preventing fetal death for pregnant diabetic women. (D.D. Reid, "The Use of Hormones in The Management of Pregnancy in Diabetics," *Lancet* 2 [October 22, 1955], 833–36.)

54. Greenhill, *The Year Book of Obstetrics and Gynecology, 1954–1955* (Chicago: Year Book Publishers, 1954), 43–44. Also see Greenhill, *Obstetrics* (Philadelphia: Saunders, 1955, 11th ed.), 441.

continued to prescribe this hormone in pregnancy from the 1950s well into the 1970s. Here Apfel and Fisher, although clearly troubled by the persistence of a discredited therapy, struggle to reconcile such professional intractability with their larger "structure of medicine" analysis. Their solution, which draws upon a recent analysis by William Silverman,[55] is to argue that many other innovations of the 1940s and 1950s—all designed to save babies—likewise remained popular even after such innovations had been found worthless or harmful. The mistaken use of prenatal DES thus becomes part of a general or "structural" pattern of error that, as Apfel and Fisher see it, inevitably accompanied the innovation process during those years.

This argument is not convincing. An initial problem is that Apfel and Fisher misunderstand Silverman, whose own analysis of "medical inflation" (medical overoptimism about unproven therapies) involves no necessary assumption of inevitability. To the contrary, Silverman identifies discrete causes of medical error, including specifically American enthusiasms of the World War II era and, to some degree, even deceptive drug company literature and advertising.[56]

Beyond this, Apfel and Fisher also miss or slide past historical realities that subvert their overriding premise of determinism. Thus, they downplay nonmedical and nonscientific biases—none of them inescapable—that figured in the continued use of prenatal DES. An example was the kind of regional loyalty to Harvard/Boston research symptomatically expressed by a critic of the Dieckmann study in 1953. "As a former Bostonian," this clinician publicly acknowledged at a medical meeting, "I would be entirely lacking in civic loyalty if I had not used stilbestrol in my private practice."[57] The highest documented rate of prenatal DES usage has in fact been found in the Northeast, and, even more specifically, at the Harvard-affiliated Boston Lying-In Hospital, where both White and the Smiths had worked.[58] This distorted usage pattern may explain the later perception, expressed by a malpractice attorney in the 1970s, that "the closer you get to Boston the more DES daughters you find, and the farther away you get, the fewer."[59]

---

55. William Silverman, *Retrolental Fibroplasia: A Modern Parable* (New York: Grune & Stratton, 1980).

56. *Ibid.*, xvi, 69–89, and *passim*. Silverman, in conversation with Bernstein, August 11, 1986, agrees that Apfel and Fisher misunderstood his work and thus incorrectly protected physicians from responsibility for their errors.

57. Frederick C. Irving, "Discussion" in Dieckmann, *et. al.*, "Does the Administration of Diethylstilbestrol," *AJOG* (1953), 1080.

58. Olli Heinonen, Boston Collaborative Drug Surveillance Program, "Diethylstilbestrol in Pregnancy: Frequency of Exposure and Usage Patterns," *Cancer* 31 (March 1973), 574, 577.

59. Seaman and Seaman, *Women and the Crisis in Sex Hormones*, p. 4. Massachusetts in fact appears to have the highest *rate* of adenocarcinoma, although as of 1980, the total *number* of cases in that state (17) were exceeded in the much larger states of New York (25) and California (34). See Herbst and Bern, *Developmental Effects*, p. 65.

For a time, adenocarcinoma would even have a reputation as the "Boston" or "Harvard" disease.[60]

Above all, however, Apfel and Fisher fail to recognize that negative research by Dieckmann and others on DES actually *did* change the prescribing habits of a substantial number of physicians. Available data suggest that the rate of prenatal DES usage in the United States peaked in 1950–1952, dropped by about 10 percent in 1953–1955, and then dropped by another 20 percent in 1956–1958. By the end of the decade, the rate had fallen to about half of what it was in 1950–1952.[61] By 1960, some leading textbooks in obstetrics and gynecology did not recommend the use of DES in pregnancy. (One major text had stopped recommending it as early as 1951 and, beginning with the 1955 edition, cited the Dieckmann study as key supporting evidence.)[62] Clearly, nothing about the "structure of medicine" prevented some scholars and practitioners of the 1950s from responding responsibly to damning scientific evidence. The rest of the medical community could have done the same.

Drug Companies and Physicians

Apfel and Fisher present a fragmentary, unsystematic, and deeply ambivalent discussion of drug company involvement in the DES episode, especially after the publication of anti-DES studies in the early 1950s. Only occasionally are the authors critical of the industry. They do point out, specifically, that manufacturer-supplied literature on prenatal DES, collected in the heavily used *Physicians' Desk Reference,* failed as late as 1961 even to mention the Dieckmann and other negative studies

60. *Ibid.* Silverman reports that retrolental fibroplasia, an iatrogenically-induced form of infant blindness common in the United States after World War II, was also called "the 'Boston disease' during the early years of the [blindness] epidemic." Silverman, *Retrolental Fibroplasia*, p. xvi.

61. Calculated from Arthur Herbst *et al.*, "Epidemiologic Aspects and Factors Relating to Survival in 384 Registry Cases of Clear Cell Adenocarcinoma of the Vagina and the Cervix," *AJOG* 135 (December 1, 1979), 876–83 and esp. p. 879 (chart). For reduced usage in the 1960s, also see Heinonen, "Diethylstilbestrol in Pregnancy," *Cancer* (1973), 573–77.

62. See, especially, Greenhill, *Obstetrics* (Philadelphia: Saunders, 1951, 10th ed.), 398 for doubts, but also p. 483 (on diabetics), and Greenhill, *Obstetrics* (1955, 11th ed.), 441, citing Dieckmann. Compare Nicholas Eastman, *Williams Obstetrics* (New York: Appleton-Century-Crofts, Inc., 1950, 10th ed.), 494, which describes prenatal DES therapy, and Eastman, *Williams Obstetrics* (New York: Appleton-Century-Crofts, Inc., 1956, 11th ed.), 1956, which does not mention such therapy. Also: Louis S. Goodman and Alfred Gilman, *The Pharmaceutical Basis of Therapeutics* (New York: Macmillan, 1956, 2nd ed.), 1601, which is largely negative on efficacy and which cites Dieckmann; and Charles C. Thomas, *A Textbook of Gynecology* (Springfield, Ill.: Charles S. Thomas, 1960), 396–97. For post-Dieckmann ambivalence about, and virtually an endorsement of, prenatal DES at a very late date, see the work of Duncan Reid, head of obstetrics/gynecology at Harvard, *A Textbook of Obstetrics* (Philadelphia: Saunders, 1962), 841–44.

459

on efficacy.[63] But they ignore, or do not know of, the evidence that some drug company salesmen ("detail men"), the key source of drug information for physicians,[64] misrepresented DES. Indeed, when one salesman was told by specialists that prenatal DES had "no value at all," he wrote back to his company, affirming his loyalty to the product and promising to "continue plugging" it.[65]

Curiously, the authors confine their only harsh charges to a brief caption they tack onto a drug company DES advertisement, reprinted in a full-page illustration in their book. This advertisement, they charge, exaggerated the claims for one medical study (by misrepresenting a sample of 200 patients as 1200), falsely stated that the advertiser's product had been used in other cited studies, and omitted any reference to the Dieckmann and other anti-DES investigations.[66] The implication is that greatly distorted and self-serving drug company information on prenatal DES misled physicians and contributed to the later iatrogenic tragedy.

Yet Apfel and Fisher neither say this explicitly nor even relate their six-line accusatory caption, cast in tiny print, to their general text and

63. Actually the brief drug descriptions in the *PDR* cite no DES-research at all, pro or con. The more telling point here is that Lilly's eleven-page physician brochure, "Diethylstilbestrol in Accidents in Pregnancy," which cited and discussed all of the pro-DES research from the 1940s (Smith, Karnaky, White, and others) and listed some negative studies, nevertheless fails to mention the major negative research of Dieckmann (1953), Ferguson (1952), and Swyer and Law (1953–1954). The Lilly pamphlet was *approved by the FDA* in late 1954, and remained in use until at least the early 1960s. See Lilly to FDA, September 27, 1954, G.A.G. and R.G.S. "Referral" 9/29/54, Smith to Lilly, Oct. 7, 1954, and brochure in NDA 7844, FDA Records.

64. Mintz, *Therapeutic Revolution*, p. 491 citing a 1959 AMA study; also see pp. 492–95.

65. Irving Sider to W.R. McHargue, November 22, 1950, in *Abel*, II, p. 510b.

66. In reality, the Grant Company's Des Plex advertisement was not *as* deceptive as Apfel and Fisher claim. They missed the fact that there were, indeed, studies of 1,200 (not 200). See Eduardo Pena, "Prevention of Abortion," *American Journal of Surgery* 87 (January 1954), 95–96 (200 cases); and Pena, "Estrogen-Vitamin Antiabortive Treatment," *Medical Times* 82 (December 1954), 921–25 (1,000 cases). Some of the cited studies may, in fact, have used the DES-vitamin combination in the advertiser's brand (DesPlex). Karl Karnaky, "Diethylstilbestrol Therapy," *Medical Times* 81 (May 1953), 315–16 used Grant's Bio-Des, which was the same combination as Grant's DesPlex but in sesame oil. Julian Ross, "Use of Diethylstilbestrol in the Treatment of Threatened Abortion," *Journal of the National Medical Association* 43 (January 1951), 20, also received his DES from Grant and it was almost certainly DesPlex. What Apfel and Fisher missed is that Ross's later claims of 100 per cent success in 200 cases and Pena's of 96 per cent in 1,200 cases are, literally, unbelievable. See Arthur King, "Threatened and Repeated Abortion," *Obstetrics and Gynecology*, (1953), 104–14 for indirect evidence on why these claims are unbelievable. Also see Julian Ross, "Further Report on the Use of Diethylstilbestrol in the Treatment of Threatened Abortion," *Journal of the National Medical Association* 45 (May 1953), 223. For a later study, using Grant's DES, see Charles Liggett, "Treatment of Threatened Abortion with Diethylstilbestrol," *Western Journal of Surgery, Obstetrics and Gynecology* 64 (January 1956), 16–21, which never mentioned any of the studies challenging the efficacy of DES. The publication of Liggett's exceptionally poor study raises serious questions about peer review and intellectual standards in this and perhaps some other medical journals. For a scathing assessment of Liggett's claims, see Greenhill, *Yearbook of Obstetrics and Gynecology, 1956–1957* (Chicago: Year Book Publishers, 1956), 23.

analysis. It is as if someone else had written their caption. Choosing not to probe deeply, they ignore such vital matters as the continuing industry-FDA relationship, and ultimately resist the implications of their own evidence. The result is that drug firms do not figure in the authors' final emphasis on inevitability and structure. In this way, their book abandons criticism and easily earns accolades, to quote the enthusiastic jacket puff, for *not* being "a condemnation of the drug industry."[67]

The Role of the FDA

Apfel and Fisher, having barely touched upon the FDA's regulation of DES in the 1930s and 1940s, provide essentially no analysis of agency actions after 1947. This is a major omission, since the FDA remained important and, beginning in the early 1960s, again assumed a central role in the unfolding drama of DES.

In 1962, under new legislation prompted by the thalidomide tragedy, the agency received explicit authority to judge the efficacy of both new and old drugs. Beginning in 1964, the FDA was empowered to reassess, using the new law's tougher standards, all of the approximately 4,000 drugs introduced since 1938 (which included DES) and to take corrective actions against drugs or drug indications found to be ineffective, or unsafe. Yet the agency waited until 1966 before even creating the necessary review panels. It then complicated the evaluation process by rejecting a straightforward "effective"-"ineffective" classification scheme in favor of one that included such blurry, intermediate categories as "probably" and "possibly" effective.[68]

This enabled the six-member Panel on Drugs Used in Disturbances of the Reproductive System to hedge, in its final 1969 report, by pronouncing DES "possibly effective" in preventing miscarriages.[69] In

67. For evidence that Apfel and Fisher may not comprehend the implications of their own analysis of industry, see Joyce Bichler's review and their response in the Winter 1985 (Bichler) and Spring 1985 (Apfel-Fisher letter) issues of *DES Action Voice*.

68. Peter Temin, *Taking Your Medicine: Drug Regulation in the United States* (Cambridge: Harvard University Press, 1980), 120–40; Milton Silverman and Philip Lee, *Pills, Profits, and Politics* (Berkeley: University of California Press, 1974), 122; and Division of Medical Sciences, National Research Council, *Drug Efficacy Study: Final Report . . .* (Washington, D.C.: National Academy of Sciences, 1969), 1–16. On relevant politics in the Kennedy years, also see Office File box 78, John F. Kennedy Library (Boston); and Series 60.3, Bureau of the Budget Papers, N.A.

69. National Academy of Sciences-National Research Council, "Drug Efficacy Study," Panel on Drugs Used in Disturbances of the Reproductive System, individual evaluation for NDA 4041 (and all other prenatal DES NDAs), ms numbers 332 and others, FDA Records. Division of Medical Sciences, *Drug Efficacy Study*, p. 6, indicates that all evaluations were "essentially completed" by mid-1968. Comments in the House Subcommittee of The Committee on Government Operations, *Regulation of Diethylstilbestrol (DES): (Its Use as a Drug for Humans and in Animal Feeds)*, Part I, 92nd Cong., 1st sess., p.79, suggest that the panel may have sent a preliminary "possibly effective" rating for prenatal DES to the FDA in 1967.

reality, this finding made little logical or scientific sense. The existing controlled-placebo studies of prenatal DES were all negative (the report actually cited Dieckmann), and the panel itself acknowledged that the "effectiveness [of prenatal DES] cannot be documented by the literature or its own experience."[70] Apparently this panel, like others, downplayed test data and drew offsetting, positive conclusions from the actual practice of physicians. Prenatal DES was found "possibly effective" simply because some doctors still had faith enough to use it; informal, unsupported judgment thus counteracted compelling clinical research. In reaching this sort of conclusion, as one critic has charged, "the [panel] experts relied upon the very market they were supposed to contain and their own subjective experience."[71]

The "possibly effective" rating came at a moment when some FDA officials had developed new concerns that DES might injure the fetus. These doubts about safety followed, and may have been motivated by, several alarming reports of hermaphroditism in a few children exposed to the drug *in utero*.[72] In 1969, agency regulators finally required one company, Eli Lilly, to add a sharp warning to its physician literature on DES: "Because of possible adverse reaction on the fetus the risk should be weighed against the possible benefits . . . in known pregnancy."[73] This warning probably had little effect, since doctors who still prescribed DES in pregnancy were not likely to be deterred by a single, cautionary sentence.

Yet by 1969, the FDA had lost some confidence in the harmlessness of DES. Clearly, a vigilant agency could have seized upon the tepid

70. NAS/NRC, "Drug Efficacy Study," NDA 4041, p. 2 of 3.

71. Temin, *Taking Your Medicine*, 129–30.

72. Alfred M. Bongiovanni, Angelo M. DiGeorge, Melvin M. Grumback, "Masculinization of the Female Infant Associated with Estrogenic Therapy Alone During Gestation: Four Cases," *Journal of Clinical Endocrinology* 19 (August 1959), 1004–11; Norman M. Kaplan, "Male Pseudohermaphroditism:" *NEJM* (1959), 641–44; and Sorrell H. Waxman, Stanley M. Gartler, and Vincent C. Kelly, "Apparent Masculinization of the Female Fetus Diagnosed as True Hermaphroditism by Chromosomal Studies," *The Journal of Pediatrics* 60 (April 1962), 540–44. For a review of 147 cases of iatrogenic female pseudohermaphroditism involving prenatal drugs, see Naotaka Ishizuka, *et al.*, "Statistical Observations on Genital Abnormalities of Newborns Following the Administration of Progestins to Their Mothers," *Journal of Japanese Obstetrical and Gynecological Society* 9 (October 1962), 271–82. For later warnings, see R. Mey, "Über Fetale Zwitterbildung durch Stilboestrol," *Gebürtshilfe und Frauenheilkunde* 26 (September 1966), 1456–64. On animal studies, see G. Pincus and Alan E. Erickson, "Sex Modifications in Hens' Eggs Following Immersion in Diethylstilbestrol Solutions," *Endocrinology* 71 (July 1962), 24–30; and Melvin M. Ketchel and Gregory Pincus, "*In Vitro* Exposure of Rabbit Ova to Estrogens," *Proceedings of the Society for Experimental Biology and Medicine* 115 (February 1964), 419–21.

73. John J. Jennings (Acting Associate Director for Marketed Drugs, Bureau of Medicine) to Lilly, February 14, 1967; Ortiz to Koustenis, July 31, 1967; Jennings to Lilly, November 21, 1967; and Armstrong to FDA, January 15, 1968—all in NDA 4041 file. For an example of the greatly diluted warning language that the FDA was willing to accept by 1970, see "Summary" of NDA 4056 (Squibb), 10/13/70, in NDA 4056 file, FDA Records. In 1969, Lilly voluntarily removed avoidance of miscarriages from its list of indications for its DES, which was still a far cry from warning *against* such prenatal use (*Physicians' Desk Reference* [New York: Medical Economics, 1969], 819–20.)

1969 endorsement ("possibly effective"), the substantial evidence of inefficacy, and the recent indications of fetal risk to contraindicate DES for use in pregnancy. The FDA did not do so. Instead, the agency dallied for years without even publishing the equivocal "possibly effective" finding that had issued from its own sponsored review of DES.

Further action had to wait until November 1971, seven months after the crucial *New England Journal* article had appeared and five months after the New York State Health Commissioner issued a DES/adenocarcinoma warning and implored the FDA to ban the use of "synthetic estrogens" in pregnancy. With congressional hearings on DES scheduled for November 11, the agency at last—belatedly—"contraindicated" the drug as a pregnancy therapy on November 10. The timing scarcely seemed fortuitous.[74]

Nevertheless, some physicians continued to prescribe prenatal DES for at least several more years. By then, ironically, researchers had discovered that the drug so long wrongly thought to *preserve* pregnancy, was usually able—if taken in large doses for a number of days after intercourse—to *prevent* it instead. Many physicians and college health services, including Harvard's (up to 1984),[75] thus began giving DES as a postcoital contraceptive, or "morning-after pill," to potentially pregnant women. Some still do so. The predictable consequence—since births sometimes occur despite the use of postcoital contraception—is that more children have been, are today, and surely will be exposed *in utero* to DES. The drug's iatrogenic threat has therefore not ended, as most assume it has, but instead persists even now, in the later 1980s, sixteen years after the cancer association came initially to light.

Anger, Guilt, and Historical Knowledge

Apfel and Fisher, as psychiatrists, are predictably more comfortable with psychological than with historical analysis. Thus, they offer some shrewd insights into physician attitudes, especially among specialists in obstetrics and gynecology. They provide arresting glimpses of DES daughters and mothers (but not of sons or fathers) responding, variously, to the "quiet trauma" of DES exposure with "denial, blame, self-accusation, rage, . . . terrible guilt," and—ideally but less often, the authors suggest—with acceptance or transcendence (pp. 66, 71, and 64). This part of their book, which also speculates about such possibly DES-related psychiatric disorders as anorexia nervosa, is potentially quite valuable.

74. House Subcommittee of the Committee on Government Operations, *Regulation of Diethylstilbestrol (DES): (Its Use as a Drug for Humans and in Animal Feeds)*, 92nd Congress, 1st Session, November 11, 1971, *passim*.

75. Harvard University Health Services to Dr. John Bunker, August 12, 1985; survey of thirty college health services conducted at Bernstein's request. Also L.H. Schilling to Bernstein, July 9, 1986, reporting Schilling's survey of DES-MAP use.

Yet even here there are problems. Apfel and Fisher give us sensitive vignettes, not hard, quantified data, so it is difficult to know which DES victim or family responses are typical and which are not. Beyond this, the authors' pessimistic historical analysis promotes an unduly negative judgment of angry or militant responses by DES daughters and mothers to a tragedy that, as Apfel and Fisher see it, could not have been prevented. Believing in an irresistible fate, the authors tend to view strong feelings of protest—"moral outrage and indignation," the attribution of "blame," a fierce determination to right past wrongs—as inappropriate, essentially irrational products of "projection" or of "guilt" (pp. 4, 87, 79–80). These unhealthy emotions, the authors imply, should be put to rest—if necessary, through expert therapy and counselling.

In fact, the historical record allows a different reading of this rage, indignation, and blame. Actions by the FDA, drug firms, and physicians, which contributed to the DES tragedy, clearly justify a degree of anger, even outrage, on the part of victims and their families. Such openly intense reactions, based upon historical realities, can actually perform a liberating function, encouraging action instead of helplessness and guilt. Many members of such groups as DES Action, for example, have effectively turned private pain and indignation into healthy, collective work on behalf of those at risk from DES. In this sense, outrage or anger grounded in good history can be both therapeutically and, as with DES Action groups, politically constructive.

A related problem is that Apfel and Fisher, in their discomfort with militancy, too easily dismiss "feminist writers" who see the DES tragedy as, in part, a product of male-dominated medicine. It is true that such interpretations can be overdone and that, as Apfel and Fisher note, "the climate that produced DES existed for many other medical phenomena that were not all gender-related" (p. 40). It nevertheless remains the case that DES was first widely used to treat female menopausal symptoms that many male physicians found "bizarre," "abnormal," or even "sickening."[76] The subsequent spread of prenatal therapy, often through ad hoc experimentation, likewise involved a larger, possibly male-biased tendency to define a female reproductive function—pregnancy—as an "illness" or "disease" requiring expert intervention. This, along with scholarship on past and present medical ideas about women's sexuality, provides some support for a feminist analysis of DES.[77] Pending further

76. See, for example, Bell, "The Synthetic Compound Diethylstilbestrol," 19–20, 59, 118, 120, 145 ff.; and Barbara Ehrenreich and Deirdre English, *Complaints and Disorders: The Sexual Politics of Sickness* (New York: Feminist Press, 1973), 5 and *passim*.

77. In addition to *ibid.*, also see Carol Smith-Rosenberg, *Disorderly Conduct: Visions of Gender in Victorian America* (New York: Knopf, 1985), especially 197–244. Carol Gilligan, *In a Different Voice* (Cambridge: Harvard University Press, 1982), and Evelyn Fox Keller, *Gender and Science* (New Haven: Yale University Press, 1985) also raise basic questions as to whether a male-dominated science is fundamentally different from a female-dominated science or a gender-unspecific science.

research, the role of sexism and especially of male paternalism in this largely female tragedy should at least remain an open question.

Is American Medicine Exceptional?

By ignoring or misconstruing many FDA actions and sliding past much of their own evidence on the drug industry, Apfel and Fisher miss essential aspects of the DES story. They fail to explain how and why DES was first approved in 1941, how it became accepted as a prenatal therapy in the 1940s, and why its use in pregnancy continued even after convincing negative studies were published in the early 1950s. They likewise downplay some physician's doubts about prenatal DES and give no attention to fetal-risk research on DES that was troubling in the 1940s and ominous by the mid-1960s. Their historical quest, flawed as it is, underscores the need to analyze biomedical problems not only in close-grained detail, but also in the larger context of culture, politics, and economics.

Such an approach to DES must consider whether American attitudes toward medical technology may be distinctive in the modern world. A crucial point, which Apfel and Fisher miss, is that prenatal DES therapy flourished in the admittedly more affluent United States as virtually nowhere else. Indeed, the drug was seldom used in pregnancy in such medically-advanced nations as England, Denmark, Switzerland, and West Germany.[78] As a result, roughly 90 percent of the documented DES-positive cases of adenocarcinoma remain confined to the United States.[79] This calls for explanation. Perhaps the United States in the early postwar years was more technologically oriented than many European nations, more confident about progress through the control of nature, and thus also more inclined to experiment heroically with new medical technologies. If this is so, then the American experience with DES and the later Dalkon Shield—as well as the American overuse of surgery—may be more significant than our luck in avoiding such European tragedies as thalidomide.

Ignoring this issue and others, Apfel and Fisher find a pattern of inevitability in history where far more contingency operated. There were missed opportunities. Not to grasp this and not to explain why plausible alternatives went unchosen is to fail to understand how and

---

78. Per H.B. Carstens and Johannes Clemmesen, "Genital Tract Cancer in Danish Adolescents," *NEJM* 287 (July 1972), 198; L.J. Kinlen, *et al.*, "A Survey of the Use of Estrogens During Pregnancy in the United Kingdom and of the Genitourinary Cancer Mortality and Incidence Rates in Young People in England and Wales," *Journal of Obstetrics and Gynecology of the British Commonwealth* 81 (November 1974), 849–55; Seaman and Seaman, *Women and the Crisis in Sex Hormones*, 28; Fenichell and Charfoos, *Daughters at Risk*, 158.

79. Herbst and Bern, *Developmental Effects*, 65.

why the DES tragedy occurred. This is also to accede, as Apfel and Fisher do, to a belief that similar events may be inevitable.[80] Perhaps the ancient Hippocratic injunction, "do no harm," need not yield so easily to the demands of "modern" medicine or the claims of fate.

80. In a remarkably brief final section on reforms in medicine necessary to avoid more iatrogenic problems, Apfel and Fisher stress the need for prudence, not changes in the structure of medicine (pp. 126–30).

ACKNOWLEDGMENTS

DeLacy, Margaret. "Puerperal Fever in Eighteenth-Century Britain." *Bulletin of the History of Medicine* 63 (Winter 1989): 521–56. Reprinted with the permission of Johns Hopkins University Press.

Holmes, Oliver Wendell. "The Contagiousness of Puerperal Fever." In *Medical Essays 1842–1882* (Boston: Houghton, Mifflin and Co., 1891): 103–72.

Wallace, Ellerslie. "Child-Bed Fever." *Clinical News* 2 (November 1881): 243–47.

Busby, M.J. and A.E. Rodin. "Relative Contributions of Holmes and Semmelweis to the Understanding of the Etiology of Puerperal Fever." *Texas Reports on Biology and Medicine* 34, Nos. 2–4 (1976): 221–37. Reprinted with the permission of the *Texas Reports on Biology and Medicine*.

Theriot, Nancy. "Diagnosing Unnatural Motherhood: Nineteenth-Century Physicians and 'Puerperal Insanity'." *American Studies* 30, No.2 (1989): 69–88. Reprinted with the permission of the University of Kansas at Lawrence.

Leavitt, Judith Walzer. "Under the Shadow of Maternity: American Women's Responses to Death and Debility Fears in Nineteenth-Century Childbirth." *Feminist Studies* 12, No.1 (1986): 129–54. Reprinted with the permission of the publisher, Feminist Studies, Inc., c/o Women's Studies Program, University of Maryland, College Park, MD 20742.

Seligman, Stanley A. "The Lesser Pestilence: Non-Epidemic Puerperal Fever." *Medical History* 35 (1991): 89–102. Reprinted with permission. Copyright The Trustee, The Wellcome Trust.

Loudon, Irvine. "Deaths in Childbed from the Eighteenth Century to 1935." *Medical History* 30 (1986): 1–41. Reprinted with permission. Copyright The Trustee, The Wellcome Trust.

Lever, John C.W. "Cases of Puerperal Convulsions." *Guy's Hospital Reports,* second series 1 (1843): 495–517.

Van Eman, J.H. "Puerperal Eclampsia." *Medical Herald* 8, No.10 (1875): 127–31.

Holland, Eardley. "The Princess Charlotte of Wales: A Triple Obstetric Tragedy." *Journal of Obstetrics and Gynaecology of the British Empire* 58, No.6 (1951): 905–19. Reprinted with the permission of Blackwell Scientific Publications Ltd.

Noeggerath, Emil. "Latent Gonorrhea, Especially with Regard to its Influence on Fertility in Women." *Transactions of the American Gynecological Society* 1 (1876): 268–300.

Tait, Lawson. "Five Cases of Extra-Uterine Pregnancy Operated Upon at the Time of Rupture." *British Medical Journal* (June 28, 1884): 1250–54. Reprinted with the permission of the British Medical Association.

Lomax, Elizabeth. "Infantile Syphilis as an Example of Nineteenth Century Belief in the Inheritance of Acquired Characteristics." *Journal of the History of Medicine and Allied Sciences* 34 (1979): 23–39. Reprinted with the permission of the *Journal of the History of Medicine and Allied Sciences*.

Williams, J. Whitridge. "The Significance of Syphilis in Prenatal Care and in the Causation of Foetal Death." *Bulletin of the Johns Hopkins Hospital* 31, No.351 (1920): 141–45.

Dekaban, Anatole, James O'Rourke, and Tillye Cornman. "Abnormalities in Offspring Related to Maternal Rubella During Pregnancy." *Neurology* 8 (1958): 387–92. Reprinted with the permission of Advanstar Communications, Inc.

Newton, Niles. "Emotions of Pregnancy." *Clinical Obstetrics and Gynecology* 6 (September 1963): 639–62. Reprinted with the permission of the J.B. Lippincott Company.

Diamond, Louis K. "The Rh Problem Through a Retrospectroscope." *American Journal of Clinical Pathology* 62 (1974): 311–24. Reprinted with the permission of J.B. Lippincott Company.

Martin, Joan C. "Drugs of Abuse during Pregnancy: Effects upon Offspring Structure and Function." *Signs* 2, No.2 (1976): 357–68. Reprinted with the permission of the University of Chicago Press, publisher. Copyright 1976 University of Chicago Press.

Longo, Lawrence D. "Environmental Pollution and Pregnancy: Risks and Uncertainties for the Fetus and Infant." *American Journal of Obstetrics and Gynecology* 137, No.2 (1980): 162–73. Reprinted with the permission of Mosby Year Book, Inc.

Smith, George Van S. and O. Watkins Smith. "Internal Secretions and Toxemia of Late Pregnancy." *Physiological Reviews* 28, No.1 (1948): 1–22. Reprinted with the permission of the American Physiological Society.

Gillam, Richard, and Barton J. Bernstein. "Doing Harm: The DES Tragedy and Modern American Medicine." *Public Historian* 9, No.1 (1987): 57–82. Reprinted with the permission of the University of California Press.

EDITORS

Series Editor

Philip K. Wilson, MA, Ph.D., is an assistant professor of the history of science at Truman State University (formerly Northeast Missouri State University) in Kirksville, Missouri. After receiving his undergraduate degree in human biology from the University of Kansas, he pursued work towards an MA in medical history at the William H. Welch Institute for the History of Medicine at The Johns Hopkins School of Medicine and received his Ph.D. in the history of medicine from the University of London. He has held postdoctoral positions at the University of Hawaii-Manoa and Yale University School of Medicine before settling in Missouri.

Wilson has received scholarly support including a Logan Clendening Summer Fellowship, an Owsei Temkin Scholarship, a Folger Shakespeare Library Fellowship, a Wellcome Trust Research Scholarship, and grants from the Hawaii and Missouri Committees for the Humanities for medical and science history projects. He was a founding member of the Hawaii Society for the History of Medicine and Public Health. Wilson has contributed chapters to volumes including *The Popularization of Medicine 1650–1850* (Routledge), *Medicine in the Enlightenment* (Rodopi), and *The Secret Malady: Venereal Disease in Eighteenth-Century Britain and France* (University Press of Kentucky), articles in the *Annals of Science,* the *London Journal,* and the *Journal of the Royal Society of Medicine,* and is a regular contributor of medical and science history entries to many dictionaries and encyclopedias. Currently, Wilson is pursuing research on women's diseases, osteopathy, and eugenics in Kirksville, Missouri, where he lives with his wife, Janice, and son, James.

Assistant Editors

Ann Dally, MA, MD, received her Master's degree from Oxford University, having been an exhibitioner in modern history at Somerville College. She then studied medicine at St. Thomas' Hospital, London, qualifying in 1953. After some years of general medical practice, she specialized in psychiatry, a specialty she practiced until her retirement in 1994. Meanwhile she pursued her interests in the history of medicine, receiving her doctorate in that subject in 1993. The book based on her doctoral thesis, *Fantasy Surgery, 1880–1930,* will shortly be published as part of the Wellcome Institute for the History of Medicine (London) series. Her most recent book, *Women Under the Knife. A History of Surgery* (Routledge), follows a long publishing history of books including *The Morbid Streak, Why Women Fail, Mothers: Their Power and Influence, Inventing Motherhood: The Consequences of an Ideal,* and a book of memoirs, *A Doctor's Story.* Currently a Research Fellow at the Wellcome Institute for the History of Medicine (London), she lives with her husband Philip Egerton in West Sussex, England and has four children and seven grandchildren.

Charles R. King, MD, MA, is a professor of obstetrics and gynecology at the Medical College of Ohio. He received his BA from Kansas State University, an MD from the University of Kansas, and has completed post graduate medical training at the University of Kansas and the University of Oregon. He has since received an MA in medical history from the University of Kansas. King has been the recipient of Rockefeller Foundation, National Endowment for the Humanities, American College of Obstetricians and Gynecologists-Ortho, and Newberry Library Fellowships for projects in medical history. He is the author of numerous publications regarding women's health, including articles in the *Bulletin of the History of Medicine, Kansas History,* and the *Great Plains Quarterly,* and has recently completed *Child Health in America* (Twain). He currently lives with his wife, Lynn, in Temperance, Michigan.

www.ingramcontent.com/pod-product-compliance
Ingram Content Group UK Ltd.
Pitfield, Milton Keynes, MK11 3LW, UK
UKHW041106040325
455677UK00032B/39